The Schlager Anthology of Women's History

A Student's Guide to Essential Primary Sources

The Schlager Anthology of Women's History

A Student's Guide to Essential Primary Sources

Kelli McCoy
Editor in Chief

Schlager

Dallas, TX

The Schlager Anthology of Women's History:
A Student's Guide to Essential Primary Sources

Schlager Group Inc.
10228 E. Northwest HWY, STE 1151
Dallas, TX 75238
USA
(888) 416-5727
info@schlagergroup.com

You can find Schlager Group online at https://www.schlagergroup.com

For Schlager Group:
Vice President, Editorial: Sarah Robertson
Vice President, Operations and Strategy: Benjamin Painter
Founder and President: Neil Schlager

Printed in the United States of America 10 9 8 7 6 5 4 3 2 1
Print ISBN: 9781961844018
eBook: 9781961844025

Library of Congress Control Number: 2023947236

Contents

Volume 2

Volume 3

Reader's Guide

About This Title and Series

Welcome to *The Schlager Anthology of Women's History: A Student's Guide to Essential Primary Sources.* This anthology marks the seventh installment in our series, "Schlager Anthologies for Students." Each title in this series aims to provide a useful anthology of primary sources for students at the high school and lower undergraduate levels as well as general researchers. In creating each title in the series, we have worked with two underlying goals: 1) to provide a diverse set of readings, including documents from often-marginalized communities and voices that are frequently ignored in other anthologies and historical accounts; 2) to provide an accessible approach to the material, one that doesn't overwhelm students and researchers with lengthy, overly difficult texts. To that end, document texts are abridged to remain brief and accessible, even to struggling readers, while activity questions range in difficulty from basic to more advanced.

Organization

The anthology is divided into three volumes, with a total of fifteen chapters covering women's history from the ancient world to the present day. Each chapter begins with an introductory essay that introduces the topic and the documents found therein; the chapter introductions end with a Further Reading section, containing books, articles, and websites for further research. The chapters follow a broadly chronological sequence, although there is some overlap of dates between chapters, and some chapters are thematic in orientation. Within each chapter, entries are likewise arranged chronologically by year. *The Schlager Anthology of Women's History* contains a total of 206 entries.

Entry Format

Each entry in *The Schlager Anthology of Women's History* is organized according to the following format:

- The **Fact Box** includes the year the document was produced, the primary author(s), the document categories, and a statement summarizing the significance of the document.

- The **Overview** provides a brief summary of the primary source document and its importance in history.

- The **Document Text** section includes the full or (more often) abridged text of the document. Abridgements are indicated by ellipses. Virtually all documents in this set are abridged to a maximum length of 1,000 words, to remain as accessible as possible to a wide readership.

- The **Glossary** defines important, difficult, or unusual terms or references in the document text.

- **Short-Answer Questions** at the end of each entry offer study questions for students.

Features

In addition to the 15 chapters and 206 entries, the set includes 175 photographs and illustrations. At the end, readers will find a list of Documents by Category and a cumulative Index.

Questions

We welcome questions and comments about the set. Readers may direct any such questions to the following address:

The Editor
Schlager Group Inc.
10228 E. Northwest Hwy, #1151
Dallas, TX 75238
USA
(888) 416-5727
info@schlagergroup.com

Contributors

Editor in Chief

Kelli McCoy
Point Loma Nazarene University

Contributors

Raymond Hylton
Virginia Union University

Matthew Jagel
Saint Xavier University

Tom Lansford
University of Southern Mississippi

Robert Malick
HACC, Central Pennsylvania's Community College

Kimberly A. Matthews
Virginia Commonwealth University

MacKenzie Mills
Boston College

Kenneth Shepherd
Henry Ford College

Ross Smeltzer
Judge Barefoot Sanders Law Magnet, Dallas Independent School District

Kenneth Alan Smith
Kansas State University

Michelle Valletta
Roger Williams University

Marcelle Wilson
Youngstown State University

Julie Yarwood
University of Mary

Acknowledgments

Adrienne Rich: "Compulsory Heterosexuality and Lesbian Experience": Reproduced by permission of Johns Hopkins University Press

Ama Ata Aidoo: "Ghana: To Be a Woman": Copyright 1984 by Robin Morgan. Excepted with permission from *Sisterhood Is Global: The International Women's Movement Anthology,* compiled and edited by Robin Morgan (1984 Doubleday publishers, New York; 2020 The Feminist Press, CUNY, New York)

Betty Friedan: *The Feminine Mystique:* Copyright © 1963 by Betty Friedan. Reprinted by permission of Curtis Brown, Ltd. All rights reserved.

Clara Zetkin: "Women's Work and the Trade Unions": Reproduced with permission of Haymarket Books.

"Combahee River Collective Statement": By permission of Zillah Eisenstein

Ella Baker: "The Black Woman in the Civil Rights Struggle": Reproduced by permission of John Wiley & Sons

Ellen Johnson Sirleaf: "A Voice for Freedom": © The Nobel Foundation 2011

Gloria Steinem: "Living the Revolution": "Living the Revolution" was originally printed in the fall 1970 issue of the *Vassar Quarterly,* the alumnae/i magazine of Vassar College. Used with permission.

Hazel V. Carby: "White Woman Listen! Black Feminism and the Boundaries of Sisterhood": Reproduced from *Empire Strikes Back,* 1st Edition by Centre for Contemporary Cultural Studies, published by Routledge. ©1982. Reproduced by arrangement with Taylor & Francis Group

Jo Ann Gibson Robinson: *The Montgomery Bus Boycott and the Women Who Started It:* From Jo Ann Gibson Robinson's *The Montgomery Bus Boycott and the Women Who Started It.* Edited, with a foreword, by David J. Garrow. Copyright © 1987 by The University of Tennessee Press. Reprinted by permission.

Juvenal: *The Satires:* Reproduced with permission of Poetry in Translation.

Lady Hong: "Diary of Lady Hong, Queen of Korea": Reproduced by permission of Taylor and Francis Group, LLC, a division of Informa plc.

Luce Irigaray: "Women on the Market": From *This Sex Which Is Not One,* by Luce Irigaray, translated by Catherine Porter, with Carolyn Burke. English translation (c) 1985 by Cornell University. Included by permission of the publisher, Cornell University Press.

Malala Yousafzai: Nobel Peace Prize Acceptance Speech: © The Nobel Foundation 2014

Margaret Cerullo: "Hidden History: An Illegal Abortion in 1968": Reproduced with permission of Margaret Cerullo.

Maria Eugenia Echenique: "The Emancipation of Women": Echenique, Maria Eugenia. The Emancipation of Women: Argentina 1876. *Journal of Women's History* 7:3 (1995), 114-116. © 1995 Journal of Women's History, Inc. Reprinted with permission of Johns Hopkins University Press.

Introduction

The Schlager Anthology of Women's History brings together more than 200 primary source documents about the lives and experiences of women, and the social, political, religious, and legal contexts that have shaped their struggles for equality in the United States and globally. This anthology uniquely brings together a diverse range of sources, giving students the opportunity to research, read carefully, think critically, and analyze historical documents.

These primary sources include letters, personal accounts, legislation, speeches, government documents, oral histories, and selections from books and essays written by and about women. The document excerpts are the ideal length for using in class or for students' own research. Concise explanatory materials written by experts accompany each document. In these, scholars identify the significance and provide the context for each source, along with providing a glossary and questions about the document to guide readers. These sources give students access to exploring first-hand the ideas, assumptions, societies, and legal systems that women have lived within and often struggled against. Through these, students can understand change over time, analyze historical arguments, assess historical interpretations, interpret past events, and understand the complexity and impact of those events.

The Schlager Anthology of Women's History is organized thematically and chronologically so that students can easily see how documents are related and can compare and contrast documents within any given section. Some of the thematic sections focus specifically on the United States, while others are global. For students in U.S. history courses, there are ample sources focusing on U.S. women's movements, including thematic sections on the suffrage movement and other reform and justice movements in the United States. For those looking to understand women's lives and rights movements in a global context, there are several thematic global sections, spanning from the ancient world to the postmodern and postcolonial eras.

Many of the sources represent milestone events in women's history and include women who were viewed as important, powerful, or world-changing in their own time. From Joan of Arc's Letter to King Henry VI of England in the fifteenth century, to Michelle Obama's remarks at the 2012 International Women of Courage Awards in the twenty-first century, readers will encounter the words of women who were widely known in their own time for working to change their worlds.

Just as importantly, this anthology also brings together sources by and about women who were not viewed as powerful or famous during their own time. Readers will find that primary sources from "ordinary" women help with understanding the real-life experiences that created the need and motivation for social, political, economic, legal, religious, and educational changes. Sources like Elizabeth Sprigs's letter to her father in the 1700s and Fabienne and Elena's oral histories in the 1900s help readers better understand the daily realities of economic and legal restraints that women have struggled within and persevered through.

The documents are organized chronologically within themes so that students can see the connections between documents. The opening chapter, "Women and Gender in the Ancient World," helps readers understand the context, assumptions, and stereotypes women faced, challenged, and sometimes embraced. From Ban Zhao's *Lessons for a Woman* during the Han Dynasty, to the Roman poet Juvenal's second-century *Satires,* readers encounter conceptions of gender in the ancient world.

This anthology intentionally includes documents from a wide array of women, including multiple world regions, various races, ethnicities, nationalities, and religious beliefs, varying degrees of political and economic power, indigenous women, LGBTQ+ women, and more. In the "Votes for Women: Suffrage in the United States" chapter, the sources from white suffragists like Elizabeth Cady Stanton's Address to the New York Legislature, are set alongside the work of suffragists of color, including Sojourner Truth's "Ain't I a Woman?," Mabel Ping-Hua Lee's "The Submerged Half," and Mary Church Terrell's "The Progress of Colored Women." When examined as a whole, they demonstrate not only the commonalities between women who fought for the right to vote but also the intersections of race, class, gender, citizenship, and more that gave differing significance to their demands for suffrage.

The final two thematic chapters bring the reader close to the present time, with sources about women's rights and justice movements around the world. The sources in these sections demonstrate that many of the issues raised by women in prior centuries are still faced by women globally today, including the demand for equal access to education, financial independence, and physical safety. Indira Gandhi's "What Educated Women Can Do" (1974) and Malala Yousafzai's Nobel Lecture (2014) remind readers of other movements for women's education, seen in earlier sources like Catherine Sawbridge Macaulay's *Letters on Education* (1790).

The final chapter, "Justice Movements in the Twenty-first Century," along with the preceding ones, demonstrates the ongoing movements for women's rights around the world and their intersection with other justice movements, including reproductive rights, economic justice, environmental justice, racial justice, movements against violence, and LGBTQ+ rights. Sources like Autumn Peltier's Address to the UN World Water Day, Greta Thunberg's "Our House Is on Fire address," and the United Nations' Sustainable Development Goal 5, all show that the future of the world is deeply connected to the future of women's equality and activism.

Through these primary sources, students encounter the voices of a diverse range of women who worked to make the world a better place, often despite great obstacles. It is notoriously difficult for historians to access the stories of ordinary people. Typically, only people viewed as important in their own time and place have their historical records and artifacts preserved. In many societies, those "important" people were disproportionately male. For everyone else, there is little historical record, and their memories are lost to time. Some, like the Cherokee women who wrote to Governor Benjamin Franklin, had power in their own societies but were ignored and silenced by others. It is therefore often difficult to find historical sources about women's thoughts, lives, and experiences. This anthology plays a crucial role in remedying that imbalance by giving students accessible sources by and about women from various times and places. Through these documents, we can hear their voices and stories.

In these accounts of women's lives and struggles for equality, students will see change over time, but they will also see the ways in which the work is ongoing. What unites these documents is that they reveal the resilience and aspirations of women in the face of legal, social, religious, political, and economic inequalities and their persistence in working toward a better future.

—Kelli McCoy, Point Loma Nazarene University

The Schlager Anthology of Women's History

A Student's Guide to Essential Primary Sources

Chapter 1

Women and Gender in the Ancient World

In the ancient world, the status of women varied across cultures, regions, and time periods. Any discussion of the topic of gender in antiquity must address several complicating factors. First, the term *ancient* encompasses a vast period stretching from the rise of Sumerian civilization (4500 to 4000 BCE) to the collapse of the Roman Empire in 476 CE. In addition, this term conceals both the geographic breadth and the diversity of the civilizations that rose, flourished, and inevitably decayed or collapsed during this time. The so-called ancient world, as it is commonly understood, encompasses the early civilizations of Europe, the Middle East, and North Africa. While these civilizations interacted with one another, they differed considerably in their outlooks and material cultures. Finally, our understanding of the status of women in antiquity is necessarily limited: nearly all source materials from the period explore gender dynamics from the perspective of social elites. Historians have precious few glimpses of everyday women's lives.

While there was considerable variability in women's status in the ancient world, there were some common themes across cultures. In most societies in antiquity, women were disadvantaged by rules and conventions made for the benefit of men. Most ancient civilizations were patriarchal, meaning that men held most of the power and authority.

Regardless of the general subordinate status of women in antiquity, women did continue to exercise influence in their societies. Women often held significant roles in religious rituals and mythology, and they served as priestesses, oracles, and living embodiments of esteemed goddesses. This religious influence sometimes extended into the political realm. While women in antiquity were commonly denied political power, there were exceptional cases of women in positions of authority. For instance, Shammuramat (811–806 BCE) was a powerful co-regent and queen of the Neo-Assyrian Empire and was among the most powerful women of the ancient Near East. Hatshepsut (r. 1479–1458 BCE) was the first female ruler of ancient Egypt. She reigned as a male and held all of the sacred and spiritual authority of pharaoh. Empress Wu Zetian, who reigned from 690 to 704 CE, was the only female emperor of Imperial China. She reigned during China's Tang Dynasty (618–907 CE) and is now regarded as one of China's most effective rulers. In the arts, many women produced books, poems, and philosophical tracts.

Ancient Mesopotamia

Between 6000 to 8000 years ago, settled agricultural societies evolved in geographically disparate regions around the world, including Ancient Egypt, around the Nile River; the Indus Valley civilization, in modern-day Pakistan; Mesopotamia, between the Tigris and Euphrates rivers in modern-day Iraq; and Ancient China, along the Yellow and Yangtze rivers. Complex civilization likely first arose in Mesopotamia, where an array of quarrelsome city-states and empires clustered around the banks of the volatile Tigris and Euphrates.

Women in ancient Sumer, the first society to develop in Mesopotamia, were subordinate to men. That said, Mesopotamian women retained significant rights. They could own businesses, buy and sell property, live autonomously, initiate divorce, and hold positions of significant religious authority. These freedoms were greatest earlier in Mesopotamia's cultural development and declined over time. This tendency can be seen by comparing two documents in this collection. The "Hymns to Inanna," written around 2300 BCE, were ancient poems believed to be written by Enheduanna, the high priestess of the moon god Nanna in the Sumerian city-state of Ur. Enheduanna was the daughter of Sargon of Akkad (r. 2334–2279 BCE), a famed Mesopotamian conqueror who made the female deity Inanna/Ishtar his personal protector. These poems elevated the goddess Inanna above all other gods in the Sumerian pantheon and are suggestive of the importance of women in Mesopotamian religious life.

Over time, women's status in Mesopotamia declined. This decline can be seen by examining the text of the Code of Assura, otherwise known as the Code of the Assyrians, promulgated in 1075 BCE. The Code expanded on earlier law codes and set harsh laws regarding interactions between men and women in the Assyrian kingdom. It was violently oppressive towards women, treating enslaved women as less than human and free-born women as little more than property.

Women in Ancient Egypt

Women were held in greater esteem in ancient Egypt than in Mesopotamia. Women in ancient Egypt enjoyed the same legal rights as men, although the extent of these rights was contingent on social class. Elite women held much more power than those from the laboring classes. All landed property in Egypt descended from the female line, passing from mother to daughter. Women were allowed to administer their own property and businesses. They could buy and sell property, execute and administer wills, serve as witnesses to the preparation of legal documents, bring action in courts, and enter into binding legal contracts. Notably, Egyptian laws recognized women as legally *capax* (competent or capable) and did not require them to be supervised by a male guardian, as was the case in the patriarchal society of ancient Greece. The deference shown to women in Egypt is best seen in the religious sphere. Feminine deities were common in Egypt's polytheistic religion, and women could serve as scribes and priests, although they were often restricted to association with cults associated with a female deity.

Women in Greece and Rome

Women in ancient Greece had few rights compared to male citizens. They were restricted from political participation, could not own land or inherit property, and were confined to a domestic role. Women were often secluded, as well, and could rarely venture out of their homes. This truncated social role contrasts with women's status in Greek religion and mythology. Athena, for instance, was the goddess of wisdom and war and was the patron deity of the powerful city-state of Athens. That said, Greek myths also abound with women cast in villainous roles. Aphrodite, the goddess of sexual love and beauty, often served as a foil to male protagonists and heroes, using her charms to make wise, honorable men lose their wits and strength. In addition, rape is a common motif in Greek mythology, with many mythic stories centering on the abduction and rape of women by male deities and heroes. These stories rarely consider the ethical implications of sexual violence.

Few women in Greece, aside from those who came from wealthy families, were taught to read and write, and most were married in their teens. There was widespread skepticism of women's abilities, and writers like Aristotle made it clear that they considered women to be unfit to make decisions for themselves. There were many authors who contested Aristotle's claim, however. The famed historian Herodotus, writing in the aftermath of the destructive Greco-Persian Wars (499–449 BCE), described the status of women in the Persian Empire. The Persian Empire, a gigantic political entity that governed the Near East in late antiquity, was a far more egalitarian society than Greece. Herodotus's attitudes towards women contrasted sharply with those of Aristotle and others. In his *Histories*, he used the perceived positive and humane virtues of women to illustrate the rash, aggressive nature of men. Women in the *Histories*, unlike in most Greek writings, have agency and can make reasonable, rational decisions. Similarly, in his *Moralia*, the Greek philosopher Plutarch describes numerous examples of virtuous and brave female figures from Greek and Roman antiquity.

While education was generally denied to women, they were active contributors to the arts and literature. Sappho, who wrote during the sixth century BCE, was a famous female Greek poet. Her poems include "Fragment 31," "Ode to Aphrodite," "Passion," and "Telesippa." These poems reveal Sappho to be a lyric poet of rare genius. Her vivid, dream-like writings were unique because they centered the poem on the poet's subjective, emotional experience and eschewed the grand historical melodramas of previous Greek poets. Sappho was held in high regard in the ancient world, but her fame should not detract from the general theme of patriarchal oppression that prevailed in ancient Greece.

Roman civilization was deeply indebted to that of Greece. It, too, was characterized by a profoundly patriarchal structure. While women were represented in Roman myths and legends, their status in society was unambiguously subordinate to that of men. Roman women were closely associated with a single social role: they were nurturers of the family. Their role in society was restricted to the bearing of legitimate offspring, which meant that they were frequently married at a young age, before they could become sexually active. Romans regarded the policing of female sexuality as a social necessity, and women with sexual histories were treated as embarrassments to their husbands and families. Within families, Roman women were subordinate to their male relatives. Roman families were male-dominated, headed by a senior male figure, revered in society as the *paterfamilias*. Women in Rome could not vote or hold political office, but they were permitted to own and inherit property and often informally held some sway over their family businesses.

The strict gender binaries that governed Roman society are particularly in evidence in the male-dominated literature produced for the Roman elite. Juvenal was a Roman satirist and author. Writing at the start of the Roman Empire, in the first century CE, he often offered a scathing critique of Rome's increasingly venal, corrupt, and materialistic society. His writings are also dripping with scorn for women and undisguised misogyny, as shown in the excerpts from his *Satires*. Juvenal's writings suggest that many Romans viewed women as lustful, untrustworthy, materialistic, and shallow. In "You're Mad to Marry," he presents Roman male readers with three alternative future lives: marriage, suicide, or a secret male lover. The latter two options are presented to the reader as superior alternatives to the first. Juvenal's writings give historians a window onto a misogynistic society where women existed in the shadow of the men in their lives.

Conclusion

The study of women's status in the ancient world is a complicated one. The writings we have from the period are nearly always written by male authors and centered on the male perspective. That said, the admittedly male-dominated literature of the period does reveal tensions and complexities in gender attitudes. The documents presented in this chapter highlight the ambiguous and contested nature of gender roles in antiquity.

Further Reading

Books

Ashton, Sally. *The Last Queens of Egypt*. London: Routledge, 2003.

Bagnall, Roger S., et al., eds. *The Encyclopedia of Ancient History*. London: Wiley-Blackwell, 2012.

Barchiesi, Alessandro. *The Oxford Handbook of Roman Studies*. Oxford University Press, USA, 2010.

Blundell, Susan. *Women in Ancient Greece*. Cambridge: Cambridge University Press, 2016.

Boys-Stones, George, et al., eds. *The Oxford Handbook of Hellenic Studies*. Oxford: Oxford University Press, 2009.

Brier, Bob, and Hoyt Hobbs. *Ancient Egypt: Everyday Life in the Land of the Nile*. London: Sterling, 2013.

David, Ann Rosalie. *Religion and Magic in Ancient Egypt*. New York: Penguin Books, 2003.

Fantham, Elaine, et al. *Women in the Classical World: Image and Text*. Oxford: Oxford University Press, 1995.

Grant, Michael. *The History of Rome*. London: Faber, 2000.

Graves-Brown, Carolyn. *Dancing for Hathor: Women in Ancient Egypt*. London: Continuum, 2010.

Hornblower, Simon. *The Oxford Classical Dictionary*. New York: Oxford University Press, 2012.

Kinzl, Konrad H. *A Companion to the Classical Greek World*. London: Wiley-Blackwell, 2016.

Lefkowitz, Mary R. and Maureen B. Fant, eds. *Women's Life in Greece and Rome: A Source Book in Translation*. Baltimore, MD: Johns Hopkins University Press, 2005.

Potter, David S. *A Companion to the Roman Empire*. London: Wiley-Blackwell, 2009.

Robins, Gay. *Women in Ancient Egypt*. Cambridge, MA: Harvard University Press, 1993.

Shaw, Ian. *The Oxford History of Ancient Egypt*. Oxford: Oxford University Press, 2016.

Tyldesley, Joyce. *Daughters of Isis: Women of Ancient Egypt*. New York: Penguin Books, 1995.

Watterson, Barbara. *The Egyptians*. London: Wiley-Blackwell, 1997.

Watterson, Barbara. *Women in Ancient Egypt*. London: Sutton Publishing Ltd, 1994.

Enheduanna: *Hymns to Inana*

Author	Significance
Enheduanna	Among the oldest surviving works of literature in the world, they placed the goddess Inana above all other gods in the Sumerian pantheon
Date	
c. 2300 BCE	
Document Type	
Poems, Plays, Fiction	

Overview

Enheduanna, the daughter of the Akkadian conqueror Sargon the Great, is thought to have authored the *Hymns to Inana*. Enheduanna was the first known high priestess of the moon god Nanna in the city of Ur and is recognized as the earliest known author in world history. Enheduanna is credited with many early temple hymns of southern Mesopotamia, including the three mentioned here: "Inana and Ebih," "The Exaltation of Inana," and "A Hymn to Inana." While there are few biographical details about Enheduanna, the historical and archaeological record indicates she was a prolific writer, having composed more than forty other poems and prayers. Although her works exhibit devotion to all the gods in the Sumerian pantheon, her attachment to Inana is particularly evident.

The *Hymns to Inana* praise and honor Inana (also spelled Inanna), who was revered by the Sumerians as the goddess of sensuality, eroticism, beauty, fertility, and war. These hymns vividly depict Inana's power and beauty, placing her at the center of the complex Sumerian sacred universe. They served an important role in Sumerian society for ceremonial and religious purposes. The hymns allowed people to express their devotion and seek Inana's favor and blessings. These poems are distinctive because they emphasize Inana's importance and relegate other gods to secondary roles in her story.

An Akkadian cylinder seal depicting Inana (Wikimedia Commons)

Document Text

Inana and Ebih

Goddess of the fearsome divine powers, clad in terror, riding on the great divine powers, Inana, made complete by the strength of the holy *ankar* weapon, drenched in blood, rushing around in great battles . . . covered in storm and flood, great lady Inana, knowing well how to plan conflicts, you destroy mighty lands with arrow and strength and overpower lands.

In heaven and on earth you roar like a lion and devastate the people. Like a huge wild bull you triumph over lands which are hostile. Like a fearsome lion you pacify the insubordinate and unsubmissive with your gall. . . .

I shall praise the lady of battle, the great child of Suen, maiden Inana.

[Inana announced:] "When I, the goddess, was walking around in heaven, walking around on earth, when I, Inana, was walking around in heaven, walking around on earth, when I was walking around in Elam and Subir, when I was walking around in the Lulubi mountains, when I turned towards the center of the mountains, as I, the goddess, approached the mountain it showed me no respect, as I, Inana, approached the mountain it showed me no respect, as I approached the mountain range of Ebih it showed me no respect.

"Since they showed me no respect, since they did not put their noses to the ground for me, since they did not rub their lips in the dust for me, I shall personally fill the soaring mountain range with my terror." . . .

My lady confronted the mountain range. She advanced step by step. She sharpened both edges of her dagger. She grabbed Ebih's neck as if ripping up esparto grass. She pressed the dagger's teeth into its interior. She roared like thunder.

The rocks forming the body of Ebih clattered down its flanks. From its sides and crevices great serpents spat venom. She damned its forests and cursed its trees. She killed its oak trees with drought. She poured fire on its flanks and made its smoke dense. The goddess established authority over the mountain. Holy Inana did as she wished. . . .

The Exaltation of Inana

At your battle-cry, my lady, the foreign lands bow low. When humanity comes before you in awed silence at the terrifying radiance and tempest, you grasp the most terrible of all the divine powers. Because of you, the threshold of tears is opened, and people walk along the path of the house of great lamentations. . . .

My lady, the great Anuna gods fly from you to the ruin mounds like scudding bats. They dare not stand before your terrible gaze. They dare not confront your terrible countenance. Who can cool your raging heart? Your malevolent anger is too great to cool. . . .

A Hymn to Inana

The great-hearted mistress, the impetuous lady, proud among the Anuna gods and pre-eminent in all lands . . . the magnificent lady who gathers up the divine powers of heaven and earth and rivals great An, is mightiest among the great gods—she makes their verdicts final. The Anuna gods crawl before her august word whose course she does not let An know; he dare not proceed against her command. She changes her own action, and no one knows how it will occur. She makes perfect the great divine powers, she holds a shepherd's crook, and she is their magnificent pre-eminent one. . . .

At her loud cries, the gods of the Land become scared. Her roaring makes the Anuna gods tremble like a solitary reed. At her rumbling, they hide all together. Without Inana great An makes no decisions, and Enlil determines no destinies. Who opposes the mistress who raises her head and is supreme over the mountains?

To open up roads and paths, a place of peace for the journey, a companion for the weak, are yours, Inana. To keep paths and ways in good order, to shatter earth and to make it firm are yours, Inana. To destroy, to build up, to tear out and to settle are yours, Inana. To turn a man into a woman and a woman into a man are yours, Inana. Desirability and arousal, bringing goods into existence and establishing properties and equipment are yours, Inana.

Mistress, you are magnificent, you are great! Inana, you are magnificent, you are great! My lady, your magnificence is resplendent. May your heart be restored for my sake!

Your great deeds are unparalleled, your magnificence is praised! Young woman, Inana, your praise is sweet!

Glossary

An: also spelled Anu, the paramount deity in Sumerian cosmology; the divine personification of the sky, king of the gods, and ancestor of many of the deities in ancient Sumer

ankar weapon: a magical weapon of great power

Anuna gods: at the time when these poems were composed, the heavenly gods of Mesopotamian cosmology; in later texts, associated with the underworld

Ebih: a Mesopotamian god representing the Hamrin Mountains

Lullubi mountains: a likely reference to the Lullubi, an ancient group of warlike hill tribes living on the rim of Sargon of Akkad's empire; throughout the poems, Inana is shown defeating rebellious lands on the edge of Mesopotamian civilization

Suen: the Mesopotamian moon god, variously known as Suen, Nanna, or Sin; an ancient god and the mythic father of the sun god Shamash and Ishtar

Short-Answer Questions

1. Describe the character of Inana as she is depicted in these poems. What traits and qualities does she display? In your response, please cite specific words or phrases to support your description.

2. How does Enheduanna show that Inana is superior to the other gods? In your response, consider the relationships the author describes between the gods and outline the kinds of powers attributed to Inana.

3. Explain what makes the depiction of Inana unusual or surprising. Consider the god's gender, and analyze what Inana's depiction suggests about gender roles in ancient Mesopotamia.

Code of Assura

Author	Significance
Unknown	Expanded on the earlier Code of Hammurabi and set harsh laws regarding interactions between men and women in the Assyrian kingdom
Date	
c. 1075 BCE	
Document Type	
Legal	

Overview

Assyrian law, as described in the Code of Assura, or Code of the Assyrians, was an ancient legal code established during the Middle Assyrian Empire, between 1450 and 1250 BCE. This law code built upon the precedents set in Sumerian and Babylonian law. Like previous law codes, the Code of the Assyrians stressed the idea of proportional retribution, especially in cases involving violent crimes. This legal approach, otherwise known as retributive justice, requires offenders receive a punishment for a crime proportional and similar to the offense committed. This idea of proportionality in punishment was reserved for free-born adult men, however. Crimes inflicted against women were punished in a much more lenient way, and female criminal offenders were punished with the utmost severity.

The Assyrian legal code retained the infamous violence of previous Near Eastern legal systems but was even harsher in its stated punishments. In addition, it was particularly oppressive toward women, treating free-born women as little more than property.

The rules listed in the Code of Assura primarily deal with sexual and romantic relations between men and women, with a substantial number of rules addressing rape, adultery, divorce, and domestic violence. The Assyrian leaders who set forth these rules were clearly concerned with the regulation of lust, marriage, and pregnancy, and they used their positions to codify the subordinate status of women in Assyrian society. The Code of Assura can be studied in the context of other Near Eastern legal codes and gives historians a window onto the ways gender hierarchies were formalized in the ancient world.

An artifact from the Middle Assyrian Empire
(Wikimedia Commons)

Document Text

I.7. If a woman bring her hand against a man, they shall prosecute her; 30 manas of lead shall she pay, 20 blows shall they inflict on her.

I.8. If a woman in a quarrel injure the testicle of a man, one of her fingers they shall cut off. And if a physician bind it up and the other testicle which is beside it be infected thereby, or take harm; or in a quarrel she injure the other testicle, they shall destroy both of her eyes. . . .

I.13. If the wife of a man go out from her house and visit a man where he lives, and he have intercourse with her, knowing that she is a man's wife, the man and also the woman they shall put to death.

I.14. If a man have intercourse with the wife of a man either in an inn or on the highway, knowing that she is a man's wife, according as the man, whose wife she is, orders to be done, they shall do to the adulterer. If not knowing that she is a man's wife he rapes her, the adulterer goes free. The man shall prosecute his wife, doing to her as he likes.

I.15. If a man catch a man with his wife, both of them shall they put to death. If the husband of the woman put his wife to death, he shall also put the man to death. If he cut off the nose of his wife, he shall turn the man into a eunuch, and they shall disfigure the whole of his face.

I.16. If a man have relations with the wife of a man at her wish, there is no penalty for that man. The man shall lay upon the woman, his wife, the penalty he wishes. . . .

I.26. If a woman be dwelling in the house of her father, and her husband have died, any gift which her husband settled upon her—if there be any sons of her husband's, they shall receive it. If there be no sons of her husband's she receives it.

I.32. If a woman be dwelling in the house of father, but has been given to her husband, whether she has been taken to the house of her husband or not, all debts, misdemeanors, and crimes of her husband shall she bear as if she too committed them. Likewise if she be dwelling with her husband, all crimes of his shall she bear as well. . . .

I.37. If a man divorce his wife, if he wish, he may give her something; if he does not wish, he need not give her anything. Empty shall she go out.

I.40. If the wives of a man, or the daughters of a man go out into the street, their heads are to be veiled. The prostitute is not to be veiled. Maidservants are not to veil themselves. Veiled harlots and maidservants shall have their garments seized and 50 blows inflicted on them and bitumen poured on their heads. . . .

I.58. Unless it is forbidden in the tablets, a man may strike his wife, pull her hair, her ear he may bruise or pierce. He commits no misdeed thereby.

Glossary

bitumen: a type of asphalt

manas: plural of *mana*, also called *mina*; an ancient Near Eastern unit of weight, commonly used to describe coinage or currency

Short-Answer Questions

1. Describe three specific ways in which the excerpts from the Code of Assura display the subordinate status of women in Assyrian society.

2. Analyze how property relations between genders are formalized in the Code of Assura. In your analysis, cite specific words, phrases, and rules from the text.

3. Analyze the legal rules on veiling in Assyrian society, which are described in I.40. Why do you think women of different statuses were expected to dress in different ways? What do you think the function of this law was in the strictly hierarchical system established by the Assyrian rulers?

Sappho: Poems and Fragments

Author Sappho	**Significance** Among the first lyric poems in the Greek tradition to adopt the subjective experience of the poet as worthy of inspiration, focusing less on epic narratives and more on identity and personal emotions
Date c. 610 BCE–c. 570 BCE	
Document Type Poems, Plays, Fiction	

Overview

Despite her enduring fame, little is known for certain about Sappho and her life. A prolific ancient Greek lyrical poet, she was likely born around 630 BCE on the island of Lesbos to a wealthy family. The author of more than 10,000 lines of poetry, of which a mere 650 still survive, Sappho's works primarily deal with internal and deeply personal emotional experiences, including jealousy, lust, and love for men and women. Sappho was a popular and well-regarded poet in her time. She was included in the canon of the Nine Lyric Poets most highly esteemed and taught by scholars in the libraries and universities of Hellenistic Alexandria. Her works have been studied by contemporary poets, including Ezra Pound and other modernists, and her elliptical style and dreamy, picturesque imagery continue to inspire readers and writers today.

Sappho is now best known as a symbol of erotic love and desire between women. The modern English words *sapphic* and *lesbian* derive from her name and her home island, respectively. Sappho's sexuality, while the subject of much speculation, remains ambiguous. While the narrators of her poems often speak openly of infatuations, admiration, and love for various women and female deities, it remains unclear if these poems are meant to be read autobiographically. Sappho's poems contain few explicit descriptions of physical relations between women. Rather, most of her works describe love as an internal passion and sensual feeling, guided by the will of Aphrodite.

Sappho was the leader of a *thiasos*, a female community with a religious and educational function. The goal of the Greek *thiasos* was the preparation of young women for marriage. In her role as an educator, Sappho served as the community's leader and as an intermediary with the group's divinity, Aphrodite. The erotic content of Sappho's poetry can, in part, be attributed to the *thiasos*'s role in the initiation of young women into the arts of grace, elegance, seduction, and love.

Document Text

Fragment 31

That man seems to me to be equal to the gods
who is sitting opposite you
and hears you nearby
speaking sweetly

and laughing delightfully, which indeed
makes my heart flutter in my breast;
for when I look at you even for a short time,
it is no longer possible for me to speak

but it is as if my tongue is broken
and immediately a subtle fire has run over my
skin,
I cannot see anything with my eyes,
and my ears are buzzing

a cold sweat comes over me, trembling
seizes me all over, I am paler
than grass, and I seem nearly
to have died.

Ode to Aphrodite
Aphrodite, subtle of soul and deathless,
Daughter of God, weaver of wiles, I pray thee
Neither with care, dread Mistress, nor with
anguish,
Slay thou my spirit!

But in pity hasten, come now if ever
From afar of old when my voice implored thee,
Thou hast deigned to listen, leaving the golden
House of thy father

With thy chariot yoked; and with doves that drew
thee,
Fair and fleet around the dark earth from heaven,
Dipping vibrant wings down the azure distance,
Through the mid-ether;

Very swift they came; and thou, gracious Vision,
Leaned with face that smiled in immortal beauty,
Leaned to me and asked, "What misfortune
threatened?

Sapho depicted in* The Parnassus *by Raphael
(Vatican Museums)

Why I had called thee?"

"What my frenzied heart craved in utter yearning,
Whom its wild desire would persuade to passion?
What disdainful charms, madly worshipped,
slight thee?
Who wrongs thee, Sappho?"

"She that fain would fly, she shall quickly follow,
She that now rejects, yet with gifts shall woo thee,
She that heeds thee not, soon shall love to
madness,
Love thee, the loth one!"

Come to me now thus, Goddess, and release me
From distress and pain; and all my distracted
Heart would seek, do thou, once again fulfilling,
Still be my ally!

Passion
Now Love shakes my soul, a mighty

Wind from the high mountain falling
Full on the oaks of the forest;

Now, limb-relaxing, it masters
My life and implacable thrills me,
Rending with anguish and rapture.

Now my heart, paining my bosom,
Pants with desire as a mænad
Mad for the orgiac revel.

Now under my skin run subtle
Arrows of flame, and my body
Quivers with surge of emotion.

Now long importunate yearnings
Vanquish with surfeit my reason;
Fainting my senses forsake me.

Telesippa
Sleep thou in the bosom
Of thy tender girl friend,
Telesippa, gentle
Maiden from Miletus.
Like twin petals shyly

Closing to the darkness,
Dewy on your drooping
Lids shall fall her kisses.

While her arms enfold you,
On your drowsy senses
Shall her soft caresses
Seal delicious languor.

Warm from her desireful
Heart the flush of passion
On your cheek unconscious,
With her sighs shall deepen.

All the long sweet night-time,
Sleepless while you slumber,
She shall lie and quiver
With her love's mad longing.

Glossary

Aphrodite: the ancient Greek goddess of sexual love, eroticism, and beauty, identified with Venus by the Romans

mænad: a female follower of Dionysus, the god of wine, ritual ecstasy, and theater

Miletus: an ancient Greek city on the western coast of Anatolia

orgiac: relating to an orgy, a secret ceremonial rite held in honor of an ancient Greek or Roman deity

surfeit: excess

Telesippa: one of Sappho's companions

Short-Answer Questions

1. How does Sappho describe love in her poetry? How do you think the poet defined love and conceptualized this emotion? As you write your response, especially consider the poems "Passion" and "Telesippa."

2. Describe the different ways that Sappho describes love in her poetry. Consider the types of love presented in the poems above, as well as the different objects of affection she describes. As you write your response, it may be useful to compare and contrast love as it is shown in "Ode to Aphrodite" and Sappho's other works.

3. Analyze the use of imagery in the poems presented here. Why do you think readers and audiences have found her work so vivid and powerful?

Herodotus:
The History of the Persian Wars

Author
Herodotus

Date
c. 430 BCE

Document Type
Essays, Reports, Manifestos

Significance
Described the events and key figures in the ancient Greco-Persian Wars and compared the Greek and Persian cultures, including the status of women in each

---

Overview

Herodotus was a Greek historian who lived from approximately 484 to 420 BCE. Much of his life was overshadowed by the Greco-Persian Wars of approximately 499–449 BCE, a series of bitter conflicts pitting the massive Persian Empire against the disunited and fractious Greek city-states. Herodotus examined these conflicts using a unique approach. Earlier Greek historians narrated events from an unscientific perspective, citing the gods as the primary agents of historical development. Herodotus, in contrast, approached the Greco-Persian Wars from a rationalist perspective, attributing the outcome of events to human agency.

Herodotus's project was complicated by the vast scope and intricacy of his subject matter. The Greco-Persian Wars were collectively made up of a series of conflicts between the city-states of classical Greece and Persia's Achaemenid Empire, which ruled most of the Near East. The struggle between these two cultures lasted for nearly half a century. At the start of the war, the Persians seemed like the more dominant power, with overwhelming advantages in resources and manpower. The Greeks, however, repeatedly defeated the Persians on land and at sea. Herodotus's account of the conflict sets out to explain the unexpected triumph of the Greeks. Herodotus's *Histories* consists of nine separate volumes, the first four of which explore the culture, history, and social structure of the Persian Empire. Herodotus argued that the social structure of the Persian Empire contributed to its defeat.

Herodotus's writings primarily deal with military confrontations, but he also compared the cultures of the Greeks and Persians. Accordingly, the *Histories* contains a great deal of information about the status of women in these two very different cultures. Women in classical

Greece were subordinate to men and largely restricted in their movements and lives. They did not hold political power and were confined to domestic roles. In contrast, women in Achaemenid Persia enjoyed more freedom, power, and respect. They held key roles in society and politics. In the *Histories*, Persian women are shown commanding kingdoms and leading armies against the Greeks. Herodotus's narrative gives historians a unique vantage point on gender dynamics in the classical Mediterranean.

Document Text

I.181: The outer wall is the main defense of the city [of Babylon]. . . . On the topmost tower there is a spacious temple, and inside the temple stands a couch of unusual size, richly adorned, with a golden table by its side. There is no statue of any kind set up in the place, nor is the chamber occupied of nights by any one but a single native woman, who, as the Chaldaeans, the priests of this god, affirm, is chosen for himself by the deity out of all the women of the land. . . .

I.184: Many sovereigns have ruled over this city of Babylon, and lent their aid to the building of its walls and the adornment of its temples, of whom I shall make mention in my Assyrian history. Among them two were women. Of these, the earlier, called Semiramis, held the throne five generations before the later princess. She raised certain embankments well worthy of inspection, in the plain near Babylon, to control the river, which, till then, used to overflow, and flood the whole country round about.

I.185: The later of the two queens, whose name was Nitocris, a wiser princess than her predecessor, not only left behind her, as memorials of her occupancy of the throne, the works which I shall presently describe, but also, observing the great power and restless enterprise of the Medes, who had taken so large a number of cities, and among them Nineveh, and expecting to be attacked in her turn, made all possible exertions to increase the defenses of her empire. . . .

I.196: Of their customs . . . the following . . . is the wisest in my judgment. Once a year in each village the maidens of age to marry were collected all together into one place; while the men stood round them in a circle. Then a herald called up

A marble bust of Herodotus
(Metropolitan Museum of Art)

the damsels one by one, and offered them for sale. He began with the most beautiful. When she was sold for no small sum of money, he offered for sale the one who came next to her in beauty. All of them were sold to be wives. The richest of the Babylonians who wished to wed bid against each other for the loveliest maidens, while the humbler wife-seekers, who were indifferent about beauty, took the more homely damsels with marriage-portions. For the custom was that when the herald had gone through the whole number of the beautiful damsels, he should then call up the ugliest—a

---

cripple, if there chanced to be one—and offer her to the men, asking who would agree to take her with the smallest marriage-portion. And the man who offered to take the smallest sum had her assigned to him.

I.199: The Babylonians have one most shameful custom. Every woman born in the country must once in her life go and sit down in the precinct of Venus [Ishtar], and there consort with a stranger.

Many of the wealthier sort, who are too proud to mix with the others, drive in covered carriages to the precinct, followed by a goodly train of attendants, and there take their station. But the larger number seat themselves within the holy enclosure with wreaths of string about their heads—and here there is always a great crowd, some coming and others going; lines of cord mark out paths in all directions the women, and the strangers pass along them to make their choice.

Glossary

Chaldaeans: a Semitic-speaking nomadic group who briefly ruled Babylon and hailed from Chaldea, a small region that existed between the tenth and early ninth centuries BCE, which was gradually absorbed into Babylonian culture and society

Nitocris: Nitocris of Babylon (c. 550 BCE), a queen of Babylon described by Herodotus in his *Histories*

Semiramis: a legendary queen of Assyria and founder of the city of Babylon; likely based on the queen regent of the Assyrian Empire Sammu-Ramat (r. 811–806 BCE); referenced in Greek, Armenian, and Jewish historical sources, although historians know little about her life and accomplishments

Short-Answer Questions

1. Describe the political status and role of women in Babylonian society, as explored by Herodotus in the excerpts above.

2. Analyze the social and religious status of women in Babylonian society, as described by Herodotus. In your response, compare the social and religious status of women with their clear political power. How do you think historians can reconcile these differences?

3. Herodotus was a Greek historian writing about the political and social customs of Near Eastern societies. What might have been his motivations for writing, and how might those motivations have influenced the accuracy of his historical writings?

Ban Zhao: *Lessons for a Woman*

Author Ban Zhao	**Significance** A Han Dynasty document that reinforced traditional Confucian ideals of filial piety and male-dominated hierarchy
Date c. 116 CE	
Document Type Essays, Reports, Manifestos	

Overview

Ban Zhao (45 CE–c. 116 CE), the daughter of one famous Chinese historian (Ban Biao) and the sister of another (Ban Gu), was the first known female Chinese historian. During the Han Dynasty, she wrote *Lessons for a Woman*, ostensibly to outline for her own daughters the position and duties of women in society. *Lessons for a Woman* would become a standard educational text in China for many centuries.

Ban Zhao instructs women to be humble in all their dealings with others, connecting this humility to the "traditional ceremonial rites and regulations" of Confucian teaching. Women are to put others' needs above their own and work tirelessly in their homes. A woman, according to Ban Zhao, must act with moral uprightness not only for her own sake but to serve her husband effectively. Ban Zhao's discussion of marriage and the relationship between husband and wife is heavily influenced by traditional Chinese values, with references to yin and yang as well as the writings of Confucian scholars. In her view, the complementary natures of women and men are innate. She considers that the natural role of husbands is to control their wives. The wives' role is to serve their husbands. Maintaining these roles, Ban Zhao asserts, will lead to balance and harmony in marriage.

But Ban Zhao seems not to have followed her own instructions. Her marriage ended with her husband's death when she was still quite young, and she devoted the rest of her life to scholarship, becoming an accomplished astronomer and mathematician. She also completed her brother's most famous work, the *History of the Han*. During much of her lifetime, she worked at the imperial court of the Han Dynasty as an advisor, librarian, and tutor.

Ban Zhao
(Shangguan Zhou)

Document Text

I, the unworthy writer, am unsophisticated, unenlightened, and by nature unintelligent, but I am fortunate both to have received not a little favor from my scholarly Father, and to have had a cultured mother and instructresses upon whom to rely for a literary education as well as for training in good manners. More than forty years have passed since at the age of fourteen I took up the dustpan and the broom in the Cao family. During this time with trembling heart I feared constantly that I might disgrace my parents and that I might multiply difficulties for both the women and the men of my husband's family. Day and night I was distressed in heart, but I labored without confessing weariness. Now and hereafter, however, I know how to escape from such fears.

Being careless, and by nature stupid, I taught and trained my children without system. Consequently I fear that my son Gu may bring disgrace upon the Imperial Dynasty by whose Holy Grace he has unprecedentedly received the extraordinary privilege of wearing the Gold and the Purple, a privilege for the attainment of which by my son, I a humble subject never even hoped. Nevertheless, now that he is a man and able to plan his own life, I need not again have concern for him. But I do grieve that you, my daughters, just now at the age for marriage, have not at this time had gradual training and advice; that you still have not learned the proper customs for married women. . . .

From this time on every one of you strive to practice these lessons.

Humility

On the third day after the birth of a girl the ancients observed three customs: first to place the baby below the bed; second to give her a potsherd with which to play; and third to announce her birth to her ancestors by an offering. Now to lay the baby below the bed plainly indicated that she is lowly and weak, and should regard it as her primary duty to humble herself before others. To give her potsherds with which to play indubitably signified that she should practice labor and consider it her primary duty to be industrious. To announce her birth before her ancestors clearly meant that she ought to esteem as her primary duty the continuation of the observance of worship in the home. . . .

No woman who observes these three fundamentals of life has ever had a bad reputation or has fallen into disgrace. If a woman fail to observe them, how can her name be honored; how can she but bring disgrace upon herself?

Husband and Wife

The Way of husband and wife is intimately connected with yin and yang and relates the individual to gods and ancestors. Truly it is the great principle of Heaven and Earth, and the great basis of human relationships. Therefore the *Rites* honor union of man and woman; and in the *Book of Poetry* the "First Ode" manifests the principle of marriage. For these reasons the relationship cannot but be an important one.

If a husband be unworthy, then he possesses nothing by which to control his wife. If a wife be unworthy, then she possesses nothing with which to serve her husband. If a husband does not control his wife, then the rules of conduct manifesting his authority are abandoned and broken. If a wife does not serve her husband, then the proper relationship between men and women and the natural order of things are neglected and destroyed. As a matter of fact the purpose of these two [the controlling of women by men, and the serving of men by women] is the same. . . .

Yet only to teach men and not to teach women—is that not ignoring the essential relation between them? . . .

Respect and Caution

. . . Now for self-culture nothing equals respect for others. To counteract firmness nothing equals com-

pliance. Consequently it can be said that the Way of respect and acquiescence is woman's most important principle of conduct. So respect may be defined as nothing other than holding on to that which is permanent; and acquiescence nothing other than being liberal and generous. Those who are steadfast in devotion know that they should stay in their proper places; those who are liberal and generous esteem others, and honor and serve them.

If husband and wife have the habit of staying together, never leaving one another, and following each other around within the limited space of their own rooms, then they will lust after and take liberties with one another. From such action improper language will arise between the two. This kind of discussion may lead to licentiousness. But of licentiousness will be born a heart of disrespect to the husband. Such a result comes from not knowing that one should stay in one's proper place. . . .

If wives suppress not contempt for husbands, then it follows that such wives rebuke and scold their husbands. If husbands stop not short of anger, then they are certain to beat their wives. The correct relationship between husband and wife is based upon harmony and intimacy, and conjugal love is grounded in proper union. Should actual blows be dealt, how could matrimonial relationship be preserved? Should sharp words be spoken, how could conjugal love exist? If love and proper relationship both be destroyed, then husband and wife are divided.

Womanly Qualifications

A woman ought to have four qualifications: (1) womanly virtue; (2) womanly words; (3) womanly bearing; and (4) womanly work. . . .

These four qualifications characterize the greatest virtue of a woman. No woman can afford to be without them. In fact they are very easy to possess if a woman only treasure them in her heart. The ancients had a saying: "Is love afar off? If I desire love, then love is at hand!" So can it be said of these qualifications. . . .

Glossary

Book of Poetry: also known as the *Book of Odes* or the *Classic of Poetry*, a collection of 305 classic poems composed and collected in ancient China early in the first millennium BCE; held to have been originally assembled by Confucius himself and, as a result, considered one of the "five classics" of Confucianism

Cao family: the family of Ban Zhao's husband, Cao Shishu

potsherd: a piece of broken pottery, here used as a metaphor for labor, in particular the type of labor a little girl might have to perform in her life

Rites: considered one of the key texts of Confucianism, consisting of descriptions and definitions of traditional ceremonies, some of them ascribed to the Zhou Dynasty (c. 1046–256 BCE)

yin and yang: the two elements out of which the universe was formed: yin, the receptive element, usually associated with femininity, and yang, the active element, usually associated with masculinity

Short-Answer Questions

1. Considering all her accomplishments, why would Ban Zhao refer to herself as "unsophisticated, unenlightened, and by nature unintelligent"?

2. If Ban Zhao debases herself, does she do the same with her son Gu? Please offer examples.

3. Ban Zhao calls for balance in relations between husbands and wives. How does she think that balance should be expressed?

Plutarch: *Moralia:* "On the Bravery of Women"

Author Plutarch	**Significance** Suggested a diversity of gender attitudes in the Greco-Roman world
Date c. 100 CE	
Document Type Essays, Reports, Manifestos	

Overview

Plutarch's *Moralia* is a collection of extended essays and dialogues written by the ancient Greek philosopher. Plutarch was born in Chaeronea in central Greece, probably around 50 CE. *Moralia* is a wide-ranging text that covers a variety of topics, including ethics, morality, leadership, education, and virtue. Throughout the text, Plutarch emphasizes the need for an individual to develop a sense of virtue by honing qualities like honesty, justice, temperance, courage, and wisdom. Like Aristotle and other Greek philosophers, he encourages his readers to seek moral excellence and strive for a life of self-improvement, learning, and introspection. While *Moralia* is little read today, Plutarch's tracts can serve as a guide for living a simple, virtuous, and fulfilling life. Greek and Roman philosophers focused on practical ethical matters. As a result, their works, though written in antiquity, remain relevant to contemporary readers and audiences.

Women in the Greek world were considered subordinate to men. Tradition and custom positioned men as superior to women and enforced a strictly misogynistic and hierarchical society. However, several ancient Greek philosophers and commentators disagreed with these social customs and argued that women deserved equal rights and access to education. Plutarch, in his *Moralia*, made the then-radical argument that women's virtues are the same as men's. Plutarch's essays in *Moralia* were composed to his friend Clea, an important priestess at the Greek ceremonial center of Delphi. In his essays, Plutarch described women as active, resourceful, virtuous, and brave. Plutarch's writings demonstrate the complexity of gender relations in the ancient world and are suggestive of the ways in which Greek philosophical and literary conventions could accommodate divergent perspectives on the status of women.

A page from **Moralia**
(Biblioteca Europea di Informazione e Cultura)

Document Text

Regarding the virtues of women, Clea, I do not hold the same opinion as Thucydides. For he declares that the best woman is she about whom there is the least talk among persons outside regarding either censure or commendation, feeling that the name of the good woman, like her person, ought to be shut up indoors and never go out. . . .

And actually it is not possible to learn better the similarity and the difference between the virtues of men and of women from any other source than by putting lives beside lives and actions beside actions, like great works of art. . . .

The Trojan Women

Most of those that escaped from Troy at the time of its capture had to weather a storm, and, because of their inexperience in navigation and ignorance of the sea, were driven upon the shores of Italy, and, in the neighbourhood of the river Tiber, they barely escaped by running in, under compulsion, where there were anchorages and havens. While the men were wandering about the country, in search of information, it suddenly occurred to the women to reflect that for a happy and successful people any sort of a settled habitation on land is better than all wandering and voyaging. . . . Thereupon, becoming of one mind, they burned the ships, one woman, Roma, taking the lead. . . .

The Trojans, apparently realizing the inevitable necessity, and after having also some experience with the native inhabitants, who received them kindly and humanely, came to be content with what had been done by the women. . . .

The Women of Argos

Of all the deeds performed by women for the community none is more famous than the struggle against Cleomenes for Argos, which the women carried out at the instigation of Telesilla the poetess. She, as they say, was the daughter of a famous house but sickly in body, and so she sent to the god to ask about health; and when an oracle was given her to cultivate the Muses, she followed the god's advice, and by devoting herself to poetry and music she was quickly relieved of her trouble, and was greatly admired by the women for her poetic art.

But when Cleomenes, king of the Spartans, having slain many Argives . . . proceeded against the city, an impulsive daring, divinely inspired, came to the younger women to try, for their country's sake, to hold off the enemy. Under the lead of Telesilla they took up arms, and, taking their stand by the battlements, manned the walls all round, so that the enemy were amazed. The result was that Cleomenes they repulsed with great loss. . . . In this way the city was saved. The women who fell in the battle they buried close by the Argive Road, and to the survivors they granted the privilege of erecting a statue of Ares as a memorial of their surpassing valour. . . .

The Celtic Women

Before the Celts crossed over the Alps and settled in that part of Italy which is now their home, a dire and persistent factional discord broke out among them which went on and on to the point of civil war. The women, however, put themselves between the armed forces, and, taking up the controversies, arbitrated and decided them with such irreproachable fairness that a wondrous friendship of all towards all was brought about between both States and families. As the result of this they continued to consult with the women in regard to war and peace, and to decide through them any disputed matters in their relations with their allies.

Glossary

Ares: one of the twelve great Olympian gods, and the Greek god of war

Argos: a large city-state in ancient Greece, and one of the oldest continuously inhabited cities in the world

Celts: tribal groups living in parts of western and central Europe in the Late Bronze Age and through the Iron Age (c. 700 BCE to c. 400 CE); a migratory culture that established a presence across the Mediterranean world, from present-day Portugal to Turkey, and shared a language as well as similar styles of art, warfare, religious, and other cultural practices

Cleomenes: Cleomenes I, the Agiad King of Sparta from c. 524 to c. 490 BCE and a significant figure in the development of Sparta into a powerful Greek city-state

the Muses: in ancient Greek religion and mythology, the inspirational goddesses of literature, science, and the arts

Thucydides: a famous Athenian historian and general whose *History of the Peloponnesian War* recounts the fifth-century BCE war between Sparta and Athens until the year 411 BCE

Tiber: a river in Italy where, according to myths, the city of Rome was founded

Troy: an ancient city located in present-day Turkey, famed primarily as the setting of the Trojan War, which in Greek mythic history was a long struggle waged by the Greeks against the city of Troy

Short-Answer Questions

1. Describe the positive qualities and virtues displayed by women in the excerpts from Plutarch's *Moralia*. In your response, cite specific phrases and examples from Plutarch's writings.

2. Explain how Plutarch contrasts the qualities of men and women in these excerpts.

3. Analyze the significance of these excerpts. How do they reveal complicated and nuanced attitudes toward gender in the male-dominated Greco-Roman world?

Soranus: *Gynaecology*

Author
Soranus

Date
Second Century CE

Document Type
Essays, Reports, Manifestos

Significance
Provided one of the few clinical and comprehensive textbooks on gynecological and obstetrics issues in the Greco-Roman world

---

Overview

Soranus of Ephesus was a Greek physician who lived during the reigns of the Roman emperors Trajan and Hadrian (98–138 CE). Little is known about his life, and what is known comes primarily from the writings of his students and notable patients, including the Roman emperor Marcus Aurelius. He practiced in Alexandria and Rome, the wealthiest and most important urban centers in the Roman world, and was an eminent representative of the so-called methodical school of medicine, a medical paradigm that prioritized simple rules of diagnostics and asserted that all diseases were the result of an adverse condition with an individual's "internal pores."

Famed as an eminent and skilled diagnostician and gynecologist, he wrote extensively during his lifetime on a variety of medical topics, addressing the rules of health and the pathology of internal diseases. Soranus's most significant publications addressed issues in childbearing,

obstetrics, feminine hygiene, and pregnancy. His writings established medical opinion concerning women's health, pregnancy, and prenatal and infant care for nearly 1,500 years. His writings offer a clinical, dispassionate, and neutral take on women's health issues. In his most important treatise, *Gynaecology*, he explored the necessary qualities of a midwife, described gynecological physiology and feminine hygiene, explored issues related to menstruation and contraception, and provided clinical commentary on pregnancy and abortion. In this wide-ranging and comprehensive work, Soranus made the then-radical argument that women experienced different conditions from men. Soranus was one of the first clinicians to concede that women could experience diseases that men could not and that they needed specialized medical care that was attuned to their needs and concerns. In many ways, Soranus's works represent the historical tendency, during the classical era, for gynecology and

---

obstetrics to transition away from being primarily the concern of midwives to becoming a formalized study of professional physicians. In addition, Soranus's writings and practices became standardized elements of Western medical practice and training, and his concepts persisted in medical discourse for centuries after the splintering of the Roman world during the fifth century CE.

Document Text
Who Are the Best Midwives?

It is necessary to tell what makes the best midwives so that on the one hand the best may recognize themselves, on the other hand, beginners may look upon them as models and the public in time of need may know who to summon. Now, generally speaking, we call a midwife faultless if she merely carries out her medical tasks, whereas we call her the best midwife if she goes further and in addition to her management of cases is well versed in theory. And more particularly we call a person the best midwife if she is trained in all branches of therapy (for some cases must be treated by diet, others by surgery, while still others must be cured by drugs). If she is moreover able to prescribe hygienic regulations for her patients to observe the general and individual features of the case and from this to find out what is expedient, not from the causes or from the repeated observations of what usually occurs or something of the kind. Now, to go into detail, she will not change her methods when the symptoms change but will give her advice in accordance with the course of the disease. She will be unperturbed, unafraid in danger, able to clearly state the reasons for her measures, she will bring reassurance to her patients and be sympathetic. And it is not absolutely essential for her to have borne children as some people contend in order that she may sympathize with the mother because of her experience with pain. . . . She must be robust on account of her duties but not necessarily young. . . . She will be well disciplined and always sober since it is uncertain when she may be summoned to those in danger. . . .

Whether Conception Is Healthful

Some people believe pregnancy to be healthful because every natural act is useful and pregnancy too is a natural action. Second, because some women menstruating with difficulty and suffering uterine pressure have been freed of their troubles after pregnancy. Opposed to such arguments one must say that menstruation too is a natural act but not a healthful one. . . . Indeed, both menstruation and pregnancy are useful for the propagation of men but certainly not beneficial for the child bearer. . . . And according to what has been laid down previously one has to point out that many inconveniences beset the pregnant woman who is heavily burdened and suffers. . . .

How to Recognize a Newborn That Is Worth Rearing

Now that the midwife having received the newborn should first put it upon the earth having examined beforehand whether the infant is male or female and should make an announcement by signs as is the custom of women. She should also consider whether it is worth rearing or not. And the infant which is suited by nature for rearing will be distinguished by the fact that its mother has spent the period of pregnancy in good health, for conditions which require medical care, especially those of the body, also harm the fetus and enfeeble the foundations of its life. Second, by the fact that it has been born at the due time, best at the end of the nine months and if it so happens later, but also after only seven months. Furthermore, by the fact that when put on the earth it immediately cries with proper vigor. . . . And by conditions contrary to those mentioned, the infant not worth rearing is recognized. . . .

Whether Women Have Conditions Peculiarly Their Own . . .

Now, a disagreement has arisen. Some assume that there are special diseases of women. . . . Others, however, assume that there are no special diseases of women. . . .

In defense of the existence of diseases peculiar to women, arguments such as the following are advanced: we call some women's physicians because they treat the conditions of women. And the public is wont to call in midwives in cases of sickness when the women suffer something peculiar which they do not have in common with men. Furthermore, the female is by nature different from the male, so much so that Aristotle and Zenon the Epicurean say that the female is imperfect, the male, however, perfect. Now, that which is different in its whole nature will also be subject to its own diseases. . . .

Now, we say that there exist natural conditions in women peculiarly their own (as conception, parturition, and lactation, if one wishes to call these conditions) whereas conditions contrary to nature are not generally different but only in a specific and particular way. For in regard to generic differences the female has her illness in common with the male, she suffers from constriction or from flux either acutely or chronically and she is subject to the same seasonal differences, to gradations of disease, to lack of strength, and to the different foreign bodies, sores, and injuries. Only as far as particulars and specific variations are concerned does the female show conditions peculiarly her own. . . . Therefore, she is subject to treatment generally the same. . . .

Glossary

Aristotle: an ancient Greek philosopher whose writings cover a broad range of subjects spanning the natural sciences, philosophy, linguistics, economics, politics, psychology, and the arts

constriction or flux: a reference to the theory promoted by so-called methodist physicians, including Soranus, that diseases could be classified as either flux-related, constriction-related, or a combination of both (and accordingly, treatments focused on either stopping the flux or releasing the constriction)

midwife: a healthcare provider who deals with pregnancy, childbirth, newborn care, and postpartum health; common in the classical world, where most issues relating to women's healthcare were addressed by midwives rather than by professional physicians

parturition: the process of giving birth

Zenon the Epicurean: also called Zeno of Sidon, a Greek Epicurean philosopher whose writings have not survived from antiquity

Short-Answer Questions

1. Describe Soranus's tone in the excerpts provided here, and explain what his text reveals about his attitudes toward women and pregnancy.

2. In the passage labeled "Whether Conception Is Healthful," which of Soranus's assertions might be considered surprising, given the time in which he was writing?

3. What does the excerpt titled "How to Recognize a Newborn That Is Worth Rearing" reveal about attitudes toward infancy and children in the classical world? In your response, consider Soranus's response and its implications for attitudes in antiquity.

Juvenal: *The Satires*

Author Juvenal **Date** c. 115 CE **Document Type** Poems, Plays, Fiction	**Significance** Offered a scathing and caustic critique of the vices, follies, and moral failings of Roman imperial society while also demonstrating the misogynistic attitudes prevalent among Romans

Overview

Juvenal was an influential Roman poet popular in the first decades of the Roman Empire, roughly from the late first until the early second centuries CE. Historians know little about his early life, though he was likely the son or adopted son of a wealthy Roman and was primarily active during the reigns of the emperors Trajan and Hadrian. Juvenal was predominantly a satirist, an artist who employed humor, irony, and exaggeration to ridicule social institutions and human failings. His writings were popular during his time and were intended for a well-educated and sophisticated audience.

He is now best known for his caustic collection of satirical poems, titled simply *The Satires*. Consisting of sixteen poems, these works were an unsparing indictment of the vices, greed, corruption, and degradation Juvenal saw in Roman imperial society. Juvenal's satirical poems address a range of topics, providing later readers and historians with an insight into how Romans commented on their own social institutions. Juvenal's works explore the decadence of the Roman political elite, the decline of traditional morality, and the moral laxity of the upper classes. The poems reveal Juvenal to be a conservative commentator, particularly in his attitudes on gender and sexuality. In his poems, Juvenal condemns both men and women and highlights the promiscuity, infidelity, and vices of Roman culture.

Juvenal's attitudes on women have been widely addressed in scholarly literature. His *Satire VI*, his most famous work, was well regarded from late antiquity until the early modern era. The text, like others in Juvenal's canon, was used to support a variety of misogynistic attitudes and practices. While Juvenal's works are little read now, they offer a unique source on Roman attitudes about women and sexuality.

A nineteenth-century representation of Juvenal
(S. H. Gimber)

Document Text
Satire VI: 25–59
"You're Mad to Marry!"

Are you, in this day and age, ready for an agreement,

A contract, the wedding vows, having your hair done

By a master-barber, your finger already wearing the pledge?

Postumus, you were sane once. Are you really taking a wife?

Which Tisiphone is it, with her snakes, driving you mad?

You surely don't have to endure it, with so much rope about,

Those vertiginous windows open, the Aemilian bridge at hand?

If none of these multiple exits please you,

wouldn't a boyfriend

Suit you better, one who would share your bed, a boyfriend

Who wouldn't quarrel all night; wouldn't demand from you

As he lies there, little gifts; and wouldn't complain that your

Body was idle, that you weren't breathing hard, as ordered.

Satire VI: 136–160
"The Rich and Beautiful"

"Then why does Caesennia's husband swear she's the perfect wife?"

She brought him ten thousand in gold, enough to call her chaste.

He's not been hit by Venus's arrows, or scorched by her torch:

It's the money he's aflame with, her dowry launched the darts.

Her freedom's bought. She can flirt, wave her love-letters in his

Face: she's a single woman still: a rich man marries for greed. . . .

Satire VI: 200–230
"The Way They Lord It over You!"

If you're not going to love the woman betrothed and joined

To you by lawful contract, there'd appear to be no reason for

Getting married, nor for wasting time on a feast with its cakes

For bloated guests at the end, or for that first night gift. . . .

But if you're simply uxorious, if your heart's given to her alone,

Then bow your head, prepare to place your neck under the yoke.

You'll not find any woman who'll spare a man who loves her.

Though she's on fire, she'll still love to torture and fleece him;

So much the less suitable as wife, then, for a man who wishes
To be a good and desirable husband. And you'll never be able
To send a gift if your bride objects, you'll never be able to sell
A thing if she happens to disagree, nor buy one if she says no. . . .

Satire VI: 286–313
"What Brought All This About?"

What brought this monstrous behaviour about, what's its source
You ask? Their lowly status used to keep Latin women chaste,
Hard work kept the corruption of vice from their humble roofs,
And lack of rest, and their hands, then, were chafed and hardened
From handling Tuscan fleeces, when Hannibal neared Rome,
When their husbands manned the towers at the Colline Gate.
Now we suffer the ills of a long peace. Worse for us than war
This luxury's stifling us, taking its revenge for an empire won. . . .

Glossary

Aemilian bridge: a famous bridge in Rome, constructed between 179 and 151 BCE

Caesennia: a Roman wife, used by Juvenal to illustrate his arguments about the relationship between greed and marriage

Colline Gate: a landmark in ancient Rome, supposed to have been built by Servius Tullius, semi-legendary king of Rome from 578 to 535 BCE

Hannibal: a Carthaginian general who commanded the forces of Carthage against the Roman Republic during the Second Punic War, and whose numerous victories over the Romans nearly resulted in Rome's defeat

Postumus: the addressee of Juvenal's poem, who has seemingly ignored Juvenal's advice to avoid marriage

Tisiphone: the Greek and Roman goddess of vengeance, and one of the three Greek Furies who, with her sisters, Alecto and Megaera, punished murder

Tuscan fleece: in Roman tradition, the rough, scratchy fleece of Tuscany (a region in central Italy) associated with frugality and hardiness

uxorious: displaying an excessive fondness for one's wife

Venus: a Roman goddess, identified with the Greek Aphrodite, with powers over love, beauty, desire, sex, fertility, prosperity, and victory

Short-Answer Questions

1. In the excerpt from Juvenal's "You're Mad to Marry," what options does Juvenal present to the hypothetical Roman male?

2. In the excerpts presented here, how does Juvenal connect marriage, lust, and materialism? What do you think was his purpose in advancing these arguments?

3. Authors and historians frequently cite Juvenal as a uniquely misogynistic author. Analyze the range of prejudices he displays in these excerpts. In your response, explain some of the various ways Juvenal's writing displays an ingrained hostility toward women. In addition, explain how studying Juvenal's work can advance historians' understanding of Roman society.

Vibia Perpetua:
The Passion of Saints Perpetua and Felicity

Author	Significance
Vibia Perpetua	Martyrdom account, from one of the first Christian female writers, of two women imprisoned in Carthage, demonstrating the significance of women in the evolution of Christianity
Date	
c. 202 CE	
Document Type	
Essays, Reports, Manifestos	

Overview

Christianity developed during the early years of the Roman Empire, when the empire was at the height of its political, economic, and military power. Most of those who lived within the empire's borders were excluded from accessing its enormous wealth and prosperity. Jesus Christ taught and attracted followers in the province of Judaea, then a provincial backwater of the empire. His teachings appealed to the disaffected and the marginalized. He was executed by Roman authorities in Jerusalem, signaling the empire's virulent hostility toward the new Christian religion. Despite Christ's execution, his disciples spread the new religion throughout the heavily populated cities of the Roman Empire. The religion appealed to several disparate communities but was particularly popular among enslaved peoples, women, and common laborers.

The Roman Empire violently persecuted Christians in the centuries after Christ's death, but eventually Roman imperial policy toward the new religion shifted. When emperor Constantine converted to Christianity, he signaled the end of the official persecution of Christians in the Roman Empire. His successors alternately tolerated and embraced Christianity, and the religion's popularity grew quickly. In 380 CE, Emperor Theodosius I made Christianity the official state religion of the Roman Empire. Eventually, the empire's institutions and those of the nascent Christian Church became inseparable, and Christianity became one of the foundational elements of late Roman imperial culture.

The Passion of Saints Perpetua and Felicity (also called *The Martyrdom of Saints Perpetua and Felicitas*) is the prison diary of Vibia Perpetua, a young woman and Christian convert martyred in the Roman city of Carthage in 202 or 203 CE. Vibia Perpetua was a recently married, well-educated young noblewoman, and a mother. She was imprisoned for her Christian faith along with Felicity, a pregnant enslaved woman. As narrated in *The Passion of Saints Perpetua and Felicity*, the two women were arrested and executed at the military games staged to celebrate the birthday of Emperor Septimius Severus. The women were subsequently commemorated and venerated by the early Christian Church. Their deaths illustrate the ways in which the early Christian faith spread across classes in the Roman Empire, as well as the resolution of the early Christians. In addition, their narrative represents the ways in which women, who were subordinate to men in the patriarchal Roman society, could gain influence through religion and spirituality.

A depiction of the martyrdom of Perpetua and Felicitas (Wikimedia Commons)

Document Text

While we were still under arrest . . . my father out of love for me was trying to persuade me and shake my resolution. "Father," said I, "do you see this vase here, for example, or waterpot or whatever?"

"Yes, I do," said he.

And I told him: "Could it be called by any other name than what it is?"

And he said: "No."

"Well, so too I cannot be called anything other than what I am, a Christian."

At this my father was so angered by the word "Christian" that he moved towards me as though he would pluck my eyes out. But he left it at that and departed, vanquished along with his diabolical arguments. . . .

One day while we were eating breakfast we were suddenly hurried off for a hearing. We arrived at the forum, and straight away the story went about the neighbourhood near the forum and a huge crowd gathered. We walked up to the prisoner's dock. All the others when questioned admitted their guilt. Then, when it came my turn, my father appeared with my son, dragged me from the step, and said: "Perform the sacrifice—have pity on your baby!"

Hilarianus the governor, who had received his judicial powers as the successor of the late proconsul Minucius Timinianus, said to me: "Have pity on your father's grey head; have pity on your infant son. Offer the sacrifice for the welfare of the emperors."

"I will not," I retorted.

"Are you a Christian?" said Hilarianus.

And I said: "Yes, I am."

When my father persisted in trying to dissuade me, Hilarianus ordered him to be thrown to the ground and beaten with a rod. I felt sorry for father, just as if I myself had been beaten. I felt sorry for his pathetic old age. . . .

[Here the editor/narrator begins to relate the story] . . .

On the day before, when they had their last meal, which is called the free banquet, they celebrated not a banquet but rather a love feast. They spoke to the mob with the same steadfastness, warned them of God's judgement, stressing the joy they would have in their suffering, and ridiculing the curiosity of those that came to see them. . . .

The day of their victory dawned, and they marched from the prison to the amphitheatre joyfully as though they were going to heaven, with calm faces, trembling, if at all, with joy rather than fear. Perpetua went along with shining countenance and calm step, as the beloved of God, as a wife of Christ, putting down everyone's stare by her own intense gaze. . . .

And so the martyrs got up and went to the spot of their own accord as the people wanted them to, and kissing one another they sealed their martyrdom with the ritual kiss of peace.

Glossary

Hilarianus: Hilarianus of Carthage, a Roman proconsul (governor) of Carthage around the year 203 CE, responsible for the sentencing and execution of Vibia Perpetua, a Christian convert who was killed for her beliefs in 203 CE

love feast: a simple meal shared among Christians, similar to the ritual meal that became known as the Lord's Supper

passion: suffering; martyrdom

Short-Answer Questions

1. Describe the character of Vibia Perpetua, explaining what traits she displays in the excerpted text.

2. Analyze how Perpetua and Felicity's steadfastness and calm might have affected Roman spectators and audiences. How might displays of these traits have benefited the early Christian faith?

3. The beginning and ending of *The Passion of Saints Perpetua and Felicity* is related by an editor and narrator whose identity remains uncertain. How does this complicate our use of this document as a primary source of information? How might the editor's perspective and intent influence the neutrality and usefulness of this source?

St. Jerome: Letter CVII to Laeta

Author	Significance
St. Jerome	Provided a guide for the education of devout religious girls in the waning years of the Roman Empire, when Christianity was expanding and becoming the established cultural framework for western Europe and the Mediterranean world
Date	
403 CE	
Document Type	
Letters/Correspondence	

Overview

St. Jerome was a church father, biblical translator, and prolific writer. His Latin commentaries, correspondences, and theological tracts have been widely published, and he is regarded as one of the most learned and knowledgeable of early Christian authors. Born in Stridon, Dalmatia, in the middle of the fourth century CE, Jerome was educated primarily in Rome, where he was baptized when he was around twenty years old. An ascetic by nature, he spent two decades traveling and living as a hermit, primarily in Chalcis and Antioch. He studied biblical texts extensively and translated works by notable theologians, including Origen and Eusebius. He eventually returned to Rome, but his prickly personality, combative and undiplomatic temperament, and tendency to engage in heated theological conflicts with his peers forced him to enter self-exile in the Holy Land. He traveled to Bethlehem late in his life, dying there in 420 CE. A formidable biblical scholar, Jerome is famed for his translation of the Bible into Latin and for translating the Old Testament from Hebrew. He is, after Augustine of Hippo, the second most published writer among the early church fathers and is now recognized by the Catholic Church as the patron saint of translators, librarians, and encyclopedists.

Jerome wrote widely on a variety of subjects and in multiple formats, including biblical works, polemical and historical essays, and letters. His letters are of unique interest, since they blend his religious thinking with his own subjective, emotive experience and provide a unique window into Roman society in the last century of the Roman Empire. Jerome's primary concern, as revealed in his letters, is on dispensing teachings that would enable readers to lead Christian moral lives in cosmopolitan urban centers like Rome. Rome was famed for its licentiousness, opulence, and decadence, and Jerome's readers sought out his guidance for living blameless Christian lives within the city's crumbling walls. Jerome's time spent among the Roman elite and upper class connected him to new Christian converts, many of whom were women who had taken vows of virginity. Many of his letters were addressed to these women, and he used his correspondence to elaborate on how female Christian converts should live their lives. Jerome's letters were published and widely circulated during his lifetime, and they helped codify Catholic teachings regarding the education of young women, establishing paradigms for gender relations that would persist for hundreds of years.

The letter excerpted here is a response to Laeta, an elite Roman woman, who has asked Jerome how she should bring up her infant daughter Paula to ensure she remains a consecrated virgin. In the Catholic Church, a consecrated virgin is considered a bride of Christ, dedicated by the church to a life of perpetual virginity, and may serve the church as either a cloistered nun or in the secular world. In his response, Jerome provides Laeta with detailed instructions on Paula's education and training.

Portrait of St. Jerome
(Albrecht Dürer)

Document Text

I wish to address you as a mother and to instruct you how to bring up our dear Paula, who has been consecrated to Christ before her birth and vowed to His service before her conception. . . .

Thus must a soul be educated which is to be a temple of God. It must learn to hear nothing and to say nothing but what belongs to the fear of God. It must have no understanding of unclean words, and no knowledge of the world's songs. Its tongue must be steeped while still tender in the sweetness of the psalms. Boys with their wanton thoughts must be kept from Paula: even her maids and female attendants must be separated from worldly associates. For if they have learned some mischief they may teach more. Get for her a set of letters made of boxwood or of ivory and called each by its proper name. Let her play with these, so that even her play may teach her something. And not only make her grasp the right order of the letters and see that she forms their names into a rhyme, but constantly disarrange their order and put the last letters in the middle and the middle ones at the beginning that she may know them all by sight as well as by sound. Moreover, so soon as she begins to use the style upon the wax, and her hand is still faltering, either guide her soft fingers by laying your hand upon hers, or else have simple copies cut upon a tablet; so that her efforts confined within these limits may keep to the lines traced out for her and not stray outside of these. Offer prizes for good spelling and draw her onwards with little gifts such as children of her age delight in. And let her have companions in her lessons to excite emulation in her, that she may be stimulated when she sees them praised. You must not scold her if she is slow to learn but must employ praise to excite her mind, so that she may be glad when she excels others and sorry when she is excelled by them. Above all you must take care not to make her lessons distasteful to her lest a dislike for them conceived in childhood may continue into her maturer years. The very words which she tries bit by bit to put together and to pronounce ought not to be chance ones, but names specially fixed upon and heaped together for the purpose, those for example of the prophets or the apostles or the list of patriarchs. . . . In this way while her tongue will be well-trained, her memory will be likewise developed. . . .

Let her very dress and garb remind her to Whom she is promised. Do not pierce her ears or paint her face consecrated to Christ with white lead or rouge. Do not hang gold or pearls about her neck or load her head with jewels, or by reddening her hair make it suggest the fires of Gehenna. . . .

When Paula comes to be a little older and to increase like her Spouse in wisdom and stature and in favor with God and man, let her go with her parents to the temple of her true Father but let her not come out of the temple with them. Let them seek her upon the world's highway amid the crowds and the throng of their kinsfolk, and let them find her nowhere but in the shrine of the scriptures, questioning the prophets and the apostles on the meaning of that spiritual marriage to which she is vowed. Let her imitate the retirement of Mary whom Gabriel found alone in her chamber and who was frightened, it would appear, by seeing a man there. . . . At no time let her go abroad, lest the watchmen find her that go about the city, and lest they smite and wound her and take away from her the veil of her chastity, and leave her naked in her blood. Nay rather when one knocketh at her door let her say: "I am a wall and my breasts like towers." . . .

Let her learn too how to spin wool, to hold the distaff, to put the basket in her lap, to turn the spinning wheel and to shape the yarn with her thumb. Let her put away with disdain silken fabrics, Chinese fleeces, and gold brocades: the clothing which she makes for herself should keep out the cold and not expose the body which it professes to cover. Let her food be herbs and wheaten bread with now and then one or two small fishes . . . let her meals always leave her hungry and able on the moment to begin reading or chanting.

When you go a short way into the country, do not leave your daughter behind you. Leave her no power or capacity of living without you, and let her feel frightened when she is left to herself. Let her not converse with people of the world or associate with virgins indifferent to their vows. Let her not be present at the weddings of your slaves and let her take no part in the noisy games of the household. As regards the use of the bath, I know that some are content with saying that a Christian virgin should not bathe along with eunuchs or with married women, with the former because they are still men, at all events in mind, and with the latter because women with child offer a revolting spectacle. For myself, however, I wholly disapprove of baths for a virgin of full age. Such an one should blush and feel overcome at the idea of seeing herself undressed. By vigils and fasts she mortifies her body and brings it into subjection. By a cold chastity she seeks to put out the flame of lust and to quench the hot desires of youth. And by a deliberate squalor she makes haste to spoil her natural good looks.

Glossary

eunuchs: men who have been castrated, especially to be guards or servants in harems or other women's quarters, and as chamberlains to kings

Gehenna: an actual valley near old Jerusalem that was, in the time of Jesus, a constantly burning urban garbage dump; later, a hypothetical place where the souls of the wicked would go after death to suffer eternal damnation or annihilation

her Spouse: Jesus Christ

"Mary, whom Gabriel found alone": a reference to the appearance of the angel Gabriel to young Mary, to tell her that she would have a son, whom she was to name Jesus

"to Whom she is promised": that is, Jesus Christ; as a consecrated virgin, Paula was considered a bride of Christ

Short-Answer Questions

1. Describe some of the suggestions St. Jerome makes for the early education and training of young women. In your response, focus on the long second paragraph of the excerpt, where Jerome expands on his ideas for early childhood development.

2. Analyze the ways in which St. Jerome's suggestions would restrict a young woman. How, in these excerpts, does he suggest Paula interact with men and with the world outside her immediate household?

3. Evaluating this text as a whole, how do you feel about St. Jerome's suggestions? In your response, consider what these suggestions indicate about St. Jerome's own attitudes on gender and sexuality. Also consider how his advice might have influenced the norms of the time in which he was writing.

Chapter 2

Women in the Early Modern Era

If there was one world-changing event that marked a break between the medieval period and the early modern period, it was the arrival of the great plague, known in Europe as the Black Death, in the middle of the fourteenth century. By the time a plague-stricken ship from the Black Sea reached Italy in 1348, the disease had already become a global pandemic. It had already caused millions of deaths in China and on the borders of Mongolia. Within a few decades, it would help bring about the collapse of the Mongol empire that had bound most of Asia together for more than a century. Over the space of a few years, the plague swept through Europe. The early Renaissance scholar and writer Giovanni Boccaccio (1313–1375) claimed to have witnessed the effects of the plague personally as it burned through Florence in 1348. Historians estimate that the plague may have caused the deaths of up to 50 percent of the population in certain areas

Women Find New Roles in Business and Religion

The high death toll had two immediate effects on the status of women in general. One was social: married women who survived their husbands were able to take their places in the public realm. The English poet Geoffrey Chaucer (c. 1342–1400) wrote about one such successful businesswoman in "The Wife of Bath's Tale," which celebrates the perspicacity of women in general. The author Christine de Pisan (1364–1430), writing in "The Treasure of the City of Ladies," provided a manual for women who were charged with running estates and stressed the ability of women to assume great social responsibilities. Joan of Arc (c. 1412–1431) addressed a letter to King Henry VI of England in which she claimed the right under God to negotiate peace or continue the ongoing war in the name of the true king of France.

Joan of Arc's position illuminates the second effect that the plague had on the status of women: it raised them as religious figures. The response of the Catholic Church to the plague was minimal at best. Contemporary documents record many instances of priests fleeing their parishes and their duty to the sick and dying to find safety on country estates and in noble houses. Faith in the church as an institution that communicated the will of God declined, and various women stepped in, speaking sometimes as representatives of church institutions and sometimes as pious individuals or mystics. Julian of Norwich (c. 1342–1416), an anchoress or female hermit who may have been a parent before entering religious life, wrote in "Revelations of Divine Love" about God's love, equating it with the love of a mother for her children. The mystic Margery Kempe (c. 1373–c. 1438) visited Julian in her seclusion and wrote about the experience—and many other spiritual experiences—in her autobiography *The Book of Margery Kempe*.

Persecution of Women as Witches

The Protestant Reformation and the later Renaissance introduced new vectors into the lives of European women. The public disillusionment with the Catholic Church expressed itself in both secular and sacred communities. The French-born German priest Heinrich Kramer (c. 1430–1505) turned his position as a hunter of heresies (deviations from official church doctrine) into a professional pursuer of witches—the vast majority of whom were elderly women, living mostly in poverty, and without the protection of relatives or close associates. Kramer viewed witchcraft as a form of heresy, and his *Malleus Maleficarum* (best known under its English title *Hammer of Witches*) prescribed ways of investigating and punishing accused witches. Despite Kramer's position as a church official and investigator of heresy, the Catholic Church condemned his book. Nonetheless, it found an enthusiastic audience among lay people.

Writing and publishing became one of the most successful ways that women were able to argue for rights and opportunities. The spread of printing throughout Europe in the late fifteenth century created new ways for literate women to communicate with one another and with a broader public. Venetian courtesan Veronica Franco (1546–1591) took a secular, and very worldly, position on the opportunities available to women in sixteenth-century Italy. A highly literate woman, Franco warned, in clear and direct language, about the dangers inherent in a lifestyle that depended on sexual attraction and the whims of powerful men in her "Letter 22: A Warning to a Mother Considering Turning Her Daughter into a Courtesan." The English philosopher Mary Astell (1666–1731) declared, in "A Serious Proposal to the Ladies for the Advancement of Their True and Greatest Interest," that men and women shared an equal capacity for intellectual pursuits, and that women deserved access to higher education on the same basis as men. Astell is regarded by some scholars as one of the earliest feminists.

Ursula de Jesus and Sor Juana Ines de la Cruz

Women in religious professions, many of them also highly literate, expressed their frustrations with the limitations of their lives both inside and outside the convent. By the seventeenth century, the Catholic Church had spread its influence throughout the Americas and into the Indo-Pacific world. The mystic Ursula de Jesus (1604–1668), the acknowledged daughter of a Spanish man and an enslaved Black African woman, spent two-thirds of her life as a slave in a household in Lima, Peru, but also recorded in "Visions of the World to Come" her hopes of escaping the brutality of racism she faced daily in the next life. But even Sor Juana Ines de la Cruz (c. 1648–1695), a well-born Hieronymite nun living in Mexico City, felt the need in "The Poet's Answer to Sor Filotea de La Cruz" to justify her literary work against the criticism of a local bishop.

From Queen Elizabeth I to Lady Hong

Many well-born women had to justify the actions they took against male chauvinism. One of the most famous was Queen Elizabeth I (1533–1603), whose "Speech to the Troops at Tilbury" used her femininity as a rallying cry for her subjects against the threat of the Spanish Armada in 1588. More than 100 years later, Lady Mary Wortley Montagu (1689–1762), wife of the English ambassador to the Ottoman Empire, used her position and her literary reputation as a writer of letters to spread the news of the Turkish practice of vaccination against smallpox. Later in the eighteenth century, Lady Hong (1735–1816), the wife of Crown Prince Sado of the Korean Joseon dynasty, spelled out the hardships she had to undergo throughout her husband's descent into violence and madness in her "Diary of Lady Hong, Queen of Korea."

Despite the many voices calling out for the equal treatment of women and, during the Enlightenment in Europe, even equal rights, women in general found themselves consistently deprived of opportunity. As late as the 1760s, the jurist William Blackstone (1723–1780), in the section of his *Commentaries on the Laws of England* called "Of Husband and Wife," declared women—married women at least—to be "feme-covert," a nonperson in the eyes of the law, with no rights outside those allowed her by her husband. The same issues that were the focus of women's complaints at the beginning of the early modern period remained in effect at its end.

Further Reading

Books

Fiero, Gloria K. *On the Threshold of Modernity: The Renaissance and Reformation.* Madison, WI: William C. Brown, 1993.

Goldstone, Nancy. *The Rival Queens: Catherine de Medici, Her Daughter Marguerite de Valois, and the Betrayal That Ignited a Kingdom.* New York: Back Bay Books, 2015.

Harrison, Kathryn. *Joan of Arc: A Life Transfigured.* New York: Doubleday, 2014.

Phillipy, Patricia, ed. *A History of Early Modern Women's Writing.* Cambridge: Cambridge University Press, 2018.

Stjerna, Kirsi I, ed. *Women Reformers of Early Modern Europe: Profiles, Texts, and Contexts.* Minneapolis, MN: Fortress Press, 2022.

Wiesner-Hanks, Merry E. *Women and Gender in Early Modern Europe.* Cambridge: Cambridge University Press, 2008.

Articles

Chappel, Carolyn Lougee. "'The Pains I Took to Save My/His Family': Escape Accounts by a Huguenot Mother and Daughter after the Revocation of the Edict of Nantes." *French Historical Studies* 22, no. 1 (Winter, 1999): 1–64.

Coclanis, Peter A. "Atlantic World or Atlantic/World." *William and Mary Quarterly*, 3rd series, 63, no. 4 (October 2006): 725–42.

Julian of Norwich:
Revelations of Divine Love

Author
Julian of Norwich

Date
c. 1373–c. 1416

Document Type
Essays, Reports, Manifestos

Significance
The earliest existing English-language book known to be written by a woman and an example of medieval Christan mysticism

Overview

Julian of Norwich (c. 1343–c. 1416) was an English mystic. Very few details are known about her life. In May 1373, when she was around thirty years of age, she was stricken by a disease and nearly died. While she was battling the illness, she experienced sixteen visions of Jesus Christ. Recovering, she vowed to dedicate her life to God. For the rest of her life, she was an anchoress, a woman who took a vow to live confined to a small cell in a church (in this case St. Julian's Church in Norwich, Norfolk) and spend her time in prayer and contemplation. She also served her community as a respected spiritual authority and advisor. She wrote an account of her visions, *Revelations of Divine Love*, shortly after her actual spiritual experience, and over time she expanded the text into a longer book of devotions by the same name.

Document Text
Chapter LVIII

"All our life is in three: 'Nature, Mercy, Grace.' The high Might of the Trinity is our Father, and the deep Wisdom of the Trinity is our Mother, and the great Love of the Trinity is our Lord"

God, the blessed Trinity, which is everlasting Being, right as He is endless from without beginning, right so it was in His purpose endless, to make Mankind. Which fair Kind first was prepared to His own Son, the Second Person. And when He would, by full accord of all the Trinity, He made us all at once; and in our making He knit us and oned us to Himself: by which oneing we are kept as clear and as noble as we were made. By the virtue of the same precious oneing, we love our Maker and seek Him, praise Him and thank Him, and endlessly enjoy Him. And this is the work which is wrought continually in every soul that shall be saved: which is the Godly Will aforesaid. And thus in our making, God, Almighty, is our Nature's Father; and God, All-Wisdom, is our Nature's Mother; with the Love and the Goodness of the Holy Ghost: which is all one God, one Lord. And in the knitting and the oneing He is our Very, True Spouse, and we His loved Wife, His Fair Maiden: with which Wife He is never displeased. For He saith: I love thee and thou lovest me, and our love shall never be disparted in two.

I beheld the working of all the blessed Trinity: in which beholding I saw and understood these three properties: the property of the Fatherhood, the property of the Motherhood, and the property of the Lordhood, in one God. In our Father Almighty we have our keeping and our bliss as anent our natural Substance, which is to us by our making, without beginning. And in the Second Person in skill and wisdom we have our keeping as anent our Sense-soul: our restoring and our saving; for He is our Mother, Brother, and Saviour. And in our good Lord, the Holy Ghost, we have our rewarding and our meed-giving for our living and our travail, and endless overpassing of all that we desire, in His marvellous courtesy, of His high plenteous grace.

For all our life is in three: in the first we have our Being, in the second we have our Increasing, and in the third we have our Fulfilling: the first is Nature, the second is Mercy, and the third is Grace.

For the first, I understood that the high Might of the Trinity is our Father, and the deep Wisdom of the Trinity is our Mother, and the great Love of the Trinity is our Lord: and all this have we in Nature and in the making of our Substance.

And furthermore I saw that the Second Person, which is our Mother as anent the Substance, that same dearworthy Person is become our Mother as anent the Sense-soul. For we are double by God's

A statue of Julian of Norwich holding **Revelations of Divine Love** (Wikimedia Commons)

making: that is to say, Substantial and Sensual. Our Substance is the higher part, which we have in our Father, God Almighty; and the Second Person of the Trinity is our Mother in Nature, in making of our Substance: in whom we are grounded and rooted. And He is our Mother in Mercy, in taking of our Sense-part. And thus our Mother is to us in diverse manners working: in whom our parts are kept undisparted. For in our Mother Christ we profit and increase, and in Mercy He reformeth us and restoreth, and, by the virtue of His Passion and His Death and Uprising, oneth us to our Substance. Thus worketh our Mother in Mercy to all His children which are to Him yielding and obedient.

And Grace worketh with Mercy, and specially in two properties, as it was shewed: which working belongeth to the Third Person, the Holy Ghost. He worketh rewarding and giving. Rewarding is a large giving-of-truth that the Lord doeth to him that hath travailed; and giving is a courteous working which He doeth freely of Grace, fulfilling and overpassing all that is deserved of creatures.

Thus in our Father, God Almighty, we have our being; and in our Mother of Mercy we have our re-forming and restoring: in whom our Parts are oned and all made perfect Man; and by [reward]-yielding and giving in Grace of the Holy Ghost, we are fulfilled.

And our Substance is [in] our Father, God Almighty, and our Substance is [in] our Mother, God, All-wisdom; and our Substance is in our Lord the Holy Ghost, God All-goodness. For our Substance is whole in each Person of the Trinity, which is one God. And our Sense-soul is only in the Second Person Christ Jesus; in whom is the Father and the Holy Ghost: and in Him and by Him we are mightily taken out of Hell, and out of the wretchedness in Earth worshipfully brought up into Heaven and blissfully oned to our Substance: increased in riches and in nobleness by all the virtues of Christ, and by the grace and working of the Holy Ghost.

Glossary

anent: about, relating to, concerning

disparted: separated, divided

meed-giving: reward, wage, compensation

oned: united or joined, following the Middle English use of the verb "to one"

shewed: showed, shown

travail: work, especially hard or painful work

Trinity: the doctrine that while there is only one God, the attributes of God are divided into the three persons of the Father, the Son, and the Holy Ghost or Holy Spirit

Short-Answer Questions

1. In what respects does Julian of Norwich differentiate between the character and functions of each person in the Holy Trinity?

2. When Julian refers to God's attributes in terms such as "Mother" or "Motherhood," to what precisely is she referring?

3. What conclusions can we draw from this document as to the nature of Julian's religious faith and understanding of the role played by gender? Are the genders complementary or contradictory?

The Schlager Anthology of Women's History

Geoffrey Chaucer: "The Wife of Bath"

Author	**Significance**
Geoffrey Chaucer	Tells the story of a popular character in *The Canterbury Tales,* remembered for her outgoing personality, her independence, and her assertion that women should seek independence in marriage
Date	
1392	
Document Type	
Poems, Plays, Fiction	

Overview

*T*he Canterbury Tales is one of the most significant surviving works of late medieval literature. Written in the fourteenth century by Geoffrey Chaucer, it relates the story of a group of pilgrims traveling from London to Canterbury. The group engages in a spirited and ribald storytelling competition to pass the time on their travels. "The Wife of Bath's Prologue and Tale" is a perennial favorite from Chaucer's collection. Ostensibly about a knight on a quest to find the object that women most desire, the narrative is memorable for the vivacity, wit, and independence of its narrator, the titular Wife of Bath, also known as Alisoun.

The Wife of Bath is a significant and enduring character. Independent, assertive, sexually promiscuous, and bawdy, she repeatedly challenges traditional gender roles and the conventions of medieval society. For instance, throughout her story, she openly admits to using her sexuality and intelligence to manipulate and gain mastery over men and acquire their wealth. She uses biblical char-acters to defend and rationalize her actions, suggesting her actions are not dissimilar to those of King Solomon. A flashy, flamboyant dresser, she refuses to comply with conventions of propriety and dress.

While Chaucer's narrative centers on the issue of sovereignty in marriage, he also uses the character of the Wife of Bath to examine a variety of topics, including marriage, sex, and gender equality. The Wife of Bath argues repeatedly that women should have control over their husbands and that they should openly seek out sexual pleasure from their partners.

Chaucer's tale is a shockingly modern one. The Wife of Bath's narrative of her life offers readers a vision of marriage as a contract between two equal parties, each of whom has mutual responsibilities and obligations to the other. Her story is not a tale of patriarchy and submission. Rather, it suggests the complexity of gender attitudes in the Middle Ages.

Geoffrey Chaucer
(National Library of Wales)

Document Text

Experience . . . were enough for me to speak of woe that is in marriage; for, lordings, since I was twelve years old. . . . I have had husbands five at church-door, for so oft have I been wedded; and in their degree all were worthy men. But in sooth it was told me not long ago that, sith Christ went never but once to a wedding . . . by the same ensample he taught me that I should be wedded but once . . . why should men speak reproach of such?

Lo, Dan Solomon! the wise king; I trow he had more wives than one, as would God I had leave to be refreshed half so oft as he! What a gift of God he had in all his wives! No man hath such now in this world. God be praised that I have wedded five, from whom I have plucked their best. Diverse schools make perfect clerks; diverse practice, in many sundry labours, maketh the workman thoroughly perfect; of five husbands am I the scholar. Welcome the sixth, whensoever he shall come. In sooth, I will not for aye keep me chaste. When mine husband is departed from the world, some Christian man shall wed me anon. . . .

I grant, in sooth, I reck not though maidenhood be preferred to bigamy; it pleaseth such to be clean, body and spirit; of mine own estate I will make no boast. For well ye know a lord in his house hath not every vessel of pure gold; some be of wood and do their lord service. God calleth folk to him in sundry ways, an his own gift, some this, some that, as it pleaseth God to bestow. Virginity is a great virtue, and continence eke, with religious folk. But Christ, that is the spring of perfection, bade not every wight that he should go sell all he hath, and give it to the poor, and in such wise follow him and his steps. He spake but to them that would live perfectly, and by your leave, lordings, I am not such. I will bestow the flower of my life in the acts and in the fruit of marriage. . . .

Thou sayest eke, if we make us gay with clothing and precious gear, that it is peril unto our chastity; and yet more, sorrow betide thee! . . . Thou saidest I was like a cat; for if a man will singe a cat's skin, then will the cat alway abide in his house; but if the cat's skin be sleek and fair, she will not dwell in house half a day, but ere any daylight be dawned, she will forth to show her skin and go a-caterwauling. This is to say if I be clad fair, sir rogue, I am running out to show my duds.

Metellius, the foul churl, the hog, that slew his wife with a staff because she drank wine,—had I been his wife, he should not have daunted me from drinking. . . . But lord! when I take remembrance upon my youth and my jollity, it tickleth me about the root of mine heart. Unto this day it doth mine heart good that I have had my world in my time.

Now, sirs, will I tell forth my story. As ever I hope to drink wine or ale, I shall say the sooth; those husbands that were mine, three of them were good and two were bad. The three were goody rich and old. They had given me their goods and their treasure; I needed no longer take pains to win their love, or do reverence to them. They loved me so well, by heaven's king, that I set no value on their love! A wise woman will ever busy her to get love where she hath none. But sith I had them wholly in hand, and sith they had given me all their goods, why should I take pains to please them, unless it were for mine own profit and my pleasure?

Glossary

alway abide: always accept or tolerate

anon: straightaway, immediately

bade not every wight: demanded not of every person

clad fair: well dressed

Dan Solomon: King Solomon, a wise and important monarch of ancient Israel

do reverence: show respect or deference

eke: also

ensample: example

ere: before a specified time

gay with clothing: flashy or flamboyant attire

go a-caterwauling: go yowling like a cat in heat

hath: has or have

jollity: lively and cheerful activity

Metellius: a Roman whose wife was fined her dowry for drinking wine

mine own estate: my own body or person

not for aye: not forever; in Middle English, "aye" was used to signify the words "ever" or "always"

reck: reckon

Glossary

running out to show my duds: showing off my fine clothes

singe: to burn (something) lightly or superficially, burn the edges

sith: since

sooth: truth

tickleth: tickles or amuses

Short-Answer Questions

1. Describe how the Wife of Bath defends her multiple marriages. In your response, please outline her attitude toward marriage.

2. How does the Wife of Bath connect relationships, marriage, sex, and materialism in these excerpts from her prologue?

3. In your view, what explains the enduring resonance and appeal of the Wife of Bath as a literary character? In your response, cite specific examples and phrases from the text to support your interpretation of this complicated, nuanced character.

Christine de Pisan:
The Treasure of the City of Ladies

<table>
<tr><td>

Author
Christine de Pisan
Date
c. 1405

Document Type
Essays, Reports, Manifestos

</td><td>

Significance
Described the role of a medieval woman in organizing and running a manor

</td></tr>
</table>

Overview

Christine de Pisan (1364–1430) is generally hailed by feminist historians as a brilliant pioneer in female literature and by all historians as an insightful, pragmatic, and shrewd commentator on the conditions of late medieval society. She was a French-Italian lady of noble birth who turned to writing as a way to make an income when her husband died of the plague. In addition to ballads, biographies, and treatises on war and governance, she also wrote moral commentaries and took up a critique of the famous *Romance of the Rose* by Jean de Meun (1240–1305), whose passages often railed against the fickleness and "falsity" of women.

In two books defending and celebrating women of history, *The Book of the City of Ladies* and *The Treasure of the City of Ladies*, she brought the first proto-feminist studies in history into vernacular French. The latter

work, from which this document is taken, is a manual for the practical education of women of various classes. This selection treats the practical matters of organizing the work of a feudal manor. De Pisan's status as a widow gave her firsthand experience with the problems of trying to run an agricultural estate in the absence of the legal lord, and her desire to reach out to women who shared her predicament demonstrates an awareness of social responsibility that belies conventional conceptions of sheltered aristocratic women whose concerns were limited to their domestic environment.

Her lucid and no-nonsense instructions regarding the management of an estate and the coordination of its seasonal operations is not merely proto-feminist; it is proto-managerial. Readers of Christine de Pisan today can gain as much from her common sense and practical knowledge as did the feudal householders of her day.

An illustration of Christine de Pisan giving her book to Margaret of Burgundy
(Wikimedia Commons)

Document Text
How ladies and young women who live on their manors ought to manage their households and estates

. . . Because barons and still more commonly knights and squires and gentlemen travel and go off to the wars, their wives should be wise and sound administrators and manage their affairs well, because most of the time they stay at home without their husbands, who are at court or abroad. They should have all the responsibility of the administration and know how to make use of their revenues and possessions. Every lady of such rank (if she is sensible) ought to know how much her annual income is and how much the revenue of her land is worth. This wise lady ought to persuade her husband . . . to discuss their finances together and try to keep to such a standard of living as their income can provide and not so far above it that at the end of the year they find themselves in debt to their own people or other creditors. There

is absolutely no shame in living within your income, however small it may be, but there is shame if creditors are always coming to your door to repossess their goods or if they are obliged to make nuisances of themselves to your men or your tenants or if they have to try by hook or by crook to get their payment.

It is proper for such a lady or young woman to be thoroughly knowledgeable about the laws related to fiefs, sub-fiefs, quit rents, *champarts*, taxes for various causes, and all those sorts of things that are within the jurisdiction of the lordship, according to the customs of the region, so that no one can deceive her about them. Since there are a great many administrators of lands and of noblemen's estates who are quite willing to deceive their masters, she ought to be well versed in all these matters and take care over them. There is nothing dishonourable about making herself familiar with the accounts. She will see them often and wish to know how they are managed in regard to her vassals. . . . Towards poor people a lady should out of love of God, be more compassionate than strict.

In addition, she will do well to be a very good manager of the estate and to know all about the work on the land and at what time and in which season one ought to perform what operations. She should know which way is the best for the furrows to go according to the lay of the land and according to whether it is in a dry or damp region. She should see that the furrows are straight and well made and of the right depth and sown at exactly the right time with such grains as are best for the land. . . . She ought to make sure that she has good workmen and overseers in these duties and not take people who change masters every quarter, because that is a bad sign. They should be neither too old, for they will be lazy and weak, nor too young, for they will always be larking about.

She is careful to have them get up early but she does not depend on anyone for it, if she is a skillful manager of the estate. She herself rises and puts on a *houppeland* and busies herself at her window so that she sees them go outside, for if they are lazy, the laziness will most likely be shown in an unwillingness to go out. She should often take time to visit the fields to see how the men are getting on with the work, for there are a good many workers who will gladly abstain from working the land and give it up for the day if they think no one is keeping an eye on them. . . . [W]hen the wheat is ripe from the month of May, she will not wait for an unrealistically high price, but will harvest her crop, having it cut by strong and industrious fellows. She will pay them in cash or in grain. . . .

The lady should get up early in the morning, for in the establishment where the lady usually lies in bed until late it is unlikely that the household will run smoothly. . . . She will have the animals brought in at the right time, take care how the shepherd looks after them and see that he is in control of them and that he is not cruel. . . . She sees that the animals are kept clean, protected from too hot a sun and from the rain and prevented from catching mange. If she is wise she will often go in the evening with one of her women to see how the sheep are being penned up, and thus the shepherd will be more careful that there is nothing for which he may be reproached. She

will have him take special care at lambing time and look after the lambs well, for they often die for lack of attention. . . .

In the winter-time, she will reflect that labour is cheap, and therefore she will have her men cut her willow or hazel groves and make vine props to sell in the season. She will set her young lads to cutting wood for heating the manor house, but if the weather is too inclement she will have them thresh in the barn. She will never let them be idle, for there is nothing more wasteful in a manor than an idle staff. Likewise, she will employ her women and her chambermaids to attend to the livestock, to feed the workmen, to seed the courtyards and work in the herb garden, even getting covered in mud. She and her girls and young women will occupy themselves in making clothing. . . . They will also make many other things that are too long to list.

In flat, arable country there is a great need to run an estate well, and the one who is most diligent and careful about it, however great she may be, is more than wise and ought to be highly praised for it. This practice of running the household wisely sometimes renders more profit than the entire income from the land. . . .

Glossary

champarts: a type of tax levied on medieval peasant tenants in France that took the form of a percentage of the harvest

"fiefs, sub-fiefs, quit rents": different forms of property rights distributed by a lord, lady, or other landowner to their tenants: a *fief*, an agreement to perform some kind of service in exchange for the use of the land; a *sub-fief*, in which the holder of the fief contracts with someone else to use the land; and a *quit rent*, in which the tenant pays money to avoid having to perform their service

furrows: trenches cut by a plow in a cultivated field to help carry water to the seedlings, directing moisture to the plants' roots

houppeland: a medieval outer garment, popular in the fourteenth century, that functioned like a modern housecoat, and whose modern descendants include the gowns worn by academics and jurists

Short-Answer Questions

1. Why does Christine de Pisan think that women need training in the management of estates?

2. Does Christine de Pisan suggest that a good manager should be sympathetic to her workers? Please offer examples.

3. According to Christine de Pisan, should a good manager be an idealist or a pragmatist? Why do you think so?

Joan of Arc:
Letter to King Henry VI of England

Author
Joan of Arc

Date
1429

Document Type
Letters/Correspondence

Significance
Demonstrated the astonishing persistence of a young woman in the medieval period who attained political and military strength enough to change the course of the Hundred Years' War

Overview

Joan of Arc was born to a peasant family in a village called Domrémy in northeastern France in 1412. She was raised in a religious household and, at the age of twelve, claimed to have had the first of many recurring visions. She told her astonished family members that an angel had directed her to lead the beleaguered French in their ongoing conflict with the English, and that she had been ordered by God to retake her homeland from English occupation. At the time of Joan's vision, much of France was under the control of the English and their Burgundian allies after repeated French defeats in the Hundred Year's War; Henry VI, still a child, had inherited the title of king of England and France in 1422 as a result of the Treaty of Troyes two years earlier. Joan was convinced that it was her divine mission to take the eldest son of France's former king Charles VI of France, also named Charles and called the Dauphin, to claim his rightful throne in the city of Rheims. For years, her claims were ignored by secular and religious authorities.

Joan continued to have religious visions through her teenage years. Eventually, as a result of her astonishing persistence and conviction, she was granted an audience with the Dauphin and the members of the French court. After convincing the Dauphin that she was a prophetess from God, Joan was given command of a small army to relieve the besieged city of Orleans, which held symbolic significance for both the English and the French. Joan astonished contemporaries and won a decisive victory over the English, shattering their myth of invincibility. She subsequently achieved a series of quick military victories, providing a much-needed morale boost to the French army and halting English expansion into France. In 1430, she was captured by Burgundian soldiers, who then gave her to her English enemies. Accused of heresy and tortured by her captors, she was publicly burned alive at the stake in Rouen in 1431. Twenty-five years later, Pope Callixtus III decreed that Joan was not a heretic, and in 1920 she was made a saint of the Catholic Church.

Joan's victories on the battlefield altered the course of the Hundred Years' War. Contemporary observers and historians alike have agreed that the English probably would have succeeded in conquering all of France if Orleans had fallen. After Joan's victories, the English quickly lost ground in France and were largely expelled from mainland Europe by 1453. The French emerged stronger from the war, becoming the most centralized state in early modern Europe.

Before her great victory in Orleans, Joan dispatched this letter to King Henry VI. Her words are notable for their boldness. Joan's words show her to be confident and authoritative, even when addressing the head of a major European power. Notably, in the text, she speaks of governments in purely sacred terms and uses a variety of words to refer to herself, including "the Maid," "she," and "I." This is suggestive of the ways in which Joan conceived of herself as both a military leader and as a vessel and messenger from God.

Joan of Arc
(Archives Nationales)

Document Text
JESUS, MARY

King of England, render account to the King of Heaven of your royal blood. Return the keys of all the good cities which you have seized, to the Maid. She is sent by God to reclaim the royal blood, and is fully prepared to make peace, if you will give her satisfaction; that is, you must render justice, and pay back all that you have taken.

King of England, if you do not do these things, I am the commander of the military; and in whatever place I shall find your men in France, I will make them flee the country, whether they wish to or not; and if they will not obey, the Maid will have them all killed. She comes sent by the King of Heaven, body for body, to take you out of France, and the Maid promises and certifies to you that if you do not leave France she and her troops will raise a mighty outcry as has not been heard in France in a thousand years. And believe that the King of Heaven has sent her so much power that you will not be able to harm her or her brave army.

To you, archers, noble companions in arms, and all people who are before Orleans, I say to you in God's name, go home to your own country; if you do not do so, beware of the Maid, and of the damages you will suffer. Do not attempt to remain, for you have no rights in France from God, the King of Heaven, and the Son of the Virgin Mary. It is Charles, the rightful heir, to whom God has given France, who will shortly enter Paris in a grand company. If you do not believe the news written of God and the Maid, then in whatever place we may find you, we will soon see who has the better right, God or you. . . .

The Maid asks you not to make her destroy you. If you do not render her satisfaction, she and the French will perform the greatest feat ever done in the name of Christianity.

Done on the Tuesday of Holy Week (March 22, 1429). HEAR THE WORDS OF GOD AND THE MAID.

Glossary

King of England: Henry VI, king of England from 1422 (at nine months old) to 1461, and disputed king of France from 1422 to 1453

the Maid: Joan's reference to herself

Short-Answer Questions

1. Describe the tone of Joan's message. What can you tell about her as a leader from her message?

2. Joan refers to herself as both the Maid and "commander of the military." Thinking of Joan's unique status and identity, what do you think her use of these varied terms suggests about her and her sense of self?

3. Considering the tone of Joan's letter and the qualities displayed in it, why do you think Joan was a uniquely effective military leader in the later years of the Hundred Years' War? Explain the ways Joan's tone could have inspired her soldiers and could have affected her English enemies.

Margery Kempe:
The Book of Margery Kempe

Author
Margery Kempe

Date
c. 1440

Document Type
Essays, Reports, Manifestos

Significance
Made an outstanding contribution to English culture as the first autobiography written in the English language

---

Overview

Margery Kempe was an important cultural figure in late medieval England. She made critical contributions to English religious life through her mystical, individualistic spirituality and was an early pioneer in the tradition of autobiographical writing. Kempe is primarily remembered for authoring *The Book of Margery Kempe*. Regarded by scholars as the first autobiography written in the English language by a woman, Kempe's words offer a novel interpretation of religious life and position faith as an intensely personal and subjective experience.

Kempe was likely born in 1373. The daughter of the mayor of Lynn, she married John Kempe in 1393 and gave birth to fourteen children. Later in her life, she took part in a series of pilgrimages to Jerusalem, Rome, Germany, and Spain. Historians know a great deal about Kempe's life because of *The Book of Margery Kempe*, a work widely regarded as the first autobiography written in English. Although Kempe herself was illiterate, she dictated the book to two clerks between 1432 and 1436. Written in the third person from Kempe's point of view, it contains detailed descriptions of her travels, mystical experiences, and religious ecstasies, as well as more prosaic accounts of her domestic troubles and illnesses, such as what is likely postpartum psychosis.

Kempe's continued relevance lies entirely in the autobiographical nature of her book. *The Book of Margery Kempe* offers historians a unique window onto the middle-class female experience in the Middle Ages. Most accounts from women in the period come from nuns and social elites; Margery was illiterate and had no connections with religious authorities. Though she was evidently pious, she held religious convictions that were starkly at odds with accepted religious dogmas.

Kempe's book also illustrates an emerging tension in the late medieval period between institutional religious orthodoxy and individual religious practices. Kempe was frequently challenged by civil and church authorities and was condemned for her departures from the standard teachings of the institutional Catholic Church. Her book suggests that by the late medieval period, many individuals were beginning to question the dogmas of Catholic authorities and starting to develop more individual and idiosyncratic approaches to spirituality.

A excerpt from **The Book of Margery Kempe** (British Library)

Document Text

When this creature was twenty year of age and some deal more, she was married to a worshipful burgess and was with child within short time, as kind would. And after that she had conceived she was labored with great accesses till the child was born, and then, what for labor she had in childing and for sickness going before, she despaired of her life, weening she might not live. And then she sent for her ghostly father, for she had a thing in conscience which she had never showed before that time in all her life. For she was ever letted by her enemy, the Devil, evermore saying to her while she was in good heal her needed no confession but [to] do penance by herself alone, and all should be forgiven, for God is merciful enow. And therefore this creature oftentimes did great penance in fasting bread and water and other deeds of alms with devout prayers, save she would not show it in confession. And when she was any time sick or diseased, the Devil said in her mind that she should be damned for she was not shriven of that default. Wherefore after that her child was born she, not trusting her life, sent for her ghostly father, as said before, in full will to be shriven of all her lifetime as near as she could. And, when she came to the point for to say that thing which she had so long concealed, her confessor was a little too hasty and gan sharply to undernim her ere that she had fully said her intent, and so she would no more say for nought he might do.

And anon for dread she had of damnation on that one side and his sharp reproving on that other side, this creature went out of her mind and was wonderly vexed and labored with spirits half year eight weeks and odd days. And in this time she saw, as her thought, devils open their mouths all inflamed with burning lows of fire as they should 'a swallowed her in, sometime ramping at her, sometime threatening her, sometime pulling her and hauling her both night and day the foresaid time. And also the devils cried upon her with great threatenings and bade her she should forsake her Christendom, her faith, and deny her God, his Mother, and all the saints in Heaven, her good works and all good virtues, her father, her mother, and all her friends. And so she did. She slandered her husband, her friends, her own self; she spoke many a reprevous word and many a shrewd word; she knew no virtue nor goodness; she desired all wickedness; like as the spirits tempted her to say and do so she said and did. . . .

. . . Then on a time as she lay alone and her keepers were from her, our merciful Lord Christ Jesus, ever to be trusted (worshiped be his name) never forsaking his servant in time of need, appeared to his creature, which had forsaken him, in likeness of a man, most seemly, most beauteous, and most amiable that ever might be seen with man's eye, clad in a mantle of purple silk, sitting upon her bed's side, looking upon her with so blessed a cheer that she was strengthened in all her spirits, said to her these words: "Daughter, why hast thou forsaken me, and I forsook never thee?" And anon as he had said these words she saw verily how the air opened bright as any levin, and he sty up into the air, not right hastily and quickly, but fair and easily that she might well behold him in the air till it was closed again. And anon the creature was stabled in her wits and in her reason as well as ever she was before. . . .

Glossary

accesses: outbursts

anon: right away

burgess: member of the English middle classes

childing: raising a child

gan: to go

ghostly father: a priest

letted: to give up or surrender

Glossary

levin: a flash of lightning

ramping: to assume a threatening stance

reprevous: reproving or blameful

shrewd: wicked, depraved, malicious, evil

shriven: having confessed or received confession

sty: ascended

this creature: Margery herself, as a lowly creation of God; this was a standard, accepted way of talking about oneself

undernim: to reprove, rebuke, or blame

weening: expecting, hoping, or intending

Short-Answer Questions

1. Describe how Kempe is treated by her confessor at the beginning of this excerpt, during what she thought was her deathbed confession. In your answer, explain how this treatment affected her.

2. Based on your understanding of this text, explain what worldly or physical factors might have prompted Kempe's visions.

3. Margery Kempe's memoirs are unique and occupy an important place in the historical record. Based on the excerpt, what features of the text, its writing style, and the character of Margery might account for its continued relevance and for the fame the author achieved during her lifetime?

Henrich Kramer: *Malleus Maleficarum*

<table>
<tr><td>

Author
Heinrich Kramer

Date
1486

Document Type
Essays, Reports, Manifestos; Legal

</td><td>

Significance
Fueled the European witch-hunting craze of the late medieval and early modern periods, and contributed to the witchcraft hysteria and trials of the sixteenth and seventeenth centuries

</td></tr>
</table>

Overview

The *Malleus Maleficarum*, commonly translated as the "Hammer of the Witches," is an infamous late medieval treatise and guidebook for the identification and punishment of alleged witches. Written by the German Catholic clergyman and inquisitor Heinrich Kramer, the book is a compendium of literature on demonology as it was understood at the time of publication. The text's significance lies in its role as the foundational text that fueled the European witch-hunting craze of the late medieval and early modern periods. In early modern Europe, roughly between 1400 and 1700, there was widespread belief that malignant Satanic witches were a clandestine threat, bent on undermining Christianity. This belief, which was buttressed by the publication of Kramer's text, had disastrous implications for European women. Witch hunting happened all throughout Europe but was conducted with special zeal in Central Europe. Collectively, this hysteria resulted in the trial, torture, humiliation, and execution of tens of thousands of victims, about three-quarters of whom were women.

The witch hunts of the early modern period took place against a backdrop of rapid social, economic, political, and religious upheaval. The collapse of the medieval social order and the fragmentation of Christianity, coupled with the development of early capitalism, caused social disorder and dislocation. This generalized social stress, which was accompanied by widespread epidemics, famine, climate change, and near constant war, directly resulted in the witch-hunting craze of the era. While the Europe of Kramer's time was fertile terrain for his paranoid misogyny, his text was initially met with skepticism. It was condemned by theologians and by the Catholic Church's own Inquisition. The book's recommendations for locating witches and extracting confessions encouraged the use of unethical and illegal practices that were inconsistent with church doctrine.

Regardless, the book found a wide readership and was used as a guidebook for identifying, persecuting, and eradicating supposed witches.

The text of the *Malleus Maleficarum* is threaded with Kramer's fevered hatred of women. In it, Kramer blames women for his own lustful impulses and demonstrates a preoccupation with the sexual habits of accused witches. Kramer argued that "women are by nature instruments of Satan—they are by nature carnal, a structural defect rooted in the original creation." Kramer's words provided the moral authority for the needless torture and abuse of tens of thousands of women. An estimated 26,000 women were executed for witchcraft in Germany alone during the early modern period. Their trials, conducted by zealous and hysterical local courts, were supported by the words contained in the *Malleus Maleficarum*.

A sixteenth-century depiction of burning alleged witches (Wikimedia Commons)

Document Text
Part 1: Question VI
Concerning Witches who copulate with Devils. Why is it that Women are chiefly addicted to Evil Superstitions.

. . . As for the first question, why a greater number of witches is found in the fragile feminine sex than among men; it is indeed a fact that it were idle to contradict, since it is accredited by actual experience, apart from the verbal testimony of credible witnesses. And without in any way detracting from a sex in which God has always taken great glory that His might should be spread abroad, let us say that various men have assigned various reasons for this fact, which nevertheless agree in principle. . . .

Now the wickedness of women is spoken of in *Ecclesiasticus* xxv: There is no head above the head of a serpent: and there is no wrath above the wrath of a woman. I had rather dwell with a lion and a dragon than to keep house with a wicked woman. And among much which in that place precedes and follows about a wicked woman, he concludes: All wickedness is but little to the wickedness of a woman. Wherefore S. John Chrysostom says on the text, It is not good to marry (*S. Matthew* xix): What else is woman but a foe to friendship, an unescapable punishment, a necessary evil, a natural temptation, a desirable calamity, a domestic danger, a delectable detriment, an evil of nature, painted with fair colours! . . . Cicero in his second book of *The Rhetorics* says: The many lusts of men lead them into one sin, but the lust of women leads them into all sins; for the root of all woman's vices is avarice. And Seneca says in his *Tragedies*: A woman either loves or hates; there is no third grade. And the tears of woman are a deception, for they may spring from true grief, or they may be a snare. When a woman thinks alone, she thinks evil. . . .

Other again have propounded other reasons why there are more superstitious women found than men. And the first is, that they are more credulous; and since the chief aim of the devil is to corrupt faith, therefore he rather attacks them. See *Ecclesiasticus* xix: He that is quick to believe is light-minded, and shall be diminished. The second reason is, that women are naturally more impressionable, and more ready to receive the influence of a disembodied spirit; and that when they use this quality well they are very good, but when they use it ill they are very evil.

The third reason is that they have slippery tongues, and are unable to conceal from the fellow-women those things which by evil arts they know; and, since they are weak, they find an easy and secret manner of vindicating themselves by witchcraft. See *Ecclesiasticus* as quoted above: I had rather dwell with a lion and a dragon than to keep house with a wicked woman. All wickedness is but little to the wickedness of a woman. And to this may be added that, as they are very impressionable, they act accordingly.

There are also others who bring forward yet other reasons, of which preachers should be very careful how they make use. For it is true that in the Old Testament the Scriptures have much that is evil to say about women, and this because of the first temptress, Eve, and her imitators. . . .

But because in these times this perfidy is more often found in women than in men, as we learn by actual experience, if anyone is curious as to the reason, we may add to what has already been said the following: that since they are feebler both in mind and body, it is not surprising that they should come more under the spell of witchcraft.

For as regards intellect, or the understanding of spiritual things, they seem to be of a different nature from men; a fact which is vouched for by the logic of the authorities, backed by various examples from the Scriptures. Terence says: Women are intellectually like children. And Lactantius (*Institutiones*, III): No woman understood philosophy except Temeste. And *Proverbs* xi, as it were describing a woman, says: As a jewel of gold in a swine's snout, so is a fair woman which is without discretion.

But the natural reason is that she is more carnal than a man, as is clear from her many carnal abominations. And it should be noted that there was a defect in the formation of the first woman, since she was formed from a bent rib, that is, a rib of the breast, which is bent as it were in a contrary direction to a man. And since through this defect she is an imperfect animal, she always deceives.

Glossary

Cicero: a Roman statesman, lawyer, scholar, philosopher, and writer, whose extensive writings include treatises on rhetoric, philosophy, and politics

***Ecclesiasticus* xxv**: chapter 25 of the book of Ecclesiasticus (also known as Sirach) in the Roman Catholic Bible, an example of sexist and misogynistic views about women in the Bible: "I would rather live with a lion and a dragon than live with an evil woman"

Lactantius: an early Christian author who became an advisor to Roman emperor Constantine I

S. John Chrysostom: an important early church father who served as archbishop of Constantinople

Seneca: a major philosophical figure of the Roman imperial period, and a central figure in the development of Stoic philosophy

Terence: a notable playwright and dramatist of the Roman republic

Short-Answer Questions

1. Describe at least three reasons Kramer provides in his response to the question of "Why is it that Women are chiefly addicted to Evil superstitions?" In addition, describe how these supposed reasons demonstrate Kramer's misogynistic attitudes.

2. Describe the nature of the "evidence" Kramer uses to support his reasoning. Why do you think readers during the early modern period found his evidence, and his arguments generally, to be so compelling?

3. Analyze this text from the lens of its historical context. What do you think the excerpt above, which is representative of Kramer's views overall, reveals about gender attitudes during the early modern period?

Veronica Franco:
A Warning to a Mother Considering Turning Her Daughter into a Courtesan

Author	**Significance**
Veronica Franco	Examined the status of men and women in sixteenth century Venice, offering critiques of gender hierarchies and the mistreatment of women
Date	
1580	
Document Type	
Letters/Correspondence	

Overview

Veronica Franco was a sixteenth-century Venetian courtesan, beauty, poet, and essayist who has been posthumously recognized as a proto-feminist. While women in the early modern era were expected to be chaste, silent, and submissive, Franco was vehement in her denunciations of gender hierarchies and was critical of the ways men subordinated the women around them.

Franco's public stance cannot be divorced from her high status in Venetian society. Franco was an Honest Courtesan, a formalized and honored occupation that denoted a sex worker who had sexual relations with members of Venice's elite and high-profile travelers to the city. Wealthy merchants, ambassadors, courtiers, and kings were all clients of Franco, and her work was considered neither shameful nor disreputable. In fact, Franco was a member of the elite of Venetian society. Born into the moneyed *cittadino* class, Franco was the daughter of a courtesan. She was given an excellent education and was married to a wealthy physician when she was young. This union ended badly, however, forcing Franco to support herself through the sex trade.

As a consequence of her elite education, Franco became a *cortigiana onesta*, an Honest Courtesan. These were refined sex workers whose status in society was a function of their cultural elegance and education. Such women needed to be beautiful, sophisticated, witty, and mannered. Consequently, Franco received a broad, humanistic education, which was normally unavailable to women, and she was expected, as a professional, to further her education by interacting with the intelligentsia and literary circles of the day. As a result of her unique status, Franco was able to befriend Domenico Venier, a patron of women writers, and to publish her writings from a position of security.

Franco was exempt from many of the restrictions imposed on Venetian women. As a member of the city's patrician class and a respected member of the social elite, she could publish with relative impunity. Protected from sexist attacks, Franco was able to publish poems, letters, and essays in which she defended other sex workers and protested their abuse by men. Franco's literary output showed her to be an elegant, engaging writer, with a confident voice and an incisive perspective. She documented the power imbalances between men and women in her city and pointedly critiqued her male contemporaries. Franco's combination of frank sensuality and intelligence comes across in her writing and demonstrates one way in which women in the early modern era were able to cultivate a space for themselves in the European social elite.

A portrait from the sixteenth century that is thought to be of Veronica Franco
(Worcester Art Museum)

Document Text

The fact that you go around complaining that I'm no longer willing for you to come to my house to see me, loving you as well as I do, bothers me less than the fact that I have a good reason for it. Since you see it as unfair and have complained about me endlessly, I would like to respond to you in this letter, making a last attempt to dissuade you from your evil intent, owing you greater friendship than ever before if you accept my truthful argument. . . .

I'm all the more eager to fulfill this duty toward you because to the extent that I clear myself of your accusations, I also fulfill a humane obligation by showing you a steep precipice hidden in the distance and by shouting out before you reach it, so that you'll have enough time to steer clear of it. Although it's mainly a question of your daughter's well-being, I'm talking about you, as well, for her ruin cannot be separated from yours. And because you're her mother, and if she should become a prostitute, you'd become her go-between and deserve the harshest punishment. . . .

You know how often I've begged and warned you to protect her virginity. And since this world is so full of dangers and so uncertain, and the houses of poor mothers are never safe from the amorous maneuvers of lustful young men, I showed you how to shelter her from danger and to help her by teaching her about life in such a way that you can marry her decently. I offered you all the help I could to assure she'd be accepted into the Casa delle Zitelle, and I also promised you, if you took her there, to help you with all the means at my disposal, as well. At first you thanked me and seemed to be listening to me and to be well disposed toward my affectionate offer. . . . Where once you made her appear simply clothed and with her hair arranged in a style suitable for a chaste girl, with veils covering her breasts and other signs of modesty, suddenly you encouraged her to be vain, to bleach her hair and paint her face. And all at once you let her show up with curls dangling around her brow and down her neck, with bare breasts spilling out of her dress, with a high uncovered forehead, and every other embellishment people use to make their merchandise measure up to the competition. . . .

Now, finally, I wanted to be sure to write these lines, urging you again to beware of what you're doing and not to slaughter in one stroke your soul and your reputation, along with your daughter's. . . . You'll break her neck expecting her to do well in the courtesan's profession, which is hard enough to succeed in even if a woman has beauty, style, good judgment, and proficiency in many skills. . . . And because, persisting in your error, you might say that such matters depend on chance, I reply first that there's nothing worse that can be done in life than to let yourself become a plaything of fortune. . . .

I'll add that even if fate should be completely favorable and kind to her, this is a life that always turns out to be a misery. It's a most wretched thing, contrary to human reason, to subject one's body and labor to a slavery terrifying even to think of. To make oneself prey to so many men, at the risk of being stripped, robbed, even killed, so that one man, one day, may snatch away from you everything you've acquired from many over such a long time, along with so many other dangers of injury and dreadful contagious diseases; to eat with another's mouth, sleep with another's eyes, move according to another's will, obviously rushing toward the shipwreck of your mind and body. . . . What wealth, what luxuries, what delights can outweigh all this?

Glossary

Casa delle Zitelle: a charitable institution founded to shelter poor, unmarried girls, to prevent their loss of virginity and ensure their access to the possibility of marriage

courtesan: a sex worker for royalty and the political and social elite, accorded high status

Short-Answer Questions

1. Describe the tone of Franco's letter. In addition, outline some of the reasons she gives for advising the woman she is addressing to steer her daughter away from a career as a courtesan.

2. Analyze the attitudes Franco displays in her letter. What does her letter reveal about the expectations concerning appropriate male and female behavior in Renaissance Venice?

3. Toward the end of this excerpt, Franco becomes more insistent about the costs of living as a courtesan, writing that it leads a woman "to eat with another's mouth, sleep with another's eyes, move according to another's will." Analyzing her language and considering her tone, interpret Franco's meaning and discuss what this reveals about the emotional toll of sex work on women.

Queen Elizabeth I:
Speech to the Troops at Tilbury

Author
Queen Elizabeth I

Date
1588

Document Type
Speeches/Addresses

Significance
In a defining moment in English history, inspired the queen's troops to resist a Spanish invasion and to recognize her right to rule England

Overview

In 1587, Queen Elizabeth I of England was faced with a predicament. She had been confronted with irrefutable evidence that her cousin, Mary, Queen of Scots, had been plotting her assassination, and Mary had been found guilty and sentenced to death by a special thirty-six-commissioner court. After much hesitation, Elizabeth signed the order of execution, though fearful that King Philip II of Spain could use it as a pretext for war \against England. This indeed occurred. Spain was at this time the leading military power in Europe, and by May of 1588, Philip had assembled a massive invasion force of 122 warships, which was dubbed the Armada Invincible (or Spanish Armada). This armada was meant to sweep aside the English fleet and transport an army of 30,000 men under command of the Duke of Parma from Flanders across the English Channel to England. The climax occurred August 7–8,

1588, off the coast of Flanders near Gravelines. The Spanish Armada lost so heavily to the English fleet that they were unable to transport Parma's army, and the threat of invasion was effectively over.

Before the news of victory reached England, Robert Dudley, Earl of Leicester, assembled a small force of some 4,000 to 5,000 men and deployed them at a fort near Tilbury on the east coast of England near the mouth of the River Thames. Their purpose was to guard London from the east against the Armada and Parma's landing force. Queen Elizabeth unexpectedly appeared and delivered a short speech on August 9 to raise the soldiers' morale. Meanwhile, more Armada ships were lost in storms trying to flee northward around the British Isles before returning to Spain, and Parma's troops never left Flanders.

Elizabeth I
(National Portrait Gallery)

Document Text

My loving people,

We have been persuaded by some that are careful of our safety to take heed how we commit ourselves to armed multitudes, for fear of treachery. But I assure you, I do not desire to live to distrust my faithful and loving people.

Let tyrants fear. I have always so behaved myself that, under God, I have placed my chiefest strength and safeguard in the loyal hearts and good-will of my subjects; and therefore I am come amongst you, as you see, at this time, not for my recreation and disport, but being resolved, in the midst and heat of the battle, to live and die amongst you all; to lay down for my God, and for my kingdom, and my people, my honour and my blood, even in the dust.

I know I have the body of a weak and feeble woman; but I have the heart and stomach of a king, and of a king of England too, and think foul scorn that Parma or Spain, or any prince of Europe, should dare to invade the borders of my realm: to which rather than any dishonour shall grow by me, I myself will take up arms, I myself will be your general, judge, and rewarder of every one of your virtues in the field.

I know already, for your forwardness you have deserved rewards and crowns; and We do assure you on a word of a prince, they shall be duly paid. In the mean time, my lieutenant general shall be in my stead, than whom never prince commanded a more noble or worthy subject; not doubting but by your obedience to my general, by your concord in the camp, and your valour in the field, we shall shortly have a famous victory over these enemies of my God, of my kingdom, and of my people.

Glossary

disport: amusement

my lieutenant general: Robert Dudley, Earl of Leicester

Parma: a reference to Alexander Farnese (1545–1592), the Duke of Parma and Piacenza, who led the invasion force that was supposed to land in England once the Spanish Armada had cleared the sea lanes

Spain: a reference to King Philip II of Spain

Short-Answer Questions

1. To what sentiments does Queen Elizabeth I appeal while addressing her audience? What, in your opinion, might resonate most strongly with her soldiers?

2. In what terms does Elizabeth describe herself and her relationship with her people? In what ways and to what extent does she cross gender boundaries?

3. What psychology does Elizabeth apply to motivate her troops? How effective do you think it might have been?

Ursula de Jesus:
"Visions of the World to Come"

Author
Ursula de Jesus

Date
1650

Document Type
Essays, Reports, Manifestos

Significance
Describes the difficulties of convent life as a woman of color in Spain's New World colonies and offers a unique perspective on baroque Catholic spirituality

Overview

Ursula de Jesus was a Roman Catholic mystic of African descent. Born into slavery in Lima, Peru, in 1604, she was taken to the Convent of Santa Clara in Lima in 1617, where she became the servant of Ines del Pulgar, a sixteen-year-old novice and the niece of the woman who owned Ursula's parents. She was enslaved for more than forty years, until one of the nuns in the convent purchased her freedom. She was denied the possibility of becoming a nun because of her race but remained at the convent for the remainder of her life, serving as a *donada*, a religious servant. This was a relatively common path for women of Afro-Indian descent in the New World colonies of Spain. Founded in 1605, the Convent of Santa Clara attracted primarily elite Spanish and creole (Spanish-descended) women. It also attracted women of color or mixed-race women who could only aspire to be peripherally involved in the convent by taking simple vows of obedience and enclosure. They would serve individual nuns and perform communal labor. This system was representative of the racialized caste system that operated throughout Spain's colonies in the Americas.

Ursula began experiencing spiritual visions after a near fatal accident in the convent. After she became a *donada* of the convent, she began to experience more frequent and intense religio-mystical visions and to communicate more directly with God. She claimed that dead souls trapped in purgatory communicated with her and begged her to serve as an intermediary on their behalf. This role was a significant one, since Catholics regarded purgatory as a punitive domain where sins were purged before souls could enter heaven. For two decades after gaining her freedom, Ursula became increasingly renowned for her mysticism and for her intimate familiarity with the souls of the dead. Saving tormented souls became her spiritual calling, and it likely presented her with an opportunity to enact her fervent baroque spirituality, to perform useful charitable labors, and to gain a religious authority commonly denied to women of color. When she died in 1666, Ursula's passing was deeply mourned.

Ursula began writing her diary in 1650, and it remains the only extant seventeenth-century spiritual autobiography written by a woman of color in Latin America. Her diary is a record of her deep religiosity and contains vivid imagery as well as probing dialogues with a variety of spiritual figures, including angels, Christ, Mary, and God. Ursula's diary is an important primary source since it contains rich details about convent life in the Spanish colonies and offers historians a rare window onto medieval and early modern female spirituality, reflected through the prism of racial inequality and the experience of enslavement.

Document Text

Stairway to Heaven

On Wednesday morning, [the nun] dona Antonia de Serrantes sent her slave to ask me to cook for her. I told her black female slave, "Go to God, your owner only remembers me to give orders." But then, I called her back again to do what she asked me. During the siesta, I went to pray, and the voices said, *If you have left the world behind, why do you complain? Was it not better to accept that without becoming angry and do it out of compassion and love of God?* and other things of this sort.

Thursday. Some days my heart races, and everything tires me out. I went before God to ask Him for His grace. There I saw a stairway extending from earth to heaven, and one path leading off to my right and another to my left. The voices explained that the stairway was the path of those who carry the cross. The right path is for those going to purgatory, and the left one for the condemned, and those who do not fear God and disobey His commandments. The latter fall into this tremendous place and drop down precipitous cliffs. I saw extreme darkness there. Moreover, they said that although these two paths came together, and those in purgatory suffered the same torture as those in hell, still they have hope because it is not forever and they are consoled. Those who climb the stairway carry the cross that our Lord Jesus Christ carried first. Only those who follow Him can take this path. . . .

Hope for Black Women

On the day of the Epiphany I was in a state of recollection after having taken communion. I do not know whether these are tricks of the big-footed one, or from my head, but I recalled María Bran, a slave of the convent who had died suddenly some fourteen years ago. I saw her in a priest's vestment, the whitest of whites, beautifully embellished and gathered together with a short cord with elegant tassels. She also wore a crown of flowers on her head. The celestial beings arranged for me to see her from the back, although I could still see her face and she was quite lovely, and her face was a resplendent black. I said, "How is it that such a good black woman, who had been neither a thief nor a liar, had spent so much time in purgatory?" She said she had gone there because of her character, and because she slept and ate at the improper time. Although she had been there a long time, her punishment had been mild. She was very thankful to God, who with His divine providence had taken her from her land and brought her down such difficult and rugged roads in order to become a Christian and be saved. I asked whether black women went to heaven and she said they did if they were thankful and heeded His beneficence, and thanked Him for it. They were saved because of His great mercy. . . .

Monday, as soon as I had gone to the choir and prostrated myself before the Lord, I saw two black women below they earth. In an instant, they were beside me. One of them said to me, "I am Lusia, the who served [the nun] Ana de San Joseph, and I have been in purgatory for this long, only because the great merciful God showed compassion towards me. No one remembers me." Very slowly, she spoke of God's goodness, power, and mercy, and how we should love and serve Him. Lusia had served this [convent] community in good faith, but sometimes they had accused her of certain things, and at times she suffered her penance when she tended to cook. For the love of God, would Ursula please commend her spirit to God. Before Lusia died, she had endured awful hardships, and because of them they had discounted much of her punishment.

Another time, after I had taken communion the voices told me to commend the spirit of a black woman to God. She had been in the convent and had been taken out to be cured because she was gravely ill but died a few days later. This had happened more than thirty years ago, and I had forgotten about her as if she had never existed. I was frightened and thought to myself, "So long in purgatory?" The voices responded, *For the things she did.* Here, the voices led me to understand that she had illicitly loved a nun and the entire convent knew about it, but that my father, Saint Francis, and my mother, Saint Claire, had gotten down on their knees and prayed to our Lady to secure the salvation of that soul from her Son. That is because she had served His house in good faith.

Glossary

big-footed one: the devil

communion: the service of Christian worship at which bread and wine are consecrated and shared

Epiphany: a Christian feast day (usually January 6) celebrating the manifestation of God in the baby Jesus and the visit of the Magi

siesta: a short nap taken in the early afternoon, often after the midday meal

Short-Answer Questions

1. Describe what we learn about Ursula's personality and inner emotional and spiritual life from these excerpts.

2. Thinking like a historian, summarize what we can learn from these excerpts about the experience of living in a convent in the Spanish colonies. In your response, consider what historians can glean about convent politics, personal struggles, and other daily matters from Ursula's diary.

3. What might this document say about race and sexuality in the convents of seventeenth-century Peru?

Juana Inés de la Cruz: "The Poet's Answer to Sor Filotea de la Cruz"

Author	**Significance**
Juana Inés de la Cruz	Often called the first feminist manifesto, a passionate declaration of the right of women to pursue intellectual and artistic interests
Date	
1691	
Document Type	
Essays, Reports, Manifestos; Letters/ Correspondence	

Overview

Sor Juana Inés de la Cruz, born Doña Inés de Asbaje y Ramírez de Santillana (c. 1648–1695), was an accomplished scholar and a contributor to the Golden Age of Spanish literature. Born the illegitimate daughter of a Spanish officer in Mexico and a wealthy lady whose family had its roots in Spain, Inés de la Cruz (she only took the name Sor Juana after entering religious life) was raised by her maternal grandparents on a hacienda near Mexico City. She was an autodidact who learned to read and write Latin by the age of three from books in her grandfather's library. Later she learned Greek philosophy, the composition of poetry, and the Aztec language Nahuatl. By the time she was sixteen, she had entered the court of the viceroy, serving as a lady in waiting to Donna Eleonora del Carretto, the vicereine (viceroy's wife), who encouraged her to further her education.

Given a choice between marriage or religious vacation, in 1667 she became a postulant at the Monastery of Saint Joseph. Two years later she joined the Hieronymite nuns at the Convent of St. Jerome in Mexico City and remained there for the next twenty-seven years until her death. Although the Hieronymites operated under the aegis of the Augustinians, Sor Juana was permitted to continue her scholarship. She was also allowed visitors; one who came to see her regularly was the polymath Don Carlos de Sigüenza y Góngora (1645–1700), sometimes called the "Mexican Da Vinci."

Sor Juana's "Poet's Answer," sometimes also called the "Reply to Sister Philotea," is one of the first declarations of the right of women not only to be educated but to be educators themselves. At the time this was considered a radical idea, and Sor Juana was reprimanded and ordered to stop writing. It is unclear if this order was carried out; some sources indicate that her books and writings were confiscated, while others say she may have sold them as well as her collection of scientific instruments. She died a few years later while caring for her sister nuns during an epidemic in the spring of 1695. Her papers were collected by her longtime friend the vicereine.

Sor Juana's letter is addressed to Sister Filotea de la Cruz, but Sor Filotea was a pseudonym used by a man, Manuel Fernández de Santa Cruz (1637–1690), the bishop of Tlaxcala. Sor Juana had written a critique of a sermon by the Portuguese Jesuit priest António Vieira (1608–1697). The bishop published Sor Juana's critique without her permission, and although he agreed with Sor Juana's assessment, he nonetheless warned her to keep to religious matters and avoid secular scholarship. Sor Juana's famous "Poet's Answer" is her response to the bishop's criticism.

Painting of Sor Juana Inés de la Cruz
(Museo Nacional de Historia)

Document Text

Most Illustrious Lady, my Lady:

It has not been my will, but my scant health and a rightful fear that have delayed my reply for so many days. Is it to be wondered that, at the very first step, I should meet with two obstacles that sent my dull pen stumbling? The first (and to me the most insuperable) is the question of how to respond to your immensely learned, prudent, devout, and loving letter. . . . The second obstacle is the question of how to render my thanks for the favor, as excessive as it was unexpected, of giving my drafts and scratches to the press: a favor so far beyond all measure as to surpass the most ambitious hopes or the most fantastic desires. . . .

I can answer nothing more to the first obstacle than that I am entirely unworthy of your gaze. To the second, I can offer nothing more than amazement, instead of thanks, declaring that I am unable to thank you for the lightest part of what I owe you. It is not false humility, my Lady, but the candid truth of my very soul, to say that when the printed letter reached my hands—that letter you were pleased to dub "Worthy of Athena"—I burst into tears. . . . For it seemed to me that your great favor was nothing other than God's reproof aimed at my failure to return His favors, and while He corrects others with punishments, He wished to chide me through benefits. . . .

[A] very saintly and simple mother superior . . . believed that study was an affair for the Inquisition and ordered that I should not read. I obeyed her (for the three months or so that her authority over

The Schlager Anthology of Women's History

us lasted) in that I did not pick up a book. But with regard to avoiding study absolutely, as such a thing does not lie within my power, I could not do it. . . . I sometimes walked back and forth along the forewall of one of our dormitories (which is a very large room), and I began to observe that although the lines of its two sides were parallel and the ceiling was flat, yet the eye falsely perceived these lines as though they approached each other and the ceiling as though it were lower in the distance than close by; from this I inferred that visual lines run straight, but not parallel, and that they form a pyramidal figure. And I conjectured whether this might be the reason the ancients were obliged to question whether the world is spherical or not. Because even though it seems so, this could be a delusion of the eye, displaying concavities where there were none.

This kind of observation has been continual in me and is so to this day, without my having control over it; rather, I tend to find it annoying, because it tires my head. Yet I believed this happened to everyone, as with thinking in verse, until experience taught me otherwise. . . .

If studies, my Lady, be merits (for indeed I see them extolled as such in men), in me they are no such thing: I study because I must. If they be a failing, I believe for the same reason that the fault is none of mine. Yet withal, I live always so wary of myself that neither in this nor in anything else do I trust my own judgment. And so I entrust the decision to your supreme skill and straightway submit to whatever sentence you may pass, posing no objection or reluctance, for this has been no more than a simple account of my inclination to letters. . . .

Now, if I turn my eyes to my much-maligned skill at writing in verse—so natural to me that indeed I must force myself not to write this very letter in rhyme, and I could observe as another did, "Whatever I tried to say came out in verse"; seeing this facility for writing poems condemned by so many and so vilified, I have sought quite deliberately to discover what harm there might be in them, and I cannot. Rather, I see them praised in the mouths of the Sibyls and sanctified by the pens of the Prophets. . . . The greater part of our sacred books are written in meter, like the Canticle of Moses; and most of Job according to the Etymologies of St. Isidore, is in heroic verse. . . . Then what harm can verses cause in and of themselves? For their misuse is no fault of the art, but of the bad practitioner who debases them, fashioning devil's snares of them. And this occurs in all the faculties and sciences.

And if the evil lies in their being used by a woman, we have just seen how many women have used them most laudable; then what evil lies in my being one? . . . If by your wisdom and sense, My Lady, you should be pleased for me to do other than what I propose, then as is only right, to the slightest motion of your pleasure I shall cede my own decision, which was as I have told you to keep still. . . .

If the style of this letter, my venerable Lady, has been less than your due, I beg your pardon. . . . But you, with your prudence and benevolence, will substitute or emend my terms; and if you think unsuitable the familiar terms of address I have employed—because it seems to me that given all the reverence I owe you, "Your Reverence" is very little reverence indeed—please alter it to whatever you think suitable. For I have not been so bold as to exceed the limits set by the style of your letter to me, nor to cross the border of your modesty.

And hold me in your own good grace, so as to entreat divine grace on my behalf; of the same, may the Lord grant you great increase, and may He keep you, as I beg of Him and as I am needful. Written at the Convent of our Father St. Jerome in Mexico City, this first day of March of the year 1691. Receive the embrace of your most greatly favored,

Sor Juana Inés de la Cruz

Glossary

Canticle of Moses: either Exodus 15:1–18, a lyric celebrating the successful crossing of the Red Sea by the Israelites that ended their exile in Egypt, or Deuteronomy 32:1–4, a set of verses Moses utters just before his death

Convent of St. Jerome: a community of cloistered (shut away from the secular world) nuns of the Order of St. Jerome (in Latin, *Ordo Sancti Hieronymi* or OSH) located in the heart of Mexico City, founded in 1585 and first admitting women in 1623

Etymologies of St. Isidore: perhaps the most influential and one of the most-copied books of the medieval period, and the greatest work of Isidore (c. 560–636), Bishop of Seville, the first encyclopedist of medieval Europe

forewall: the outer wall of a building

Short-Answer Questions

1. What is the core of Sor Juana's justification for writing poetry or verse?

2. Why does Sor Juana make a point of the style of her letter?

3. Based on what she says in her "Poet's Answer," is Sor Juana sincere when she thanks "Sor Filotea" for publishing her work?

Mary Astell:
A Serious Proposal to the Ladies for the Advancement of Their True and Greatest Interest

Author
Mary Astell

Date
1697

Document Type
Essays, Reports, Manifestos

Significance
Argued for greater education for women in Great Britain in the seventeenth century

Overview

Educational and economic opportunities for women were limited in seventeenth-century Great Britain. In a groundbreaking work published in 1697, the feminist author Mary Astell pointed out that most women simply became wives and mothers. Their principal goal was to learn to dress well and conduct themselves properly in public. Because the male-dominated society limited the opportunities for women, it inhibited their spiritual and intellectual potential. It also reinforced the false impression that women were frivolous and shallow. Astell strongly disagreed with this conventional view of gender and asserted that females were as smart, rational, and capable as their male counterparts.

To create an atmosphere that would allow women to thrive, Astell proposed the establishment of an all-women's college, which she termed a monastery. She conceived of the institution as an area where women could withdraw from the pressures and problems of the society of the day to study both religion and non-religious subjects. It would also free them from the accepted gender roles of the day. Astell contended that women needed their own facilities to prevent male domination in the classroom. Through education, women would be able to gain the independence that would free them from the male-dominated world and allow them to make choices and decisions for themselves.

Astell's proposal did not meet with much success. Many male commentators of the day ridiculed her ideas. She was unable to find the financial or public support for an all-women's college. However, in 1709, Astell was appointed to run an all-female Christian school for the poor. She was able to create her own curriculum and named other women to various posts in the school.

Astell was ahead of her time. Her ideas and proposals did not resonate with the public at the time, but they were significant in the development of modern feminism. It is important to note that Astell's characterization of society applied mainly to the wealthy and elite. It also downplayed the role many women, both poor and wealthy, played in managing businesses or households.

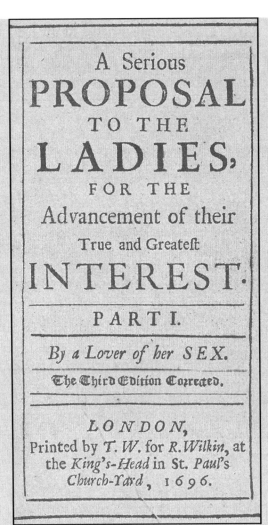

A Serious
PROPOSAL
TO THE
LADIES,
FOR THE
Advancement of their
True and Greateſt
INTEREST.
PART I.
By a Lover of her SEX.
The Third Edition Corrected.
LONDON,
Printed by T. W. for R. Wilkin, at
the King's-Head in St. Paul's
Church-Yard, 1696.

Title page from **A Serious Proposal to the Ladies** (Wikimedia Commons)

Document Text

When a poor Young Lady is taught to value her self on nothing but her Cloaths, and to think she's very fine when well accoutred; When she hears say, that 'tis Wisdom enough for her to know how to dress her self, that she may become amiable in his eyes, to whom it appertains to be knowing and learned; who can blame her if she lay out her Industry and Money on such Accomplishments, and sometimes extends it farther than her misinformer desires she should? When she sees the vain and the gay, making Parade in the World and attended with the Courtship and admiration of the gazing herd, no wonder that her tender Eyes are dazled with the Pageantry, and wanting Judgment to pass a due Estimate on them and their Admirers, longs to be such a fine and celebrated thing as they? What tho' she be sometimes told of another World, she has however a more lively perception of this, and may well think, that if her Instructors were in earnest when they tell her of *hereafter*, they would not be so busied and concerned about what happens *here*. She is it may be, taught the Principles and Duties of Religion, but not Acquainted with the Reasons and Grounds of them; being told 'tis enough for her to believe, to examine why, and wherefore, belongs not to her. And therefore, though her Piety may be tall and spreading, yet because it wants foundation and Root, the first rude Temptation overthrows and blasts it, or perhaps the short liv'd Gourd decays and withers of its own accord. But why should she be blamed for setting no great value on her Soul, whose noblest Faculty her Understanding is render'd useless to her? Or censur'd for relinquishing a course of Life, whole Prerogatives she was never acquainted with, and tho' highly reasonable in it self, was put upon the embracing it with as little reason as she now forsakes it? For if her Religion it self be taken up as the Mode of the Country, 'tis no strange thing that she lays it down again in conformity to the Fashion. . . .

Now as to the Proposal, it is to erect a *Monastery*, or if you will (to avoid giving offence to the scrupulous and injudicious, by names which tho' innocent in themselves, have been abus'd by superstitious Practices,) we will call it a *Religious Retirement*, and such as shall have a double aspect, being not only a Retreat from the World for those who desire that advantage, but likewise, an Institution and previous discipline, to fit us to do the greatest good in it; such an Institution as this (if I do not mightily deceive my self) would be the most probable method to amend the present and improve the future Age. For here those who are convinc'd of the emptiness of earthly Enjoyments, who are sick of the vanity of the world and its impertinencies, may find more substantial and satisfying entertainments, and need not be confin'd to what they justly loath. Those who are desirous to know and fortify their weak side, first do good to themselves, that hereafter they may be capable of doing more good to others; or for their greater security are willing to avoid *temptation*, may get out of that danger which a continual stay in view of the Enemy, and the familiarity and unwearied application of the Temptation may expose them to; and gain an opportunity to look into themselves to be acquainted at home and no longer the greatest strangers to their own hearts. Such as are willing in a more peculiar and undisturb'd manner, to attend the great business they came into the world about, the service of GOD and improvement of their own Minds, may find a convenient and blissful recess from the noise and hurry of the world. A world so cumbersom, so infectious, that altho' thro' the grace of GOD and their own strict watchfulness, they are kept from sinking down into its corruptions, 'twill however damp their flight to heav'n, hinder them from attaining any eminent pitch of Vertue.

You are therefore Ladies, invited into a place, where you shall suffer no other confinement, but to be kept out of the road of sin: You shall not be depriv'd of your grandeur, but only exchange the vain Pomps and Pageantry of the world, empty Titles and Forms of State, for the true and solid Greatness of being able to despise them. You will only quit the Chat of insignificant people for an ingenious Conversation; the froth of flashy Wit for real Wisdom; idle tales for instructive discourses. The deceitful Flatteries of those who under pretence of loving and admiring you, really served their *own* base ends for the seasonable Reproofs and wholesome Counsels of your hearty well-wishers and affectionate Friends, which will procure you those perfections your feigned lovers pretended you had, and kept you from obtaining. No uneasy task will be enjoyn'd you, all your labour being only to prepare for the highest degrees of that Glory, the very lowest of which is more than at present you are able to conceive, and the prospect of it sufficient to out-weigh all the Pains of Religion, were there any in it, as really there are none. All that is requir'd of you, is only to be as Happy as possibly you can, and to make sure of a Felicity that will fill all the capacities of your Souls!

Glossary

accoutred: well-dressed with the proper articles of clothing or dress

cumbersom: alternate spelling of cumbersome; difficult to handle; overly heavy or burdensome

monastery: a facility to allow people to seclude themselves from society to live a pious life and concentrate on religious study

Short-Answer Questions

1. When this was written, what were the main occupations to which women were supposed to direct their energies? How did these priorities limit their opportunities?

2. Why did the author believe that women needed a separate facility for their education? Why not simply integrate women into the existing male colleges?

3. What role did religion play in Astell's proposed women's institution? What benefits could women gain from the study of religion, in the opinion of the author?

Lady Mary Wortley Montagu: Smallpox Vaccination in Turkey

Author Lady Mary Wortley Montagu **Date** c. 1717 **Document Type** Letters/Correspondence	**Significance** Described efforts in the eighteenth century to inoculate people against smallpox

Overview

Smallpox was a deadly and highly contagious disease that ravaged the world until the widespread use of vaccinations essentially eradicated the illness in the late twentieth century. Victims of the disease suffered a high fever and a skin rash characterized by pustules. These typically left dramatic scarring. The disease was transmitted mainly by skin-to-skin contact with an infected person. Approximately one in three people who became infected with smallpox died.

In areas of Central Asia, India, the Middle East, and China, physicians had some success preventing the disease through inoculation. Doctors would intentionally infect a person with a mild form of smallpox through a process known as variolation. Variolation stimulated a person's immune system to fight the disease. If the inoculation worked, it gave a person lifetime immunity to smallpox. However, in some cases, variolation caused a person to develop a full and even fatal case of the disease.

Lady Mary Wortley Montagu was the wife of the British ambassador to the Ottoman Empire (an Islamic empire that ruled most of the Middle East and North Africa until the 1900s). During her stay in what is now modern Turkey, beginning in 1717, Lady Montagu observed Ottoman physicians using variolation. In letters to friends and family back in Great Britain, she praised variolation and argued strongly for its use in her native country. Lady Montagu described the process and reported that it was generally effective and resulted in much less scarring than the disease caused. Usually the inoculations were given to children. The ambassador's wife even noted that she intended to have her son inoculated. Lady Montagu wrote that she hoped to introduce the system to Britain even if there was resistance to the new approach by doctors there.

By the 1720s, partially thanks to Lady Montagu's advocacy, a growing number of people in Britain and the rest of Western Europe were being inoculated through variolation. However, in 1796, a British physician, Edward Jenner, found a new system of inoculation. Jenner discovered that he could inject patients with cow pox, a mild disease related to smallpox, and achieve immunity in those people. Jenner's discovery led to extensive vaccination campaigns that eventually suppressed the disease.

Lady Mary Wortley Montagu
(Wikimedia Commons)

Document Text

I am going to tell you a thing, that will make you wish yourself here. The small-pox, so fatal, and so general amongst us, is here entirely harmless, by the invention of engrafting, which is the term they give it. There is a set of old women, who make it their business to perform the operation, every autumn, in the month of September, when the great heat is abated. People send to one another to know if any of their family has a mind to have the small-pox; they make parties for this purpose, and when they are met (commonly fifteen or sixteen together) the old woman comes with a nut-shell full of the matter of the best sort of small-pox, and asks what vein you please to have opened. She immediately rips open that you offer to her, with a large needle (which gives you no more pain than a common scratch) and puts into the vein as much matter as can lie upon the head of her needle, and after that, binds up the little wound with a hollow bit of shell, and in this manner opens four or five veins. The Grecians have commonly the superstition of opening one in the middle of the forehead, one in each arm, and one on the breast, to mark the sign of the Cross; but this has a very ill effect, all these wounds leaving little scars, and is not done by those that are not superstitious, who chuse to have them in the legs, or that part of the arm that is concealed. The children or young patients play together all the rest of the day, and are in perfect health to the eighth. Then the fever begins to seize them, and they keep their beds two days, very seldom three. They have very rarely above twenty or thirty in their faces, which never mark, and in eight days' time, they are as well as before their illness. Where they are wounded, there remains running sores during the distemper, which I don't doubt is a great relief to it. Every year, thousands undergo this operation, and the French Ambassador says pleasantly, that they take the small-pox here by way of diversion, as they take the waters in other countries. There is no example of any one that has died in it, and you may believe I am well satisfied of the safety of this experiment, since I intend to try it on my dear little son.

I am patriot enough to take the pains to bring this useful invention into fashion in England, and

I should not fail to write to some of our doctors very particularly about it, if I knew any one of them that I thought had virtue enough to destroy such a considerable branch of their revenue, for the good of mankind. But that distemper is too beneficial to them, not to expose to all their resentment, the hardy wight that should undertake to put an end to it. Perhaps if I live to return, I may, however, have courage to war with them. Upon this occasion, admire the heroism in the heart of your friend. . . .

Glossary

chuse: alternate spelling of choose

distemper: disease or malady, or symptoms of disease

engrafting: an early form of inoculation that involved injecting diseased material into the skin to stimulate a person's immune system

Grecians: Greeks

wight: soul or person

Short-Answer Questions

1. Why did the Greeks use a different system for their inoculations? What were the potential problems with the Greek system?

2. Why would Ottoman women in the eighteenth century have parties for smallpox inoculation? Was this a good approach to encourage more people to get inoculated, or could there have been better methods to expand the use of variolation?

3. Why does Lady Montagu believe that some physicians in Great Britain would be opposed to inoculating people against smallpox?

Lady Hong:
"Diary of Lady Hong, Queen of Korea"

Author
Lady Hong

Date
c. 1750

Document Type
Essays, Reports, Manifestos

Significance
Described the challenges of life as a crown princess in the gilded palaces of Korea's neo-Confucian Joseon Dynasty court, Lady Hong's husband's descent into madness, and the killings for which he was eventually put to death

Overview

Lady Hong, also known as Lady Hyegyeong, was born in 1735. A Korean writer and a crown princess during the neo-Confucian Joseon Dynasty, she reveals in her memoirs the tortured life of a high-status, elite woman in Korea's conservative society. Lady Hong was married to Crown Prince Sado when she was just nine years old and spent most of her life in the palaces of modern-day Seoul. In 1744, a royal edict was dispatched throughout the Joseon realm requesting that families with eligible young girls submit their names for the selection of a spouse for the son of King Yeongjo. The Hong family was not wealthy, but Lady Hong was selected to be betrothed to Crown Prince Sado. When she was nine years old, Lady Hong was separated from her family and ensconced in Changdeokgung Palace, "The Palace of Prospering Virtue." She was married to Prince Sado in elaborate ceremonies held over seven days in early 1744.

The marriage was not a happy one. Early in their marriage, the Crown Prince showed signs of increasingly severe mental illness. He was notorious for his "clothing phobia," which caused him to burn whole collections of outfits before selecting one to wear. Eventually, his episodes became violent. At one point, he presented the severed head of one of his eunuchs (castrated servants, often used to guard women's living areas in Asian court societies) to Lady Hong's ladies-in-waiting, forcing them to view it with him. Prince Sado was eventually executed for his crimes, and Lady Hong's only son took the throne as King Chongjo in 1776.

This excerpt from Lady Hong's diaries reveals her sensitivity and her insights into the hierarchical, conservative workings of the Korean court. It also amply demonstrates that the wealth and status she gained from her marriage proved to be far from liberating. Elite women in Korean society suffered under patriarchal norms and stifling rules of behavior that could be every bit as oppressive as those that tyrannized women of lower status and wealth.

Document Text

Although what follows is something I should not record, I cannot help but do so. When I was pregnant with Uiso, I often saw [my sister-in-law] Princess Hwap'yong in my dreams. She would come into my bedroom, sit beside me, and laugh. In my immature way I thought it was because Princess Hwap'yong had died in childbirth and since she appeared so regularly in my dreams, I was concerned about my own well-being, for I understood that the spirit of delivery is merciless. When Uiso was born and washed, I found he had a red spot on his shoulder and a blue spot on his stomach. At first I did not pay special attention to this, but King Yongjo was supposed to proceed to Onyang on 11 October 1750, and on the tenth he and Lady Sonhui came to see us, their faces half happy and half sad. Suddenly, they undid the baby's coat collar and bared his shoulders, discovering the red spot immediately. They seemed to be very moved really to think that Princess Hwap'yong had been reincarnated. From that time, they treasured the baby just as they had treasured my sister-in-law, Hwap'yong. . . .

One hundred days after the baby's birth, the king ordered repairs to be made to the Hwan'gyong-Jon Mansion, where he used to give audience to the people and moved the baby into this palace. As King Yongjo loved the baby so much, I implored him to treat the baby's father [Lady Hong's husband, the crown prince] better. But the fact is that the king loved the baby because he thought it was the reincarnation of Hwap'yong and, as its parents, we were treated no better than before . . . and when

Uiso died in the spring of 1752, the king's agony exceeded description.

In January 1752, with the help and influence of heaven and the royal ancestors, I again became pregnant and in the ninth month, 1752, I bore another son. This was the future King Chonjo. In view of the few blessings I had received up till then, it was an unexpected happiness. When the baby was born, his appearance was impressive, his bone structure outstanding, and he really was the True Man of Taoism, the heaven-sent one. . . .

After the bitter loss of Uiso, King Yongjo was delighted to regain a foundation for the state, and said to me, "Since the royal grandson is so outstanding, he must be a blessing sent by the divine spirits of the royal ancestors. You, a descendent of Princess Chongmyong, became the crown prince's consort, and your body was blessed so that you were able to make this meritorious contribution to the state." He also said, "Please rear the child carefully yet modestly, for in this way you may spin out his happiness." Naturally, I held these royal instructions in high regard, never forgetting such royal favor and keeping these in mind all the time. The crown prince too was overjoyed, and everyone in the country rejoiced, even more so than before. . . . I was very happy and proud to think that at the age of twenty, my body had been blessed that I was able to ensure the happiness of the state, and that my future was secured. I prayed that in my old age I might long be able to enjoy my son's filial devotion.

Glossary

Hwan'gyong-Jon Mansion: also transcribed Hwangyeongjeon, a structure in Changgyeong Palace in Seoul, South Korea, first built in 1484 during the reign of King Seongjong

King Yongjo: Yeongjo of Joseon (1694–1776), the twenty-first monarch of the Joseon Dynasty of Korea; has earned a positive reputation in Korean history due to his sincere efforts to rule by Confucian ethics despite a reign marked by political infighting and the controversial execution of his own son

Lady Sonhui: Royal Noble Consort Yeong, alternatively known as Lady Seonhui, a concubine of King Yeongjo of Joseon and the mother of Crown Prince Sado

Princess Chongmyong: also transcribed Princess Cheonmyeong, a princess of Silla, one of the Three Kingdoms of early Korea

Princess Hwap'yong: also transcribed Princess Hwapyeong (1727–1748), the eldest daughter of King Yeongjo of Joseon

True Man of Taoism: known as *zhenren* in Chinese, a term meaning "authentic person" or "Taoist spiritual master"; mythologized in religious Taoism, in which *zhenren* occupy various places in the celestial hierarchy

Short-Answer Questions

1. Describe the roles of religion, prophecy, and spirituality in the life of Lady Hong. Use specific examples from the excerpt in your response.

2. Explain what you think this passage reveals about the status of elite women in Korean society during this time period. Use specific examples from the excerpt to support your interpretations and analysis.

3. Based on this excerpt, analyze Lady Hong's status in the eyes of the Korean King and his subjects. Why was she valued, and what was she valued for? In your response, consider the role of her body and reproductive capacities in Korea's political system.

William Blackstone: *Commentaries on the Laws of England:* "Of Husband and Wife"

Author	Significance
William Blackstone	An influential interpretation of English common law that was written in the eighteenth century and highlighted existing gender inequalities in marriage laws
Date	
1765	
Document Type	
Essays, Reports, Manifestos	

Overview

Common law formed the basis for the U.S. legal system, which evolved to incorporate the U.S. Constitution, court precedent, local statues and regulations, and other sources as well. Common law arose in England and was then exported to the various British colonies around the world, including those in North America that would eventually become the United States. In the 1760s, Sir William Blackstone, a noted English legal scholar, wrote a highly detailed and comprehensive four-volume overview of common law titled *Commentaries on the Laws of England*. The collection became the basis for the study of law in English-speaking countries. It was used to train lawyers and to guide judges as they reviewed cases.

One chapter of Blackstone's work, "Of Husband and Wife," reviewed the legal framework surrounding marriage. At the time, the laws were extraordinarily unfair toward women. When a woman married, she lost her individual identity. She ceased to be considered a separate person in the eyes of the law. A woman was unable to enter into contracts without her husband's consent, nor was she able to sue or seek damages without the permission of her spouse. When a women married, all of her property or wealth became that of her husband.

While these discriminatory traits existed in English common law at the time, Blackstone's work reinforced their importance in legal matters. This approach toward women was generally echoed in laws on marriage and women's property rights in the new states and territories of the United States after the Revolutionary War. However, even before the rebellion against Great Britain, some North American colonies had begun to grant women some minimal rights over property and wealth. For instance, in the early 1770s, New York and Maryland approved laws that required married women to approve property sales or transfers by their husbands. After the Revolution, Massachusetts adopted a similar measure that also gave women the right buy or sell property or engage in other business transactions if their husband was out of the state or overseas.

Nonetheless, despite limited progress in some states, women remained limited in property rights among most of the colonies. These limitations were also used by various state governments to justify denying women the right to vote. Opponents of women's suffrage argued that husbands could easily coerce their wives into voting for whoever they favored. It was only in the 1800s that U.S. women began to gain greater property and political rights resulting from the first wave of feminism that began with the Women's Rights Convention of 1848.

William Blackstone
(National Portrait Gallery)

Document Text

By marriage, the husband and wife are one person in law: that is, the very being or legal existence of the woman is suspended during the marriage, or at least is incorporated and consolidated into that of the husband: under whose wing, protection, and *cover*, she performs every thing; and is therefore called in our law-french a *feme-covert*; is said to be *covert-baron*, or under the protection and influence of her husband, her *baron*, or lord; and her condition during her marriage is called her *cover-ture*. Upon this principle, of an union of person in husband and wife, depend almost all the legal rights, duties, and disabilities, that either of them acquire by the marriage. I speak not at present of the rights of property, but of such as are merely *personal*. For this reason, a man cannot grant any thing to his wife, or enter into covenant with her: for the grant would be to suppose her separate existence; and to covenant with her, would be only to covenant with himself: and therefore it is also generally true, that all compacts made between husband and wife, when single, are voided by the intermarriage. A woman indeed may be attorney for her husband; for that implies no separation from, but is rather a representation of, her lord. And a husband may also bequeath any thing to his wife by will; for that cannot take effect till the coverture is determined by his death. The husband is bound to provide his wife with necessaries by law, as much as himself; and if she contracts debts for them, he is obliged to pay them; but for any thing besides necessaries, he is not chargeable. Also if a wife elopes, and lives with another man, the husband is not chargeable even for necessaries; at least if the person, who furnishes them, is sufficiently apprized of her elopement. If the wife be indebted before marriage, the husband is bound afterwards to pay the debt; for he has adopted her and her circumstances together. If the wife be injured in her person or her property, she can bring no action for redress without her husband's concurrence, and in his name, as well as her own: neither can she be sued, without making the husband a defendant. There is indeed one case where the wife shall sue and be sued as a *feme sole*, viz. where the husband has abjured the realm, or is banished: for then he is dead in law; and, the husband being thus disabled to sue for or defend the wife, it would be most unreasonable if she had no remedy, or could make no defence at all. In criminal prosecutions, it is true, the wife may be indicted and punished separately; for the union is only a civil union. But, in trials of any sort, they are not allowed to be evidence for, or against, each other: partly because it is impossible their testimony should be indifferent; but principally because of the union of person: and therefore, if they were admitted to be witnesses *for* each other, they would contradict one maxim of law . . . and if *against* each other, they would contradict another maxim. . . . But where the offence is directly against the person of the wife, this rule has been usually dispensed with: and therefore, by statute . . . in case a woman be forcibly taken away, and married, she may be a witness against such her husband, in order to convict him of felony. For in this case she can with no propriety be reckoned his wife; because a main ingredient, her consent, was wanting to the contract: and also there is another maxim of law, that no man shall take advantage of his own wrong; which the ravisher here would do, if by forcibly marrying a woman, he could prevent her from being a witness, who is perhaps the only witness, to that very fact. . . .

But, though our law in general considers man and wife as one person, yet there are some instances in which she is separately considered; as inferior to him, and acting by his compulsion. And therefore all deeds executed, and acts done, by her, during her coverture, are void, or at least voidable; except it be a fine, or the like matter of record, in which case she must be solely and secretly examined, to learn if her act be voluntary. She cannot by will devise lands to her husband, unless under special circumstances; for at the time of making it she is supposed to be under his coercion. And in some felonies, and other inferior crimes, committed by her, through constraint of her husband, the law excuses her: but this extends not to treason or murder.

The husband also (by the old law) might give his wife moderate correction. For, as he is to answer for her misbehaviour, the law thought it reasonable to intrust him with this power of restraining her, by domestic chastisement, in the same moderation that a man is allowed to correct his servants or children; for whom the master or parent is also liable in some cases to answer. But this power of correction was confined within reasonable bounds, and the husband was prohibited to use any violence to his wife. . . . The civil law gave the husband the same, or a larger, authority over his wife. . . . But, with us, in the politer reign of Charles the second, this power of correction began to be doubted: and a wife may now have security of the peace against her husband; or, in return, a husband against his wife. Yet the lower rank of people, who were always fond of the old common law, still claim and exert their antient privilege: and the courts of law will still permit a husband to restrain a wife of her liberty, in case of any gross misbehavior.

These are the chief legal effects of marriage during the coverture; upon which we may observe, that even the disabilities, which the wife lies under, are for the most part intended for her protection and benefit. So great a favourite is the female sex of the laws of England.

Glossary

Charles the second: Charles II, monarch of England from 1660 to 1685

chastisement: pain or other forms of punishment in response to bad or unacceptable behavior

covert-baron: a married woman

coverture: the restrictions and rights of a married women in the common law system

elopement: the act of leaving one partner for another

feme-covert: a married woman

feme sole: an unmarried woman

law-french: the language of the court

Short-Answer Questions

1. Under common law, what happened to a women's property or wealth when she married? Why?

2. Why were women not allowed to testify against their husbands in trials or other legal matters? Was this fair? Were there any situations in which a female spouse could act to represent her husband?

3. Under common law in the 1700s, could a husband restrain or use other physical measures against his wife? What were the guidelines or limitations on the actions of the husband in these circumstances?

Chapter 3

Women in Colonial and Revolutionary America

When Europeans began arriving in large numbers in the Americas, they brought not only their animals, plants, and diseases with them, they also brought their assumptions and beliefs about how society ought to operate. That included ideas about the roles and status of women, ideas that had been slowly changing for centuries. The process of colonization accelerated those changes. By the early seventeenth century, when English colonies began to spread across the coast of what is now the United States, European-born men and women were experimenting with new ways of running their society and new understandings of how social roles ought to operate.

Women Seek Religious and Property Rights

Many of these experiments were rooted in questions about the free practice of religion within the colonies. In the colonies of New England, many Protestant settlers were willing to redefine their roles toward traditional institutions, especially the established Church of England. They were far less willing to allow women to practice and preach their religion on an equal basis with men. That intransigence emerged in the Massachusetts

Bay Colony's (1637) trial of Anne Hutchinson (1591–1643), a woman accused of hosting worship services in her own home. Scandalized by Hutchinson's assertion of a woman's right to preach the Gospel, the all-male court expelled her from the community.

Only eleven years later, a Maryland woman named Margaret Brent (c. 1601–c. 1671) made what the all-male Maryland Assembly considered an extraordinary request: she asked that the assembly acknowledge her right to vote as a landowner (on an equal basis with all members of the assembly) and as Lord Baltimore's representative. A successful businessperson, Brent not only managed property for herself and her brothers, but she also sued to protect their interests—and Lord Calvert's—in court. When Lord Calvert died, however, his heir took steps to undercut Brent's position, and after a few years Brent was forced out of the colony, eventually settling in Virginia.

Laws Continue to Constrict Lower-Class Women and Slaves

Brent's example, however, is an outlier. Most women did not have her advantages of position of wealth and were more concerned with problems associated with everyday life: death, marriage, and birth, such as the one the poet Anne Bradstreet (1612–1672) wrote about in "Before the Birth of One of Her Children." Enslaved women of color faced an even bleaker future, especially after 1662 in Virginia, where the colony's Act XII established that children born to an enslaved Black mother would themselves be slaves. As late as 1756 in Maryland, an indentured servant named Elizabeth Sprigs wrote in a letter addressed to her father in England, complaining bitterly about cruel treatment, lack of food, and poor clothing. "If you have any Bowels of Compassion left," Sprigs said, "show it by sending me some Relief, Clothing is the principle thing wanting."

One of the most notorious examples of ill-treatment of ordinary women during the colonial period was the witch trials that took place in Salem, Massachusetts, in 1692. The vast majority of those accused of witchcraft were women, as were those who were executed. Although there are many examples of misogyny throughout the trial records, there are very few that offer an exoneration, or even a defense, of the accused. The sole exception is Deodat Lawson, a former minister at Salem, who wrote *A Further Account of the Tryals of the New England Witches, Sent in a Letter from Thence, to a Gentleman in London* (1692). Lawson pointed out that one accused, whom he identified as a woman by the name of Dayton, had a sterling reputation, and no credible evidence was produced against her—an indictment of the misogyny that characterized the trials. "Upon the whole," Lawson concluded, "there was not prov'd against her any thing worthy of Reproof, or just admonition, much less so heinous a Charge."

The Revolutionary Era

During the Revolutionary era, as their ancestors had done 150 years earlier, women recognized the battle for rights and added their voices to the patriot cause. In 1775 the poet Phillis Wheatley addressed an ode to "His Excellency General Washington," celebrating Washington's appointment as commander in chief of the patriot forces seeking to liberate the town of Boston from its British occupiers. Wheatley, an enslaved Black woman, sent a copy of the poem to Washington—one of the most prominent slaveholders in Virginia—along with a letter addressed to him. The following year Abigail Adams, the wife of then-representative John Adams of Massachusetts, wrote her husband a letter enjoining him to "Remember the Ladies" (1776). She reminded him that, if American men were oppressed by British power, American women were equally oppressed by their husbands and had inalienable rights as well. Eleven years later, in 1787, a group of Cherokee women wrote to Governor Benjamin Franklin of Pennsylvania, exercising the right to speak for their nation. Franklin, despite his reputation as a lover of liberty, did not respond.

It remained for the Pennsylvania physician and Enlightenment philosopher Benjamin Rush (1746–1816) to establish a position on the treatment of women that acknowledged some—but far from all—the rights that Revolutionary-era women had demanded. Rush's 1787 essay "Thoughts upon Female Education" helped establish the idea of "Republican motherhood": the concept that women's role in the American republic was primarily one of nurturing and educating the next generation of patriotic Americans. Rush argued for women's access to higher education but also felt that such an education ought to be limited to the subjects of religion, morality, history, and poetry. He also advocated for separate educational institutions for men and women; he himself was a cofounder of the Young Ladies' Academy of Philadelphia, the city's first institution for higher education. Rush's vision acknowledged some rights for women (at least, for women of higher social status). But it did not come anywhere near the goals that women like Abigail Adams, her friend Mercy Otis Warren, and Phillis Wheatley imagined for themselves. Male patriots had achieved many of their dreams at the end of the Revolutionary period. For American women, however, the struggle was just beginning.

Further Reading

Books

Baker, Emerson M. *A Storm of Witchcraft: The Salem Trials and the American Experience.* New York: Oxford University Press, 2015.

Berkin, Carol. *First Generations: Women in Colonial America.* New York: Hill & Wang, 1996.

Block, Sharon. *Rape and Sexual Power in Early America.* Chapel Hill: University of North Carolina Press, 2006.

Brown, Kathleen. *Good Wives, Nasty Wenches, and Anxious Patriarchs: Gender, Race, and Power in Colonial Virginia.* Chapel Hill: University of North Carolina Press, 1996.

Fischer, Kirsten. *Suspect Relations: Sex, Race, and Resistance in Colonial North Carolina.* Ithaca, NY: Cornell University Press, 2002.

Foster, Thomas A., ed. *Women in Early America.* New York: New York University Press, 2015.

Lyons, Clare A. *Sex among the Rabble: An Intimate History of Gender and Power in the Age of Revolution, Philadelphia, 1730–1830.* Chapel Hill: University of North Carolina Press, 2006.

Norton, Mary Beth. *Liberty's Daughters: The Revolutionary Experience of American Women, 1750–1800.* Ithaca, NY: Cornell University Press, 1996.

Perdue, Theda. *Cherokee Women: Gender and Culture Change, 1700–1835.* Lincoln: University of Nebraska Press, 1998.

Online

"Adams Family Papers: An Electronic Archive." Massachusetts Historical Society, accessed September 22, 2023, https://www.masshist.org/digitaladams/archive/index.

"Salem Witch Trials Documentary Archive and Transcription Project" (2018). University of Virginia website, accessed September 22, 2023, https://salem.lib.virginia.edu/home.html.

Massachusetts Bay Colony Trial against Anne Hutchinson

Author
Massachusetts Bay Colony General Court

Date
1637

Document Type
Legal

Significance
Challenged the patriarchal norms of Puritan society and advanced the then-radical idea of freedom of worship

Overview

On November 7, 1637, Anne Hutchinson, a member of the Puritan community of Massachusetts Bay, faced a tribunal led by Massachusetts governor John Winthrop. Hutchinson, who was deeply religious, thought that the religious leaders of her community had lost their way and argued that the strict religious decrees that governed Massachusetts conflicted with the doctrine of predestination. In essence, she argued that members of the public could ignore the dictates of the colony's leaders and seek salvation on their own. The Puritan ministers were deeply threatened by Hutchinson and had her brought before the colony's General Court. Hutchinson's response to Winthrop has become a landmark statement on freedom of worship and freedom of conscience. Historians also see Hutchinson herself as a woman who challenged the male patriarchy of both colony and church.

The trial against Anne Hutchinson arrived at a sensitive time for the Massachusetts Bay Colony. The colony was being threatened by forces from three different directions: from the French in Canada, from the largest group of Native Americans in the area, and from the English government in London, which was reportedly considering recalling Massachusetts Bay's charter and turning it into a royal colony. Both ministers and governor saw the challenge to their authority as a threat to the very existence of Massachusetts Bay.

Winthrop was also angry because he thought Hutchinson's behavior was threatening what he believed to be the colony's divine mission. Winthrop thought that Massachusetts Bay had a duty to be the epitome of Christian life and service—to be, in effect, a new Jerusalem. Winthrop claimed that Hutchinson was disrupting the rule of God in the colony and thwarting his political agenda. For her part, Hutchinson responded that she was, in fact, following holy law herself, and if disruption was occurring it was the fault of Winthrop and his supporters. Their back-and-forth dialogue demonstrates clearly how disagreements, even within a tight-knit community of Christian believers, caused political and social unrest in early New England.

Document Text

Gov. John Winthrop: Mrs. Hutchinson, you are called here as one of those that have troubled the peace of the commonwealth and the churches here; you are known to be a woman that hath had a great share in the promoting and divulging of those opinions that are the cause of this trouble, and to be nearly joined not only in affinity and affection with some of those the court had taken notice of and passed censure upon, but you have spoken divers things, as we have been informed, very prejudicial to the honour of the churches and ministers thereof, and you have maintained a meeting and an assembly in your house that hath been condemned by the general assembly as a thing not tolerable nor comely in the sight of God nor fitting for your sex. . . .

Mrs. Anne Hutchinson: I am called here to answer before you but I hear no things laid to my charge.

Gov. John Winthrop: I have told you some already and more I can tell you.

Mrs. Anne Hutchinson: Name one, Sir.

Gov. John Winthrop: Have I not named some already?

Mrs. Anne Hutchinson: What have I said or done?

Gov. John Winthrop: Why for your doings, this you did harbor and countenance those that are parties in this faction that you have heard of.

Mrs. Anne Hutchinson: That's matter of conscience, Sir.

Gov. John Winthrop: Your conscience you must keep, or it must be kept for you.

Mrs. Anne Hutchinson: Must not I then entertain the saints because I must keep my conscience.

The trial of Anne Hutchinson
(Wikimedia Commons)

Gov. John Winthrop: Say that one brother should commit felony or treason and come to his brother's house, if he knows him guilty and conceals him he is guilty of the same. . . .

Gov. John Winthrop: Why do you keep such a meeting at your house as you do every week upon a set day?

Mrs. Anne Hutchinson: It is lawful for me to do so, as it is all your practices, and can you find a warrant for yourself and condemn me for the same thing? The ground of my taking it up was, when I first came to this land because I did not go to such meetings as those were, it was presently reported that I did not allow of such meetings but held them unlawful and therefore in that regard they said I was proud and did despise all ordinances. . . .

Gov. John Winthrop: . . . By what warrant do you continue such a course?

Mrs. Anne Hutchinson: I conceive there lies a clear rule in Titus that the elder women should instruct the younger and then I must have a time wherein I must do it.

Gov. John Winthrop: All this I grant you, I grant you a time for it, but what is this to the purpose that you Mrs. Hutchinson must call a company together from their callings to come to be taught of you?

Mrs. Anne Hutchinson: If you look upon the rule in Titus it is a rule to me. . . .

Gov. John Winthrop: . . . But you must take it in this sense that elder women must instruct the younger about their business and to love their husbands and not to make them to clash Mrs. Hutchinson. . . .

Mrs. Anne Hutchinson: . . . If any come to my house to be instructed in the ways of God what rule have I to put them away? . . . Do you think it not lawful for me to teach women and why do you call me to teach the court?

Gov. John Winthrop: We do not call you to teach the court but to lay open yourself. . . .

Mrs. Anne Hutchinson: If you please to give me leave I shall give you the ground of what I know to be true. Being much troubled to see the falseness of the constitution of the Church of England, I had like to have turned Separatist. Whereupon I kept a day of solemn humiliation and pondering of the thing; this scripture was brought unto me—he that denies Jesus Christ to be come in the flesh is antichrist. This I considered of and in considering found that the papists did not deny him to be come in the flesh, nor we did not deny him—who then was antichrist? Was the Turk antichrist only? The Lord knows that I could not open scripture; he must by his prophetical office open it unto me. So after that being unsatisfied in the thing, the Lord was pleased to bring this scripture out of the Hebrews. He that denies the testament denies the testator, and in this did open unto me and give me to see that those which did not teach the new covenant had the spirit of antichrist, and upon this he did discover the ministry unto me; and ever since, I bless the Lord, he hath let me see which was the clear ministry and which the wrong.

Since that time I confess I have been more choice and he hath left me to distinguish between the voice of my beloved and the voice of Moses, the voice of John the Baptist and the voice of antichrist, for all those voices are spoken of in scripture. Now if you do condemn me for speaking what in my conscience I know to be truth I must commit myself unto the Lord. . . .

Mr. Nowel (assistant to the Court): How do you know that was the spirit?

Mrs. Anne Hutchinson: How did Abraham know that it was God that bid him offer his son, being a breach of the sixth commandment?

Dep. Gov. Thomas Dudley: By an immediate voice.

Mrs. Anne Hutchinson: So to me by an immediate revelation.

Dep. Gov. Thomas Dudley: How! an immediate revelation.

Mrs. Anne Hutchinson: By the voice of his own spirit to my soul. . . .

Glossary

rule in Titus: Titus 2:3–4: "The aged women likewise, that they be in behavior as becometh holiness, not false accusers, not given to much wine, teachers of good things; That they may teach the young women to be sober, to love their husbands, to love their children"

Separatist: a Protestant who wished to separate from the Church of England

sixth commandment: "Thou shalt not kill"

the Turk: a Muslim, especially a subject of the sultan of Turkey

Short-Answer Questions

1. Describe the character traits and qualities Anne Hutchinson exhibits in the excerpted text. In your response, please outline what type of individual you imagine Hutchinson was.

2. How does Anne Hutchinson use scriptural texts and religious principles to justify her actions and argue for her then-radical concept of freedom of conscience? How effective are her arguments?

3. Based on the excerpt above, analyze the social and political threat Anne Hutchinson presented to the male leadership of the Massachusetts Bay Colony. Why do you think the leaders of the colony found her so dangerous that they ultimately elected to banish her?

Margaret Brent's Request for Voting Rights

Author
Assembly of Maryland

Date
1648

Document Type
Legal; Legislative

Significance
Recorded the first effort of a woman in North America to attain the right to vote

Overview

Margaret Brent was an early colonist in Maryland, at the time an English colony where any Christian—Catholic, Anglican, or otherwise—could live freely. Brent's family was Catholic, arriving in 1638, and she, her sister, and two brothers worked to make a life for themselves as traders in St. Mary's City, deep in the Chesapeake Bay. Since there were so few colonists in the new colony, everyone knew everyone else, and Margaret made a name for herself quickly as a responsible businesswoman and landowner. She was very well known to the Calvert family, who owned the colony as a private, religiously tolerant concern. Though it was not the norm, it was hardly unusual in English North America—at the time a pestilential climate full of hostile Native inhabitants, unsafe water, and exceedingly hard work and living—for a single woman to hold an important role in maintaining her family and its profits; after all, anyone could die off at any time, so all hands were necessary. What was unusual was that Margaret (as opposed to one of her brothers) was the head of her household and a confidant of the Calvert family. When Leonard Calvert, the governor

of Maryland, died in the middle of the English Civil War in 1647, he left Margaret as the executor of his will, charging her with using his family's fortune to pay his soldiers fighting for Charles I. Because Leonard Calvert's estate was not sufficient to pay his soldiers, Margaret Brent got the Maryland General Assembly to grant her control over his brother's estate too—that of George Calvert, the reigning Lord Baltimore. To pay the soldiers, she sold some of Lord Baltimore's cattle.

To be sure that her actions were approved by the General Assembly, she asked to be allowed to vote in its proceedings—in fact, she asked for two votes: one as herself, and one as Lord Baltimore's attorney. The assembly turned her down, to her eventual downfall: despite the assembly's later defense of her actions, Lord Baltimore himself was angered at his loss of cattle to pay soldiers, and the Brent family migrated to Virginia in disgrace. Nevertheless, Margaret Brent's petition to the Maryland General Assembly is the first recorded instance of a woman calling for the right to vote in the history of what would eventually become the United States.

Document Text

Friday 21 Jan

The freemen bound to attend the Assembly appeared except Mr. Fenwick, Mr. Borneborough, Mr Brookes & George Saphyer

Summons to George Saphyer to be at the Assembly forthwith upon sight &c was read certain orders to be observed in the house during the Assembly

Came Mrs Margaret Brent and requested to have vote in the house for her self and voice also for that at the last Court 3rd Jan: it was ordered that the said Mrs Brent was to be looked upon and received as his Lordship's Attorney. The Government denyed that the said Mrs Brent should have any vote in the house. And the said Mrs Brent protested against all proceedings in this present Assembly, unless she may be present and have vote as aforesaid.

Painting of Margaret Brent
(Wikimedia Commons)

Glossary

freemen: a title distinguishing the assembly's members from indentured servants, slaves, women, and so on.

his Lordship: Lord Baltimore, brother of Leonard Calvert, then owner and governor of the colony of Maryland

Short-Answer Questions

1. Describe the proceedings of the Maryland General Assembly on January 21, 1648.

2. Why do you think the General Assembly turned down Margaret Brent's petition to vote?

3. If the Maryland General Assembly had accepted Margaret Brent's petition to vote, how do you think American history might have turned out differently?

Virginia's Act XII: Negro Women's Children to Serve according to the Condition of the Mother

Author
Virginia House of Burgesses

Date
1662

Document Type
Legislative; Legal

Significance

Made the child of an enslaved mother a slave for life, departing from the English tradition in which a child received their status from their father

Overview

In December 1662 the Virginia House of Burgesses met for the second time that year and approved a set of twenty-three statutes that focused on various facets of colonial life. The most infamous of these laws, Act XII: Negro Women's Children to Serve according to the Condition of the Mother, made the civil status of enslaved African and African American women inheritable by their offspring. The burgesses, convened by the governor, Sir William Berkeley, and presided over by the speaker, Captain Robert Wynne, acted in response to their perceptions of the colonists' needs and interests. Other legislation passed during that session included the commission for a new city to be built at Jamestown, various attempts at regulating trade, several taxes and tax reforms, a law aimed at controlling brabbling (squabbling) or gossiping women, and six statutes governing the behavior and status of indentured servants.

Act XII represented a unique departure from the English tradition regarding the heritability of slavery. Traditionally, a child received his or her enslaved status from his or her father. It also imposed greater fines for sexual relations between "any christian" (referring to colonists of European descent) and Africans or descendants of Africans.

Document Text

Whereas some doubts have arisen whether children got by any Englishman upon a negro woman should be slave or free, *Be it therefore enacted and declared by this present grand assembly,* that all children borne in this country shall be held bond or free only according to the condition of the mother, *And* that if any christian shall commit fornication with a negro man or woman, he or she so offending shall pay double the fines imposed by the former act.

Glossary

fornication: sexual intercourse between people who are not married

got: produced

held bond: enslaved

Short-Answer Questions

1. What do you think was the intended purpose of the Virginia House of Burgesses passing this statute? Consider both elements of the statute in your response.

2. How might slaveholders—many of whom were members of the Virginia House of Burgesses—have used the heritability of slavery and the formation of enslaved families to their advantage?

3. Despite living in a patriarchal society, African men or men of African descent were denied the right to determine the legal status of their children, according to the statute. How might this have affected them?

Anne Bradstreet: "Before the Birth of One of Her Children"

Author	**Significance**
Anne Bradstreet	Reflections by the first American poet on every-day life in Massachusetts Bay Colony
Date	
1678	
Document Type	
Poems, Plays, Fiction	

Overview

Anne Bradstreet (1612–1672) is acknowledged as the first English poet writing in the North American colonies—the first poet in U.S. history. She was the daughter of a prominent Puritan named Thomas Dudley, and she married another Puritan, her father's assistant, Simon Bradstreet. In 1630 the entire Dudley family, including Anne and her husband, immigrated to Massachusetts Bay Colony, similar to many Puritans at the time. Despite her misgivings, Bradstreet dutifully followed her father and husband to Salem, Massachusetts, where they immediately found a life of hardships as opposed to a religious Promised Land. However, over time, the Dudley and Bradstreet clans built successful lives for themselves in Massachusetts Bay. Both Thomas Dudley and Simon Bradstreet became governors of the colony, and Bradstreet found a level of contentment in being a wife and mother. What was interesting about Bradstreet was how she expressed her contentment, along with her occasional discontents—she wrote poetry. Her brother-in-law copied her poetry collection without her knowledge and brought the copies back to England, to publish them as *The Tenth Muse Lately Sprung Up in America, By a Gentlewoman in Those Parts* (1650). The collection was immediately successful; it mostly detailed Anne Bradstreet's Puritan beliefs, emulated her poetic heroes in rhyme and structure, and reflected on her duties as a wife and mother.

After her death in 1672, one of her sons collected the more recent poems and published a second edition of *The Tenth Muse* in 1678. The newer poems are generally regarded by literary historians as superior in quality to the older ones; more important for historical purposes, they illuminate Anne Bradstreet's inner life, particularly her sense of herself as an educated woman expected to know her place in society. As such, her later poems are seen by historians as a valuable insight into the hardships and rewards of colonial life and the life of a woman in North America. In this poem, Bradstreet addresses her fears of dying in childbirth—a very real concern at the time, and an issue eight times in her life.

Document Text

All things within this fading world hath end,
Adversity doth still our joyes attend;
No ties so strong, no friends so dear and sweet,
But with death's parting blow is sure to meet.
The sentence past is most irrevocable,
A common thing, yet oh inevitable.
How soon, my Dear, death may my steps attend,
How soon't may be thy Lot to lose thy friend,
We are both ignorant, yet love bids me
These farewell lines to recommend to thee,
That when that knot's untied that made us one,
I may seem thine, who in effect am none.
And if I see not half my dayes that's due,
What nature would, God grant to yours and you;
The many faults that well you know I have
Let be interr'd in my oblivious grave;
If any worth or virtue were in me,
Let that live freshly in thy memory
And when thou feel'st no grief, as I no harms,
Yet love thy dead, who long lay in thine arms.
And when thy loss shall be repaid with gains
Look to my little babes, my dear remains.
And if thou love thyself, or loved'st me,
These o protect from step Dame's injury.
And if chance to thine eyes shall bring this verse,
With some sad sighs honour my absent Hearse;
And kiss this paper for thy love's dear sake,
Who with salt tears this last Farewel did take.

A posthumous depiction of Anne Bradstreet
(Wikimedia Commons)

Glossary

step Dame: in this context, a future stepmother to Bradstreet's children

Tenth Muse: a reference to the Nine Muses of Greek mythology, who represented the arts; Bradstreet's brother-in-law gave her the name as a similar promoter of the arts in North America

Short-Answer Questions

1. Describe what this poem is about.

2. What does Bradstreet's emphasis on her own death reveal about life in Massachusetts Bay Colony in the seventeenth century?

3. Analyze the literary devices (word choice, repetition, metaphor, etc.) that Bradstreet uses to explore the theme of death.

Deodat Lawson:
"A Further Account of the Tryals of the New England Witches, Sent in a Letter from Thence, to a Gentleman in London"

Author Deodat Lawson **Date** 1692 **Document Type** Letters/Correspondence; Essays, Reports, Manifestos	**Significance** A sensationalized account of the Salem witch trials that attempted to justify the mass prosecutions in seventeenth-century Massachusetts

Overview

In the early months of 1692, several young girls in Salem, Massachusetts, underwent a series of unexplainable outbursts and convulsions. A local doctor diagnosed them as being bewitched by evil after the girls claimed to be under the influence of satanic forces. At the time, colonial Massachusetts was controlled by the Puritans, an extremist Protestant sect that had left England to avoid religious persecution. Once in New England, the Puritans enacted a series of strict religious laws to punish those who did not conform to their beliefs. The result was a society that enforced rigid gender roles and believed that women were weaker than men and therefore inherently more likely to sin. The Puritans had very little tolerance for those who did not behave like everyone else. It was also a community in which many believed in the supernatural and blamed problems and unexplained events on the devil, witches, or other evil spirits.

The initial group of girls accused three women of being witches and casting spells on them. One of those accused, Tituba, an enslaved woman, confessed that she was a witch in an apparent attempt to save herself. Tituba also claimed there were other witches in the community. Along with additional accusations by the original accusers, the new allegations sparked a wave of hysteria. Friends and neighbors accused each other, and some used the opportunity to attack enemies or people they did not like or trust. There were wild rumors and unsubstantiated claims about the powers of the alleged witches. Many claimed that they had witnessed manifestations of evil. Ultimately, more than 200 people were accused of witchcraft, the majority of whom were women. One of those accused was a four-year-old girl. Another woman was almost eighty.

The colony's governor, William Phips, created a special court to investigate the allegations and try those

Deodat Lawson: "A Further Account of the Tryals of the New England Witches, Sent in a Letter from Thence, to a Gentleman in London"

111

accused of witchcraft. During the trials, the accusers often acted as if they were possessed and blamed their strange behavior on the supposed witches. They seemed to undergo fits and conniptions that even included self-mutilation, such as stabbing themselves with pins or needles. Known as "spectral" evidence, these acts exerted a major impact on the judges, although there was no way to conclusively prove whether the defendants had any control over their accusers. Nineteen people, including fourteen women, were hung after they were convicted of being witches. Another victim was killed while being tortured in an effort to get him to confess. At least seven people died in prison while awaiting trial.

By late 1692, the excesses of the trials and punishments led to increasing criticism by religious and civil leaders. The special court was terminated, and by May 1693, those still imprisoned for witchcraft were released with a pardon by the governor. The survivors and heirs of those executed received compensation from the colonial government in 1711. Yet some continued to support the trials and believed that they helped rid the colony of evil.

The trials were a demonstration of the worst excesses of mass hysteria combined with destructive gender stereotypes. They have come to symbolize how members of a community can turn against each other, and they highlight the dangers of religious or social intolerance. This fragment of a letter describing the trials, said to have been sent to a Mr. Nathaniel Higginson in London, appeared in a pamphlet called *A Brief and True Narrative* published by a minister in New England named Deodat Lawson in 1692, not long after the events described.

Examination of a Witch, *a painting inspired by the* **Salem Witch Trials** (Peabody Essex Museum)

Document Text

Here were in Salem, June 10, 1692, about 40 persons that were afflicted with horrible torments by Evil Spirits, and the afflicted have accused 60 or 70 as Witches, for that they have Spectral appearances of them, tho the Persons are absent when they are tormented. When these Witches were Tried, several of them confessed a contract with the Devil, by signing his Book, and did express much sorrow for the same, delareing also thir Confederate Witches, and said the Tempters of them desired 'em to sign the Devils Book, who tormented them till they did it. There were at the time of Examination, before many hundreds of Witnesses, strange Pranks play'd; such as the taking Pins out of the Clothes of the afflicted, and thrusting them into their flesh; many of which were taken out again by the Judges own hands. Thorns also in like kind were thrust into their flesh; the accusers were sometimes struck dumb, deaf, blind, and sometimes lay as if they were dead for a while, and all foreseen and declared by the afflicted just before 'twas done. Of the afflicted there were two Girls, about 12 or 13 years of age, who saw all that was done, and were therefore called the Visionary Girls; they would say, Now he, or she, or they, are going to bite, or pinch the Indian; and all there present in Court saw the visible marks on the Indians arms; they would also cry out, Now look, look, they are going to bind such an ones Legs, and all present saw the same person spoken of, fall with her Legs twisted in an extraordinary manner; Now say they, we shall all fall, and immediately 7 or 8 of the afflicted fell down, with terrible shrieks and Out-crys; at the time when one of the Witches was sentenc'd, and pinnion'd with a Cord, at the same time was the afflicted Indian Servant going home, being about 2 or 3 miles out of town, and had both his Wrists at the same instant bound about with a like Cord, in the same manner as she was when she was sentenc'd, but with that violence, that the Cord entered into his flesh, not to be untied, not hardly cut'. Many Murders are suppos'd to be in this way committed; for these Girls, and others of the afflicted, say, they see Coffins, and bodies in Shrowds, rising up, and looking on the accused, crying, Vengeance, Vengeance on the Murderers— Many other strange things were transacted before the Court in the time of their Examination; and especially one thing which I had like to have forgot, which is this, One of the accus'd, whilst the rest were under Examination, was drawn up by a Rope to the Roof of the house where he was, and would have been choak'd in all probability, had not the Rope been presently cut; the rope hung at the Roof by some invisible tye, for there was no hole where it went up; but after it was cut the remainder of it was found in the Chamber just above, lying by the very place where it hung down.

In December 1692, the Court sate again at Salem in New-England, and cleared about 40 persons suspected for Witches, and Condemned three. The Evidence against these three was the same as formerly, so the Warrant for their Execution was sent, and the Graves digged for the said three, and for about five more that had been Condemned at Salem formerly, but were Repreived by the Governour.

In the beginning of February 1693, the Court sate at Charles-Town, where the Judge exprest himself to this effect.

That who it was that obstructed the Execution of Justice, or hindered those good proceedings they had made, he knew not, but thereby the Kingdom of Satan was advanc'd, &c and the Lord have mercy on this Country; and so declined coming any more into Court. In his absence Mr. D— sate as Chief Judge 3 several days, in which time 5 or 6 were clear'd by Proclamation, and almost as many by Trial; so that all are acquitted.

The most remarkable was an Old Woman named Dayton, of whom it was said, If any in the World were a Witch, she was one, and had been so accounted 30 years. I had the Curiosity to see her tried; she was a decrepid Woman of about 80 years of age, and did not use many words in her own defence. She was accused by about 30 Witnesses; but

Deodat Lawson: "A Further Account of the Tryals of the New England Witches, Sent in a Letter from Thence, to a Gentleman in London"

113

the matter alledged against her was such as needed little apology, on her part not one passionate word, or immoral action, or evil, was then objected against her for 20 years past, only strange accidents falling out, after some Christian admonition given by her, as saying, God would not prosper them, if they wrong'd the Widow. Upon the whole, there was not prov'd against her any thing worthy of Reproof, or just admonition, must less so heinous a Charge.

So that by the Goodness of God we are once more out of present danger of this Hobgoblin Monster; the standing Evidence used at Salem were called, but did not appear.

There were others also at Charles-town brought upon their Tryals, who had formerly confess'd themselves to be Witches; but upon their tryals deny'd it, and were all clear'd; So that at present there is no further prosecution of any Cases.

Glossary

Charles-town: a village in colonial Massachusetts and a current neighborhood in modern Boston

Confederate Witches: fellow witches; colleagues; accomplices

hobgoblin: an evil, mischievous monster

spectral: ghostly, other worldly

Short-Answer Questions

1. Why were more women than men accused, convicted, and executed for witchcraft during the trials? What did the trails reveal about the status of women at the time?

2. What was the main evidence used to convict those accused of witchcraft? Why were people willing to believe or accept such evidence?

3. Why does the author view the trials positively? What does he feel they accomplished? Was his attitude shared by others at the time?

The Schlager Anthology of Women's History

Letter from Elizabeth Sprigs to Her Father

Author		Significance
Elizabeth Sprigs		Offered a personal account of the miserable treatment of indentured servants in the American colonies
Date		
1756		
Document Type		
Letters/Correspondence		

Overview

Indentured servitude, in which a person agrees to work for a specified number of years in exchange for transportation to the American colonies, was used as a way to import labor and boost the population in the English settlements of North America. Following the creation of the settlement at Jamestown, the practice of indentured servitude became increasingly popular in the Chesapeake region. Typically, indentured servants would work for about five years in exchange for their passage, lodging, board, and eventual freedom. Depending on the colony, indentured servants were protected by a series of laws, particularly in Virginia, that regulated the treatment of servants. This fascinating document, a letter from Elizabeth Sprigs to her father, tells the story of a young woman who worked as an indentured servant in the colonies. In exchange for her passage from England, Sprigs would have signed a contract to work as an indentured domestic servant. The practice is typically regarded as a seventeenth-century one, but this letter illustrates that indenture was still being utilized into the eighteenth century.

On September 22, 1756, Elizabeth Sprigs wrote to her father, John Sprigs of London, about her experiences in Maryland. In her letter, Elizabeth details the harsh treatment she faced at the hands of her master and begged her father for aid. Throughout the letter, Elizabeth complains about her treatment, food, and clothing, among her many sufferings in this new life. Although not much is known about Elizabeth, it can be decerned from the letter that she was banished from her father's house, leading her to seek work in the American colonies. Referring to herself as Betty, Elizabeth asks her father specifically to send clothing through ships traveling to Baltimore. Sprigs's insight is significant as it details the treatment that some indentured servants experienced.

Document Text

Honored Father

My being for ever banished from your sight, will I hope pardon the Boldness I now take of troubling you with these, my long silence has been purely owning to my undutifullness to you, and well knowing I had offended in the highest Degree, put a tie to my tongue and pen, for fear I should be extinct from your good Graces and add a further Trouble to you, but too well knowing your care and tenderness for me so long as I retain'd my Duty to you, induced me once again to endeavor if possible, to kindle up that flame again. O Dear Father, believe what I am going to relate the words of truth and sincerity, and Balance my former bad Conduct my sufferings here, and then I am sure you'll pity your Destress Daughter, What we unfortunate English People suffer here is beyond the probability of you in England to Conceive, let it suffice that I one of the unhappy Number, am toiling almost Day and Night, and very often in the Horses drudgery, with only this comfort that you Bitch you do not halfe enough, and then tied up and whipp'd to that Degree that you'd not serve an Animal, scarce any thing but Indian Corn and Salt to eat and that even begrudged nay many Negroes are better used, almost naked no shoes nor stockings to wear, and the comfort after slaving during Masters pleasure, what rest we can get is to rap ourselves up in a Blanket and ly upon the Ground, this is the deplorable Condition your poor Betty endures, and now I beg if you have any Bowels of Compassion left show it by sending me some Relief, Clothing is the principal thing wanting, which if you should condiscend to, may easily send them to me by any of the ships bound to Baltimore Town Patapsco River Maryland, and give me leave to conclude in Duty to you and Uncles and Aunts, and Respect to all Friends

Honored Father
Your undutifull and Disobedient Child
Elizabeth Sprigs

Glossary

better used: better treated

condiscend: deign to do; agree to do

destress: distressed

Short-Answer Questions

1. Explain in brief detail how Elizabeth Sprigs views her treatment from what she has written in this letter.

2. Summarize the chief complaints that Elizabeth Sprigs makes to her father in the letter.

3. Why might Elizabeth compare her treatment to that of enslaved people? Who does she believe is being treated "better," and why?

Phillis Wheatley: "His Excellency General Washington"

Author Phillis Wheatley **Date** 1775 **Document Type** Poems, Plays, Fiction	**Significance** Demonstrated the literary prowess of a once-enslaved woman and served as an early example of patriotic poetry honoring the American Revolution

Overview

Phillis Wheatley was born in the West African nation of Senegal in about 1753. As a young child, she was enslaved and transported to Boston, Massachusetts, where she served the Wheatley family. Early on, the family recognized Phillis's sharp intelligence and accordingly provided her with an extensive classical education. When she was around twenty years of age, in 1773, she published a collection of poetry, *Poems on Various Subjects, Religious and Moral*, making her the first-ever African American poet to be published. The collection won widespread admiration from such figures as King George III of England and Benjamin Franklin. That year, too, she was granted her freedom.

After the outbreak of the American Revolution in 1775, Wheatley wrote "To His Excellency General Washington," a passionately patriotic poem that addressed the recently appointed commander of the Continental Army, praising the American Revolution and the "great chief, with virtue on thy side." The poem reflects Wheatley's classical education, for it includes numerous allusions to the mythology of ancient Greece and Rome and embodies classical philosophical concepts relevant to the eighteenth century. Thus, she conceives of the fledgling nation as a classical goddess named Columbia and sees her as an embodiment of freedom; the poem marked the first appearance of "Columbia" in reference to the nation, and the name became a fixture in American culture and tradition. Wheatley sent the poem to Washington in a letter, prompting him to respond: "However undeserving I may be of such encomium . . . the style and manner exhibit a striking proof of your great poetical Talents." Wheatley died in 1784.

Engraving featuring Phillis Wheatley
(Library of Congress)

Document Text

Celestial choir! enthron'd in realms of light,
Columbia's scenes of glorious toils I write.
While freedom's cause her anxious breast alarms,
She flashes dreadful in refulgent arms.
See mother earth her offspring's fate bemoan,
And nations gaze at scenes before unknown!
See the bright beams of heaven's revolving light
Involved in sorrows and the veil of night!
The Goddess comes, she moves divinely fair,
Olive and laurel binds Her golden hair:
Wherever shines this native of the skies,
Unnumber'd charms and recent graces rise.
Muse! Bow propitious while my pen relates
How pour her armies through a thousand gates,
As when Eolus heaven's fair face deforms,
Enwrapp'd in tempest and a night of storms;
Astonish'd ocean feels the wild uproar,
The refluent surges beat the sounding shore;
Or think as leaves in Autumn's golden reign,
Such, and so many, moves the warrior's train.
In bright array they seek the work of war,
Where high unfurl'd the ensign waves in air.
Shall I to Washington their praise recite?
Enough thou know'st them in the fields of fight.
Thee, first in peace and honors—we demand
The grace and glory of thy martial band.
Fam'd for thy valour, for thy virtues more,
Hear every tongue thy guardian aid implore!
One century scarce perform'd its destined round,
When Gallic powers Columbia's fury found;
And so may you, whoever dares disgrace
The land of freedom's heaven-defended race!
Fix'd are the eyes of nations on the scales,
For in their hopes Columbia's arm prevails.
Anon Britannia droops the pensive head,
While round increase the rising hills of dead.
Ah! Cruel blindness to Columbia's state!
Lament thy thirst of boundless power too late.
Proceed, great chief, with virtue on thy side,
Thy ev'ry action let the Goddess guide.
A crown, a mansion, and a throne that shine,
With gold unfading, WASHINGTON! Be thine.

Glossary

Anon Britannia: Great Britain

Columbia: historical and poetic name used for America, as well as the female personification of America

ensign: a flag flown as a symbol of nationality

Eolus: Aeolus; in Greek mythology, the ruler of the winds

Gallic: of or relating to Gaul/France; likely referring to the French and Indian War

the Goddess: Wheatley's poem incorporates both allusions to Greco-Roman myth and concepts from classical philosophy; for this poem, Wheatley conceived a classically styled goddess of the American Revolution named "Columbia," an embodiment of freedom

laurel: a type of aromatic evergreen plant

propitious: giving or indicating good chance or favor

refluent: flowing back; ebbing

refulgent: shining brightly

tempest: a storm

Short-Answer Questions

1. Consider the impact of Wheatley's use of divine imagery throughout this poem. What does it suggest about her intent and her central idea?

2. Interpret the meaning of lines 33 and 34 of the poem: "Fix'd are the eyes of the nations on the scales, / For in their hopes Columbia's arm prevails." In your response, consider what Wheatley is suggesting about the international impact of the American Revolution.

3. Using evidence from the text, explain how Wheatley's poem might have contributed to an emerging sense of American patriotism during the Revolutionary War. In your response, consider how Wheatley characterizes both America and its people.

Abigail Adams:
"Remember the Ladies" Letter
to John Adams

Author
Abigail Adams

Date
1776

Document Type
Letters/Correspondence

Significance
Urged John Adams and the Continental Congress to consider the legal position and rights of the women of the American colonies

---

Overview

Abigail Adams's letter of March 31, 1776, was written from Braintree, Massachusetts, to her husband, John Adams, who was in Philadelphia at the Continental Congress urging the case for American independence. The letter, commonly referred to by her admonition to John to "remember the ladies," first speaks of the fighting in Virginia and the recent British troop withdrawal from Boston. The British position had become indefensible after General George Washington placed fortifications at Dorchester Heights, overlooking the city. Abigail voices optimism about a "temporary peace" in the spring. She then turns to the outlook for the more distant future, anticipating the formation of the new republic. In almost revolutionary language, she implores her husband in this context to keep in view the legal position of women and grant them more liberty.

Document Text

Braintree, 31 March, 1776

. . . I have sometimes been ready to think that the passion for liberty cannot be equally strong in the breasts of those who have been accustomed to deprive their fellow creatures of theirs. Of this I am certain, that it is not founded upon that generous and Christian principle of doing to others as we would that others should do unto us. . . .

I long to hear that you have declared an independency. And, by the way, in the new code of laws which I suppose it will be necessary for you to make, I desire you would remember the ladies and be more generous and favorable to them than your ancestors. Do not put such

---

The Schlager Anthology of Women's History

unlimited power into the hands of the husbands. Remember, all men would be tyrants if they could. If particular care and attention is not paid to the ladies, we are determined to foment a rebellion, and will not hold ourselves bound by any laws in which we have no voice or representation.

That your sex are naturally tyrannical is a truth so thoroughly established as to admit of no dispute; but such of you as wish to be happy willingly give up the harsh title of master for the more tender and endearing one of friend. Why, then, not put it out of the power of the vicious and the lawless to use us with cruelty and indignity with impunity? Men of sense in all ages abhor those customs which treat us only as the vassals of your sex; regard us then as beings placed by Providence under your protection, and in imitation of the Supreme Being make use of that power only for happiness.

Painting of Abigail Adams
(National Gallery of Art)

Glossary

vassals: completely dependent subjects

Short-Answer Questions

1. Analyze Abigail Adams's approach to her argument, considering especially how she draws a parallel between the plight of American women and the political status of the colonies.

2. Interpret the text of the paragraph in which Adams says "such of you [men] as wish to be happy willingly give up the harsh title of master for the more tender and endearing one of friend."

3. Interpret Adams's precise political demands. What is she requesting from her husband? What do you think Adams means when she encourages men to "regard us then as beings placed by Providence under your protection"?

Cherokee Women: Letter to Governor Benjamin Franklin

<table>
<tr><td>Author
Katteuha and three other Cherokee women</td><td>Significance
Illustrated opposing assumptions about female political power by contrasting the importance of women in Cherokee society with the patriarchal norms of colonial American culture</td></tr>
<tr><td>Date
1787</td><td></td></tr>
<tr><td>Document Type
Letters/Correspondence</td><td></td></tr>
</table>

Overview

On September 8, 1787, Katteuha and three other Cherokee women sent a letter to Benjamin Franklin, the governor of Pennsylvania at the time and a delegate to the Constitutional Convention. Their letter asked him to consider the negotiation of a peace treaty between the Cherokee and the new American nation.

Franklin disregarded the letter and did not even deign to respond to its authors.

The historical significance of this document lies in what it reveals about Cherokee social structure and what it suggests about contrasting attitudes toward female status in colonial America. Cherokee society, like that of many Native American groups, was matrilineal, meaning that each person in Cherokee society was identified with their matriline—their mother's lineage—and inherited property and social status based on their mother. Obviously,

in a matrilineal society like the Cherokee, women held considerable familial, economic, and political power. Cherokee women had control over children and property and were included in key roles in the councils and religious ceremonies that guided Cherokee life. Certain women were sometimes granted the title of *ghighua* or Beloved Woman. This was an esteemed position in Cherokee society, and it entitled Ketteuha to act as the Cherokee ambassador to the emerging United States.

Franklin was likely unaware of the intricacies of gender norms among the Cherokee and did not understand Ketteuha's significance among her people. Her letter to him, with its forthright, direct tone and its assumption of equality, diverged markedly from his probable expectations about correct female behavior. Ketteuha's letter assumes an equality between sexes, and she grounds her political legitimacy in her intimate connection to nature and childbearing. Moreover, she cites the physical and emotional bonds between mothers and children as a reason to cultivate peaceful relations between political rivals. Ultimately, while Ketteuha's letter was ignored by Franklin, its contents reveal stark differences between the Cherokee and colonial American societies, especially in how these two cultures constructed and performed gender. The Cherokee assumed the presence of women in their power structure; the Americans did not.

Document Text

Brother,

8th Sept., 1787.

I am in hopes my Brothers and the Beloved men near the water side will heare from me. This day I filled the pipes that they smoaked in piece, and I am in hopes the smoake has Reached up to the skies above. I here send you a piece of the same Tobacco, and am in hopes you and your Beloved men will smoake it in Friendship—and I am glad in my heart that I am the mother of men that will smoak it in piece.

I am in hopes if you Rightly consider it that woman is the mother of All—and that woman Does not pull Children out of Trees or Stumps nor out of old Logs, but out of their Bodies, so that they ought to mind what a woman says, and look upon her as a mother—and I have Taken the privelage to Speak to you as my own Children, and the same as if you had sucked my Breast—and I am in hopes you have a beloved woman amongst you who will help to put her Children Right if they do wrong, as I shall do the same—the great men have all promised to Keep the path clear and straight, as my Children shall Keep the path clear and white so that the Messengers shall go and come in safety Between us—the old people is never done Talking to their Children—which makes me say so much as I do. The Talk you sent to me was to talk to my Children, which I have done this day, and they all liked my Talk well, which I am in hopes you will heare from me Every now and then that I keep my Children in piece—tho' I am a woman giving you this Talk, I am in hopes that you and all the Beloved men in Congress will pay particular Attention to it, as I am Delivering it to you from the Bottom of my heart. . . .

From Katteuha, The Beloved woman of Chota.

Moses Price & Tom Ben, Linchesters.

Endorsed: From Kaattahee, Scolecutta and Kaattahee, Indian Women. His Excellency, Benjamin Franklin, Governor of the State of Pennsylvania.

Glossary

"My Brothers and the Beloved men near the water side": a reference to Benjamin Franklin and the other colonial leaders

piece: alternate spelling of "peace"

"pipes that they smoaked in piece": reference to smoking tobacco as a ceremonial and religious ritual to mark important occasions, such as prayers and peace treaties

smoaked: alternate spelling of "smoked"

Short-Answer Questions

1. Describe the reasons Katteuha cites for why women should be listened to.

2. What makes the arguments made by Katteuha so revolutionary? Consider the centrality of childbearing and motherhood to her reasoning.

3. Consider the perspective of Benjamin Franklin as the recipient of this letter. How do you think he likely reacted to it and interpreted its arguments? Consider the social context in which this document was written, as well as Franklin's perspective as a wealthy man in a patriarchal society.

The Schlager Anthology of Women's History

Benjamin Rush: "Thoughts upon Female Education"

Author
Benjamin Rush

Date
1787

Document Type
Speeches/Addresses

Significance
Promoted a specific curriculum of female education as a way of supporting American society and government

Overview

Benjamin Rush (1746–1813) was an educator, physician, humanitarian, and Founding Father of the United States. In his speech, given before the Young Ladies' Academy in Philadelphia in 1787, Benjamin Rush promotes the education of women as a way of preserving and promoting the American form of government. He begins by pointing out differences between British and American women. Rush argues that American women, because they marry at a younger age, must focus on useful forms of education that will aid them in their primary role, that of wife and mother. Women in the United States served as the "guardians of their husbands' property." In Britain, educated servants oversaw the homestead and property, while in the United States this role was predominantly played by the wife. Being educated helped in this role. Rush also points out that mothers acted as the next generation's first and most important teachers. For the American nation to survive and thrive, ideas supporting the American democratic-republican form of government must be passed down from mother to child, generation to generation. Rush is encouraging the education of women as a way of accomplishing this.

Rush lays out a specific course of study for women in their roles as wives and mothers. This includes such things as English grammar and writing along with readings in history, geography, and biographies. Singing and dancing are encouraged as ways to promote better health. Religious education is also strongly promoted as a way of promoting morality and reason.

While encouraging specific education studies, Rush also points out areas to be avoided as unnecessary for women in their social roles or simply a waste of time. These include reading novels, drawing, learning to play instruments, and learning French.

Rush concludes by stating again the benefits of educating American women. Educated wives would better their husbands and sons. The dangers of adhering to British traditions and customs, he says, will eventually lead to the degradation and decline of America. He concludes by encouraging his female listeners to prove the benefits of education within society.

Benjamin Rush
(Charles Willson Peale)

Document Text
GENTLEMEN,

I have yielded with diffidence to the solicitations of the Principal of the Academy, in undertaking to express my regard for the prosperity of this seminary of learning by submitting to your candor a few thoughts upon female education.

The first remark that I shall make upon this subject is that female education should be accommodated to the state of society, manners, and government of the country in which it is conducted.

This remark leads me at once to add that the education of young ladies in this country should be conducted upon principles very different from what it is in Great Britain and in some respects different from what it was when we were a part of a monarchical empire.

There are several circumstances in the situation, employments, and duties of women in America which require a peculiar mode of education.

I. The early marriages of our women . . . renders it necessary to contract its plan and to confine it chiefly to the more useful branches of literature.

II. The state of property in America renders it necessary for the greatest part of our citizens to employ themselves in different occupations for the advancement of their fortunes. This cannot be done without the assistance of the female members of the community. They must be the stewards and guardians of their husbands' property. That education, therefore, will be most proper for our women which teaches them to discharge the duties of those offices with the most success and reputation.

III. From the numerous avocations to which a professional life exposes gentlemen in America from their families, a principal share of the instruction of children naturally devolves upon the women. . . .

IV. The equal share that every citizen has in the liberty and the possible share he may have in the government of our country make it necessary . . . to concur in instructing their sons in the principles of liberty and government.

V. In Great Britain the business of servants is a regular occupation, but in America this humble station is the usual retreat of unexpected indigence; hence the servants in this country possess less knowledge and subordination than are required from them;

and hence our ladies are obliged to attend more to the private affairs of their families than ladies generally do of the same rank in Great Britain. . . .

The branches of literature most essential for a young lady in this country appear to be:

I. A knowledge of the English language. . . .

II. Pleasure and interest conspire to make the writing of a fair and legible hand a necessary branch of female education. . . .

III. Some knowledge of figures and bookkeeping is absolutely necessary to qualify a young lady for the duties which await her in this country. There are certain occupations in which she may assist her husband with this knowledge, and should she survive him and agreeably to the custom of our country be the executrix of his will, she cannot fail of deriving immense advantages from it.

IV. An acquaintance with geography and some instruction in chronology will enable a young lady to read history, biography, and travels, with advantage, and thereby qualify her not only for a general intercourse with the world but to be an agreeable companion for a sensible man. To these branches of knowledge may be added, in some instances, a general acquaintance with the first principles of astronomy and natural philosophy, particularly with such parts of them as are calculated to prevent superstition by explaining the causes or obviating the effects of natural evil.

V. Vocal music should never be neglected in the education of a young lady in this country. Besides preparing her to join in that part of public worship which consists in psalmody it will enable her to soothe the cares of domestic life. The distress and vexation of a husband, the noise of a nursery, and even the sorrows that will sometimes intrude into her own bosom may all be relieved by a song, where sound and sentiment unite to act upon the mind. . . .

VI. Dancing is by no means an improper branch of education for an American lady. It promotes health and renders the figure and motions of the body easy and agreeable. . . .

VII. The attention of our young ladies should be directed as soon as they are prepared for it to the reading of history, travels, poetry, and moral essays. These studies are accommodated, in a peculiar manner, to the present state of society in America, and when a relish is excited for them in early life, they subdue that passion for reading novels which so generally prevails among the fair sex. I cannot dismiss this species of writing and reading without observing that the subjects of novels are by no means accommodated to our present manners. They hold up life, it is true, but it is not yet life in America. Our passions have not as yet "overstepped the modesty of nature," nor are they "torn to tatters," to use the expressions of the poet, by extravagant love, jealousy, ambition, or revenge. As yet the intrigues of a British novel are as foreign to our manners as the refinements of Asiatic vice. . . .

VIII. It will be necessary to connect all these branches of education with regular instruction in the Christian religion. For this purpose the principles of the different sects of Christians should be taught and explained, and our pupils should early be furnished with some of the most simple arguments in favor of the truth of Christianity. . . .

From two to four hours in a day, for three or four years, appropriated to music are an immense deduction from that short period of time which is allowed by the peculiar circumstances of our country for the acquisition of the useful branches of literature that have been mentioned. How many useful ideas might be picked up in these hours from history, philosophy poetry, and the numerous moral essays with which our language abounds, and how much more would the knowledge acquired upon these subjects add to the consequence of a lady with her husband and with society than the best performed pieces of music upon a harpsichord or a guitar! Of the many ladies whom we have known who have spent the most important years of their lives in learning to play upon instruments of music, how few of them do we see amuse themselves or their friends with them after they become mistresses of families! Their harpsichords serve only as sideboards for their parlors and prove by their silence that necessity and circumstances will always prevail over fashion and false maxims of education.

Let it not be supposed from these observations that I am insensible of the charms of instrumental music or that I wish to exclude it from the education of a lady where a musical ear irresistibly disposes to it, and affluence at the same time affords a prospect of such an exemption from the usual cares and duties of the mistress of a family as will enable her to practice it. These circumstances form an exception to the general conduct that should arise upon this subject, from the present state of society and manners in America.

I beg leave further to bear a testimony against the practice of making the French language a part of female education in America. . . . It certainly comports more with female delicacy, as well as the natural politeness of the French nation, to make it necessary for Frenchmen to learn to speak our language in order to converse with our ladies than for our ladies to learn their language in order to converse with them. . . .

It is with reluctance that I object to drawing as a branch of education for an American lady. . . .

The influence of female education would be still more extensive and useful in domestic life. The obligations of gentlemen to qualify themselves by knowledge and industry to discharge the duties of benevolence would be increased by marriage; and the patriot—the hero—and the legislator would find the sweetest reward of their toils in the approbation and applause of their wives. Children would discover the marks of maternal prudence and wisdom in every station of life, for it has been remarked that there have been few great or good men who have not been blessed with wife and prudent mothers. . . .

Thus, gentlemen, have I briefly finished what I proposed. If I am wrong in those opinions in which I have taken the liberty of departing from the general and fashionable habits of thinking I am sure you will discover and pardon my mistakes. But if I am right, I am equally sure you will adopt my opinions for to enlightened minds truth is alike acceptable, whether it comes from the lips of age or the hand of antiquity or whether it be obtruded by a person who has no other claim to attention than a desire of adding to the stock of human happiness. . . .

Glossary

indigence: extreme poverty; implying that the position of servant is a desirable and skilled occupation in Great Britain but only a last-resort job for extremely poor people in the United States

psalmody: reading or singing the biblical psalms

sects: denominations; branches of Christianity

Short-Answer Questions

1. Compare and contrast the roles of women in the United States and Great Britain.

2. Explain why Rush believes singing to be a beneficial skill for women while learning an instrument is not. How does singing contribute to the roles women are expected to perform?

3. Why does Rush believe a woman's education is important?

Chapter 4

Women's Rights in the Late Modern Era

The ideals of the American Revolution challenged the existing political, economic, and social structure of Western Europe. These principles also contributed to the first wave of organized feminism in which women in the United States and Europe sought to end overt discrimination and genderism. From the late 1700s into the 1900s, women struggled to gain basic equality under the law and political rights, including the right to vote and hold elected office. Many of the leaders of the first wave of feminism were women from the upper classes, and their priorities and goals reflected their elite backgrounds. They also faced intense criticism for their ideas. Nonetheless, the work of early feminists such as Olympe de Gouges helped pave the way for achievements such as women's suffrage.

Revolutions in America and France

The U.S. Declaration of Independence (1776) explicitly stated that "all men were created equal," and the document emphasized the importance of individual rights. The new nation's Constitution (1789) and Bill of Rights (1791) promised a new political system based on equality and liberty that offered new social and economic opportunities. These qualities were in direct contrast to the monarchies of Europe that were dominated at the time by inequalities and a rigid class system. The American Revolution inspired a revolution in France that toppled that country's monarchy and a wave of uprisings in 1848 against autocratic rule in Europe. However, after the American Revolution, more than half the U.S. population was unable to partake of the stated freedoms of the new system. Slavery continued in the southern states and remained legal until the end of the Civil War in 1865. Furthermore, women of all races and classes continued to face legal, political, social, and economic barriers to equality. For instance, many nations had specific rules prohibiting women from owning land or property. Women also faced legal and social barriers to education and were not allowed to vote or participate in politics in any meaningful way.

The need for full equality between the sexes was a central theme in the aftermath of the American and French Revolutions. Writing in 1792, in *Declaration of the Rights of Woman and of the Female Citizen*, the French playwright Olympe de Gouges (1748–1793) responded to the *Declaration of the Rights of Man and of the Citizen* (1789), which extolled the virtues of universal liberty and was one of the main documents of the French Revolution. In her response, de Gouges highlighted the hypocrisy of the 1789 declaration, which called for full equality but failed to address gender inequalities in society. De Gouges's work was echoed by Englishwoman Mary Wollstonecraft's *A Vindication of the Rights of Women* (1792). In her influential work, Wollstonecraft (1759–1797) criticized existing societal values that denigrated women and restricted them to narrow roles in their homes and families. She asserted that the best way to overcome the pervasive gender inequalities in society was through education. Wollstonecraft would later be credited as the "mother" (or for some, the "grandmother") of feminism.

Catharine Sawbridge Macauley and Savitribai Phule

Education was a major concern for eighteenth and nineteenth century feminists. The noted English historian Catharine Sawbridge Macauley's (1731–1791) *Letters on Education* (1790) made the argument that the lack of education among women allowed men to dominate them into accepting subservient roles. Savitribai Phule's (1831–1897) poem "Go, Get Education" highlighted that education was a concern in non-European areas as well.

In the late 1700s and early 1800s, many societies had very unequal educational systems for boys and girls. Upper class boys could benefit from extensive educational opportunities that included the arts, sciences, history, and politics. They also had access to elite boarding schools and the potential to attend college. Less affluent children attended public or religious schools, typically for a much more limited time. Meanwhile, the curriculum for girls often emphasized lessons in comportment, dance and music, and religion. Argentine author Maria Eugenia Echenique (1851–1878) criticized this approach in an essay in 1876 in which she argued strongly that women should have an education that emphasized science and mathematics.

In the United States, educational opportunities for girls varied greatly among the states. Nonetheless, by the 1830s public schools were becoming increasingly common and the United States had one of the highest literacy rates in the world among both males and females. The oldest girls' school in the United States was Ursuline Academy, founded in New Orleans in 1727, while the oldest women's college was Bethlehem Female Seminary (which later became Moravian University), established in 1742. By the late 1800s, thanks in part to the advocacy of feminists, the United States and most Western European nations had compulsory public education.

Women Advocate for Equality Beyond the Educational Sphere

While seeking educational equality, women's rights advocates sought to end economic and legal inequalities. In her 1798 work, *Reflection on the Present Condition of the Female Sex*, Priscilla Bell Wakefield (1751–1832) argued both for better education but also more economic opportunity for women. Mary Hays (1754–1832) argued that women were trapped in a system that kept them subservient to men. One way to loosen male dominance, especially in family and household issues, was to make it easier to end marriages. Divorce laws in countries such as Great Britain, France, and the United States were extremely rigid. Caroline Norton (1808–1877) lamented the difficulty of divorce in Great Britain in the 1800s in a letter to Queen Victoria. Before divorces were made easier in 1857, only four women in British history had been able to gain a legal divorce.

Among other efforts, voting rights was one of the main goals of feminists in the 1800s. Suffragist Emmeline Pankhurst's (1858–1928) 1913 speech, "Freedom, or Death," on the importance of the vote is often regarded as one of the most important addresses of the twentieth century. Pankhurst's speech is especially notable for its militancy, and it reflects the frustration that many feminists felt in the early 1900s as efforts to secure the vote were stymied in the United States, Great Britain, and other Western democracies. Yet even after women secured the right to vote in the United States in 1920 and in Britain in 1928 (women did not gain suffrage in France until 1945), writers such as Virginia Woolf (1882–1941) highlighted the continuing inequalities that would prompt the emergence of a second wave of feminism in the 1950s and 1960s.

The Schlager Anthology of Women's History

Further Reading

Books

Hill, Bridget. *The Republican Virago. The Life and Times of Catharine Macaulay, Historian.* Oxford: Clarendon Press, 1992.

Hughes, Christina. *Key Concepts in Feminist Theory and Research.* Santa Barbara, CA: SAGE Publications, 2002.

Johnson, Claudia, ed. *The Cambridge Companion to Mary Wollstonecraft.* Cambridge: Cambridge University Press, 2002.

Kelly, Gail P., ed. *International Handbook of Women's Education.* Westport, CT: Greenwood Press, 1989.

Moore, Lisa L., Joanna Brooks, and Caroline Wigginton. *Transatlantic Feminisms in the Age of Revolutions.* Oxford: Oxford University Press, 2012.

Mousset, Sophie. *Women's Rights and the French Revolution: A Biography of Olympe de Gouges.* London: Transaction Publishers, 2007.

Phillips, Roderick. *Untying the Knot: A Short History of Divorce.* Cambridge: Cambridge University Press, 1991.

Simonton, Deborah, ed. *The Routledge History of Women in Europe since 1700.* New York: Routledge, 2006.

Todd, Janet. *Mary Wollstonecraft: A Revolutionary Life.* London: Weidenfeld & Nicolson, 2000.

Tong, Rosemarie. *Feminist Thought: A More Comprehensive Introduction.* New York: Routledge, 2018.

Walker, Alice. *In Search of Our Mothers' Gardens: Womanist Prose.* New York: Harcourt Brace Jovanovich, 2004.

Weedon, Chris. *Gender, Feminism, & Fiction in Germany, 1840–1914.* New York: Peter Lang, 2006.

Articles

Gershon, Livia. "This Was the Struggle for Female Education in the U.S." World Economic Forum and *Quartz* (January 3, 2020). Available at https://www.weforum.org/agenda/2020/01/girls-gender-equality-education-history/.

Hill, Bridget, and Christopher Hill. "Catharine Macaulay's *History* and Her 'Catalogue of Tracts'." *Seventeenth Century* 8, no. 2 (1993).

Purvis, June. "Emmeline Pankhurst (1858–1928), Suffragette Leader and Single Parent in Edwardian Britain." *Women's History Review* 20, no. 1 (2011).

Further Reading

Webites

"Feminism: The First Wave." National Women's History Museum website, April 5, 2001, https://www.womenshistory.org/exhibits/feminism-first-wave-0.

Hardy, James. "The History of Divorce Law in the USA." History Cooperative website, May 29, 2015, https://historycooperative.org/the-history-of-divorce-law-in-the-usa/.

Catherine Sawbridge Macaulay Graham:
Letters on Education

Author	Significance
Catherine Sawbridge Macaulay Graham	Repudiated Jean-Jacques Rousseau's theory concerning the differences between the sexes
Date	
1790	
Document Type	
Letters/Correspondence; Essays, Reports, Manifestos	

Overview

Catherine Sawbridge Macaulay Graham (1731–1791) was a prominent British historian and political thinker noted especially for her eight-volume *History of England* (1763–83). She was an avowed liberal, and her support for radical ideas led her to support both the American and French revolutions. Her views also contributed to her friendship with many of America's founders, including Benjamin Franklin, George Washington, Benjamin Rush, and John and Abigail Adams.

Graham published her collection *Letters on Education: With Observations on Religious and Metaphysical Subjects* in 1790. In Letter 22, "No Characteristic Difference in Sex," Graham argues against the commonly held belief in the intellectual differences between males and females. Intellectually, she says, there is no difference between the two. Graham proposes that men have traditionally been both bolder and physically stronger than women, and this combination led to the subservient status of women. Graham believes that since no intellectual difference exists between the sexes, both should strive toward virtue. There should be no difference in their education. Women should not be distracted by petty things and instead should strive for betterment.

In her letter, Graham disputes the ideas of Jean-Jacques Rousseau, one of the most influential thinkers of the day. Rousseau argued that Nature intended the subjugation of one sex by the other and therefore instilled in women an intellectual deficiency. To make up for this intellectual gap, he claimed, women are instilled with attractiveness and feminine grace. These two halves, male intellect and female grace, compose a moral whole and thus a natural balance.

Graham challenges Rousseau's belief as absurd and goes so far as to label the philosopher prideful and obscene.

The only difference, Graham argues, is a physical ability that has enabled men to dominate Europe's savage history. With the coming of the Enlightenment and the weakening of male control, she asserted, women may now exert their influence to achieve what has been denied to them previously.

Eighteenth-century painting of Catherine Sawbridge Macaulay (National Portrait Gallery)

Document Text
Letter XXII: No Characteristic Difference in Sex

The great difference that is observable in the characters of the sexes, Hortensia, as they display themselves in the scenes of social life, has given rise to much false speculation on the natural qualities of the female mind.

It is a long time before the crowd give up opinions they have been taught to look upon with respect. . . . It is from such causes that the notion of a sexual difference in the human character has, with a very few exceptions, universally prevailed from the earliest times, and the pride of one sex, and the ignorance and vanity of the other, have helped to support an opinion which a close observation of Nature, and a more accurate way of reasoning, would disprove.

It must be confessed, that the virtues of the males among the human species, though mixed and blended with a variety of vices and errors, have displayed a bolder and a more consistent picture of excellence than female nature has hitherto done. It is on these reasons that, when we compliment the appearance of a more than ordinary energy in the female mind, we call it masculine; and hence it is, that Pope has elegantly said a perfect woman's but a softer man. And if we take in the consideration, that there can be but one rule of moral excellence for beings made of the same materials, organized after the same manner, and subjected to similar laws of Nature, we must either agree with Mr. Pope, or we must reverse the proposition, and say, that a perfect man is a woman formed after a coarser mold.

Among the most strenuous asserters of a sexual difference in character, Rousseau is the most conspicuous, both on account of that warmth of sentiment which distinguishes all his writings, and the eloquence of his compositions: but never did enthusiasm and the love of paradox, those enemies to philosophical disquisition, appear in more strong opposition to plain sense than in Rousseau's definition of this difference. He sets out with a supposition, that Nature intended the subjection of the one sex to the other; that consequently there must be an inferiority of intellect in the subjected party; but as man is a very imperfect being, and apt to play the capricious tyrant, Nature, to bring things nearer to an equality, bestowed on the woman such attractive graces, and such an insinuating address, as to turn the balance on the other scale. Thus Nature, in a giddy mood, recedes from her purposes, and subjects prerogative to an influence which must produce confusion and disorder in the system of human affairs. Rousseau saw this objection; and in order to obviate it, he has made up a moral person of the union of the two sexes, which, for contradiction and absurdity, outdoes every metaphysical riddle that was ever formed in the schools. In short, it is not reason, it is not wit; it is pride and sensuality that speak in Rousseau, and, in this instance, has lowered the man of genius to the licentious pedant.

But whatever might be the wise purpose intended by Providence in such a disposition of things, certain it is, that some degree of inferiority, in point of corporal strength, seems always to have existed between the two sexes; and this advantage, in the barbarous ages of mankind, was abused to such a degree, as to destroy all the natural rights of the female species, and reduce them to a state of abject slavery. What accidents have contributed in Europe to better their condition, would not be to my purpose to relate; for I do not intend to give you a history of women; I mean only to trace the sources of their peculiar foibles and vices; and these I firmly believe to originate in situation and education only: for so little did a wise and just Providence intend to make the condition of slavery an unalterable law of female nature, that in the same proportion as the male sex have consulted the interest of their own happiness, they have relaxed in their tyranny over women; and such is their use in the system of mundane creation, and such their natural influence over the male mind, that were these advantages properly exerted, they might carry every point of any importance to their honour and happiness. However, till that period arrives in which women will act wisely, we will amuse ourselves in talking of their follies.

The situation and education of women, Hortensia, is precisely that which must necessarily tend to corrupt and debilitate both the powers of mind and body. From a false notion of beauty and delicacy, their system of nerves is depraved before they come out of their nursery; and this kind of depravity has more influence over the mind, and consequently over morals, than is commonly apprehended. But it would be well if such causes only acted towards the debasement of the sex; their moral education is, if possible, more absurd than their physical. The principles and nature of virtue, which is never properly explained to boys, is kept quite a mystery to girls. They are told indeed, that they must abstain from those vices which are contrary to their personal happiness, or they will be regarded as criminals, both by God and man; but all the higher parts of rectitude, every thing that ennobles our being, and that renders us both innoxious and useful, is either not taught, or is taught in such a manner as to leave no proper impression on the mind. This is so obvious a truth, that the defects of female education have ever been a fruitful topic of declamation for the moralist; but not one of this class of writers have laid down any judicious rules for amendment. Whilst we still retain the absurd notion of a sexual excellence, it will militate against the perfecting a plan of education for either sex. The judicious Addison animadverts on the absurdity of bringing a young lady up with no higher idea of the end of education than to make her agreeable to a husband, and confining the necessary excellence for this happy acquisition to the mere graces of person.

Glossary

animadverts: speaks out against

follies: foolishness

licentious pedant: perverse know-it-all

militate: make the case for or against

Providence: God's care

Short-Answer Questions

1. What quality does Graham attribute to men? In her view, how has this quality influenced the established social order of her day?

2. Describe how Rousseau explains the subjugation of one sex over the other.

3. What arguments does Graham use to counter Rousseau's theory? Explain the reasons Graham offers for the subjugation of women.

The Schlager Anthology of Women's History

Olympe de Gouges:
Declaration of the Rights of Woman and of the Female Citizen

Author
Olympe de Gouges (Marie Gouze)

Date
1791

Document Type
Essays, Reports, Manifestos

Significance
Advocated for a set of issues and social prescriptions using the language of later feminist activists and thinkers, and influenced activists to consider the status of women in Western societies

Overview

In September 1791, approximately two years after the *Declaration of the Rights of Man and the Citizen* was promulgated in France, Marie Gouze wrote the *Declaration of the Rights of Woman and of the Female Citizen*. A self-educated butcher's daughter from the south of France, she wrote a number of pamphlets, plays, and speeches under the name Olympe de Gouges. Her preamble was a call to arms to all women, including the Queen of France, Marie-Antoinette. Calling on the Supreme Being for guidance, de Gouge lists seventeen rights of women and female citizens. Ending with a sample marriage contract designed to ensure more equitable treatment of women, the *Declaration of the Rights of Woman and of the Female Citizen* was never accepted or promulgated.

Most of the prominent radicals of the French Revolution held conservative attitudes about gender and the status of women. In response to the *Declaration of the Rights of Woman and of the Female Citizen*, de Gouges was immediately suspected of treason. In addressing her pamphlet to the Queen of France, de Gouges had opened herself up to accusations of Royalist sympathies. Declared a "political enemy," she was quickly tried and convicted of treason and was executed by the guillotine. Although de Gouge's political activism directly led to her death and her ideas found few supporters in France, her writings spread abroad, influencing many women to begin questioning the prevailing patriarchal norms of the day. In England, Mary Wollstonecraft wrote *A Vindication of the Rights of Woman: With Strictures on Political and Moral Subjects* in 1792, and in the United States, Elizabeth Cady Stanton cited the text heavily in her *Declaration of Sentiments*. De Gouge's militant and uncompromising tone thus created a template for later generations of feminist thinkers.

Olympe de Gouges
(Wikimedia Commons)

Document Text
The Rights of Woman

Man, are you capable of being just? It is a woman who poses the question; you will not deprive her of that right at least. Tell me, what gives you sovereign empire to oppress my sex? Your strength? Your talents? Observe the Creator in his wisdom; survey in all her grandeur that nature with whom you seem to want to be in harmony, and give me, if you dare, an example of this tyrannical empire. Go back to animals, consult the elements, study plants, finally glance at all the modifications of organic matter, and surrender to the evidence when I offer you the means; search, probe, and distinguish, if you can, the sexes in the administration of nature. Everywhere you will find them mingled; everywhere they cooperate in harmonious togetherness in this immortal masterpiece.

Man alone has raised his exceptional circumstances to a principle. Bizarre, blind, bloated with science and degenerated—in a century of enlightenment and wisdom—into the crassest ignorance, he wants to command as a despot a sex which is in full possession of its intellectual faculties; he pretends to enjoy the Revolution and to claim his rights to equality in order to say nothing more about it. . . .

Preamble

Mothers, daughters, sisters [and] representatives of the nation demand to be constituted into a national assembly. Believing that ignorance, omission, or scorn for the rights of woman are the only causes of public misfortunes and of the corruption of governments, [the women] have resolved to set forth a solemn declaration the natural, inalienable, and sacred rights of woman in order that this declaration, constantly exposed before all members of the society, will ceaselessly remind them of their rights and duties. . . .

Article I. Woman is born free and lives equal to man in her rights. Social distinctions can be based only on the common utility. . . .

Article IV. Liberty and justice consist of restoring all that belongs to others; thus, the only limits on the exercise of the natural rights of woman are perpetual male tyranny; these limits are to be reformed by the laws of nature and reason. . . .

Article VI. The law must be the expression of the general will; all female and male citizens must contribute either personally or through their representatives to its formation; it must be the same for all: male and female citizens, being equal in the eyes of the law, must be equally admitted to all honors, positions, and public employment according to their capacity and without other distinctions besides those of their virtues and talents. . . .

Article XIII. For the support of the public force and the expenses of administration, the contributions of woman and man are equal; she shares all the duties and all the painful tasks; therefore, we must have the same share in the distribution of positions, employment, offices, honors, and jobs. . . .

Postscript

Woman, wake up; the tocsin of reason is being heard throughout the whole universe; discover your rights. The powerful empire of nature is no longer surrounded by prejudice, fanaticism, superstition, and lies. The flame of truth has dispersed all the clouds of folly and usurpation. Enslaved man has multiplied his strength and needs recourse to yours to break his chains. Having become free, he has become unjust to his companion. Oh, women, women! When will you cease to be blind? What advantage have you received from the Revolution? A more pronounced scorn, a more marked disdain. In the centuries of corruption you ruled only over the weakness of men. The reclamation of your patrimony, based on the wise decrees of nature—what have you to dread from such a fine undertaking? . . .

Regardless of what barriers confront you, it is in your power to free yourselves; you have only to want to.

Glossary

despot: tyrannical ruler

tocsin: alarm; warning bell

Short-Answer Questions

1. Describe the tone of de Gouge's pamphlet. In your response, use specific words and phrases to support your conclusions.

2. Analyze de Gouge's arguments. How does she use the Enlightenment language of science, reason, and appeals to nature to support her positions?

3. De Gouge was executed for authoring this text. Why do you think the male leaders of the French Revolution would have found her writing so deeply and profoundly threatening?

Mary Wollstonecraft:
A Vindication of the Rights of Woman

Author
Mary Wollstonecraft

Date
1792

Document Type
Essays, Reports, Manifestos

Significance
Placed women on equal terms with men in regard to their intellectual abilities, restrained only by educational limitations

Overview

Her personal experiences with her controlling father, work as a teacher and private tutor, and familiarity with the philosophical and political issues of her day all spurred Mary Wollstonecraft (1759–1797) to take an interest in gender roles. She read or was acquainted with leading Enlightenment theorists such as Thomas Paine, Jean-Jacques Rousseau, William Wordsworth, and William Godwin, the latter of whom she married. Much political discussion centered on citizens' rights and the importance of reason in the development of human character, which she felt contrasted sharply with prevailing philosophies of women's education and their social reality.

Wollstonecraft advocated the extension of rights and acknowledgment of reason to women in her treatise *A Vindication of the Rights of Woman*, published in 1792 on the heels of *A Vindication of the Rights of Men*, her response to Edmund Burke's *Reflections on the French Revolution*. Burke attributed the inevitable failure of the French Revolution to its failure to maintain traditional social structures. Wollstonecraft countered this view in 1790 in *A Vindication of the Rights of Men*, where she states that the rights of citizens cannot be dependent on traditions. *A Vindication of the Rights of Woman* extends the argument from male citizens' rights to women's rights. Promoting educational reform as a way to promote the betterment of women in society, Wollstonecraft is also critical of women for being overly concerned with beauty and marriage.

Wollstonecraft's work is widely regarded as one of the first feminist writings. At the time of its publication, it was met with a mixed response. Among her liberal circles, Wollstonecraft's work was met positively. Her opponents and the general public, however, were highly critical of her tone and views.

Document Text

Introduction

After considering the historic page, and viewing the living world with anxious solicitude, the most melancholy emotions of sorrowful indignation have depressed my spirits, and I have sighed when obliged to confess, that either nature has made a great difference between man and man, or that the civilization which has hitherto taken place in the world has been very partial. I have turned over various books written on the subject of education, and patiently observed the conduct of parents and the management of schools; but what has been the result?—a profound conviction that the neglected education of my fellow-creatures is the grand source of the misery I deplore; and that women, in particular, are rendered weak and wretched by a variety of concurring causes, originating from one hasty conclusion. The conduct and manners of women, in fact, evidently prove that their minds are not in a healthy state; for, like the flowers which are planted in too rich a soil, strength and usefulness are sacrificed to beauty; and the flaunting leaves, after having pleased a fastidious eye, fade, disregarded on the stalk, long before the season when they ought to have arrived at maturity. One cause of this barren blooming I attribute to a false system of education, gathered from the books written on this subject by men who, considering females rather as women than human creatures, have been more anxious to make them alluring mistresses than affectionate wives and rational mothers; and the understanding of the sex has been so bubbled by this specious homage, that the civilized women of the present century, with a few exceptions, are only anxious to inspire love, when they ought to cherish a nobler ambition, and by their abilities and virtues exact respect.

In a treatise, therefore, on female rights and manners, the works which have been particularly written for their improvement must not be overlooked; especially when it is asserted, in direct terms, that the minds of women are enfeebled by false refinement; that the books of instruction, written

Portrait of Mary Wollstonecraft
(Tate Britain)

by men of genius, have had the same tendency as more frivolous productions; and that . . . they are treated as a kind of subordinate beings, and not as a part of the human species. . . .

Yet, because I am a woman, I would not lead my readers to suppose that I mean violently to agitate the contested question respecting the equality or inferiority of the sex; but as the subject lies in my way, and I cannot pass it over without subjecting the main tendency of my reasoning to misconstruction, I shall stop a moment to deliver, in a few words, my opinion. In the government of the physical world it is observable that the female in point of strength is, in general, inferior to the male. This is the law of nature; and it does not appear to be suspended or abrogated in favour of woman. A degree of physical superiority cannot, therefore, be denied—and it is a noble prerogative! But not content with this natural pre-eminence, men endeavour to sink us still lower, merely to render us alluring objects for a moment; and women, intoxicated by the adoration which men, under the influence of their senses, pay them, do not seek to obtain a durable interest in their hearts, or to become the friends of the fellow creatures who find amusement in their society.

I am aware of an obvious inference: from every quarter have I heard exclamations against masculine women; but where are they to be found? If by this appellation men mean to inveigh against their ardour in hunting, shooting, and gaming, I shall most cordially join in the cry; but if it be against the imitation of manly virtues, or, more properly speaking, the attainment of those talents and virtues, the exercise of which ennobles the human character, and which raise females in the scale of animal being, when they are comprehensively termed mankind; all those who view them with a philosophic eye must, I should think, wish with me, that they may every day grow more and more masculine. . . .

I wish also to steer clear of an error which many respectable writers have fallen into . . . but, addressing my sex in a firmer tone, I pay particular attention to those in the middle class, because they appear to be in the most natural state. Perhaps the seeds of false-refinement, immorality, and vanity, have ever been shed by the great. Weak, artificial beings, raised above the common wants and affections of their race, in a premature unnatural manner, undermine the very foundation of virtue, and spread corruption through the whole mass of society! As a class of mankind they have the strongest claim to pity; the education of the rich tends to render them vain and helpless, and the unfolding mind is not strengthened by the practice of those duties which dignify the human character. They only live to amuse themselves, and by the same law which in nature invariably produces certain effects, they soon only afford barren amusement.

But as I purpose taking a separate view of the different ranks of society, and of the moral character of women, in each, this hint is, for the present, sufficient; and I have only alluded to the subject, because it appears to me to be the very essence of an introduction to give a cursory account of the contents of the work it introduces.

My own sex, I hope, will excuse me, if I treat them like rational creatures, instead of flattering their fascinating graces, and viewing them as if they were in a state of perpetual childhood, unable to stand alone. I earnestly wish to point out in what true dignity and human happiness consists—I wish to persuade women to endeavour to acquire strength, both of mind and body, and to convince them that the soft phrases, susceptibility of heart, delicacy of sentiment, and refinement of taste, are almost synonymous with epithets of weakness, and that those beings who are only the objects of pity and that kind of love, which has been termed its sister, will soon become objects of contempt.

Dismissing then those pretty feminine phrases, which the men condescendingly use to soften our slavish dependence, and despising that weak elegancy of mind, exquisite sensibility, and sweet docility of manners, supposed to be the sexual characteristics of the weaker vessel, I wish to shew that elegance is inferior to virtue, that the first object of laudable ambition is to obtain a character as a human being, regardless of the distinction of sex; and that secondary views should be brought to this simple touchstone.

This is a rough sketch of my plan; and should I express my conviction with the energetic emotions that I feel whenever I think of the subject, the dictates of experience and reflection will be felt by some of my readers. Animated by this important object, I shall disdain to cull my phrases or polish my style; I aim at being useful, and sincerity will render me unaffected; for, wishing rather to persuade by the force of my arguments, than dazzle by the elegance of my language, I shall not waste my time in rounding periods, or in fabricating the turgid bombast of artificial feelings, which, coming from the head, never reach the heart. I shall be employed about things, not words!—and, anxious

The Schlager Anthology of Women's History

to render my sex more respectable members of society, I shall try to avoid that flowery diction which has slided from essays into novels, and from novels into familiar letters and conversation. . . .

The education of women has, of late, been more attended to than formerly; yet they are still reckoned a frivolous sex, and ridiculed or pitied by the writers who endeavour by satire or instruction to improve them. It is acknowledged that they spend many of the first years of their lives in acquiring a smattering of accomplishments; meanwhile strength of body and mind are sacrificed to libertine notions of beauty, to the desire of establishing themselves, the only way women can rise in the world, by marriage. And this desire making mere animals of them, when they marry they act as such children may be expected to act: they dress; they paint, and nickname God's creatures. Surely these weak beings are only fit for a seraglio! Can they be expected to govern a family with judgment, or take care of the poor babes whom they bring into the world?

If then it can be fairly deduced from the present conduct of the sex, from the prevalent fondness for pleasure which takes place of ambition and those nobler passions that open and enlarge the soul; that the instruction which women have hitherto received has only tended, with the constitution of civil society, to render them insignificant objects of desire—mere propagators of fools!—if it can be proved that in aiming to accomplish them, without cultivating their understandings, they are taken out of their sphere of duties, and made ridiculous and useless when the short-lived bloom of beauty is over, I presume that rational men will excuse me for endeavouring to persuade them to become more masculine and respectable.

Indeed the word masculine is only a bugbear: there is little reason to fear that women will acquire too much courage or fortitude; for their apparent inferiority with respect to bodily strength, must render them, in some degree, dependent on men in the various relations of life; but why should it be increased by prejudices that give a sex to virtue, and confound simple truths with sensual reveries? . . .

Glossary

ardour: enthusiasm or passion

bugbear: an irritant; a made-up problem

exact: to obtain

libertine: without morals or responsibilities

melancholy: sad or depressed mood

rounding periods: a rhetorical device involving complex sentences

seraglio: harem

Glossary

shew: show

specious: deceptive

virtue: good moral qualities

Short-Answer Questions

1. According to the text, what is the purpose of education? In what ways have women been denied access to education?

2. Explain what Wollstonecraft means when she refers to masculine women.

3. Identify stereotypes Wollstonecraft associates with men and with women. Can you compare these to any current stereotypes common today among the sexes?

Mary Hays:
Appeal to the Men of Great Britain in Behalf of Women

Author
Mary Hays

Date
1798

Document Type
Essays, Reports, Manifestos

Significance
Punctures the contemporary arguments made by men about their supposed superiority to women

---

Overview

Although not as well-known as Mary Wollstonecraft (1759–1797), her friend and fellow women's rights advocate, London native Mary Hayes (1760–1843) was her equal in passion for obtaining justice for women. Hayes came from a family of Rational Dissenters, a group of Christians who followed the practices of the Church of England in principle but rejected certain aspects of that faith, including its reliance on unquestioning obedience to authority. Hays was an autodidact; she educated herself through correspondence with a fellow Dissenter and through contact with some of the leading Dissenters of the day. These included the scientist Joseph Priestley and Theophilus Lindsey, the founder of the Unitarian sect. She wrote a tract in defense of Unitarianism and became famous as the author of novels that caused scandals because of their forthright depiction of feminist ideals, including *Memoirs of Emma Courtney* (1796) and *The Victim of Prejudice* (1799). Perhaps her best-known work is *Female Biography* (1803), one of the earliest works of women's history.

Her *Appeal to the Men of Great Britain in Behalf of Women* was a political tract first published anonymously in 1798. In 1792 Hays had become friends with Mary Wollstonecraft and her husband William Godwin (1756–1836). The two women were close until Wollstonecraft's death in childbirth in 1797. The following year, however, after Godwin published his late wife's *Memoirs*—which, among other things, revealed her several extramarital affairs and her suicide attempts—Hays broke with Godwin. Although she continued to hold strong views about women's rights, she voiced them less frequently. Her opinions were reined in by the conservative backlash that started with the publication of Godwin's book. However, Hays's *Appeal to the Men of Great Britain in Behalf of Women* stands with Wollstonecraft's *A Vindication of the Rights of Women* as one of the most forthright and passionate arguments against male double standards and for women's liberty.

Document Text

It may at first sight appear absurd to address the following pages in behalf of women, to the men of Great Britain; whose apparent interest it perhaps is, in common with that of all other men, that things should remain on the footing they are. But as the men of Great Britain, to whom in particular I chuse to appeal, have to their everlasting honor always been remarkable for an ardent love of liberty, and high in their pretensions to justice with regard to themselves, it is not to be believed, if the subject of the present work were taken into their serious consideration, but that the same sentiments would be freely and generously extended to that class of beings, in whose cause I though unworthy appear. A class, upon whom the Almighty has stamped so sublime, so unequivocal marks of dignity and importance, that it is difficult to conceive why men should wish to counteract the benevolent designs of Providence in their favour by leading in chains, too often galling to their sensible and tender natures, those, whom heaven having in its wisdom formed their equals, could never surely, save in its wrath, doom to be the slaves of man.

Arguments Adduced from Reason against the Subjection of Women

. . . That "most women have no character at all" it is feared men in general endeavour to make themselves believe; and that too perhaps, not from the most upright motives. For confirming and disseminating this pleasant idea, the women of Great Britain are much indebted to the very silly line of Pope's which I have just quoted;—and who by the way, with all his wit, had a great many silly ones on that subject. upon this principle however, such as it is, men have formed a standard, to which they would willingly reduce the whole sex. Like the barbarous tyrant, who is reported to have stretched or of his subjects, or strangers, to suit his miserable caprice; so men, not contented with women as they come from the hands of the all-wise Creator, with that endless variety of character, that variety which is the soul of beauty, the most potent charm in society men will not allow their companions to be, what Heaven has made them, and intended them to remain; but must model them anew after their own fashion; to suit their passions and prejudices; and so as to give the least check possible to that unbounded freedom to which they have always aspired, and the least chance possible for women to emancipate themselves. . . .

What Men Would Have Women to Be

Of all the systems,—if indeed a bundle of contradictions and absurdities may be called a system,—which human nature in its moments of intoxication has produced, that which men have contrived with a view to forming the minds, and regulating the conduct of women, is perhaps the most completely absurd. And, though the consequences are often very serious to both sexes, yet if one could for a moment forget these, and consider it only as a system, it would rather be found a subject of mirth and ridicule than serious anger.

What Women Are

. . . It must be confessed, that even those who consider the human species, in a more liberal and extensive point of view,—who do not see sufficient grounds for those claims so haughtily advanced on the part of the men,—yet suppose the necessity of subordination on one side unavoidable. They therefore fear, that women, were their eyes opened to their natural equality and consequence, would not so tamely submit to the cruel injustice with which they are treated, in many of the leading points in life. And they know that nothing would tend so much to this *éclaircissement*, as an education, which by exercising their reason, and unfolding their talents, should point out to themselves, how they might exert them to the utmost. Such a development of mind would undoubtedly enable them to see and reason upon what principles, all the other regulations of society were formed,—which however they may deviate in execution, are evidently founded on justice and humanity,—and would consequently enable them to bring home and apply those principles to the situation of their sex in general. Thus awakened to a sense of their injuries, they would behold with astonishment and indignation, the arts which had been employed, to keep them in a state of PERPETUAL BABYISM. . . .

And this is precisely a case in point. For, in the first place it cannot be proved, that men are fitter to govern women, than women are to govern themselves, in the unlimited sense that men aspire to; except comparative experiment had been fairly and repeatedly made. Or, except superiority of mind had from the beginning, been so completely, so distinctly, and so uniformly marked, that it could bear no more dispute, that men should take the whole command into their own hands, than that mature age, should care for helpless infancy.

Men however, having taken for granted, and endeavoured to establish without proof, that they have some degree of intellectual superiority over women; have the consequences of their government, been equal to their declarations of superior wisdom, or answerable to their wishes, or to their ideas, of the possible perfection of the female sex, even in that secondary view in which they chuse to consider them? I apprehend they will not say so. Or if they do, the sex will by no means join them. For chained and blindfolded as they most certainly are, with respect to their own rights;—they know,—they feel conscious—of capability of greater degrees of perfection, than they are permitted to arrive at. Yes they see—there is not an individual among them, who does not at times see,—and feel too with keenest anguish,—that mind, as has been finely said, is of no sex. . . .

Glossary

chuse: alternate spelling of "choose"

éclaircissement: French term meaning "clarification"

"silly line of Pope's": a reference to Alexander Pope (1688–1744), a famous poet and satirist of the Enlightenment, who suggests that since women have no character, one should concentrate only on their appearance, especially their hair

Short-Answer Questions

1. What, according to Hays, is the worst form of discrimination men practice against women?

2. What is Hays's central complaint about the way that men—even men who embrace liberal Enlightenment ideas—think about and behave toward women?

3. Why does Hays think an appeal to men on behalf of women's rights might have an impact?

Priscilla Bell Wakefield: *Reflections on the Present Condition of the Female Sex; with Suggestions for Its Improvement*

Author Priscilla Bell Wakefield	**Significance** An early comment about unequal job opportunities and pay rates between women and men
Date 1798	
Document Type Essays, Reports, Manifestos	

Overview

The Quaker author, economist, and philanthropist Priscilla Bell Wakefield (1751–1832) was a polymath who is remembered today for her role in promoting savings banks for ordinary people. She referred to the institutions she championed as "frugality banks," and she urged that women and children be permitted to invest their small savings in them. As a philanthropist, in 1791 Wakefield founded a charity center—the Lying-In Charity for Women—in which poor pregnant women could give birth in relative safety. The recipients of the charity also received basic supplies for their babies, including clothing.

Wakefield went on to create a School for Industry, a trade school that taught girls skills such as sewing and knitting and also provided education in reading, writing, and math. She was also a prolific author of books for children, many of them educational, which won her widespread recognition; subjects ranged from *Juvenile Anecdotes, Founded on Facts* (1795–98) to *An Introduction to Botany* (1796), *The Juvenile Travellers* (1801), and *An Introduction to the Natural History and Classifications of Insects* (1816).

Reflections on the Present Condition of the Female Sex; with Suggestions for Its Improvement was one of Wakefield's only works aimed specifically at an adult audience. It serves in part as a criticism of economist Adam Smith's *The Wealth of Nations* (1776), the first articulation of capitalism. Wakefield points out that his work ignored the contributions that women and children made to their countries' economies. *Reflections* is also notable because, although it argues for women's economic independence, it does so without embracing the goals of contemporary feminists, suggesting that educating women would better prepare them for roles as wives and mothers.

Wakefield's husband, Edward, died in 1826. Following his death, Priscilla Wakefield retired to her daughter's home in Ipswich, a town some sixty miles north and east of London. She died there in September of 1832.

Document Text
Chapter I

. . . In civilized nations it has ever been the misfortune of the [female] sex to be too highly elevated, or too deeply depressed; now raised above the condition of mortals, upon the score of their personal attractions, and now debased below that of reasonable creatures, with respect to their intellectual endowments. The result of this improper treatment has been a neglect of the mental powers, which women really possess, but know not how to exercise; and they have been contented to barter the dignity of reason, for the imaginary privilege of an empire, of the existence of which they can entertain no reasonable hope beyond the duration of youth and beauty.

Of the few who have raised themselves to pre-eminence by daring to stray beyond the accustomed path, the envy of their own sex, and the jealousy or contempt of the other, have too often been the attendants; a fate which doubtless has deterred others from attempting to follow them, or emulate, even in an inferior degree, the distinction they have attained.

But notwithstanding these disadvantages, and others of less perceptible influence, the diffusion of christianity, and the progress of civilization, have raised the importance of the female character; and it has become a branch of philosophy, not a little interesting, to ascertain the offices which the different ranks of women are required to fulfil. Their rights and their duties have lately occupied the pens of writers of eminence; the employments which may properly exercise their faculties, and fill up their time in a useful manner, without encroaching upon those professions, which are appropriate to men, remain to be defined. There are many branches of science, as well as useful occupations, in which women may employ their time and their talents, beneficially to themselves and to the community, without destroying the peculiar characteristic of their sex, or exceeding the most exact limits of modesty and decorum. Whatever

Priscilla Bell Wakefield
(Wikimedia Commons)

obliges them to mix in the public haunts of men, or places the young in too familiar a situation with the other sex, whatever is obnoxious to the delicacy and reserve of the female character, or destructive, in the smallest degree, to the strictest moral purity, is inadmissible. The sphere of feminine action is contacted by numberless difficulties, that are no impediments to masculine exertions. Domestic privacy is the only sure asylum for the juvenile part of the sex, nor can the grave matron step far beyond that boundary with propriety. Unfitted, by their relative situation in society, for many honourable and lucrative employments, those

Priscilla Bell Wakefield: *Reflections on the Present Condition of the Female Sex; with Suggestions for Its Improvement*

151

only are suitable for them, which can be pursued without endangering their virtue, or corrupting their manners.

But, under these restrictions, there may be found a multitude of objects adapted to the useful exertions of female talents, which it will be the principal design of these Reflections to point out, after making some remarks upon the present state of female education, and suggesting some improvements towards its reformation.

Chapter IV

. . . Another heavy discouragement in the industry of women, is the inequality of the reward of their labour, compared with that of men, an injustice which pervades every species of employment performed by both sexes! In employments which depend upon bodily strength the distinction is just; for it cannot be pretended that the generality of women can earn as much as men, where the produce of their labour is the result of corporeal exertion; but it is a subject of great regret, that this inequality should prevail, even where an equal share of skill and application are exerted. Male stay-makers, mantua-makers, and hair-dressers are better paid than female artists of the same professions; but surely it will never be urged as an apology for this disproportion, that women are not as capable of making stays, gowns, dressing hair, and similar arts, as men; if they are not superior to them, it can only be accounted for upon this principle, that the prices they receive for their labour are not sufficient to repay them for the expence of qualifying themselves for their business, and that they sink under the mortification of being regarded as artizans of inferior estimation, whilst the men, who supplant

them, receive all the encouragement of large profits and full employment, which is ensured to them by the folly of fashion. The occasion for this remark is a disgrace upon those who patronize such a brood of effeminate beings in the garb of men; when sympathy with their humbler sisters should direct them to act in a manner exactly opposite, by holding out every incitement to the industry of their own sex. This evil indeed calls loudly upon women of rank and fortune for redress: they should determine to employ women only, wherever they can be employed, they should procure female instructors for their children; they should frequent no shops that are not served by women; they should wear no clothes that are not made by them; they should reward them as liberally as they do the men who have hitherto supplanted them. . . .

The serving of retail shops, which deal in articles of female consumption, should be exclusively appropriated to women. For were the multitudes of men, who are constantly employed in measuring linen, gauze, ribbons, and lace; selling perfumes and cosmetics; setting a value on feathers and trinkets; and displaying their talents in praising the elegance of bonnets and caps, to withdraw, they might benefit the community, by exchanging such frivolous avocations for something more worthy of the masculine character, and by this measure afford an opportunity of gaining a creditable livelihood to many destitute women, whom a dreadful necessity drives to the business of prostitution.—The attendance of women in shops, need not be entirely confined to haberdashers, perfumers, and milliners; there are other trades in which they may be employed behind the counter: the familiar offices of trying on gloves and shoes, are more suitably performed by persons of the same sex. . . .

Glossary

artizans: variant spelling of "artisans"; people who make items and sell them themselves (as opposed to wage workers who work for an employer)

haberdashers: in Britain, sellers of goods used for sewing; in North America, sellers of men's clothing

hair-dressers: creators of the elaborate wigs that were just going out of style at the time Wakefield was writing

mantua-makers: creators of a specific type of gown designed for wear at court functions

milliners: those who make and sell hats for women

stay-makers: those who design and sells corsets, a type of women's undergarment

Short-Answer Questions

1. Why does Wakefield think that women's work is underpaid and underappreciated?

2. What does Wakefield suggest as a remedy for the lack of appreciation for women's work?

3. How does Wakefield show that she is more socially conservative than other feminists of her generation?

Priscilla Bell Wakefield: *Reflections on the Present Condition of the Female Sex; with Suggestions for Its Improvement*

153

Savitribai Phule:
"Go, Get Education"

<table>
<tr><td>

Author
Savitribai Phule

Date
mid-1800s

Document Type
Poems, Plays, Fiction

</td><td>

Significance
Urged female readers to emancipate themselves from oppression, ignorance, and superstition by obtaining a modern education

</td></tr>
</table>

Overview

Savitribai Phule (1831–1897), a social reformer and author, is recognized as the first female teacher in India. Through tireless advocacy and educational initiatives, she played an instrumental role in establishing some of the first girls' schools in India. In addition, she advanced several broadly feminist and progressive causes, including pushing for the abolition of India's notorious caste system. Although it was officially abolished in 1850, the Indian caste system still exists today. The system is a class structure in which one's location in the social hierarchy is determined at birth and is unchangeable. In the India of Phule's time, opportunities, access, and treatment were dependent entirely on the status of one's family.

Movements for the education of women and girls in India began in the nineteenth century but were largely connected with the efforts of English Christian missionaries. The London Missionary Society founded the first school exclusively for girls in Chinsurgh, Bengal, in 1818, for instance. These schools reached relatively few Indians, but those educated in them would often go on to become catalysts for change in Indian society.

Savitribai Phule was born on January 3, 1831, at the village of Naigaon in Maharashtra. She was only nine years old when she was married to Jyotiba Phule, who was thirteen at the time of their marriage. Both were members of the socially ostracized Mali caste. Jyotiba was educated at an English school run by Christian missionaries, and he encouraged Savitribai to obtain her own education. Soon after she completed her studies, she established the first girls' school in Pune, a city in Maharashtra state in Western India. The school, which used innovative inquiry-based teaching methods, was widely opposed by conservative elements in the city. Savitribai herself, was widely ostracized and was physically harassed for providing girls and lower-caste Indians with educational opportunities. Undeterred by this harassment, Savitribai established more schools and even set up night schools for members of the predominantly working-class Shudra and Dalit communities.

In addition to her teaching and social advocacy, Savitribai was a poet. She published her first collection of poetry in 1854, when she was twenty-three years old. Her literary voice was deeply connected with her social concerns, and most of her writings reveal an unconcealed hostility toward India's conservative Brahman priesthood. Savitribai Phule died in 1897 after visiting a clinic for those stricken with the bubonic plague. Phule's activist agenda was truly radical. She insisted on the need to abandon the caste system and demanded absolute equality for all Indians. Moreover, as is indicated by the contents of her poem "Go, Get Education," she connected her educational concerns with an insistence that Indians discard the religious and cultural traditions of their ancestors.

Savitribai Phule depicted on an Indian postage stamp (Wikimedia Commons)

Document Text

Be self-reliant, be industrious
Work, gather wisdom and riches,
All gets lost without knowledge
We become animal without wisdom,
Sit idle no more, go, get education

End misery of the oppressed and forsaken,
You've got a golden chance to learn
So learn and break the chains of caste.
Throw away the Brahman's scriptures fast.

Glossary

Brahman: a member of the highest Hindu caste, that of the priesthood

caste: inherited social class or rank

Short-Answer Questions

1. Describe the tone of Phule's poem. In your response, cite specific word choices or phrases used by the author.

2. What does Phule suggest will be the benefits of an education? How does she indicate that educated individuals can help those around them?

3. Analyze the social reaction to Phule's radical poetry. Why do you think conservative elements of Indian society were so opposed to her educational advocacy and her writings?

Caroline Norton:
Letter to the Queen on Lord Chancellor Cranworth's Marriage and Divorce Bill

---

Author
Caroline Norton

Date
1855

Document Type
Letters/Correspondence; Essays, Reports,
Manifestos

Significance
Styled as a letter written to Queen Victoria,
described a married woman's legal status in the
nineteenth century as non-existent and pressed
for legal reforms

Overview

Caroline Sheridan Norton (1808–1877) published her *Letter to the Queen on Lord Chancellor Cranworth's Marriage and Divorce Bill* in 1855, providing an articulate description of married women's legal situation in mid-nineteenth-century Great Britain. Caroline, an impoverished granddaughter of the actor Richard Sheridan, entered into a loveless marriage with George Norton, a lawyer and member of Parliament, in 1827. Abused by her husband and later in dire financial straits, Caroline Norton turned to writing prose and poetry. By the mid-1830s, Norton was well known as both an author and political salonnière and had tried on several occasions to leave her husband.

In 1836, in a highly publicized case, George Norton accused the prime minister, Lord Melbourne, of having an affair with his wife. Although her own reputation was at stake, Caroline Norton could not even testify in *Norton v. Melbourne*, which determined that no adultery had occurred. Without proof of a wife's adultery,

however, it was nearly impossible to divorce under English law, and a woman could not divorce her husband for any reason. Furthermore, a wife had no legal rights to her children, which George Norton used to his advantage in a prolonged custodial battle with his wife. As a result, Caroline Norton wrote political pamphlets that called for changes to the existing laws.

Norton's published letter to Queen Victoria (r. 1837–1901) addresses the ways in which married women were denied the most basic rights. Although she makes clear, well-reasoned arguments, Norton also gives emotional details of her own experiences throughout their marriage. The letter is a powerful, impassioned plea for changing the "non-existent" legal status of married women in England and a good example of the reasons Norton has been credited with successfully campaigning for such social reforms as the Matrimonial Causes Act (1857) and the Married Women's Property Act (1870).

Painting of Caroline Norton
(National Portrait Gallery)

Document Text

I connect your Majesty's name with these pages . . . for two reasons: of which one, indeed, is a sequence to the other. First, because I desire to point out the grotesque anomaly which ordains that married women shall be "non-existent" in a country governed by a female Sovereign; and secondly, because, whatever measure for the reform of these statutes may be proposed, it cannot become "the law of the land" without your Majesty's assent. . . .

A married woman in England has *no legal existence*: her being is absorbed in that of her husband. Years of separation or desertion cannot alter this position. Unless divorced by special enactment in the House of Lords, the legal fiction holds her to be "*one*" with her husband, even though she may never see or hear of him.

She has no possessions, unless by special settlement; her property is *his* property. . . .

An English wife has no legal right even to her clothes and ornaments; her husband may take them and sell them if he pleases. . . .

An English wife cannot make a will. She may have children or kindred whom she may earnestly desire to benefit;—she may be separated from her husband, who may be living with a mistress; no matter: the law gives what she has to him, and no will she could make would be valid.

An English wife cannot legally claim her own earnings. Whether wages for manual labour, or payment for intellectual exertion, whether she weed potatoes, or keep a school, her salary is *the husband's.* . . .

If the wife sue for separation for cruelty, it must be "cruelty that endangers life or limb," and if she has once forgiven, or, in legal phrase, "*condoned*" his offences, she cannot plead them; though her past forgiveness only proves that she endured as long as endurance was possible.

If her husband take proceedings for a divorce, she is not, in the first instance, allowed to defend herself. She has no means of proving the falsehood of his allegations. She is not represented by attorney, nor permitted to be considered a party to the suit between him and her supposed lover, for "damages." . . .

If an English wife be guilty of infidelity, her husband can divorce *her* so as to marry again; but she cannot divorce the husband. . . . No law court can divorce in England. A special Act of Parliament annulling the marriage, is passed for each case. The House of Lords grants this almost as a matter of course to the husband, but not to the wife. In only four instances (two of which were cases of incest), has the wife obtained a divorce to marry again.

She cannot prosecute for a libel. . . .

She cannot sign a lease, or transact responsible business.

She cannot claim support, as a matter of personal right, from her husband. The general belief and nominal rule is, that her husband is "bound to maintain her." That is not the law. He is not bound to *her*. He is bound to his country; bound to see that she does not cumber the parish in which she resides. . . .

She cannot bind her husband by any agreement, except through a third party. A contract formally drawn out by a lawyer,—witnessed, and signed by her husband,—is *void in law*; and he can evade payment of an income so assured, by the legal quibble that "a man cannot contract with his own wife."

Separation from her husband by consent, or for his ill usage, does not alter their mutual relation. He retains the right to divorce her *after* separation,—as before,—though he himself be unfaithful. . . .

Of course an opposite picture may be drawn. There are bad, wanton, irreclaimable women, as there are vicious, profligate, tyrannical men: but the difference is *this*: that to punish and restrain bad wives, there are laws, and very severe laws (to say nothing of social condemnation); while to punish or restrain bad husbands, there is, in England, no adequate law whatever. Indeed, the English law holds out a sort of premium on infidelity; for there is no doubt that the woman who is divorced for a lover and marries him, suffers less (except in conscience) than the woman who *does not deserve to suffer at all*. . . .

Why is England the only country obliged to confess that she cannot contrive to administer justice to women? Why is it more difficult than in France? Why more difficult than in Scotland? . . . They never will satisfy, with measures that give one law for one sex and the rich, and another law for the other sex and the poor. Nor will they ever succeed in acting on the legal fiction that married women are "non-existent," and man and wife are still "one," in cases of alienation, separation, and enmity; when they are about as much "one" as those ingenious twisted groups of animal death we sometimes see in sculpture; one creature wild to resist, and the other fierce to destroy. . . .

While the laws that women appeal to, are administered by men, we need not fear that their appeals will be too carelessly granted. No statement can be more incontrovertible than the Lord Chancellor's *dictum*, that the profligate husband "suffers little in the opinion of the world at large." It were well if he were held harmless only by public opinion: but he is also held harmless by *LAW*. . . .

A third case (to which I shall recur) is my own: in which, after personal violence, ill-usage, an "action for damages," and a long separation, the husband—being desirous to raise money,—procured a contract to be signed between himself and his wife, containing certain provisions as to his trust-funds, and as to her income, both before and after the death of certain parties. . . .

When the income so secured (or supposed to be secured), was claimed for creditors, the husband, in this case, refused to pay it. The law of England proved to be, that the wife being "non-existent," or one with the husband, *could not legally make any contract with him*. The signature of the husband, the signature of the brother of those other distinguished persons in your Majesty's service,—and the signature of the lawyer who drew up the agreement,—all failed to make it more valuable than a sheet of blank paper. The wife, who might have compelled the execution of such a contract had she been a menial servant, was left without a remedy, *because she was a wife*; and without further explanation than that "the law" would hold her husband harmless, for mocking her and mocking the gentlemen who had added their signatures, by offering this fictitious security. . . .

Mr. Gladstone, speaking on the Marriage Amendment Bill, says that "when the gospel came into the world, woman was elevated to an equality with her stronger companion,"—and that there is "per-

---

fect equality between man and woman as far as the marriage tie is concerned,"—and he asks whether it is now "intended to have one marriage code for men and another for women?" But I say, there is *already* one marriage code for men and another for women. . . . A sneer is the only answer to Mr. Gladstone's "gospel" doctrine; and the only text on the subject acknowledged by Parliament, is the Old Testament text: "*and he shall rule over her.*" . . .

The law was, (and I thank God I believe I was greatly instrumental in changing that law), that a man might take children from the mother at any age, and without any fault or offence on her part. . . . Mr Norton, then, took my little children (aged two, four, and six years); and I traced them to the house of that vile woman [to whom they had been delivered], who threatened to give me "to the police" when I went there and claimed them.

It was not till six weeks *after* the stealing of my children,—after a long, angry correspondence—and after having attempted to condition that "if my family would retract all that had been said against *him*, he would retract all he had said against *me*"— that Mr Norton took higher ground than his real cause of anger,—and appeared before the world in the character of "an injured husband." . . .

And here, again, *MONEY* was his avowed motive; for he first affirmed that the residence of these infants with me might make him liable for the debts of my household; and then, that "others" on whom he himself depended, would not permit him to send back his children, as it would appear to justify me. . . .

One of my children was afterwards killed, for want of the commonest care a mother would have given to her household. Mr Norton allowed this child to lie ill a week before he sent to tell me he was dying; and, when I arrived, I found the poor little creature already in his coffin.

. . . What I suffered respecting those children, God knows, and He only: what I endured, and yet lived past,—of pain, exasperation, helplessness, and despair, under the evil law which suffered any man, for vengeance or for interest, to take baby children from the mother, I shall not even try to explain. I believe *men* have no more notion of what that anguish is, than the blind have of colours; and I bless God that at least mine was *one* of the cases which called attention to the state of the law as it then existed. . . .

I consulted counsel whether *I* could not now divorce my husband: whether a divorce "by reason of cruelty" might not be pleaded for me; and I laid before my lawyers the many instances of violence, injustice, and ill-usage, of which the trial was but the crowning example. I was then told that no divorce *I* could obtain would break my marriage; that I could not plead cruelty *which I had forgiven*; that by returning to Mr. Norton I had "*condoned*" all I complained of. I was an *ENGLISH WIFE*, and for me there was no possibility of redress. The answer was always the same. The *LAW*. "Have I no remedy?"—"No remedy in *LAW*. The *LAW* can do nothing for you: your case is one of singular, of incredible hardship; but there is no possible way in which the *LAW* could assist you." . . .

The natural position of woman is inferiority to man. Amen! That is a thing of God's appointing, not of man's devising. I believe it sincerely, as a part of my religion: and I accept it as a matter proved to my reason. I never pretended to the wild and ridiculous doctrine of equality. I will even hold that (as one coming under the general rule that the wife must be inferior to the husband), *I* occupy that position. . . . I am Mr Norton's inferior. . . . Put me then—(my ambition extends no further)—in the same position as all his other inferiors! In that of his housekeeper, whom he could not libel with impunity, and without possible defence; of an apprentice whom he could not maltreat lawlessly. . . . Put me under *some* law of protection; and do not leave me to the mercy of one who has never shewn me mercy. For want of such a law of protection, all other protection has been vain! . . .

But let the recollection of what I write, remain with those who read; and above all, let the recollection remain with your Majesty, to whom it is addressed; the one woman in England who *cannot* suffer wrong; and whose royal assent will be formally necessary to any Marriage Reform Bill which the Lord Chancellor, assembled Peers, and assembled Commons, may think fit to pass, in the Parliament of this free nation; where, with a Queen on the throne, all other married women are legally "*NON-EXISTENT*." . . .

Glossary

cumber: to burden

dictum: a statement from an individual in authority

Gladstone: William Ewart Gladstone, Liberal British politician who served as Prime Minister four times (1868–1874, 1880–1885, 1886, and 1892–1894)

libel: false publication or statement that causes damage to one's reputation

Peers: Members of the British House of Lords

profligate: extravagant and wasteful

shewn: shown

vain: useless; ineffective

Short-Answer Questions

1. Explain what Norton means when she defines married women as "non-existent."

2. Identify the reasons Norton believes underlie a married woman's status.

3. Norton writes that equality is "wild and ridiculous." Show how she can support reforms to the rights of women while not supporting sexual equality.

Maria Eugenia Echenique: "The Emancipation of Women"

Author Maria Eugenia Echenique **Date** 1876 **Document Type** Essays, Reports, Manifestos	**Significance** Argued forcefully for women's emancipation and for the inclusion of women in Argentina's national economy

Overview

Maria Eugenia Echenique (1851–1878) was an Argentine feminist author. Although she died young, likely of cancer, she was a significant voice for women's emancipation in Latin America during a period of immense social, political, and economic transition. The countries of Latin America changed enormously during the nineteenth century, transforming` from colonial outposts of Spain and Portugal into independent industrializing nations with rapidly growing populations and urban centers. In this climate of ferment, small groups of women, often well-educated and from the nascent middle class, attempted to change the patriarchal gender norms dominant in their societies. These groups did not represent a large political movement, but they nonetheless agitated forcefully for the rights of women and stressed that women needed to be included in national economies and political deliberations.

Echenique wrote primarily for publications in her native Argentina and argued for her feminist principles using the language of modernization, scientific rationalism, and economics. Echenique, like other feminist thinkers of the time, contended that the logical status of men and women in society was absolute equality. Her beliefs put her at odds with the prevailing opinion in Argentine society. In the late nineteenth century, most men and women in Argentina supported a strictly patriarchal social system. Many women supported traditional roles, fearing the fracturing of the family if equality became the norm. Men, who had substantial legal, cultural, economic, and political advantages over women, were largely unmoved by the feminist arguments for equality.

Although she lived in a relatively conservative political and cultural climate, Echenique advanced remarkably forceful positions about gender equality. She contended that there were enormous economic benefits to the inclusion of women in the workforce and suggested that women had an inalienable right to be economically self-sufficient. Dispelling the objections of her critics, she suggested that women's equality would produce a harmonious and prosperous society and would promote public morality. Overall, Echenique's writing is indicative of the global nature of feminist thought in the late nineteenth century.

Document Text

When emancipation was given to men, it was also given to women in recognition of the equality of rights, consistent with the principles of nature on which they are founded, that proclaim the identity of soul between men and women. Thus, Argentine women have been emancipated by law for a long time. The code of law that governs us authorizes a widow to defend her rights in court, just as an educated woman can in North America, and like her, we can manage the interests of our children, these rights being the basis for emancipation. What we lack is sufficient education and instruction to make use of them. . . .

So let the debate be there, on the true point where it should be: whether or not it is proper for women to make use of those granted rights, asking as a consequence the authorization to go to the university so as to practice those rights or make them effective. . . .

Are all women going to marry? Are all going to be relegated to a life of inaction during their youth or while they remain single? Is it so easy for all women to look for a stranger to defend their offended dignity, their belittled honor, their stolen interests? Don't we see every day how the laws are trodden underfoot, and the victim, being a woman, is forced to bow her head because she does not know how to defend herself, exposed to lies and tricks because she does not know the way to clarify the truth?

Far from causing the breakdown of the social classes, the emancipation of women would establish morality and justice in them; . . . generous and abnegated by nature, women would teach men humanitarian principles and would condemn the frenzy and insults that make a battlefield out of the courtroom. . . .

Men as much as women are victims of the indifference that ignorance, not science, produces. Men are more slaves of women who abuse the prestige of their weakness and become tyrants in their home, than of the schooled and scientific women who understand their duties and are capable of something.

The ignorant woman, the one who voluntarily closes her heart to the sublime principles that provoke sweet emotions in it and elevate the mind, revealing to men the deep secrets of the All-Powerful; the woman incapable of helping her husband in great enterprises for fear of losing the prestige of her weakness and ignorance; the woman who only aspires to get married and reproduce, and understands maternity as the only mission of women on earth—she can be the wife of a savage, because in him she can satisfy all her aspirations and hopes, following that law of nature that operates even on beasts and inanimate beings. . . .

I would renounce and disown my sex if the mission of women were reduced only to procreation; yes, I would renounce it. But the mission of women in the world is much more grandiose and sublime, it is more than the beasts', it is the one of teaching humankind, and in order to teach it is necessary to know. A mother should know science in order to inspire in her children great deeds and noble sentiments, making them feel superior to the other objects in the universe, teaching them from the cradle to become familiar with great scenes of nature where they should go to look for God and love Him. And nothing more sublime and ideal than the scientific mother who, while her husband goes to cafés or to the political club to talk about state interests, she goes to spend some of the evening at the astronomical observatory, with her children by the hand to show them Jupiter, Venus, preparing in that way their tender hearts for the most legitimate and sublime aspirations that could occupy men's minds. This sacred mission in the scientific mother who understands emancipation—the fulfillment of which, far from causing the abandonment of the home, causes it to unite more closely—instead of causing displeasure to her husband, she will cause his happiness.

The abilities of men are not so miserable that the carrying out of one responsibility would make it impossible to carry out others. There is enough time and competence for cooking and mending, and a great soul such as that of women, equal to that of their mates, born to embrace all the beauty that exists in Creation of divine origin and end, should not be wasted all on seeing if the plates are clean and rocking the cradle.

Glossary

Jupiter: the chief deity of the Roman Republic and Empire, the god of the sky and thunder, and king of the gods in ancient Roman mythology; now primarily recognized as the fifth planet from the sun and the largest in the solar system

Venus: a Roman goddess of love, beauty, desire, sex, fertility, prosperity, and victory; the second planet from the sun and the hottest and brightest planet in the solar system

---

Short-Answer Questions

1. Describe Echenique's position on the importance of education to women. Cite specific evidence from the text above to support your response.

2. Examine the last paragraphs of the excerpt. Analyze how Echenique rebuts the common argument that women's education will result in the fragmentation of the traditional family. How does she connect education with successful mothering?

3. Analyze the nuances of Echenique's argument and consider how she suggests that Argentine men will benefit from women's education. In your response, consider her purposes for making this argument. Why do you think she would suggest that men could be the beneficiaries of a more egalitarian society?

Emmeline Pankhurst: "Freedom or Death"

Author	Significance
Emmeline Pankhurst	Encouraged militant action to achieve women's right to vote
Date	
1913	
Document Type	
Speeches/Addresses	

Overview

One of the most important figures in the fight for women's rights in Great Britain, Emmeline Pankhurst (1858–1928) promoted militant action, protest, and violence to achieve her goals. In 1903, Pankhurst founded the Women's Social and Political Union (WSPU). The group disrupted political gatherings, challenged British politicians who did not support women's right to vote, and conducted public protests involving vandalism and arson. Under the motto "Deeds, not Words," the WSPU's actions helped to publicize their cause. On numerous occasions, Pankhurst and fellow suffragists faced arrest and imprisonment. Those imprisoned would continue their protests, this time by hunger strikes. Under Britain's Prisoner Act of 1913 (the Cat and Mouse Law), women who were physically weak (from not eating) could be released only to be rearrested once they regained their strength. This law resulted in Pankhurst being arrested and released twelve times in one year.

Pankhurst toured the United States numerous times to speak and raise funds. Her 1903 visit included a speech in Hartford, Connecticut. Introduced by Katharine Houghton Hepburn, the mother of future film star Katherine Hepburn, Pankhurst's ninety-minute speech is both defiant and aggressive. Referring to herself as a soldier, Pankhurst describes the fight for women's suffrage as a civil war. Addressing her American crowd, she refers to the American Revolution and its fight against taxation without representation and points out that women, who pay taxes, are not represented. Pankhurst asks why such liberal ideals, espoused in both Great Britain and the United States, only apply to men. Displaying a pragmatic viewpoint, she explains the reasons for the use of violence and protests to achieve the right to vote. Harkening back to Patrick Henry's famous line "Give me liberty or give me death," Pankhurst declares that the war for women's suffrage can end in only one of two ways; granting women the right to vote or killing them.

Although criticized at the time for its militarism, Pankhurst's "Freedom or Death" is today remembered as an important speech in the struggle for women's rights.

Pankhurst never lived to see equal voting rights for women in Great Britain, dying on June 14, 1928, a few weeks prior to the passing of the Representation of the People Act.

A 1913 portrait of Emmeline Pankhurst
(Library of Congress)

Document Text

I am here as a soldier who has temporarily left the field of battle in order to explain . . . what civil war is like when civil war is waged by women. I am not only here as a soldier temporarily absent from the field at battle; . . . I am here as a person who, according to the law courts of my country, it has been decided, is of no value to the community at all: and I am adjudged because of my life to be a dangerous person, under sentence of penal servitude in a convict prison. . . .

If I were a man and I said to you, "I come from a country which professes to have representative institutions and yet denies me, a taxpayer, an inhabitant of the country, representative rights," you would at once understand that that human being, being a man, was justified in the adoption of revolutionary methods to get representative institutions. But since I am a woman it is necessary in the twentieth century to explain why women have adopted revolutionary methods in order to win the rights of citizenship.

You see, in spite of a good deal that we hear about revolutionary methods not being necessary for American women, because American women are so well off, most of the men of the United States quite calmly acquiesce in the fact that half of the community are deprived absolutely of citizen rights, and we women, in trying to make our case clear, always have to make as part of our argument, and urge upon men in our audience the fact . . . that women are human beings. It is quite evident you do not all realise we are human beings or it would not be necessary to argue with you that women may, suffering from intolerable injustice, be driven to adopt revolutionary methods.

A great many of you have been led to believe . . . that in England there is a strange manifestation taking place, a new form of hysteria being swept across part of the feminist population of those Isles, and this manifestation takes the shape of irresponsible breaking of windows, burning of letters, general inconvenience to respectable, honest business people. . . . It is very irrational you say: even if these women had sufficient intelligence to understand what they were doing, and really did want the vote, they have adopted very irrational means for getting the vote. "How are they going to persuade people that they ought to have the vote by breaking their windows?" you say. Now, if you say that, it shows you do not understand the meaning of our revolution at all, and I want to show you that when damage is done to property it is not done in order to convert people to woman suffrage at all. It is a practical political means, the only means we consider open to voteless persons to bring about a political situation, which can only be solved by giving women the vote. . . .

We know what happened when your forefathers decided that they must have representation for taxation, many, many years ago. When they felt they couldn't wait any longer, when they laid all the arguments before an obstinate British government that they could think of, and when their arguments were absolutely disregarded, when every other means had failed, they began by the tea party at Boston, and they went on until they had won the independence of the United States of America. . . .

It is perfectly evident to any logical mind that when you have got the vote . . . you can get out of any legislature whatever you want, or . . . you can send them about their business and choose other people who will be more attentive to your demands. But, it is clear to the meanest intelligence that if you have not got the vote, you must either submit to laws just or unjust, administration just or unjust, or the time inevitably comes when you will revolt against that injustice and use violent means to put an end to it. . . .

. . . When women asked questions in political meetings and failed to get answers, they were not doing anything militant. To ask questions at political meetings is an acknowledged right of all people who attend public meetings; certainly in my country, men have always done it, and I hope they do it in America, because it seems to me that if you allow people to enter your legislatures without asking them any questions as to what they are going to do when they get there you are not exercising your citizen rights and your citizen duties as you ought. At any rate in Great Britain it is a custom, a time-honoured one, to ask questions of candidates for parliament and ask questions of members of the government. No man was ever put out of a

public meeting for asking a question until Votes for Women came onto the political horizon. The first people who were put out of a political meeting for asking questions, were women; they were brutally ill-used; they found themselves in jail before twenty-four hours had expired.

We found that all the fine phrases about freedom and liberty were entirely for male consumption, and that they did not in any way apply to women. When it was said taxation without representation is tyranny—when it was "taxation of men without representation is tyranny"—everybody quite calmly accepted the fact that women had to pay taxes and even were sent to prison if they failed to pay them—quite right. We found that "government of the people, by the people and for the people," which is also a time-honoured Liberal principle, was again only for male consumption. . . .

Well now, let me come to the situation as we find it. We felt we had to rouse the public to such a point that they would say to the government, you must give women the vote. . . . You now can understand why we women thought we must attack the thing that was of most value in modern life in order to make these people wake up and realise that women wanted the vote, and that things were going to be very uncomfortable until women got the vote, because it is not by making people comfortable you get things in practical life, it is by making them uncomfortable. . . .

That is what we women have been doing, and in the course of our desperate struggle we have had to make a great many people very uncomfortable. . . . Women broke some windows as a protest: they broke a good many shopkeepers' windows: they broke the windows of shopkeepers where they spent most of their money when they bought their hats and their clothing. They also broke the windows of many of the clubs, the smart clubs in Piccadilly. . . .

Well, then the shopkeepers . . . could not understand why we should break the shopkeepers' windows. Why should we alienate the sympathy of the shopkeepers? Well, there is the other side of the question, gentlemen—why should the shopkeepers alienate the sympathy of their customers by refusing to help them to get political power, some power to make the condition of the woman who helps to earn the shopkeepers money by serving in his shop, easier than it is at the present time? Those women broke shopkeepers' windows, and what was the situation? Just at the beginning of the winter season when all the new winter hats and coats were being shown, the shopkeepers had to barricade all their windows with wood and nobody could see the new winter fashions. Well, there again is an impossible situation. The shopkeeper cannot afford to quarrel with his customers, and we have today far more practical sympathy amongst the shopkeepers of London than we ever had when we were quiet, gentle, ladylike suffragists asking nicely for a vote. . . .

But this experience will show you that if you really want to get anything done, it is not so much a matter of whether you alienate sympathy; sympathy is a very unsatisfactory thing if it is not practical sympathy. It does not matter to the practical suffragist whether she alienates sympathy that was never of any use to her. What she wants is to get something practical done, and whether it is done out of sympathy or whether it is done out of fear, or whether it is done because you want to be comfortable again and not be worried in this way, doesn't particularly matter so long as you get it. . . . We would rather have an angry man going to the government and saying, my business is interfered with and I won't submit to its being interfered with any longer because you won't give women the vote, than to have a gentleman come onto our platforms year in and year out and talk about his ardent sympathy with woman suffrage. . . .

"Put them in prison," they said, "that will stop it." But it didn't stop it. They put women in prison for long terms of imprisonment, for making a nuisance of themselves . . . and they thought that by sending them to prison, giving them a day's imprisonment, would cause them to all settle down again and there would be no further trouble. But it didn't happen so at all: instead of the women giving it up, more women did it, and more and more and more women did it until there were three hundred women at a time. . . .

Well then they felt they must do something else, and they began to legislate. I want to tell men in this meeting that the British government, which is not remarkable for having very mild laws to administer, has passed more stringent laws to deal with this agitation than it ever found it necessary during all the history of political agitation in my country. . . . They have had to pass special legislation, and now they are on the point of admitting that that special legislation has absolutely failed. . . .

Now, I want to say to you who think women cannot succeed, we have brought the government of England to this position, that it has to face this alternative: either women are to be killed or women are to have the vote. . . . Well, there is only one answer to that alternative; there is only one way out of it, unless you are prepared to put back civilisation two or three generations: you must give those women the vote. Now that is the outcome of our civil war.

Glossary

acquiesce: passively accept

adjudged: judged; condemned

Liberal principle: political belief centered on individualism, equality, and representative forms of government

meanest: dullest; most mentally ill-equipped

Short-Answer Questions

1. Summarize the arguments Emmeline Pankhurst makes for a women's right to vote.

2. Pankhurst compares the fight for suffrage with a soldier's fight in a civil war. Do you believe her comparison is accurate?

3. Illustrate how Pankhurst sought to connect with her American audience. In what ways did she use U.S. history to further her argument?

Virginia Woolf:
A Room of One's Own

Author
Virginia Woolf

Date
1929

Document Type
Essays, Reports, Manifestos

Significance
Accused a male-dominated society of suppressing women's creative development and called for economic equality as a way to gain social and cultural equality

Overview

Born in London, England, in 1882, Virginia Woolf was one of the most influential writers of the twentieth century. Her use of stream-of-thought writing and nonlinear storytelling influenced the development of modernist literature. A founding member of the Bloomsbury Group, a gathering of writers, intellectuals, and artists who challenged social norms and standards, Woolf addressed such issues in her writings as women's rights, mental illness, war, and fascism.

Woolf's *A Room of One's Own* emerged out of two lectures on women and fiction given at Cambridge College in 1928. Challenging the common belief in the inferiority of women writers, Woolf argues it is not ability but education and society that have kept women from achieving their full potential. Using a mixture of reality and fiction, Woolf accuses society and literature of being male-dominated and designed to marginalize and limit women and their abilities. She believes women need financial security and their own room in which to work in order to experiment and develop their talents. Deeply influenced by World War I, Woolf criticizes the patriarchal society that led to such destruction.

Woolf's feminist critique is one of her best-remembered nonfiction works. Her call for economic equality as a way to gain social and cultural equality influenced future generations of feminist activists and writers.

Document Text

That, more or less, is how the story would run, I think, if a woman in Shakespeare's day had had Shakespeare's genius. But for my part . . . it is unthinkable that any woman in Shakespeare's day should have had Shakespeare's genius. For genius like Shakespeare's is not born among labouring, uneducated, servile people. It was not born in England among the Saxons and the Britons. It is not born to-day among the working classes. How, then, could it have been born among women whose work began . . . almost before they were out of the nursery, who were forced to it by their parents and held to it by all the power of law and custom? Yet genius of a sort must have existed among women as it must have existed among the working classes. Now and again an Emily Brontë or a Robert Burns blazes out and proves its presence. But certainly it never got itself on to paper. When, however, one reads of a witch being ducked, of a woman possessed by devils, of a wise woman selling herbs, or even of a very remarkable man who had a mother, then I think we are on the track of a lost novelist, a suppressed poet, of some mute and inglorious Jane Austen, some Emily Brontë who dashed her brains out on the moor or mopped and mowed about the highways crazed with the torture that her gift had put her to. Indeed, I would venture to guess that Anon, who wrote so many poems without signing them, was often a woman. . . .

This may be true or it may be false—who can say?—but what is true in it, so it seemed to me, reviewing the story of Shakespeare's sister as I had made it, is that any woman born with a great gift in the sixteenth century would certainly have gone crazed, shot herself, or ended her days in some lonely cottage outside the village, half witch, half wizard, feared and mocked at. For it needs little skill in psychology to be sure that a highly gifted girl who had tried to use her gift for poetry would have been so thwarted and hindered by other people, so tortured and pulled asunder by her own contrary instincts, that she must have lost her health and sanity to a certainty. No girl could have

Virginia Woolf
(Wikimedia Commons)

walked to London and stood at a stage door and forced her way into the presence of actor-managers without doing herself a violence and suffering an anguish which may have been irrational—for chastity may be a fetish invented by certain societies for unknown reasons—but were none the less inevitable. Chastity had then, it has even now, a religious importance in a woman's life, and has so wrapped itself round with nerves and instincts that to cut it free and bring it to the light of day demands courage of the rarest. To have lived a free life in London in the sixteenth century would have meant for a woman who was poet and playwright a nervous stress and dilemma which might well have killed her. Had she survived, whatever she had written would have been twisted and deformed, issuing from a strained and morbid imagination. And undoubtedly, I thought, looking at the shelf where there are no plays by women, her work would have gone unsigned. That refuge she would have sought certainly. It was the relic of the sense of chastity that dictated anonymity to women even so late as the nineteenth century. Currer Bell, George Eliot, George Sand, all the victims of inner strife as their writings prove, sought ineffectively to veil themselves by using the name of a man. Thus they did homage to the convention, which if not implanted by the other sex was liberally encouraged by them (the chief glory of a woman is not to be talked of, said Pericles, himself a much-talked-of man) that publicity in women is detestable. Anonymity runs in their blood. The desire to be veiled still possesses them. They are not even now as concerned about the health of their fame as men are, and, speaking generally, will pass a tombstone or a signpost without feeling an irresistible desire to cut their names on it. . . .

And one gathers from this enormous modern literature of confession and self-analysis that to write a work of genius is almost always a feat of prodigious difficulty. Everything is against the likelihood that it will come from the writer's mind whole and entire. Generally material circumstances are against it. Dogs will bark; people will interrupt; money must be made; health will break down. Further, accentuating all these difficulties and making them harder to bear is the world's notorious indifference. It does not ask people to write poems and novels and histories; it does not need them. It does not care whether Flaubert finds the right word or whether Carlyle scrupulously verifies this or that fact. Naturally, it will not pay for what it does not want. And so the writer, Keats, Flaubert, Carlyle, suffers, especially in the creative years of youth, every form of distraction and discouragement. . . .

But for women, I thought, looking at the empty shelves, these difficulties were infinitely more for-midable. In the first place, to have a room of her own, let alone a quiet room or a sound-proof room, was out of the question, unless her parents were exceptionally rich or very noble, even up to the beginning of the nineteenth century. Since her pin money, which depended on the goodwill of her father, was only enough to keep her clothed, she was debarred from such alleviations as came even to Keats or Tennyson or Carlyle, all poor men, from a walking tour, a little journey to France, from the separate lodging which, even if it were miserable enough, sheltered them from the claims and tyrannies of their families. Such material difficulties were formidable; but much worse were the immaterial. The indifference of the world which Keats and Flaubert and other men of genius have found so hard to bear was in her case not indifference but hostility. The world did not say to her as it said to them, Write if you choose; it makes no difference to me. The world said with a guffaw, Write? What's the good of your writing? Here the psychologists of Newnham and Girton might come to our help, I thought, looking again at the blank spaces on the shelves. For surely it is time that the effect of discouragement upon the mind of the artist should be measured, as I have seen a dairy company measure the effect of ordinary milk and Grade A milk upon the body of the rat. They set two rats in cages side by side, and of the two one was furtive, timid and small, and the other was glossy, bold and big. Now what food do we feed women as artists upon? I asked, remembering, I suppose, that dinner of prunes and custard. . . . I will quote, however, Mr. Oscar Browning, because Mr. Oscar Browning was a great figure in Cambridge at one time, and used to examine the students at Girton and Newnham. Mr. Oscar Browning was wont to declare "that the impression left on his mind, after looking over any set of examination papers, was that, irrespective of the marks he might give, the best woman was intellectually the inferior of the worst man." . . .

Glossary

Anon: anonymous; the signature on works whose author is unknown

chastity: refraining from immoral activity

Currer Bell: pen name used by English writer Charlotte Brontë (1816–1855)

George Eliot: pen name used by English writer Mary Ann Evans (1819–1880)

George Sand: pen name used by French writer Amantine Lucile Aurore Dupin (1804–1876)

Girton: Girton College of the University of Cambridge in England

Newnham: Newnham College of the University of Cambridge in England

Oscar Browning: English educational reformer at Cambridge University in the late nineteenth and early twentieth centuries

Pericles: ancient Athenian politician (495–429 BCE) remembered for his promotion of the arts

Short-Answer Questions

1. Based on the text, what is the result of creative women living in a male-dominated society?

2. Based on the text, describe restrictions that were imposed on women in the sixteenth century.

3. Woolf utilizes "a room of one's own" as a metaphor. Explain her meaning. Construct a modern metaphor that one could use to convey the meaning to a contemporary audience.

Chapter 5

American Women's Lives in the Nineteenth Century

The nineteenth century was an era of growth, education, and technological advancements. Revolutionary changes occurred; by the end of the 1800s the world was vastly different. Women's lives and roles evolved as groups debated different ideas regarding slavery and freedom, work and family, education and opportunity. Class, race, and gender were still the predominant hallmarks that guided behavior. The beginning of the century saw American women fulfilling their perceived destiny as "creatures of reproduction." Depending on one's economic rank, many women also worked outside the domestic sphere. Women living in the upper and middle classes had the luxury of servants who alleviated much of the labor associated with maintaining a home and family, duties such as cleaning, cooking, mending, childcare, and the like. Women in working- and lower-class families assumed more tasks than those simply considered the domain of every female. They engaged in the gendered roles of wives and mothers as well as paid employment to help sustain the family.

As technology improved and the population began its transition from largely agricultural advocations to industrial pursuits in cities, some women concentrated on more than domestic pursuits. Exciting possibilities opened for women to take their skills and improve society. Reform movements motivated women to work in areas of religion, poverty, immorality and vice, drinking, antislavery, and education.

Women in the Abolition Movement

Some northern women worked in abolitionist societies, the Underground Railroad, and advocated for the end of slavery. Many helped to educate slaves and championed for their equality. This awareness of slaves as human beings with rights, intellect, and ability can be seen in Frances Anne Kemble's *Journal of a Resident on a Georgia Plantation*. During her brief stay on the plantation of her husband, Pierce Mease Butler, Kemble (1809–1893) recorded her observations about enslaved people, their qualities, and abilities. She was a woman of the era and provided contradictory accounts and statements that received criticism by historians in the twentieth century. In some passages she mentions the apologists' view and refutes it. Her perceptive thoughts are akin to many of those used to justify education and rights for women. The work that female abolitionists did would link the ideology that not only are people of color human and deserve rights and respect, so too were women. They recognized societal and legal limitation on their sex. This led to the development of women's suffrage and women's rights campaigns.

Catharine Beecher and Margaret Fuller

Catharine Esther Beecher's *Treaties on Domestic Economy* is an example of prescriptive literature reenforcing women's stereotypical roles. Primarily written for an upper-class audience of white women, Beecher (1800–1878) used the framework of a primer to teach the proper roles of women. Her text embodies elements of the burgeoning reform ideologies for women's roles as wives and mothers. Margaret Fuller's *Woman in the Nineteenth Century* is a seminal feminist tract justifying full emancipation of American women. Using transcendental principles, Fuller (1810–1850) argued that women need the freedom of introspection and educational enlightenment to achieve their highest level of evolution. Reflecting on examples from politics, history, philosophy, and religion, Fuller criticized the paternalistic nature that European tradition instilled in Americans, for the horrendous treatment on American Indians and slaves and American Indian policies. She associated the plight of woman with that of the slave, a common tactic of the day. It is a radical document that espouses many of the same types of feminism found in the modern era.

Continuing the theme of equality in *Alas, Poor Adam*, Amelia Jenks Bloomer (1818–1894) used the Bible and common sense to render the claim that God appointed man to wield power and authority over woman false. She questioned why God would want woman to be inferior but give her intellect and ability. She analyzed the edicts of St. Paul and provided strong arguments against his strictures. Her most convincing rational for woman's equality is that not all husbands wanted to restrict their wives, and if a woman were single or widowed, she had no husband to constrain her or her actions. Why should woman listen to a man if he is not her husband and the Bible does not implore her to do so?

The Page Act and Chinese Exclusion Act

Touted as a protective measure, the Page Act of 1875 was part and parcel of the anti-Asian feelings circulating in America. It prohibited Chinese women from immigrating to this country, claiming they were entering the country for immoral purposes. It was soon followed by the Chinese Exclusion Act of 1882. Long-term effects of this law included attaching an unsavory, sexually permissive reputation to Asian women.

"The Status of Woman, Past, Present, and Future" by Susan B. Anthony (1820–1906), published in 1897, discusses the progress women made in the realms of education, professions, property ownership, wages, and the like. Anthony looked at conditions of women fifty years prior and declared that most of the demands made in the 1848 Seneca Falls Declaration of Sentiments had been met. She identified politics as one of the last bastions still hostile toward women. It is interesting to look at what Anthony considered progress and success, while knowing that so many of the rights women received and exercised were the direct result of other women striving for change. It is also clear that Anthony was writing for a middle- and upper-class audience who would have the economic support and leisure time possible to pursue education and careers. The vote was only one of many rights and privileges that women lacked, and Anthony believed it was only a matter of time before they gained it. Victoria Woodhull (1838–1927) contributed to this literature on suffrage in *Lecture on Constitutional Equality*. As the first woman to appear before a Congressional Committee, Woodhull used the Fourteenth and Fifteenth Amendments to demonstrate that women already had the right to vote as citizens and as a pursuit of their civil liberties granted in the Constitution. A right was not to be rescinded unless the person committed a crime that needed to be adjudicated through due process. Simply by being born female, woman as a class and species had not violated any law. Woodhull argued that to be truly free, women must have the ability to participate in the franchise by which men are elected and pass laws and taxes affecting them. To deny this right was analogous to slavery.

Sarah Winnemucca Exposes Stereotypes Applied to Native Americans

Sarah Winnemucca's 1883 *Life Among the Paiutes* is a powerful account of the history and struggles of her people. Written in the flowery, Victorian language of the era, Winnemucca (?–1891) attempted to enlighten white readers of the negative and long-lasting effects of their white settlements. Primarily political, this treatise was dedicated to changing the hearts and minds of Americans. She worked to explain the harmful stereotypes applied to American Indians as a means of developing empathy and effecting change. Her account is significant because she was living a variety of intersectionalities that typically prevented such people from gaining recognition and a national platform.

Elinore Pruitt Stewart (1876–1933) wrote of her adventures on a ranch in Wyoming in *Letters of a Woman Homesteader*, published in 1914. She not only chronicled her experiences but also served as inspiration for other women who craved independence, autonomy, and freedom. The feminist elements that Stewart pursued and valued were achieved by her hard work and sacrifice. Her letters portray her as single, living on a ranch although she was married and in an equal partnership atypical of the time. She desired independence as a woman and showed women's capabilities.

In these documents, shared ideals resound in subtle ways to highlight the abilities of women, societal limitations, and their constant striving to effect change. Equality is their goal, even when unstated, and is evident by their intellect and their ability to state their beliefs and defend their humanity.

Further Reading

Books

Blackwell, Alice Stone. *Lucy Stone: Pioneer of Woman's Rights*. Charlottesville: University Press of Virginia, 2001.

Cott, Nancy F. *The Grounding of Modern Feminism*. New Haven, CT: Yale University Press, 1989.

Rothman, Joshua D. *Reforming America, 1815–1860: A Norton Documents Reader*. New York: W.W. Norton & Company, 2010.

Schneir, Miriam. *Feminism: The Essential Historical Writings*. New York: Vintage, 1994.

Wellman, Judith. *The Road to Seneca Falls: Elizabeth Cady Stanton and the First Woman's Rights Convention*. Champaign: University of Illinois Press, 2004.

Articles

Brah, Avtar, and Ann Phoenix. "Ain't I a Woman? Revisiting Intersectionality." *Journal of International Women's Studies* (2004): 75–86.

Cruea, Susan M. "Changing Ideals of Womanhood During the Nineteenth-Century Woman Movement." *University Writing Program Faculty Publications* (2005).

Lawrence, Amanda. "The Power of Intersectionality to Transcend National Identity in the United States." *Studies in Ethnicity and Nationalism* (December 1, 2017). Available at https://onlinelibrary.wiley.com/doi/full/10.1111/sena.12235.

McCall, Leslie. "The Complexity of Intersectionality." *Signs* 30, no. 3 (Spring 2005): 1771–1800.

Offen, Karen. "Defining Feminism: A Comparative Historical Approach." *Signs* 14, no. 1 (1988): 119–57.

Setzer, Claudia. "The Bible and the Legacy of First Wave Feminism," in Philip Goff, Arthur Farnsley, and Peter Thuesen, eds., *The Bible in American Life*. New York: Oxford University Press, 2017.

Catherine E. Beecher:
Treatise on Domestic Economy

Author
Catharine E. Beecher

Date
1841

Document Type
Essays, Reports, Manifestos

Significance
Justified education for women and girls and addressed the influence of the domestic role of women on American society

Overview

Catharine E. Beecher (1800–1878) was the daughter of the Reverend Henry Ward Beecher and the elder sister of the novelist Harriet Beecher Stowe. She is best known for her advocation of education for women. She received a formal education at a girls' school in Connecticut but taught herself subjects that were not thought suitable for young ladies at the time. When she was twenty-one, she opened a school for girls in Hartford, Connecticut. She also organized a protest against the attempts by the administration of President Andrew Jackson to expel Native Americans from their lands in the Southeast—the Indian Removal Act (1830). When her father was called to a new post in Cincinnati, Ohio, in 1832, Catharine (sometimes spelled "Catherine") went with him and

established a ladies' seminary. Although she retired in 1837 because of poor health, she continued advocating for women's education for forty years.

Beecher's *Treatise on Domestic Economy* was one of the first single-volume textbooks used in girls' schools. The book is most remarkable for the way it justifies female education. In the first chapter, excerpted here, Beecher presents the argument that American women held interests and roles in society. By connecting American democracy with Christianity and without directly challenging male authority, she suggests that American women, through education and morality, can have an influence on American life in ways that far outstrips their limited nineteenth-century roles.

Document Text

Chapter I: The Peculiar Responsibilities of American Women

There are some reasons why American women should feel an interest in the support of the democratic institutions of their Country, which it is important that they should consider. The great maxim, which is the basis of all our civil and political institutions, is, that "all men are created equal," and that they are equally entitled to "life, liberty, and the pursuit of happiness." But it can readily be seen, that this is only another mode of expressing the fundamental principle which the Great Ruler of the Universe has established, as the law of His eternal government. "Thou shalt love thy neighbor as thyself"; and "Whatsoever ye would that men should do to you, do ye even so to them." . . . The principles of democracy, then, are identical with the principles of Christianity. But, in order that each individual may pursue and secure the highest degree of happiness within his reach, unimpeded by the selfish interests of others, a system of laws must be established, which sustain certain relations and dependencies in social and civil life. . . .

For this purpose, it is needful that certain relations be sustained, which involve the duties of subordination. There must be the magistrate and the subject, one of whom is the superior, and the other the inferior. There must be the relations of husband and wife, parent and child, teacher and pupil, employer and employed, each involving the relative duties of subordination. The superior, in certain particulars, is to direct, and the inferior is to yield obedience. . . .

But who shall take the higher, and who the subordinate, stations in social and civil life? This matter, in the case of parents and children, is decided by the Creator. He has given children to the control of parents, as their superiors, and to them they remain subordinate, to a certain age, or so long as they are members of their household. . . .

In most other cases, in a truly democratic state, each individual is allowed to choose for himself,

Catharine Beecher
(Flickr)

who shall take the position of his superior. No woman is forced to obey any husband but the one she chooses for herself; nor is she obliged to take a husband, if she prefers to remain single. So every domestic, and every artisan or laborer, after passing from parental control, can choose the employer to whom he is to accord obedience, or, if he prefers to relinquish certain advantages, he can remain without taking a subordinate place to any employer. . . .

The tendencies of democratic institutions, in reference to the rights and interests of the female sex, have been fully developed in the United States; and it is in this aspect, that the subject is one of peculiar interest to American women. In this Country, it is established, both by opinion and by practice, that woman has an equal interest in all social and civil concerns; and that no domestic, civil, or political, institution, is right, which sacrifices her interest to promote that of the other sex. But in order to secure her the more firmly in all these privileges, it is decided, that, in the domestic relation, she take a subordinate station, and that, in civil and political concerns, her interests be intrusted to the other sex, without her taking any part in voting, or in making and administering laws. . . .

. . . The Americans have applied to the sexes the great principle of political economy, which governs the manufactories of our age by carefully dividing the duties of man from those of woman, in order that the great work of society may be the better carried on.

In no country has such constant care been taken, as in America, to trace two clearly distinct lines of action for the two sexes, and to make them keep pace one with the other, but in two pathways which are always different. . . .

As for myself, I do not hesitate to avow, that, although the women of the United States are confined within the narrow circle of domestic life, and their situation is, in some respects, one of extreme dependence, I have nowhere seen women occupying a loftier position; and if I were asked . . . to what the singular prosperity, and growing strength of that people ought mainly to be attributed, I should reply,—to the superiority of their women. . . .

It appears, then, that it is in America, alone, that women are raised to an equality with the other sex; and that, both in theory and practice, their interests are regarded as of equal value. They are made subordinate in station, only where a regard to their best interests demands it, while, as if in compensation for this, by custom and courtesy, they are always treated as superiors. Universally, in this Country, through every class of society, precedence is given to woman, in all the comforts, conveniences, and courtesies, of life.

In civil and political affairs, American women take no interest or concern, except so far as they sym-pathize with their family and personal friends; but in all cases, in which they do feel a concern, their opinions and feelings have a consideration, equal, or even superior, to that of the other sex.

In matters pertaining to the education of their children . . . and in all questions relating to morals or manners, they have a superior influence. In such concerns, it would be impossible to carry a point, contrary to their judgement and feelings; while an enterprise, sustained by them, will seldom fail of success.

If those who are bewailing themselves over the fancied wrongs and injuries of women in this Nation, could only see things as they are, they would know, that, whatever remnants of a barbarous or aristocratic age may remain in our civil institutions, in reference to the interests of women, it is only because they are ignorant of them, or do not use their influence to have them rectified; for it is very certain that there is nothing reasonable, which American women would unite in asking, that would not readily be bestowed.

The preceding remarks, then, illustrate the position, that the democratic institutions of this Country are in reality no other than the principles of Christianity carried into operation, and that they tend to place woman in her true position in society, as having equal rights with the other sex; and that, in fact, they have secured to American women a lofty and fortunate position. . . .

No American woman, then, has any occasion for feeling that hers is an humble or insignificant lot. The value of what an individual accomplishes is to be estimated by the importance of the enterprise achieved, and not by the particular position of the laborer. . . . The builders of a temple are of equal importance, whether they labor on the foundations, or toil upon the dome.

Thus, also, with those labors which are to be made effectual in the regeneration of the Earth. And it is by forming a habit of regarding the apparently insignificant efforts of each isolated laborer, in a comprehensive manner, as indispensable portions of a grand result, that the minds of all, however humble their sphere of service, can be invigorated and cheered. The woman who is rearing a family of children; the woman who labors in the schoolroom . . . even the humble domestic, whose example and influence may be moulding and forming young minds, while her faithful services sustain a prosperous domestic state;—each and all may be animated by the consciousness, that they are agents in accomplishing the greatest work that ever was committed to human responsibility. . . .

Glossary

manufactories: factories

maxim: a truth or principle expressed in a short statement

peculiar: distinctive; special

subordinate: under the control of another

Short-Answer Questions

1. In what way does Beecher argue that American democracy mirrors Christian principles?

2. In her writing, Beecher proposes that women are equal while at the same time subordinate to men. Describe how she believes this is possible. In what ways are women equal, according to Beecher, and in what ways are they not?

3. Based on the reading, do you believe the author was a feminist? Why or why not?

Margaret Fuller:
Woman in the Nineteenth Century

Author
Margaret Fuller

Date
1845

Document Type
Essays, Reports, Manifestos

Significance
Encouraged women to obtain an education and achieve independence from the home

---

Overview

Margaret Fuller gained wide notice during the 1840s as one of the American Transcendentalist movement's leading voices. Her work shared ideas in common with Ralph Waldo Emerson, Bronson Alcott, and Henry David Thoreau, among other writers who promoted the power of individual knowledge to transcend the concerns of society, yet it reflected distinctive concerns that were Fuller's own. Through her published work, she sought to influence public opinion beyond the intellectual confines of her native New England. Fuller advocated freedom of expression tempered by high critical standards as a literary reviewer. As a journalist and travel writer, she sought to apply her reformist ideals to factual reportage. Her desire to advance women's rights in American society led her to take on the conventions of her time as an essayist and author. Fuller's works demonstrate her wide scope as a writer and her forward-thinking views about artistic, philosophical, and social questions.

Woman in the Nineteenth Century was first published in July 1843 as an essay titled "The Great Lawsuit" in the Transcendentalist journal *Dial*, which Fuller herself edited. She later expanded and republished her thoughts in book form in 1845. *Woman in the Nineteenth Century*, the first major work of feminism in the United States, examines the role of women in American democracy. Fuller believed women should seek to fulfill their potential by being whatever they wanted to be. To reach their potential, women needed to obtain an education and achieve independence from the home. At the time of its publication, the work was considered to be both brilliant and deeply radical.

Document Text

It may well be an Anti-Slavery party that pleads for Woman, if we consider merely that she does not hold property on equal terms with men; so that, if a husband dies without making a will, the wife, instead of taking at once his place as head of the family, inherits only a part of his fortune, often brought him by herself, as if she were a child, or ward only, not an equal partner.

We will not speak of the innumerable instances in which profligate and idle men live upon the earnings of industrious wives; or if the wives leave them, and take with them the children, to perform the double duty of mother and father, follow from place to place, and threaten to rob them of the children, if deprived of the rights of a husband, as they call them, planting themselves in their poor lodgings, frightening them into paying tribute by taking from them the children, running into debt at the expense of these otherwise so overtasked helots. . . . I have seen the husband who had stained himself by a long course of low vice, till his wife was wearied from her heroic forgiveness, by finding that his treachery made it useless, and that if she would provide bread for herself and her children, she must be separate from his ill fame—I have known this man come to install himself in the chamber of a woman who loathed him, and say she should never take food without his company. . . .

But to return to the historical progress of this matter. Knowing that there exists in the minds of men a tone of feeling toward women as toward slaves, such as is expressed in the common phrase, "Tell that to women and children"; that the infinite soul can only work through them in already ascertained limits; that the gift of reason, Man's highest prerogative, is allotted to them in much lower degree; that they must be kept from mischief and melancholy by being constantly engaged in active labor, which is to be furnished and directed by those better able to think. . . .

That can never be necessary, cry the other side. All men are privately influenced by women; each has

Portrait of Margaret Fuller
(National Portrait Gallery)

his wife, sister, or female friends, and is too much biased by these relations to fail of representing their interests; and, if this is not enough, let them propose and enforce their wishes with the pen. The beauty of home would be destroyed, the delicacy of the sex be violated, the dignity of halls of legislation degraded, by an attempt to introduce them there. . . .

But if, in reply, we admit as truth that Woman seems destined by nature rather for the inner circle, we must add that the arrangements of civilized life have not been, as yet, such as to secure it to her. Her circle, if the duller, is not the quieter. If kept from "excitement," she is not from drudgery. Not only the Indian squaw carries the burdens of the camp, but the favorites of Louis XIV accompany him in his journeys, and the washerwoman stands at her tub, and carries home her work at all seasons, and in all states of health. Those who think the physical circumstances of Woman would make a part in the affairs of national government unsuitable, are by no means those who think it impossible for the negresses to endure field work, even during pregnancy, or for the sempstresses to go through their killing labors. . . .

As to the possibility of her filling with grace and dignity any such position, we should think those who had seen the great actresses, and heard the Quaker preachers of modern times, would not doubt that woman can express publicly the fulness of thought and creation, without losing any of the peculiar beauty of her sex. . . .

As to her home, she is not likely to leave it more than she now does for balls, theatres, meetings for promoting missions, revival meetings, and others to which she flies, in hope of an animation for her existence commensurate with what she sees enjoyed by men. . . . If men look straitly to it, they will find that, unless their lives are domestic, those of the women will not be. A house is no home unless it contain food and fire for the mind as well as for the body. . . .

As to men's representing women fairly at present, while we hear from men who owe to their wives not only all that is comfortable or graceful, but all that is wise, in the arrangement of their lives, the frequent remark, "You cannot reason with a woman," when from those of delicacy, nobleness, and poetic culture, falls the contemptuous phrase "women and children," and that in no light sally of the hour, but in works intended to give a permanent statement of the best experiences, when not one man, in the million, shall I say? no, not in the hundred million, can rise above the belief that woman was made for man, when such traits as these are daily forced upon the attention, can we feel that man will always do justice to the interests of woman. . . .

Under these circumstances, without attaching importance, in themselves, to the changes demanded by the champions of woman, we hail them as signs of the times. We would have every arbitrary barrier thrown down. We would have every path laid open to woman as freely as to man. Were this done, and

a slight temporary fermentation allowed to subside, we should see crystallizations more pure and of more various beauty. We believe the divine energy would pervade nature to a degree unknown in the history of former ages, and that no discordant collision, but a ravishing harmony of the spheres, would ensue.

Yet, then and only then will mankind be ripe for this, when inward and outward freedom for woman as much as for man shall be acknowledged as a right, not yielded as a concession. As the friend of the negro assumes that one man cannot by right hold another in bondage, so should the friend of Woman assume that Man cannot by right lay even well-meant restrictions on Woman. If the negro be a soul, if the woman be a soul, appareled in flesh, to one Master only are they accountable. There is but one law for souls, and, if there is to be an interpreter of it, he must come not as man, or son of man, but as son of God. . . .

That now the time has come when a clearer vision and better action are possible. When man and woman may regard one another as brother and sister, the pillars of one porch, the priests of one worship.

I have believed and intimated that this hope would receive an ampler fruition, than ever before, in our own land.

And it will do so if this land carry out the principles from which sprang our national life.

I believe that, at present, women are the best helpers of one another.

Let them think; let them act; till they know what they need.

We only ask of men to remove arbitrary barriers. Some would like to do more. But I believe it needs that woman show herself in her native dignity, to teach them how to aid her; their minds are so encumbered by tradition. . . .

You ask, what use will she make of liberty, when she has so long been sustained and restrained?

I answer; in the first place, this will not be suddenly given. I read yesterday a debate of this year on the subject of enlarging women's rights over property. . . . With their wives at home, and the readers of the paper, it was the same. And so the stream flows on; thought urging action, and action leading to the evolution of still better thought.

But, were this freedom to come suddenly, I have no fear of the consequences. Individuals might commit excesses, but there is not only in the sex a reverence for decorums and limits inherited and enhanced from generation to generation, which many years of other life could not efface, but a native love, in Woman as Woman. . . .

But if you ask me what offices they may fill, I reply—any. I do not care what case you put; let them be sea-captains, if you will. I do not doubt there are women well fitted for such an office, and, if so, I should be as glad to see them in it. . . .

I think women need, especially at this juncture, a much greater range of occupation than they have, to rouse their latent powers. A party of travellers lately visited a lonely hut on a mountain. There they found an old woman, who told them she and her husband had lived there forty years. "Why," they said, "did you choose so barren a spot?" She "did not know; it was the man's notion."

And, during forty years, she had been content to act, without knowing why, upon "the man's notion." I would not have it so.

In families that I know, some little girls like to saw wood, others to use carpenters' tools. Where these tastes are indulged, cheerfulness and good-humor are promoted. Where they are forbidden, because "such things are not proper for girls," they grow sullen and mischievous. . . .

I have no doubt, however, that a large proportion of women would give themselves to the same employments as now, because there are circumstances that must lead them. Mothers will delight to make the nest soft and warm. Nature would take care of that; no need to clip the wings of any bird that wants to soar and sing, or finds in itself the strength of pinion for a migratory flight unusual to its kind. The difference would be that all need not be constrained to employments for which some are unfit. . . .

I have urged on woman independence of man, not that I do not think the sexes mutually needed by one another, but because in Woman this fact has led to an excessive devotion, which has cooled love, degraded marriage, and prevented either sex from being what it should be to itself or the other.

I wish woman to live, first, for God's sake. Then she will not make an imperfect man her god, and thus sink to idolatry. Then she will not take what is not fit for her from a sense of weakness and poverty. Then, if she finds what she needs in Man embodied, she will know how to love, and be worthy of being loved.

Glossary

helots: enslaved people in ancient Sparta

profligate: extravagant and wasteful

sempstresses: seamstresses; dressmakers

squaw: Native American woman

Short-Answer Questions

1. Explain what Fuller means by a "greater range of occupation." Why does she say that women need a greater range of occupation? What would be the benefits?

2. Can you provide a definition for the inner circle referred to by Fuller? Do you believe Fuller's belief that most women will wish to remain in their inner circle?

3. Describe what benefits Fuller believes will occur with the expansion of women's rights.

Frances Anne Kemble:
Journal of a Residence on a Georgian Plantation in 1838–1839

Author Frances Anne Kemble **Date** 1863 **Document Type** Essays, Reports, Manifestos; Letters/Correspondence	**Significance** Offers a detailed account of the conditions of enslaved women and girls on a Southern plantation

Overview

Born in London, England, Frances Anne "Fanny" Kemble (1809–1893) was an actress, writer, and abolitionist. While touring the United States, Kemble met Pierce Butler, whom she wed in 1834. Butler was part of one of the wealthiest families in America at the time. Although they lived in Philadelphia, their holdings included cotton and rice plantations in Georgia. Butler inherited the plantations in 1836 and in 1838, and Butler, Kemble, and their children traveled south to the properties.

While spending four months in the South, Kemble witnessed the harsh conditions of slavery firsthand. During that time, she kept a journal of her experiences. Upon returning to the North, Kemble's abolitionist sentiments led to tension with her pro-slavery husband. The couple divorced in 1848.

Fearful that Butler would use her writings against her and keep her from her children, Kemble refrained from publishing her accounts of life on the Georgian plantations. When the American Civil War erupted in 1861, Kemble and daughter Sarah remained loyal to the North, while Butler and their other daughter, Frances, supported the Confederacy. Concerned with British support for the South, Kemble allowed the publication of her journal as a way of showing the inhumanity of the Southern system of enslavement. Her work, published in 1863 as *Journal of a Residence on a Georgian Plantation in 1838–1839*, stands as the most detailed account of slavery written by a northern abolitionist.

An engraving of Fanny Kemble
(Wikimedia Commons)

Document Text

Before closing this letter, I have a mind to transcribe to you the entries for to-day recorded in a sort of daybook, where I put down very succinctly the number of people who visit me, their petitions and ailments, and also such special particulars concerning them as seem to me worth recording. You will see how miserable the physical condition of many of these poor creatures is; and their physical condition, it is insisted by those who uphold this evil system, is the only part of it which is prosperous, happy, and compares well with that of northern labourers. Judge from the details I now send you; and never forget, while reading them, that the people on this plantation are well off, and consider themselves well off, in comparison with the slaves on some of the neighbouring estates.

Fanny has had six children, all dead but one. She came to beg to have her work in the field lightened.

Nanny has had three children, two of them are dead; she came to implore that the rule of sending them into the field three weeks after their confinement might be altered.

Leah, Caesar's wife, has had six children, three are dead.

Sophy, Lewis' wife, came to beg for some old linen; she is suffering fearfully, has had ten children, five of them are dead. The principal favour she asked was a piece of meat, which I gave her.

Sally, Scipio's wife, has had two miscarriages and three children born, one of whom is dead. She came complaining of incessant pain and weakness in her back. This woman was a mulatto daughter of a slave called Sophy, by a white man of the name of Walker, who visited the plantation.

Charlotte, Renty's wife, had had two miscarriages, and was with child again. She was almost crippled with rheumatism, and showed me a pair of poor swollen knees that made my heart ache. I have promised her a pair of flannel trowsers, which I must forthwith set about making.

Sarah, Stephen's wife,—this woman's case and history were, alike, deplorable, she had had four miscarriages, had brought seven children into the world, five of whom were dead, and was again with child. She complained of dreadful pains in the back, and an internal tumour which swells with the exertion of working in the fields; probably, I think, she is ruptured. She told me she had once been mad and ran into the woods, where she contrived to elude discovery for some time, but was at last tracked and brought back, when she was tied up by the arms and heavy logs fastened to her feet, and was severely flogged. After this she contrived to escape again, and lived for some time skulking in the woods, and she supposes mad, for when she was taken again she was entirely naked. She subsequently recovered from this derangement, and seems now just like all the other poor creatures who come to me for help and pity. I suppose her constant child-bearing and hard labour in the fields at the same time may have produced the temporary insanity.

Sukey, Bush's wife, only came to pay her respects. She had had four miscarriages, had brought eleven children into the world, five of whom are dead.

Molly, Quambo's wife, also only came to see me; hers was the best account I have yet received; she had had nine children, and six of them were still alive.

This is only the entry for to-day, in my diary, of the people's complaints and visits. Can you conceive a more wretched picture than that which it exhibits of the conditions under which these women live? Their cases are in no respect singular, and though they come with pitiful entreaties that I will help them with some alleviation of their pressing physical distresses, it seems to me marvellous with what desperate patience (I write it advisedly, patience of utter despair) they endure their sorrow-laden existence. Even the poor wretch who told that miserable story of insanity and lonely hiding in the swamps and scourging when she was found, and of her renewed madness and flight, did so in a sort of low, plaintive, monotonous murmur of misery, as if such sufferings were all "in the day's work."

I ask these questions about their children because I think the number they bear as compared with the number they rear a fair gauge of the effect of the system on their own health and that of their offspring. There was hardly one of these women, as you will see by the details I have noted of their ailments, who might not have been a candidate for a bed in an hospital, and they had come to me after working all day in the fields.

Glossary

flogged: severely beaten

mulatto: someone with mixed African and European ancestry

petitions: requests for help

ruptured: that is, the amniotic sac has ruptured (her water has broken), suggesting an impending miscarriage

scourging: whipping; severe punishment

trowsers: trousers

Short-Answer Questions

1. What does the above text tell us concerning the role of enslaved women on plantations?

2. Infer the reasons for such high child mortality among the women Kemble met.

3. Explain what Kemble means when she remarks that the suffering of the enslaved women's suffering was all "in the day's work."

Amelia Jenks Bloomer: "Alas! Poor Adam" Speech

Author	Significance
Amelia Jenks Bloomer	Challenged women's submission to men

Date
1870

Document Type
Speeches/Addresses

Overview

Throughout the 1840s and early 1850s, Amelia Jenks Bloomer (1818–1894) emerged as a leader of the reform movements centered in Seneca Falls, New York. These included women's rights, temperance, and various humanitarian causes. As editor of the temperance newspaper *The Lily*, Bloomer was heavily influenced by Elizabeth Cady Stanton and introduced issues concerning women's rights to *The Lily*'s female readers. Today, she is best remembered for championing women's dress reforms and her promotion of a short dress worn over trousers. Wearers of the Bloomer suit, or simply Bloomers, showed their support for women's rights.

In 1854, Bloomer and her husband, Dexter Bloomer, moved to Council Bluff, Iowa. With the passing of the Fifteenth Amendment in 1869 and the enfranchisement of African American men, women's suffragists escalated efforts. In Iowa, Bloomer received resistance from both Republicans and Democrats. On June 1, 1870, in Des Moine, Bloomer spoke at the city's first suffrage meeting. In "Alas! Poor Adam," Bloomer challenges long-held religious beliefs in women's inferiority and subservience to men. An active member of the Episcopalian Church, she believed women in the Bible had been misinterpreted. Addressing such topics as the fall of Adam and Eve and the letters of St. Paul (who advised women to keep quiet in church), Bloomer argues that traditional sexual inequality and biblical interpretations (or misinterpretations) had no bearing on contemporary society and women's role in it.

Divisions within the Iowa suffragist movement, in particular those involving free love, and growing antifeminist sentiment hampered the movement and eventually led to Bloomer's withdrawal from it. Despite Bloomer's influence in bringing the suffragists' movement to Iowa and neighboring states, the vote for women in Iowa would not be achieved until the passing of the Nineteenth Amendment in 1920.

Sketch of Amelia Bloom
(Wikimedia Commons)

Document Text

Among the many obstacles thrown in the way of woman's progress and enfranchisement, there is a very serious one in the minds of many which I wish briefly to consider this evening. It is one that has not only made her submissive and in a measure contented in her inferior, subject state, but has in numberless instances caused her untold sorrow and made her life one of extreme bitterness. I allude to the prevalent idea and teaching that woman was created subject to man—an inferior being, incapable of self government—needing a protector and supporter, and that man was to rule over and govern her for all time. . . .

This idea and this teaching has, in my view, brought untold misery into the world by making that rela-

tion which should be an equal partnership, where the rights and feelings and interests of each should be considered and respected, a relation instead of master and slave—of tyrant and subject—of superior and inferior. Made the woman, who is often superior in intellect, in morals, in benevolence, in every good thing, to her husband, the victim of his whims and caprices, of his blows and curses and lusts. . . .

First, then, we will go back to Genesis, . . . "God said, 'let us make man in our image, after our likeness, and let them have dominion over the fish of the sea, and over the fowl of the air, and over every creeping thing that creepeth upon the earth.' So God created man in his own image, in the image of God created He him; male and female created He them. And God blessed them, and God said unto them, 'be fruitful and multiply, and replenish the earth, and subdue it, and have dominion over the fish of the sea, and over the fowl of the air, and over every living thing that moveth upon the earth'" (Genesis 1:26–28).

In all this we find nothing to show that God created the man superior to the woman, or that he gave him greater right, or power, or dominion than he gave to her, or that he assigned them to different spheres of action. On the contrary, we are clearly told that he gave her equal power and dominion, and united her jointly and equally with him in the great commission given for the temporal government of the earth.

But farther on we are told . . . of the fall of this first pair—of Eve eating of the forbidden fruit, after the serpent had overcome her scruples by promises of great knowledge and good to follow—and of Adam, who was with her, also eating, without any scruples of conscience or promises from her of great reward (Genesis 3). Certainly in this transaction he manifested no superiority of intellect or goodness.

In reading this account of the fall of Adam and Eve, I cannot see wherein Eve committed the greater sin or showed the greater weakness. The command not to eat of the tree of knowledge was given to Adam by God himself before the creation of Eve, and we have no evidence that this command was repeated to her by the Creator. She probably received it secondhand from Adam. He being the one to whom the command was directly given, first created, and according to popular belief, endowed with superior intelligence, it was doubly binding on him to observe and keep it.

. . . Alas! poor Adam, while it required all the persuasive powers and eloquence of the subtle tempter, all the promises of wisdom, and knowledge, and power to seduce the so-called "weaker vessel" from the right path, all that was necessary to secure his downfall was simply to offer him the apple. He not only stood by and saw her eat, without a warning word, but ate himself without remonstrance or objection. And then, when enquired of by God concerning what he had done, instead of standing up like a man and honestly acknowledging his fault, he weakly tried to shield himself by throwing the blame on his wife. . . .

To the woman he said, "Thy desire shall be to thy husband and he shall rule over thee" (Genesis 3:16). This is generally regarded as a command, and binding for all time. . . . Can we believe that it was God's will, and pleasure, and command that such a state of things should exist in the marriage relation? If so, then we make Him responsible for all the quarrels and contentions and murders that ensue between husband and wife. . . . It can hardly be claimed that the Creator intended the woman to be always the meek, patient, silent subject . . . else He would have made her more patient under wrongs and dumb before her master, instead of endowing her with intellect, a keen sense of right, and in all respects like passions with man. . . .

God has placed no ruler between woman and himself. If this were so—if it be true that man is her ruler and master, to whom she is to yield obedience, then she is answerable to man and not to God for her actions. Her own conscience and the will of her husband may sometimes conflict—who then is she to serve? Her husband, of course, if

he is her ruler and she bound to obey him. It is a question with some whether woman has a soul! . . . If she has a soul, and if this doctrine of implicit obedience to the husband be true, then the husband must be answerable to God for her. She cannot justly be held accountable to two masters.

We pass to the New Testament, and there we find several passages from St. Paul, which in the minds of the opponents of woman's cause condemn woman to everlasting silence, submission, and nonentity. "Let the woman learn in silence with all subjection. I suffer not a woman to teach nor to usurp authority over the man, but to be in silence" (1 Timothy 2:11–12). "Let your women keep silence in the churches, for it is not permitted unto them to speak, but to be under obedience, and if they will learn anything let them ask their husbands at home, for it is a shame for women to speak in the church" (1 Corinthians 14:34–35). "Wives obey your husbands. The man is head of the wife as Christ is head of the Church" (Ephesians 5:22–23).

These I believe comprise all the utterances and rules laid down to govern woman's action, and they have been a terror to awe her into a state of fear and submission during all the centuries that have passed since they were proclaimed. To me they have no such terror, for I regard none of them as spoken to, or of, me. Whatever rules may have been necessary for the action of women eighteen hundred years ago, has little to do with the women of our day. As well say that the men of this generation shall be, and do, as were, and did, the men of that olden time, as to say that the women of these days shall be bound by laws and customs in force eighteen centuries before their existence. . . .

"Wives obey your husbands!" Oh! what a bugbear those four words have been to woman! How they have crushed, and belittled, and enslaved her! What a power for evil they have been to man, and how cruelly he has sometimes exercised it, domineering over and beating, even unto death, her whom he has chosen for a life partner and whom he is commanded to love even as his own self. To say nothing of the condition of women in past ages, and in pagan countries at this day, the newspapers of our own country and time teem with accounts of the most brutal tyranny, the most cruel oppression, and heartrending incidents growing out of the exercise of this power. . . .

Admitting for the sake of argument this passage to have been a command, binding upon woman for all time, as is the general belief, yet it does not have the weight that is usually given it. It only reaches women who have husbands. Unmarried women and widows are free from it. And since married women are to be in obedience to the will of their own husbands only, if a woman's husband approves of her preaching and talking in public, and of her voting and holding office, as very many husbands do, she is just as much bound by St. Paul's injunction to do all this, as another woman is to refrain from doing it at her husband's command. If my husband tells me that it is right for me to vote, and it is his wish that I exercise that right, I am as much bound to listen to and obey that wish as my neighbor is to obey her husband who denies her that right and forbids her exercising it. . . .

But, my friends, the passages we have been reviewing have nothing whatever to do with the question of Woman Suffrage—nothing to do with her talking and acting outside the church. Search the Bible through and you can find nothing against her sharing in political affairs, or enjoying political rights. They relate only to the church—and to the church of other times. Let woman set her heart at rest on this point, and cease to feel that God created her an inferior and subject. . . .

Some argue that because man was first created he was therefore superior. "Adam first, then Eve," they say. To this we reply, "animals first, then Adam." If things first created were superior, then Adam must give way to the life which preceded him. . . .
Clearly, all this is a matter with which we have nothing to do in our advocacy of Woman Suffrage. Whatever rules St. Paul found it necessary to lay down for the women of certain churches eighteen centuries ago, we are no more bound by them in this matter than men are bound to observe all the laws and customs of the same period, which we know that they do not.

Men are commanded to "love their wives even as their own selves," but somehow they very often overlook or forget this command. If they would observe it, women would not find it hard to obey, for as all men love themselves, and do not willingly inflict any wrong upon themselves, so if they loved their wives as themselves they would do them no wrong, but ever treat them with kindness, consideration and respect, and regard them as in all things their equals. . . .

Glossary

bugbear: a source of irritation; a made-up problem

enfranchisement: endowment with the rights of citizenship, especially the right to vote

St. Paul: important leader in early Christianity whose letters form much of the New Testament

Short-Answer Questions

1. Explain the traditional interpretation of Adam and Eve's story as one of women's subservience to men, and how Bloomer counters this interpretation.

2. Bloomer claims that the exhortation "Wives obey your husbands" can be used to promote equality and women's rights. Explain how this can be so.

3. Explain how a woman's possession of a soul, according to Bloomer, is an argument against male dominance over women.

Victoria Woodhull:
Lecture on Constitutional Equality

Author Victoria Woodhull	**Significance** Asserted in 1871 that women already had the right to vote because the Fourteenth and Fifteenth Amendments implicitly granted that right to all citizens
Date 1871	
Document Type Essays, Reports, Manifestos	

Overview

In January 1871, Victoria Woodhull became the first women to appear before a congressional committee when she addressed the House Judiciary Committee in a bid to persuade Congress to enact female suffrage. Benjamin Butler—a high-ranking Massachusetts Republican who would later chair the panel—allowed her to deliver her plea in person. Woodhull based her arguments on her belief that women already had the right to vote, in that the Fourteenth and Fifteenth Amendments to the Constitution implicitly granted that right to all citizens. The congressional majority did not accept her arguments and voted to dismiss the request, but the minority report written by just two of the committee's members, Butler and William Loughridge, supported the cause, saying that women were "competent voters." Woodhull went on to deliver fiery lectures on the constitutional enfranchisement of women, notably at Lincoln Hall in Washington, D.C., in February 1871. This expansion of her argument was published that same year in pamphlet form as *Lecture on Constitutional Equality*.

Document Text

I have no doubt it seems strange to many of you that a woman should appear before the people in this public manner for political purposes. . . .

On the 19th of December 1870, I memorialized Congress, setting forth what I believed to be the truth and right regarding Equal Suffrage for all citizens. This memorial was referred to the Judiciary Committees of Congress. On the 12th of January I appeared before the House Judiciary Committee and submitted to them the Constitutional and Legal points upon which I predicated such equality. January 20th Mr. Bingham, on behalf of the majority of said Committee, submitted his report to the House in which, while he admitted all my basic propositions, Congress was recommended to take no action. . . .

Public opinion is against Equality, but it is simply from prejudice, which requires but to be informed to pass away. No greater prejudice exists against equality than there did against the proposition that the world was a globe. This passed away under the influence of better information, so also will present prejudice pass. . . .

I come before you, to declare that my sex are entitled to the inalienable right to life, liberty and the pursuit of happiness. The first two I cannot be deprived of except for cause and by due process of law; but upon the last, a right is usurped to place restrictions so general as to include the whole of my sex, and for which no reasons of public good can be assigned. I ask the right to pursue happiness by having a voice in that government to which I am accountable. . . . I have the right to life, to liberty, unless I forfeit it by an infringement upon others' rights. . . . I also have the right to pursue happiness, unless I forfeit it in the same way, and am denied it accordingly. It cannot be said, with any justice, that my pursuit of happiness in voting for any man for office, would be an infringement of one of his rights as a citizen or as an individual. I hold, then, that in denying me this right without my having forfeited it, that departure is made from

1874 photograph of Victoria Woodhull
(Harvard Art Museum/Fogg Museum)

the principles of the Constitution, and also from the true principles of government, for I am denied a right born with me, and which is inalienable. . . .

I *am* subject to tyranny! I am taxed in every conceivable way . . . to *all* these must I submit, that *men's* government may be maintained, a government in the administration of which I am denied a voice, and from its edicts there is no appeal. . . . To be compelled to submit to *these* extortions . . . is bad enough: but to be compelled to submit to them, and also denied the right to cast my vote *against* them, is a tyranny *more* odious than that which, being rebelled against, gave this country independence. . . .

The formal abolition of slavery created several millions of male negro citizens, who, a portion of the acknowledged citizens assumed to say, were *not* entitled to equal rights with themselves. To get over this difficulty, Congress in its wisdom saw fit to propose a XIV Amendment to the Constitution. . . . After the adoption of the XIV Amendment it was found that still more legislation [XV Amendment] was required to secure the exercise of the right to vote to all who by it were declared to be citizens. . . .

It is not the women who are happily situated, whose husbands hold positions of honor and trust, who are blessed by the bestowal of wealth, comforts and ease that I plead for. These do not feel their condition of servitude any more than the happy, well-treated slave felt her condition. Had slavery been of this kind it is at least questionable if it would not still have been in existence; but it was not all of this kind. Its barbarities, horrors and inhumanities roused the blood of some who were free, and by their efforts the male portion of a race were elevated by Congress to the exercise of the rights of citizenship. Thus would I have Congress regard woman, and shape their action, *not* from the condition of those who are so well cared for as not to wish a change to enlarge their sphere of action, but for the *toiling female millions*, who have human rights which should be respected. . . .

We are now prepared to dispose of the sex argument. If the right to vote shall not be denied to any person of any race, how shall it be denied to the female part of all races? Even if it could be denied on account of sex, I ask, what warrant men have to presume that it is the *female* sex to whom such denial can be made instead of the *male* sex? Men,

you are wrong, and you stand convicted before the world of denying me, a woman, the right to vote, not by any right of law, but simply because you have usurped the power so to do, just as all other tyrants in all ages have, to rule their subjects. The extent of the tyranny in either case being limited only by the power to enforce it. . . .

We will have our rights. . . . We have besought, argued and convinced, but we have failed; *and we will not* fail.

We will try you *just once more*. If the very next Congress refuse women all the legitimate results of citizenship; if they indeed merely so much as fail by a proper declaratory act to withdraw every obstacle to the most ample exercise of the franchise, then we give here and now, deliberate notification of what we will do next.

There is one alternative left, and we have resolved on that. . . . As surely as one year passes, from this day, and this right is not fully, frankly and unequivocally considered, we shall proceed to call another convention expressly to frame a new constitution and to erect a new government, complete in all its parts, and to take measures to maintain it as effectually as men do theirs. . . .

We mean treason; we mean secession, and on a thousand times grander scale than was that of the South. We are plotting revolution; we will overthrow this bogus republic and plant a government of righteousness in its stead, which shall not only profess to derive its power from the consent of the governed, but shall do so in reality.

Glossary

besought: asked for; begged for

Bingham: John Bingham, Ohio congressman

franchise: a right or set of rights; in particular, the right to vote

prejudice: adverse opinion based on insufficient knowledge

usurped: used without permission; stolen

XIV Amendment to the Constitution: the Fourteenth Amendment, which granted citizenship and equal protection of the law to "all persons, born or naturalized in the United States," including those formerly enslaved

XV Amendment: the Fifteenth Amendment: "The right of citizens of the United States to vote shall not be denied or abridged by the United States or by any State on account of race, color or previous condition of servitude"

Short-Answer Questions

1. How does Woodhull bring the analogy of slavery, including the Fourteenth and Fifteenth Amendments, into her argument for women's suffrage?

2. How persuasive a case does Woodhull make? Does her militant tone and appeal to revolution at the end of the manifesto help or weaken it? Explain.

3. Consider the manifesto's text from a logical and constitutional point of view. How would you reinforce her claim to the rights she feels are being denied to women? Would you add to or omit any of the points that were put forward?

Page Act of 1875

<table>
<tr><td>Author
Forty-Third U.S. Congress</td><td>Significance
Prohibited the immigration of contracted Asian labor and Asian women</td></tr>
<tr><td>Date
1875</td><td></td></tr>
<tr><td>Document Type
Legislative</td><td></td></tr>
</table>

Overview

Passed in 1875 and named after California's Republican House Representative Horace Page, the Page Act (or An Act Supplementary to the Acts in Relation to Immigration) empowered U.S. consuls-general and consuls to oversee and deny immigration to the United States from Asian countries. Japan, China, and "Oriental" nations were specifically referred to in the legislation. Two groups were targeted. Laborers who were deemed not "free and voluntary" and Asian women believed to be immigrating for immoral purposes, such as prostitution, were prohibited.

The growth of anti-Chinese racism was prevalent along the western coast of the United States in the latter half of the nineteenth century. The belief was that Chinese women were overly sexual, and fears of prostitution and race-mixing abounded. Chinese women who wished to move to the United States had to first prove they were not prostitutes. This act of legislation severely decreased female Chinese immigration and was later followed by other laws based on moral stereotypes that excluded immigration and allowed deportation. Later restrictions, such as the Chinese Exclusion Act of 1882, extended restrictions on all Asian immigrants.

Document Text

FORTY-THIRD CONGRESS. SESS. II. CH. 141. 1875.

CHAP. 141.—An act supplementary to the acts in relation to immigration.

Be it enacted by the Senate and House of Representatives of the United States of America in Congress assembled, That in determining whether the immigration of any subject of China, Japan, or any Oriental country, to the United States, is free and voluntary, as provided by section two thousand one hundred and sixty-two of the Revised Code, title "Immigration," it shall be the duty of the consul-general or consul of the United States residing at the port from which it is proposed to convey such subjects, in any vessels enrolled or licensed in the United States, or any port within the same, before delivering to the masters of any such vessels the permit or certificate provided for in such section, to ascertain whether such immigrant has entered into a contract or agreement for a term of service within the United States, for lewd and immoral purposes; and if there be such contract or agreement, the said consul-general or consul shall not deliver the required permit or certificate.

SEC. 2. That if any citizen of the United States, or other person amenable to the laws of the United States shall take, or cause to be taken or transported, to or from the United States any subject of China, Japan, or any Oriental country, without their free and voluntary consent, for the purpose of holding them to a term of service, such citizen or other person shall be liable to be indicted therefore, and, on conviction of such offense, shall be punished by a fine not exceeding two thousand dollars and be imprisoned not exceeding one year; and all contracts and agreements for a term of service of such persons in the United States, whether made in advance or in pursuance of such illegal importation, and whether such importation shall have been in American or other vessels, are hereby declared void.

The Page Act effectively prohibited the entry of Chinese women into the United States.
(The Bancroft Library, University of California, Berkeley)

SEC. 3. That the importation into the United States of women for the purposes of prostitution is hereby forbidden; and all contracts and agreements in relation thereto, made in advance or in pursuance of such illegal importation and purposes, are hereby declared void; and whoever shall knowingly and willfully import, or cause any importation of, women into the United States for the purposes of prostitution, or shall knowingly or willfully hold, or attempt to hold, any woman to such purposes, in pursuance of such illegal importation and contract or agreement, shall be deemed guilty of a felony, and, on conviction thereof, shall be imprisoned not exceeding five years and pay a fine not exceeding five thousand dollars.

SEC. 4. That if any person shall knowingly and willfully contract, or attempt to contract, in advance or in pursuance of such illegal importation, to supply to another the labor of any cooly or other person brought into the United States in violation of section two thousand one hundred and fifty-eight of the Revised Statutes, or of any other section of the laws prohibiting the cooly-trade or of this act, such person shall be deemed guilty of a felony, and, upon conviction thereof, in any United States court, shall be fined in a sum not exceeding five hundred dollars and imprisoned for a term not exceeding one year.

SEC. 5. That it shall be unlawful for aliens of the following classes to immigrate into the United States, namely, persons who are undergoing a sentence for conviction in their own country of felonious crimes other than political or growing out of or the result of such political offenses, or whose sentence has been remitted on condition of their emigration, and women "imported for the purposes of prostitution." Every vessel arriving in the United States may be inspected under the direction of the collector of the port at which it arrives, if he shall have reason to believe that any such obnoxious persons are on board; and the officer making such inspection shall certify the result thereof to the master or other person in charge of such vessel, designating in such certificate the person or persons, if any there be, ascertained by him to be of either of the classes whose importation is hereby forbidden. . . .

Glossary

consul/consul-general: government officials representing their country in another country

cooly: derogatory term for a laborer from Asia

immigrant: a person moving from one country to another of which they are not a citizen

obnoxious: censured

Oriental: a term, now considered derogatory, referring to Asia or a person from Asia

remitted: withdrawn; pardoned

Short-Answer Questions

1. How were U.S. citizens discouraged from transporting Asian workers "without their free and voluntary consent"?

2. Identify how the Page Act was used to stop Chinese women from immigrating.

3. Explain how racism and stereotypes play into this law.

Sarah Winnemucca Hopkins:
Life among the Piutes

Author	Significance
Sarah Winnemucca Hopkins	Described the violent seizure of the Paiutes' homelands by the U.S. government, corrupt Indian agents, and white settlers
Date	
1883	
Document Type	
Essays, Reports, Manifestos	

Overview

Sarah Winnemucca Hopkins (1844–1891) was a Northern Paiute (also spelled Piute) woman, the daughter of a chief, and a tireless advocate for her people. The Northern Paiute faced pressure from white settlers and corrupt Indian agents who violently dispossessed them of their homelands in what is now Nevada.

When Winnemucca Hopkins was young, she learned English, Spanish, and three Indian dialects, and she used her command of language to help her people. At one point in her life, she worked for the Bureau of Indian Affairs as an interpreter. However, the work that Winnemucca Hopkins is most known for is her advocacy for her people. As an adult, she traveled the United States giving hundreds of speeches, interviews, and public addresses. She also wrote letters to public officials and testified in Congress to expose how her people had been treated by Indian agents, especially how they had been unjustly and violently removed from their homeland. Ultimately, she wrote and published a book (the first Native woman to do so) called

Life among the Piutes: Their Wrongs and Claims. Like all of her advocacy work, this book was intended for white audiences. She wanted them to see the ways that Indigenous Americans were being unjustly treated and dispossessed of their lands by a corrupt federal Indian agency. Her work exposed the hypocrisy of the government's policy to "civilize" Native peoples, showing that this was simply a justification to take Native land in the process of resettling and re-creating an American West for white people.

Winnemucca Hopkins's story is the story of many Native Americans in the United States during the period of expansion across the continent. It is a story of unprovoked massacres and of resistance to the ideology of manifest destiny and the force of white westward expansion. This excerpt, from a chapter in *Life among the Piutes* called "Reservation of Pyramid and Muddy Lakes," describes the kind of violent attacks her people faced in the later part of the nineteenth century as they fought to keep their homeland and way of life.

Sarah Winnemucca Hopkins
(Wikimedia Commons)

Document Text

This reservation, given in 1860, was at first sixty miles long and fifteen wide. The line is where the railroad now crosses the river, and it takes in two beautiful lakes, one called Pyramid Lake, and the one on the eastern side, Muddy Lake. No white people lived there at the time it was given us. We Piutes have always lived on the river, because out of those two lakes we caught beautiful mountain trout, weighing from two to twenty-five pounds each, which would give us a good income if we had it all, as at first. Since the railroad ran through in 1867, the white people have taken the best part of the reservation from us, and one of the lakes also. . . .

In 1865 we had another trouble with our white brothers. It was early in the spring, and we were then living at Dayton, Nevada, when a company of soldiers came through the place and stopped and spoke to some of my people, and said, "You have been stealing cattle from the white people at Harney Lake." They said also that they would kill everything that came in their way, men, women, and children. That captain's name was [Almond B.] Wells. The place where they were going to is about three hundred miles away. The days after they left were very sad hours, indeed. Oh, dear readers, these soldiers had gone only sixty miles away to Muddy Lake, where my people were then living and fishing, and doing nothing to anyone. The soldiers rode up to their encampment and fired into it, and killed almost all the people that were there. Oh, it is a fearful thing to tell, but it must be told. Yes, it must be told by me. It was all old men, women and children that were killed; for my father had all the young men with him, at the sink of Carson on a hunting excursion, or they would have been killed too. After the soldiers had killed all but some little children and babies still tied up in their baskets, the soldiers took them also, and set the camp on fire and threw them into the flames to see them burn alive. I had one baby brother killed there. My sister jumped on father's best horse and ran away. As she ran, the soldiers ran after her; but, thanks be to the Good Father in the Spirit-land, my dear sister got away. This almost killed my poor papa. But my people kept peaceful.

That same summer another of my men was killed on the reservation. This name was Truckee John. He was an uncle of mine, and was killed by a man named Flamens, who claimed to have had a brother killed in the war of 1860, but of course that had nothing to do with my uncle. About two weeks after this, two white men were killed over at Walker Lake by some of my people, and of course soldiers were sent for from California, and a great many companies came. They went after my people all over Nevada. Reports were made everywhere throughout the whole country by the white settlers, that the red devils were killing their cattle, and by this lying of the white settlers the trail began which is marked by the blood of my people from hill to hill and from valley to valley. . . . These reports were only made by those white settlers so that they could sell their grain, which they could not get rid of any other way. The only way the cattle-men and farmers get to make money is to start an Indian war, so that the troops may come and buy their beef, cattle, horses, and grain. The settlers get fat by it.

Glossary

Pyramid Lake and Muddy Lake: two lakes on the Paiute reservation that were historically important for fishing; an attack and massacre of some Paiutes took place on Muddy Lake

reservation: plot of land set up by the U.S. government for Native Americans removed from their homelands, overseen by Indian agents charged with making sure annuities and goods (such as food, blankets, education, and healthcare) were distributed

Short-Answer Questions

1. Why do you think Sarah Winnemucca Hopkins uses the phrase "white brothers" when describing the Muddy Lake massacre? Considering that she is writing for a white audience, what response might she have hoped to elicit from her reader?

2. Winnemucca Hopkins writes that the massacre at Muddy Lake "must be told by me." Why do you think she emphasizes that this "must be told"?

3. Consider what "westward expansion" meant to the Paiute and other Native peoples in this period? How does looking at westward expansion from the point of view of Sarah Winnemucca Hopkins, and all Native Americans, change the story?

Susan B. Anthony: "The Status of Woman, Past, Present, and Future"

Author Susan B. Anthony **Date** 1897 **Document Type** Essays, Reports, Manifestos	**Significance** Recounted the progress toward women's enfranchisement since the Seneca Falls Convention of 1848 and encouraged women to continue to work together to gain the vote

Overview

In her speeches and writings, abolitionist, education reform activist, and suffragist Susan B. Anthony displayed her devotion to the cause of women's rights—particularly the right to vote. Over the years, she honed her arguments until the success of the cause of suffrage and women's rights became inevitable. This major shift in public opinion was the result in large part of Anthony's carefully crafted arguments. In her 1897 article for *Arena* magazine, "The Status of Woman, Past, Present, and Future," Anthony reflects on the progress made to change the status of women since the Seneca Falls Convention of 1848 and encourages women to continue to work together to gain the vote.

Document Text

Fifty years ago woman in the United States was without a recognized individuality in any department of life. . . .

In those days the women of the family were kept closely at home, carding, spinning, and weaving, making the butter and cheese, knitting and sewing, working by day and night, planning and economizing, to educate the boys of the family. Thus the girls toiled so long as they remained under the home roof, their services belonging to the father by law and by custom. . . . When the boy was twenty-one, the father agreed to pay him a fixed sum per annum, thenceforth, for his services, or, in default of this, he was free to carry his labor where it would receive a financial reward. No such agreement ever was made with the girls of the family. . . . When they married, their services were transferred to the husband. . . .

Cases were frequent where fathers willed all of their property to the sons. . . . Where, however, the daughters received property, it passed directly into the sole possession of the husband. . . . At his death he could dispose of it by will, depriving the wife of all but what was called the "widow's dower." . . . The wife could neither sue nor be sued, nor testify in the courts. . . . According to the English common law . . . a man might beat his wife up to the point of endangering her life, without being liable to prosecution.

Fifty years ago no occupations were open to women except cooking, sewing, teaching, and factory work. . . . Every woman must marry, either with or without love, for the sake of support, or be doomed to a life of utter dependence . . . without any financial recompense, and usually looked upon with disrespect by the children. . . . Is it any wonder that a sour and crabbed disposition was universally ascribed to spinsterhood, or that those women should be regarded as most unfortunate? . . .

Such was the helpless, dependent, fettered condition of women when the first Women's Rights Convention was called just forty-nine years ago, at Seneca Falls, N.Y., by Elizabeth Cady Stanton and Lucretia Mott. . . . While there had been individual demands, from time to time, the first organized body to formulate a declaration of the rights of women was the one which met at Seneca Falls, July 19–20, 1848. . . . In the Declaration of Sentiments and the Resolutions there framed, every point was covered that . . . has been contended for by the advocates of equal rights for women. Every inequality of the existing laws and customs was carefully considered and a thorough and complete readjustment demanded. The only resolution that was not unanimously adopted was the one urging the elective franchise for women. . . . But Mrs. Stanton and Frederick Douglass, seeing that the

Susan B. Anthony
(Wikimedia Commons)

power to make laws and choose rulers was the right by which all others could be secured, persistently advocated the resolution and at last carried it by a good majority. . . .

The close of this nineteenth century finds every trade, vocation, and profession open to women, and every opportunity at their command. . . . The ban of social ostracism has been largely removed from the woman wage-earner. . . . Woman is no longer compelled to marry for support, but may herself make her own home and earn her own financial independence.

With but few exceptions, the highest institutions of learning in the land are as freely opened to girls as to boys. . . . In the world of literature and art women divide the honors with men;

and our civil-service rules have secured for them many thousands of remunerative positions under the Government. . . .

There has been a radical revolution in the legal status of women. In most States the old common law has been annulled by legislative enactment. . . . In nearly every State they may retain and control property owned at marriage and all they may receive by gift or inheritance thereafter. . . . They may sue and be sued, testify in the courts, and carry on business in their own name. . . . In six or seven States have equal guardianship of the children. . . .

The department of politics has been slowest to give admission to women. Suffrage is the pivotal right. . . . If women could make the laws or elect those who make them, they would be in the position of sovereigns instead of subjects. Were they the political peers of man they could command instead of having to beg, petition, and pray. . . .

But even this stronghold is beginning to yield to the long and steady pressure. In twenty-five States women possess suffrage in school matters; in four States they have a limited suffrage in local affairs; in one State they have municipal suffrage; in four States they have full suffrage, local, State, and national. Women are becoming more and more interested in political questions and public affairs. . . . Especial efforts are made by politicians to obtain the support of women. . . . Some of the finest political writing in the great newspapers of the day is done by women. . . . In many of the large cities women have formed civic clubs and are exercising a distinctive influence in municipal matters. In most of the States of the Union women are eligible for many offices, State and County Superintendents, Registers of Deeds, etc. They are Deputies to State, County, and City officials, notaries public, State Librarians, and enrolling and engrossing clerks in the Legislatures.

It follows, as a natural result, that in the States where women vote they are eligible to all offices. They have been sent as delegates to National Conventions, made Presidential electors, and are sitting to-day as members in both the Upper and Lower Houses of the Legislatures. . . . These radical changes have been effected without any social upheaval or domestic earthquakes, family relations have suffered no disastrous changes, and the men of the States where women vote furnish the strongest testimony in favor of woman suffrage. . . .

From that little convention at Seneca Falls, with a following of a handful of women scattered through half-a-dozen different States, we have now the great National Association. . . . The Legislatures of Washington and South Dakota have submitted woman-suffrage amendments to their electors for 1898. . . . For a quarter of a century Wyoming has stood as a conspicuous object-lesson in woman suffrage, and is now reinforced by the three neighboring States of Colorado, Utah, and Idaho. . . .

Until woman has obtained "that right protective of all other rights—the ballot," this agitation must still go on. . . . The day will come when man will recognize woman as his peer, not only at the fireside, but in the councils of the nation. . . . Only good can come to the individual or the nation through the rendering of exact justice.

Glossary

carding: brushing fabric to disentangle fibers

common law: law created over the centuries, based on court decisions, royal decrees, and local customs, some dating back to Anglo-Saxon England, rather than on statutes passed by a legislative body such as the U.S. Congress

crabbed: irritable; crabby

elective franchise: the right to vote

electors: elected representatives from each state whose vote, in the Electoral College, decides presidential elections

fettered: shackled; hobbled, as a horse

"fifty years ago": at the time of the Seneca Falls Convention of 1848

Frederick Douglass: abolitionist, writer, statesman, social reformer, and supporter of women's rights

National Association: the National American Women Suffrage Association

remunerative: for a wage; profitable

suffrage: the right to vote

Upper and Lower Houses of the Legislatures: here, a reference to state senates and houses of representatives

Wyoming: the first territory (in 1869) and then state (in 1890) to grant women's suffrage

Short-Answer Questions

1. What are the changes over the course of the fifty years since the Seneca Falls Convention that Susan B. Anthony describes? How did women's rights progress over that time span?

2. What importance does Anthony ascribe to the Seneca Falls Convention? Is her assessment justified? Why or why not?

3. How justified is Anthony's selection of suffrage as "the pivotal right"? How does she argue in support of this?

Elinore Pruitt Stewart:
Letters of a Woman Homesteader

Author
Elinore Pruitt Stewart

Date
1909–1914

Document Type
Letters/Correspondence

Significance
Championed female independence and the opportunities available to those willing to homestead

Overview

Born on June 3, 1876, in White Bead Hill in the Chickasaw Nation, Indian Territory, Elinore Pruitt knew hard times from an early age. Her father died when she was three, and she was raised by her mother, Josephine Elizabeth, and her mother's new husband (the brother of her first husband), Thomas Pruitt. Her parents died by the time she reached age eighteen and orphaned her and her seven surviving half-siblings. Two of the girls were married off, and the rest, along with Elinore, went to live with a grandmother. By 1902 Pruitt had married, and she and her husband, Harry C. Rupert, had filed for a homestead claim. It was during this period that she began writing for the *Kansas City Star*. Four years later, she had a daughter, Jerrine, and claimed to be a widow, although she was probably divorced.

Pruitt ventured to Denver with her daughter and eventually became the housekeeper for Juliet Coney, a widow and retired teacher. In 1909 Pruitt answered an advertisement for a housekeeper written by Clyde Stewart of Burnt Fork, Wyoming. She arrived in Wyoming in the spring, promptly filed a homestead claim adjacent to Clyde Stewart, and married him on May 5.

The new Mrs. Stewart wrote regularly to her former employer, Juliet Coney. Portions of her correspondence were eventually published in serial form in the *Atlantic Monthly* and then as two books, *Letters of a Woman Homesteader* (1914) and *Letters on an Elk Hunt* (1915). Her missives were unfailingly optimistic in tone and championed female independence and the opportunities available to those willing to homestead. While Stewart addressed her letters to Coney, she clearly had a larger audience in mind and wrote to entertain and fascinate her largely female, middle-class, and urban readers.

Document Text
The Joys of Homesteading
January 23, 1913.

Dear Mrs. Coney,—

. . . I am very enthusiastic about women homesteading. It really requires less strength and labor to raise plenty to satisfy a large family than it does to go out to wash, with the added satisfaction of knowing that their job will not be lost to them if they care to keep it. Even if improving the place does go slowly, it is that much done to stay done. Whatever is raised is the homesteader's own, and there is no house-rent to pay. This year Jerrine cut and dropped enough potatoes to raise a ton of fine potatoes. She wanted to try, so we let her, and you will remember that she is but six years old. We had a man to break the ground and cover the potatoes for her and the man irrigated them once. That was all that was done until digging time, when they were ploughed out and Jerrine picked them up. Any woman strong enough to go out by the day could have done every bit of the work and put in two or three times that much, and it would have been so much more pleasant than to work so hard in the city and then be on starvation rations in the winter.

To me, homesteading is the solution of all poverty's problems, but I realize that temperament has much to do with success in any undertaking, and persons afraid of coyotes and work and loneliness had better let ranching alone. At the same time, any woman who can stand her own company, can see the beauty of the sunset, loves growing things, and is willing to put in as much time at careful labor as she does over the washtub, will certainly succeed; will have independence, plenty to eat all the time, and a home of her own in the end.

. . . I would not, for anything, allow Mr. Stewart to do anything toward improving my place, for I want the fun and the experience myself. And I want to be able to speak from experience when I tell others what they can do. Theories are very beautiful, but facts are what must be had, and what I intend to give some time. . . .

Yours affectionately,
Elinore Rupert Stewart.

. . .

Success

November, 1913.

Dear Mrs. Coney,—

. . . Now, this is the letter I have been wanting to write you for a long time, but could not because until now I had not actually proven all I wanted to prove. Perhaps it will not interest you, but if you see a woman who wants to homestead and is a little afraid she will starve, you can tell her what I am telling you.

I never did like to theorize, and so this year I set out to prove that a woman could ranch if she wanted to. We like to grow potatoes on new ground, that is, newly cleared land on which no crop has been grown. Few weeds grow on new land, so it makes less work. So I selected my potato-patch, and the man ploughed it, although I could have done that if Clyde would have let me. . . .

I raised a great many flowers and I worked several days in the field. In all I have told about I have had no help but Jerrine. Clyde's mother spends each summer with us, and she helped me with the cooking and the babies. Many of my neighbors did better than I did, although I know many town people would doubt my doing so much, but I did it. I have tried every kind of work this ranch affords, and I can do any of it. Of course I am extra strong, but those who try know that strength and knowledge come with doing. I just love to experiment, to work, and to prove out things, so that ranch life and "roughing it" just suit me.

Glossary

homestead: to settle with the intention of farming and building a house

Short-Answer Questions

1. How does Pruitt depict life on the homestead?

2. How would Pruitt's determination as a homesteader be influential to other single women? Explain.

3. How does Pruitt's life as a homesteader blur the traditional roles of gender of the time? Explain.

Chapter 6

Votes for Women: Suffrage in the United States

Suffrage, the right to vote in elections, was fought for by women beginning with the founding of the United States. In her March 31, 1776, letter to husband John Adams, Abigail Adams warned that "If perticuliar care and attention is not paid to the Laidies we are determined to foment a Rebelion, and will not hold ourselves bound by any Laws in which we have no voice, or Representation." Her words, however, failed to move the framers of the new American government. A woman's role in society was believed to be in the home, educating the next generation of Americans in republican values and exerting influence on their husbands. Voting was not guaranteed in the U.S. Constitution. It fell to the individual states to decide suffrage. Most states excluded large portions of men, in particular, those not owning land, in addition to women.

The Quest for Women's Suffrage Begins

In the early 1800s the restrictions limiting white male suffrage fell away. At the same time, the quest for women's suffrage also began to evolve, merging with the growing abolition movement. Women took prominent roles at abolitionist meetings, drawing parallels between slavery and their legal status. Women like Sarah Grimke, who in her response to Congregational Ministers of Massachusetts argued for the rights of both slaves and women. The leadership and organizational experience gained in the abolition movement helped to prepare women to advocate for their own rights.

The Seneca Falls Convention

In 1848, 300 women and men gathered in Seneca Falls, New York. Remembered as the first women's rights convention, the Seneca Falls event was attended by Elizabeth Cady Stanton, Lucretia Mott, and Frederick Douglass. The resulting Declaration of Sentiments, written by Stanton and containing twelve resolutions, called for educational access for women and the right to own property and maintain one's own money. Women's suffrage, believed to be too controversial, was the only resolution that failed to pass unanimously.

Following Seneca Falls, the women's rights movement continued to expand. Mott, in 1849, promoted greater social equality between the sexes while at the same time timidly encouraging suffrage. In 1854 Stanton became the first woman to lobby the New York Legislature. In her "Address to the New York Legislature," Stanton encouraged amending New York's Married Women's Property Law to allow women the right to control their finances, conduct business, and have greater legal rights over their children. African American women also began to make their voices heard, as exemplified by Sojourner Truth's 1851 speech, "Ain't I a Woman?"

The Civil War and Establishment of Competing Suffrage Organizations

With the outbreak of the Civil War in 1861, the struggle for political equality became secondary to the struggle to preserve the Union and end slavery. The defeat of the Confederacy in April 1865 was followed by the passing of the Thirteenth Amendment, which abolished slavery in the United States in December 1865. The passing of the Fourteenth Amendment in 1868 guaranteed citizenship to all individuals born in the United States. The inclusion of the right of all "male" citizens (the first reference to gender in the Constitution) to vote dashed the hopes for women's suffrage. As a result, a split emerged within the suffrage movement. Some believed that supporting the Fourteenth (and later the Fifteenth) Amendment was key in establishing African American equality and full citizenship. It was believed that women's suffrage would follow shortly. Others, such as Stanton and Susan B. Anthony, argued that both amendments were a betrayal. Rival factions within the movement emerged: the National Women's Suffrage Association (NWSA), led by Stanton and Anthony, worked for a constitutional amendment guaranteeing a women's right to vote and social equality, while the American Woman Suffrage Association (AWSA) promoted women's suffrage state-by-state. Both organizations worked towards the same goal, just by different means. The two organizations remained split until merging in 1890 to form the National American Woman Suffrage Association (NAWSA). With the merger, the NAWSA coordinated the national and local fight to achieve the vote.

The court system was another path utilized by the suffragists to achieve their goals. Arguing that the Fourteenth Amendment granted equal protection to all citizens, NAWSA members attempted to register to vote across the nation. In Virginia, Reese Happersett was stopped from registering, resulting in her suing. In 1874, the U.S. Supreme Court ruled on *Minor v. Happersett*. In a setback for women's rights, the Court declared that suffrage was not a right of citizens.

In addition to legal setbacks, anti-suffrage organizations sought to halt the movement. Many stated that most women did not want to vote or that they were too busy raising children and maintaining a home to keep up to date with politics. In *Some of the Reasons against Woman Suffrage*, Francis Parkman argued voting was harmful to a woman's health.

African American Women Advocate for Equal Rights

African American women also continued to organize and struggle for the vote following the Civil War. Women like Josephine St. Pierre Ruffin and Mary Church Terrell argued that African American women not only had to overcome sexual prejudices but also racial ones. Their efforts, however, were ignored or marginalized by the major white-led organizations.

With the emergence of the Progressive Era in the late nineteenth and early twentieth century, women's involvement in social movements and organizations continued to expand. As it had with abolition prior to the Civil War, the fight for women's suffrage connected with other reform movements. Anna Howard Shaw combined the right to vote with the Temperance Movement. Charlotte Perkins Gilman's promotion of women's rights revolved around the emerging sciences of Darwin and evolution. Jane Addams discussed the practicality of women voting, arguing that in the modern world, women need to vote and be politically engaged. Addressing Chinese immigrants, Mabel Ping-Hua Lee encouraged the support of women's suffrage and educational rights. Others, influenced by the British suffragist movement, turned to more militant and direct methods to achieve the right to vote. Attracting attention through parades and strikes, militant suffragettes broke from the NAWSA and under the leadership of Alice Paul formed the National Women's Party (NWP) in 1917.

State Actions Pave the Way to the Nineteenth Amendment

By 1890 the movement began to see success. That year, Wyoming became the first state to grant women the right to vote. Colorado (1893), Utah (1896), Idaho (1896), Washington (1910), and California (1911) followed. Political pressure supporting women's suffrage continued to grow. Ida Husted Harper testified before

The Schlager Anthology of Women's History

the U.S. Senate Select Committee on Woman Suffrage in 1908. In 1915 Alice Paul testified before the House Judicial Committee. Each victory, protest, or parade further encouraged the growth of the movement. Carrie Chapman Catt, who assumed leadership of the NAWSA in 1915, unified the fractured organization and formulated a dual push on both the federal and state levels to obtain the vote.

The United States entered World War I in 1917. NAWSA members rushed to support the war effort, while at the same time the NWP picketed the White House. President Woodrow Wilson, who initially opposed the vote for women, in 1918 shifted his view to support the right of women to vote. The Nineteenth Amendment, ratified in 1920, guaranteed the right to vote for women.

The Nineteenth Amendment can be viewed as a victory, but the fight for suffrage continued following its passing. In 1920 NAACP President William Pickens addressed the disenfranchisement of African American women in the Jim Crow South. Alice Moore Dunbar-Nelson, in 1927, encouraged African American women voters to exercise their power as they had done previously in support of the Dyer Anti-Lynching Bill. This idea of women organizing as voters was echoed by Elenor Roosevelt in 1928, in which she argued that women "must learn to play the game as men do."

Further Reading

Books

Cahill, Cathleen D. *Recasting the Vote: How Women of Color Transformed the Suffrage Movement.* Chapel Hill: University of North Carolina Press, 2020.

DuBois, Ellen Carol. *Suffrage: Women's Long Battle for the Vote.* New York: Simon & Shuster, 2020.

Tetrault, Lisa. *The Myth of Seneca Falls: Memory and the Women's Suffrage Movement, 1848–1898.* Chapel Hill: University of North Carolina, 2017.

Weiss, Elaine F. *The Woman's Hour: The Great Fight to Win the Vote.* New York: Penguin Books, 2019.

Articles

McCammon, Holly J., Karen E. Campbell, Ellen M. Granberg, and Christine Mowery. "How Movements Win: Gendered Opportunity Structures and U.S. Women's Suffrage Movements, 1866 to 1919." *American Sociological Review* 66, no. 1 (2001): 49–70.

Miller, Joe C. "Never A Fight of Woman against Man: What Textbooks Don't Say about Women's Suffrage." *History Teacher* 48, no. 3 (2015): 437–82.

Websites

"History of U.S. Woman's Suffrage." History of U.S. Woman's Suffrage website, accessed July 27, 2023, https://www.crusadeforthevote.org/.

"National American Woman Suffrage Association Records." Library of Congress website, accessed July 27, 2023, https://www.loc.gov/collections/national-american-woman-suffrage-association-records/.

"Woman Suffrage and the 19th Amendment." National Archives and Records Administration website, accessed July 27, 2023, https://www.archives.gov/education/lessons/woman-suffrage.

Sarah M. Grimké: Reply to the Pastoral Letter the General Association of Congregational Ministers of Massachusetts

Author
Sarah M. Grimké

Date
1837

Document Type
Letters/Correspondence; Essays, Reports, Manifestos

Significance
Refuted arguments that restrictions on women's rights were based on Christian scriptural teachings

Overview

Sarah Moore Grimké (1792–1873) was a true anomaly. The daughter of a very rich South Carolina plantation owner and lawyer-politician, she began rebelling against her environment at an early age—bringing her father's anger down on her for teaching some of the slaves how to read. In 1819 her father died, and Grimké moved to Philadelphia and in 1821 joined the Quaker denomination. In partnership with her sister Angelina, Sarah Grimké became active in both the abolitionist and women's rights causes. In 1837, a letter critical of women's rights circulating within the General Association of Congregational Ministers of Massachusetts came to her attention and so roused her indignation that she wrote this fiery reply for gender equality.

Document Text

Dear Friend—

When I last addressed thee, I had not seen the Pastoral Letter of the General Association. . . . I am persuaded that when the minds of men and women become emancipated from the thralldom of superstition and "traditions of men," the sentiments contained in the Pastoral Letter will be recurred to us with as much astonishment as the opinions of Cotton Mather and other distinguished men of his day, on the subject of witchcraft; nor will it be deemed less wonderful, that a body of divines should gravely assemble and endeavor to prove that woman has no right to "open her mouth for the dumb," than it now is that judges should have sat on the trials of witches, and solemnly condemned nineteen persons and one dog to death for witchcraft.

But to the letter.

It says, "We invite your attention to the dangers which at present threaten the FEMALE CHARACTER with widespread and permanent injury.". . . I believe if woman investigates it, she will soon discover that danger is impending, though from a totally different source from which the Association apprehends,—danger from those who, having long held the reins of usurped authority, are unwilling to permit us to fill that sphere which God created us to move in. . . .

. . . No one can desire more earnestly than I do, that woman may move exactly in the sphere which her Creator has assigned her; and I believe her having been displaced from that sphere has introduced confusion into the world. It is therefore, of vast importance to herself and to all rational creation, that she should ascertain what are her duties and her privileges as a responsible and immortal being.

The New Testament has been referred to, and I am willing to abide by its decisions, but must enter my protest against the false translation of some passages by the MEN who did that work, and against the perverted interpretation by the MEN who undertook to write commentaries thereon. I am inclined to think, when we are admitted to the honor of studying Greek and Hebrew, we shall produce some various readings of the Bible a little different from those we now have.

The Lord Jesus defines the duties of his followers in his Sermon on the Mount. . . . I follow him through all his precepts, and find him giving the same directions to women as to men, never even referring to the distinction now so strenuously insisted upon between masculine and feminine virtues: this in one of the anti-christian "traditions of men" which are taught instead of the "commandments of God." Men and women were CREATED EQUAL; they are both moral and accountable be-

Sarah Grimké
(Library of Congress)

ings, and whatever is right for man to do, is right for woman.

But the influence of woman, says the Association, is to be private and unobtrusive; her light is not to shine before man like that of her brethren; but she is passively to let the lords of the creation, as they call themselves, put the bushel over it, lest peradventure it might appear that the world has been benefitted by the rays of her candle so that her quenched light, according to their judgement, will be of more use than if it were set on a candlestick. . . .

This doctrine of dependence upon man is utterly at variance with the doctrine of the Bible. In that book I find nothing like the softness of woman, nor the sternness of man: both are equally commanded to bring forth the fruits of the Spirit, love, meekness, gentleness, etc. But we are told, "the power of woman is in her dependence, flowing from a consciousness of that weakness which God has given her for her protection."

If physical weakness is alluded to, I cheerfully concede that superiority; if brute force is what my brethren are claiming, I am willing to let them have all the honor they desire; but if they mean to intimate, that mental or moral weakness belongs to woman more than to man, I utterly disclaim the charge. Our powers of mind have been crushed, as far as man could do it, our sense of morality has been impaired by his interpretation of our duties; but no where does God say that he made any distinction between us, as moral and intelligent beings. . . .

But woman may be permitted to lead religious inquirers to the PASTORS for instruction. Now this is assuming that all pastors are better qualified to give instruction than woman. This I utterly deny. I have suffered too keenly from the teaching of man, to lead anyone to him for instruction. The Lord Jesus says, "Come unto me and learn of me." He points his followers to no man; and when woman is made the favored instrument of rousing a sinner to his lost and helpless condition, she has no right to substitute any teacher for Christ. . . .

The General Association say, that "when woman assumes the place and tone of man as a public reformer, our care and protection of her seem unnec-essary; we put ourselves in self-defense against her, and her character becomes unnatural."

Here again the unscriptural notion is held up, that there is a distinction between the duties of men and women as moral beings; that what is virtue in man, is vice in woman; and women who dare to obey the command of Jehovah, "Cry aloud, spare not, lift up thy voice like a trumpet, and show my people their transgressions," are threatened with having the protection of brethren withdrawn. . . .

Our trust is in the Lord Jehovah, and in him is everlasting strength. The motto of woman, when she is engaged in the great work of public reformation should be, "The Lord is my light and my salvation; whom shall I fear? The Lord is the strength of my life; of whom shall I be afraid?" She must feel, if she feels rightly, that she is fulfilling one of the important duties laid upon her as an accountable being, and that her character, instead of being "unnatural," is in exact accordance with the will of Him to whom, and to no other, she is responsible for the talents and gifts confided to her. . . .

Ah! How many of my sex feel in the dominion, thus unrighteously exercised over them, under the gentle appellation of protection that what they have leaned upon has proved a broken reed at best, and oft a spear.

Thine in the bonds of womanhood,

SARAH M. GRIMKÉ

Glossary

Cotton Mather: Puritan minister (1663–1728) notorious for his role in the Salem, Massachusetts, witchcraft trials of 1692, and who was often cited as an example of religious extremism and misogyny

disclaim: deny

Jehovah: Hebrew biblical name for God, literally translated "I am that I am"; sometimes rendered as "Yahweh"

peradventure: by chance; possibly

recurred: brought back in reminder; shown

thralldom: captivity; fascination with

usurped: stolen

Short-Answer Questions

1. What, according to Grimké, is woman's rightful "sphere," and how does she justify her perceptions?

2. How does Grimké use sarcasm to drive home her points? Give specific examples.

3. In what significant ways does Grimké's ideas on religion, women's rights, and "protection" differ from those in the Pastoral Letter?

Elizabeth Cady Stanton: Seneca Falls Convention Declaration of Sentiments

Author
Elizabeth Cady Stanton

Date
1848

Document Type
Essays, Reports, Manifestos

Significance
Modeled after the Declaration of Independence, announced that women in the United States would no longer stand for being treated inequitably

Overview

The Declaration of Sentiments was written by Elizabeth Cady Stanton and was presented to the participants at a convention in Seneca Falls, New York, on July 19–20, 1848. Modeling her work on the Declaration of Independence, the author sought to address the wrongs perpetrated against womankind and called for redress of those wrongs. The Seneca Falls meeting was the first convention specifically devoted to the issue of women's rights. Organized by Stanton, Lucretia Coffin Mott, Mary Ann McClintock, Martha Wright, and Jane Hunt, the convention's goal was to address "the social, civil and religious rights of women," according to the *Seneca County Courier* of July 14, 1848. The Declaration of Sentiments summed up the current state of women's rights in the United States and served notice that women would no longer stand for being treated inequitably.

While antebellum reformers, many of whom were abolitionists, connected the situation of women with that of slaves, in that neither could vote, hold office, sit on juries, or have property rights, the Seneca Falls Convention marked the first time that men and women publicly discussed the issue of women's rights. The people who gathered at Seneca Falls realized that they were taking an unprecedented—not to mention controversial—step in calling for full citizenship for American women. The Declaration of Sentiments was considered radical for its time, especially in the clause calling for suffrage of women. In the context of antebellum America, this document is indeed a radical one. While it took seventy-two years after this for women to get the vote and even longer to abolish other forms of discrimination, the Declaration of Sentiments marked an important step in the long struggle for women's rights.

Document Text
The Declaration of Sentiments

When, in the course of human events, it becomes necessary for one portion of the family of man to assume among the people of the earth a position different from that which they have hitherto occupied, but one to which the laws of nature and of nature's God entitle them, a decent respect to the opinions of mankind requires that they should declare the causes that impel them to such a course.

We hold these truths to be self-evident: that all men and women are created equal; that they are endowed by their Creator with certain inalienable rights; that among these are life, liberty, and the pursuit of happiness; that to secure these rights governments are instituted, deriving their just powers from the consent of the governed. Whenever any form of government becomes destructive of these ends, it is the right of those who suffer from it to refuse allegiance to it, and to insist upon the institution of a new government, laying its foundation on such principles, and organizing its powers in such form, as to them shall seem most likely to effect their safety and happiness. Prudence, indeed, will dictate that governments long established should not be changed for light and transient causes; and accordingly all experience hath shown that mankind are more disposed to suffer, while evils are sufferable, than to right themselves by abolishing the forms to which they are accustomed. But when a long train of abuses and usurpations, pursuing invariably the same object, evinces a design to reduce them under absolute despotism, it is their duty to throw off such government, and to provide new guards for their future security. Such has been the patient sufferance of the women under this government, and such is now the necessity which constrains them to demand the equal station to which they are entitled. The history of mankind is a history of repeated injuries and usurpations on the part of man toward woman, having in direct object the establishment of an absolute tyranny over her. To prove this, let facts be submitted to a candid world.

Elizabeth Cady Stanton wrote the Declaration of Sentiments. (Wikimedia Commons)

The history of mankind is a history of repeated injuries and usurpations on the part of man toward woman, having in direct object the establishment of an absolute tyranny over her. To prove this, let facts be submitted to a candid world.

He has never permitted her to exercise her inalienable right to the elective franchise.

He has compelled her to submit to laws, in the formation of which she had no voice.

He has withheld from her rights which are given to the most ignorant and degraded men—both natives and foreigners.

Having deprived her of this first right of a citizen, the elective franchise, thereby leaving her without representation in the halls of legislation, he has oppressed her on all sides.

He has made her, if married, in the eye of the law, civilly dead.

He has taken from her all right in property, even to the wages she earns.

He has made her, morally, an irresponsible being, as she can commit many crimes with impunity, provided they be done in the presence of her husband. In the covenant of marriage, she is compelled to promise obedience to her husband, he becoming, to all intents and purposes, her master—the law giving him power to deprive her of her liberty, and to administer chastisement.

He has so framed the laws of divorce, as to what shall be the proper causes, and in case of separation, to whom the guardianship of the children shall be given, as to be wholly regardless of the happiness of women—the law, in all cases, going upon a false supposition of the supremacy of man, and giving all power into his hands.

After depriving her of all rights as a married woman, if single, and the owner of property, he has taxed her to support a government which recognizes her only when her property can be made profitable to it.

He has monopolized nearly all the profitable employments, and from those she is permitted to follow, she receives but a scanty remuneration. He closes against her all the avenues to wealth and distinction which he considers most honorable to himself. As a teacher of theology, medicine, or law, she is not known.

He has denied her the facilities for obtaining a thorough education, all colleges being closed against her.

He allows her in church, as well as state, but a subordinate position, claiming apostolic authority for her exclusion from the ministry, and, with some exceptions, from any public participation in the affairs of the church.

He has created a false public sentiment by giving to the world a different code of morals for men and women, by which moral delinquencies which exclude women from society, are not only tolerated, but deemed of little account in man.

He has usurped the prerogative of Jehovah himself, claiming it as his right to assign for her a sphere of action, when that belongs to her conscience and to her God.

He has endeavored, in every way that he could, to destroy her confidence in her own powers, to lessen her self-respect, and to make her willing to lead a dependent and abject life.

Now, in view of this entire disfranchisement of one-half the people of this country, their social and religious degradation—in view of the unjust laws above mentioned, and because women do feel themselves aggrieved, oppressed, and fraudulently deprived of their most sacred rights, we insist that they have immediate admission to all the rights and privileges which belong to them as citizens of the United States.

Glossary

candid: impartial

chastisement: discipline, especially physical punishment

The Schlager Anthology of Women's History

Glossary

constrains: forces; compels

covenant: formal agreement of legal validity

disfranchisement: denial of a right, especially the right to vote

franchise: the right to vote

hitherto: up to this time; until now

impunity: immunity from punishment

inalienable: incapable of being repudiated or transferred to another

Jehovah: a name for God in the Old Testament

prerogative: exclusive entitlement

prudence: caution regarding practical matters

remuneration: wages; payment or consideration received for services or employment

sufferance: capacity to endure hardship

supposition: an assumption

usurped: used without authority or right; employed

Short-Answer Questions

1. Compare and contrast the Declaration of Sentiments with the Declaration of Independence. How do these documents differ, and how are they alike? In your response, consider the time they were written, the audience, and the reaction.

2. Why was the demand for the vote so radical when first proposed at Seneca Falls?

3. How would you summarize the major principles presented in the Declaration of Sentiments? What arguments might be leveled either in support of or against them? In either case, defend your position.

Lucretia Mott: "Discourse on Women"

Author	Significance
Lucretia Mott	Used arguments based in Christian scripture to support women's right to vote
Date	
1849	
Document Type	
Poems, Plays, Fiction	

Overview

Lucretia Coffin Mott (1793–1880) was the prototypical and quintessential social activist of the nineteenth century. She was brought up in the Quaker faith and in 1821 became a minister. Married to businessman James Mott, she reared six children and found the time to help found the American Anti-Slavery Society, organize her home as a station on the Underground Railroad, and put together the Seneca Falls Convention in 1849 in partnership with her close friend Elizabeth Cady Stanton. Her role in the convention made her a national celebrity, and Mott delivered her "Discourse on Women" in Philadelphia on December 17, 1849. In 1866, she was elected as first president of the American Equal Rights Association, which focused on securing the right to vote for women and African Americans.

Document Text

There is nothing of greater importance to the well-being of society at large—of man as well as woman—than the true and proper position of woman. . . .

This subject has claimed my earnest interest for many years. I have long wished to see woman occupying a more elevated position than that which custom for ages has allotted to her. It was with great regret, therefore, that I listened a few days ago to a lecture upon this subject, which, though replete with intellectual beauty, and containing much that was true and excellent, was yet fraught with sentiments calculated to retard the progress of woman to the high elevation destined by her Creator. . . .

Free discussion upon this, as upon all other subjects, is never to be feared; nor will be, except by such as prefer darkness to light. "Those only who are in the wrong dread discussion. The light alarms those only who feel the need of darkness." It was sound philosophy, uttered by Jesus, "He that doeth truth cometh to the light, that his deeds may be made manifest, that they are wrought in God." . . .

The laws given on Mount Sinai for the government of man and woman were equal, the precepts of Jesus make no distinction. Those who read the Scriptures, and judge for themselves, not resting satisfied with the perverted application of the text, do not find the distinction, that theology and ecclesiastical authorities have made, in the condition of the sexes. . . .

Numbers of women were the companions of Jesus,—one going to the men of the city, saying, "Come, see a man who told me all things that ever I did; is not this the Christ?" Another, "Whatsoever he saith unto you, do it." . . .

If these scriptures were read intelligently, we should not so learn Christ, as to exclude any from a position, where they might exert an influence for good to their fellow-beings. . . .

These things are too much lost sight of. They should be known, in order that we may be prepared to meet the assertion, so often made, that woman is stepping out of her appropriate sphere, when she shall attempt to instruct public assemblies. . . . Women as well as men are interested in these works of justice and mercy. They are efficient co-workers, their talents are called into profitable exercise, their labors are effective in each department of reform. The blessing to the merciful, to the peacemaker is equal to man and to woman. It is greatly to be deplored, now that she is increasingly qualified for usefulness, that any view should be presented, calculated to retard her labors of love. . . .

A new generation of women is now upon the stage, improving the increased opportunities fur-

Painting of Lucretia Mott
(National Portrait Gallery)

nished for the acquirement of knowledge. Public education is coming to be regarded the right of the children of a republic. The hill of science is not so difficult of ascent as formerly represented by poets and painters; but by fact and demonstration smoothed down, so as to be accessible to the assumed weak capacity of woman. She is rising in the scale of being through this, as well as other means, and finding heightened pleasure and profit on the right hand and on the left. . . .

These duties are not to be limited by man. Nor will woman fulfill less her domestic relations, as the faithful companion of her chosen husband, and the fitting mother of her children, because she has a right estimate of her position and her responsibilities. Her self-respect will be increased; preserving the dignity of her being, she will not suffer herself to be degraded into a mere dependent. Nor will her feminine character be impaired. Instances are not few, of woman throwing off the encumbrances which bind her, and going forth in a manner worthy of herself, her creation, and her dignified calling. . . .

The question is often asked, "What does woman want, more than she enjoys? What is she seeking to obtain? Of what rights is she deprived? What privileges are withheld from her? I answer, she asks nothing as favor, but as right, she wants to be acknowledged a moral, responsible being. She is seeking not to be governed by laws, in the making of which she has no voice. . . .

It is with reluctance that I make the demand for the political rights of woman, because this claim is so distasteful to the age. Woman shrinks, in the present state of society, from taking any interest in politics. The events of the French Revolution, and the claim for woman's rights are held up to her as a warning. But let us not look at the excesses of women alone, at that period; but remember that the age was marked with extravagances and wickedness in men as well as women. . . . If woman's judgment were exercised, why might she not aid in making the laws by which she is governed? . . .

Far be it from me to encourage woman to vote, or to take an active part in politics, in the present state of our government. Her right to the elective franchise however, is the same, and should be yielded to her, whether she exercise that right or not. Would that man too, would have no participation in a government based upon the life-taking principle—upon retaliation and the sword. It is unworthy a Christian nation. But when, in the diffusion of light and intelligence, a convention shall be called to make regulations for self-government on Christian, non-resistant principles, I can see no good reason, why woman should not participate in such an assemblage, taking part equally with man. . . .

In conclusion, let me say, "Credit not the old fashioned absurdity, that woman's is a secondary lot, ministering to the necessities of her lord and master! It is a higher destiny I would award you. If your immortality is as complete, and your gift of mind as capable as ours, of increase and elevation, I would put no wisdom of mine against God's evident allotment. I would charge you to water the undying bud, and give it healthy culture, and open its beauty to the sun—and then you may hope, that when your life is bound up with another, you will go on equally, and in a fellowship that shall pervade every earthly interest."

Glossary

elective franchise: the right to vote

French Revolution: a revolution (1789–1799), in which some women took an active role, generally viewed as a time of chaos, war, and the committing of atrocities, including executions on the guillotine

Mount Sinai: a reference to the Ten Commandments, which Moses was said to have received from God on Mount Sinai to govern the Israelites

usurped: used without authority or right; employed

Short-Answer Questions

1. Bearing in mind that Lucretia Mott was a minister, how does she employ religion to support her ideas and amplify her points?

2. In what ways is Mott revolutionary in the ideas she expresses, and in what ways conservative? Explain fully.

3. From the tone of her presentation, is Mott directing her arguments more toward the men or the women in her audience? To what extent, and how?

Sojourner Truth:
"Ain't I a Woman?"

<table>
<tr><td>

Author
Sojourner Truth

Date
1851

Document Type
Speeches/Addresses

</td><td>

Significance
Fused women's rights and abolitionist arguments to forcefully condemn the second-class treatment of both women and Blacks in the United States

</td></tr>
</table>

Overview

The acknowledged formal beginning of the feminist movement took place in the summer of 1848 at a gathering of women's rights advocates in Seneca Falls, New York. It was at this convention that the Declaration of Sentiments, written by the activists Elizabeth Cady Stanton and Lucretia Mott, was first presented. The motivation behind the writing of the document, which is modeled on the Declaration of Independence, was Mott's being refused permission to speak at the world antislavery convention in London, England, despite the fact that she was an official delegate to the convention. Sixty-eight women and thirty-two men signed the document, which stated that women, as human beings with the same "unalienable rights" as men and as citizens of the United States of America, should have those rights recognized and respected.

After this conference came others, and support—from men and women, both Black and white—began to grow.

Although some women wanted their movement to be recognized on its own, entirely separate from that of abolition, the majority of women's rights supporters viewed the movements as equally important calls for reform.

Sojourner Truth, as both a woman and a former slave, turned her efforts to the twin causes of women's rights and abolition, serving as a living symbol of both. As slavery in the 1840s and 1850s became a distinctly southern institution, Truth was often characterized in articles and reports as speaking with a southern dialect; she objected to this stereotypical depiction, as her experience was not of southern slavery but of *American* slavery, and her accent reflected her Dutch heritage. Because she had been a slave in the notionally free North, Truth felt it was her duty to agitate for abolition across the whole United States. Her memorable speech before the Women's Rights Convention in 1851 demonstrates her commitment to equality in all areas and marries her outrage over Black oppression with her anger over the second-class status of American women in the mid-nineteenth century.

There is some controversy regarding Truth's famous speech. There are, in fact, different versions of the speech. The most popular version of the speech was first published by Frances Gage in 1863, twelve years after it was delivered. Another version was published by the *Anti-Slavery Bugle* a month after the speech was delivered. This speech was transcribed by the Rev. Marius Robinson. In Robinson's version, which is presented here, the phrase "Ain't I a Woman" is not present.

Document Text

I want to say a few words about this matter. I am a woman's rights. I have as much muscle as any man, and can do as much work as any man. I have plowed and reaped and husked and chopped and mowed, and can any man do more than that? I have heard much about the sexes being equal. I can carry as much as any man, and can eat as much too, if I can get it. I am as strong as any man that is now.

As for intellect, all I can say is, if a woman have a pint, and a man a quart—why can't she have her little pint full? You need not be afraid to give us our rights for fear we will take too much,—for we can't take more than our pint'll hold.

The poor men seems to be all in confusion, and don't know what to do. Why children, if you have woman's rights, give it to her and you will feel better. You will have your own rights, and they won't be so much trouble.

I can't read, but I can hear. I have heard the Bible and have learned that Eve caused man to sin. Well, if woman upset the world, do give her a chance to set it right side up again. The lady has spoken about Jesus, how he never spurned woman from him, and she was right. When Lazarus died, Mary and Martha came to him with faith and love and besought him to raise their brother. And Jesus wept—and Lazarus came forth. And how came Jesus into the world? Through God who created him and the woman who bore him. Man, where was your part?

But the women are coming up blessed be God and a few of the men are coming up with them. But man is in a tight place, the poor slave is on him, woman is coming on him, and he is surely between a hawk and a buzzard.

Sojourner Truth
(National Portrait Gallery)

Glossary

woman have a pint: "pint" and "quart" are used here to mean capacity for knowledge

Lazarus: Lazarus of Bethany, the subject of a prominent sign of Jesus in the Gospel of John, in which Jesus restores him to life four days after his death

between a hawk and a buzzard: idiom meaning that one is caught between two extremes or two factions

usurped: used without authority or right; employed

Short-Answer Questions

1. Summarize the central argument Sojourner Truth presents in this speech and evaluate the effectiveness of her argument.

2. How does Sojourner Truth support her claim that men shouldn't fear women getting rights? Explain why you think she included this claim in her speech.

3. In the second paragraph of this speech, Sojourner Truth points out that there is no connection between rights and intellect. What purpose does this claim serve in the context of her overall argument?

Elizabeth Cady Stanton:
Address to the New York Legislature

Author Elizabeth Cady Stanton **Date** 1854 **Document Type** Speeches/Addresses	**Significance** Demanded of the New York Legislature the opportunity for women to vote and exercise all other rights of citizenship

Overview

Elizabeth Cady Stanton's education, unorthodox for a woman of that era, is apparent in her writing. Her articles and speeches are full of classical and biblical references and demonstrate her knowledge of history. In turn, Stanton's early conversations with her father and his law clerks are apparent in the logical development of her arguments. She backs up her positions with engaging examples and uses wit and down-to-earth common sense to capture her audience. This background is apparent in her Address to the New York Legislature, which Stanton delivered on February 14, 1854, to the New York State Woman's Rights Convention. In it, she asks for the vote for women and, in fact, for the opportunity for women to exercise all the other rights of citizenship.

Document Text

Gentlemen, in republican America, in the 19th century, we, the daughters of the revolutionary heroes of '76, demand at your hands the redress of our grievances—a revision of your state constitution—a new code of laws. Permit us then . . . to call your attention to the legal disabilities under which we labor.

1st. Look at the position of woman as woman. It is not enough for us that by your laws we are permitted to live and breathe, to claim the necessaries of life from our legal protectors. . . . We demand the full recognition of all our rights as citizens of the Empire State. We are . . . native, free-born citizens; property-holders, tax-payers; yet are we denied the exercise of our right to the elective franchise. We support our-

Photograph of Elizabeth Cady Stanton
(Boston Public Library)

selves, and, in part, your schools, colleges, churches, your poor-houses, jails, prisons, the army, the navy, the whole machinery of government, and yet we have no voice in your councils. We have every qualification required by the constitution, necessary to the legal voter, but the one of sex. We are moral, virtuous and intelligent, and in all respects quite equal to the proud white man himself . . . but we . . . are denied the most sacred rights of citizens, because . . . we came not into this republic crowned with the dignity of manhood! . . . Now, gentlemen, we would fain know by what authority you have disfranchised one-half the people of this state? . . .

We demand, in criminal cases, that most sacred of all rights, trial by a jury of our own peers. . . . At this moment among the hundreds of women who are shut up in prisons in this state, not one has enjoyed that most sacred of all rights. . . .

2d. Look at the position of woman as wife. Your laws relating to marriage . . . are in open violation of our enlightened ideas of justice. . . . If you take the highest view of marriage, as a Divine relation, which love alone can constitute and sanctify, then of course human legislation can only recognize it. Man can neither bind nor loose its ties, for that prerogative belongs to God alone. . . . But if you regard marriage as a civil contract, then let it be subject to the same laws which control all other contracts. Do not make it a kind of half-human, half-divine institution, which you may build up but cannot regulate. . . .

So long as . . . the parties in all mere civil contracts retain their identity and all the power and independence they had before contracting, with the full right to dissolve all partnerships and contracts for any reason, . . . upon what principle of civil jurisprudence do you permit the boy of fourteen and the girl of twelve, . . . to make a contract more momentous in importance than any other, and then hold them to it, . . . the whole of their natural lives, in spite of disappointment, deception and misery? . . . The signing of this contract is instant civil death to one of the parties. . . . The wife who inherits no property holds about the same legal position that does the slave on the southern plantation. She can own nothing, sell nothing. She has no right even to the wages she earns; her person, her time, her services are the property of another. . . .

3d. Look at the position of woman as widow. . . . Behold the magnanimity of the law in allowing the widow to retain a life interest in one-third the landed estate, and one-half the personal property of her husband, and taking the lion's share to itself! Had she died first, the house and land would all have been the husband's. . . .

4th. Look at the position of woman as mother. . . . Behold how cruel and ruthless are your laws touching this most sacred relation.

Nature has clearly made the mother the guardian of the child; but man, in his inordinate love of power, does continually set nature and nature's laws at open defiance. The father may apprentice his child, bind him out to a trade or labor, without the mother's consent—yea, in direct opposition to her most earnest entreaties. . . .

He may apprentice his son to a gamester or rum-seller, and thus cancel his debts of honor. By the abuse of this absolute power, he may bind his daughter to the owner of a brothel, and, by the degradation of his child, supply his daily wants. . . .

In case of separation, the law gives the children to the father; no matter what his character or condition. At this very time we can point you to noble, virtuous, well educated mothers in this state, who have abandoned their husbands for their profligacy and confirmed drunkenness. All these have been robbed of their children, who are in the custody of the husband, . . . whilst the mothers are permitted to see them but at stated intervals. . . .

By your laws, all these abominable resorts are permitted. . . . But when woman's moral power shall speak through the ballot-box, then shall her influence be seen and felt. . . .

Here, gentlemen, is our difficulty: When we plead our cause before the law makers . . . of the republic, they cannot take in the idea that men and women are alike; and so long as the mass rest in this delusion, the public mind will not be so much startled by the revelation made of the injustice and degradation of woman's position as by the fact that she should at length wake up to a sense of it. . . .

We ask no better laws than those you have made for yourselves. We need no other protection than that which your present laws secure to you. . . .

You may say that the mass of the women of this state do not make the demand; it comes from a few sour, disappointed old maids and childless women. You are mistaken; the mass speak through us. . . . Do you candidly think these wives do not wish to control the wages they earn—to own the land they buy—the houses they build? To have at their disposal their own children, without being subject to the constant interference and tyranny of an idle, worthless profligate? . . .

For all these, then, we speak. . . .

Glossary

elective franchise: the vote

Empire State: nickname of New York State, apparently in common use by 1850, possibly arising from a letter written by George Washington in 1785 referring to New York as the "seat of Empire"

fain: eagerly; gladly

gamester: a gambler

profligate: a self-indulgent person

Short-Answer Questions

1. What methods and examples does Stanton employ to persuade the New York law makers to her point of view?

2. Which of her arguments would, in your estimation, have been the most effective? Which would have been least effective? Please explain your rationale.

3. How is Stanton's background of legal knowledge apparent in her speech? Cite specific examples and passages to support your position.

Minor v. Happersett

Author	Significance
Morrison Waite	Held that citizenship did not guarantee a right to vote, so state laws barring women from voting were valid
Date	
1875	
Document Type	
Legal	

Overview

Virginia Minor (1824–1894) was active in the suffrage movement in St. Louis County, Missouri, and in 1867 cofounded and became president of the Women's Suffrage Association of Missouri. Knowing that she would be rejected but determined to take the suffrage issue to court, Minor tried to vote in St. Louis in 1872. When this was predictably refused, she sued the St. Louis Registrar, Reese Happersett. The case went to the Supreme Court, which rejected the appeal on March 29, 1875, by a 9–0 vote. Minor's argument that her citizenship rights under the Fourteenth Amendment entitled her to vote was countered by the Court's ruling that citizenship did not necessarily carry with it the right to vote. This decision contributed to a push to enfranchise women by a separate constitutional amendment (eventually the Nineteenth Amendment in 1919).

Document Text

ERROR to the Supreme Court of Missouri; the case being thus:

The fourteenth amendment to the Constitution of the United States, in its first section, thus ordains:

"All persons born or naturalized in the United States, and subject to the jurisdiction thereof, are citizens of the United States, and of the State wherein they reside. No State shall make or enforce any law, which shall abridge the privileges or immunities of citizens of the United States. Nor shall any State deprive any person of life, liberty, or property, without due process of law; nor deny to any person within its jurisdiction, the equal protection of the laws."

Chief Justice Morrison Waite wrote the unanimous majority opinion in **Minor v. Happersett.**
(Library of Congress)

And the constitution of the State of Missouri thus ordains:

"Every male citizen of the United States shall be entitled to vote." . . .

. . . On the 15th of October, 1872, . . . Mrs. Virginia Minor, a native born, free, white citizen of the United States, . . . over the age of twenty-one years, wishing to vote . . . applied to one Happersett, the registrar of voters, to register her as a lawful voter, which he refused to do, assigning for cause that she was not a "male citizen of the United States." . . . She thereupon sued him in one of the inferior State courts of Missouri. . . .

The registrar demurred, and the court in which the suit was brought sustained the demurrer, and gave judgment in his favor. . . . Mrs. Minor now brought the case here on error.

Mr. Francis Minor, . . . for the plaintiff in error, went into an elaborate argument. . . .
1st. As a citizen of the United States, the plaintiff was entitled to any and all the "privileges and immunities" that belong to such position however defined; and as are held, exercised, and enjoyed by other citizens of the United States.

2d. The elective franchise is a "privilege" of citizenship, in the highest sense of the word. . . .

3d. The denial or abridgment of this privilege . . . must be sought only in . . . the Constitution of the United States. . . .

4th. But the Constitution of the United States, so far from recognizing or permitting any denial or abridgment of the privileges of its citizens, expressly declares that "no State shall make or enforce any law which shall abridge the privileges or immunities of citizens of the United States."

5th. If follows that the provisions of the Missouri constitution and registry law before recited, are in conflict with and must yield to the paramount authority of the Constitution of the United States

The CHIEF JUSTICE delivered the opinion of the court.

The question is presented in this case, whether, since the adoption of the fourteenth amendment, a woman, who is a citizen of the United States and of the State of Missouri, is a voter in that State. . . . We might, perhaps, decide the case upon other grounds, but this question is fairly made. . . . We have concluded to waive all other considerations and proceed at once to its determination. . . .

There is no doubt that women may be citizens. They are persons, and by the fourteenth amendment "all persons born or naturalized in the United States and subject to the jurisdiction thereof" are expressly declared to be "citizens of the United States and of the State wherein they reside." . . .

. . . Sex has never been made one of the elements of citizenship in the United States. In this respect men have never had an advantage over women. The same laws precisely apply to both. The fourteenth amendment did not affect the citizenship of women any more than it did of men. In this particular, therefore, the rights of Mrs. Minor do not depend upon the amendment. She has always been a citizen from her birth. . . . The amendment prohibited the State, of which she is a citizen, from abridging any of her privileges and immunities as a citizen of the United States; but it did not confer citizenship on her. That she had before its adoption.

. . . The direct question is, therefore, presented whether all citizens are necessarily voters.

The Constitution does not define the privileges and immunities of citizens. For that definition we must look elsewhere. In this case we need not determine what they are, but only whether suffrage is necessarily one of them. . . .

. . . The Constitution has not added the right of suffrage to the privileges and immunities of citizenship as they existed at the time it was adopted. This makes it proper to inquire whether suffrage was coextensive with the citizenship of the States at the time of its adoption. If it was, then it may with force be argued that suffrage was one of the rights which belonged to citizenship, and in the enjoyment of which every citizen must be protected. But if it was not, the contrary may with propriety be assumed.

And still again, after the adoption of the fourteenth amendment, it was deemed necessary to adopt a fifteenth, as follows: "The right of citizens of the United States to vote shall not be denied or abridged by the United States, or by any State, on account of race, color, or previous condition of servitude." The fourteenth amendment had already provided that no State should make or enforce any law which should abridge the privileges or immunities of citizens of the United States. If suffrage was one of these privileges or immunities, why amend the Constitution to prevent its being denied on account of race, &c.? . . .

. . . No new State has ever been admitted to the Union which has conferred the right of suffrage upon women, and this has never been considered a valid objection to her admission. On the contrary . . . the right of suffrage was withdrawn from women as early as 1807 in the State of New Jersey, without any attempt to obtain the interference of the United States to prevent it. Since then the governments of the insurgent States have been reorganized under a requirement that before their representatives could be admitted to seats in Congress they must have adopted new constitutions, republican in form. In no one of these constitutions was suffrage conferred upon women, and yet the States have all been restored to their original position as States in the Union. . . .

. . . If the law is wrong, it ought to be changed; but the power for that is not with us. . . . Our duty is at an end if we find it is within the power of a State to withhold.

Being unanimously of the opinion that the Constitution of the United States does not confer the right of suffrage upon any one, and that the constitutions and laws of the several States which commit that important trust to men alone are not necessarily void, we

AFFIRM THE JUDGMENT.

Glossary

demurred: disagreed or objected to something

elective franchise: the right to vote

on error: maintaining that the law or ruling was incorrect or invalid

suffrage: the right to vote

sustained: ruled in favor of

Short-Answer Questions

1. What distinction does the Supreme Court see between citizenship and the right to suffrage?

2. Regardless of the outcome, what is your opinion regarding the strengths of the arguments on both sides? Explain in detail.

3. According to the document, what does being a citizen of the United States seem to entail, and who might be classified as a "citizen"?

Francis Parkman:
Some of the Reasons against Woman Suffrage

Author Francis Parkman **Date** c. 1883 **Document Type** Essays, Reports, Manifestos	**Significance** Presented arguments against extending the vote to women and was considered in the U.S. Senate as evidence against women's suffrage

Overview

Francis Parkman Jr. (1823–1893) was a well-known American historian of the nineteenth century, noted especially for his works on the history of the American frontier, including *The Oregon Trail: Sketches of Prairie and Rocky-Mountain Life* and *England and France in North America*. Also among his writings were essays rejecting the idea of women's suffrage. One of these, *Some of the Reasons against Woman Suffrage*, was printed as a pamphlet around 1883, and the essay was read in the U.S. Senate and considered in arguments concerning women's suffrage. Because of his prestige as a scholar and member of the Boston Athenaeum, one of the United States' first independent libraries, his anti-suffrage works were republished and used by groups opposed to extending the franchise to women well into the twentieth century.

Document Text

Cruelty of Woman Suffrage

The frequent low state of health among American women is a fact as undeniable as it is deplorable. In this condition of things, what do certain women demand for the good of their sex? To add to the excitements that are wasting them other and greater excitements, and to cares too much for their strength other and greater cares. Because they cannot do their own work, to require them to add to it the work of men, and launch them into turmoil where the most robust sometimes fail. It is much as if a man in a state of nervous exhaustion were told by his physician to enter at once for a foot-race or a boxing match.

Power Should Go with Responsibility

To hold the man responsible and yet deprive

him of power is neither just nor rational. The man is the natural head of the family, and is responsible for its maintenance and order. Hence he ought to control the social and business agencies which are essential to the successful discharge of the trust imposed upon him. If he is deprived of any part of this control, he should be freed also in the same measure from the responsibilities attached to it.

Alternatives to Woman Suffrage

Woman suffrage must have one of two effects. If, as many of its advocates complain, women are subservient to men, and do nothing but what they desire, then woman suffrage will have no other result than to increase the power of the other sex; if, on the other hand, women vote as they see fit, without regarding their husbands, then unhappy marriages will be multiplied and divorces redoubled. We cannot afford to add to the elements of iidomestic unhappiness.

Political Dangers of Woman Suffrage

One of the chief dangers of popular government is that of inconsiderate and rash legislation. In impatience to be rid of one evil, ulterior consequences are apt to be forgotten. In the haste to redress one wrong, a door may be opened to many. This danger would be increased immeasurably if the most impulsive and excitable half of humanity had an equal voice in the making of laws, and in the administration of them. Abstract right would then be made to prevail after a fashion somewhat startling. A lady of intelligence and admirable intentions, an ardent partisan on principles of pure humanitarianism, confessed that, in the last presidential election, Florida had given a majority, for the Democrats; but insisted it was right to count it for Hayes, because other states had been wrongfully counted for Tilden. It was impossible to make her comprehend that government conducted on such principles would end in anarchy. In politics, the virtues of women would sometimes be as dangerous as their faults.

If the better class of women flatter themselves that they can control the others, they are doomed to disappointment. They will be outvoted in their own kitchens, without reckoning the agglomerations of poverty, ignorance and vice that form a startling proportion of our city populations. It is here that the male vote alone threatens our system with its darkest perils. The female vote would enormously increase the evil, for it is often more numerous, always more impulsive and less subject to reason, and almost devoid of the sense of responsibility. Here the bad politician would find his richest resources. He could not reach the better class of female voters, but the rest would be ready to his hand. Three-fourths of them, when not urged by some pressing need or contagious passion, would be moved, not by principles, but by personal predilections.

The Female Politician

It is not woman's virtues that would be prominent or influential in the political arena. They would shun it by an invincible repulsion; and the opposite qualities would be drawn into it. The Washington lobby has given us some means of judging what we may expect from the woman "inside politics." If politics are to be purified by artfulness, effrontery, insensibility, a pushing self-assertion, and a glib tongue then we may look for regeneration; for the typical female politician will be richly endowed with all these gifts.

Thus accoutered for the conflict, she may fairly hope to have the better of her masculine antagonist. A woman has the inalienable right of attacking without being attacked in turn. She may strike, but must not be struck, either literally or figuratively. Most women refrain from abusing their privilege of non-combatants; but there are those in whom the sense of impunity breeds the cowardly courage of the virago.

In reckoning the resources of the female politicians, there is one which can by no means be left out. None know better than women the potency of feminine charms aided by feminine arts. The woman "inside politics" will not fail to make use of an influence so subtle and strong, and of which the management is peculiarly suited to her talents. If—and the contingency is in the highest degree probable—she is not gifted with charms of her own, she will have no difficulty in finding and using others of her sex who are. . . . When "woman" is fairly "inside politics," the sensation press will reap a harvest of scandals more lucrative to itself than profitable to public morals. . . .

Men Will Give Women the Suffrage If They Want It

Again, one of the chief arguments of the agitators is that government without the consent of the governed is opposed to inalienable right. But most women, including those of the best capacity and worth, fully consent that their fathers, husbands, brothers or friends shall be their political representatives; no exhortation or teasing has induced them to withhold their consent. Nor is this surprising; for a woman is generally represented in a far truer and more intimate sense by her male relative. . . .

Nothing is more certain than that women will have the suffrage if they ever want it; for when they want it, men will give it to them regardless of consequences. . . .

Glossary

accoutered: dressed or equipped for

agglomeration: a collection or concentration of items

Florida: a reference to the controversial 1876 presidential election when the Democratic candidate, Samuel J. Tilden, received more popular votes than his Republican rival, Rutherford B. Hayes, but Hayes won the election based on disputed electoral votes in three states, of which Florida was one

Hayes: Republican candidate Rutherford B. Hayes in the 1876 U.S. presidential election

impunity: freedom from consequence

predilections: preferences or biases

Tilden: Democratic candidate Samuel J. Tilden in the 1876 U.S. presidential election

virago: an overbearing woman; a shrew

Washington lobby: likely a reference to lobby groups urging congressmen to support women's suffragev

Short-Answer Questions

1. What stereotypes does Parkman attribute to women that, according to him, should disqualify them from voting?

2. How would you counter Parkman's arguments?

3. In what ways does Parkman's pamphlet reflect fears that he might harbor, and what might those fears be?

Josephine St. Pierre Ruffin: "Address to the First National Conference of Colored Women"

Author Josephine St. Pierre Ruffin **Date** 1895 **Document Type** Speeches/Addresses	**Significance** Demonstrated a self-imposed call to action and noted the crucial role of Black women in the women's rights movement

Overview

Josephine St. Pierre Ruffin was an African American publisher, journalist, civil rights leader, and suffragist. Her "Address to the First National Conference of Colored Women" opened the proceedings for a group of 100 African American women who met in Boston at the Charles Street African Methodist Episcopal Church in July 1895. Ruffin was the president of the Women's Era Club in Boston, founded two years previously, and it was her work with this group that inspired her to found the National Federation of Afro-American Women. She organized and convened the Boston conference with a view to bringing together African American club women from across the nation to join with her in that effort. Attending the conference as representatives from clubs around the nation, the participants convened to assert their position as a critical component of the women's movement, to discuss the issues and challenges facing Black women, and to debate how best to move forward in light of those challenges. The "Address to the First National Conference of Colored Women" was a call to action. Ruffin's remarks were brief, but they served to inspire a generation of African American women to active involvement in the women's movement and to challenge all women to "bring in a new era to the colored women of America."

Josephine St. Pierre Ruffin
(L. A. Scruggs)

Document Text

It is with especial joy and pride that I welcome you all to this, our first conference. . . . Although rather hastily called, you as well as I can testify how long and how earnestly a conference has been thought of and hoped for and even prepared for. These women's clubs, which have sprung up all over the country, built and run upon broad and strong lines, have all been a preparation, small conferences in themselves, and their spontaneous birth and enthusiastic support have been little less than inspirational on the part of our women and a general preparation for a large union such as it is hoped this conference will lead to. . . . It shows that we are truly American women, with all the adaptability, readiness to seize and possess our opportunities, willingness to do our part for good as other American women.

The reasons why we should confer are so apparent that it would seem hardly necessary to enumerate them, and yet there are none of them but demand our serious consideration. In the first place we need to feel the cheer and inspiration of meeting each other; we need to gain the courage and fresh life that comes from the mingling of congenial souls, of those working for the same ends. Next, we need to talk over those things that are of especial interest to us as colored women, the training of our children . . . in order to prepare them to meet the peculiar conditions in which they shall find themselves, how to make the most of our own, to some extent, limited opportunities. . . .

I have left the strongest reason for our conferring together until the last. All over America there is to be found a large and growing class of earnest, intelligent, progressive colored women, women who, if not leading full, useful lives, are only waiting for the opportunity to do so, many of them warped and cramped for lack of opportunity, not only to do more but to be more; and yet, if an estimate of the colored women of America is called for, the inevitable reply, glibly given is, "For the most part ignorant and immoral, some exceptions of course, but these don't count." . . .

Too long have we been silent under unjust and unholy charges; we cannot expect to have them removed until we disprove them through ourselves. It is not enough to try to disprove unjust charges through individual effort, that never goes any further. Year after year southern women have protested against the admission of colored women into any national organization on the ground of the immorality of these women. . . . Now with an army of organized women standing for purity and mental worth, we in ourselves deny the charge and open the eyes of the world to a state of affairs to which they have been blind, often willfully so, and the very fact that the charges, audaciously and flippantly made, as they often are, are of so humiliating and delicate a nature, serves to protect the accuser by driving the helpless accused into mortified silence. It is to break this silence, not by noisy protestations of what we are not, but by a dignified showing of what we are and hope to become that we are impelled to take this step, to make of this gathering an object lesson to the world. . . .

Our woman's movement is woman's movement in

that it is led and directed by women for the good of women and men, for the benefit of all humanity, which is more than any one branch or section of it. We want, we ask the active interest of our men, and, too, we are not drawing the color line; we are women, American women, as intensely interested in all that pertains to us as such as all other American women; we are not alienating or withdrawing, we are only coming to the front, willing to join any others in the same work and cordially inviting and welcoming any others to join us. . . .

It is hoped and believed that from this will spring an organization that will in truth bring in a new era to the colored women of America.

Glossary

audacious: showing an impudent lack of respect; rude; out of line

color line: refers to racial segregation that existed in the United States after the abolition of slavery

congenial: compatible; having similar qualities or interests

women's clubs: social or political organizations founded on the idea that women had a moral duty to transform public policy

Short-Answer Questions

1. Josephine St. Pierre Ruffin mentions many reasons why this meeting was necessary. What are the main three reasons she gives? Why does she assign them different levels of importance?

2. Ruffin states that meeting with congenial souls is important to the women's movement and that the movement's goals benefit all of humanity. What evidence does she use in her speech to support the necessity of group efforts? Are these efforts limited to women of color?

3. When Ruffin says "we are not drawing the color line," what does she mean? How does this statement fit in with the overall message of the address?

Mary Church Terrell: "The Progress of Colored Women"

Author	Significance
Mary Church Terrell	Asserted the importance of education and urged national women's groups to support free kindergarten for less-fortunate children in Black communities
Date	
1898	
Document Type	
Speeches/Addresses	

Overview

On February 18, 1898, at a meeting of the National American Woman Suffrage Association (NAWSA), Mary Church Terrell delivered an address titled "The Progress of Colored Women." She states in the address that the occasion marks the fiftieth anniversary of the NAWSA, but this is only partly true. This meeting of the association was held in conjunction with the fiftieth anniversary of the Seneca Falls Convention of 1848 in New York, which many historians regard as the official start of the women's suffrage movement in the United States. In part as a result of the Seneca Falls Convention, various suffrage organizations were formed, including the National Woman Suffrage Association and the American Woman Suffrage Association. The NAWSA in turn was formed in 1890 as a merger of the two organizations.

Terrell, one of the nation's first African American women to earn a college degree, was active in the NAWSA and numerous other organizations. In 1896, for example, she had cofounded the National Association of College Women, which later became the National Association of University Women, an organization that has continued to this day. That year, too, she was named the first president of the National Association of Colored Women's Clubs (NACWC). This group, known more simply as the National Association of Colored Women (the name Terrell uses in her address), united the National Federation of Afro-American Women, the Women's Era Club of Boston, and the Colored Women's League of Washington, D.C., as well as other groups that had taken part in the African American women's club movement. Thus, she was eminently qualified to speak about the status of African American women, and her speech was later published as a pamphlet.

Document Text

Fifty years ago a meeting such as this, planned, conducted and addressed by women would have been an impossibility. Less than forty years ago, few sane men would have predicted that either a slave or one of his descendants would in this century at least, address such an audience in the Nation's Capital at the invitation of women representing the highest, broadest, best type of womanhood, that can be found anywhere in the world. Thus to me this semi-centennial of the National American Woman Suffrage Association is a double jubilee, rejoicing as I do, not only in the prospective en-franchisement of my sex but in the emancipation of my race. . . . Consider if you will, the almost insurmountable obstacles which have confronted colored women in their efforts to educate and cultivate themselves since their emancipation, and I dare assert, not boastfully, but with pardonable pride, I hope, that the progress they have made and the work they have accomplished, will bear a fa-vorable comparison at least with that of their more fortunate sisters, from whom the opportunity of acquiring knowledge and the means of self-culture have never been entirely withheld. . . . Though the slaves were liberated less than forty years ago, pen-niless, and ignorant, with neither shelter nor food, so great was their thirst for knowledge and so her-culean were their efforts to secure it, that there are today hundreds of negroes, many of them women, who are graduates, some of them having taken de-grees from the best institutions of the land. . . .

With this increase of wisdom there has sprung up in the hearts of colored women an ardent desire to do good in the world. No sooner had the favored few availed themselves of such advantages as they could secure than they hastened to dispense these blessings to the less fortunate of their race. With tireless energy and eager zeal, colored women have, since their emancipation, been continuously pros-ecuting the work of educating and elevating their race, as though upon themselves alone devolved the accomplishment of this great task. Of the teachers engaged in instructing colored youth, it is perhaps

Mary Church Terrell
(Library of Congress)

no exaggeration to say that fully ninety per cent are women. . . . By banding themselves together in the interest of education and morality, by adopting the most practical and useful means to this end, colored women have in thirty short years become a great power for good. Through the National Associa-tion of Colored Women, which was formed by the union of two large organizations in July, 1896, and which is now the only national body among colored women, much good has been done in the past, and more will be accomplished in the future, we hope. Believing that it is only through the home that a people can become really good and truly great, the National Association of Colored Women has en-tered that sacred domain. . . .

As an organization of women nothing lies near-er the heart of the National Association than the children, many of whose lives, so sad and dark, we might brighten and bless. It is the kindergarten we need. Free kindergartens in every city and hamlet of this broad land we must have, if the children are to receive from us what it is our duty to give. Already during the past year kindergartens have been established and successfully maintained by several organizations, from which most encouraging reports have come. May their worthy example be emulated, till in no branch of the Association shall the children of the poor, at least, be deprived of the blessings which flow from the kindergarten alone. The more unfavorable the environments of children, the more necessary is it that steps be taken to counteract baleful influences on innocent victims. . . .

And so, lifting as we climb, onward and upward we go, struggling and striving, and hoping that the buds and blossoms of our desires will burst into glorious fruition ere long. With courage, born of success achieved in the past, with a keen sense of the responsibility which we shall continue to assume, we look forward to a future large with promise and hope. Seeking no favors because of our color, nor patronage because of our needs, we knock at the bar of justice, asking an equal chance.

Glossary

baleful: threatening harm; menacing

emulate: match, copy, or follow

hamlet: a small settlement

jubilee: a special anniversary of an event, normally after either twenty-five or fifty years; also, biblically, a year of emancipation or restoration of rights or ownership

Short-Answer Questions

1. What is Terrell referring to when she describes a "double jubilee"?

2. According to Terrell, what role does education play in the efforts of the National Association of Colored Women?

3. Why does Terrell consider "free kindergartens in every city and hamlet" a necessity? How does this relate to the lack of educational opportunities for Black children in America?

Anna Howard Shaw: Address on the Place of Women in Society

Author Anna Howard Shaw **Date** 1905 **Document Type** Speeches/Addresses	**Significance** Asserted that giving women voting rights would not hinder their effectiveness as mothers and homemakers

Overview

Anna Howard Shaw (1847–1919) was a leader in the women's suffrage movement. She had overcome poverty and misogyny to become a Methodist minister in 1873, and she earned an M.D. from Boston University in 1886. Shortly afterward, Dr. Shaw became proactive in temperance and women's suffrage organizations, being elected president of the National Women Suffrage Association. She served in this capacity until 1915. During her tenure of office, she made numerous speeches. She was particularly renowned for her oratory, and this short address, delivered during the early months of her presidential administration, answered those critics who maintained that giving women voting rights would work to the detriment of their effectiveness as mothers and homemakers. It also mirrors some of the societal reform principles of the progressive movement of the time.

Document Text

When the cry of race-suicide is heard, and men arraign women for race decadence, it would be well for them to examine conditions and causes, and base their attacks upon firmer foundations of fact. Instead of attacking women for their interest in public affairs and relegating them to their children, their kitchen, and their church, they will learn that the kitchen is in politics; that the children's physical, intellectual, and moral well-being is controlled and regulated by law; that the real cause of race decadence is not the fact that fewer children are born, but to the more fearful fact that, of those born, so few live, not primarily because of the neglect of the mother, but because men themselves neglect their duty as citizens and public officials. If

1915 photograph of Anna Howard Shaw
(National Portrait Gallery)

playing in the streets and alleys and viler places, until they have learned the lessons which take them to ever-growing numbers of reformatories, whose inmates are increasing four times as rapidly as the population. Let them follow the children who survive all these ills of early childhood, until they enter the sweat-shops and factories, and behold there the maimed, dwarfed, and blighted little ones, 500,000 of whom under 14 years of age are employed in these pestilential places. Let them behold the legalized saloons and the dens of iniquity where so many of the voting population spend the money that should be used in feeding, housing, and caring for their children. Then, if these mentors of women's clubs and mothers' meetings do not find sufficient cause for race degeneracy where they have power to control conditions, let them turn to lecturing women. It is infinitely more important that a child shall be well born and well reared than that more children shall be born. It is better that one well-born child shall live than that two shall be born and one die in infancy. That which is desirable is not that the greatest possible number of children should be born into the world; the need is for more intelligent motherhood and fatherhood, and for better born and better educated children. . . .

The great fear that the participation of women in public affairs will impair the quality and character of home service is irrational and contrary to the tests of experience. Does an intelligent interest in the education of a child render a woman less a mother? Does the housekeeping instinct of woman, manifested in a desire for clean street, pure water, and unadulterated food, destroy her efficiency as a home-maker? Does a desire for an environment of moral and civic purity show neglect of the highest good of the family? It is the "men must fight and women must weep" theory of life which makes men fear that the larger services of women will impair the high ideal of home. The newer ideal, that men must cease fighting and thus remove one prolific cause for women's weeping, and that they shall together build up a more perfect home and a more ideal government, is infinitely more

men honestly desire to prevent the causes of race decadence, let them examine the accounts of food adulteration, and learn that from the effect of impure milk alone, in one city 56,000 babies died in a single year. Let them examine the water supply, so impregnated with disease that in some cities there is continual epidemic of typhoid fever. Let them gaze upon the filthy streets, from which perpetually arises contagion of scarlet fever and diphtheria. Let them examine the plots of our great cities, and find city after city with no play places for children, except the streets, alleys, and lanes. Let them examine the school buildings, many of them badly lighted, unsanitary, and without yards. Let them turn to the same cities, and learn that from five to a score or thousand children secure only half-day tuition because there are not adequate schoolhouse facilities. Let them watch these half-day children sane and desirable. Participation in the larger and broader concerns of the State, will increase instead of decreasing the efficiency of motherhood, and tend to develop that self-control, that more perfect judgment which is wanting in much of the home training of to-day.

Glossary

arraign: to blame or condemn someone

race decadence: a reference either to the human race generally or to the white population, both of which were popularly said during the late nineteenth and early twentieth centuries to be in danger of moral and physical decay

typhoid fever: a serious illness caused by food or water contaminated by sewage, or by person-to-person contact

Short-Answer Questions

1. What specific rights does Shaw advocate for women that she feels are being denied?

2. How do Shaw's medical knowledge and support for the temperance movement figure in her arguments?

3. Analyze the issues that the speaker raises and the target audience she is addressing. How effective was the speech in making the case for women's rights? What are the strengths and weaknesses of the arguments she presents?

Ida Husted Harper:
Statement before the U.S. Senate Select Committee on Woman Suffrage

---

Author
Ida Husted Harper

Date
1908

Document Type
Speeches/Addresses

Significance
Contrasted progress in women's suffrage in countries around the world with the lack of advancement in the United States

---

Overview

By the late 1800s, women in several countries had gained the ability to vote in local or national elections. This was the result of a global feminist movement to secure the right to vote. In the United States, Wyoming and Utah became the first U.S. territories to enact women's suffrage (Utah also became the first state to grant women the vote). However, efforts to secure voting rights for women at the national level were repeatedly blocked in Congress or by the states.

Ida Husted Harper (1851–1931) was an early leader of the U.S. women's suffrage movement. She became famous as a writer and reporter. In addition, Harper was a leading figure of the International Council of Women (ICW), which advocated for women's suffrage around the world. On March 3, 1908, she testified before Congress on the need for women's suffrage. Harper emphasized recent advancements in suffrage in Europe. For instance, women in Finland had been given full voting rights and the ability to seek elected offices. She also noted that her counterparts in countries such as Denmark and Great Britain were on the verge of obtaining the vote for national elections. Meanwhile, the suffragist pointed out that women had already been elected to local and national office in some European nations. There were women serving as mayors, municipal council members, and members of parliaments.

In contrast, Harper noted, little or no progress had been made in the United States. Indeed, women had full suffrage in only four U.S. states at the time, and those voting rights had been granted in the 1890s. She strongly condemned the lack of progress in her country and described the shame U.S. women faced when confronted by the progress in voting rights made in other areas of the world. Harper highlighted the contradiction whereby the United States was founded on the promise individual rights and freedoms yet lagged behind nations such as Russia that were generally perceived to be autocratic and undemocratic.

Although her testimony in 1908 did not have an immediate impact, Harper would later play a major role in the successful campaign to gain the vote through the ratification of the Nineteenth Amendment in 1920.

Document Text

Gentlemen and members of the committee: Since the representatives of the National Woman Suffrage Association last appeared before this committee, two years ago, two nations of Europe have conferred the complete franchise on their women and one has practically granted municipal suffrage. Finland in 1906 enfranchised all women on exactly the same terms as men and made them eligible to all offices including the parliamentary. This measure was the result of great deliberation and careful procedure, decided upon by a carefully selected commission, passed by all the four chambers of the Diet with but one dissenting voice, and signed by the Czar. About 300,000 women were thus enfranchised. At the next election all parties put women on their tickets and one year ago this month 19 were elected to Parliament and are now sitting in that body. At this election fully as large a proportion of women as of men voted, and in some districts it was larger.

The women of Norway, since 1901, have possessed the complete municipal franchise and eligibility to the city councils. Several hundred have been elected as aldermen, 6 in Christiana at the recent election. A very large number use the franchise; in some places 90 per cent. In 1907 the full parliamentary suffrage was conferred with a tax-paying qualification so small that even domestic servants can meet it, and the wife may vote on the husband's income. About 350,000 women thus became electors.

At last accounts the Parliament of Denmark had given the third reading to a bill for the municipal franchise for women, and it is doubtless now a law. In Sweden the movement for woman suffrage is so far advanced as to insure its success within the next year or two. In the Netherlands, the full franchise

Ida Husted Harper
(Library of Congress)

for women has been placed in the proposed new constitution, and only the overthrow of the present Government will prevent its adoption. Women of Great Britain have had municipal suffrage for nearly forty years, and within a few months the Parliament has made them eligible as mayors, as town and county councilors, and as presidents of the councils. This bill passed the conservative House of Lords by a vote of 73 to 46, while there were only 15 votes against it in the House of Commons. At the first election thereafter 7 cities elected women to their councils. . . .

These statements illustrate the actual political progress of women in European countries within the past two years, and many steps forward in others might be cited if time permitted.

During this period what have been the concrete gains for women in the United States, the nation alleged to give them more rights than any on the face of the earth? The answer can be given in a very few words: "There has not been one." How many political privileges have been secured within the past ten years? Not one. There is the shameful record in all its nakedness, and let those who boast of this glorious Republic make the best of it. While the legislative bodies of most of the progressive nations throughout the world are moving forward toward the political recognition of women, those of the United States are standing stock-still, just where they were at the beginning of their existence, and resisting every effort to move them from their medieval position.

When we women go abroad to our great international meetings we meet there the delegates from New Zealand, who have been fully enfranchised since 1893; from Australia, who have had the complete suffrage and the right to sit in Parliament for the past six years, ever since their States were federated into a commonwealth; from Finland and Norway, with their full political rights; from Great Britain, with the municipal vote and rights to office; from Denmark, and from our neighbor, Canada, with the municipal franchise; yes, and even the women of Russia, who tell us that representatives in the douma of every political party are in favor of giving votes to women. What are we to answer to the amazed inquiries when we of the United States have no voice in a Government whose greatest pride is that of being founded on individual representation? Shall we say it is because our men are not as just and generous as those of other nations? Or shall we take the other horn of the dilemma and say it is because our women are not so capable of being trusted with it!? No one can truthfully say it is because our women do not want it, for they have worked far longer and harder for it than have those of all these other countries combined.

This year the suffragists of the United States will observe the sixtieth anniversary of the first woman's rights convention ever held in all history, that one which met in Seneca Falls, N.Y., the home of Elizabeth Cady Stanton, in 1848. First among the rights which it demanded women was that of suffrage. After three-score years' continuous agitation, education, and organization what are the meager results we face to-day? In one State, Kansas, women have a limited municipal franchise; in Iowa, Louisiana, Montana and the villages of New York a shred of tax-payers' suffrage; in about one-half of the States a partial school vote. Not in one have women the same voice in school affairs that men have, and in order to exercise what they do possess they must comply with all the formalities required of men to vote for every official up to President of the United States. In 4 out of 46 States—Wyoming, Colorado, Idaho, and Utah—women are fully enfranchised on exactly the same terms as men. All of these 4 States took this action within six years, from 1890 to 1896, and it looked as if the time had come when woman suffrage would sweep the western part of the country. . . .

Glossary

czar: the monarch of Russia, which until 1917 included Finland as a principality

diet: a parliament or legislature

douma: variant spelling of *duma*; the Russian parliament during that country's monarchy

franchise: the right to vote

municipal suffrage/municipal franchise: the right to vote in local elections

third reading: one of the final steps in the legislative process before a bill becomes law

Short-Answer Questions

1. Why had women in some other nations achieved more progress in voting rights than those in the United States? Analyze why some autocratic governments might have been more willing to grant women the right to vote than a democracy such as the United States.

2. Was Harper's contrast of the United States with other nations an effective way to convince Congress to grant women's suffrage? Discuss possible reasons why did it not work.

3. What happened in other nations when women were granted the right to vote? What were some of the results? How did those results justify women's suffrage?

Charlotte Perkins Gilman: "The Humanness of Women"

Author	Significance
Charlotte Perkins Gilman	Criticized contemporary ideas about gender and the role of women in society and helped rally support for women's suffrage and equal rights
Date	
1910	
Document Type	
Speeches/Addresses	

Overview

Women's suffrage was one aspect of a broader movement that has been dubbed first-wave feminism in the United States in the nineteenth and early twentieth centuries. Women sought to remove legal and political barriers to equality. The right to vote emerged as one of the key goals of the movement, both in the United States and abroad, but women also endeavored to end formal and informal obstacles to education, property rights, and economic empowerment.

Charlotte Perkins Gilman (1860–1935) exerted a lasting influence on feminism through her writings, lectures, and advocacy for women's rights. Her 1892 semi-autobiographical short story "The Yellow Wallpaper" was widely regarded as one of the major literary works of first-wave feminism, and her address "The Humanness of Women" was an influential critique of gender stereotypes that predated the social condemnations of U.S. society in the later twentieth century.

In her speech, Gilman emphasized the importance of the vote for women as a means to end other forms of discrimination. The celebrated feminist attacked prevailing views that the world was marked by competition and strife. She argued that this perspective was part of the foundation for gender inequality. It was part of a narrative that women were too weak or otherwise ill-suited to compete in the brutal, daily battles that marked society and the marketplace. Gilman rejected this view of life. She instead argued that life was not a "battlefield" but rather a garden in which men and women could work together equally to advance society. To not allow women full equality meant that the nation missed the input and efforts of half its population. Furthermore, Gilman asserted that women were natural teachers who emphasized cooperation and collaboration over conflict. She ended her lecture with a call for women's suffrage.

Gilman delivered her lecture "The Humanness of Women" on a number of occasions in a variety of venues in the Northeast in 1909 and 1910. The speech helped rally support for women's suffrage and the broad effort for equal rights.

Document Text

For a little over a century we have become increasingly conscious of a stir, an uprising, and protest among women. The long-suppressed "better half" of humanity has begun to move and push and lift herself. This Woman's movement is as natural, as beneficial, as irresistible as the coming of spring; but it has been misunderstood and opposed from the first by the glacial moraine of old ideas, the inert force of sheer blank ignorance, and prejudice as old as Adam.

At first the women strove for a little liberty, for education; then for some equality before the law, for common justice; then, with larger insight, for full equal rights with men in every human field; and as essential base of these, for the right of suffrage.

Woman suffrage is but one feature of the movement, but it is a most important one. The opposition to it is wholly one of sex-prejudice, of feeling, not of reason; the opposition of a masculine world; and of an individualism also masculine. The male is physiologically an individualist. It is his place in nature to vary, to introduce new characteristics, and to strive mightily with his rivals for the favor of the females. A world of males must fight.

With the whole of history of this combative sort; with masculinity and humanity identical in the average mind; there is something alien, unnatural, even revolting, in the claim of woman to her share in the work and management of the world. Against it he brings up one constant cry—that woman's progress will injure womanhood. All that he sees in woman is her sex; and he opposes her advance on the ground that "as a woman" she is unfit to take part in "a man's world"—and that if she did, it would mysteriously but inevitably injure her "as a woman."

Suggest that she might be able to take part in "a woman's world,"—and has as much right to a world made her way as he has to his man-made world! Suggest that without any such extreme reversal, she has a right to half the world; half the

Charlotte Perkins Gilman
(Library of Congress)

work, half pay, half the care, half the glory!

To all this replies the Male-Individualist:

"The World has to be as it is. It is a place to fight in; fight for life, fight for money. Work is for slaves and poor people generally. Nobody would work unless they had to. You are females and no part of the world at all. Your place is at home; to bear and rear children—and to cook."

Now what is the position toward women of this new philosophy that sees Society as one thing, and the main thing to be considered; that sees the world as a place open to ceaseless change and improvement; that sees the way so to change and improve it that the major part of our poor silly sins and sorrows will disappear utterly for lack of cause?

From this viewpoint male and female fall into two lower positions, both right and proper; useful, beautiful, essential for the replenishment of the race on earth. From this viewpoint men and women rise, together, from that lower relation, to the far higher one of Humanness, that common Humanness which is hers as much as his. Seeing Society as the real life-form; and our individual lives as growing in glory and power as we serve and develop Society; the movement of women becomes of majestic importance. It is the advance of an entire half the race, from a position of arrested development, into full humanness.

The world is no longer seen as a battlefield, where it is true, women do not belong; but as a garden—a school—a church—a home, where they visibly do belong. In the great task of cultivating the earth they have an equal interest and an equal power. Equality is not identity. There is work of all kinds and sizes—and half of it is woman's.

In that vast labor of educating humanity, till all of us understand one another; till the thoughts and feelings necessary to our progress can flow smooth and clear through the world-mind, women have pre-eminent part. They are the born teachers, by virtue of their motherhood, as well as in the human joy of it.

In the power of organization which is essential to our progress we have special need of women, and their rapid and universal movement in this direction is one of the most satisfactory proofs of our advance. In every art, craft and profession they have the same interests, the same power. We rob the world of half its service when we deny women their share in it.

In direct political action there is every reason for women's voting that there is for men's; and every reason for a spreading universal suffrage that there is for democracy. As far as any special power in government is called for, the mother is the natural ruler, the natural administrator and executive. The functions of democratic government may be wisely and safely shared between men and women.

Here we have our great position fairly before us:—the improvement of the world is ours to make; women are coming forward to help make it; women are human with every human power; democracy is the highest form of government—so far; and the use of the ballot is essential to democracy; therefore women should vote!

Glossary

individualist: someone who believes strongly in the individual, self-reliance, and self-responsibility; the opposite of someone who emphasizes the importance of the group, cooperation, or society

masculine: qualities that have been historically associated with males

moraine: an area of rocks, boulders, or other materials at the edge of a glacier

Short-Answer Questions

1. What characteristics were common in the "man's world" according to the author? What potential problems could these traits cause to society?

2. Why was the right to vote an important first step for women to gain other rights? How would voting help end other forms of discrimination in the United States?

3. Why does the author refer to women as "natural leaders"? What characteristics or approaches does she suggest women bring to solving problems?

Jane Addams:
"Why Women Should Vote"

Author
Jane Addams

Date
1910

Document Type
Essays, Reports, Manifestos

Significance
Argued to readers of a popular ladies' magazine that women should have the right to vote because of changes in society and women's responsibility to children

Overview

Jane Addams (1860–1935) was a celebrated social activist and reformer. She helped draw attention to a range of social problems in the United States in the late 1800s and early 1900s. Addams was a cofounder of Hull House in Chicago, which offered assistance and aid to the poor and disadvantaged. She was also a staunch advocate for women's suffrage.

In this widely read article for the popular magazine *Ladies' Home Journal*, Addams endeavored to link voting with the conduct of traditional gender roles. For instance, she wrote that one of the main duties that was expected of a woman at the time was to maintain the cleanliness of her home. Increasingly, however, the order and maintenance of a residence depended on government policies and action. Cities wrote codes to ensure that water and sanitation systems were safe. People were also dependent on municipal governments to collect trash and clean the streets and sidewalks. Therefore, if society was going to continue to expect women to fulfill these traditional roles, it was important for them to be able to influence decisions on health and safety.

Addams was not endorsing the common gender stereotypes of her day. She was instead using the basic premises of those opposed to women's suffrage to show that those very beliefs actually justified granting women the right to vote. Addams also noted that by continuing to deny women the vote, men were preventing women from fulfilling their responsibilities. The author concluded her essay by pointing out the need for effective government to include all viewpoints and perspectives. Otherwise, cities and municipalities throughout the United States would be unbalanced. They would emphasize trade and commerce and neglect the other aspects that make a healthy and vibrant community.

After women gained the right to vote, Addams continued to fight for reform in other aspects of U.S. life. She was one of the founders of the American Civil Liberties Union (ACLU), which promoted free speech and other civil liberties. In 1931, she won the Nobel Peace Prize, the first U.S. woman to receive the award. Until her death in 1935, Addams worked to improve the lives of disadvantaged groups and break down traditional stereotypes.

Document Text

This paper is an attempt to show that many women to-day are failing to discharge their duties to their own households properly simply because they do not perceive that as society grows more complicated it, is necessary that woman shall extend her sense of responsibility to many things outside of her own home if she would continue to preserve the home in its entirety. One could illustrate in many ways. A woman's simplest duty, one would say, is to keep her house clean and wholesome and to feed her children properly. Yet if she lives in a tenement house, as so many of my neighbors do, she cannot fulfill these simple obligations by her own efforts because she is utterly dependent upon the city administration for the conditions which render decent living possible. Her basement will not be dry, her stairways will not be fireproof, her house will not be provided with sufficient windows to give light and air, nor will it be equipped with sanitary plumbing, unless the Public Works Department sends inspectors who constantly insist that these elementary decencies be provided. Women who live in the country sweep their own dooryards and may either feed the refuse of the table to a flock of chickens or allow it innocently to decay in the open air and sunshine. In a crowded city quarter, however, if the street is not cleaned by the city authorities, no amount of private sweeping will keep the tenement free from grime; if the garbage is not properly collected and destroyed a tenement house mother may see her children sicken and die of diseases from which she alone is powerless to shield them, although her tenderness and devotion are unbounded. She cannot even secure untainted meat for her household, she cannot provide fresh fruit, unless the meat has been inspected by city officials, and the decayed fruit, which is so often placed upon sale in the tenement districts, has been destroyed in the interests of public health. In short, if woman would keep on with her old business of caring

Jane Addams
(Library of Congress)

for her house and rearing her children she will have to have some conscience in regard to public affairs lying quite outside of her immediate household. The individual conscience and devotion are no longer effective. . . .

If women follow only the lines of their traditional activities, here are certain primary duties which belong to even the most conservative women, and which no one woman or group of women can adequately discharge unless they join the more general movements looking toward social amelioration through legal enactment.

The first of these, of which this article has already treated, is woman's responsibility for the members of her own household that they may be properly fed and clothed and surrounded by hygienic conditions. The second is a responsibility for the education of children: (a) that they may be provided with good books; (b) that they may be kept free from vicious influences on the street; (c) that when working they may be protected by adequate child-labor legislation. . . .

Public-spirited women who wish to use the ballot, as I know them, do not wish to do the work of men nor to take over men's affairs. They simply want an opportunity to do their own work and to take care of those affairs which naturally and historically belong to women, but which are constantly being overlooked and slighted in our political institutions. In a complex community like the modern city all points of view need to be represented; the resultants of diverse experiences need to be pooled if the community would make for sane and balanced progress. If it would meet fairly each problem as it arises, whether it be connected with a freight tunnel having to do largely with business men, or with the increasing death rate among children under five years of age, a problem in which women are vitally concerned, or with the question of more adequate streetcar transfers, in which both men and women might be said to be equally interested, it must not ignore the judgments of its entire adult population. To turn the administration of our civic affairs wholly over to men may mean that the American city will continue to push forward in its commercial and industrial development, and continue to lag behind in those things which make a City healthful and beautiful. After all, woman's traditional function has been to make her dwelling-place both clean and fair. Is that dreariness in city life, that lack of domesticity which the humblest farm dwelling presents, due to a withdrawal of one of the naturally co-operating forces? If women have in any sense been responsible for the gentler side of life which softens and blurs some of its harsher conditions, may they not have a duty to perform in our American cities? In closing, may I recapitulate that if woman would fulfill her traditional responsibility to her own children; if she would educate and protect from danger factory children who must find their recreation on the street; if she would bring the cultural forces to bear upon our materialistic civilization; and if she would do it all with the dignity and directness fitting one who carries on her immemorial duties, then she must bring herself to the use of the ballot—that latest implement for self-government. May we not fairly say that American women need this implement in order to preserve the home?

Glossary

amelioration: the act or action of making something more tolerable or acceptable

child-labor legislation: rules and regulations that govern the conditions in which children can work

materialistic: emphasizing possessions or personal fortune

public-spirited: interested in the laws and policies that oversee public life

The Schlager Anthology of Women's History

Short-Answer Questions

1. List some examples of how changes in society affected the ability of women to accomplish their traditional tasks. What steps could women undertake to overcome these obstacles?

2. What audience is Addams addressing? Why does she use traditional gender stereotypes as part of her argument? Could she have made her main points without using examples that could be seen as degrading to women?

3. What would happen to U.S. cities and communities if women were denied the right to vote? Would they operate efficiently? What were the main drawbacks of operating municipalities in which only half the population could vote?

Alice Paul:
Testimony before the
House Judiciary Committee

Author
Alice Paul

Date
1915

Document Type
Speeches/Addresses

Significance
Urged the House Judiciary Committee to refer the Anthony Amendment—which five years later would be ratified as the Nineteenth Amendment—to the floor of the House of Representatives for a vote

Overview

Alice Paul (1885–1977), one of the nation's most outspoken suffragists and feminists in the early twentieth century and beyond, did not produce a large body of written documents. Modern students of the woman's suffrage and early feminist movements can gain insight into Paul's values and beliefs from oral sources, including her testimony to the House Judiciary Committee on the question of female suffrage. Along with three of her fellow suffragists, Paul appeared before the committee on December 16, 1915, to speak on behalf of the Congressional Union for Woman Suffrage in support of an amendment to the U.S. Constitution granting voting rights to women.

In her statements and responses to members of Congress, Paul expressed the hope that her organization, the Congressional Union for Woman Suffrage, would cease to exist before the next legislative election. She expected that Congress would enact a constitutional amendment to grant women the right to vote and thereby make the union unnecessary. Her group had made a strategic decision to pressure Congress since action at the national level would be the quickest way to secure voting rights.

Paul was very critical of the Democratic Party for its failure to support suffrage. She noted that the Congressional Union had opposed congressional candidates who would not endorse the right to vote for women, and the majority of those candidates had not been reelected. In response, the Democratic Party ceased blocking efforts in Congress to enact suffrage.

Earlier during the month of Paul's testimony, the Anthony Amendment (named for Susan B. Anthony) had been introduced (not for the first time) in the House by Franklin Wheeler Mondell and in the Senate by George Sutherland. In the ensuing years, the amendment was repeatedly tabled, postponed, or rejected. It was not until June of 1919 that Congress voted 56 to 25 to pass it as the Nineteenth Amendment. It took effect on August 18, 1920, when Tennessee became the thirty-sixth state to ratify it.

After women gained the right to vote, Paul continued to campaign for gender equality. She backed the Equal Rights Amendment (ERA), which forbade discrimination based on gender. Paul also was instrumental in securing the inclusion of women as part of the 1964 Civil Rights Act.

Document Text

In closing the argument before this committee, may I summarize our position? We have come here to ask one simple thing: that the Judiciary Committee refer this Suffrage Amendment, known as the Susan B. Anthony Amendment, to the House of Representatives. We are simply asking you to do what you can do—that you let the House of Representatives decide this question. We have tried to bring people to this hearing from all over the United States to show the desire of women that this should be done.

I want to emphasize just one point, in addition, that we are absolutely non-partisan. We are made up of women who are strong Democrats, women who are strong Republicans, women who are Socialists, Progressives—every type of women. We are all united on this one thing—that we put Suffrage before everything else. In every election, if we ever go into any future elections, we simply pledge ourselves to this—that we will consider the furtherance of Suffrage and not our party affiliations in deciding what action we shall take.

Mr. Williams, of Illinois: Is it your policy to fight this question out only as a national issue? Do you make any attempt to secure relief through the States?

Miss Paul: The Congressional Union is organized to work for an Amendment to the National Constitution. We feel that the time has come, because of the winning of so many Suffrage States in the West, to use the votes of women to get Suffrage nationally. In the earlier days in this country, all the Suffrage work was done in the States, but the winning of the Western States has given us a power which we did not have before, so we have now

American suffragist Alice Paul
(Library of Congress)

turned from State work to national work. We are concentrating on the national government.

Mr. Gard: Miss Paul, is it true that you prefer to approach this through the State legislatures than to approach it directly through the people?

Miss Paul: We prefer the quickest way, which we believe is by Congressional action.

Mr. Taggart: Why did you oppose the Democrats in the last election?

Alice Paul: Testimony before the House Judiciary Committee

Miss Paul: We came into existence when the administration of President Wilson first came in. We appealed to all members of Congress to have this Amendment put through at once. We did get that measure out upon the floor of the House and Senate, but when it came to getting a vote in the House we found we were absolutely blocked. We went again and again, week after week, and month after month to the Democratic members of the Rules Committee, who controlled the apportioning of the time of the House, and asked them to give us five or ten minutes for the discussion of Suffrage. Every time they refused. They told us that they were powerless to act because the Democrats had met in caucus and decided that Suffrage was a matter to be decided in the States and should not be brought up in Congress. (Here Miss Paul, moving the papers in front of her, deftly extracted a letter.) I have here a letter from Mr. Henry, Chairman of the Rules Committee, in which he says: "It would give me great pleasure to report the Resolution to the House, except for the fact that the Democratic caucus, by its direct action, has tied my hands and placed me in a position where I will not be authorized to do so unless the caucus is reconvened and changes its decision. I am sure your good judgment will cause you to thoroughly understand my attitude." . . .

After we had been met for months with the statement that the Democratic Party had decided in caucus not to let Suffrage come up in Congress, we said, "We will go out to the women voters in the West and tell them how we are blocked in Washington, and ask them if they will use their vote for the very highest purpose for which they can use it—to help get votes for other women."

We campaigned against every one of the forty-three men who were running for Congress on the Democratic ticket in any of the Suffrage States; and only nineteen of those we campaigned against came back to Washington. In December, at the close of the election, we went back to the Rules Committee. They told us then that they had no greater desire in the world than to bring the Suffrage Amendment out. They told us that we had misunderstood them in thinking that they were opposed to having Suffrage come up in Congress. They voted at once to bring Suffrage upon the floor for the first time in history. The whole opposition of the Democratic Party melted away and the decision of the party caucus was reversed.

The part we played in the last election was simply to tell the women voters of the West of the way the Democratic Party had blocked us at Washington and of the way the individual members of the Party, from the West, had supported their Party in blocking us. As soon as we told this record they ceased blocking us and we trust they will never block us again.

Question: But what about next time?

Miss Paul: We hope we will never have to go into another election. We are appealing to all Parties and to all men to put this Amendment through this Congress and send it on to the State Legislatures. What we are doing is giving the Democrats their opportunity. We did pursue a certain policy which we have outlined to you as you requested. As to what we may do we cannot say. It depends upon the future situation. . . .

The Schlager Anthology of Women's History

Glossary

caucus: a coalition formed by members of a legislature to coordinate policy

Congressional Union: formally known as the Congressional Union for Woman Suffrage, an organization established by Alice Paul and other suffragists to advocate for the right to vote for women

non-partisan: not endorsing or supporting a single political party

Progressives: people who supported government reform in the late 1800s and early 1900s

Socialists: people who support government involvement in the economy, including collective or public ownership of certain corporations, farms, and other economic activities

Short-Answer Questions

1. Why was Alice Paul critical of the Democratic Party in her testimony? What had the Democrats done to earn the ire of suffragists?

2. What actions did the Congressional Union take to oppose those members of Congress who did not support women's suffrage? Was the strategy successful?

3. What was the purpose of the Congressional Union? Why were the suffragists trying to gain the right to vote through Congress instead of working through the states?

Mabel Ping-Hua Lee: "The Submerged Half"

Author
Mabel Ping-Hua Lee

Date
c. 1915

Document Type
Speeches/Addresses

Significance
Highlighted continuing gender discrimination in China and called for equal rights in all aspects of society

Overview

A revolution in China in 1911 toppled that country's monarchy. China's new government initiated a series of reforms, including outlawing a variety of forms of gender discrimination. However, enforcement of the new laws proved to be uneven, and Chinese women continued to be excluded from gaining their full civil, political, and economic rights.

Born in China in 1896, Mabel Ping-Hua Lee (1896–1966) immigrated to the United States in 1905. While attending college, Lee emerged as a passionate advocate for women's rights, especially the right to vote. In 1915, she gave an address that acknowledged that the Chinese government had taken steps to end some of the more repressive customs that undermined women's rights, but she called for stronger measures.

In her speech, Lee pointed out that Western Christian missionaries had helped initiate reforms. They were especially important in establishing schools for Chinese girls. Though thankful for the efforts of the missionaries, Lee stated that it was time for the Chinese people to take the lead in female education and other gender reforms. She asserted that Chinese women had already been part of the broad struggle to modernize their country. Women had even fought in the Chinese Revolution. Lee also accepted that the new government had endeavored to modernize the country. However, the Chinese American feminist detailed the main obstacles that still confronted women. Lee pointed out that rules and regulations that outlawed discriminatory practices such as foot-binding and polygamy were rarely enforced. Women continued to be treated unequally, especially in matters such as education and politics. Lee ended her address with a warning that no country could achieve its true potential without the participation of all of its citizens.

Lee was a staunch suffragist while attending college in the early 1900s. In 1917, she became the first Chinese woman to earn a doctorate in economics. A devout Christian, Lee established a Baptist mission society in New York. Because of U.S. laws restricting the number of Chinese immigrants, Lee was unable to cast a ballot even after other U.S. women gained the right to vote in 1920. It was not until 1943 that a law was passed that granted her access to the ballot.

Document Text

I plead for a wider sphere of usefulness for the long submerged women of China. I ask for our girls the open door to the treasury of knowledge, the same opportunities for physical development as boys and the same rights of participation in all human activities of which they are individually capable.

By the beginning of the 20th century the conditions of the great masses of Chinese women may be thus briefly summarized. Politically, of course, they were nonentities. The scheme of education left them out of consideration because learning was deemed unnecessary for the discharge of their duties as wives and mothers. Those who obtained the rudiments of learning were so rare as to attract notice. The custom which dictated the seclusion of women forbade social intercourse with the other sex. The custom of foot-binding robbed them of freedom of movement and crippled them from their girlhood to the time when earthly sufferings end.

Except in rural communities where they worked like the men and alongside of them, the Chinese women's sphere was enclosed by the walls of their homes. . . .

An old custom based on a false philosophy deprived her of the choice of her mate. An iniquitous law made it easier for the husband to divorce his wife than for her to divorce him. In no country is the double standard of morals so deeply entrenched as in China. . . .

After China opened five ports under the treaty with England in 1848, the education and uplift of Chinese women was taken up by missionaries. After they had devoted 55 years of patient and

Mabel Ping-Hua Lee
(Library of Congress)

persevering labours to this noble cause, the work was undertaken by the Chinese themselves, who established the first school for girls in Foochow in 1897. . . .

A new day has dawned [for the hitherto secluded and uneducated women of China] and no patriot or friend of China can fail to rejoice at the change. Hampered by crippling foot-bandages and the ever more rigid bonds of old social customs, our women have known no horizon beyond the four walls of their houses. They have received so little education, if any at all, that even in thought they have been practically limited to the area within these walls. That they, in spite of these limitations, have exercised such undeniable influence from time to time, is significant of the power which will be exercised by the Chinese women of the future, who with unbound feet and untrammeled minds, will face a new and dazzling era in the history of her sex.

Edicts have been issued against slavery and foot-binding, schools are being established for women and girls, and polygamy has been condemned as incompatible with modern civilization. These are evidences of the change of attitude toward women and her place in life. In the past she had no recognized place in society. To-day, not a few appear as equals in social and public gatherings and voice their sentiments. . . .

The missionaries came in their turn. They not only wished and prayed, but they labored. And it is largely due to their untiring efforts in the face of obstacles well-nigh insurmountable, that the present interest in women's education owes its existence.

Now it is our turn. What are we going to do in answer to the call of duty?

What good are laws and edicts if they are not enforced? Who of us does not know that at this very day foot-binding is still going on unhindered, that educational opportunities for girls are few and far behind those for boys, and that polygamy is an everyday practice even among some officials?

The Great Charter was wrung from King John 700 years ago—but the fight for freedom and human rights is still going on in England itself. How many years will it take for us to fully raise the submerged half of our country?

Friends and fellow-students: China's submerged half has begun to emerge and when you recall that a battalion of Chinese young women was orga-nized and drilled for service in the late revolution, and that a militant woman suffragist used violence towards a deputy of the Nanking Assembly for refusing to vote for woman suffrage, you will agree with me that a part of that half has emerged with a vengeance.

Still, all that is but a beginning. The great mass of the people has yet to be aroused to the necessity for action. The neglect and indifference to women's welfare in the past must be remedied—Not only laws must be passed in the interest of the future mothers of the new Republic, but they must be religiously enforced. Prejudice must be removed and a healthy public sentiment created to support the progressive movement.

In furtherance of such a cause we students should take a leading part. To us girls especially, who are among the first to emerge, will fall the duties of pioneers and, if we do our share, ours will be the honor and the glory.

The welfare of China and possibly its very existence as an independent nation depends on rendering tardy justice to its womankind. For no nation can ever make real and lasting progress in civilization unless its women are following close to its men if not actually abreast with them.

In the fierce struggle for existence among the nations, that nation is badly handicapped which leaves undeveloped one half of its intellectual and moral resources.

If, according to President Lincoln, the Federal Union could not endure half free, half slave, how can China maintain her position among independent nations half free and taught, half shackled in body and in mind?

Glossary

foot-binding: the practice of wrapping women's feet in cloths to inhibit their growth

Great Charter: the Magna Carta, a 1215 royal proclamation in which King John granted a series of rights to English aristocrats and in turn accepted limits on royal power

insurmountable: impossible to overcome

Nanking Assembly: the parliament of the Chinese government after the 1911 revolution

polygamy: marriage to more than one spouse

Short-Answer Questions

1. What were some of the discriminatory customs that the post-1911 Chinese government attempted to end? How did these practices prevent women from gaining equality or equal rights?

2. What is the significance of the Great Charter (Magna Carta) in the address? How does Mabel Ping-Hua Lee use the document from English history to illustrate her points?

3. How would Lee's experiences as a Chinese immigrant in the United States affect her views on her own country? Would she be more, or less, likely to advocate for broader reforms in the United States?

Carrie Chapman Catt: "Equal Suffrage"

Author Carrie Chapman Catt **Date** 1916 **Document Type** Speeches/Addresses	**Significance** Argued in favor of a West Virginia initiative to grant women the right to vote in that state

Overview

As part of the effort to gain the vote, advocates for women's suffrage campaigned to secure the right to vote in state and local elections across the country. Individual states had the authority to enact legislation granting women's suffrage in all balloting, except for national elections. Suffrage leaders believed that if enough states granted women the right to vote, it would be easier to win that right at the national level. One challenge was to convince the men of these states to vote in favor of women's suffrage. Nonetheless, through the 1910s, women won the ability to vote in a succession of states, including Arizona, California, Kansas, Nevada, Oregon, and Montana.

Carrie Chapman Catt was one of the leaders of the struggle for women's suffrage. She served as president of the National American Woman Suffrage Association (NAWSA) on two occasions. Under her leadership, NAWSA undertook successful fundraising campaigns and became better organized and more efficient. One of Catt's strategies was to concentrate on state referendums on suffrage. She and fellow suffrage advocates crisscrossed the country to bolster support for women's voting rights.

On August 3, 1916, Catt spoke to an audience in West Virginia as men in that state prepared to vote in a referendum on whether to grant women the right to vote. She used an example from a small town in Idaho that voted to expand legalized gambling. She told her listeners that most of the men in the community supported the measure to loosen restrictions on gambling, while most women opposed it. Since only men could vote, the initiative passed. However, soon, even the mayor realized the referendum was a mistake and wished that it had not been enacted. Catt argued if women had the vote, the measure would have been defeated and it would have saved the town considerable trouble.

Despite the efforts of Catt and NAWSA, West Virginia voters rejected the proposal to grant women suffrage. Later, however, in March 1920, West Virginia would become the 34th state to ratify the Nineteenth Amendment, which granted women the right to vote.

Document Text

It was my privilege to be present in Idaho when women got the vote, and I visited the town of Caldwell. Nobody thought well of woman suffrage, and I had a little bit of a meeting there, but the town went against it, but the state was carried. Later I had a letter from a friend of mine. They had submitted what we call a local option law for gambling in the state and it was passed by the legislature, so they had a license. I don't know whether you ever had anything like this in the East or not, but there were places where small boys could get a nickel, go in and do a little of this gambling, and become fascinated with it, and it was the dismay of the mothers of their town, and the moment the question came up, what they call the business men of the town circulated petitions reading: "We customers of yours, we buy our goods here, we help you to maintain your business, now you help us to keep ours." And so in one way and another they got the men to sign.

Then the women started a petition, and more nearly than at any instance that I know of that has ever arisen were the women lined up on one side and the men on the other. The men's petition was read first, and it was formulated in the regular way: "We, the undersigned, do hereby pray your honorable body to do this, etc." Then the women's. They had had no opportunity to cast their vote yet, but their petition began: "We, the undersigned voters do hereby demand," and so these two petitions were read, the men's to keep the license, and the women's against it.

The chairman said: "You know last November when I voted against it, and I have never been converted to it until tonight, but so far this is the first time that I know where gamblers came to pray and mother to demand" and the license was taken away.

All the way around the world we find that this is the way to get things. Why, over across the sea in Norway, the women wanted to do a thing for the good of humanity. They said: "If we can only get a home for the poor girls of the streets, we will sell

Carrie Chapman Catt
(Library of Congress)

the productions of their labor, we will save them and the country the disaster of their downfall," and they asked the premier, and every time were told that Norway was too poor, but be it known by all men that whenever a woman sets her mind to do a thing they keep at it until it is done. And so they got the vote. The woman who was head of this movement again sent a note to the premier, saying "We ask a hearing before you and your cabinet in behalf of our measure." The premier replied: "We will grant your hearing, but you needn't bother to come if you don't want to, because we have already selected the lands for the home. We are going to do it anyway, but if you wish to come to the hearing we will be glad to have you."

So you may not see anything to be done in this world. You may like to live in it. You may not like the idea of voting but it is the means by which we are climbing upward. Perhaps when 25,000 years have passed by, we will arrive at a better order. If you want to accomplish anything, you must vote. What is a vote? It is a prayer. There is a political Divinity who hears and who answers prayers, but they are not recorded in the ballot box, and when they are not the prayers of voters, they are not heard nor answered.

It is not a question of right, nor of freedom, but a duty, and I believe that to be the duty of every woman. I ask the men of West Virginia to do this great thing for the women of this state. Across the sea when they crown a king they have a ceremony, and beside the king there is a queen and in a certain point he lifts his crown and touches the queen's head to show that she also shares his power and his honor.

In American every man is a king and every woman is a slave. Gentlemen, we ask you next November to take the crown from your head just a moment and to touch it to the head of the wife by your side, that you may lift her up and seat her upon the throne that you may rule together.

Glossary

petition: a request by voters or citizens for action to be taken on an issue or policy

premier: the leader of a country

suffrage: the right to vote

Short-Answer Questions

1. Why did suffragists concentrate their efforts on securing the right for women to vote at the state level? What were the advantages and disadvantages of this approach?

2. How does Carrie Chapman Catt's example of the vote on gambling in Idaho illustrate the importance of women voting? Why would the issue be one in which women supported one side and men the other?

3. Why does Catt argue that voting is not just a right but a duty? Is she correct? Please explain.

Nineteenth Amendment to the U.S. Constitution

Author Aaron A. Sargen, Susan B. Anthony	**Significance** Granted women in the United States the constitutional the right to vote
Date 1920	
Document Type Legislative	

Overview

After more than a century of activism, women in the United States won the right to vote through the Nineteenth Amendment to the Constitution in 1920. The amendment was initially introduced in Congress in 1878 by Senator Aaron A. Sargent, a Republican from California, who was passing along the measure as written by his friend Susan B. Anthony, who in turn based the language on the Fifteenth Amendment. However, it failed to secure passage after it was defeated in the Senate in 1886. Over the next three decades, the amendment was introduced by others and either blocked from consideration or defeated. For instance, it failed to pass the Senate in both 1913 and 1918. Many members of Congress clung to outdated stereotypes about gender roles, while others were afraid that male voters did not back increased rights for women.

Meanwhile, several states in the West, beginning with Wyoming, granted women the right to vote as support for women's suffrage grew across the country. The National American Woman Suffrage Association led the campaign to gain voting rights for women. In 1912, former president Theodore Roosevelt announced his support for granting women the right to vote as part of his presidential campaign. Then in 1916, Jeannette Rankin became the first women elected to Congress. She served as a member of the House of Representatives from Montana.

Support for suffrage further increased during the U.S. involvement in World War I in 1917 and 1918 as many women took on new responsibilities and roles while a large number of men served in the military. Incumbent president Woodrow Wilson endorsed women's suffrage in 1918 as part of his effort to unite Americans behind the war effort. By the end of the war, fifteen states allowed women to vote.

In May 1919, the Nineteenth Amendment was reintroduced in Congress. The measure passed the House on a vote of 304 to 89 on May 21. The Senate approved the measure on June 4, on a vote of 56–25. Although Congress had approved the measure, the amendment required the endorsement of two-thirds of the states to become law. Tennessee was the 36th state to ratify the amendment on August 18. The amendment then became part of the Constitution on August 26. Despite the passage of the Nineteenth Amendment, women would continue to struggle for full political equality into the twenty-first century.

Document Text

The right of citizens of the United States to vote shall not be denied or abridged by the United States or by any State on account of sex.

Congress shall have power to enforce this article by appropriate legislation.

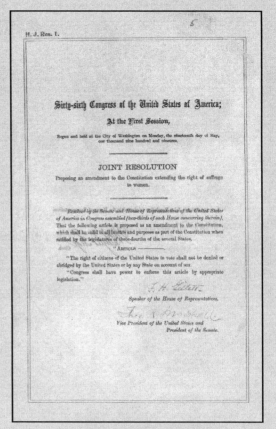

The Nineteenth Amendment
(National Archives)

Glossary

abridged: restricted or constrained

suffrage: the right to vote

Short-Answer Questions

1. Why did it take so long for women to secure the right to vote in the United States? What were the main obstacles women faced in their struggle to gain suffrage?

2. What were some of the factors that increased support for the Nineteenth Amendment in the early 1900s?

3. Why did the amendment grant Congress, and not the executive branch, the authority to oversee suffrage? Why did the framers of the amendment foresee that there might be a need for additional laws to secure the right to vote for women?

William Pickens: "The Woman Voter Hits the Color Line"

Author William Pickens	**Significance** Highlighted the troubles Black women faced when attempting to register to vote after the passage of the Nineteenth Amendment
Date 1920	
Document Type Essays, Reports, Manifestos	

Overview

William Pickens (1881–1954), the son of freed slaves, was an American orator, educator, journalist, and essayist who produced numerous publications during his lifetime. His academic and professional work centered on the African American experience throughout the nation's history. Pickens was also an active and vocal member of the National Association for the Advancement of Colored People (NAACP). Late in his life, he was the director of the interracial section of the Treasury Department's Saving Bonds Division, where he worked to sell World War II bonds to a largely Black audience. His article "The Woman Voter Hits the Color Line" examines events in his home state of South Carolina after the passage of the Nineteenth Amendment.

Document Text

The Nineteenth Amendment has become the law of the land and it is constitutionally possible for twenty-five million women to vote. How many of these will actually vote? Three million are colored, and more than three fourths of them live below Mason and Dixon's Line. There the colored man has been cheated out of nine-tenths of his votes, and only a small proportion of the white men vote because of the indirect reaction of this political dishonesty. Will the colored women of the South be similarly shut out? The recent registration of voters in South Carolina may be taken as a fair example, as this State has been ever representative of the South. In common with other Southern States, it has, by administration and manipulation of suffrage laws, practically nullified the Fourteenth and Fifteenth amendments, which enfranchised colored men. The black race slightly outnumbers the white in South Carolina, and colored women outnumber colored men. The colored woman is accordingly the largest class in the State, and her right to vote gives a new concern to the maintainers of "white supremacy." . . .

On the first day of the registration in September the colored women who presented themselves evidently took the registrars by surprise, as the latter seemed to have no concerted plan for dealing with colored women except to register them like the white women; and this they were doing without any test or question whatsoever, save such necessary inquiries as to name, age and residence. The registrars had evidently believed that few colored women would have the nerve to attempt to register, and there was visible disappointment when many colored women, bright and intelligent, in some cases armed with the necessary tax receipt, appeared the first day. While there was apparently no preconcerted plan not to register them, one ready-made discrimination of the South was freely used, that of "white people first." The registrars would keep numbers of colored women standing for hours while they registered every white person in sight, man or woman, even the late-comers. . . . Yet many of these colored women bravely stayed and patiently stood from 11:30 in the morning till 8:00 at night in order to register to vote! The attitude and the disappointed calculation of the white men can be best expressed by quoting one of them: "Who stirred up all these colored women to come up here and register?" Such persistent courage, however, was too ominous to the white registrars, the guardians of racial supremacy and party success; for although they seemed to have no plan of repulse for the first day, they evidently held a council of war at night—and things looked different on the morrow. . . .

One can register if one pays taxes on at least three hundred dollars' worth of property, or can read from the State or the Federal Constitution some

William Pickens
(Library of Congress)

passage selected by the registrar. It would seem the purpose of such a law merely to determine the general fitness and intelligence of the candidate, or to make a bona fide test of his literacy. . . .

Well educated colored women were denied the right to register. Some of the questions actually put to the inexperienced colored applicant were: "Explain a mandamus." "Define civil code." "How would you appeal a case?" "If presidential votes are tied, how would you break the tie?" "How much revenue did the State hospital pay the State last year?" "How much revenue does the Baptist Church pay the State?" South Carolina law requires only that one shall read, and not the passing of any examination in law or civil government. If a colored woman mispronounced a word in the opinion of the half-educated registrar, she was disqualified. . . .

Every method has been employed against the colored man, up to "red shirt," "Ku Klux" campaigns and less picturesque but equally forceful terrorism. In some districts a colored man seals his death warrant by even attempting to register. Nothing in the code of "Southern chivalry" will prevent similar treatment of colored women. Will the women of the United States who know something at least of disfranchisement tolerate such methods to prevent intelligent colored women from voting?

Glossary

civil code: a codification of private law relating to property, family, and obligations

"Ku Klux" campaigns: referring to the Ku Klux Klan, a white supremacist organization, formed in 1866, that mounted a campaign of violence and intimidation against African Americans, Jews, and others

morrow: referring to next day

mandamus: a judicial writ issued as a command to an inferior court or ordering a person to perform a public or statutory duty

"red shirt": a Democratic Party paramilitary group that emerged in South Carolina during the late nineteenth century; members wore red shirts as a uniform and carried weapons to intimidate Black voters

Short-Answer Questions

1. What did the Nineteenth Amendment do? How did it threaten the maintainers of "white supremacy" in South Carolina?

2. Pickens describes the different treatment that Black women received in comparison to their white counterparts. Briefly explain what the registrars did to get around the Nineteenth Amendment. How did measures of wealth or intelligence play a role?

3. Pickens makes it clear that "Southern chivalry" would not protect Black women. However, he issues a question to white women. What is it? Why does he mention disfranchisement?

Alice Moore Dunbar-Nelson: "The Negro Woman and the Ballot"

Author	Significance
Alice Moore Dunbar-Nelson	Argued that Black women needed to exercise their voting power by voting in their best interests, resisting outside pressures from men and the Republican Party
Date	
1927	
Document Type	
Essays, Reports, Manifestos	

Overview

In 1927 the writer, educator, and activist Alice Moore Dunbar-Nelson published an article titled "The Negro Woman and the Ballot" in the African American magazine *The Messenger*. In the article, she posed the question, "What have Black women done with their vote?" Dunbar-Nelson believed that Black women had not accomplished nearly enough since their enfranchisement in 1920. She encouraged them to start exercising their power as voters without bowing to pressure from their male peers or remaining loyal to the Republican Party, which at that time held the allegiance of most Black Americans. She noted that Af-

rican American women had already demonstrated their power as a group in the congressional elections of 1922, in which their votes had helped oust Republican legislators in Delaware, New Jersey, and Michigan who had failed to support the anti-lynching legislation known as the Dyer Bill. Dunbar-Nelson noted that if Black women realized that their children's futures could be helped or hindered by the way they voted, perhaps they would set aside allegiance to the Republican Party and use their ballot power to improve the condition of all African Americans.

Document Text

It has been six years since the franchise as a national measure has been granted women. The Negro woman has had the ballot in conjunction with her white sister, and friend and foe alike are asking the question, What has she done with it?

Six years is a very short time in which to ask for results from any measure or condition, no matter how simple. In six years a human being is barely able to make itself intelligible to listeners; is a feeble, puny thing at best, with undeveloped understanding, no power of reasoning, with a slight contributory value to the human race, except in a sentimental fashion. Nations in six years are but the beginnings of an idea. It is barely possible to erect a structure of any permanent value in six years, and only the most ephemeral trees have reached any size in six years. . . .

It has been six years since the franchise as a national measure has been granted women. The Negro woman has had the ballot in conjunction with her white sister, and friend and foe alike are asking the question, What has she done with it?

Six years is a very short time in which to ask for results from any measure or condition, no matter how simple. In six years a human being is barely able to make itself intelligible to listeners; is a feeble, puny thing at best, with undeveloped understanding, no power of reasoning, with a slight contributory value to the human race, except in a sentimental fashion. Nations in six years are but the beginnings of an idea. It is barely possible to erect a structure of any permanent value in six years, and only the most ephemeral trees have reached any size in six years. . . . Cheap political office and little political preferment had dazzled their eyes so that they could not see the great issues affecting the race. They had been fooled by specious lies, fair promises and large-sounding words. Pre-election promises had inflated their chests, so that they could not see the post-election failures at their feet. . . .

But all that is neither here nor there. The Negro woman got the vote along with some tens of million other women in the country. And has it made any appreciable difference in the status of the race? . . . The Negro woman was going to be independent, she had averred. She came into the political game with a clean slate. No Civil War memories for her, and no deadening sense of gratitude to influence her vote. She would vote men and measures, not parties. She could scan each candidate's record and give him her support according to how he had stood in the past on the question of race. She owed no party allegiance. The name of Abraham Lincoln was not synonymous with her for blind G.O.P. allegiance. She would show the Negro man how to make his vote a power, and not a joke. She would break up the tradition that one could tell a Black man's politics by the color of his skin.

And when she got the ballot she slipped quietly, safely, easily, and conservatively into the political party of her male relatives. . . .

In other words the Negro woman has by and large been a disappointment in her handling of the ballot. She has added to the overhead charges of the political machinery, without solving racial problems. . . .

As the younger generation becomes of age it is apt to be independent in thought and in act. But it is soon whipped into line by the elders, and by the promise of plums of preferment or of an amicable position in the community or of easy social relations—for we still persecute socially those who disagree with us politically. What is true of the men is true of the women. The very young is apt to let father, sweetheart, brother, or uncle decide her vote. . . .

Whether women have been influenced and corrupted by their male relatives and friends is a moot question. . . .

All this is rather a gloomy presentment of a well-known situation. But it is not altogether hopeless.

The fact that the Negro woman CAN be roused when something near and dear to her is touched and threatened is cheering. Then she throws off the influence of her male companion and strikes out for herself. Whatever the Negro may hope to gain for himself must be won at the ballot box, and quiet "going along" will never gain his end.

When the Negro woman finds that the future of her children lies in her own hands—if she can be made to see this—she will strike off the political shackles she has allowed to be hung upon her, and win the economic freedom of her race.

Perhaps some Joan of Arc will lead the way.

Glossary

averred: asserted or affirmed with confidence

cajoled: persuaded (someone) to do something by sustained coaxing or flattery

ephemeral tree: tree that has a short life cycle

puny: small and weak

Short-Answer Questions

1. The author asserts that African American women have "by and large been a disappointment in her handling of the ballot." What are her reasons for saying this?

2. Why is the author critical of the excuses used by African American women to explain why they are hesitant to vote?

3. What reasons does the author give to explain why the time is now for African American women to exercise their voting power?

Eleanor Roosevelt: "Women Must Learn to Play the Game as Men Do"

Author
Eleanor Roosevelt

Date
1928

Document Type
Essays, Reports, Manifestos

Significance
Highlighted, to readers of a popular ladies' magazine, the necessity for women to seek political office, support female candidates, and adopt the strategies that men used to gain political power

Overview

Eleanor Roosevelt (1884–1962) was arguably the most active and outspoken of the nation's First Ladies, one who hurled herself into the national political arena and into international issues such as human rights. The more she observed the welter of events through which she lived, the more roles she assumed and the more articulate, more public, and more insistent her voice became. In the process, she used a wide variety of media, including print, radio, film, and television, to make her case, generating twenty-seven books, more than eight thousand columns, over 550 articles, and an average of seventy-five lectures a year. Her 1928 article "Women Must Learn to Play the Game as Men Do," written five years before she became First Lady and published in the popular ladies' magazine *Red Book*, gives insight into her views of the role of women in politics. She argues for party-based organization at all levels and states that women have a both "right and duty in political life."

Roosevelt writes that even though the nation's political parties actively seek the votes of women, they actually discourage female participation in the party leadership bodies. This occurs even though the parties claim, falsely, to seek women for top roles. The future First Lady highlights some of the stereotypical excuses male party members give to justify their discrimination. These justifications typically reveal outdated and prejudicial views of women.

Roosevelt argues that women need to do several things to overcome these obstacles. First, women need to seek elected office and leadership positions in the parties. Second, to accomplish the first goal, women need to support female candidates for those positions. Finally, women need to adopt the tactics and strategies that men use within the parties. This might mean abandoning some of the expectations of society about how women are supposed to behave. However, if women are going to compete with men, they have to approach politics the way men do.

Document Text

Women have been voting for ten years. But have they achieved actual political equality with men? No. They go through the gesture of going to the polls; their votes are solicited by politicians; and they possess the external aspect of equal rights. But it is mostly a gesture without real power. With some outstanding exceptions, women who have gone into politics are refused serious consideration by the men leaders. Generally they are treated most courteously, to be sure, but what they want, what they have to say, is regarded as of little weight. In fact, they have no actual influence or say at all in the consequential councils of their parties. . . .

In those circles which decide the affairs of national politics, women have no voice or power whatever. On the national committee of each party there is a woman representative from every State, and a woman appears as vice-chairman. Before national elections they will be told to organize the women throughout the United States, and asked to help in minor ways in raising funds. But when it comes to those grave councils at which possible candidates are discussed, as well as party policies, they are rarely invited in. At the national conventions no woman has ever been asked to serve on the platform committee. . . .

The machinery of party politics has always been in the hands of men, and still is. Our statesmen and legislators are still keeping in form as the successors of the early warriors gathering around the campfire plotting the next day's attack. Yes, they have made feints indicating they are willing to let the women into the high councils of the parties. But, in fact, the women who have gone into the political game will tell you they are excluded from any actual kind of important participation. They are called upon to produce votes, but they are kept in ignorance of noteworthy plans and affairs. Their requests are seldom refused outright, but they are put off with a technique that is an art in itself. The fact is that generally women are not taken seriously. With certain exceptions, men still as a class dismiss their consequence and value

Eleanor Roosevelt in 1933
(Library of Congress)

in politics, cherishing the old-fashioned concept that their place is in the home. . . .

Beneath the veneer of courtesy and outward show of consideration universally accorded women, there is a widespread male hostility—age-old, perhaps—against sharing with them any actual control.

How many excuses haven't I heard for not giving nominations to women! "Oh, she wouldn't like the kind of work she'd have to do!" Or, "You know she wouldn't like the people she'd have to associate with—that's not a job for a nice, refined woman." Or more usually: "You see, there is so little patronage nowadays. We must give every appointment the most careful consideration. We've got to consider the good of the party." "The good of the party" eliminates women!

When no women are present at the meetings, the leaders are more outspoken. "No, we're not going to have any woman on the ticket," declared one leader according to a report once made to me. . . .

It is a strong and liberal man, indeed, who speaks on behalf of the women at those secret conclaves, and endeavors to have them fairly treated.

To many women who fought so long and so valiantly for suffrage, what has happened has been most discouraging. For one reason or another, most of the leaders who carried the early fight to success have dropped out of politics. This has been in many ways unfortunate. Among them were women with gifts of real leadership. They were exceptional and high types of women, idealists concerned in carrying a cause to victory, with no idea of personal advancement or gain. In fact, attaining the vote was only part of a program for equal rights—an external gesture toward economic independence, and social and spiritual equality with men. . . .

How, then, can we bring the men leaders to concede participation in party affairs, adequate representation and real political equality?

Our means is to elect, accept and back women political bosses. . . .

If women believe they have a right and duty in political life today, they must learn to talk the language of men. They must not only master the phraseology, but also understand the machinery which men have built up through years of practical experience. Against the men bosses there must be women bosses who can talk as equals, with the backing of a coherent organization of women voters behind them. . . .

I should not want the average woman, or the exceptional woman for that matter, who for one reason or another could not do a public job well, to take one at present. For just now a woman must do better than a man, for whatever she does in the public eye reflects on the whole cause of women. There are women in the United States I would gladly see run for any office. But if we cannot have the best I should prefer to wait and prepare a little longer until women are more ready to make a fine contribution to public life in any office they might hold. . . .

Certain women profess to be horrified at the thought of women bosses bartering and dickering in the hard game of politics with men. But many more women realize that we are living in a material world, and that politics cannot be played from the clouds. To sum up, women must learn to play the game as men do. If they go into politics, they must stick to their jobs, respect the time and work of others, master a knowledge of history and human nature, learn diplomacy, subordinate their likes and dislikes of the moment and choose leaders to act for them and to whom they will be loyal. They can keep their ideals; but they must face facts and deal with them practically.

Glossary

conclaves: secret meetings

feints: deceptive moves

idealist: a person whose life is guided by abstract principles and goals

material: physical; earthly

phraseology: the words, sayings, or expressions of speech of a particular group

platform committee: the central body of a political party that decides policy and strategy for elections

veneer: behavior that hides a person's real motives or objectives

Short-Answer Questions

1. What were some of the ways that political parties took advantage of women in the 1920s? What tactics did the parties use to make it appear that they valued the input and interests of women?

2. What were some of the excuses men in U.S. political parties used to justify discrimination against women? What was the basis for many of these justifications?

3. What steps did Roosevelt argue were necessary for women to gain access to political power and influence within the parties? How did she suggest they be implemented?

The Schlager Anthology of Women's History

A Student's Guide to Essential Primary Sources

The Schlager Anthology of Women's History

A Student's Guide to Essential Primary Sources

Kelli McCoy
Editor in Chief

Dallas, TX

The Schlager Anthology of Women's History:
A Student's Guide to Essential Primary Sources

Schlager Group Inc.
10228 E. Northwest HWY, STE 1151
Dallas, TX 75238
USA
(888) 416-5727
info@schlagergroup.com

You can find Schlager Group online at https://www.schlagergroup.com

For Schlager Group:
Vice President, Editorial: Sarah Robertson
Vice President, Operations and Strategy: Benjamin Painter
Founder and President: Neil Schlager

Printed in the United States of America 10 9 8 7 6 5 4 3 2 1
Print ISBN: 9781961844018
eBook: 9781961844025

Library of Congress Control Number: 2023947236

Contents

Volume 2

Volume 3

The Schlager Anthology of Women's History

A Student's Guide to Essential Primary Sources

Chapter 7

Women's Reform and Justice Movements in the United States

During the 1800s and 1900s, American women embraced a variety of reform and justice movements. Some of the efforts were intertwined with feminism, while others addressed other longstanding societal problems. The priorities of these campaigns evolved and changed over time as the movements achieved success or adopted new objectives. Ultimately, the success of many of these movements depended on the leadership and support of American women, who embraced the need for fundamental societal changes to move closer to the goal of full equality.

Public Education and Educational Reform

Educational reform was one of the early priorities for U.S. women in the late 1700s and early 1800s. Male and female reformers sought to expand educational opportunities for young Americans through the establishment of a system of public education. However, women were particularly interested in ensuring that young girls were not constrained by educational systems that emphasized traditional female roles. For instance, in a series of lectures in the early 1800s, Scottish feminist author Frances Wright urged Americans to allow girls

the right to "free enquiry" or free thought so that women could develop their intellects to the same degree as men. Wright and many early feminists argued that disparities in education between males and females resulted in a male-dominated society in which women were treated as inferiors. To build a society that made full use of the talents and skills of all of its citizens, female reformers struggled to secure equality for all, both men and women.

Women Leaders in the Abolition Movement

The goal of equality led many early feminists to support the abolition of slavery and other changes to ensure that African Americans were treated the same as other races in the United States. In the aftermath of the American Revolution, the northern states abolished slavery. For many Americans, the principles of the revolution, including the idea that "all men are created equal," could not be reconciled with slavery. However, slavery remained legal in the South. Feminist abolitionists such as Lucretia Mott played a major role in the struggle to end the institution. Mott also emerged as a leader in the suffrage movement, demonstrating the links between the two efforts. Many notable figures in women's rights movements believed that females could not gain full equality, including the right to vote, until all men had equal opportunities. Feminist leaders such as the author Lydia Maria Childs campaigned vigorously for the abolition of slavery. Childs's 1833 work, *An Appeal in Favor of That Class of Americans Called Africans,* denounced slavery and highlighted the inequalities of education for African Americans at the time. In 1861 Childs published Harriet Jacobs's narrative, *Incidents in the Life of a Slave Girl,* which recounted the many abuses that the author faced while she was a slave.

Even after slavery was abolished in 1865 through the Thirteenth Amendment, women's rights advocates continued to campaign against racial discrimination. The abolition movement evolved into a broader effort to secure civil rights and end legal forms of racial discrimination. Ida B. Wells emerged as one of the foremost advocates for African American equality in the late 1800s and early 1900s through works such as *Southern Horrors: Lynch Law in All its Phases* (1898) and her famous speech "Lynching: Our National Crime" (1909). Wells was not afraid to criticize her fellow feminists when they engaged in racist speech or supported racist laws or policies. As such, she was a champion of both women's rights and African American rights. The work of women's groups in the 1800s laid the foundation for the modern civil rights movement of the 1900s.

Jane Addams, Nellie Bly, Clara Barton, and Rachel Carson

Even as the main focus of women's rights groups in the late 1800s remained suffrage, women also led campaigns to improve the social conditions of Americans. For instance, Jane Addams, who won the Nobel Peace Prize in 1931, endeavored to draw attention to the need for better housing for the indigent, along with more training and education for those who were displaced. Meanwhile, journalist Elizabeth Cochran Seaman (better known as "Nellie Bly") attempted to expose the problems and abuses at mental health facilities in the late 1800s in her work *Ten Days in a Mad-House* (Bly

had gone undercover at an asylum). Bly helped permanently change the way people with mental illnesses were treated. Meanwhile, Clara Barton's experiences in the Civil War led her to create the American Red Cross to provide assistance during crises and disasters. The Red Cross emerged as one of the most significant humanitarian organizations in modern history, as Barton detailed in her 1898 work, *The Red Cross in War and Peace.*

As part of the effort to gain full equality for females, women's rights leaders embraced temperance, a ban on the sale and consumption of alcohol. Some in the temperance movement naively believed that the root of sexism among males was alcoholism, while others condemned alcohol as the cause for physical or emotional abuse toward women and as a cause for financial problems. Frances Willard discussed the arguments in favor of prohibition of alcohol in a speech before the Women's Christian Temperance Union (WCTU). Founded in 1873, the WTCU played a major role in the passage in 1919 of the Eighteenth Amendment, which prohibited the sale of alcohol in the United States. That amendment was overturned by the Twenty-first Amendment in 1933, after prohibition proved to be unpopular and difficult to enforce (prohibition was also associated with a rise in organized crime).

In 1962 Rachel Carson published her book *Silent Spring.* The book helped launch the modern environmental movement in the United States. Carson highlighted the problems associated with the widespread use of chemical pesticides. *Silent Spring* helped make Americans aware of the importance of the environment and the need for government action to protect natural spaces and both plant and animal species. It also helped create the momentum that culminated in the creation of government bodies such as establishment in 1970 of the Environmental Protection Agency (EPA), the federal organization that oversees environmental policy. Contemporary efforts to combat climate change trace their roots to Carson's work and her attempts to educate Americans on environmental issues.

Further Reading

Books

Bay, Mia. *To Tell the Truth Freely: The Life of Ida B. Wells.* New York: Hill & Wang, 2009.

Berg, Barbara J. *The Remembered Gate: The Origins of American Feminism—The Woman and the City, 1800–1860.* New York: Oxford University Press, 1980.

Berson, Robin Kadison. *Jane Addams: A Biography.* Westport, CT: Greenwood Press, 2004.

Blocker, Jack S. *American Temperance Movements: Cycles of Reform.* Boston: Twayne Publishers, 1989.

Ginzberg, Lori D. *Women and the Work of Benevolence: Morality, Politics, and Class in the Nineteenth-Century United States.* New Haven, CT: Yale University Press, 1990.

Hunter, Tera W. *To Joy My Freedom: Southern Black Women's Lives and Labors after the Civil War.* Cambridge, MA: Harvard University Press, 1997.

Karcher, Carolyn L. *The First Woman in the Republic: A Cultural Biography of Lydia Maria Child.* Durham, NC: Duke University Press, 1994.

Kroeger, Brooke. *Nellie Bly: Daredevil, Reporter, Feminist.* New York: Three Rivers Press, 1994.

Lytle, Mark Hamilton. *The Gentle Subversive: Rachel Carson, Silent Spring, and the Rise of the Environmental Movement.* New York: Oxford University Press, 2007.

Ross, Ishbel. *Angel of the Battlefield: The Life of Clara Barton.* New York: Harper and Brothers Publishers, 1956.

Salerno, Beth A. *Sister Societies: Women's Antislavery Organizations in Antebellum America.* DeKalb: Northern Illinois University Press, 2005.

Schechter, Patricia. *Ida B. Wells–Barnett and American Reform: 1880–1930.* Chapel Hill: University of North Carolina Press, 2003.

Articles

Dannenbaum, Jed. "The Origins of Temperance Activism and Militancy among American Women." *Journal of Social History* 14 (1981).

Gidlow, Liette. "The Sequel: The Fifteenth Amendment, the Nineteenth Amendment, and Southern Black Women's Struggle to Vote." *Journal of the Gilded Age and Progressive Era* 17 (July 2018).

Shields, Patricia M. "Democracy and the Social Feminist Ethics of Jane Addams: A Vision for Public Administration." *Administrative Theory & Praxis* 28, no. 3 (September 2006).

Further Reading

Websites

"Clara Barton: Visionary Leader and Founder of the American Red Cross." American Red Cross website, accessed September 1, 2023, https://www.redcross.org/about-us/who-we-are/history/clara-barton.html.

Lear, Linda. "The Life and Legacy of Rachel Carson." Rachel Carson website, accessed September 1, 2023, https://www.rachelcarson.org/.

"Women's Rights Emerges within the Abolitionist Movement." National Women's History Museum website, accessed September 1, 2023, https://www.crusadeforthevote.org/abolition.

Frances Wright:
"Of Free Enquiry"

Author	Significance
Frances Wright	Called for gender equality at a time when women faced widespread discrimination
Date	
1828	
Document Type	
Speeches/Addresses	

Overview

Frances Wright was born in Scotland in 1795 and settled in the United States in 1824. She became a U.S. citizen the following year. By that point, Wright was already famous in France and England as an advocate for women's equality. She was also a staunch opponent of slavery and a proponent of public education. Many of her ideas were considered radical at the time, and Wright often faced criticism and hostility from conservative segments of society.

Wright was a gifted author who wrote works on politic, equality, and religion. To garner public support for gender equality and the abolition of slavery, she embarked on a series of speaking engagements in 1828. Her addresses were later collected as essays in the book *Course of Public Lectures as Delivered by Frances Wright* (1829).

Wright presented her lecture "Of Free Enquiry" in several cities in 1828, including New York, Baltimore, and Philadelphia. Her speech called for equality between men and women. Wright asserted that a society could not progress or improve if half of its population was unequal to the other half. She dismissed the idea that the United States was a republic where the people held political power. She also called into question the principle of equality as one of the nation's core values. Instead, the strident feminist noted that the United States was highly unequal because of gender and racial prejudices. In addition, the wealthy had numerous advantages over the average person. The result was that a small group of people dominated the country.

To overcome the power of elites, Wright emphasized the importance of education for all people. She argued that the right to education and free thought was the main way to reduce inequality. In her address, she also contended that the contemporary system of education in the United States at the time was unfair and unequal because the rich were able to attend more advanced schools that had better funding. Wright concluded by asserting that the divisions within society would eventually result in strife and conflict. Therefore, only by granting equal educational opportunities to all people could the nation progress and grow in a healthy manner.

Frances Wright
(Wikimedia Commons)

Document Text

However novel it may appear, I shall venture the assertion, that, until women assume the place in society which good sense and good feeling alike assign to them, human improvement must advance but feebly. It is in vain that we would circumscribe the power of one half of our race, and that half by far the most important and influential. If they exert it not for good, they will for evil; if they advance not knowledge, they will perpetuate ignorance. Let women stand where they may in the scale of improvement, their position decides that of the race. Are they cultivated?—so is society polished and enlightened. Are they ignorant?—so is it gross and insipid. Are they wise?—so is the human condition prosperous. Are they foolish?—so is it unstable and unpromising. Are they free?—so is the human character elevated. Are they enslaved?—so is the whole race degraded. . . .

It is my object to show, that, before we can engage successfully in the work of enquiry, we must engage in a body; we must engage collectively; as human beings desirous of attaining the highest excellence of which our nature is capable; as children of one family, anxious to discover the true and the useful for the common advantage of all. It is my farther object to show that no co-operation in this matter can be effective which does not embrace the two sexes on a footing of equality; and, again, that no co-operation in this matter can be effective, which does not embrace human beings on a footing of equality. Is this a republic—a country whose affairs are governed by the public voice—while the public mind is unequally enlightened? Is this a republic, where the interests of the many keep in check those of the few—while the few hold possession of the courts of knowledge, and the many stand as suitors at the door? Is this a republic, where the rights of all are equally respected, the interests of all equally secured, the ambitions of all equally regulated, the services of all equally rendered? Is this such a republic—while we see endowed colleges for the rich, and barely common schools for the poor; while but one drop of colored blood shall stamp a fellow creature for a slave, or, at the least, degrade him below sympathy; and while one half of the whole population is left in civil bondage, and, as it were, sentenced to mental imbecility?

Let us pause to enquire if this be consistent with the being of a republic. Without knowledge, could your fathers have conquered liberty? and without knowledge, can you retain it? Equality! where is it, if not in education? Equal rights! they cannot exist without equality of instruction. "All men are born free and equal!" they are indeed so born, but do they so live? Are they educated as equals? and, if not, can they be equal? and, if not equal, can they be free? Do not the rich command instruction? and they who have instruction, must they not possess the power? and when they have the power, will they not exert it in their own favor? I will ask more; I will ask, do they not exert it in their own favor? I will ask if two professions do not now rule the land and its inhabitants? I will ask, whether your legislatures are not governed by lawyers and your households by priests? And I will farther ask, whether the deficient instruction of the mass of your population does not give to lawyers their political ascendancy; and whether the ignorance of women be not the cause that your domestic hearths are invaded by priests? . . .

Your political institutions have taken equality for their basis; your declaration of rights, upon which your institutions rest, sets forth this principle as vital and inviolate. Equality is the soul of liberty; there is, in fact, no liberty without it—none that cannot be overthrown by the violence of ignorant anarchy, or sapped by the subtilty of professional craft. That this is the case your reasons will admit; that this is the case your feelings do admit—even those which are the least amiable and the least praiseworthy. The jealousy betrayed by the uncultivated against those of more polished address and manners, has its source in the beneficial principle to which we advert, however, (in this, as in many other cases,) misconceived and perverted. Cultivation of mind will ever lighten the countenance and polish the exterior. This external superiority, which is but a faint emanation of the superiority within, vulgar eyes can see and ignorant jealousy will resent. This, in a republic, leads to brutality; and, in aristocracies, where this jealously is restrained by fear, to servility. Here it will lead the wagoner to dispute the road with a carriage; and, in Europe, will make the foot passenger doff his hat to the lordly equipage which spatters him with mud, while there he mutters curses only in his heart. The unreasoning observer will refer the conduct of the first to the republican institutions—the reflecting observer, to the anti-republican education. The instruction befitting free men is that which gives the sun of knowledge to shine on all; and which at once secures the liberties of each individual, and disposes each individual to make a proper use of them.

Glossary

aristocracies: governments ruled by a small group, often based on heredity

bondage: slavery

circumscribe: to restrict or limit

common schools: public schools with limited budgets and resources

endowed colleges: elite institutions of higher learning funded by wealthy donors

imbecility: a lack of intelligence

republic: a form of government in which the people elect representatives to make decisions for them, constrained by a constitution or other basic set of laws

Short-Answer Questions

1. Why is education so important, according to Frances Wright? How are education and equality related? Did the United States have an equal system of education in the 1800s?

2. According to the address, which two professions dominated contemporary U.S. society? Why did these occupations exert so much power over government and the home?

3. How could the inequalities in U.S. society lead to strife in the country? What could be done to reduce the potential for conflict?

Lydia Maria Child:
An Appeal in Favor of That Class of Americans Called Africans

---

Author
Lydia Maria Child

Date
1833

Type
Essays, Reports, Manifestos

Significance
Offered a blistering critique of slavery that shocked many readers by insisting upon abolishing slavery without further delay, making formerly enslaved people U.S. citizens, and granting mixed-race marriages

---

Overview

The daughter of white Massachusetts abolitionists, Lydia Maria Child deepened her commitment to the elimination of slavery upon making the acquaintance of famed abolitionist leader William Lloyd Garrison in 1831. Already a successful and esteemed author of historical novels, Child drew upon her writing skills to better educate the northern population about the evils of slavery and further the cause of abolition. To this end, in 1833 she produced *An Appeal in Favor of That Class of Americans Called Africans*, her most well-known work, which serves as both a history of slavery in America and a fierce condemnation of it. Reflecting the outlook of Garrison, the book calls for the immediate cessation of slavery rather than a gradual one, as recommended by more cautious abolitionists. While the controversial nature of the book cost Child a significant portion of her readership, it had the intended effect of informing many white people of the insidiousness of slavery and furthering the cause of abolitionism. This passage, from chapter eight, questions why laws existed throughout the country that prohibited marriages between individuals identified as members of different races.

Engraving of Lydia Maria Child
(Wikimedia Commons)

Document Text

While we bestow our earnest disapprobation on the system of slavery, let us not flatter ourselves that we are in reality any better than our brethren of the South. Thanks to our soil and climate, and the early exertions of the Quakers, the *form* of slavery does not exist among us; but the very spirit of the hateful and mischievous thing is here in all its strength. The manner in which we use what power we have, gives us ample reason to be grateful that the nature of our institutions does not intrust us with more. Our prejudice against colored people is even more inveterate than it is at the South. The planter is often attached to his negroes, and lavishes caresses and kind words upon them, as he would on a favorite hound: but our cold-hearted, ignoble prejudice admits of no exception—no intermission.

The Southerners have long continued habit, apparent interest and dreaded danger, to palliate the wrong they do; but we stand without excuse. They tell us that Northern ships and Northern capital have been engaged in this wicked business; and the reproach is true. Several fortunes in this city have been made by the sale of negro blood. If these criminal transactions are still carried on, they are done in silence and secrecy, because public opinion has made them disgraceful. But if the free States wished to cherish the system of slavery forever, they could not take a more direct course than they now do. Those who are kind and liberal on all other subjects, unite with the selfish and the proud in their unrelenting efforts to keep the colored population in the lowest state of degradation; and the influence they unconsciously exert over children early infuses into their innocent minds the same strong feelings of contempt.

The intelligent and well informed have the least share of this prejudice; and when their minds can be brought to reflect upon it, I have generally observed that they soon cease to have any at all. But such a general apathy prevails and the subject is so seldom brought into view, that few are really aware how oppressively the influence of society is made to bear upon this injured class of the community. When I have related facts, that came under my own observation, I have often been listened to with surprise, which gradually increased to indignation. In order that my readers may not be ignorant of the extent of this tyrannical prejudice, I will as briefly as possible state the evidence, and leave them to judge of it, as their hearts and consciences may dictate.

In the first place, an unjust law exists in this Commonwealth, by which marriages between persons of different color is pronounced illegal. And while this injustice exists with regard to honest, industrious individuals, who are merely guilty of differing from us in a matter of taste, neither the legislation nor customs of slave-holding States exert their influence against *immoral* connexions.

In one portion of our country this fact is shown in a very peculiar and striking manner. There is a numerous class at New Orleans, called Quateroons, or Quadroons, because their colored blood has for several successive generations been intermingled with the white. The women are much distinguished for personal beauty and gracefulness of motion; and their parents frequently send them to France for the advantages of an elegant education. White gentlemen of the first rank are desirous of being invited to their parties, and often become seriously in love with these fascinating but unfortunate beings. Prejudice forbids matrimony, but universal custom sanctions temporary connexions, to which a certain degree of respectability is allowed, on account of the peculiar situation of the parties. These attachments often continue for years—sometimes for life—and instances are not unfrequent of exemplary constancy and great propriety of deportment.

What eloquent vituperations we should pour forth, if the contending claims of nature and pride produced such a tissue of contradictions in some other country, and not in our own!

Glossary

disapprobation: condemnation or disapproval

ignoble: disgraceful, immoral

palliate: to ease the symptoms of an illness

Quakers: religious sect founded in England in the mid-1600s committed to peace and abolition that established communities in colonial America

Quateroons/Quadroons: individuals who are one-quarter Black and three-quarters white

vituperations: condemnations, criticisms

Short-Answer Questions

1. Why does Child consider people living in the North, where slavery was illegal, to be just as culpable for the horrors of slavery as southerners?

2. What is Child's approach to condemning restrictions on marriages between individuals identified as belonging to different races?

3. What aspects of Child's positions on slavery and race might have seemed particularly radical in the early 1830s?

Harriet Jacobs:
Incidents in the Life of a Slave Girl

Author
Harriet Jacobs

Date
1861

Type
Essays, Reports, Manifestos

Significance
Demonstrates the impact of the 1850 Fugitive Slave Law on self-emancipated men and women in the northern states

Overview

Harriet Jacobs's *Incidents in the Life of a Slave Girl: Written by Herself* (1861) is a personal narrative published as the author was approaching fifty years of age on the cusp of the Civil War. Jacobs was born enslaved in North Carolina, but she managed to escape and gain her freedom as well as the freedom of her two children. While the book is autobiographical, it changes the names of the participants, with Jacobs writing under the pseudonym Linda Brent. Her narrative details her life as a young enslaved girl, focusing on the unrelenting sexual advances she endured from her enslaver. She surveys the time that she spent as a fugitive, including seven years hiding in her grandmother's attic.

In detailing her time spent in the North while she was still a fugitive, she emphasizes her efforts to keep her children, who were born into slavery, out of the hands of slave catchers.

The book originally began appearing in serial form in the *New York Tribune*, a newspaper edited by the abolitionist Horace Greeley. Many of the incidents of sexual abuse, however, as well as Jacobs's out-of-wedlock motherhood, were regarded as too shocking for newspaper readers, so Greeley suspended publication before the narrative was completed. It was eventually published in book form in Boston.

Document Text
XL: The Fugitive Slave Law

One day, when I had been requested to do an errand for Mrs. Bruce, I was hurrying through back streets, as usual, when I saw a young man approaching, whose face was familiar to me. As he came nearer, I recognized Luke. I always rejoiced to see or hear of any one who had escaped from the – pit; but, remembering this poor fellow's extreme hardships, I was peculiarly glad to see him on Northern soil, though I no longer called it free soil. I well remembered what a desolate feeling it was to be alone among strangers, and I went up to him and greeted him cordially. At first, he did not know me; but when I mentioned my name, he remembered all about me. I told him of the Fugitive Slave Law, and asked him if he did not know that New York was a city of kidnappers. . . .

All that winter I lived in a state of anxiety. When I took the children out to breathe the air, I closely observed the countenances of all I met. I dreaded the approach of summer, when snakes and slaveholders make their appearance. I was, in fact, a slave in New York, as subject to slave laws as I had been in a Slave State. Strange incongruity in a State called free!

Spring returned, and I received warning from the south that Dr. Flint knew of my return to my old place, and was making preparations to have me caught. I learned afterwards that my dress, and that of Mrs. Bruce's children, had been described to him by some of the Northern tools, which slaveholders employ for their base purposes, and then indulge in sneers at their cupidity and mean servility.

I immediately informed Mrs. Bruce of my danger, and she took prompt measures for my safety. My place as nurse could not be supplied immediately, and this generous, sympathizing lady proposed that I should carry her baby away. It

Portrait of Harriet Jacobs
(Gilbert Studios)

was a comfort to me to have the child with me; for the heart is reluctant to be torn away from every object it loves. But how few mothers would have consented to have one of their own babes become a fugitive, for the sake of a poor, hunted nurse, on whom the legislators of the country had let loose the bloodhounds! When I spoke of the sacrifice she was making, in depriving herself of her dear baby, she replied, "It is better for you to have baby with you, Linda; for if they get on your track, they will be obliged to bring the child to me; and then, if there is a possibility of saving you, you shall be saved."

This lady had a very wealthy relative, a benevolent gentleman in many respects, but aristocratic and pro-slavery. He remonstrated with her for harboring a fugitive slave; told her she was violating the laws of her country; and asked her if she was aware of the penalty. She replied, "I am very well aware of it. It is imprisonment and one thousand dollars fine. Shame on my country that it *is* so! I am ready to incur the penalty. I will go to the state's prison, rather than have any poor victim torn from *my* house, to be carried back to slavery."

The noble heart! The brave heart! The tears are in my eyes while I write of her. May the God of the helpless reward her for her sympathy with my persecuted people!

I was sent into New England, where I was sheltered by the wife of a senator, whom I shall always hold in grateful remembrance. This honorable gentleman would not have voted for the Fugitive Slave Law, as did the senator in "Uncle Tom's Cabin;" on the contrary, he was strongly opposed to it; but he was enough under its influence to be afraid of having me remain in his house many hours. So I was sent into the country, where I remained a month with the baby. When it was supposed that Dr. Flint's emissaries had lost track of me, and given up the pursuit for the present, I returned to New York.

Glossary

Fugitive Slave Law: controversial 1850 law requiring men and women who escaped slavery to be returned and mandating that officials and citizens in the free states cooperate in that return

kidnappers: individuals who acted to seize African Americans in northern free states and bring them before fugitive slave courts where they might be ordered returned to slavery

Uncle Tom's Cabin: 1852 novel by Harriet Beecher Stowe depicting plantation slavery and widely credited with leading many to oppose slavery

Short-Answer Questions

1. How did the Fugitive Slave Law impact the lives of Harriet Jacobs and her friend Luke?

2. Summarize the relationship between Mrs. Bruce and the author. What actions was she willing to take to help Jacobs?

3. Analyze the impact of Jacobs's slave narrative on readers in 1861. How might it influence readers' views of slavery?

Nellie Bly:
Ten Days in a Mad-House

Author	Significance
Nellie Bly	Exposed the wretched treatment and mismanagement of patients at a lunatic asylum on Blackwell's Island in New York
Date	
1887	
Type	
Essays, Reports, Manifestos	

Overview

In 1887 muckraking journalist Elizabeth Cochran, who wrote under the pen name Nellie Bly, went undercover to expose the inner workings of the Women's Lunatic Asylum on Blackwell's Island in New York City for the *New York World*. Impersonating a "crazy immigrant Cuban girl" named Nellie Brown, Bly spent ten days and ten nights at the asylum to learn how inmates were treated. She wrote of her experience in a series of articles that was later published as the book *Ten Days in a Mad-House*.

Bly's work shed light on the dehumanization of the institutionalized, whom she often referred to as the "others." The exposé chronicled the filthy conditions of the asylum along with the systematic violence used against patients. Bly learned that many women who were institutionalized were not insane but were immigrants, poor, disobedient to their husbands, or noncompliant with social gender roles, and thus institutionalized.

Nativist Americans—that is, white Americans of European ancestry who opposed new immigration, particularly from southern and central Europe, Asia, and the Caribbean—promoted the idea that the rising numbers of immigrants of the era were linked to criminal activity. American political authorities often used their power to eliminate people who were considered a burden or dangerous to American society, including new immigrants, poor people, or disabled people. Bly, a white woman, easily convinced a judge that she was insane by pretending to also be an immigrant. Upon admittance to the asylum, she learned that many women were "disposed of" in the same fashion because they were immigrants who were misunderstood or struggled to assimilate into society.

Bly's narrative not only drew public attention to the corrupt practices at the asylum but also convinced a Grand Jury in New York to increase funding for the care of the insane.

Elizabeth Cochran Seaman, known by the pen name Nellie Bly (Library of Congress)

Document Text

I was asked by the *World* if I could have myself committed to one of the asylums for the insane in New York, with a view to writing a plain and unvarnished narrative of the treatment of the patients therein and the methods of management, etc. Did I think I had the courage to go through such an ordeal as the mission would demand? . . . I said I could and I would. And I did. . . .

I shall never forget my first walk. . . . We had not gone many paces when I saw . . . long lines of women guarded by nurses. . . . Vacant eyes and meaningless faces, and their tongues uttered meaningless nonsense. One crowd passed and I noted by nose as well as eyes, that they were fearfully dirty.

"Who are they?" I asked of a patient near me.

"They are considered the most violent on the island," she replied. . . . A long cable rope fastened to wide leather belts, and these belts locked around the waists of fifty-two women. At the end of the rope was a heavy iron cart, and in it two women—one nursing a sore foot. . . . One woman had on a straightjacket, and two women had to drag her along. Crippled, blind, old, young, homely, and pretty. . . .

I had been watching and talking with a fair-complexioned woman for several days, and I was at a loss to see why she had been sent there, she was so sane. . . .

"Are you sick mentally?" I urged.

"Oh, no; what gave you such an idea? I had been overworking myself, and I broke down. Having some family trouble, and being penniless and nowhere to go, I applied to the commissioners to be sent to the poorhouse until I would be able to go to work."

"But they do not send poor people here unless they are insane," I said. . . .

"I believed them when they told me this was the place they sent all the poor who applied for aid." . . .

On bathing day the tub is filled with water, and the patients are washed, one after the other, vwithout a change of water. . . . The same towels are used on all the women, those with eruptions as well as those without. . . . If the patient has a visitor, I have seen the nurses hurry her out and change her dress before the visitor comes in. This keeps up the appearance of careful and good management. . . .

I made the acquaintance of Bridget McGuinness, who seems to be sane at the present time. She said she was . . . put on the "rope gang." "The beating I got there were something dreadful. I was pulled around by the hair, held under the water until I strangled, and I was choked and kicked. The nurses would always keep a quiet patient stationed at the window to tell them when any of the doctors were approaching. It was hopeless to complain to the doctors, for they always said it was the imagination of our diseased brains, and besides we would get another beating for telling. . . . Among other beating I got there, the nurses jumped on me once and broke two of my ribs. . . .

"They inject so much morphine and chloral that the patients are made crazy. I have seen the patients wild for water from the effect of the drugs, and the nurses would refuse it to them. I have heard women beg for a whole night for one drop and it was not given them. I myself cried for water until my mouth was so parched and dry that I could not speak." . . .

Soon after I had bidden farewell to the Blackwell's Island Insane Asylum, I was summoned to appear before the Grand Jury. . . .

I swore to the truth of my story, and then I related all. . . . The jurors then requested that I should accompany them on a visit to the Island. . . .

The trip to the island was vastly different to my first. . . .

Some of the nurses were examined by the jury, and made contradictory statements to one another, as well as to my story. . . . Dr. Dent confessed that he had no means by which to tell positively if the bath was cold and of the number of women put into the same water. . . .

If nurses were cruel to their patients, had he any positive means of ascertaining it? No, he had not.

"I am glad you did this now, and had I known your purpose, I would have aided you. We have no means of learning the way things are going except to do as you did. Since your story was published I found a nurse at the Retreat who had watches set for our approach, just as you had stated. She was dismissed."

Miss Anne Neville was brought down. . . . She was not sworn, but her story must have convinced all hearers of the truth of my statements.

"When Miss Brown and I were brought here the nurses were cruel and the food was too bad to eat. We did not have enough clothing. . . . Strange to say, ever since Miss Brown has been taken away everything is different. The nurses are very kind and we are given plenty to wear. The doctors come to see us often and the food is greatly improved." . . .

We found the halls in the finest order. The beds were improved, and . . . the buckets in which we were compelled to wash had been replaced by bright new basins. . . .

I hardly expected the grand jury to sustain me, after they saw everything different from what it had been while I was there. Yet they did, and their report to the court advises all the changes made that I had proposed.

I have one consolation for my work—on the strength of my story the committee of appropriation provides $1,000,000 more than was ever before given, for the benefit of the insane.

Glossary

asylum: an institution offering shelter and support for people who are mentally ill

Miss Brown: Miss Nellie Brown, the pseudonym Nellie Bly used in the asylum

Glossary

chloral: chloral hydrate, a sedative

committed: involuntarily placed in an institution like an insane asylum

Miss Anne Neville: a patient at the asylum

sworn: giving testimony under oath

Short-Answer Questions

1. Why did medical staff treat patients so brutally? What was the purpose of the abuse?

2. Why did nonconformist or immigrant women find themselves committed to asylums?

3. Explain how the asylum was changed as a result of Bly's exposé.

Jane Addams:
"The Subjective Necessity
for Social Settlements"

Author
Jane Addams

Date
1892

Type
Speeches/Addresses; Essays, Reports, Manifestos

Significance
Depicted settlement houses as a means to foster social progress, education, and democracy as daily experiences for the urban poor, urban youth, and immigrants

Overview

Jane Addams was part of the Progressive movement, a broad and diverse middle-class coalition that, at the turn of the twentieth century, tried to reform American society and reconcile democracy with capitalism. The steady industrialization and urbanization of the 1880s and 1890s had deeply transformed American society, spurring harsh conflicts between labor and management. The middle class had supported the process of industrialization by espousing the Victorian values of laissez-faire individualism, domesticity, and self-control. Yet by the 1890s it was apparent that these values had trapped the middle class between the warring demands of big business and the working classes. Growing consumerism, a new wave of immigration, and tensions between the sexes further challenged bourgeois existence. In the face of these confrontations, the Progressives tried to reform the American capitalist system and its institutions from within, seeking to strike a compromise between radical demands and the preservation of established interests.

Addams's concern with the major issues of Progressivism and her own agenda for social reform clearly emerge in her speech "The Subjective Necessity for Social Settlements," in which she catalogs the beliefs and convictions that led to the foundation of Hull House, the second settlement house established in the United States. The speech later became the sixth chapter of Addams's autobiography, *Twenty Years at Hull-House*.

Painting of Jane Addams
(National Portrait Gallery)

Document Text

This paper is an attempt to analyze the motives which underlie a movement based, not only upon conviction, but upon genuine emotion, wherever educated young people are seeking an outlet for that sentiment for universal brotherhood, which the best spirit of our times is forcing from an emotion into a motive. . . . They have been shut off from the common labor by which they live which is a great source of moral and physical health. They feel a fatal want of harmony between their theory and their lives, a lack of coordination between thought and action. I think it is hard for us to realize how seriously many of them are taking to the notion of human brotherhood, how eagerly they long to give tangible expression to the democratic ideal. . . .

We have in America a fast-growing number of cultivated young people who have no recognized outlet for their active faculties. They hear constantly of the great social maladjustment, but no way is provided for them to change it. . . . These young people have had advantages of college, of European travel, and of economic study, but they are sustaining this shock of inaction. . . . Many of them dissipate their energies in so-called enjoyment. Others not content with that, go on studying and go back to college for their second degrees; not that they are especially fond of study, but because they want something definite to do, and their powers have been trained in the direction of mental accumulation. Many are buried beneath this mental accumulation with lowered vitality and discontent. . . .

This young life . . . seems to me as pitiful as the other great mass of destitute lives. One is supplementary to the other, and some method of communication can surely be devised. Mr. Barnett, who urged the first Settlement—Toynbee Hall, in East London—recognized this need of outlet for the young men at Oxford and Cambridge, and hoped that the Settlement would supply the communication. It is easy to see why the Settlement movement originated in England, where the years of education are more constrained and definite than they are here, where class distinctions are more rigid. . . . We are fast feeling the pressure of the need and meeting the necessity for Settlements in America. Our young people feel nervously the need of putting theory into action, and respond quickly to the Settlement form of activity. . . .

The Settlement then, is an experimental effort to aid in the solution of the social and industrial problems which are engendered by the modern conditions of life in a great city. It insists that these problems are not confined to any one portion of a city. It is an attempt to relieve, at the same time, the overaccumulation at one end of society and the destitution at the other; but it assumes that this overaccumulation and destitution is most sorely felt in the things that pertain to social and educational privileges. . . . The only thing to be dreaded in the Settlement is that it loses its flexibility, its power of quick adaptation, its readiness to change its methods as its environment may demand. It must be open to conviction and must have a deep and abiding sense of tolerance. It must be hospitable and ready for experiment. . . . Its residents must be emptied of all conceit of opinion and all self-assertion, and ready to arouse and interpret the public opinion of their neighborhood. They must be content to live quietly side by side with their neighbors, until they grow into a sense of relationship and mutual interests. . . . In short, residents are pledged to devote themselves to the duties of good citizenship and to the arousing of the social energies which too largely lie dormant in every neighborhood given over to industrialism. . . .

It is always easy to make all philosophy point one particular moral and all history adorn one particular tale; but I may be forgiven the reminder that the best speculative philosophy sets forth the solidarity of the human race; that the highest moralists have taught that without the advance and improvement of the whole, no man can hope for any lasting improvement in his own moral or material individual condition; and that the subjective necessity for Social Settlements is therefore identical with that necessity, which urges us on toward social and individual salvation.

Glossary

maladjustment: failure to cope with the demands of a normal social environment

settlement house/social settlement: an institution in an inner-city area providing educational, recreational, and other social services to the community, primarily focusing on the urban poor, urban youth, and immigrants

Toynbee Hall: a settlement house in London, England, used as a model for similar establishments in the United States

Short-Answer Questions

1. Describe Jane Addams's goals for settlement houses.

2. How were settlement houses meant to help "cultivated young people"? How were they meant to help poor people and immigrants?

3. How could settlement housing, such as the Hull House in Chicago, Illinois, help prepare urban youth, many of them the children of immigrants, for assimilation into American culture and society?

Ida B. Wells:
Southern Horrors

Author
Ida B. Wells

Date
1892

Type
Essays, Reports, Manifestos

Significance
Called attention to lynching and documented its prevalence throughout the United States, particularly the South

Overview

The public record of lynchings in the United States shows that during the post–Civil War era, lynching and other acts of mob violence steadily increased. While the victims of lynchings across the nation still included whites, Native Americans, Chicanos, and Asians, by 1892 the majority of victims were African American, and the majority of these murders were in the South. Through newspaper articles in the *New York Age* and later in the *Chicago Conservator*, in her 1892 book *Southern Horrors: Lynch Law in All Its Phases*, and in lectures throughout the United States and Great Britain, journalist Ida B. Wells demanded that the United States confront and put an end to lynching.

After the end of Reconstruction, southern whites confronted what they called the "Negro problem." Solving that problem meant prohibiting Blacks from voting and segregating Blacks from whites socially. In 1883 the U.S. Supreme Court overturned the Civil Rights Act of 1875, which had outlawed racial discrimination in public accommodations. In 1890, in what would become a pattern in the South, the state of Mississippi adopted a new constitution that disenfranchised Blacks. To evade the equal protection clauses of the Fourteenth and Fifteenth Amendments, southern states usually did not specifically cite race. Instead, they passed laws requiring voters to pay a poll tax and pass a literacy test administered by white registrars as a way to disenfranchise most Black voters. A flood of Jim Crow laws followed.

In the meantime, neither the federal nor state governments took any steps to stem the rising occurrence of violence against Blacks. Black men and women were killed without having been tried and convicted of any capital crime. Being politically active could cause a Black activist to be killed by an angry white mob.

One common justification of white supremacists for lynching was to punish Black men for raping white women. But Wells discovered that only a minority of Black victims had ever actually been accused of rape; even when rape was the charge, it was rarely true.

White-on-Black violence was, she argued, all about maintaining power and control. Lynching, driven by racial prejudice, was a form of intimidation designed to keep Black men from challenging (politically, economically, or socially) white supremacy.

Photograph of Ida B. Wells
(Wikimedia Commons)

Document Text
THE OFFENSE

Wednesday evening May 24, 1892, the city of Memphis was filled with excitement. Editorials in the daily papers of that date caused a meeting to be held in the Cotton Exchange Building; a committee was sent for the editors of the Free Speech, an Afro-American journal published in that city, and the only reason the open threats of lynching that were made were not carried out was because they could not be found. The cause of all this commotion was the following editorial published in the Free Speech May 21, 1892, the Saturday previous.

Eight negroes lynched since last issue of the Free Speech one at Little Rock, Ark., last Saturday morning where the citizens broke(?) into the penitentiary and got their man; three near Anniston, Ala., one near New Orleans; and three at Clarksville, Ga., the last three for killing a white man, and five on the same old racket—the new alarm about raping white women. The same programme of hanging, then shooting bullets into the lifeless bodies was carried out to the letter.

Nobody in this section of the country believes the old thread-bare lie that Negro men rape white women. If Southern white men are not careful, they will overreach themselves and public sentiment will have a reaction; a conclusion will then be reached which will be very damaging to the moral reputation of their women.

Glossary

penitentiary: prison

racket: illegal or dishonest scheme

Short-Answer Questions

1. What does Wells mean when she says "a conclusion will then be reached which will be very damaging to the moral reputation of their women"?

2. Describe what justifications Wells says were given for lynching the eight African Americans mentioned in the account.

3. Why does Wells refer to the allegation of the rape of white women as "the same old racket"? Please explain.

Frances Willard:
Address before the Woman's Christian Temperance Union

<table>
<tr><td>

Author
Frances Willard

Date
1893

Type
Speeches/Addresses

</td><td>

Significance
Urged the temperance movement to broaden the scope of its reform efforts to address education, labor, poverty, and more

</td></tr>
</table>

Overview

By the time she addressed the Second Biennial Convention of the World's Woman's Christian Temperance Union (WCTU) in 1893, Frances Elizabeth Caroline Willard was one of the most famous social reformers in the United States. Raised in Wisconsin, Willard completed her schooling at North Western Female College in Evanston, Illinois, and then taught science at several institutions. In 1871 she served as president of the newly established Evanston College for Ladies, which merged with Northwestern University in 1872. Willard was the university's first dean of women but resigned in 1874 to become the corresponding secretary for the WCTU. This national organization, founded in the same year in Cleveland, Ohio, advocated abstinence from alcohol as a method of protecting the home and family. In many ways, the WCTU used its crusade to promote women's rights. Certainly, this was true after Willard became the

second national president of the WCTU in 1879, a position she held until her death in 1898.

While her predecessor, Annie Wittenmyer, had followed a one-policy platform during her presidency, Willard wanted to broaden the WCTU's scope of reform efforts. An active reformer and president of the National Council of Women of the United States, Willard led the WCTU to promote social reform in the areas of education, labor, prisons, care of orphans, homelessness, and prostitution. The association also lobbied for female suffrage. In pursuing these goals, Willard promoted a "Do Everything Policy," which is at the heart of the address excerpted here. The speech was delivered to delegates of the World's WCTU, an international organization founded by Willard in 1883, and provides insight to the state of the temperance movement at that time.

Frances Willard (Library of Congress)

Document Text

A one-sided movement makes one-sided advocates. Virtues, like hounds, hunt in packs. Total abstinence is not the crucial virtue in life that excuses financial crookedness, defamation of character, or habits of impurity. The fact that one's father was, and one's self is, a bright and shining light in the total abstinence galaxy, does not give one a vantage ground for high-handed behaviour toward those who have not been trained to the special virtue that forms the central idea of the Temperance Movement. . . .

Concerning the Temperance Movement in our land and throughout the world to-day, the pessimist says—and says truly—"There was never so much liquor manufactured in any one year since time began as in the year 1893, and as a consequence never did so much liquor flow down the people's throats as in this same year of grace." "But," says the optimist, "there is each year a larger acreage from which the brewer and distiller may gather the golden grain and luscious fruits, there are more people to imbibe the exhilarating poison; but, per contra, there was never so much intelligent thinking in any one year as to the drink delusion, there were never so many children studying in the schools the laws written in their members, there were never such gatherings together of temperance people to consult on the two great questions what to do and what not to do as in this year; there was never such a volume of experience and expert testimony and knowledge so varied, so complete, as we have had this year at the International Congress; there were never so many total abstainers in proportion to the population, never so many intelligent people who could render a reason scientific, ethical, aesthetic, for their total abstinence faith as now; there were never so many pulpits from which to bombard the liquor traffic and the drink habit; there were never so many journalists who had a friendly word to say for the Temperance Reform; there was never such a stirring up of temperance politics; for the foremost historic nation of the world, Great Britain, has this year, for the first time, adopted as a plank in the platform of the dominant party the principle that the people shall themselves decide whether or not they want the public house; and as a natural consequence of this political action there was never a public sentiment so respectful toward the Temperance Reform. The great world-brain is becoming saturated with the idea that it is reasonable and kind to let strong drink alone. The vastness of these changes can only be measured by the remembrance that a few generations ago these same drinks were the accredited emblems in cot and palace alike, of hospitality, kindness, and good-will." . . .

The Prohibition agitation in America has not been as great in the past year as formerly, and the reasons are not far to seek. A presidential campaign always lowers the moral atmosphere for a year before it begins and a year after it is over. Legislators become timid, politicians proceed to "hedge," journalists, with an eye to the loaves and fishes, furl their sails concerning issues that have at best only a fighting chance; the world, the flesh, and the devil get their innings, and the time is not yet. In the past year the attention of the nation has been focused on the World's Fair and the endless difficulties to which that has given birth. There has been an incalculable amount of ill-will set in motion as the result of personal financial interest and ignoble ambition. All this savours not the things of God or of humanity. The re-adjustment of political parties is still inchoate; men's hearts are failing them for fear; leaders in the traditional party of moral ideas have thrown off all disguises and grounded any weapons of rebellion they may once have lifted against the liquor traffic. The financial panic has rivetted the attention of the public on their own dangers and disasters, and the spirit of money-making has lamentably invaded the ranks of the temperance army itself; but Prohibition is as lively an issue to-day as emancipation was in 1856; an issue that stirs such deadly hatred is by no means dead. It is still quick with fighting blood, and its enemies know this even better than its friends.

Glossary

Emancipation of 1865: refers to the passing of the 13th Amendment, which abolished slavery on the United States

Prohibition: the prevention of the manufacture, sale, and transportation of alcohol in the United States from 1920 to 1933

Temperance Movement: a reform movement which focused on the promotion of abstaining from alcoholic consumption

World's Fair: an international exhibition that held a variety of exhibits of science, industry, and culture

Short-Answer Questions

1. Summarize the argument that Frances Willard is making concerning the temperance movement.

2. What might Willard have meant in her assertion that temperance was a "one-sided movement"?

3. Analyze the meaning of Willard's statement about the World's Fair and how it related to the temperance movement.

Clara Barton:
The Red Cross in Peace and War

Author
Clara Barton

Date
1898

Type
Essays, Reports, Manifestos

Significance
Highlights the development of the Red Cross into an organization that responds to domestic and international crises during war and peacetime

---

Overview

The American Civil War resulted in a profound shift on society and individuals, including the nurse and humanitarian Clara Barton (1821–1912). From the first bloodshed in Maryland in the first year of the war, she was committed to helping wounded soldiers, some of whom she had known personally. She provided medical assistance, dressed wounds, provided food and aid, and offered emotional support to those who needed it. After the war, she helped open the Office of Missing Soldiers to locate, identify, and bury soldiers who had been killed or missing in action. It was her experience during the American Civil War that led her to start the American Red Cross, the American branch of the International Committee of the Red Cross. During peacetime, she coordinated efforts with local officials in the United States and abroad to offer assistance wherever the Red Cross was needed. This evolution of the Red Cross is apparent during the Spanish–American War, as the Red Cross came to the aid not just of U.S. soldiers but also of refugees and prisoners of war. *The Red Cross in Peace and War* depicts the evolution of the Red Cross and the stories and accounts that helped develop the Red Cross into what it is today.

Clara Barton in 1904
(Library of Congress)

Document Text

. . . The plain, simple services told in repeated sentences the heart gratitude of a stricken people to God for what he had put into the hearts of America to do. She had remembered them when all was gone, when hunger, pain and death alone remained to them; and when that assemblage of pale, hollow faces and attenuated forms knelt on the rough stone floor in praise to the Great Giver, one felt if this was not acceptable, no worship might ever hope to be. From the church to the house of the mayor, the judge, the doctor and other principal men of the town. It now remained to see what we had "gone for to see." Two hours' wandering about in the hot sunshine from hovel to hovel dark and damp, thatched roof and ground floor, no furniture, sometimes a broken bench, a few rags of clothing; some of the people could walk about, some could not, but all had something to eat. Thank God, if not *all* their lean bodies might crave, still *something*, and while they showed their skeleton bodies and feet swollen to bursting, they still blessed the people of the country that had remembered them with food.

The line of march was long and weary, and ended with the "hospital." What shall I say of it? If only a sense of decency were consulted one would say nothing; but truth and facts demand a record. We tried to enter, to reach a poor, wretched looking human being on a low cot on the far side of the room, but were driven back by the stench that met us, not alone the smell one might expect in such a place of neglect, but the dead had evidently lain there unremoved until putrefaction had taken place. There were perhaps four wrecks of men in the various rooms, doubtless left there to die. Like a body of retreating soldiers, driven but not defeated, we went a few rods out and rallied, and calling for volunteers and picked men for service, determined to "storm the works."

Jaruco is one of the great points of devastation; it is said that more people have died there than the entire town numbers in time of peace; it is still almost a city of reconcentrados.

Naturally, the inhabitants who survive have given all they had many times over in these terrible months. Everything is scarce and dear; even water has to be bought. This was the first point of attack. Twenty good soldiers, with only dirt and filth as enemies, can make some progress. Water by the dray load, lime by the barrel, brushes, brooms, blue for whitewash, hatchets, buckets and things most needful, made up the equipment; and late in the afternoon, when Mr. Elwell, who might well be termed the "Vigilant," returned to look after the work, preparatory to leaving for home, he found the four poor patients in clean clothes, on clean beds, in the sunshine, eating crackers and milk, the house cleaned, scrubbed, limed, and being whitewashed from ceiling to floor.

It will be finished to-morrow. Sunday and to-day (Monday), we ship cots, blankets, sheets, pillow-slips, all the first utensils needed to make a plain hospital for twenty-five, to be increased to fifty—the food to go regularly. The sick, lying utterly helpless in the hovels, to be selected with care and sent to the hospital, a nurse placed with them, the doctor already there in Jaruco to attend them, and send frequent reports of condition and needs. In two weeks time we may hope to see, not only a hospital that may bear the name, but progress of its patients that may be noted.

I am writing this at length, because it is the first of hundreds that should follow throughout the island, and a type of what we shall endeavor to accomplish. It will naturally be asked if we expect the Spanish authorities to permit us to do this. Judging from to-day, we have reason to expect every co-operation. The commandant of the town was one of the men who welcomed us; and so far as they had the materials desired, offered them for our use; it was very well, as there were some we could get in no other way.

Glossary

commandant: an officer in charge of a particular force

dray: sturdy cart used for hauling

Jaruco: a city in Cuba

putrefaction: the process of decay or rotting in a body or other organic matter

reconcentrados: during the Spanish–American War, the noncombatants who were concentrated by the military authorities in areas surrounding the fortified towns, and later were concentrated in the smaller limits of the towns themselves

Short-Answer Questions

1. Describe the role of the Red Cross in Cuba. How does its role reflect the attitude of American intervention?

2. "The plain, simple services told in repeated sentences the heart gratitude of a stricken people to God for what he had put into the hearts of America to do." Explain what this quote says about Cuban attitudes toward the United States and the Red Cross.

3. Describe the conditions in Jaruco. How might these depictions explain the relationship between the United States and Cuba?

The Schlager Anthology of Women's History

Ida B. Wells:
"Lynching: Our National Crime"

Author
Ida B. Wells

Date
1909

Type
Speeches/Addresses; Essays, Reports, Manifestos

Significance
Highlighted lynching as a national crime that required a national solution in the form of federal anti-lynching legislation

Overview

As an early activist in the civil rights movement and founding member of the National Association for the Advancement of Colored People (NAACP), Ida B. Wells worked tirelessly to call attention to the rising number of lynchings, particularly of Black men, occurring in the United States, particularly in the South, at the close of the nineteenth century. Wells advocated for the congressional passage of laws that would allow the federal government to investigate lynchings and punish those found responsible for these heinous killings.

Born in bondage in Mississippi in 1862, Wells and her four younger siblings relocated to Memphis, Tennessee, in 1882, following the deaths of their parents during a yellow fever epidemic. She became a journalist four years later, quickly gaining a reputation as a tenacious investigator and passionate advocate for racial reform. Her commitment to ending lynchings developed in response to the 1892 murder of her friend Thomas Moss, a Black grocery store owner, and two of his employees, also African Americans, at the hands of a white mob. As a part-owner of the *Free Speech* newspaper, Wells turned to her writing skills to craft a scathing editorial condemning the recent murders, which resulted in an arson attack against her press office.

Wells relocated to New York City and then Chicago in 1893, all the while continuing her crusade to raise national awareness about Southern lynchings and press for federal action, authoring educational pamphlets and statistical reports. In 1909 Wells attended a conference that set into motion the creation of the NAACP. She delivered a short address in which she outlined the history of the practice of lynching and identified its uniquely American characteristics. While her letters to presidents and members of Congress influenced the drafting of anti-lynching bills, one would not be passed until 2020, nearly ninety years after Wells's death.

Photograph of Ida B. Wells (Mary Garrity)

Document Text

The lynching record for a quarter of a century merits the thoughtful study of the American people. It presents three salient facts:

First: Lynching is color line murder.

Second: Crimes against women is the excuse, not the cause.

Third: It is a national crime and requires a national remedy.

Proof that lynching follows the color line is to be found in the statistics which have been kept for the past twenty-five years. During the few years preceding this period and while frontier lynch law existed, the executions showed a majority of white victims. Later, however, as law courts and authorized judiciary extended into the far West, lynch law rapidly abated and its white victims became few and far between.

Just as the lynch law régime came to a close in the West, a new mob movement started in the South. This was wholly political, its purpose being to suppress the colored vote by intimidation and murder. Thousands of assassins banded together under the name of Ku Klux Klans, "Midnight Raiders," "Knights of the Golden Circle," etc., spread a reign of terror, by beating, shooting and killing colored people by the thousands. In a few years, the purpose was accomplished and the Black vote was suppressed. But mob murder continued.

From 1882, in which year 52 were lynched, down to the present, lynching has been along the color line. Mob murder increased yearly until in 1892 more than 200 victims were lynched and statistics show that 3,284 men, women and children have been put to death in this quarter of a century. During the last ten years from 1899 to 1908 inclusive the number lynched was 959. Of this number 102 were white while the colored victims numbered 857. No other nation, civilized or savage, burns its criminals; only under the stars and stripes is the human holocaust possible. Twenty-eight human beings burned at the stake, one of them a woman and two of them children, is the awful indictment against American civilization—the gruesome tribute which the nation pays to the color line.

Why is mob murder permitted by a Christian nation? What is the cause of this awful slaughter? This question is answered almost daily—always the same shameless falsehood that "Negroes are lynched to protect womanhood." . . . John Temple Graves, at once champion of lynching and apologist for lynchers, said: "The mob stands today as the most potential bulwark between the women of the South and such a carnival of crime as would infuriate the world and precipitate the annihilation of the Negro race." This is the never varying answer of lynchers and their apologists. All know it is untrue. The cowardly lyncher revels in murder, then seeks to shield himself from public execration by claiming devotion to woman. But truth is mighty and the lynching record discloses the hypocrisy of the lyncher as well as his crime.

The Springfield, Illinois, mob rioted for two days, the militia of the entire state was called out, two men were lynched, hundreds of people driven from their homes, all because a white woman said a Negro had assaulted her. A mad mob went to the jail, tried to lynch the victim of her charge and, not being able to find him, proceeded to pillage and burn the town and to lynch two innocent men. Later, after the police had found that the woman's charge was false, she published a retraction, the indictment was dismissed and the intended victim discharged. But the lynched victims were dead. Hundreds were homeless and Illinois was disgraced. . . .

This nation must assert itself and defend its federal citizenship at home as well as abroad. The strong arm of the government must reach across state lines whenever unbridled lawlessness defies state laws. . . .

Federal protection of American citizenship is the remedy for lynching. . . .

Glossary

John Temple Graves: newspaper editor and politician from Georgia

holocaust: mass destruction through fire; mass murder, usually directed against a racial, ethnic, or religious group

Ku Klux Klan: a white supremacist organization, formed in 1866, that mounted a campaign of violence and intimidation against African Americans, Jews, and others

lynching: a term used to describe mob violence against an individual

Short-Answer Questions

1. What does Wells mean when she says that lynching is "color line murder"? What evidence does she use in the piece to support this assertion? Explain how she makes her case.

2. How did people historically justify lynching, according to Wells? What evidence does she use to dispute those justifications?

3. What does Wells say must be done to end lynching in America?

Rachel Carson:
Silent Spring

Author
Rachel Carson

Date
1962

Document Type
Essays, Reports, Manifestos

Significance
Helped spark the environmental movement in the United States by highlighting the damage done by the excessive use of pesticides

Overview

In 1947, the U.S. federal government and thirteen state governments launched a broad campaign to eliminate malaria in the southeastern region of the country by reducing the mosquito population. The initiative relied heavily on the use of the chemical pesticide dichloro-diphenyl-trichloroethane (DDT). Developed in the 1940s, DDT was one of the first widely used insecticides. It was highly effective at killing mosquitos and other insects. However, over time it was discovered that the chemical was poisonous to humans and other mammals. DDT also became less effective over time as insect populations became immune to the pesticide.

A popular author and marine biologist at the time, Rachel Carson began studying the harmful impact of DDT in the 1950s. What she found shocked her. Among other problems, DDT was responsible for almost causing the bald eagle to become extinct. Eagles, falcons, pelicans, and other birds of prey consumed fish contaminated with DDT. The chemical caused damage to the birds' eggs, making it difficult for their young to survive. The biologist also found evidence that DDT caused cancer in humans who ate fruit or vegetables that had been sprayed with the insecticide. Carson subsequently wrote a book about DDT and how the widespread use of chemicals severely damaged the environment and human health.

Published in 1962, Carson's book *Silent Spring* was a powerful condemnation of the way most Americans treated and viewed the environment. Carson called for dramatic changes in U.S. environmental policy, including transitioning away from the use of chemical pesticides such as DDT. In the introduction to her book, the author wrote that the country was at a crossroads. Americans needed to seek new, non-harmful solutions to deal with insects and other pests. Carson noted that there were many natural approaches that could be used in place of chemical insecticides.

Silent Spring was extremely popular and widely read. It helped launch the modern environmental movement in the United States by dramatically changing public perceptions about environmental policy. One result was the creation of the Environmental Protections Agency (EPA) in 1970. In 1972, the commercial use of DDT was banned in the United States. Other nations would also ban the chemical in later decades.

Rachel Carson in 1944
(U.S. Fish and Wildlife Service)

Document Text

The history of life on earth has been a history of interaction between living things and their surroundings. To a large extent, the physical form and the habits of the earth's vegetation and its animal life have been molded by the environment. Considering the whole span of earthly time, the opposite effect, in which life actually modifies its surroundings, has been relatively slight. Only within the moment of time represented by the present century has one species—man—acquired significant power to alter the nature of his world.

During the past quarter century this power has not only increased to one of disturbing magnitude but it has changed in character. The most alarming of all man's assaults upon the environment is the contamination of air, earth, rivers, and sea with dangerous and even lethal materials. This pollution is for the most part irrecoverable; the chain of evil it initiates not only in the world that must support life but in living tissues is for the most part irreversible. In this now universal contamination of the environment, chemicals are the sinister and little-recognized partners of radiation in changing the very nature of the world—the very nature of its life. Strontium 90, released through nuclear explosions into the air, comes to earth in rain or drifts down as fallout, lodges in soil, enters into the grass or corn or wheat grown there, and in time takes up its abode in the bones of a human being, there to remain until his death. Similarly, chemicals sprayed on croplands or forests or gardens lie long in soil, entering into living organisms, passing from one to another in a chain of poisoning and death. Or they pass mysteriously by underground streams until they emerge and, through the alchemy of air and sunlight, combine into new forms that kill vegetation, sicken cattle, and work unknown harm on those who drink from once pure wells. . . .

To adjust to these chemicals would require time on the scale that is nature's; it would require not merely the years of a man's life but the life of generations. And even this, were it by some miracle possible, would be futile, for the new chemicals come from our laboratories in an endless stream; almost five hundred annually find their way into actual use in the United States alone. The figure is staggering and its implications are not easily grasped—500 new chemicals to which the bodies of men and animals are required somehow to adapt each year, chemicals totally outside the limits of biologic experience.

Among them are many that are used in man's war against nature. Since the mid-1940's over 200 basic chemicals have been created for use in killing insects, weeds, rodents, and other organisms described in the modern vernacular as "pests"; and they are sold under several thousand different brand names.

These sprays, dusts, and aerosols are now applied almost universally to farms, gardens, forests, and home—nonselective chemicals that have the power to kill every insect, the "good" and the "bad," to still the song of birds and the leaping of fish in the streams, to coat the leaves with a deadly film, and to linger on in soil—all this though the intended target may be only a few weeds or insects. Can anyone believe it is possible to lay down such a barrage of poisons on the surface of the earth without making it unfit for all life? They should not be called "insecticides," but "biocides." . . .

The whole process of spraying seems caught up in an endless spiral. Since DDT was released for civilian use, a process of escalation has been going on in which ever more toxic materials must be found. This has happened because insects, in a triumphant vindication of Darwin's principle of the survival of the fittest, have evolved super races immune to the particular insecticide used, hence a deadlier one has always to be developed and then a deadlier one than that. It has happened also because, for reasons to be described later, destructive insects often undergo a "flareback," or resurgence, after spraying, in numbers greater than before. Thus the chemical war is never won, and all life is caught in its violent crossfire. . . .

The Other Road

We stand now where two roads diverge. . . . The road we have long been traveling is deceptively easy, a smooth superhighway on which we progress with great speed, but at its end lies disaster. . . .

A truly extraordinary variety of alternatives to the chemical control of insects is available. Some are already in use and have achieved brilliant success. Others are in the stage of laboratory testing. Still others are little more than ideas in the minds of imaginative scientists, waiting for the opportunity to put them to the test. All have this in common: they are biological solutions, based on understanding of the living organisms they seek to control, and of the whole fabric of life to which these organisms belong. Specialists representing various areas of the vast field of biology are contributing entomologists, pathologists, geneticists, physiologists, biochemists, ecologists all pouring their knowledge and their creative inspirations into the formation of a new science of biotic controls. . . .

The "control of nature" is a phrase conceived in arrogance, born of the Neanderthal age of biology and philosophy, when it was supposed that nature exists for the convenience of man. The concepts and practices of applied entomology for the most part date from that Stone Age of science. It is our alarming misfortune that so primitive a science has armed itself with the most modem and terrible weapons, and that in turning them against the insects it has also turned them against the earth.

Glossary

alchemy: the transformation of chemicals into other materials

biotic: involving living or natural materials

Darwin: Charles Darwin (1809–1882), a British naturalist who helped popularize the concept of biological evolution based on the notion that, over time, superior organisms are more likely to thrive through adaptive change ("survival of the fittest")

entomology: the study of insects and their environments

Neanderthal: an early human species; a term used to describe actions or policies that are primitive or simple

Stone Age: an early period of human evolution before the widespread use of metals for tools or weapons; a term used to describe something primitive or simple

Strontium 90: a radioactive material that results from atomic explosions and causes a variety of health problems, including cancer in humans and animals

Short-Answer Questions

1. Why are chemical pesticides such as DDT bad for the environment? What are some examples of the damage these insecticides do to plants, insects, and humans?

2. How can the use of insecticides actually make it more difficult to control insects? What long-term problems are associated with the use of chemical pesticides?

3. Are there approaches that would allow humans to control insects and other "pests" without damaging the environment? What do these non-chemical methods have in common?

Chapter 8

Women's Work and Labor Movements

Women have historically struggled to secure equal treatment in the workplace. They have faced formal and informal barriers to different forms of occupation, often being denied employment because of their gender. The phrase *women's work* refers to domestic chores such as cooking, cleaning, and raising children. Such work was historically not only unpaid, but it was also often demeaning and unrewarding. Yet many women were confined to such roles because of discriminatory societal customs. Indeed, for much of the history of the United States, females who were able to obtain employment outside of the home were often confined to low-paying jobs as domestic workers or childcare providers. In addition, women faced continuing disparities in pay and compensation even as new employment opportunities emerged in the nineteenth and twentieth centuries. Discrimination also prevented women from being promoted or appointed to senior positions, a phenomenon known as the "glass ceiling" (referring to the widespread invisible barrier that constrained women's advancement in business). While considerable progress was made, the struggle for equal rights in the workplace continued into the twenty-first century.

Traditional Views of Women's Work

The traditional view of women's work was often reinforced by popular culture in the 1800s and 1900s. *Mrs. Beeton's Book of Household Management*, first published in 1861 in Great Britain, became a national bestseller in that country. The publication was mainly a cookbook, but it also offered advice and guidance on how to manage a home. Marketed to women, the book was based on existing gender stereotypes.

In the 1800s state laws in the United States created barriers to women in certain professions. For instance, Illinois and other states had laws that forbade women from becoming lawyers. The authority of states to do this was confirmed by the 1873 Supreme Court decision *Bradwell v. Illinois*. The case sparked a backlash against these types of restrictions, and in the late 1800s states, including Illinois, rescinded prohibitions on women being doctors or lawyers or engaging in most other professions.

Mary S. Paul and Clara Lemlich Argue for Better Pay and Conditions

The onset of the Industrial Revolution created the need for more workers. One result was an increase in employment for women in manufacturing. However, such work was low-paid, dangerous, and usually provided little security or long-term stability. In a series of letters, Mary S. Paul recounted the challenges of working in textile mills in Massachusetts in the 1840s. Paul described how difficult it was to live on her limited pay. She also reported on the dangers of the work and her fear that wages would be cut. Clara Lemlich, a Russian immigrant, echoed many of Paul's challenges in an essay she wrote in 1909 about working in a clothing factory. The low pay and ill treatment Lemlich faced prompted her to help organize a strike whereby workers collectively stopped working in an effort to force their employers to grant concessions, including higher pay.

Like Lemlich, many women turned to the newly forming trade unions in an effort to improve their lives and working conditions. Unions were organizations formed to advocate for worker's rights in specific industries or occupations. A range of women's rights activists urged females to join unions. For example, Clara Zetkin wrote a compelling tract, *Women's Work and the Trade Unions*, in 1887 in which the German feminist argued that without unions, workers were abused and taken advantage of by their employers. This was especially true of disadvantaged groups such as African Americans, as noted in the 1906 work "The Economic Handicap of the Negro in the North." Much later, in 1969, Dolores Huerta in testimony to the U.S. Senate Subcommittee on Migratory Labor recounted the struggles of Hispanic migrant workers.

The Triangle Shirtwaist Factory Fire

Among the most glaring examples of workers' mistreatment was the 1911 Triangle Shirtwaist Factory fire. On March 26, 1911, a fire swept through a clothing factory in New York, killing 146 workers. Most of those that died were young women. The loss of life was so high because the factory owners had blocked exits to prevent workers from taking unauthorized breaks and had failed to repair faulty fire escapes. In a powerful 1911 speech, Rose Schneiderman called for workers to unite in order to prevent future tragedies.

Efforts to organize workers into unions were often resisted by employers, especially if employees attempted to strike. In 1913 workers at various silk mills in Patter-

son, New Jersey, walked off of their jobs and went on strike. The strikers sought reforms such as an eight-hour work day and higher pay, but they met with fierce resistance by factory owners. More than 1,800 strikers were arrested between February and July 1913. Although the strike was considered a failure since the demands of the workers were not met, labor leader Elizabeth Gurley Flynn gave a speech in January 1914 in which she argued that the effort helped galvanize workers elsewhere to stand up for their rights.

A Changing Environment, Post-War

World War I dramatically changed working conditions for many women in the United States. Because large numbers of American men served in the military during the conflict (more than 4 million) there was a worker shortage. Women gained new opportunities to work in industrial positions and engage in other forms of work that had traditionally been dominated by males. The National Women's Trade Union League highlighted some of the changes that occurred during the conflict and argued for reforms to labor practices in a 1918 essay, "Women's Work and War."

After World War I ended, many women lost the jobs they had acquired during the conflict. A similar pattern happened in World War II, when once again women were asked to take on new jobs as men were conscripted into the military (more than 350,000 U.S. women also served in the military during the war). By the end of the war, approximately one out of every four adult women were employed outside of the home and outside of traditional women's work.

The rise of women in the workforce after World War II created new momentum for workplace reforms. In 1963 Congress enacted the Equal Pay Act, which required most companies to pay men and women the same for comparable work. This was followed in 1965 by President Lyndon B. Johnson's Executive Order No. 11246, which prohibited workplace discrimination based on race, ethnicity, religion, gender, or sexual orientation by federal contractors. Although actions such as these helped dramatically reduce gender discrimination and bias in the workplace, women continued to face a range of employment-related challenges, including a lingering pay-gap when compared with men.

Further Reading

Books

Anderson, Karen. *Wartime Women: Sex Roles, Family Relations, and the Status of Women During World War II.* Westport, CT: Greenwood Press, 1981.

Balser, Diane. *Sisterhood and Solidarity: Feminism and Labor in Modern Times.* Boston: South End Press, 1987.

Blewett, Mary H. *Men, Women and Work: Class, Gender, and Protest in the New England Shoe Industry, 1780–1910.* Champaign: University of Illinois Press, 1988.

Bordin, Ruth Birgitta Anderson. *Frances Willard: A Biography.* Chapel Hill: University of North Carolina Press, 1986.

Cobble, Dorothy Sue. *The Other Women's Movement: Workplace Justice and Social Rights in Modern America.* Princeton: Princeton University Press, 2004.

Cott, Nancy F. *The Grounding of Modern Feminism.* New Haven, CT: Yale University Press, 1987.

Gabin, Nancy. *Feminism in the Labor Movement: Women and the United Auto Workers, 1935–1970.* Ithaca, NY: Cornell University Press, 1990.

Gómez-Quiñones, Juan. *Mexican American Labor, 1790–1990.* Albuquerque: University of New Mexico Press, 1994.

Greenwald, Maurine Weiner. *Women, War, and Work: The Impact of World War I on Women Workers in the United States.* Westport, CT: Greenwood Press, 1980.

Hattam, Victoria C. *Labor Visions and State Power: The Origins of Business Unionism in the United States.* Princeton: Princeton University Press, 1993.

Levine, Susan. *Labor's True Women: Carpet Weavers, Industrialization, and Labor Reform in the Gilded Age.* Philadelphia: Temple University Press, 1984.

Orleck, Annelise. *Common Sense and a Little Fire: Women and Working-Class Politics in the United States, 1900–1965.* Chapel Hill: University of North Carolina Press, 1995.

Articles

Bronfenbrenner, Kate. "Organizing Women: The Nature and Process of Union Organizing Efforts Among U.S. Women Workers since the 1990s." *Work and Occupations* 32, no. 4 (2005).

MacLean, Nancy. "The Hidden History of Affirmative Action: Working Women's Struggles in the 1970s and the Gender of Class." *Feminist Studies* 25, no. 1 (Spring 1999).

Further Reading

Articles

Rose, Evan. "The Rise and Fall of Female Labor Force Participation during World War II in the United States." *Journal of Economic History* 78, no. 3 (September 2018).

Websites

"Women in the Labor Movement." National Park Service website, accessed September 1, 2023, https://www.nps.gov/subjects/womenshistory/women-in-the-labor-movement.htm.

"Women in the Work Force during World War II." National Archives website, accessed September 1, 2023, https://www.archives.gov/education/lessons/wwii-women.html.

Mary S. Paul:
Letters from Lowell Mills

Author
Mary S. Paul

Date
1845

Document Type
Letters/Correspondence

Significance
From a young textile worker's point of view, described the problems and working conditions of the Industrial Revolution in New England in the mid-nineteenth century

Overview

In Massachusetts in the early 1800s, entrepreneur Francis Cabot Lowell developed a new system of manufacturing that became common throughout New England. Named for its founder, the Lowell system attempted to cut costs and make textile production more efficient while also eliminating some of the worst labor practices of the Industrial Revolution.

Lowell revolutionized textile manufacturing in New England by centralizing all steps of cotton production in one mill and expanding the use of machines in the process. Instead of using different facilities or independent workers to complete the steps required to turn raw cotton into finished cloth, the new approach reduced time and costs since there was no need to transport products from one location to another. In addition, managers could better monitor the quality of their products when work was done under their direct supervision instead of being farmed out to outside workers.

Lowell also wanted to create a system that was more humane to workers. While on a trip to England in 1811, the New Englander had been shocked by the widespread use of child labor in factories. Lowell decided to employ young women instead. The women were housed together in company-owned dormitories where they were under the supervision of monitors. The girls were encouraged to improve their education and future prospects by attending classes and lectures. There were strict rules about behavior, and workers were required to attend church services. Lowell envisioned a system in which women would work at his factory for a few years before moving on to better-paying jobs.

The Lowell system was initially successful. It did reduce manufacturing costs, and it produced a better-quality product. It was widely copied through the region. However, by the 1840s, the system had begun to break down. The female workers had to work six days a week, usually for twelve hours. Most were unable to find better-paying jobs or positions and instead continued to work in the mills. Meanwhile, imports of cheaper textiles from other countries made the New England mills less profitable and caused many to reduce the number of workers or even go out of business.

Mary Paul was a young woman from Vermont who went to work at textile mills in New England. Beginning in 1845, she wrote a series of letters to her father, Bela Paul, that described her struggles in the mills. Her writing provided an important view of what life was like for the "Lowell girls" and a good summary of the events that led to the demise of the Lowell system.

Lowell Mills girls circa 1870
(University of Massachusetts Lowell Librarie)

Document Text
Lowell Nov 20th 1845
Dear Father

An opportunity now presents itself which I improve in writing to you. I started for this place at the time I talked of which was Thursday. I left Whitneys at nine o'clock stopped at Windsor at 12 and staid till 3 and started again. Did not stop again for any length of time till we arrived at Lowell. Went to a boarding house and staid until Monday night. On Saturday after I got here Luthera Griffith went round with me to find a place but we were unsuccessful. On Monday we started again and were more successful. We found a place in a spinning room and the next morning I went to work. I like very well have 50 cts first payment increasing every payment as I get along in work have a first rate overseer and a very good boarding place. I work on the Lawrence Corporation. Mill is No 2 spinning room. l was very sorry that you did not come to see me start. I wanted to see you and Henry but I suppose that you were otherways engaged. I hoped to see Julius but did not much expect to for I sposed he was engaged in other matters. He got six dollars for me which I was very glad of. It cost me $3.25 to come. Stage fare was $3.00 and lodging at Windsor, 25 cts. Had to pay only 25 cts for board for 9 days after I got here before I went into the mill. Had 2.50 left with which I got a bonnet and some other small articles. . . .

excuse bad writing and mistakes

This from your own daughter
Mary

Lowell Dec 21st 1845

Dear Father

I received your letter on Thursday the 14th with much pleasure. I am well which is one comfort. My life and health are spared while others are cut off. Last Thursday one girl fell down and broke her neck which caused instant death. She was going in or coming out of the mill and slipped down it being very icy. The same day a man was killed by the [railroad] cars. Another had nearly all of his ribs broken. Another was nearly killed by falling down and having a bale of cotton fall on him. Last Tuesday we were paid. In all I had six dollars and sixty cents paid $4.68 for board. . . . Next payment I am to have a dollar a week beside my board. We have not had much snow the deepest being not more than 4 inches. It has been very warm for winter. Perhaps you would like something about our regulations about going in and coming out of the mill. At 5 o'clock in the morning the bell rings for the folks to get up and get breakfast. At half past six it rings for the girls to get up and at seven they are called into the mill. At half past 12 we have dinner are called back again at one and stay till half past seven. . . . I get along very well with my work. I can doff as fast as any girl in our room. I think I shall have frames before long. The usual time allowed for learning is six months but I think I shall have frames before I have been in three as I get along so fast. I think that the factory is the best place for me and if any girl wants employment I advise them to come to Lowell. Tell Harriet that though she does not hear from me she is not forgotten. I have little time to devote to writing that I cannot write all I want to. There are half a dozen letters which I ought to write to day but I have not time. Tell Harriet I send my love to her and all of the girls. Give my love to Mrs. Clement. Tell Henry this will answer for him and you too for this time.
This from
Mary S Paul

Lowell Nov 5th 1848

Dear Father

Doubtless you have been looking for a letter from me all the week past. I would have written but wished to find whether I should be able to stand it—to do the work that I am now doing. I was unable to get my old place in the cloth room on the Suffolk or on any other corporation. I next tried the dressrooms on the Lawrence Cor[poration], but did not succeed in getting a place. I almost concluded to give up and go back to Claremont, but thought I would try once more. So I went to my old overseer on the Tremont Cor. I had no idea that he would want one, but he *did*, and I went to work last Tuesday warping—the same work I used to do.

It is *very* hard indeed and sometimes I think I shall not be able to endure it. I never worked so hard in my life but perhaps I shall get used to it. I shall try hard to do so for there is no other work that I can do unless I spin and that I shall not undertake on any account. I presume you have heard before this that the wages are to be reduced on the 20th of this month. It is *true* and there seems to be a good deal of excitement on the subject but I can not tell what will be the consequence. The companies pretend they are losing immense sums every *day* and therefore they are obliged to lessen the wages, but this seems perfectly absurd to me for they are constantly making *repairs* and it seems to me that this would not be if there were really any danger of their being obliged to *stop* the mills. . . .

Write soon. Yours affectionately
Mary S Paul

Glossary

cts: cents

doff: change the spindles on a spinning machine

overseer: manager; someone who supervises other employees

spinning room: an area in a factory where raw cotton fibers were twisted together to make thread through the use of spindles

stage: stagecoach; horse-drawn passenger carriage

staid: stayed

warping: controlling the threads on a spinning loom

Short-Answer Questions

1. Francis Cabot Lowell's system of manufacturing centralized the steps of cotton production in one mill, expanded the use of machines, and employed young women rather than children. What were the advantages of such a system, and to whom? What were the disadvantages, and to whom? Was the system successful?

2. What were the main reasons that young women like Mary Paul wanted to work in the textile mills? What challenges did Mary and other young women face at the mills?

3. Mary mentions her employer's plan to reduce wages. Why would the textile companies reduce wages? Why does Mary not believe the reasons stated by the owners of the businesses?

Isabella Beeton:
Mrs. Beeton's Book of Household Management

Author Isabella Beeton	**Significance** Shows assumptions about the roles played by middle-class employers and their domestic servants in the nineteenth century
Date 1861	
Document Type Essays, Reports, Manifestos	

Overview

Isabella Beeton (1836–1865) was an author, editor, and journalist best known for *Mrs. Beeton's Book of Household Management*, a set of recipes, domestic hints, and other useful tips for managing a Victorian home. Beeton was born Isabella Mason in London in 1836, the eldest daughter of a merchant and his wife. Her father died when she was only four years old, whereupon her mother sent her two eldest daughters to live with relatives. Isabella moved in with her grandfather in Cumberland, in the far northwestern corner of England. By the time her mother remarried, in about 1843, Isabella had returned to London to live with her stepfather, her sisters, and her four stepsiblings. They relocated from London to Surrey, where her mother and stepfather had thirteen more children. As the eldest child, Isabella assumed many responsibilities in their rural English home. She put that experience to good use in writing magazine articles about cooking and household management.

By 1854, Isabella had entered a relationship with Samuel Orchart Beeton, the son of a former neighbor and an up-and-coming publisher. He had contracted to publish an English edition of the runaway American bestseller *Uncle Tom's Cabin* by Harriet Beecher Stowe. He also published two prominent magazines: *Boys' Own*, the first of a long series of magazines designed to appeal to male adolescents, and the *Englishwoman's Domestic Magazine*, a periodical intended to appeal to middle-class women. The latter was enormously successful, selling as many as 50,000 issues a month. Isabella Beeton contributed to the magazine from its launch in 1854, sometimes as a translator of French fiction and later as a supplier of recipes and household hints. The latter were collected in 1861 as *Mrs. Beeton's Book of Household Management*. The volume was a steady seller and has remained in print for more than 150 years.

Isabella Beeton (National Portrait Gallery)

Document Text

Masters and Mistresses.—It has been said that good masters and mistresses make good servants, and this to a great extent is true. There are certainly some men and women in the wide field of servitude whom it would be impossible to train into good servants, but the conduct of both master and mistress is seldom without its effect upon these dependents. They are not mere machines, and no one has a right to consider them in that light. The sensible master and the kind mistress know, that if servants depend on them for their means of living, in their turn they are dependent on their servants for very many of the comforts of life; and that, with a proper amount of care in choosing servants, and treating them like reasonable beings, and making slight excuses for the shortcomings of human nature, they will, save in some exceptional case, be tolerably well served, and, in most instances, surround themselves with attached domestics. . . .

The Lady's-Maid.—The qualifications a lady's maid should possess are a thorough knowledge of hair dressing, dressmaking and repairing and restoring clothes. She should be able to pack well, and her taste, being often called into requisition in matters of dress, should be good. It is also essential that she be well spoken, quiet in manner and quick; that she should be clean and honest goes without saying. A lady's maid having so much more intercourse with her mistress than any other servant should not only possess, but learn, discretion from day to day. To know when to speak and when to be silent, and to be willing to bear with patience any little caprices of taste and temper with which she may have to contend.

Her first duty in the morning, after having performed her own toilet, is to prepare the bath and everything for dressing for her mistress, taking her an early cup of tea if she requires one. She then examines the clothes put off by her mistress the evening before, either to put them away, or to see that they are all in order to put on again. During the winter and in wet weather, the dresses should be carefully examined, and the mud removed. Dresses of tweed, and other woolen materials may be laid out on a table and brushed all over; but in general, even in woolen fabrics, the lightness of the tissues renders brushing unsuitable to dresses, and it is better to remove the dust from the folds by beating them lightly with a handkerchief or thin cloth. Silk dresses should never be brushed, but rubbed with a piece of merino, or other soft material, of a similar color, kept for the purpose. Summer dresses . . . simply require shaking; but if the muslin be tumbled, it must be ironed afterwards. If the dresses require slight repair, it should be done at once: "a stitch in time saves nine." . . .

Duties of the Housemaid.—"Cleanliness is next to godliness," saith the proverb, and "order" is in the next degree; the housemaid, then, may be said to be the handmaiden to two of the most prominent virtues. Her duties are very numerous, and many of the comforts of the family depend on their performance; but they are simple and easy to a person naturally clean and orderly, and desirous of giving satisfaction. In all families, whatever the habits of the master and mistress, servants will find it advantageous to rise early; their daily work will thus become easy to them. If they rise late, there is a struggle to overtake it, which throws an air of haste and hurry over the whole establishment. Where the master's time is regulated by early business or professional engagements, this will, of course, regulate the hours of the servants; but even where that is not the case, servants will find great personal convenience in rising early and getting through their work in an orderly and methodical manner. The housemaid who studies her own ease will certainly be at her work by six o'clock in the summer, and, probably, half-past six or seven in the winter months, having spent a reasonable time in her own chamber in dressing. Earlier than this would, probably, be an unnecessary waste of coals and candle in winter. . . .

The first duty of the housemaid in winter is to open the shutters of all the lower rooms in the house and take up the hearthrugs of those rooms which she is going to "do" before breakfast. In some families, where there is only a cook and housemaid kept, and where the drawing-rooms are large, the cook has the care of the dining-room, and the housemaid that of the breakfast-room, library, and drawing-rooms. After the shutters are all opened, she sweeps the breakfast-room, sweeping the dust towards the fireplace, of course previously removing the fender. She should then lay a cloth (generally made of coarse wrappering) over the carpet in front of the stove, and on this should place her housemaid's box, containing blacklead brushes, leathers, emery-paper, cloth, black lead, and all utensils necessary for cleaning a grate, with the cinder-pail on the other side. She now sweeps up the ashes, and deposits them in her cinder-pail, which is a japanned tin pail, with a wire-sifter inside, and a closely-fitting top. In this pail the cinders are sifted, and reserved for use in the kitchen. . . .

Breakfast served, the housemaid proceeds to the bed-chambers, throws up the sashes, if not already done, pulls up the blinds, throwing back curtains at the same time, and opens the beds, by removing the clothes, placing them over a horse, or, failing that, over the backs of chairs. She now proceeds to empty the slops. In doing this, everything is emptied into the slop-pail, leaving a little scalding-hot water for a minute in such vessels as require it; adding a drop of turpentine to the water, when that is not sufficient to cleanse them. . . .

Glossary

black lead: graphite, the same substance used in pencils, widely used in the Victorian era as a polish for cast-iron appliances, including cooking stoves and fireplace grates

caprices: impulsive or unpredictable actions or moods

fender: a kind of external fence surrounding a fireplace, meant to keep burning logs in the fireplace and children and pets out of it

horse: clotheshorse; an item used to air out and dry fabrics

intercourse: speech and professional interaction

japanned: finished in a varnish known as *japan*

Glossary

merino: a light, fine wool, woven from the fleeces of merino sheep

slops: a euphemism for the urine and feces in a chamber pot

toilet: personal grooming

Short-Answer Questions

1. What are the major differences between a lady's maid and a housemaid?

2. Does Mrs. Beeton think that there is such a thing as a bad servant? If so, how might she describe such a servant?

3. How does Mrs. Beeton describe the relationship between employer and domestic servant? In what ways is it similar to or different from the modern relationship between employer and employee?

Bradwell v. the State of Illinois

Author
Samuel Freeman Miller (Majority Opinion);
Joseph P. Bradley (Concurring Opinion)

Date
1873

Document Type
Legal

Significance
Ruled that women did not have a right to a specific occupation and highlighted the extraordinary degree of discrimination that women faced at the time

Overview

In the 1860s, women could not become lawyers under Illinois law. Nonetheless, in 1869, Myra Bradwell passed the Illinois bar exam, the test required to become a lawyer. When she formally applied to practice law, the state rejected her request. At the time, married women were not permitted to sign contracts or conduct other legal actions without the consent of their husband. Therefore, the state argued that married women could not be lawyers since they would have to rely on the assent of their spouses when interacting with clients or the courts.

Bradwell sued the state. She argued that under the Fourteenth Amendment all Americans had to be treated equally. The amendment held that the government could not infringe on the privileges and immunities of citizens. In other words, states could not treat someone differently just because they came from another state. Bradwell had been born in Vermont and claimed that part of the reason for her rejection was because she had

moved to Illinois. The Illinois Supreme Court rejected Bradwell's appeal. The would-be lawyer then took her case to the U.S. Supreme Court.

The Supreme Court heard arguments in the case on January 19, 1873. The Court issued its opinion on April 15, 1873. Eight of the nine justices rejected Bradwell's arguments (only Chief Justice Salmon Chase voted in her favor). In a majority opinion, Justice Samuel Freeman Miller wrote that the Fourteenth Amendment did not guarantee that Americans had the right to a specific occupation. Instead, states could set conditions that had to be met before someone was allowed to be a lawyer or doctor. In addition, Miller rejected the privileges and immunities argument. He wrote that Bradwell was a citizen of Illinois since she had lived in that state for several years. Four other justices joined Chase in his written opinion. Of course, Bradwell met all of the qualifications to be a lawyer, with the exception of her gender.

Meanwhile, Justice Joseph P. Bradley issued a concurring opinion backed by two other justices. Bradley's arguments were rooted in sexism and discrimination. He asserted that women were unsuited to be lawyers. He also reiterated the argument of the Illinois Supreme Court that women did not have an independent legal existence but were instead dependent on their husbands in legal matters.

The Bradwell case caused an uproar in Illinois and eventually prompted the state legislature to adopt a law that banned gender discrimination in licensing lawyers.

Bradwell became an attorney in 1890. Meanwhile, other states also ended restrictions on women joining the legal profession, although it was not until 1880 that the first woman lawyer argued a cases before the U.S. Supreme Court.

Over time, the Supreme Court has upheld the principle that no one has a basic right to a profession. However, beginning in the 1900s, the Court increasingly used the Fourteenth Amendment to ban gender discrimination, effectively rejecting and overturning Bradley's arguments.

Myra Bradwell (Wikimedia Commons)

Document Text
Majority Opinion
MR. JUSTICE MILLER delivered the opinion of the Court. . . .

The Fourteenth Amendment declares that citizens of the United States are citizens of the state within which they reside; therefore the plaintiff was, at the time of making her application, a citizen of the United States and a citizen of the State of Illinois. . . .

In regard to that amendment counsel for the plaintiff in this Court truly says that there are certain privileges and immunities which belong to a citizen of the United States as such; otherwise it would be nonsense for the Fourteenth Amendment to prohibit a state from abridging them, and he proceeds to argue that admission to the bar of a state of a person who possesses the requisite learning and character is one of those which a state may not deny.

In this latter proposition we are not able to concur with counsel. We agree with him that there are privileges and immunities belonging to citizens of the United States, in that relation and character, and that it is these and these alone which a state is forbidden to abridge. But the right to admission to practice in the courts of a state is not one of them. This right in no sense depends on citizenship of the United States. It has not, as far as we know, ever been made in any state, or in any case, to depend on citizenship at all. Certainly many prominent and distinguished lawyers have been admitted to practice, both in the state and federal courts, who were not citizens of the United States or of any state. But on whatever basis this right may be placed, so far as it can have any relation to citizenship at all, it would seem that, as to the courts of a state, it would relate to citizenship of the state, and as to federal courts, it would relate to citizenship of the United States.

Concurring Opinion
MR. JUSTICE BRADLEY:

I concur in the judgment of the Court in this case, by which the judgment of the Supreme Court of Illinois is affirmed, but not for the reasons specified in the opinion just read.

The claim of the plaintiff, who is a married woman, to be admitted to practice as an attorney and counselor at law is based upon the supposed right of every person, man or woman, to engage in any lawful employment for a livelihood. The Supreme Court of Illinois denied the application on the ground that, by the common law, which is the basis of the laws of Illinois, only men were admitted to the bar, and the legislature had not made any change in this respect, but had simply provided that no person should be admitted to practice as attorney or counselor without having previously obtained a license for that purpose from two justices of the Supreme Court, and that no person should receive a license without first obtaining a certificate from the court of some county of his good moral character. In other respects, it was left to the discretion of the court to establish the rules by which admission to the profession should be determined. The court, however, regarded itself as bound by at least two limitations. One was that it should establish such terms of admission as would promote the proper administration of justice, and the other that it should not admit any persons, or class of persons, not intended by the legislature to be admitted, even though not expressly excluded by statute. In view of this latter limitation the court felt compelled to deny the application of females to be admitted as members of the bar. Being contrary to the rules of the common law and the usages of Westminster Hall from time immemorial, it could not be supposed that the legislature had intended to adopt any different rule.

The claim that under the Fourteenth Amendment of the Constitution, which declares that no state shall make or enforce any law which shall abridge the privileges and immunities of citizens of the United States, the statute law of Illinois, or the common law prevailing in that state, can no longer be set up as a barrier against the right of females to pursue any lawful employment for a livelihood (the practice of law included), assumes that it is one of the privileges and immunities of women as citizens to engage in any and every profession, occupation, or employment in civil life.

It certainly cannot be affirmed, as an historical fact, that this has ever been established as one of the fundamental privileges and immunities of the sex. On the contrary, the civil law, as well as nature herself, has always recognized a wide difference in the respective spheres and destinies of man and woman. Man is, or should be, woman's protector and defender. The natural and proper timidity and delicacy which belongs to the female sex evidently unfits it for many of the occupations of civil life. The Constitution of the family organization, which is founded in the divine ordinance as well as in the nature of things, indicates the domestic sphere as that which properly belongs to the domain and functions of womanhood. The harmony, not to say identity, of interest and views which belong, or should belong, to the family institution is repugnant to the idea of a woman adopting a distinct and independent career from that of her husband. So firmly fixed was this sentiment in the founders of the common law that it became a maxim of that system of jurisprudence that a woman had no legal existence separate from her husband, who was regarded as her head and representative in the social state, and, notwithstanding some recent modifications of this civil status, many of the special rules of law flowing from and dependent upon this cardinal principle still exist in full force in most states. One of these is that a married woman is incapable, without her husband's consent, of making contracts which shall be binding on her or him. This very incapacity was one circumstance which the Supreme Court of Illinois deemed important in rendering a married woman incompetent fully to perform the duties and trusts that belong to the office of an attorney and counselor.

It is true that many women are unmarried and not affected by any of the duties, complications, and incapacities arising out of the married state, but these are exceptions to the general rule. The paramount destiny and mission of woman are to fulfill the noble and benign offices of wife and mother. This is the law of the Creator. And the rules of civil society.

Glossary

abridge: limit or restrict

bar: an informal term for the license to practice law

common law: a legal system based on traditional English law and court decisions known as precedents

concurring opinion: a legal judgment that agrees with another decision, but for different reasons

Fourteenth Amendment: an amendment from 1868 that defined citizenship for the United States and guaranteed that all U.S. citizens should be treated equally

majority opinion: a legal decision that has the support of the majority of judges of a court

privileges and immunities: rights and protections granted by one state that have to be respected by other states

Westminster Hall: one of the buildings of the British parliament and the site of trials and other legal proceedings

Short-Answer Questions

1. Did the majority opinion of the Supreme Court interpret the Fourteenth Amendment correctly in the Bradwell case? Should people have a right to engage in a specific profession such as the law? Please explain.

2. What were the main flaws or problems with the concurring opinion? What does that opinion reveal about gender discrimination at the time and the legal status of women in the United States?

3. In what way did Bradwell decision actually help reduce gender discrimination?

Lucy Parsons:
"The Negro:
Let Him Leave Politics to the Politician and Prayers to the Preacher"

Author
Lucy Parsons

Date
1886

Type
Letters/Correspondence

Significance
Blamed capitalism, rather than race, for the oppression of African Americans and other wage earners

Overview

Lucy Parsons was a Black labor activist who supported anarcho-communism and Black rights. She wrote many pamphlets and articles, including "The Negro: Let Him Leave Politics to the Politician and Prayers to the Preacher," published April 3, 1886, in *The Alarm*, an anarchist newspaper edited by her husband, Albert Parsons. The article was written in response to the lynching of thirteen African Americans in Carrollton, Mississippi. Parsons blames capitalism, rather than race, for the African Americans' oppression and their lynching and states that they were targets because they were poor.

Document Text

Who has stood upon the seashore and watched the weird dash of the ceaseless waves and has not become tired of their monotonous sameness? . . .

Yet, like the waves, there arises amid all this monotony a wrong sometimes as much or more glaring in all its details that not only is our attention attracted but our sympathies are enlisted.

Who . . . is to depict the wrongs to which the propertyless class are subjected, . . . as they read the graphic account flashed to ·us of the awful massacre of the poor and defenseless wage-slaves in Carrolton, in the state of Mississippi? . . .

Are there any so stupid as to believe these outrages have been . . . heaped upon the Negro

Photograph of Lucy Parsons from the 1920s
(Wikimedia Commons)

because he is Black? Not at all. It is because he is poor. It is because he is dependent. Because he is poorer as a class than his white wage-slave brother of the North. And to the Negro himself we would say your deliverance lies mainly in your own hands. . . . You sow but another reaps. You till the soil but for another to enjoy. . . .

The same land which you once tilled as a chattel slave you still till as a wage-slave, and in the same cabin which you then entered at eve not knowing but what you would be sold from wife and little ones before the morrow's setting sun, you now enter with dread lest you will be slain by the assassin hand of those who once would simply have sold you if they did not like you. . . .

Will the soft, smooth words of the bidder for your vote emancipate you from these conditions? . . . Will prayer stay the hand of the oppressor? Who has prayed with more zeal than you? . . . Then clearly your road to redemption lies not along these paths. But your course in future, if you value real freedom, is to leave politics to the politician, and prayer to those who can show wherein it has done them more good than it has ever done for you, and join hands with those who are striving for economic freedom. . . .

As to those local, periodical, damnable massacres to which you are at all times liable, these you must revenge in your own way. Are you deaf, dumb and blind to the atrocities that you are subjected to? . . . Is your heart a heart of stone, or its palpitations those of cowards, that you slink to your wretched abode and offer no resistance? Do you need something to nerve you to action? Then look in the tear-stained eye of your sorrowing wife and hungry children, or think of your son, who has been sent to the chain-gang or perhaps murdered upon your door-steps. . . . And this is the beginning of respect! Do you ask me what I would do if I were like you, poor, unarmed and defenseless? You are not absolutely defenseless.

Glossary

chattel slave: person owned as property

till: to prepare land for growing crops

wage-slave: person dependent on wages for survival

Short-Answer Questions

1. What is Lucy Parsons implying by her opening line, "Who has stood upon the seashore and watched the weird dash of the ceaseless waves and has not become tired of their monotonous sameness?" How does this relate to the treatment of Blacks?

2. Why does Parsons believe the problems Blacks faced were the result of poverty?

3. Why does Parsons stress that Blacks are not defenseless? What power does she believe Blacks have to improve their lives?

Clara Zetkin:
"Women's Work and the Trade Unions"

Author	**Significance**
Clara Zetkin	One of the earliest examples of an attempt to look at the ways gender and class struggle intersect
Date	
1893	
Document Type	
Essays, Reports, Manifestos	

Overview

Clara Josephin Eissner Zetkin (1857–1933) was a German Marxist theorist, activist, and advocate for women's rights. In 1911, she served as one of the organizers of the first International Women's Day, a global recognition of gender equality and the fight for equal rights and pay. Zetkin, who had trained as a journalist and teacher, became interested in socialism while attending school in Leipzig. By 1878, however, a nationwide ban on socialist activities forced her to flee the country. Zetkin left Germany for Switzerland and eventually ended up in Paris, where she became the companion of the Marxist organizer Ossip Zetkin (1850–1889), with whom she had two children.

After Ossip Zetkin's death in 1889, Clara Zetkin married an artist named Georg Friedrich Zundel and returned to Germany. Under the Weimar Republic—the government that controlled Germany from the end of World War I until the rise of the Nazi party—she served as a representative in the Reichstag, the lower body of the Weimar Parliament. With the rise of the Nazi party, however, she was forced into exile again. She found shelter in the Soviet Union and died there in 1933.

It was while married to Zundel that Clara Zetkin assumed the editorship of the socialist and feminist journal *Gleichhheit* (*Equality*), a magazine dedicated to themes that supported women's and workers' equality. Zetkin edited the journal for twenty-five years, from 1892 to 1917. She published the essay "Women's Work and the Trade Unions" in the magazine on November 1, 1893, during her second year as editor.

1897 photograph of Clara Zetkin
(Wikimedia Commons)

Document Text

. . . It is not just the women workers who suffer because of the miserable payment of their labor. The male workers, too, suffer because of it. As a consequence of their low wages, the women are transformed from mere competitors into unfair competitors who push down the wages of men. Cheap women's labor eliminates the work of men and if the men want to continue to earn their daily bread, they must put up with low wages. Thus women's work is not only a cheap form of labor, it also cheapens the work of men and for that reason it is doubly appreciated by the capitalist, who craves profits. . . .

The economic advantages of the industrial activity of proletarian women only aid the tiny minority of the sacrosanct guild of coupon clippers and extortionists of profit. . . .

Given the fact that many thousands of female workers are active in industry, it is vital for the trade unions to incorporate them into their movement. In individual industries where female labor plays an important role, any movement advocating better wages, shorter working hours, etc., would be doomed from the start because of the attitude of those women workers who are not organized. Battles which began propitiously enough, ended up in failure because the employers were able to play off non-union female workers against those that are organized in unions. These non-union workers continued to work (or took up work) under any conditions, which transformed them from competitors in dirty work to scabs. . . .

Certainly one of the reasons for these poor wages for women is the circumstances that female workers are practically unorganized. They lack the strength which comes with unity. They lack the courage, the feeling of power, the spirit of resistance, and the ability to resist which is produced by the strength of an organization in which the individual fights for everybody and everybody fights for the individual. Furthermore, they lack the enlightenment and the training which an organization provides. . . .

Glossary

capitalist: in Marxist theory, someone who owns the means to produce goods, who hires other people to do the work that produces those goods, and who takes the surplus generated from the sale of those goods

guild: another word for union

proletarian: a person who does not own the means to make products but has only their labor to sell, effectively putting them under the control of capitalists

propitiously: auspiciously, hopefully

"sacrosanct guild of coupon clippers": a reference to bourgeois women—the wives of capitalists—who benefit from the labor of proletarian women but whose own work is limited to finding ways to save themselves and their families money

scabs: nonunion workers who are hired when union workers are striking specifically to break the union's strike

Short-Answer Questions

1. What role do capitalists play in the situation of working-class women?

2. What does Zetkin suggest that working women should do to survive in the workplace?

3. Why does Zetkin suggest that men should advocate for higher wages for working women?

Jack London:
The People of the Abyss

Author Jack London **Date** 1903 **Document Type** Essays, Reports, Manifestos	**Significance** Challenged the social and economic structures that perpetuated the crippling conditions of the working-class experience, humanized people living in poverty, and confronted the prevailing view of the era that poverty was solely a result of personal failings

Overview

The Industrial Revolution of the late nineteenth century sparked immense scientific and technological innovation, rapid economic growth, and great power for its nations and elites. At the same time, it took a hard toll on the poor working class.

In its day, *The People of the Abyss* was one of several books that documented the dismal and disturbing conditions endured by poor urban workers in America and England. This book offered a blunt account of poverty in the East End of London, England. Its author, Jack London, was an accomplished American author best known for writing travel and survival adventure stories such as *The Call of the Wild* and *White Fang*. He also worked as an investigative journalist interested in political and social issues concerning workers' rights, the plight of marginalized people, and socialism. In *The People of the Abyss*, he captured in great detail the extent of overpopulation, filth, poverty, crime, and hopelessness. Upon its publication, the book ignited public debate and controversy. It contributed to the growing social and political movements of the time that questioned capitalism and advocated for social reforms.

Author Jack London
(Wikimedia Commons)

Document Text
Chapter XIX. The Ghetto

. . . Today the dominant economic class . . . has confined the undesirable yet necessary workers into ghettos of remarkable meanness and vastness. East London is such a ghetto, where the rich and the powerful do not dwell, and the traveller cometh not, and where two million workers swarm, procreate, and die. . . .

It must not be supposed that all the workers of London are crowded into the East End, but the tide is setting strongly in that direction. . . .

While it is not a city of slums . . . it may well be said to be one gigantic slum. . . . Where sights and sounds abound which neither you nor I would care to have our children see and hear is a place where no man's children should live, and see, and hear.

Where you and I would not care to have our wives pass their lives is a place where no other man's wife should have to pass her life. . . . What is not good enough for you is not good enough for other men. . . .

The law demands 400 cubic feet of space for each person. In army barracks each soldier is allowed 600 cubic feet. . . . Yet in London there are 900,000 people living in less than the 400 cubic feet prescribed by the law. . . .

But with 900,000 people actually living under illegal conditions, the authorities have their hands full. When the overcrowded folk are ejected they stray off into some other hole; . . . it is next to impossible to keep track of them. If the Public Health Act of 1891 were suddenly and completely enforced, 900,000 people would receive notice to clear out of their houses and go on to the streets, and 500,000 rooms would have to be built before they were all legally housed again. . . .

The mean streets merely look mean from the outside, but inside the walls are to be found squalor, misery, and tragedy. . . .

A short while back died an old woman of seventy-five years of age. At the inquest the coroner's officer stated that "all he found in the room was a lot of old rags covered with vermin." . . . The doctor said: "Deceased was very badly nourished and was very emaciated. She had extensive sores on her legs." . . .

It is notorious that here in the Ghetto the houses of the poor are greater profit earners than the mansions of the rich. Not only does the poor worker have to live like a beast, but he pays proportionately more for it than does the rich man for his spacious comfort. . . . Not only are houses let, but they are sublet, and sub-sublet down to the very rooms. . . .

This Ghetto crowding is not through inclination, but compulsion. Nearly fifty percent of the workers pay from one-fourth to one-half of their earnings for rent. The average rent . . . is from four to six shillings per week for one room. . . . And rents are going up all the time. . . .

Class supremacy can rest only on class degradation; and when the workers are segregated in the Ghetto, they cannot escape the consequent degradation. A short and stunted people is created. . . .

To make matters worse, the men of the Ghetto are the men who are left—a deteriorated stock, left to undergo still further deterioration. . . . Those who are lacking, the weak of heart and head and hand, as well as the rotten and hopeless, have remained to carry on the breed. And year by year, in turn, the best they breed are taken from them. Wherever a man of vigour and stature manages to grow up, he is haled forthwith into the army. . . .

This constant selection of the best from the workers has impoverished those who are left. . . . They become indecent and bestial. When they kill, they kill with their hands, and then stupidly surrender themselves to the executioners. . . . Wife-beating is the masculine prerogative of matrimony. . . . And when they have polished off the mother of their children with a black eye or so, they knock her down and proceed to trample her very much as a Western stallion tramples a rattlesnake. . . .

A woman of the lower Ghetto classes is as much the slave of her husband as is the Indian squaw. . . . The men are economically dependent on their masters, and the women are economically dependent on the men. The result is, the woman gets the beating the man should give his master, and she can do nothing. There are the kiddies, and he is the bread-winner, and she dare not send him to jail and leave herself and children to starve. Evidence to convict can rarely be obtained when such cases come into the courts; as a rule, the trampled wife and mother is weeping and hysterically beseeching the magistrate to let her husband off for the kiddies' sakes. . . .

It would be enough to condemn modern society as hardly an advance on slavery or serfdom, if the permanent condition of industry were to be that which we behold, that ninety percent of the actual producers of wealth have no home that they can call their own beyond the end of the week; have no bit of soil, or so much as a room that belongs to them; have nothing of value of any kind, except as much old furniture as will go into a cart; have the precarious chance of weekly wages, which barely suffice to keep them in health; are housed, for the most part, in places that no man thinks fit for his horse; are separated by so narrow a margin from destitution that a month of bad trade, sickness, or unexpected loss brings them face to face with hunger and pauperism. . . . If this is to be the permanent arrangement of modern society, civilization must be held to bring a curse on the great majority of mankind. . . .

It used to be the proud boast that every Englishman's home was his castle. . . . The Ghetto folk have no homes. . . .

Glossary

dominant economic class: upper-class and some middle-class people with economic and political power; politicians, bankers, industrialists, and the like

ghetto: a portion of a city occupied by a minority group, particularly due to social, racial, or economic pressure

meanness: austerity; shabbiness

Short-Answer Questions

1. Identify the audience or audiences for whom author Jack London wrote this account.

2. Describe the explicit and implicit conditions that East End workers experienced.

3. What groups of people does the author seem to hold responsible for East End workers' problems? Why?

Florence Kelley:
"Child Labor and Women's Suffrage"

Author
Florence Kelley

Date
1905

Document Type
Speeches/Addresses

Significance
Served as a catalyst for increased awareness and action against child labor and emphasized the connections between women's suffrage and labor rights

Overview

From the late nineteenth and early twentieth centuries, child labor grew exponentially in every corner of urban working-class America. The 1870 U.S. census recorded 750,00 children under the age of fifteen working in mines, factories, and other mass industries. By 1905, the number more than doubled, including children as young as five years old. Employers subjected children to long hours, low wages, and hazardous environments, which often resulted in injuries, illness, and mental health conditions.

Florence Kelley, a prominent social reformer and advocate for labor rights, became a champion in the fight against child labor and a fierce women's suffrage supporter. Kelley's speech "Child Labor and Women's Suffrage" was delivered on July 22, 1905, at the National American Woman Suffrage Association Convention in Philadelphia. The speech played a significant role in advocating for the abolition of child labor and for women's right to vote. The speech highlighted the exploitation of children in factories, the urgent need for social and political reforms, and the connection between child labor reform and women's suffrage. Kelley argued that women's suffrage was vital to achieving child labor reforms because empowered and enfranchised women would be able to influence legislation and advocate for the welfare of children. In this way, Kelly helped foster a broader understanding of the importance of women's empowerment to bring about meaningful societal and political change.

In addition, Kelley's speech addressed the detrimental effects of child labor on both the children themselves and society as a whole. She emphasized that child labor was not just a labor issue but also a human rights issue. Kelley argued that children, as the future citizens of the nation, deserved the opportunity to receive an education and develop their physical and mental capacities rather than being trapped in exploitative labor. This argument implored unions and workers to support child labor reform and women's suffrage.

Document Text

We have, in this country, two million children under the age of sixteen years who are earning their bread. They vary in age from six and seven years (in the cotton mills of Georgia) and eight, nine and ten years (in the coal-breakers of Pennsylvania), to fourteen, fifteen and sixteen years in more enlightened states.

No other portion of the wage earning class increased so rapidly from decade to decade as the young girls from fourteen to twenty years. Men increase, women increase, youth increase, boys increase in the ranks of the breadwinners; but no contingent so doubles from census period to census period (both by percent and by count of heads), as does the contingent of girls between twelve and twenty years of age. They are in commerce, in offices, in manufacturing.

Tonight while we sleep, several thousand little girls will be working in textile mills, all the night through, in the deafening noise of the spindles and the looms spinning and weaving cotton and wool, silks and ribbons for us to buy.

In Alabama the law provides that a child under sixteen years of age shall not work in a cotton mill at night longer than eight hours, and Alabama does better in this respect than any other southern state. North and South Carolina and Georgia place no restriction upon the work of children at night; and while we sleep little white girls will be working tonight in the mills in those states, working eleven hours at night.

In Georgia there is no restriction whatever! A girl of six or seven years, just tall enough to reach the bobbins, may work eleven hours by day or by night. And they will do so tonight, while we sleep.

Nor is it only in the South that these things occur. Alabama does better than New Jersey. For Alabama limits the children's work at night to eight hours, while New Jersey permits it all night long. Last year New Jersey took a long backward step. A good

Florence Kelley (Library of Congress)

law was repealed which had required women and [children] to stop work at six in the evening and at noon on Friday. Now, therefore, in New Jersey, boys and girls, after their 14th birthday, enjoy the pitiful privilege of working all night long.

In Pennsylvania, until last May it was lawful for children, 13 years of age, to work twelve hours at night. A little girl, on her thirteenth birthday, could start away from her home at half past five in the afternoon, carrying her pail of midnight luncheon as happier people carry their midday luncheon, and could work in the mill from six at night until six in the morning, without violating any law of the Commonwealth.

If the mothers and the teachers in Georgia could vote, would the Georgia Legislature have refused at every session for the last three years to stop the work in the mills of children under twelve years of age?

Would the New Jersey Legislature have passed that shameful repeal bill enabling girls of fourteen years to work all night, if the mothers in New Jersey were enfranchised? Until the mothers in the great industrial states are enfranchised, we shall none of us be able to free our consciences from participation in this great evil. No one in this room tonight can feel free from such participation. The children make our shoes in the shoe factories; they knit our stockings, our knitted underwear in the knitting factories. They spin and weave our cotton underwear in the cotton mills. Children braid straw for our hats, they spin and weave the silk and velvet wherewith we trim our hats. They stamp buckles and metal ornaments of all kinds, as well as pins and hat-pins. Under the sweating system, tiny children make artificial flowers and neckwear for us to buy. They carry bundles of garments from the factories to the tenements, little beasts of burden, robbed of school life that they may work for us.

We do not wish this. We prefer to have our work done by men and women. But we are almost powerless. Not wholly powerless, however, are citizens who enjoy the right of petition. For myself, I shall use this power in every possible way until the right to the ballot is granted, and then I shall continue to use both.

What can we do to free our consciences? There is one line of action by which we can do much. We can enlist the workingmen on behalf of our enfranchisement just in proportion as we strive with them to free the children. No labor organization in this country ever fails to respond to an appeal for help in the freeing of the children.

For the sake of the children, for the Republic in which these children will vote after we are dead, and for the sake of our cause, we should enlist the workingmen voters, with us, in this task of freeing the children from toil!

Glossary

abolition: an act of bringing something to an end

enfranchised: extended the right to vote

suffrage: political voting rights

workingmen: members of labor unions

Short-Answer Questions

1. Describe the explicit and implicit effects of child labor.

2. What rhetorical devices or persuasive words does Kelly use in her speech to connect with the sympathies of the audience? Why might she have specified that "white girls" were working at night in cotton mills?

3. Describe the connection between child labor reform and women's suffrage that Florence Kelly describes.

Kelly Miller:
"The Economic Handicap of the Negro in the North"

Author Kelly Miller **Date** 1906 **Type** Essays, Reports, Manifestos	**Significance** Asserted that fewer Black southerners than anticipated moved to northern cities in the early 1900s, despite rampant racial discrimination in the South, because economic conditions could not support such a move

Overview

In an article published in the May 1906 issue of *The Annals of the American Academy of Political and Social Science*, Kelly Miller takes stock of the reasons why, despite a marked increase in racially motivated violence in the South, surprisingly few African Americans were relocating to the North. A professor of sociology at Howard University for close to four decades, Miller sought to reconcile the opposing positions of the two most prominent African American leaders of the late nineteenth and early twentieth centuries, Booker T. Washington and W. E. B. Du Bois. Miller advocated for a system of education that would offer both the vocational training that Washington promoted and the more traditional liberal arts curriculum championed tirelessly by Du Bois.

In this article, Miller exhibits a similar sort of pragmatism in his comparison of the employment prospects for Black Americans in the southern and northern states, finding that economic realities superseded political aspirations and discouraged the sort of mass exodus from the South by that one might have expected of African Americans. The Great Migration, which got underway roughly a decade after the publication of Miller's article, bears out his thesis; millions of Black southerners relocated to northern and western destinations primarily for employment opportunities.

Document Text

The economic problem growing out of the negro's presence in the North borrows importance from the prevailing dread of an overwhelming influx from the South. This conclusion is founded on fear rather than on careful consideration of the facts and factors entering into the premises. . . . The total number of negroes in the thirty-one free States of the North and West does not equal the negro population of the single State of Alabama . . . . If we make the slightest marginal allowance for the increase of the negroes who were in the North in 1900, it will be seen that the entire Northern influx which occasions so much frantic discussion would be less than the growth in a single Southern State. . . .

Seven-tenths of the Northern negroes are found in the cities. The Northern influx during the last decade was mainly to the large cities of that section. Outside of these centers the tendency is to diminish rather than to increase. From 1890 to 1900 there was an actual decrease of the negro population in seven Northern States. . . .

Surprise is sometimes expressed that this race does not in larger numbers remove itself from the political and civil restrictions of the South to the more liberal regime of the freer States. But it is economic rather than political motives that influence the movement of modern population. A conservative tendency disposes all people to endure political ills at home rather than fly to industrial conditions they know not of. If we except the more restless and ambitious spirit, the twenty million foreigners who have come to this country since 1820 have not been attracted by an asylum from political oppression, but have come in quest of better economic opportunity and outlook. . . .

In the North it is true that the negro enjoys the fullest political prerogative, his educational facilities are the best that the world affords, and yet these things attract not the mass of the race, simply because they do not carry with them corresponding industrial opportunity. . . .

The broad distinction between the negro workman in the North and in the South is that in one section he is confined generally to agricultural pursuits, whereas in the other he is shut in to personal and domestic service. It is also true that in the South, especially in the lower and hotter tier of Southern States, where white competition is not energetic, he is largely engaged in mechanical pursuits, a calling from which he is all but absolutely excluded in the North. . . .

The negro is being driven even from the domain of domestic and semi-domestic service as fast as white men fill up the higher fields of mechanical skill and press downwards into the lower stratum of occupation. Pursuits once monopolized by the negro in the North are rapidly passing from him. The white waiter, barber, and coachman poaches defiantly upon the Black man's industrial preserves. . . . The attitude of the trade union towards the negro is that of intolerance and exclusion. . . .

I cannot agree with Dr. Booker T. Washington that these pursuits are passing from the Black man because of his shiftlessness and inefficiency. It is rather the case of the stronger competitor pushing the weak to the wall. The strong man enters into the house of the weak, binds him and takes his possessions, and heeds not his wail of entreaty. The smallness of his numbers is the negro's industrial weakness in the North. . . .

As meager as are his earning opportunities, when it comes to renting a house, which in the nature of the case must absorb a large part of his earnings, he is often forced to pay a higher rate of rental than his white competitor for like accommodations. . . .

The negro in the North, by reason of his hard industrial lot, is forced to live in the alleys and shady places, the breeders of vice and crime, of disease and death, and the feeders of jails, hospitals and penitentiaries. When these cities are threatened with such frightful death rate and crime rate among this neglected class they should remember that it is but the logical outcome of the hard industrial lot. . . .

Glossary

entreaty: a plea for help

influx: movement of a large group of people

shiftlessness: laziness

stratum: layer

Short-Answer Questions

1. Based on Miller's analysis, why were African Americans moving into northern states in such unexpectedly small numbers?

2. How does Miller compare and contrast the challenges faced by African Americans living in the northern states with those confronting African Americans in the South?

3. How does Miller take issue with Booker T. Washington's claim that the supposed "shiftlessness and inefficiency" of Black men was holding them back?

Muller v. Oregon

Author David J. Brewer	**Significance** Upheld a state law limiting working hours for female but not male workers, thereby reinforcing sex discrimination against women in the workplace and hindering the campaign for equality
Date 1908	
Document Type Legal	

Overview

In the late 1800s and early 1900s, political progressives pursued economic and political reforms. Many pushed hard to improve working conditions for men, women, and children laboring in shops and factories. At the same time, the women's movement pressed for the right to vote and the right to exercise autonomy in legal and economic affairs just as men enjoyed. They did not want the government policing them based on their sex. However, some argued there were inherent differences between men and women, and considering women's physique and their maternal and societal roles, they needed to be protected in the workplace. The State of Oregon passed an act that aligned with this idea and limited the hours a woman could work in a twenty-four-hour period to ten hours.

In 1908, in *Muller v. Oregon*, the U.S. Supreme Court heard a case challenging Oregon state law that regulated the employment of women. The case arose when the owner of a laundry in Portland, Oregon, violated a state law limiting the number of hours a woman could work in his shop. The man challenged the constitutionality of this protective legislation; the direction the Supreme Court was taking in cases of this sort at the time portended a victory for the laundry owner. However, defenders of the Oregon state law presented a mountain of evidence that demonstrated the danger to women workers posed by industrial practices if left unregulated. As a result, the U.S. Supreme Court unanimously upheld Oregon's law. This victory for progressives supporting worker protections thus came at a cost, as the Court's decision upholding protective legislation undermined women's rights.

Document Text

Mr. Justice Brewer Delivered the Opinion of the Court:

On February 19, 1903, the legislature of the state of Oregon passed an act (Session Laws 1903, p. 148) the first section of which is in these words:

Sec. 1. That no female (shall) be employed in any mechanical establishment, or factory, or laundry in this state more than ten hours during any one day. The hours of work may be so arranged as to permit the employment of females at any time so that they shall not work more than ten hours during the twenty-four hours of any one day. . . .

A trial resulted in a verdict against the defendant, who was sentenced to pay a fine of $10. The supreme court of the state affirmed the conviction . . . whereupon the case was brought here on writ of error.

The single question is the constitutionality of the statute under which the defendant was convicted, so far as it affects the work of a female in a laundry. That it does not conflict with any provisions of the state Constitution is settled by the decision of the supreme court of the state.

The contentions of the defendant, now plaintiff in error, are thus stated in his brief:

(1) Because the statute attempts to prevent persons sui juris from making their own contracts, and thus violates the provisions of the 14th Amendment, as follows:

No state shall make or enforce any law which shall abridge the privileges or immunities of citizens of the United States; nor shall any state deprive any person of life, liberty, or property, without due process of law; nor deny to any person within its jurisdiction the equal protection of the laws.

Justice David Josiah Brewer wrote the unanimous opinion in **Muller v. Oregon.**
(Library of Congress)

(2) Because the statute does not apply equally to all persons similarly situated, and is class legislation.

(3) The statute is not a valid exercise of the police power. The kinds of work prescribed are not unlawful, nor are they declared to be immoral or dangerous to the public health; nor can such a law be sustained on the ground that it is designed to protect women on account of their sex. There is no necessary or reasonable connection between the limitation prescribed by the act and the public health, safety, or welfare. . . .

It is the law of Oregon that women, whether married or single, have equal contractual and personal rights with men. As said by Chief Justice Wolverton, . . .

". . . The current runs steadily and strongly in the direction of the emancipation of the wife, and the policy, as disclosed by all recent legislation upon the subject in this state, is to place her upon the same footing as if she were a feme sole, not only with respect to her separate property, but as it affects her right to make binding contracts." . . .

It is undoubtedly true, as more than once declared by this court, that the general right to contract in relation to one's business is part of the liberty of the individual, protected by the 14th Amendment to the Federal Constitution; yet it is equally well settled that this liberty is not absolute and extending to all contracts, and that a state may, without conflicting with the provisions of the 14th Amendment, restrict in many respects the individual's power of contract. . . .

That woman's physical structure and the performance of maternal functions place her at a disadvantage in the struggle for subsistence is obvious. This is especially true when the burdens of motherhood are upon her. Even when they are not, by abundant testimony of the medical fraternity continuance for a long time on her feet at work, repeating this from day to day, tends to injurious effects upon the body, and, as healthy mothers are essential to vigorous offspring, the physical well-being of woman becomes an object of public interest and care in order to preserve the strength and vigor of the race.

Still again, history discloses the fact that woman has always been dependent upon man. He established his control at the outset by superior physical strength, and this control in various forms, with diminishing intensity, has continued to the present. . . . Education was long denied her, and while now the doors of the schoolroom are opened and her opportunities for acquiring knowledge are great, yet even with that and the consequent increase of capacity for business affairs it is still true that in the struggle for subsistence she is not an equal competitor with her brother. Though limitations upon personal and contractual rights may be removed by legislation, there is that in her disposition and habits of life which will operate against a full assertion of those rights. She will still be where some legislation to protect her seems necessary to secure a real equality of right. Doubtless there are individual exceptions, and there are many respects in which she has an advantage over him; but looking at it from the viewpoint of the effort to maintain an independent position in life, she is not upon an equality. . . .

Even though all restrictions on political, personal, and contractual rights were taken away, and she stood, so far as statutes are concerned, upon an absolutely equal plane with him, it would still be true that she is so constituted that she will rest upon and look to him for protection; that her physical structure and a proper discharge of her maternal functions—having in view not merely her own health, but the well-being of the race—justify legislation to protect her from the greed as well as the passion of man. The limitations which this statute places upon her contractual powers, upon her right to agree with her employer as to the time she shall labor, are not imposed solely for her benefit, but also largely for the benefit of all. . . .

. . . We are of the opinion that it cannot be adjudged that the act in question is in conflict with the Federal Constitution, so far as it respects the work of a female in a laundry, and the judgment of the Supreme Court of Oregon is affirmed.

Glossary

feme sole: in the English-American common law tradition, an unmarried woman in charge of her separate estate and against whom legal obligations are enforceable; the term is of French origin

sui juris: of age and capacity to take full possession of one's rights; not under the authority of another

Short-Answer Questions

1. Summarize the Supreme Court's arguments concerning the rights women possess.

2. Summarize the Supreme Court's arguments concerning the rights women do not possess.

3. Evaluate the Supreme Court's justification for ruling that women are not equal to men.

Clara Lemlich:
"Life in the Shop"

<table>
<tr><td>

Author
Clara Lemlich

Date
1909

Type
Essays, Reports, Manifestos

</td><td>

Significance
Described the abysmal working conditions in which garment workers toiled that helped justify the New York shirtwaist strike of 1909

</td></tr>
</table>

Overview

Clara Lemlich, a Ukranian Jewish immigrant, at twenty-three years old, was largely responsible for igniting the 1909 walkout of shirtwaist makers in New York City with her call for a general strike. The walkout came to be known as the Uprising of the Twenty Thousand and lasted more than two months. In this article published in the *New York Evening Journal* on November 28, 1909, she describes the working conditions in a shirtwaist factory. Lemlich later married an activist for a printer's union and continued to act on behalf of labor and other causes.

Document Text

First let me tell you something about the way we work and what we are paid. There are two kinds of work—regular, that is salary work, and piecework. The regular work pays about $6 a week and the girls have to be at their machines at 7 o'clock in the morning and they stay at them until 8 o'clock at night, with just one-half hour for lunch in that time.

The work is all divided up. No girl ever makes a whole waist. There are examiners and finishers. They all get different pay for their work, but it runs only from $3 or $4 a week; the finishers make [it] to the $6 or sometimes $7 a week the cutters and some others make. The shops. Well, there is just one row of ma-

Portrait of Clara Lemlich
(Wikimedia Commons)

chines that the daylight ever gets to—that is the front row, nearest the window. The girls at all the other rows of machines back in the shops have to work by gaslight, by day as well as by night. Oh, yes, the shops keep the work going at night, too.

The bosses in the shops are hardly what you would call educated men, and the girls to them are part of the machines they are running. They yell at the girls and they "call them down" even worse than I imagine the Negro slaves were in the South. They don't use very nice language. They swear at us and sometimes do worse—they call us names that are not pretty to hear.

There are no dressing rooms for the girls in the shops. They have to hang up their hats and coats—such as they are—on hooks along the walls. Sometimes a girl has a new hat. It never is much to look at because it never costs more than 50 cents, but it's pretty sure to be spoiled after it's been at the shop.

We're human, all of us girls, and we're young. We like new hats as well as any other young women. Why shouldn't we? And if one of us gets a new one, even if it hasn't cost more than fifty cents, that means that we have gone for weeks on two-cent lunches—dry cake and nothing else.

I have known many girls who were never able to buy a hat at all. Lots of them don't wear any, Winter or Summer. They are the ones who earn $3 a week. They take the clothes of the girls better off—those who earn $6 or $7 a week—after they have really been worn out. That's how they manage to get along. They never buy any clothes of their own.

Seventy-five cents is the most a girl can pay for a pair of shoes. And she has to wear them a long time—and she does. Some girls can buy only one, perhaps two shirtwaists a year—while they help to make thousands of them. They make their own dresses after they have worked thirteen or fourteen hours a day, made with remnants that cost altogether $1 or $1.50.

The shops are unsanitary—that's the word that is generally used, but there ought to be a worse one used. Whenever we tear or damage any of the goods we sew on, or whenever it is found damaged after we are through with it, whether we have done it or not, we are charged for the piece and sometimes for a whole yard of the material— perhaps $1 or $1.50.

At the beginning of every slow season, $2 is deducted from our salaries. We have never been able to find out what this is for.

Glossary

shirtwaist: a tailored blouse for women that resembles a men's shirt in terms of its collar and buttons

Short-Answer Questions

1. What is the nature of the work Lemlich describes? How might those performing the jobs be impacted physically and emotionally over time?

2. Besides the low wage, what aspects of the jobs in the shirtwaist factories prevented workers from escaping poverty?

3. How might readers of this piece in 1909 have been particularly enraged about the fact that the workers were women? What does this reveal about notions of gender in the early twentieth century?

Rose Schneiderman:
Speech on the Triangle Shirtwaist Fire

Author
Rose Schneiderman

Date
1911

Document Type
Speeches/Addresses

Significance
Pointed out that labor conflicts do not just involve workers and management but that citizens, politicians, and police play roles as well

Overview

Many New York City garment manufacturers were known for exploiting their workers in the early twentieth century. Female workers were especially vulnerable. Low wages, long hours, hazardous working conditions, workplace safety violations, and sexual harassment were among the workers' complaints. Workers often tried to organize labor unions to negotiate with factory owners.

The Triangle Shirtwaist Factory was located on the eighth, ninth, and tenth floors of the Asch Building in Greenwich Village, New York City. The company made women's blouses and employed approximately 500 employees. The workers were mostly young Jewish and Italian immigrant women and girls. They worked six days a week for low wages in an unsafe building. Management locked doors and staircase exits to surveil workers and keep union organizers out. On March 25, 1911, a devasting fire at the factory killed 146 workers—123 females and 23 males. Many people jumped 100 feet to their deaths as an alternative to being burned alive.

Rose Schneiderman, a Jewish immigrant from Poland, worked as a labor union organizer and advocated for women's suffrage. On April 2, 1911, she delivered this speech at the Metropolitan Opera House during a meeting organized to protest the fire and garner support for unionization.

Rose Schneiderman
(Library of Congress)

Document Text

I would be a traitor to these poor burned bodies if I came here to talk good fellowship. We have tried you good people of the public and we have found you wanting. The old Inquisition had its rack and its thumbscrews and its instruments of torture with iron teeth. We know what these things are today; the iron teeth are our necessities, the thumbscrews are the high powered and swift machinery close to which we must work, and the rack is here in the firetrap structures that will destroy us the minute they catch on fire.

This is not the first time girls have been burned alive in the city. Every week I must learn of the untimely death of one of my sister workers. Every year thousands of us are maimed. The life of men and women is so cheap and property is so sacred. There are so many of us for one job it matters little if 146 of us are burned to death.

We have tried you citizens; we are trying you now, and you have a couple of dollars for the sorrowing mothers, brothers and sisters by way of a charity gift. But every time the workers come out in the only way they know to protest against conditions which are unbearable the strong hand of the law is allowed to press down heavily upon us.

Public officials have only words of warning to us—warning that we must be intensely peaceable, and they have the workhouse just back of all their warnings. The strong hand of the law beats us back, when we rise, into the conditions that make life unbearable.

I can't talk fellowship to you who are gathered here. Too much blood has been spilled. I know from my experience it is up to the working people to save themselves. The only way they can save themselves is by a strong working-class movement.

Glossary

Inquisition: reference to the Spanish Inquisition, famous for the use of torture

shirtwaist: a woman's tailored blouse

tried: tested one's patience

Short-Answer Questions

1. Describe the challenges workers face, according to Schneiderman.

2. Identify the groups that work against factory workers.

3. Who is Schneiderman addressing? What is the purpose of her speech?

Leonora O'Reilly: Statement to the U.S. House Judiciary Committee

Author
Leonora O'Reilly

Date
1912

Document Type
Speeches/Addresses

Significance
Advocated for a constitutional amendment giving women the right to vote, positing that access to education and training opportunities, the economic and political empowerment of women, and achieving equality and justice for working women hinged on women's suffrage

Overview

Leonora O'Reilly, nicknamed "the agitator," was a significant leader in the labor and women's suffrage movements of the early twentieth century. Born in New York City in 1870 to Irish immigrant parents, she started working in a shirt factory at age eleven and experienced firsthand the hardship of poverty and the many challenges working-class families faced. Throughout her teen years, she became especially focused on the exploitation of working women and children.

By the age of sixteen, she joined the Knights of Labor, a prominent labor organization of the time. She organized and participated in strikes, demonstrations, and campaigns for better wages, shorter work hours, and improved working conditions. In addition, she was a strong supporter of women's suffrage. In 1911, she cofounded the Wage Earner's Suffrage League in New York City, and she played a vital role in organizing suffrage campaigns among working-class women. She believed that the fight for workers' rights and women's rights were intertwined.

On March 13, 1912, O'Reilly testified, along with a delegation of suffragists, before the U.S. House Judiciary Committee in support of a constitutional amendment giving women the right to vote.

Document Text

Mr. Chairman and gentlemen of the committee. I ask this committee in all seriousness to understand that we working women are not asking for the vote for fun; we need the vote for self-protection. Gentlemen, you may tell us that our place is in the home. Do not make fun of us, please. There are 8,000,000 of us in these United States who must earn our daily bread. Now, . . . because we must earn that bread, we come to tell you that while we are working in the mills, the mines, the factories, and the mercantile houses, we have not the protection that we should have. Gentlemen, you have been making laws for us; now, we want to make laws for ourselves, because the laws you have made have not been good for us. Year after year working women have gone to the legislature in every State; they have tried to tell their story of need in the same old way. They have gone to you, believing as they do believe, in the strength of the big brother; believing that the big brother could do for them what they should, as citizens, do for themselves.

They have seen . . . the power of the big interest come behind the big brother and say to him: "If you grant the request of these working women you die, politically." It is because the working women have seen this that they now demand the ballot. In New York, and in every other State, we plead for shorter hours. When the legislators learn that women to-day in every industry are being overspeeded and overworked most legislators would, if they dared, vote protective legislation for the women. Why do they neglect the women? We answer, because those who have the votes have the power to take the legislators' political ladder away from them, a power that we, who have no votes, do not have. The getting of the vote and the use of the vote for self-protection as a class is another thing we working women are going to do; we are going to do it as well as we have done our work in the factory, mill, office, and shop. The world to-day knows that the women in industry are making good. But we working women maintain that the rest of the world are not keeping faith with us, in that they are driving us like mad, burning us alive, or working us to death for profits. We . . . remember the Triangle fire cases; we saw our women burned alive, and then when our people appealed to the courts and tried to get justice we got instead the same old verdict from the courts, "Nobody to blame." The ballot is a matter of necessity with working women. We come to you to-day to say we want you to put behind you all your prejudice against votes for women; we ask you for fair play. Deal with us as you would want to be dealt by. When the workingmen come to you with the power of the ballot they make you listen. We want the power of the ballot for the same reason. If there is a man who will not be just, we mean to put him out of politics. If there is a man in office who is serving humanity fairly, we will keep him in office to help make our land what it ought to be.

. . . Working women want the power to protect themselves. Working women want the opportunity to work effectively for decent factory laws, sane labor laws. Working women know that we will never have a universal child-labor law until we have the heart of all the women of the land behind the framing and the enforcing of such a law.

While the doors of the colleges have been opened to the fortunate women of our country, only one woman in a thousand goes into our college, while one woman in five must go into industry to earn her living. And it is for the protection of this one woman in every five that I speak.

You may say the vote was never given as a right, but rather as an expedient to any group of people. Then we demand it as an expedient. It is time that these women who work in the factories, or wherever they work, contracting the diseases known as occupational diseases, were given the opportunity to clean our political house of its disease germs. It is in a wretchedly unhealthy condition to-day. Men, let the women come in and help you in this political house cleaning. You have got it into an awful mess; we only ask you to do the thing you have done since Adam, namely, turn the burden of responsibility over to woman when it gets too big for you or you fear the consequences. Let us help you now, or if you will not it will look as if you are afraid of the kind of house cleaning we will give you. Well, we will give it to you, as sure as fate, because we are on this job to win. . . . We see that there is not a thing in the way of this right which we are asking but prejudice or fear; we are pleading for the right to use our intelligence, as you use yours at the ballot box. You believe you protect us. You say you want to take care of the women. I can tell you as a working woman we know you have made a very bad job of the protection and care-taking. . . . A working woman has to deal with the facts of life; she knows when she is overtired, when her finger is taken off by a machine just because she was too tired to take it out. That is what one of my girls calls a "fac'." Now, men, we working women deal in "fac's." We want the ballot in order that we may straighten out all of this economic and political mess that your superior intelligence has gotten us into. Is that straight? Well, that is what the working woman wants.

Glossary

overspeeded: refers to factory and manufacturing efficiency practices that increased the speed of machines to make human workers work faster

Triangle fire cases: refers to the court cases regarding the March 25, 1911, Triangle Shirtwaist Company fire where 146 workers (mostly young immigrant women) perished.

Short-Answer Questions

1. Summarize the arguments O'Reilly makes to give women the right to vote.

2. What are the obstacles to women getting the right to vote that O'Reilly points out?

3. Of the conditions and demands O'Reilly describes, which have been resolved? Which have not?

The Schlager Anthology of Women's History

Elizabeth Gurley Flynn:
"The Truth about the Paterson Strike"

Author	Significance
Elizabeth Gurley Flynn	Reflects on an important strike that involved 25,000 workers who had to overcome nationality, gender, and occupational differences to maintain solidarity
Date	
1914	
Document Type	
Speeches/Addresses	

Overview

Paterson, New Jersey, became known as Silk City because it produced nearly 50 percent of U.S. silk and was home to 300 silk mills and dye houses. Tensions between workers and management occurred regularly over several decades. Overworked silk workers generally labored fifty-five hours a week: ten hours Monday through Friday and five hours on Saturdays. Management historically paid wages well below national averages. Many children as young as nine worked in the mills.

Conflict between workers and mill owners came to a boiling point when management told workers they had to run four silk looms instead of the traditional two looms. In essence, workers would be required to do even more work with fewer workers and feared there would be layoffs. As a result, beginning February 25, 1913, around 25,000 silk workers in Paterson conducted a work stoppage that lasted five months. The workers wanted higher wages, improved working conditions, and to maintain the two silk loom assignments.

The strike gained national attention because of the number of workers involved, the tactics used to organize and maintain solidarity, and the involvement of the Industrial Workers of the World (IWW), who helped the workers. The IWW, known for its militant tactics and socialist and anarchist ideology, was a force to be reckoned with. Elizabeth Gurley Flynn, an IWW labor organizer, played a significant role in organizing the protests, uniting the strikers, and giving speeches to maintain their resolve. She delivered this speech to the New York Civic Club Forum on January 31, 1914. The strikers clashed with police, and Flynn and others were arrested. Throughout the work stoppage, strikers faced harsh criticism from politicians and businessmen.

Ultimately, the strikers were not totally successful. They did not get the factory owners to agree to better working conditions or higher wages, but management did refrain from increasing the loom assignments.

Labor leader, activist, and feminist Elizabeth Gurley Flynn (Library of Congress)

Document Text

Comrades and Friends:

The reason why I undertake to give this talk at this moment, one year after the Paterson strike was called, is that the flood of criticism about the strike is unabated, becoming more vicious all the time, drifting continually from the actual facts, and involving as a matter of course the policies and strike tactics of the I.W.W. To insure future success in the city of Paterson it is necessary for the past failure to be understood, and not to be clouded over by a mass of outside criticism. Many of our critics are people who never went to Paterson, or who went

on a holiday; who did not study the strike as a day-by-day process. . . .

What is a labor victory? I maintain that it is a two-fold thing. Workers must gain economic advantage, but they must also gain revolutionary spirit, in order to achieve a complete victory. For workers to gain a few cents more a day, a few minutes less a day, and go back to work with the same psychology, the same attitude toward society is to have achieved a temporary gain and not a lasting victory. For workers to go back with a class-conscious spirit, with an organized and a determined attitude toward society means that even if they have made no economic gain they have the possibility of gaining in the future. In other words, a labor victory must be economic and it must be revolutionizing. Otherwise it is not complete. . . .

So a labor victory must be twofold, but if it can only be one it is better to gain in spirit than to gain economic advantage. . . . We have certain general principles; their application differs as the people, the industry, the time and the place indicate. It is impossible to conduct a strike among English-speaking people in the same way that you conduct a strike among foreigners, it is impossible to conduct a strike in the steel industry in the same manner you conduct a strike among the textile workers where women and children are involved in large numbers. . . . We realize that we are dealing with human beings and not with chemicals. And we realize that our fundamental principles of solidarity and class revolt must be applied in as flexible a manner as the science of pedagogy. . . .

In the beginning of last year, 1913, there was a strike in the Doherty mill against the four-loom system. There had been agitation for three months by the Eight-Hour League of the I.W.W. for the eight-hour day, and it had stimulated a general response from the disheartened workers. So we held a series of mass meetings calling for a general strike, and that strike broke on the 25th of February, 1913. It was responded to mostly by the unorganized workers. We had three elements to deal with in the Paterson strike; the broad silk weavers and the dyers, who were unorganized and who were as you might say, almost virgin material, easily brought forth and easily stimulated to aggressive activity. But on the other hand we had the ribbon weavers, the English-speaking conservative people, who had behind them craft antecedents, individual crafts unions that they had worked through for thirty years. These people responded only after three weeks, and then they formed the complicating element in the strike, continually pulling back on the mass through their influence as the English-speaking and their attitude as conservatives. The police action precipitated the strike of many workers. They came out because of the brutal persecution of the strike leaders and not because they themselves were so full of the strike feeling that they could not stay in any longer. This was the calling of the strike. . . .

The first period of the strike meant for us persecution and propaganda, those two things. Our work was to educate and stimulate. Education is not a conversion, it is a process. One speech to a body of workers does not overcome their prejudices of a lifetime. We had prejudices on the national issues, prejudices between crafts, prejudices between competing men and women,—all these to overcome. We had the influence of the minister on the one side, and the respect that they had for government on the other side. We had to stimulate them. Stimulation, in a strike, means to make that strike and through it the class struggle their religion; to make them forget all about the fact that it's for a few cents or a few hours, but to make them feel it is a "religious duty" for them to win that strike. Those two things constituted our work, to create in them a feeling of solidarity and a feeling of class-consciousness. . . .

I contend that there was no use for violence in the Paterson strike. . . . This is not a moral or legal objection but a utilitarian one. I don't say that violence should not be used, but where there is no call for it, there is no reason why we should resort to it. In the Paterson strike, for the first four months there wasn't a single scab in the mills. The mills were shut down. . . .

Mass action is far more up-to-date than personal or physical violence. Mass action means that the workers withdraw their labor power, and paralyze the wealth production of the city, cut off the means of life, the breath of life of the employers. Violence may mean just weakness on the part of those workers. Violence occurs in almost every American Federation of Labor strike, because the workers are desperate, because they are losing their strike. . . . Physical violence is dramatic. It's especially dramatic when you talk about it and don't resort to it. But actual violence is an old fashioned method of conducting a strike. And mass action, paralyzing all industry, is a new-fashioned and a much more feared method of conducting a strike. That does not mean that violence shouldn't be used in self-defense. Everybody believes in violence for self-defense. . . . But the actual fact is that in spite of our theory that the way to win a strike is to put your hands in your pocket and refuse to work, it was only in the Paterson strike of all the strikes in 1913 that a strike leader said what Haywood said: "If the police do not let up in the use of violence against the strikers the strikers are going to arm themselves and fight back." . . .

Glossary

Comrades: fellow workers

I.W.W.: Industrial Workers of the World, a general labor union with subdivisions in various industries

mass action: coordinated activity in pursuit of a goal

pedagogy: education

scab: a worker who accepts work from an employer during a strike

Short-Answer Questions

1. According to Flynn, what is needed for a labor victory?

2. Summarize Flynn's defense of the Patterson strike. In what ways was it unsuccessful? In what ways was it successful?

3. Analyze Flynn's views regarding violence during a strike.

Helena Swanwick:
The War in Its Effect upon Women

Author	Significance
Helena Swanwick	Explained how World War I impacted the lives and futures of British women
Date	
1916	
Document Type	
Essays, Reports, Manifestos	

Overview

Helena Maria Lucy Swanwick (1864–1939) was a German-born British writer, editor, and journalist. She spent much of her career arguing for women's rights, but because of her fervent pacifist beliefs she was also occasionally critical of violence in the suffragist movement of the early twentieth century. She was a forthright opponent of World War I, calling throughout the war for both sides to negotiate a peace. In the 1920s she served as an alternative delegate to the League of Nations. In 1939, however, deeply depressed by the increasing tensions in Europe, including the rise of Nazism and the outbreak of World War II, Swanwick committed suicide at her home in Berkshire.

Swanwick was born in Munich, the only daughter of the artist Oswald Sickert and his wife, Eleanor. The Sickerts brought their children to England in 1868, settling in London. Unlike many girls of her generation, Helena received an extensive education, attending Notting Hill High School and Girton College, Cambridge. In

1888 she married a fellow academic, the mathematician Frederick Tertius Swanwick (1851–1931).

Helena Swanwick began her career in journalism through her association with C. P. Scott, a Member of Parliament and publisher of the Manchester *Guardian*. By 1906 she had joined the National Union of Women's Suffrage Societies (NUWSS) in support of the goal of winning women the right to vote. By 1909 she was serving as the editor of the organization's journal, *The Common Cause*, which argued for the need for working men and women to unite in pursuit of their goals. By 1912, however, she had broken with the organization over what she felt was its embracing of violence in pursuit of its goals.

Swanwick wrote *The War in Its Effect upon Women* in 1916 and initially issued it as an individual pamphlet, but it received much broader circulation after it was published along with another long essay, *Women and War*. This excerpt is taken from the original publication.

Document Text

How has the war affected women? How will it affect them? Women, as half the human race, are compelled to take their share of evil and good with men, the other half. The destruction of property, the increase of taxation, the rise of prices, the devastation of beautiful things in nature and art—these are felt by men as well as by women. Some losses doubtless appeal to one or the other sex with peculiar poignancy, but it would be difficult to say whose sufferings are the greater, though there can be no doubt at all that men get an exhilaration out of war which is denied to most women. When they see pictures of soldiers encamped in the ruins of what was once a home, amidst the dead bodies of gentle milch cows, most women would be thinking too insistently of the babies who must die for need of milk to entertain the exhilaration which no doubt may be felt at "the good work of our guns." When they read of miles upon miles of kindly earth made barren, the hearts of men may be wrung to think of wasted toil, but to women the thought suggests a simile full of an even deeper pathos; they will think of the millions of young lives destroyed, each one having cost the travail and care of a mother, and of the millions of young bodies made barren by the premature death of those who should have been their mates. The millions of widowed maidens in the coming generation will have to turn their thoughts away from one particular joy and fulfillment of life. While men in war give what is, at the present stage of the world's development, the peculiar service of men, let them not forget that in rendering that very service they are depriving a corresponding number of women of the opportunity of rendering what must, at all stages of the world's development, be the peculiar service of women. After the war, men will go on doing what has been regarded as men's work; women, deprived of their own, will also have to do much of what has been regarded as men's work. These things are going to affect women profoundly, and one hopes that the reconstruction of society is going to be met by the whole people—men and women—with a sympathetic understanding of each other's circumstances. When what are known as men's questions are discussed, it is generally assumed that the settlement of them depends upon men only; when what are known as women's questions are discussed, there is never any suggestion that they can be settled by women independently of men. Of course they cannot. But, then, neither can "men's questions" be rightly settled so. In fact, life would be far more truly envisaged if we dropped the silly phrases "men's and women's questions"; for, indeed, there are no such matters, vand all human questions affect all humanity. . . .

It would be wise to remember that the dislocation of industry at the outbreak of the war was easily met; first, because the people thrown out by the cessation of one sort of work were easily absorbed by the increase of another sort; second, because there was ample capital and credit in hand; third, because the State was prepared to shoulder many risks and to guarantee stability; fourth, because there was an untapped reservoir of women's labor to take the place of men's. The problems after the war will be different, greater, and more lasting. . . . Because it will obviously be impossible for all to find work quickly (not to speak of the right kind of work), there is almost certain to be an outcry for the restriction of work in various directions, and one of the first cries (if we may judge from the past) will be to women: "Back to the Home!" This cry will be raised whether the women have a home or not. . . . We must understand the unimpeachable right of the man who has lost his work and risked his life for his country, to find decent employment, decent wages and conditions, on his return to civil life. We must also understand the enlargement and enhancement of life which women feel when they are able to live by their own productive work, and we must realize that to deprive women of the right to live by their work is to send them back to a moral imprisonment (to say nothing of physical and intellectual starvation), of which they have become now for the first time fully conscious. And we must realize the exceeding danger that conscienceless employers may regard women's labor as preferable, owing to its cheapness and its docility, and that women, if unsympathetically treated by their male relatives and fellow workers, may be tempted to continue to be cheap and docile in the hands of those who have no desire except that of exploiting them and the community. The kind of man who likes "to keep women in their place" may find he has made slaves who will be used by his enemies against him. Men need have no fear of free women; it is the slaves and the parasites who are a deadly danger. . . .

What the war has put in a fresh light, so that even the dullest can see, is that if the State may claim women's lives and those of their sons and husbands and lovers, if it may absorb all private and individual life, as at present, then indeed the condition of those who have no voice in the State is a condition of slavery, and Englishmen don't feel quite happy at the thought that their women are still slaves, while their Government is saying they are waging a war of liberation, Many women had long ago become acutely aware of their ignominious position, but the jolt of the war has made many more aware of it.

Glossary

ignominious: something that is shameful or causes a loss of public esteem

milch cow: dairy cow

"one particular joy and fulfillment of life": a reference to marriage and childbirth

travail: labor (in the sense of either childbirth or work)

unimpeachable: undoubtable; absolutely trustworthy

Short-Answer Questions

1. What does Swanwick fear might happen to the women who have joined the public workforce during the war?

2. How does Swanwick describe the relationship between war and men? Between war and women?

3. What organization does Swanwick hold responsible for redressing any wrongs that women might suffer at the end of the war?

National Women's Trade Union League: Women's Work and War

Author National Women's Trade Union League **Date** 1919 **Document Type** Essays, Reports, Manifestos	**Significance** Argued for the establishment of laws for the care of women and children, and for the provision of social welfare and public resources for these marginalized populations

Overview

Established in 1903, the National Women's Trade Union League (WTUL) advocated for improved wages and working conditions for women. The WTUL was composed of both working-class and more prosperous women, many of whom were white and Protestant and had gained experience in advocacy and social work as part of the settlement house movement. The settlement house movement was a reformist social movement that fought for the creation of large-scale urban housing and for social services to support the swelling numbers of working-class urban poor. The women who participated in this movement developed an intimate understanding of the plight of working-class women in America's growing cities, and they also began to appreciate that the settlement house model of charity and philanthropic efforts had distinct limitations. The WTUL was born of a recognition that only legislation and political advocacy could address the needs of the urban poor.

At the turn of the twentieth century, many women were employed in garment and textile factories, where they often faced dangerous and abusive working conditions and received little compensation for their work. Female factory workers, like men, faced long hours and terrible conditions in unregulated and unsafe workplaces. Compared to men, though, they received lower wages and struggled uniquely with workplace discrimination and harassment. Finally, women had the double burden of doing all household work and caregiving.

Recognizing that uplifting the conditions of working-class women required legislation and political activity, the WTUL was founded with the express purpose of organizing labor unions and eliminating sweatshop conditions. At its founding, the WTUL proclaimed that its primary goal was to organize women into trade unions and ensure that these unions had the collective bargaining muscle to be successful.

In addition, the WTUL also advocated for the passing of labor standardization laws, pushed for the education of women in the workforce, and promoted women's suffrage.

While the organization existed until 1950, its greatest successes occurred in the first decades of the twentieth century. It played a key role in the organization of a series of strikes that resulted in the creation of the International Ladies' Garment Workers' Union and the Amalgamated Clothing Workers of America. The WTUL was enormously successful and achieved many of its legislative goals, including an eight-hour workday, a minimum wage, the abolition of child labor, and the establishment of new industrial safety regulations. Published in 1919, in the aftermath of World War I, this document provides a window into the ambitious goals of the WTUL—then at the height of the organization's power and influence. These goals showcase the ambition and confidence of the organization.

Document Text

The French Federation of Women's Trade Unions has recently issued its reconstruction program and it is interesting to note the points on which the French women place their emphasis. They open their program as do their English and American sisters by fixing the working age for children. In their program it is fourteen years. Vocational training is asked, also the eight-hour day and no night work for women.

They make one interesting point in asking for a minimum weekly rest of forty-eight consecutive hours, by preference including Saturday and Sunday, or when that is impossible Sunday and Monday morning.

The provisions in which the French women are obviously most interested are those relating to the care of mothers and children. They are stated thus:

7. Protection of women during childbirth. That they be given all the State aid for 30 days after the birth of the child and two-thirds of the minimum wage established by the industry to which the young woman belongs, provided that she does not return to work.

8. A minimum wage to be fixed for each trade on the basis of the cost of living and the value of the work done.

9. Equal pay for equal work for men and women where the quality and the output of work are equal.

Women's Trade Union League logo (Wikimedia Commons)

10. Family endowment. The establishment by trades of family endowment funds, subscribed to by the employer in proportion to the number of employees, the remainder of the fund allowed by the State. The heads of the family, parents, are to be allowed for one child a sum equivalent to a quarter of their wages; for two children two-fifths, and for each additional child one-eighth of the wages.

11. Sickness, unemployment and old-age pensions, obligatory social insurance the funds for which shall be provided by the employer, the workers and

the State. These pensions shall be allowed in case of maternity, during the months which precede the birth of the child.

12. An international advisory commission for women's work. This commission shall be composed of two representatives of each country where there are women's trade unions. The organized women workers may only be represented by delegates elected by the unions.

Both the English and the French women are much more generally interested than are we in the State care of mothers and children. Maternity benefits and family allowances have been outlined by both the French and English women. In this country, on the other hand, State aid for mothers is seldom mentioned in labor programs, while equality of pay and of opportunity are arousing the keenest interest among working women of all groups.

Glossary

equal pay for equal work: a central concept in labor rights organizing based on the premise that individuals in the same workplace doing the same work be given the same pay; a phrase first used in publication by Carrie Ashton Johnson, an American suffragist and labor rights advocate

keenest: most enthusiastic

Short-Answer Questions

1. Describe three of the demands outlined in the document above. Please select the demands that you consider to be the most radical or most beneficial for women and children.

2. The demands made by labor organizations like the WTUL were met with widespread hostility. What classes or interest groups would probably have been hostile to these demands, and what might have been the motivations or reasons for their hostility?

3. Imagine the WTUL still existed and still advocated for the rights of women and children in the workplace. Outline at least one proposal the WTUL would demand in our current political, social, and economic environment. In your outlined proposal, please explain why the WTUL would support this proposal.

The Schlager Anthology of Women's History

Equal Pay Act

Author Esther Peterson	**Significance** Made substantial legal corrections to several centuries of gender-wage discrimination practices in the United States
Date 1963	
Document Type Legislative	

Overview

On June 10, 1963, President John F. Kennedy signed into law the Equal Pay Act, a law passed to amend the Fair Labor Standards Act of 1938. Labor activist Esther Peterson, as head of the Women's Bureau in the Department of Labor, had submitted the draft bill to Congress in February that year. The goal of the law was simple: to ensure that in the matter of pay, employers do not discriminate on the basis of gender, generally meaning that they do not pay women less than men for the same work. The Equal Pay Act was intended to provide a broad remedial framework for ending gender discrimination. Within the framework, the U.S. Supreme Court has had to adjudicate claims of gender discrimination. In doing so, the Supreme Court applies a three-part test: First, are higher wages paid to employees of the opposite sex? Second, do the employees perform substantially equal work on jobs requiring equal effort, skill, and responsibility? And third, are the jobs performed under similar conditions? If the answers to these questions are yes, the employer is strictly liable, regardless of the employer's intent.

The Equal Pay Act arose in the context of what became known as second-wave feminism in the 1960s. While first-wave feminism dealt with such issues as the right to vote, second-wave feminism took on more subtle forms of discrimination and prejudice, including gender discrimination with regard to pay. While estimates vary, the gender disparity in pay for full-time year-round employees at the time meant that women were paid less than 60 percent of what men were paid.

President John F. Kennedy signs the Equal Pay Act into law alongside American Association of University Women members. (JFK Presidential Library and Museum)

Document Text
Sec. 206. Minimum Wage . . .
(d) Prohibition of sex discrimination

(1) No employer having employees subject to any provisions of this section shall discriminate, within any establishment in which such employees are employed, between employees on the basis of sex by paying wages to employees in such establishment at a rate less than the rate at which he pays wages to employees of the opposite sex in such establishment for equal work on jobs the performance of which requires equal skill, effort, and responsibility, and which are performed under similar working conditions, except where such payment is made pursuant to

(i) a seniority system;

(ii) a merit system;

(iii) a system which measures earnings by quantity or quality of production; or

(iv) a differential based on any other factor other than sex:

The Schlager Anthology of Women's History

Provided, That an employer who is paying a wage rate differential in violation of this subsection shall not, in order to comply with the provisions of this subsection, reduce the wage rate of any employee.

(2) No labor organization, or its agents, representing employees of an employer having employees subject to any provisions of this section shall cause or attempt to cause such an employer to discriminate against an employee in violation of paragraph (1) of this subsection.

(3) For purposes of administration and enforcement, any amounts owing to any employee which have been withheld in violation of this subsection shall be deemed to be unpaid minimum wages or unpaid overtime compensation under this chapter.

(4) As used in this subsection, the term "labor organization" means any organization of any kind, or any agency or employee representation committee or plan, in which employees participate and which exists for the purpose, in whole or in part, of dealing with employers concerning grievances, labor disputes, wages, rates of pay, hours of employment, or conditions of work.

Glossary

seniority: privilege based on length of employment

wage rate differential: a difference in wages

Short-Answer Questions

1. Who are the intended audiences for this document?

2. Analyze why this law is necessary.

3. Summarize the circumstances in which pay for similar jobs may be different.

Executive Order 11246: Equal Employment Opportunity

Author Lyndon B. Johnson	**Significance** Advanced equal employment opportunity and affirmative action and for the first time included sex in the list of protected designations
Date 1965	
Document Type Poems, Plays, Fiction	

Overview

Just fourteen months after signing the landmark Civil Rights Act of 1964, President Lyndon B. Johnson issued Executive Order 11246. Executive Order 11246 is just one of several presidential executive orders established to regulate contractors who complete work for the federal government and to support the long history of federal affirmative action. This executive order amended existing legislation with the addition of the word *sex* in the list of protected attributes, thereby extending discrimination protections to women.

It prohibited federal contractors, subcontractors, and their affiliated labor unions from discriminating against any qualified employee or applicant for employment based on race, color, religion, sex, or national origin. The executive order gave the secretary of labor the authority to enforce equal opportunity for minorities when federal contractors engaged in employment practices such as recruiting, hiring, training, and other employment-related matters. It also obligated federal contractors and subcontractors to take affirmative action to ensure that applicants and employees were treated fairly and without discrimination. It mandated specific obligations on the contractors and subcontractors, such as implementing nondiscriminatory hiring policies that would increase the representation of minority groups and women, requiring transparency of their records, and establishing affirmative action programs to eliminate barriers to equal opportunity. The order's impact has been far-reaching, promoting diversity and helping to level the playing field for historically marginalized groups in the American workforce.

Document Text

Under and by virtue of the authority vested in me as President of the United States by the Constitution and statutes of the United States, it is ordered as follows: . . .

Part II—Nondiscrimination in Employment by Government Contractors and Subcontractors
Subpart B—Contractors' Agreements
Sec. 202. Except in contracts exempted in accordance with Section 204 of this Order, all Government contracting agencies shall include in every Government contract hereafter entered into the following provisions:

"During the performance of this contract, the contractor agrees as follows:

"(1) The contractor will not discriminate against any employee or applicant for employment because of race, color, religion, sex, or national origin. The contractor will take affirmative action to ensure that applicants are employed, and that employees are treated during employment, without regard to their race, color, religion, sex or national origin. Such action shall include, but not be limited to the following: employment, upgrading, demotion, or transfer; recruitment or recruitment advertising; layoff or termination; rates of pay or other forms of compensation; and selection for training, including apprenticeship. The contractor agrees to post in conspicuous places, available to employees and applicants for employment, notices to be provided by the contracting officer setting forth the provisions of this nondiscrimination clause.

"(2) The contractor will, in all solicitations or advertisements for employees placed by or on behalf of the contractor, state that all qualified applicants will receive consideration for employment without regard to race, color, religion, sex or national origin.

"(3) The contractor will send to each labor union or representative of workers with which he has a collective bargaining agreement or other contract

President Lyndon B. Johnson signed Executive Order 11246 into law. (Wikimedia Commons)

or understanding, a notice, to be provided by the agency contracting officer, advising the labor union or workers' representative of the contractor's commitments under Section 202 of Executive Order No. 11246 of September 24, 1965, and shall post copies of the notice in conspicuous places available to employees and applicants for employment.

"(4) The contractor will comply with all provisions of Executive Order No. 11246 of Sept. 24, 1965, and of the rules, regulations, and relevant orders of the Secretary of Labor.

"(5) The contractor will furnish all information and reports required by Executive Order No. 11246 of September 24, 1965, and by the rules, regulations, and orders of the Secretary of Labor, or pursuant thereto, and will permit access to his books, records, and accounts by the contracting agency and the Secretary of Labor for purposes of investigation to ascertain compliance with such rules, regulations, and orders.

"(6) In the event of the contractor's noncompliance with the nondiscrimination clauses of this contract or with any of such rules, regulations, or orders, this contract may be cancelled, terminated or suspended in whole or in part and the contractor may be declared ineligible for further Government contracts in accordance with procedures authorized in Executive Order No. 11246 of Sept. 24, 1965, and such other sanctions may be imposed and remedies invoked as provided in Executive Order No. 11246 of September 24, 1965, or by rule, regulation, or order of the Secretary of Labor, or as otherwise provided by law." . . .

Sec. 204. The Secretary of Labor may, when he deems that special circumstances in the national interest so require, exempt a contracting agency from the requirement of including any or all of the provisions of Section 202 of this Order in any specific contract, subcontract, or purchase order. The Secretary of Labor may, by rule or regulation, also exempt certain classes of contracts, subcontracts, or purchase orders (1) whenever work is to be or has been performed outside the United States and no recruitment of workers within the limits of the United States is involved; (2) for standard commercial supplies or raw materials; (3) involving less than specified amounts of money or specified numbers of workers; or (4) to the extent that they involve subcontracts below a specified tier. . . .

Subpart D—Sanctions and Penalties
Sec. 209. (a) In accordance with such rules, regulations, or orders as the Secretary of Labor may issue or adopt, the Secretary may:

(1) Publish, or cause to be published, the names of contractors or unions which it has concluded have complied or have failed to comply with the provisions of this Order or of the rules, regulations, and orders of the Secretary of Labor.

(2) Recommend to the Department of Justice that, in cases in which there is substantial or material violation or the threat of substantial or material violation of the contractual provisions set forth in Section 202 of this Order, appropriate proceedings be brought to enforce those provisions, including the enjoining, within the limitations of applicable law, of organizations, individuals, or groups who prevent directly or indirectly, or seek to prevent directly or indirectly, compliance with the provisions of this Order.

(3) Recommend to the Equal Employment Opportunity Commission or the Department of Justice that appropriate proceedings be instituted under Title VII of the Civil Rights Act of 1964.

(4) Recommend to the Department of Justice that criminal proceedings be brought for the furnishing of false information to any contracting agency or to the Secretary of Labor as the case may be.

(5) After consulting with the contracting agency, direct the contracting agency to cancel, terminate, suspend, or cause to be cancelled, terminated, or suspended, any contract, or any portion or portions thereof, for failure of the contractor or subcontractor to comply with equal employment opportunity provisions of the contract. Contracts may be cancelled, terminated, or suspended absolutely or continuance of contracts may be conditioned upon a program for future compliance approved by the Secretary of Labor. . . .

Part III—Nondiscrimination Provisions in Federally Assisted Construction Contracts . . .
(b) In the event an applicant fails and refuses to comply with the applicant's undertakings pursuant to this Order, the Secretary of Labor may, after consulting with the administering department or agency, take any or all of the following actions: (1) direct any administering department or agency to cancel, terminate, or suspend in whole or in part the agreement, contract or other arrangement with such applicant with respect to which the failure or refusal occurred; (2) di-

rect any administering department or agency to refrain from extending any further assistance to the applicant under the program with respect to which the failure or refusal occurred until satisfactory assurance of future compliance has been received by the Secretary of Labor from such applicant; and (3) refer the case to the Department of Justice or the Equal Employment Opportunity Commission for appropriate law enforcement or other proceedings.

Glossary

affirmative action: policies aimed to correct the injustices caused by historic discrimination against minorities

collective bargaining agreement: a written contract between an employer and employees, arrived at through negotiations between the employer and a labor union or unions

executive order: a written and issued proclamation signed by the president of the United States that does not require approval from Congress

government contractors and subcontractors: companies that provide products and services to the federal government via a contract

Short-Answer Questions

1. Summarize in what circumstances the regulations of Executive Order 11246 can be excused.

2. Describe what measures have been established in the executive order to ensure contractor and subcontractor agencies follow the rules of the agreement.

3. In a detailed response, analyze how you think Executive Order 11246 helped women achieve employment opportunities and workplace equality.

Dolores Huerta:
Statement to the Senate Subcommittee on Migratory Labor

Author
Dolores Huerta

Date
1969

Document Type
Speeches/Addresses

Significance
Highlighted the abysmal working conditions endured by migrant laborers and encouraged boycotts as an effective way to support farm worker organization and union recognition

Overview

The civil rights movement of the 1950s and 1960s helped inspire other marginalized groups to organize and fight for their rights. The farm workers' movement, for example, advocated for farm workers' civil and employment rights, and Dolores Huerta—a self-proclaimed "born-again feminist," prominent American labor leader, civil rights activist—was a champion of the cause. Huerta became an activist in the 1950s when she witnessed the poor working conditions and exploitation endured by agricultural workers, particularly those of Mexican descent. She and fellow workers' rights activist Cesar Chavez fought for better wages, safer working conditions, and labor protections for farm workers. They founded the National Farm Workers Association, which was later renamed the United Farm Workers (UFW).

Huerta appeared before the Senate Subcommittee on Migratory Labor on July 15, 1969, and provided a prepared statement and gave oral testimony. The subcommittee hearings, titled "Migrant and Seasonal Farmworker Powerlessness," focused on workers' lack of political and economic agency, workers' cultural identity, and the grim labor conditions in the agricultural industry. Most of these concerns dealt directly with the struggles between agribusinesses and their workers and how the increased purchasing of grapes by the Department of Defense (DOD) was involved in the situation. Huerta's detailed and impassioned testimony shed light on the unsafe and harsh realities farm workers faced. But she also argued that the DOD was harming the farm workers as well. The DOD became a focus of the UFW's campaign because it was a significant purchaser of grapes for military consumption, including in the commissaries and mess halls of military bases. The UFW reasoned that by purchasing grapes from growers who mistreated their workers, the DOD was indirectly supporting and perpetuating labor exploitation. Overall, Huerta described the abysmal working conditions endured by migrant laborers, such as exposure to dangerous pesticides and no access to toilets or washing facilities. Additionally, she argued that conditions in the grape fields were connected to the U.S. soldiers fighting in Vietnam.

Document Text

My name is Dolores Huerta. I am the Vice-President of the United Farm Workers Organizing Committee (UFWOC), AFL-CIO. It is a pleasure to come before your committee to discuss a very serious matter for our union and for all farm workers—obstacles to farm worker organizing.

. . . UFWOC has undertaken an international boycott of all California-Arizona table grapes in order to gain union recognition for striking farm workers. We did not take up the burden of the boycott willingly. It is expensive. It is a hardship on the farm worker families who have left the small valley towns. . . . But, because of the table grape growers' refusal to bargain with their workers, the boycott is our major weapon and our last line of defense against the growers who use foreign labor to break our strikes. It is only through the pressure of the boycott that UFWOC has won contracts with major California wine grape growers. . . .

Our boycott has been met with well-organized and well-financed opposition by the growers and their sympathizers. Most recently, several major California grape growers joined with other agribusiness interests . . . to form an employer-dominated "union," the Agricultural Workers Freedom to Work Association, for the sole purpose of destroying UFWOC. . . .

In spite of this type of anti-union activity, our boycott of California-Arizona table grapes is successful. It is being successful for the simple reason that millions of Americans are supporting the grape workers strike by not buying table grapes.

After six weeks of the 1969–1970 table grape harvest, California table grape shipments to 36 major United States cities are down 20 percent from last year. . . . It is because of the successful boycott that, on Friday, June 13, 1969, ten major California growers offered to meet with UFWOC under the auspices of the Federal Mediation Service. UF-

Dolores Huerta in 2019
(Wikimedia Commons)

WOC representatives and ranch committee members met with the growers for two weeks. Progress is being made in these negotiations, which are presently recessed over the issue of pesticides.

U.S. Department of Defense Table Grape Purchases
Now that the boycott has brought us so close to a negotiated settlement of this three-year-old dispute, we learn that the United States Department of Defense (DOD) has doubled its purchases of table grapes. We appear to be witnessing an all-out effort by the military to bail out the growers and break our boycott. . . .

These are the facts as to how the Grapes of Wrath are being converted into the Grapes of War by the world's richest government in order to stop farm workers from waging a successful boycott and organizing campaign against grape growers. . . .

. . . DOD purchases of table grapes . . . , at a critical point in the UFWOC boycott, are permitting many growers to stand firm in their refusal to negotiate with their workers.

It is obvious that the DOD is taking sides with the growers in this dispute. The DOD Fact Sheet states . . . "The basic policy of the DOD with regard to awarding defense contracts to contractors involved in labor disputes is to refrain from taking a position on the merits of any labor dispute. This policy is based on the premise that it is essential to DOD procurement needs to maintain a sound working relationship with both labor and management." . . . AFL-CIO News of June 14, 1969, notes that "union observers point out, however, that DOD does become involved in a labor dispute when it so greatly increases its purchase of boycotted grapes." It seems that the DOD is violating its own policy and endangering its working relationship with labor, and we hope that the committee will explore this fully.

DOD Table Grape Purchases: A National Outrage
The history of our struggle against agribusiness is punctuated by the continued violations of health and safety codes by growers, including many table grape growers. . . . Such violations are so well documented that Superior Judge Irving Perluss recently ruled that a jobless worker was within his rights when he refused to accept farm labor work offered him through the California Department of Employment on grounds that most of such jobs are in violation of state health and sanitation codes. . . .

If the federal government and the DOD is not concerned about the welfare of farm workers, they must be concerned with protecting our servicemen from contamination and disease carried by grapes picked in fields without toilets or washstands. Recent laboratory tests have found DDT residues on California grapes. Economic poisons have killed and injured farm workers. Will they also prove dangerous to U.S. military personnel? Focusing on other forms of crime in the fields, we would finally ask if the DOD buys table grapes from the numerous growers who daily violate state and federal minimum wage and child labor laws, who employ illegal foreign labor, and who do not deduct social security payments from farm worker wages?

The DOD increasing purchase of table grapes is nothing short of a national outrage. It is an outrage to the millions of American taxpayers who are supporting the farm workers' struggle for justice by boycotting table grapes. How can any American believe that the U.S. Government is sincere in its efforts to eradicate poverty when the military uses its immense purchasing power to subvert the farm workers' nonviolent struggle for a decent, living wage and a better future?

Many farm workers are members of minority groups. They are Filipino- and Mexican-Americans and black Americans. These same farm workers are on the front lines of battle in Vietnam. It is a cruel and ironic slap in the face to these men who have left the fields to fulfill their military obligation to find increasing amounts of non-union grapes in their mess kits.

In conclusion let me say that our only weapon is the boycott. Just when our boycott is successful the U.S. military doubles its purchases of table grapes, creating a major obstacle to farm worker organization and union recognition. The DOD is obviously acting as a buyer of last resort for scab grapes and is, in effect, providing another form of federal subsidy for anti-union growers who would destroy the efforts of the poor to build a union. UFWOC calls on all concerned Americans and on the members of the Senate Subcommittee on Migratory Labor to protest this anti-union policy of the military and the Nixon administration.

Glossary

AFL-CIO: American Federation of Labor and Congress of Industrial Organizations, the primary federation of U.S. labor unions

agribusiness: refers to businesses engaged in the production and processing-manufacturing of plants, animals, equipment, and chemicals used for farming

DDT: dichlorodiphenyltrichloroethane, an insecticide used to control harmful insects such as mosquitos that spread malaria, which also has adverse effects on wildlife and potential human health risks

scab grapes: slang term referring to grapes picked by non-union workers employed by business owners to subvert striking union workers

table grapes: grapes that are grown to be eaten fresh, not processed for wine or preservation

Short-Answer Questions

1. Who are the intended audiences for this document? How do you know?

2. Describe the obstacles UFWOC faced during their strike and boycott.

3. Describe the connection between UFWOC farm workers and soldiers fighting in Vietnam. Why might this be significant?

Pauline Newman:
A Worker Recalls Her Time at the
Triangle Shirtwaist Factory

Author
Joan Morrison (interviewer); Pauline Newman
(interviewee)

Date
c. 1980

Document Type
Essays, Reports, Manifestos

Significance
Offers a firsthand account of what it was like to
work at the Triangle Shirtwaist Factory

Overview

In 1902, the Triangle Shirtwaist Factory was located
on the eighth, ninth, and tenth floors of the Asch
building in Greenwich Village, New York City. The
company manufactured women's blouses and employed
approximately 500 employees. The workers were primarily young Jewish and Italian immigrant women and
girls, some in their early teen years. The factory owners
were known for exploiting their workers. They required
workers to labor six days a week for low wages and in
an unsafe building. They oppressively watched workers
and locked factory doors to keep union organizers out.
Some workers were sexually harassed and threatened by
management. In November 1909, the workers at the
Triangle Shirtwaist Factory, along with workers of the
Leiserson and the Rosen Brothers factories, went on
strike for better wages and working conditions, repair of
building hazards, and unionization. The strike went on
for nearly four months. Leiserson and Rosen Brothers
reached an agreement with their workers, but Triangle
owners refused to allow unionization. Triangle workers

did get adjusted hours and slight wage increases, but
they returned to work with no union representation
and the same deathtrap safety hazards in the factory.
Two years later, a fire at the Triangle factory occurred.

The Triangle Shirtwaist Company fire on March 26,
1911, was one of the deadliest industrial tragedies in U.S.
history. The fire claimed the lives of 146 workers (123
females and 23 males). Scores of workers leaped 100 feet
to their deaths in an attempt to avoid being burned alive.

Historian Joan Morrison interviewed Pauline Newman, a former Triangle Shirtwaist Factory worker, for
a firsthand account from someone who understood the
conditions there. Newman, a Lithuanian immigrant,
began working at the factory when she was thirteen
years old. She was not working when the fire occurred
but knew many of the people who died that day. Later
in life, Newman became a union organizer and leader
of the International Ladies' Garment Workers' Union.

Document Text

Joan Morrison: So, back to the early days when you first came, and you lived in this flat, with the toilet in the street, and the coal stove. Did you go right to work then? And your mother? Do you remember your first job, how you got it?

Pauline Newman: We got here in May and . . . a cousin of mine worked for the Triangle Shirtwaist Company. And by the time she got me in there it was October. So between May and October I did various jobs off and on, you know? But in October she got me to the Triangle basement.

Morrison: Do you remember your first impressions of going in there?

Newman: What, the Triangle Shirtwaist Company? You don't forget a situation of that kind, because . . . in the first place, it was probably the largest shirtwaist factory in the city of New York. By the time I got there, they had something like two, more than two hundred operators. And they had collars, examiners, finishers. All together, probably, they had about four hundred people. And that was a large staff. And they had two floors. The fire took place on one floor. . . . We started work at 7:30, and during the busy season, we worked until nine o'clock in the evening. They didn't pay any overtime and didn't give you anything for supper money. At times they would give you—in those days, the bakery had a little apple pie, not very much bigger than this, and they would give you that for your supper. Very generous.

Morrison: A small child, then, like you, would go in and work all day with that and . . . ?

Newman: You'd work until you got your regular pay from six to nine in those times.

Morrison: And what did they pay you?

Newman: And what, ah, what they did—as I said, at times they'd be generous. You could even get a little apple pie.

The Triangle Shirtwaist Factory fire
(Wikimedia Commons)

Morrison: Yes.

Newman: The wage scales. You forget nothing, as long as your memory still serves, and mine does. My own wages when I got to the Triangle Shirtwaist Company was a dollar and a half a week. And by the time I left during the shirtwaist workers' strike in 1909 I worked myself up to six dollars.

Morrison: Ah, magnificent.

Newman: But you see, hours didn't change. The hours remained, no matter how much you got. The operators, their average wage, as I recall—because two of my sisters worked there—they averaged around six, seven dollars a week. If you were very fast—because they worked piece work—if you were very fast and nothing happened to your machine, no breakage or anything, you could make around ten dollars a week. But most of them, as I remember—and I do remember them very well—they averaged about seven dollars a week. Now the collars are the skilled men in the trade. Twelve dollars was the maximum.

Morrison: And that was piece work, also?

Newman: Yes. You were considered well paid, twelve dollars a week!

Morrison: And what about what you did? What did you do for your dollar and a half?

Newman: Well, what I did really was not difficult. . . . When you fitted the shirtwaist at the machine, there are some threads that are left. And I wasn't the only one. We was, we had the corner on the floor. It resembled a kindergarten: we were all youngsters. And we were given a little scissors to cut the threads off, like so. It wasn't heavy work. It was monotonous, 'cause you did that from 7:30 till nine o'clock at night. You had one half hour for lunch and nothing for supper or anything like that. Before I left, I was promoted to the cutting department. You'd cut the embroidery, which was inserted into the front of the shirtwaist in those days, and that was— They were the kind of employers who didn't recognize anyone working for them as a human being. You were not allowed to sing. Operators would like to have sung, because they, too, had the same thing to do, and weren't allowed to sing. You were not allowed to talk to each other. Oh, no! They would sneak up behind you, and if you were found talking to your next colleague, you were admonished. If you'd keep on, you'd be fired. If you went to the toilet, and you were there more than the forelady or foreman thought you should be, you were threatened to be laid off for half a day, and sent home, and that meant, of course, no pay, you know. You were not allowed to use the passenger elevator, only a freight elevator. And, ah, you were watched every minute of the day by the foreman, forelady. Employers would sneak behind your back. And you were not allowed to have your lunch on the fire escape in the summertime. And that door was locked. And that was proved during the investigation of the fire. They were mean people. There were two partners, Blanck and Harris, and one was worse than the other. People were afraid, actually. And finally, it took from the time I got there, October 1901 to November 1909, for the people to really rise and proclaim that they cannot work under such condition any longer. And we had 20,000 of them coming out here, and 15,000 in Philadelphia, you know. And that was the strike, . . . from November 1909 to the end of March 1910.

Glossary

Blanck and Harris: Max Blanck and Isaac Harris, known as the "Shirtwaist kings," founders of the Triangle Shirtwaist Company

piece work: work done for a per-unit rate

shirtwaist: a woman's tailored blouse

Short-Answer Questions

1. Summarize Newman's description of the working conditions at the Triangle Shirtwaist Factory.

2. Evaluate the possible effects of such factory work on the girls working in these conditions.

3. Analyze the consequences of the safety hazards in the factory in the event of a fire.

Chapter 9

Feminism and Equal Rights in the United States

Despite the significant advancements made after the ratification in 1920 of the Nineteenth Amendment, which gave women the right to vote, society generally supported and maintained the patriarchal status quo. Gender equality was still far from achieved in areas such as employment, wages, education, and reproductive rights. Although there were challenges to broad societal views of the role of women, such as those made by Edith M. Stern (1901–1975), gaining sufficient political power to remove the institutionalized roadblocks to equality was a long, slow process. With a renewed focus on the capabilities of the individual to work for change, however, progress was made. By 1960, for example, women comprised over one-third of college enrollments, and nearly 40 percent worked outside the home. The social movements of the 1960s, following in the footsteps of the civil rights movement, empowered women in various ways and inspired many to create their own movement for liberation. These women agitated for change from the bottom, creating a grassroots effort to influence change at the heights of political power. Yet they also faced many obstacles to progress, leaving many to feel that for every two steps forward, they took one step back.

The Equal Pay Act and *The Feminine Mystique*

Both inspired by and pressured by grassroots activists, President John F. Kennedy appointed the Commission on the Status of Women in 1961. Issued two years later, the Commission's report, *American Woman*, laid the groundwork for the passage of the Equal Pay Act (1963), which required employers to provide men and women equal pay for equal work. In passing the bill, Congress stated that sex discrimination "depresses wages and living standards for employees necessary for their health and efficiency; prevents the maximum utilization of the available labor resources; tends to cause labor disputes, thereby burdening, affecting, and obstructing commerce; burdens commerce and the free flow of goods in commerce; and constitutes an unfair method of competition." The next year, a significant portion of the Civil Rights Act prohibited gender bias in employment and created the Equal Employment Opportunity Commission. Together, these substantial legislative accomplishments ignited debate on the Equal Rights Amendment, which had been originally proposed in 1923.

Betty Friedan's highly influential 1963 work, *The Feminine Mystique,* offered a new analysis of the role of women in the household. According to Friedan's findings, women experienced feelings of isolation and alienation, and they sought to transcend the societal norms and expectations imposed on them. In 1966 Friedan and a group of women came together to form the National Organization for Women (NOW) with the aim of advancing gender equality. Their goals included advocating for the Equal Rights Amendment, supporting maternity leave, increasing the accessibility of childcare centers, and defending reproductive rights. Although the organization predominantly attracted members who were of white, middle-class backgrounds, women of color also advocated for gender equality. Ella Baker's "The Black Woman in the Civil Rights Struggle" gave voice to the overlooked role that African American women played in both the feminist and the civil rights movements.

In the 1970s feminists achieved several significant accomplishments. These included the enactment of the Educational Amendments Act, which included Title IX, a significant step forward for women's involvement in college sports. Women also sought justice for employment discrimination by utilizing the Equal Employment Opportunity Commission. Furthermore, the formation of the National Women's Political Caucus in 1971 opened new doors for women to engage and participate in politics. Although advances for women of color proved to be more of a challenge, Shirley Chisholm became the first African American to run for a major political party's nomination for president in 1972, and the first woman to run for president as a member of the Democratic Party.

The Battle over the ERA

Feminists also promoted the passage of the Equal Rights Amendment. Broadly supported by both Democrats and Republicans, it passed both houses of Congress and succeeded in getting thirty-five states to ratify. By the mid-1970s, however, conservatives began to take hold in the Republican Party, with advocates claiming a pro-family mantra, notably Phyllis Schlafly, leading a fight against the ERA. She and others argued that passage of the ERA would bring about a dramatic and negative shift in American cultural values. The measure was stopped just short of the thirty-eight needed to ratify the amendment.

The Supreme Court and Abortion Rights

One of the most controversial legacies of the feminist movement of this period was the 1973 Supreme Court ruling in *Roe v. Wade* that states could not ban abortion within the first three months of pregnancy. In this case, the Court ruled for a women's right to privacy under the Due Process Clause of the Fourteenth Amendment. The 7–2 Court ruling triggered widespread, long-lasting resistance. Despite the Court upholding the decision in 1992 (*Planned Parenthood v. Casey*), and after decades of conservative activists trimming away at the margins, the Supreme Court in 2022 ultimately overturned precedent and rejected the *Roe* decision.

Although the 1970s were in some ways the highwater mark of success for second-wave feminists, additional progress in the fight for equality was made in the following decades. In the 1990s, for example, the Violence Against Women Act and the *United States v. Virginia* Supreme Court decision built upon the foundations of progress of prior generations. In response to these successes, conservative political forces grew ascendant after the 1970s. Because of this, the next generation of feminists often finds itself not only fighting and relitigating previously won battles but attempting to forge ahead in the grand war for gender equality in the United States.

Further Reading

Books

Collins, Patricia Hill. *Black Feminist Thought: Knowledge, Consciousness, and the Politics of Empowerment.* New York: Routledge, 2002.

Felsenthal, Carol. *Sweetheart of the Silent Majority: The Biography of Phyllis Schlafly.* New York: Doubleday & Company, 1981.

Heilbrun, Carolyn F. *The Education of a Woman: The Life of Gloria Steinem.* New York: Random House, 2011.

Levine, Suzanne Braun and Mary Thom. *Bella Abzug: How One Tough Broad from the Bronx Fought Jim Crow and Joe McCarthy, Pissed Off Jimmy Carter, Battled for the Rights of Women and Workers, Rallied Against War and for the Planet, and Shook Up Politics Along the Way.* New York: Farrar, Straus and Giroux, 2007.

Melich, Tanya. *The Republican War Against Women: An Insider's Report From Behind the Lines.* New York: Random House, 1998.

Randolph, Sherie M. *Florynce "Flo" Kennedy: The Life of a Black Feminist Radical.* Chapel Hill: University of North Carolina Press, 2015.

Sherman, Janann, ed. *Interviews with Betty Friedan.* Jackson: University Press of Mississippi, 2002.

Spruill, Marjorie J. *Divided We Stand: The Battle Over Women's Rights and Family Values That Polarized American Politics.* New York: Bloomsbury, 2017.

Articles

Gay, Roxane. "Fifty Years Ago, Protesters Took on the Miss America Pageant and Electrified the Feminist Movement." Smithsonian.com, January 1, 2018. Available at https://www.smithsonianmag.com/history/fifty-years-ago-protestors-took-on-miss-america-pageant-electrified-feminist-movement-180967504/.

Gordon, Linda. "The Women's Liberation Movement," in Dorothy Sue Cobble, Linda Gordon, and Astrid Henry, eds. *Feminism Unfinished: A Short, Surprising History of American Women's Movements.* New York: Liveright Publishing Corporation, 2014.

Websites

"Feminism: The Second Wave." National Women's History Museum website, accessed September 13, 2023, https://www.womenshistory.org/exhibits/feminism-second-wave.

National Organization for Women website, accessed September 13, 2023, https://now.org.

Further Reading

Websites

"Women in the Civil Rights Movement." Library of Congress website, accessed September 13, 2023, https://www.loc.gov/collections/civil-rights-history-project/articles-and-essays/women-in-the-civil-rights-movement/.

"Women in Congress." U.S. House of Representatives website, accessed September 13, 2023, https://history.house.gov/Exhibition-and-Publications/WIC/Women-in-Congress/.

Edith M. Stern:
"Women Are Household Slaves"

Author
Edith M. Stern

Date
1949

Document Type
Essays, Reports, Manifestos

Significance
An early indicator of the second-wave feminist movement that grew into public form in the 1960s

---

Overview

During World War II, more than nineteen million women in America worked in various industries while men went to fight the war. Several hundred thousand women worked or volunteered in the military service. Many filled blue-collar jobs that traditionally were male occupations, while others applied their skills in the civil service, medical field, office work, retail, and service industries.

However, after the war ended, securing jobs for returning soldiers became a national priority. As a result, a cultural shift occurred that demised women's value and intellectual capabilities. A large majority of women lost their employment and were relegated back to domestic life. Some writers and feminist-minded advocates raised their pens and voices to bring attention to the inequality and devaluation women experienced.

Edith M. Stern (1901–1975) spent years working as a novelist and journalist. By the 1940s, she had published several "how to cope" and self-help books dealing with the effects of stress and illness, especially in families. She published her essay "Women Are Household Slaves" in January 1949 as postwar optimism and economic security, at least for white suburbanites, were on the rise. Challenging prevailing views of the era that claimed women's lives were easy and carefree, Stern pointed to all the ways women's work as housewives and mothers were complex, underappreciated, unpaid, and sometimes unfulfilling.

Stern challenged prevailing notions about housewives (Library of Congress)

Document Text

HELP WANTED: DOMESTIC: FEMALE. All cooking, cleaning, laundering, sewing, meal planning, shopping, weekday chauffeuring, social secretarial service, and complete care of three children. Salary at employer's option. Time off if possible.

No one in her right senses would apply for such a job. No one in his right senses, even a desperate widower, would place such an advertisement. Yet it correctly describes the average wife and mother's situation, in which most women remain for love, but many because they have no way out.

A nauseating amount of bilge is constantly being spilled all over the public press about the easy, pampered existence of the American woman. . . .

Housewifery is a complex of housekeeping, household management, housework, and childcare. Some of its elements, such as budgeting, dietetics, and above all, the proper upbringing of children, involve the higher brain centers; indeed, home economics has quite as respectable an academic status as engineering, and its own laboratories, dissertations, and hierarchy of degrees. . . .

The role of the housewife is . . . analogous to that of the president of a corporation who would not only determine policies and make overall plans but also spend the major part of his time and energy in such activities as sweeping the plant and oiling machines.

Industry, of course, is too thrifty of the capacities of its personnel to waste them in such fashion. . . .

Organized labor and government afford workers certain standardized legal or customary protections. But in terms of enlightened labor practice, the housewife stands out blackly as the Forgotten Worker.

She is covered by no minimum wage law; indeed, she gets no wages at all. Like the bondservant of another day, or the slave, she receives maintenance; but anything beyond that, whether in the form of a regular "allowance" or sporadic largesse, is ruggedly individualistic. . . .

No state or county health and sanitation inspectors invade the privacy of the home, as they do that of the factory; hence kitchens and domestic dwellings may be ill-ventilated, unsanitary and hazardous without penalty. That many more accidents occur in homes than in industry is no coincidence. Furthermore, when a disability is incurred, such as a bone broken in a fall off a ladder or legs scalded by the overturning of a kettle of boiling water, no beneficent legislation provides for the housewife's compensation.

Rest periods are irregular, . . . night work is frequent and unpredictably occasioned by a wide variety of factors such as the mending basket, the gang gathering for a party, a sick child, or even more pressing, a sick husband. The right to a vacation, thoroughly accepted in business and industry, is non-existent in the domestic sphere. When families go to beach bungalows or shacks in the woods, Mom continues on almost the same old treadmill; there are still little garments to be buttoned and unbuttoned, three meals a day to prepare, beds to be made and dishes to be washed. Even on jolly whole-family motor trips with the blessings of life in tourist camps or hotels, she still has the job considered full time by paid nurses and governesses.

Though progressive employers make some sort of provision for advancement, the housewife's opportunities for advancement are nil; the nature and scope of her job, the routines of keeping a family fed, clothed and housed remain always the same. If the male upon whom her scale of living depends prospers, about all to which she can look forward is a larger house—and more work. . . .

According to another line of unreasoning, the housewife has the advantage of being "her own boss" and unlike the gainfully employed worker can arrange her own schedules. This is pure balderdash. . . . If there is anything more inexorable than children's needs, from an infant's yowls of hunger and Junior's shrieks that he has just fallen down the stairs to the subtler need of an adolescent for a good listener during one of his or her frequent emotional crises, it is only the pressure of Dad's demand for supper as soon as he gets home. . . . Many a housewife drags through her performances in a state of semi-invalidism that would send any gainfully employed man or woman to bed on sick leave. . . .

Perhaps even more deplorable is the loss to society when graduate nurses, trained teachers, lawyers, physicians, artists, and other gifted women are unable to utilize their prolonged and expensive educations for the common good. Buried in the homemade cakes the family loves, lost among the stitches of patches, sunk in the suds of the week's wash, are incalculable skilled services.

But just as slaves were in the service of individual masters, not of the community or state or nation in general, so are housewives bound to the service of individual families. . . . Only a psychology of slavery can put women at the service of grown men. Ironically, the very gentlemen scrupulous about opening a door for a lady, carrying her packages, or helping her up onto a curb, take it for granted that at mealtimes, all their lives long, ladies should carry their food to them and never sit through a meal while they never get up. A wife, when she picks up the soiled clothing her husband has strewn on the floor, lugs his garments to the tailor, makes his twin bed, or sews on his buttons, acts as an unpaid body-servant. . . . Free individuals, in a democracy, perform personal services for themselves or, if they have the cash, pay other free individuals to wait on them. It is neither freedom nor democracy when such service is based on color or sex.

As long as the institution of housewifery in its present form persists, both ideologically and practically it blocks any true liberation of women. The vote, the opportunity for economic independence, and the right to smoke cigarettes are all equally superficial veneers over a deep-rooted, ages-old concept of keeping woman in her place. Unfortunately, however, housewives not only are unorganized, but also, doubtless because of the very nature of their brain-dribbling, spirit-stifling vocation, conservative. There is therefore little prospect of a House-wive's Rebellion. There is even less, in the light of men's comfortable setup under the present system, of a male-inspired movement for Abolition!

Glossary

analogous: similar

bilge: slang for nonsense

mending basket: a basket with clothing or household goods that needed to be repaired

unorganized: not organized into a labor union

Short-Answer Questions

1. Who is the intended audience of this essay?

2. What rhetorical devices (words that persuade or invoke sympathetic responses) does Stern use in her essay to invoke the sympathies of the audience?

3. Summarize Stern's claims of hypocrisy regarding women as equal to men, as free persons, and as persons to be respected.

Hoyt v. Florida

Author
John M. Harlan II

Date
1961

Document Type
Legal

Significance
Upheld the constitutionality of a Florida statute exempting women from mandatory jury duty

---

Overview

In 1957, Gwendolyn Hoyt was arrested in Florida for the murder of her husband. She pleaded not guilty by reason of temporary insanity. A Florida state court convicted her of second-degree murder. First, she appealed to the Florida Supreme Court, asserting that her right to an impartially selected jury was violated because the jurors were all men. During this time, a Florida jury statute exempted women from jury duty due to their domestic and maternal roles, but women could volunteer for jury duty. Her defense argued that women jurors would have been better suited to understand the aspects of the case, but the Florida Supreme Court upheld the conviction. Next, a second appeal was filed with the U.S. Supreme Court asking to rule if the Florida statute violated the equal protection clause of the Fourteenth Amendment. Hoyt lost the appeal; the Supreme Court unanimously upheld the Florida statute as constitutional.

During this era, despite some shifts in societal norms and laws that granted more equity to women, long-standing narrow views concerning the roles of women persisted, as reflected in the Florida jury duty statute.

Document Text

Appellant, a woman, killed her husband and was convicted in a Florida state court of second-degree murder. She claimed that her trial before an all-male jury violated her rights under the Fourteenth Amendment. A Florida statute provides, in substance, that no woman shall be taken for jury service unless she volunteers for it.

Held: The Florida statute is not unconstitutional on its face or as applied in this case. . . .

(a) The right to an impartially selected jury assured by the Fourteenth Amendment does not entitle one accused of crime to a jury tailored to the circumstances of the particular case. It requires only that the jury be indiscriminately drawn from among those in the community eligible for jury service, untrammelled by any arbitrary and systematic exclusions. . . .

(b) The Florida statute is not unconstitutional on its face, since it is not constitutionally impermissible for a State to conclude that a woman should be relieved from jury service unless she herself determines that such service is consistent with her own special responsibilities. . . .

(c) It cannot be said that the statute is unconstitutional as applied in this case, since there is no substantial evidence in the record that Florida has arbitrarily undertaken to exclude women from jury service. . . .

MR. JUSTICE HARLAN delivered the opinion of the Court.

. . . On this appeal . . . from the Florida Supreme Court's affirmance of the judgment of conviction, . . . we noted probable jurisdiction, . . . to consider appellant's claim that her trial before an all-male jury violated rights assured by the Fourteenth Amendment. The claim is that such jury was the product of a state jury statute which works an unconstitutional exclusion of women from jury service.

Justice John Marshall Harlan II wrote the unanimous opinion in **Hoyt v. Florida.**
(Oyez)

The jury law primarily in question is Fla.Stat., 1959, § 40.01(1). This Act . . . requires that grand and petit jurors be taken from "male and female" citizens of the State possessed of certain qualifications, . . . "provided, however, that the name of no female person shall be taken for jury service unless said person has registered with the clerk of the circuit court her desire to be placed on the jury list."

Showing that since the enactment of the statute, only a minimal number of women have so registered, appellant challenges the constitutionality of the statute both on its face and as applied in this case. For reasons now to follow we decide that both contentions must be rejected.

At the core of appellant's argument is the claim that the nature of the crime of which she was convicted peculiarly demanded the inclusion of persons of her own sex on the jury. . . .

As described by the Florida Supreme Court, the affair occurred in the context of a marital upheaval involving, among other things, the suspected infidelity of appellant's husband, and culminating in the husband's final rejection of his wife's efforts at reconciliation. It is claimed, in substance, that women jurors would have been more understanding or compassionate than men in assessing the quality of appellant's act and her defense of "temporary insanity." . . .

. . . Florida's § 40.01(1) does not purport to exclude women from state jury service. Rather, the statute "gives to women the privilege to serve, but does not impose service as a duty." . . .

In the selection of jurors, Florida has differentiated between men and women. . . . It has given women an absolute exemption from jury duty based solely on their sex, no similar exemption obtaining as to men. . . . And it has provided for its effectuation in a manner less onerous than that governing exemptions exercisable by men: women are not to be put on the jury list unless they have voluntarily registered for such service; men, on the other hand, even if entitled to an exemption, are to be included on the list unless they have filed a written claim of exemption as provided by law. . . .

In neither respect can we conclude that Florida's statute is not "based on some reasonable classification," and that it is thus infected with unconstitutionality. Despite the enlightened emancipation of women from the restrictions . . . and protections of bygone years, and their entry into many parts of community life formerly considered to be reserved to men, woman is still regarded as the center of home and family life. We cannot say that it is constitutionally impermissible for a State, acting in pursuit of the general welfare, to conclude that a woman should be relieved from the civic duty of jury service unless she herself determines that such service is consistent with her own special responsibilities.

. . . Women are now eligible for jury service in all but three States of the Union. . . . Of the forty-seven States where women are eligible, seventeen besides Florida, as well as the District of Columbia, have accorded women an absolute exemption based solely on their sex, exercisable in one form or another. . . . In two of these States, as in Florida, the . . . exemption is automatic, unless a woman volunteers for such service. . . .

Appellant argues that whatever may have been the design of this Florida enactment, the statute . . . results in an exclusion of women from jury service, because women, like men, can be expected to be available for jury service only under compulsion. In this connection, she points out that, by 1957, when this trial took place, only some 220 women out of approximately 46,000 registered female voters in Hillsborough County . . . had volunteered for jury duty. . . .

This argument, however, is surely beside the point. Given the reasonableness of the classification involved in § 40.01(1), the relative paucity of women jurors does not carry the constitutional consequence appellant would have it bear. . . .

We cannot hold this statute, as written, offensive to the Fourteenth Amendment.

II

Appellant's attack on the statute as applied in this case fares no better.

In the year here relevant Fla.Stat., 1955, § 40.10, in conjunction with § 40.02, required the jury commissioners, with the aid of the local circuit court judges and clerk, to compile annually a jury list of 10,000 inhabitants qualified to be jurors. In 1957, the existing Hillsborough County list had become exhausted to the extent of some 3,000 jurors. The new list was constructed by taking over from the old list the remaining some 7,000 jurors, including 10 women, and adding some 3,000 new male jurors to build up the list to the requisite 10,000. At the time, some 220 women had registered for jury duty in this county, including those taken over from the earlier list. . . .

Finding no substantial evidence whatever in this record that Florida has arbitrarily undertaken to exclude women from jury service, a showing which it was incumbent on appellant to make, . . . we must sustain the judgment of the Supreme Court of Florida.

Glossary

appellant: a person asking for an appeal; that is, requesting that a higher court reverse the ruling of a lower court

second-degree murder: murder with intent but not premeditated

untrammelled: free from restriction

Short-Answer Questions

1. Summarize what female citizens in Hillsborough County, Florida, need to know and do if they want to be added to the jury duty list.

2. Analyze the reasons the Supreme Court ruled to uphold the Florida statute exempting women from jury duty in Florida.

3. Evaluate the potential consequences this ruling might have had on women in Florida.

Betty Friedan:
The Feminine Mystique

Author Betty Friedan	**Significance** Challenged women to consider their identities and their role in society and ushered in the second wave of the feminist movement
Date 1963	
Document Type Essays, Reports, Manifestos	

Overview

The Feminine Mystique, by Betty Friedan (1921–2006), is one of a relative handful of modern books that can truly be said to have altered dramatically the course of thinking—in this case, about the role of women. After the book was published in 1963, it touched off a national debate about women's roles and quickly became a central text in modern feminism. Indeed, that debate sometimes became fierce, for Friedan and her family were forced to move out of their New York City neighborhood because of threats from angry neighbors.

Friedan earned a bachelor's degree in psychology from Smith College and continued her studies in psychology at the University of California at Berkeley. She then moved to New York City, where, in addition to writing freelance magazine articles, she married, had children, and adopted the traditional role of homemaker. The genesis of *The Feminine Mystique* was her

fifteen-year class reunion at Smith. She later distributed a questionnaire to two hundred of her classmates (all women, since Smith is a women's college, and all or mostly white, since only about 1 percent of the students at Smith by the late 1960s were African American). The results of the questionnaire led her to the conclusion that many of her classmates—and by implication many suburban American women—were unhappy and did not know why, causing her to title the first chapter of her book "The Problem That Has No Name." Initially she had difficulty finding a publisher for a magazine article she wrote based on her findings, but after several years of further research and writing, she published her results in *The Feminine Mystique*.

After defining the problem in the first chapter, Friedan provides a detailed analysis of the root causes of the problem. In her view, the problem stems from an idealized image of what it means to be a woman. Women, she says, have been encouraged, if not forced, to adopt the roles of mother and "housewife," in the process abandoning their education and any career goals they might have had. These roles prevented women from developing their unique identities. She sees the problem as an outgrowth of World War II and the Cold War that followed, which pro-

duced the baby boom and the sprawling suburbs that limited and defined womanhood. The overwhelming response to *The Feminine Mystique* turned Betty Friedan into a household name and launched her career as a leading feminist speaker, writer, and co-founder and president of the National Organization for Women.

Document Text

Chapter 1: "The Problem That Has No Name"

The problem lay buried, unspoken, for many years in the minds of American women. It was a strange stirring, a sense of dissatisfaction, a yearning that women suffered in the middle of the twentieth century in the United States. Each suburban wife struggled with it alone. As she made the beds, shopped for groceries, matched slipcover material, ate peanut butter sandwiches with her children, chauffeured Cub Scouts and Brownies, lay beside her husband at night—she was afraid to ask even of herself the silent question—"Is this all?"

For over fifteen years there was no word of this yearning in the millions of words written about women, for women, in all the columns, books and articles by experts telling women their role was to seek fulfillment as wives and mothers. . . .

The suburban housewife—she was the dream image of the young American women and the envy, it was said, of women all over the world. The American housewife—freed by science and labor-saving appliances from the drudgery, the dangers of childbirth and the illnesses of her grandmother. She was healthy, beautiful, educated, concerned only about her husband, her children, her home. She had found true feminine fulfillment. . . .

In the fifteen years after World War II, this mystique of feminine fulfillment became the cherished and self-perpetuating core of contemporary American culture. Millions of women lived their lives in the image of those pretty pictures of the American suburban housewife, kissing their husbands good-

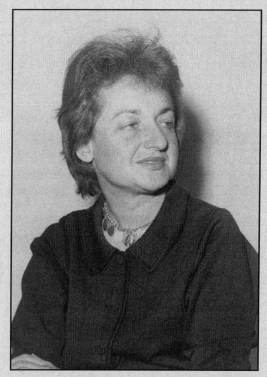

American feminist and writer Betty Friedan
(Library of Congress)

bye in front of the picture window, depositing their stationwagonsful of children at school, and smiling as they ran the new electric waxer over the spotless kitchen floor. . . . Their only dream was to be perfect wives and mothers; their highest ambition to have five children and a beautiful house, their only fight to get and keep their husbands. . . .

If a woman had a problem in the 1950's and 1960's, she knew that something must be wrong with her marriage, or with herself. Other women were satisfied with their lives, she thought. What kind of a woman was she if she did not feel this mysterious fulfillment waxing the kitchen floor? She was so ashamed to admit her dissatisfaction that she never knew how many other women shared it. . . .

For over fifteen years women in America found it harder to talk about the problem than about sex. . . .

But on an April morning in 1959, I heard a mother of four, having coffee with four other mothers in a suburban development fifteen miles from New York, say in a tone of quiet desperation, "the problem." And the others knew, without words, that she was not talking about a problem with her husband, or her children, or her home. Suddenly they realized they all shared the same problem, the problem that has no name. They began, hesitantly, to talk about it. . . .

Just what was this problem that has no name? What were the words women used when they tried to express it? Sometimes a woman would say "I feel empty somehow . . . incomplete." Or she would say, "I feel as if I don't exist." . . .

In 1960, the problem that has no name burst like a boil through the image of the happy American housewife. In the television commercials the pretty housewives still beamed over their foaming dishpans. . . . But the actual unhappiness of the American housewife was suddenly being reported—from the *New York Times* and *Newsweek* to *Good Housekeeping* and CBS Television ("The Trapped Housewife"), although almost everybody who talked about it found some superficial reason to dismiss it. . . .

The problem was dismissed by telling the housewife she doesn't realize how lucky she is. . . . The problem was also, and finally, dismissed by shrugging that there are NO solutions: this is what being a woman means, and what is wrong with American women that they can't accept their role gracefully? . . .

It is NO longer possible to ignore that voice, to dismiss the desperation of so many American women. This is not what being a woman means, no matter what the experts say. For human suffering there is a reason; perhaps the reason has not been found because the right questions have not been asked, or pressed far enough. . . .

It is no longer possible today to blame the problem on loss of femininity: to say that education and independence and equality with men have made American women unfeminine. I have heard so many women try to deny this dissatisfied voice within themselves because it does not fit the pretty picture of femininity the experts have given them. I think, in fact, that this is the first clue to the mystery; the problem cannot be understood in the generally accepted terms by which scientists have studied women, doctors have treated them, counselors have advised them, and writers have written about them. Women who suffer this problem, in whom this voice is stirring, have lived their whole lives in the pursuit of feminine fulfillment. . . .

Can the problem that has no name be somehow related to the domestic routine of the housewife? When a woman tries to put the problem into words, she often merely describes the daily life she leads. What is there in this recital of comfortable domestic detail that could possibly cause such a feeling of desperation?

It is easy to see the concrete details that trap the suburban housewife, the continual demands on her time. But the chains that bind her in her trap are chains in her own mind and spirit. They are chains made up of mistaken ideas and misinterpreted facts, of incomplete truths and unreal choices. They are not easily seen and not easily shaken off. . . .

If I am right, the problem that has no name stirring in the minds of so many American women today is not a matter of loss of femininity or too much education, or the demands of domesticity. It is far more important than anyone recognizes.

It is the key to these other new and old problems which have been torturing women and their husbands and children, and puzzling their doctors and educators for years. It may well be the key to our future as a nation and a culture. We can no longer ignore that voice within women that says: "I want something more than my husband and my children and my home."

Glossary

Brownies: the youngest members of the Girl Scouts

Cub Scouts: the youngest members of the Boy Scouts

feminine: relating to or characteristic of women

mystique: air of mystery; special skill

stationwagonsful: referring to the station wagon, a popular suburban family vehicle in the mid-twentieth century

Short-Answer Questions

1. How does the author describe the suburban housewife? What are some of the characteristics she highlights?

2. Define the "problem that has no name." What is it, and why does the author claim it can no longer be ignored?

3. Evaluate the language and images used by the author, focusing specifically on how she paints a picture of women and their circumstances. What effect do you think this text had on readers in the 1960s?

President's Commission on the Status of Women: "American Women"

Author	**Significance**
President's Commission on the Status of Women	Provided a summary of findings regarding the status of discrimination against women and suggestions for ways to eliminate such discrimination
Date 1963	
Document Type Presidential/Executive; Essays, Reports, Manifestos	

Overview

President John F. Kennedy established the President's Commission on the Status of Women by Executive Order 10980, issued on February 28, 1961. The commission was a bipartisan organization given the task of examining the status of discrimination against women in the nation and proposing ways to eliminate it. Eleanor Roosevelt served as chair of the commission, and the twenty-six members were comprised of a range of individuals, including cabinet members, senators, U.S. representatives, union leaders, educators, and leaders in women's organizations. Seven committees were established, each focusing on a different area: Education, Federal Employment Policies and Practices, Home and Community, Political and Civil Rights, Private Employment, Protective Labor Legislation, and Social Insurance and Taxes.

Each committee conducted extensive research, compiled official reports of their findings, and made specific recommendations for federal policy changes. They also advocated for changes in discriminatory state laws such as laws excluding women from serving on juries, from owning property, from legal control of their earnings, or from owning a business. Numerous legislative and executive actions can find their roots in the work of the commission. For example, the commission officially endorsed the Equal Pay Act, which Kennedy signed into law in 1963. It also led to the establishment of similar commissions in every state within a few years to conduct similar studies considering the current status of women.

The commission submitted its final report, "American Women," to President Kennedy on October 11, 1963. This included the final findings and recommendations of each committee and an overall assessment of the currents status of women in the nation. After receiving the report, Kennedy disestablished the commission and issued an executive order establishing two new groups to continue the work they had started: the Citizen's Advisory Council on the Status of Women and the Interdepartmental Committee on the Status of Women.

Document Text
Women Under the Law

Jury Service

The right to a trial by a jury that reflects the community is a bulwark of justice. Women became eligible to serve on all Federal juries only by virtue of the Civil Rights Act of 1957. The Commission regards further Federal legislation as necessary to assure that procedure for selecting the names of qualified persons to be placed in the jury box shall not systematically or deliberately exclude any group from the jury panel on account of race, sex, political or religious affiliation, or economic or social status.

In 3 States, women still may not serve on juries of the State courts, and in 26 others and the District of Columbia, women who are called on for jury service may claim exemptions that are not available to men.

Appropriate action, including enactment of legislation, where necessary, should be taken to achieve equal jury service in the States.

It is also desirable for appropriate agencies like the Federal Judicial Conference and the National Conference of State Chief Justices, as well as national and State civic organizations, to give continuing attention to assuring equal jury service without distinction as to sex. Women and men alike should assume their responsibilities for making juries representative of the communities in which they live.

Personal and Property Rights

In many specific areas of State law, the disabilities of married women are considerable. State statutes affecting family law and personal and property rights of women should be modernized.

Single women enjoy equality of legal treatment with men in respect to property and contract law, the only general exception being the lower minimum age at which they may contract to marry. But married women, over much broader legal range, are denied such equality.

John F. Kennedy established the President's Commission on the Status of Women.
(National Archives and Records Administration)

Limitations on the rights of married women derive from a long history: some go back to concepts of the common law brought to this continent by its English settlers; some, particularly those related to concepts of community property, derive from the law traditional among the settlers from France and Spain. In practically all of these areas of law, remedial action lies under the jurisdiction of the States. Many States have already removed most inequities, but in every State, one kind of disability or another limits the legal rights of married women.

State legislatures and other groups concerned with the improvement of State statutes affecting family law and personal and property rights of married women, including the National Conference of Commissioners on Uniform State Laws, the Council of State

Governments, the American Law Institute, and State Commissions on the State of Women, should move to eliminate laws which impose legal disabilities on women.

Specifically, the Commission directs their attention to these considerations:

• The civil capacity of married women and married men should be equalized through the elimination of legal restrictions on the rights of married women to contract, convey, or own real or personal property, to engage in business, to act as surety or fiduciary, to receive and control their own earnings, and to dispose of their own property by will; the law governing domicile for purposes such as voting, holding public office, jury service, taxation, and probate should be the same for married women as it is for married men.

• Marriage as a partnership in which each spouse makes a different but equally important contribution is increasingly recognized as a reality in this country and is already reflected in the laws of some other countries. During marriage, each spouse should have a legally defined substantial right in the earnings of the other, in the real and personal property acquired through those earnings, and in their management. Such a right should be legally recognized as surviving the marriage in the event of termination by divorce, annulment, or death. Appropriate legislation should safeguard either spouse and protect the surviving spouse against improper alienation of property by the other. Surviving children as well as the surviving spouse should be protected from disinheritance.

• The prevailing rule in the United States is for guardianship of children during marriage to be vested jointly in both parents; all States should make their statutes conformable to it.

• In line with the partnership view of marriage, while the husband should continue to have primary responsibility for support of his wife and minor children, the wife should be given legal responsibility for sharing in the support of herself and the children to the extent she has means to do so.

Modernization of State law in these respects should be initiated now.

The Commission found that in several areas, legal research and analysis are essential before firm proposals for reform can be recommended. These include:

• The effect of according married women the same right as married men to establish a separate domicile on marital status, rights, and obligations, on alimony and support, on custody and visitation of children.

• Minimum age of marriage for males and females.

• Alimony, support, and property settlements. Such a study should include not only the law and practice pertaining to the rendition of alimony and support decrees, but also methods of locating persons responsible for the support of dependents.

• Differences in substantive law and procedure as between men and women in the field of criminal law and administration, including correction.

The Commission notes the great progress that women have achieved during the last few decades as the result of the efforts of civic and other organizations, including women's groups, to focus public attention on the problem of discrimination based on sex and believes that continuance and increase of these efforts constitute an indispensable condition to the achievement of equal rights for women. Such groups can likewise render service by helping women of all groups and income levels to know their rights; while rights accorded women frequently lag behind those accorded men, many women are inadequately aware of what their current rights actually are.

A know-your-rights pamphlet should be published, under either public or private auspices, to enable more women to become aware of their legal position.

Glossary

Civil Rights Act of 1957: the first federal civil rights legislation passed since Reconstruction; allowed federal prosecution of anyone who tried to prevent someone from voting and established a commission to investigate voter fraud; also established uniform qualifications for jurors in federal courts, allowing women to serve on juries in federal courts even in states that did not permit women to serve on juries in state courts

common law: a body of unwritten laws, rules, or customs based on tradition or legal precedents

substantive law: laws that govern conduct (as compared to procedural law, which governs how substantive laws are made or enforced)

Short-Answer Questions

1. Describe the status of women reported here in regard to jury service. What actions does the commission recommend should be taken to improve the situation?

2. The report claims "the disabilities of married women are considerable" in regard to personal and property rights. Describe two examples it provides to support this claim.

3. In a detailed response, analyze the recommendations given for how personal and property law could be reformed specifically regarding marriage and the guardianship of children. What arguments could be made to support these recommendations? To challenge them?

Fannie Lou Hamer:
Testimony at the
Democratic National Convention

Author Fannie Lou Hamer	**Significance** Brought to national attention the threats, indignities, and horrific beatings Hamer and others endured for registering to vote
Date 1964	
Type Speeches/Addresses	

Overview

In 1964 at the Democratic National Convention, Fannie Lou Hamer testified before the party's Credentials Committee to explain the atmosphere of fear in which civil rights workers lived in Mississippi and to challenge the moral legitimacy of the state's "regular" delegation to the convention. Hamer and her colleagues from the civil rights movement in Mississippi had generated momentum that year through the Freedom Summer project, which accomplished widespread education and registration of African American voters. The activists used this momentum to launch a new political institution, the Mississippi Freedom Democratic Party (MFDP), to challenge the legitimacy of the state's traditional Democratic Party (in the one-party Solid South, the Democratic Party was the only one that mattered). They did so in part simply to bring national attention to Mississippi, but they also held hopes that their gambit would result in the national Democratic Party's stripping the state's traditional branch of its status and recognizing MFDP members instead as the representatives of the Magnolia State.

Hamer emerged as the group's most eloquent spokesperson. She had distinguished herself as a homegrown leader in the civil rights movement, one who excelled at describing the plight of rural Black Mississippians and the changes they sought to bring about in a way rural Black Mississippians could understand. When the Democratic National Committee held its quadrennial convention in Atlantic City, New Jersey, at the end of the summer, Hamer was a natural choice to speak on behalf of the MFDP. The Freedom Democrats lodged a formal complaint with the national party over the seating of the "regulars," and the complaint would be adjudicated by the national convention's Credentials Committee. The labor lawyer and Democratic Party insider Joseph L. Rauh Jr. of Washington, D.C., who represented the MFDP in Atlantic City, called on Hamer to testify before the committee on August 22, 1964.

Fannie Lou Hamer
(Library of Congress)

Document Text

Mr. Chairman, and the Credentials Committee, my name is Mrs. Fannie Lou Hamer. . . .

It was the 31st of August in 1962 that 18 of us traveled twenty-six miles to the county courthouse in Indianola to try to register to try to become first-class citizens. We was met in Indianola by Mississippi men, highway patrolmens and they only allowed two of us in to take the literacy test at the time. After we had taken this test . . . we was held up by the City Police and the State Highway Patrolmen and carried back to Indianola, where the bus driver was charged that day with driving a bus the wrong color.

After we paid the fine among us . . . and Reverend

Jeff Sunny carried me four miles in the rural area where I had worked as a timekeeper and sharecropper for eighteen years. I was met there by my children, who told me that the plantation owner was angry because I had gone down to try to register.

After they told me, my husband came, and said that the plantation owner was raising cain because I had tried to register. . . . The plantation owner came, and said, "Fannie Lou, do you know—did Pap tell you what I said?"

And I said, "yes, sir."

He said, "I mean that. . . . If you don't go down and withdraw your registration, you will have to leave." . . .

And I addressed him . . . and said, "I didn't try to register for you. I tried to register for myself." I had to leave that same night. . . .

And in June, the 9th, 1963, I had attended a voter registration workshop. . . . Ten of us was traveling by the Continental Trailway bus. When we got to Winona, Mississippi, . . . four of the people got off to use the washroom. . . . The four people that had gone in to use the restaurant was ordered out. . . . I got off of the bus to see what had happened, and one of the ladies said, "It was a State Highway Patrolman and a chief of police ordered us out."

I got back on the bus. . . . I saw when they began to get the four people in a highway patrolman's car. I stepped off of the bus to see what was happening and somebody screamed from the car that the four workers was in and said, "Get that one there," and when I went to get in the car, when the man told me I was under arrest, he kicked me.

I was carried to the county jail. . . . After I was placed in the cell I began to hear the sound of kicks and horrible screams, and I could hear somebody say, "Can you say, yes sir, n*****?" . . . She would say, "Yes, I can say yes, sir." . . .

They beat her, I don't know how long. . . .

And it wasn't too long before three white men came to my cell. One of these men was a State Highway Patrolman. . . . He said, "We are going to make you wish you was dead."

I was carried out of that cell into another cell where they had two Negro prisoners. The State Highway Patrolmen ordered the first Negro to take the blackjack. . . . The first Negro began to beat . . . , and I was holding my hands behind me at that time on my left side because I suffered from polio when I was six years old. After the first Negro had beat until he was exhausted the State Highway Patrolman ordered the second Negro to take the blackjack.

The second Negro began to beat and I began to work my feet, and the State Highway Patrolman ordered the first Negro . . . to set on my feet. . . . I began to scream and one white man got up and began to beat me my head and told me to hush. One white man—my dress had worked up high, he walked over and pulled my dress down—and he pulled my dress back, back up. . . .

I was in jail when Medgar Evers was murdered.

All of this is on account we want to register, to become first-class citizens. . . . I question America, is this America, the land of the free and the home of the brave where we have to sleep with our telephones off of the hooks because our lives be threatened daily because we want to live as decent human beings, in America?

Glossary

blackjack: a baton or truncheon used by police as a weapon; a billy club

Medgar Evers: civil rights activist, field secretary for the NAACP, and World War II veteran who was assassinated in 1963 by Byron De La Beckwith, a member of the White Citizen's Council, in Jackson, Mississippi

Short-Answer Questions

1. Why do you think Fannie Lou Hamer told the plantation owner that she had registered to vote knowing she would be forced to leave?

2. Why would the state patrolman have ordered the Black prisoners to beat Hamer instead of doing it himself?

3. Hamer poses a question at the end of her speech: "I question America, is this America, the land of the free and the home of the brave where we have to sleep with our telephones off of the hooks because our lives be threatened daily because we want to live as decent human beings, in America?" What is the significance of this question?

Title VII of the Civil Rights Act of 1964

Author
Robert Kennedy, Burke Marshall, Nicholas
Katzenbach, Harold Greene, Howard W. Smith,
and others

Date
1964

Document Type
Legislative

Significance
Prohibits employment discrimination based on
race, color, religion, sex, and national origin,
and created the Equal Employment Opportunity Commission to implement the law

Overview

President John F. Kennedy was instrumental in the passage of the Civil Rights Act of 1964. Acknowledging the increased tension across the nation as the civil rights movement (and the opposition to it) continued to gain momentum, recognizing the widespread white resistance to desegregation, and in direct response to the highly publicized murder of civil rights leader Medgar Evers, Kennedy asked Congress to draft a comprehensive civil rights bill in June 1963. Congress complied with this request, and the Civil Rights Act of 1964 was signed into law by President Lyndon B. Johnson on July 2, 1964. This landmark piece of legislation marked a significant shift in the United States. It included provisions to extend the Commission on Civil Rights, to prevent discrimination in federally assisted programs, to prohibit discrimination in public facilities and in public education, and to prohibit employment discrimination.

Passage of the law was not simple. Numerous individuals were involved in the drafting and revision of the bill. The original bill was crafted and drafted in the Department of Justice, headed by Attorney General Robert Kennedy. The drafting group almost certainly included Robert Kennedy and his assistant attorneys general, Burke Marshall and Nicholas Katzenbach, as well as the Justice Department lawyer Harold Greene (who later became a judge). As the bill moved through the committee process in the House of Representatives, it was significantly redrafted and strengthened by members and staff of the House Judiciary Committee, including Representatives Emanuel Celler (D-N.Y.) and William McCulloch (R-Ohio) and their aides. Many amendments were added from the floor of the House, with one of the most momentous being the addition of a provision including sex discrimination in Title VII of the Civil Rights Act of 1964.

Title VII outlawed discrimination in employment on the basis of race, religion, national origin, and sex. The provision including sex discrimination as a prohibited mode of discrimination was added to the bill by Howard W. Smith (D-Va.), chairman of the House Rules Committee, seemingly in an attempt to derail the bill and stop its passage. The amended text passed, however, solidifying the protection against sex discrimination in employment. Title VII also created the Equal Employment Opportunity Commission (EEOC) to implement the law.

President Lyndon B. Johnson signs the 1964 Civil Rights Act. (White House Press Office)

Document Text
Unlawful Employment Practices
SEC. 2000e-2. *[Section 703]*

(a) Employer practices

It shall be an unlawful employment practice for an employer—

(1) to fail or refuse to hire or to discharge any individual, or otherwise to discriminate against any individual with respect to his compensation, terms, conditions, or privileges of employment, because of such individual's race, color, religion, sex, or national origin; or

(2) to limit, segregate, or classify his employees or applicants for employment in any way which would deprive or tend to deprive any individual of employment opportunities or otherwise adversely affect his status as an employee, because of such individual's race, color, religion, sex, or national origin. . . .

Equal Employment Opportunity Commission

SEC. 2000e-4. *[Section 705]*

(a) Creation; composition; political representation; appointment; term; vacancies; Chairman and Vice Chairman; duties of Chairman; appointment of personnel; compensation of personnel

There is hereby created a Commission to be known as the Equal Employment Opportunity Commission, which shall be composed of five members, not more than three of whom shall be members of the same political party. Members of the Commission shall be appointed by the President by and with the advice and consent of the Senate for a term of five years. Any individual chosen to fill a vacancy shall be appointed only for the unexpired term of the member whom he shall succeed, and all members of the Commission shall continue to serve until their successors are appointed and qualified, except that no such member of the Commission shall continue to serve (1) for more than sixty days when the Congress is in session unless a nomination to fill such vacancy shall have been submitted to the Senate, or (2) after the adjournment sine die of the session of the Senate in which such nomination was submitted. The President shall designate one member to serve as Chairman of the Commission, and one member to serve as Vice Chairman. The Chairman shall be responsible on behalf of the Commission for the administrative operations of the Commission, and, except as provided in subsection (b) of this section, shall appoint, in accordance with the provisions of Title 5 *[United States Code]* governing appointments in the competitive service, such officers, agents, attorneys, administrative law judges *[originally, hearing examiners]*, and employees as he deems necessary to assist it in the performance of its functions. . . .

Enforcement Provisions
SEC. 2000e-5. *[Section 706]*

(a) Power of Commission to prevent unlawful employment practices

The Commission is empowered, as hereinafter provided, to prevent any person from engaging in any unlaw-ful employment practice as set forth in section 2000e-2 or 2000e-3 of this title *[section 703 or 704]*.

(b) . . . Whenever a charge is filed by or on behalf of a person claiming to be aggrieved, or by a member of the Commission, alleging that an employer, employment agency, labor organization, or joint labor management committee controlling apprenticeship or other training or retraining, including on-the-job training programs, has engaged in an unlawful employment practice, the Commission shall serve a notice of the charge (including the date, place and circumstances of the alleged unlawful employment practice) on such employer, employment agency, labor organization, or joint labor-management committee (hereinafter referred to as the "respondent") within ten days, and shall make an investigation thereof. Charges shall be in writing under oath or affirmation and shall contain such information and be in such form as the Commission requires. Charges shall not be made public by the Commission. If the Commission determines after such investigation that there is not reasonable cause to believe that the charge is true, it shall dismiss the charge and promptly notify the person claiming to be aggrieved and the respondent of its action. In determining whether reasonable cause exists, the Commission shall accord substantial weight to final findings and orders made by State or local authorities in proceedings commenced under State or local law. . . . If the Commission determines after such investigation that there is reasonable cause to believe that the charge is true, the Commission shall endeavor to eliminate any such alleged unlawful employment practice by informal methods of conference, conciliation, and persuasion. Nothing said or done during and as a part of such informal endeavors may be made public by the Commission, its officers or employees, or used as evidence in a subsequent proceeding without the written consent of the persons concerned. Any person who makes public information in violation of this subsection shall be fined not more than $1,000 or imprisoned for not more than one year, or both. The Commission shall make its determination on reasonable cause as promptly as possible and, so far as practicable, not later than one hundred and twenty days from the filing of the charge. . . .

Glossary

discriminate against: to treat worse

sine die: without a future date being arranged

Short-Answer Questions

1. What categories of discrimination in employment are prohibited in Title VII of the Civil Rights Act of 1964?

2. Describe the process that would occur if a person filed a charge accusing an employer of engaging in unlawful employment practices. How would the EEOC proceed once the charge were filed?

3. Briefly explain why you think the inclusion of "sex" in this list of prohibited categories for discrimination was significant at the time. What effect do you think this had on the women's rights movement?

Pauli Murray and Mary O. Eastwood: "Jane Crow and the Law: Sex Discrimination and Title VII"

Author	Significance
Pauli Murray and Mary O. Eastwood	Introduced arguments that would become foundational in women's rights advocacy and litigation, drawing comparisons between sex-based discrimination and Jim Crow laws
Date 1965	
Document Type Essays, Reports, Manifestos; Legal	

Overview

Before 1964, federal laws and regulations designed to eliminate discrimination did not include sex as a protected category. Title VII of the Civil Rights Act of 1964, however, included "sex" with race, color, religion, and national origin in the list of categories that were to be protected against discrimination in employment. This significant step marked the beginning of a new consideration of sex discrimination in United States law and in practice.

In 1965, Pauli Murray and Mary Eastwood coauthored the article "Jane Crow and the Law: Sex Discrimination and Title VII," which was published in the *George Washington Law Review*. Murray was a lawyer, civil rights advocate, and leading voice in the women's movement. The question of sexism within the civil rights movement was a central focus of Murray's legal career, leading to the development of a feminist critique known as "Jane Crow." Mary Eastwood was also a lawyer and committed civil rights advocate. She served as an attorney advisor to the Justice Department's Office of Legal Counsel. The two were both members of the President's Commission on the Status of Women established by President John F. Kennedy. They served on the Civil and Political Rights Committee of the commission, conducting research and making recommendations for federal policy changes to improve the status of women. Their landmark article draws from their experiences on this committee and from a variety of legal sources. In it, they make comparisons between sex-based discrimination and Jim Crow laws through Murray's "Jane Crow" critique. This was the first comprehensive treatment of sex discrimination in an American law review.

In "Jane Crow and the Law," they call for the protection of women against discrimination based on the United States Constitution, specifically the Fourteenth Amendment, and the newly passed Title VII of the Civil Rights Act of 1964. Murray and Eastwood argue that these sources must be interpreted to prohibit discrimination against women by both the government and by private employers. Specific arguments and legal interpretations introduced in this article became foundational in civil rights litigation and advocacy for more than a decade after its initial publication.

Document Text

During the 1960's, more concern for the legal status of women has been demonstrated than at any time since the adoption of the nineteenth amendment. . . . Despite all of this activity, there are problem areas that need to be clarified.

Equality of Rights under the Constitution

. . . Early and definitive court pronouncement, particularly by the U.S. Supreme Court, is urgently needed with regard to the validity under the 5th and 14th amendments of laws and official practices discriminating against women, to the end that the principle of equality become firmly established in constitutional doctrine. . . .

Both proponents and opponents of the equal rights amendment, unlike the Commission, generally have assumed there is a constitutional gap with respect to women, a view also expressed by the Senate Judiciary Committee in reporting favorably on the proposed amendment. . . .

The courts generally have over-simplified the question of reasonableness of classification by sex by applying the principle that "sex is a valid basis for classification." The blanket application of such a doctrine totally defeats the meaning of equal protection of the law for women. . . .

Although the Supreme Court has in no case found a law distinguishing on the basis of sex to be a violation of the fourteenth amendment, the amendment may nevertheless be applicable to sex discrimination. . . . Recent Supreme Court decisions in cases involving school desegregation, reapportionment, the right to counsel, and the extension of the concept of state action illustrate the modern trend towards insuring equality of status and recognizing individual rights. Courts have not yet fully realized that women's rights are a part of human rights; but the climate appears favorable to renewed judicial attacks on sex discrimination as suggested by the President's Commission on the Status of Women. . . .

The difficulty in asserting women's rights lies not in the limited reach of the fourteenth amendment, but in the failure of the courts to isolate and analyze the discriminatory aspect of differential treatment based on sex. . . .

Before attempting to formulate any principle of equal protection of the laws, certain assumptions that have confused the issue must be reexamined. The first is the assumption that equal rights for women is tantamount to seeking identical treatment with men. This is an oversimplification. As individuals, women seek equality of opportunity for education, employment, cultural enrichment, and civic participation without barriers built upon the myth of the stereotyped "woman." As women, they seek freedom of choice: to develop their maternal and familial functions primarily, or to develop different capacities at different stages of life, or to pursue some combination of these choices. . . .

The second assumption confusing the "woman problem" is that, because of inherent differences between the sexes, differential treatment does not imply inequality or inferiority. The inherent differences between the sexes, according to this view, make necessary the application of different principles to women than to minority groups. . . .

Although the "classification by sex" doctrine was useful in sustaining the validity of progressive labor legislation in the past, perhaps it should now be shelved alongside the "separate but equal" doctrine. It could be argued that, just as separate schools for Negro and white children by their very nature cannot be "equal," classification on the basis of sex is today inherently unreasonable and discriminatory. . . .

If laws classifying persons by sex were prohibited by the Constitution, and if it were made clear that laws recognizing functions, *if performed*, are not based on sex per se, much of the confusion as to the legal status of women would be eliminated. . . .

The Committee on Civil and Political Rights suggested several possible subjects for constitutional attack: for example, state laws excluding women from jury service, domiciliary rules that restrict a married woman's right to vote, and discrimination in public employment.

The administration of the sex discrimination provisions of Title VII of the Civil Rights Act of 1964 should create new interest in constitutional equality of rights. Insofar as certain types of sex discrimination in private employment might be officially sanctioned through interpretations by the Equal Employment Opportunity Commission under Title VII, this most important area of discrimination against women may be brought within the reach of the fifth amendment. The issue of constitutionality under the fourteenth amendment of a state labor standards law that applies only to women might be relitigated in state efforts to enforce a law that an employer believes would require him to violate Title VII. . . .

The Civil Rights Act of 1964, Title VII

The Committee on Private Employment of the President's Commission on the Status of Women noted in its report that "increased employment of women and the need for their services has brought forcefully to public attention the necessity for equal employment opportunities for that one-third of the Nation's work force composed of women." . . .

Conclusion

According women equality of rights under the Constitution and equal employment opportunity, through positive implementation of Title VII of the Civil Rights Act of 1964, would not likely result in any immediate, drastic change in the pattern of women's employment. But great scientific and social changes have already taken place, such as longer life span, smaller families, and lower infant death rate, with the result that motherhood consumes smaller proportions of women's lives. Thus, the effects of sex discrimination are felt by more women today.

The recent increase in activity concerning the status of women indicates that we are gradually coming to recognize that the proper role of the law is not to protect women by restrictions and confinement, but to protect both sexes from discrimination.

We are entering the age of human rights. In the United States, perhaps our most important concerns are with the rights to vote and to representative government and with equal rights to education and employment. Hopefully, our economy will outgrow concepts of class competition, such as Negro v. white, youth v. age, or male v. female, and, at least in matters of employment, standards of merit and individual quality will control rather than prejudice.

Glossary

Committee on Civil and Political Rights: one of the seven committees that comprised the President's Commission on the Status of Women

Nineteenth Amendment: guarantees women's right to vote

President's Commission on the Status of Women: sometimes referred to simply as the Commission, a bipartisan group established by President Kennedy in 1961 to examine the status of discrimination against women in the nation and propose ways to eliminate it

Title VII of the Civil Rights Act of 1964: prohibits employment discrimination based on race, color, religion, sex, or national origin; also created the Equal Employment Opportunity Commission (EEOC) to implement the law

Short-Answer Questions

1. What do you think is the primary goal of the authors? What are they hoping to accomplish with this article?

2. The authors claim that several assumptions need to be cleared up before formulating any "principle of equal protection of the laws." Describe one of the assumptions they identify. Why is this significant?

3. Analyze the authors' use the term "Jane Crow." What connection are they hoping to make for the reader? Do you think this is helpful? Appropriate? Why or why not?

Casey Hayden and Mary King: "Sex and Caste"

<table>
<tr><td>

Author
Casey Hayden and Mary King

Date
1965

Document Type
Essays, Reports, Manifestos; Letters/
Correspondence

</td><td>

Significance
A foundational document of second-wave
feminism, identifying recurring social issues im-
pacting women and various forms of unofficial
inequality women were facing

</td></tr>
</table>

Overview

It could be argued that the modern feminist movement began with the publication of "Sex and Caste,"
described by its authors, Casey Hayden and Mary
King, as a "kind of memo" sent to a number of women
active in the civil rights and anti–Vietnam War movements in 1965 and published in the pacifist magazine
Liberation in 1966. Prior to 1965 the authors had been
involved in the civil rights struggle as members of the
Student Nonviolent Coordinating Committee (SNCC,
pronounced "snick"). Earlier, in 1964, King had written
a paper, cosigned by Hayden, in which she outlined her
dissatisfaction with what she perceived to be the sexism
of the SNCC. The paper was dismissed by the SNCC's
male leadership. The SNCC, despite its commitment to
racial equality, fell lamentably short in matters of gender
equality and generally expected the organization's idealis-
tic women volunteers to perform such tasks as cooking,
typing, taking notes, running errands, operating mimeo-
graph machines, and deferring to the male leadership. At
a SNCC staff meeting in 1964, the organization's leader,
Stokely Carmichael, is alleged to have said that "the only
position for women in SNCC is prone."

Casey Hayden was born Sandra Cason in highly segregated East Texas. She was one of the founding members of SNCC and a member of the Students for a
Democratic Society (SDS). In 1961 she married Tom
Hayden, the president of the Students for a Democratic
Society. Mary Elizabeth King, too, was affiliated with
SNCC and was frequently at the side of Martin Luther
King Jr. during civil rights demonstrations in the late
1950s and early 1960s. Although the two would not
know it at the time, "Sex and Caste" would come to
be widely discussed in feminist circles and is considered a foundational document of "second-wave feminism" (the feminist movement of the 1960s and 1970s,
which focused not on the legal inequalities attacked by
first-wave feminism but on unofficial inequalities and
a range of social issues affecting women). Indeed, the
authors themselves state that "the chances seem nil that
we could start a movement," yet that is precisely what
they did.

Document Text

We've talked a lot, to each other and to some of you, about our own and other women's problems in trying to live in our personal lives and in our work as independent and creative people. In these conversations we've found what seems to be recurrent ideas or themes. Maybe we can look at these things many of us perceive, often as a result of insights learned from the movement:

Sex and Caste

There seem to be many parallels that can be drawn between treatment of Negroes and treatment of women in our society as a whole. But in particular, women we've talked to who work in the movement seem to be caught up in a common-law caste system that operates, sometimes subtly, forcing them to work around or outside hierarchical structures of power which may exclude them. Women seem to be placed in the same position of assumed subordination in personal situations too. It is a caste system which, at its worst, uses and exploits women.

This is complicated by several facts, among them: (1) The caste system is not institutionalized by law (women have the right to vote, to sue for divorce, etc.); (2) Women can't withdraw from the situation (a la nationalism) or overthrow it; (3) There are biological differences (even though those biological differences are usually discussed or accepted without taking present and future technology into account so we probably can't be sure what these differences mean). Many people who are very hip to the implications of the racial caste system, even people in the movement, don't seem to be able to see the sexual caste system and if the question is raised they respond with: "That's the way it's supposed to be. There are biological differences." Or with other statements which recall a white segregationist confronted with integration.

Women and Problems of Work

The caste system perspective dictates the roles assigned to women in the movement, and certainly even more to women outside the movement. Within the movement, questions arise in situations ranging from relationships of women organizers to men in the community, to who cleans the freedom house, to who holds leadership positions, to who does secretarial work, and who acts as a spokesman for groups. Other problems arise between women with varying degrees of awareness of themselves as being as capable as men but held back from full participation, or between women who see themselves as needing more control of their work than other women demand. And there are problems with relationships between white women and black women.

Women and Personal Relations with Men

Having learned from the movement to think radically about the personal worth and abilities of people whose role in society had gone unchallenged before, a lot of women in the movement have begun trying to apply those lessons to their own relations with men. . . .

Institutions

Nearly everyone has real questions about those institutions which shape perspectives on men and women: marriage, child rearing patterns, women's (and men's) magazines, etc. People are beginning to think about and even to experiment with new forms in these areas.

Men's Reactions to the Questions Raised Here

A very few men seem to feel, when they hear conversations involving these problems, that they have a right to be present and participate in them, since they are so deeply involved. At the same time, very few men can respond non-defensively, since the whole idea is either beyond their comprehension or threatens and exposes them. . . .

The problems we're listing here, and what others have said about them, are therefore largely drawn from conversations among women only—and that difficulty in establishing dialogue with men is a recurring theme among people we've talked to.

Lack of Community for Discussion

Nobody is writing, or organizing or talking publicly about women, in any way that reflects the problems that various women in the movement come across and which we've tried to touch above. . . .

The reason we want to try to open up dialogue is mostly subjective. Working in the movement often intensifies personal problems, especially if we start trying to apply things we're learning there to our personal lives. Perhaps we can start to talk with each other more openly than in the past and create a community of support for each other so we can deal with ourselves and others with integrity and can therefore keep working.

Objectively, the chances seem nil that we could start a movement based on anything as distant to general American thought as a sex-caste system. Therefore, most of us will probably want to work full time on problems such as war, poverty, race.

The very fact that the country can't face, much less deal with, the questions we're raising means that the movement is one place to look for some relief. Real efforts at dialogue within the movement and with whatever liberal groups, community women, or students might listen are justified. That is, all the problems between men and women and all the problems of women functioning in society as equal human beings are among the most basic that people face. We've talked in the movement about trying to build a society which would see basic human problems (which are now seen as private troubles) as public problems and would try to shape institutions to meet human needs rather than shaping people to meet the needs of those with power. To raise questions like those above illustrates very directly that society hasn't dealt with some of its deepest problems and opens discussion of why that is so. (In one sense, it is a radicalizing question that can take people beyond legalistic solutions into areas of personal and institutional change.) The second objective reason we'd like to see discussion begin is that we've learned a great deal in the movement and perhaps this is one area where a determined attempt to apply ideas we've learned there can produce some new alternatives.

Glossary

caste system: a class structure determined by birth

common-law: a body of unwritten laws, rules, or customs based on tradition or legal precedents

the movement: the civil rights and antiwar movement

---

1. Who was the intended audience for this piece? How might that impact the content and tone of the memo?

2. Describe some characteristics of the "sex-caste system" the authors assert women are subject to. How does it impact women and their role in society?

3. In a detailed response, analyze the authors' objectives for opening this conversation about women. What were they hoping to accomplish? What effect do you think this document had on the women who received the memo?

National Organization for Women Statement of Purpose

Author	Significance
Betty Friedan and Pauli Murray	Articulated the purpose of the National Organization for Women, which was to work for the professional, political, and educational equality of women
Date	
1966	
Document Type	
Essays, Reports, Manifestos	

Overview

The National Organization for Women (NOW) adopted its statement of purpose when gathering for its first national conference in Washington, DC. The statement, which was officially approved on October 29, 1966, was written by Betty Friedan (1921–2006), author of the foundational feminist book *The Feminine Mystique* (1963), and Pauli Murray (1910–1985), a civil rights activist and, later in life, Episcopal priest. Just four months earlier, on June 30, 1966, NOW had been founded by delegates to the Third National Conference of Commissions on the Status of Women. This commission was the successor to the Presidential Commission on the Status of Women, which President John F. Kennedy had created by executive order on December 14, 1961, and which was chaired by Eleanor Roosevelt. In 1963 the commission had reported its findings that women were the victims of gender inequality. Among the twenty-eight founders of NOW were Friedan, Murray, and Shirley Chisholm,

an American politician who in 1972 became the first Black woman to mount a serious presidential bid. The purpose of the organization, articulated in the Statement of Purpose, was to work for professional, political, and educational equality for women—to become a public voice for women and their aspirations.

NOW's Statement of Purpose was written at a time of massive change in the political and social landscape of America. Three years earlier, on June 10, 1963, Kennedy had signed into law the Equal Pay Act to ensure that in the matter of compensation, employers did not discriminate on the basis of gender, generally meaning that they would not pay women less than men for the same work. A year after that, Congress enacted the landmark Civil Rights Act of 1964, which outlawed various forms of discrimination against African Americans and women and was a major victory in the civil rights movement. In 1965 the U.S. Supreme Court, in *Griswold v. Con-*

necticut, ruled 7–2 that a Connecticut ban on the use of contraceptives violated the "right of marital privacy." Thus, by 1966, the women's liberation movement was well underway and would gather increasing momentum in the years that followed. NOW would emerge as both the most powerful women's organization and the largest, with half a million members and nearly six thousand local chapters.

Betty Friedan
(Lynn Gilbert)

Document Text

We, men and women who hereby constitute ourselves as the National Organization for Women, believe that the time has come for a new movement toward true equality for all women in America, and toward a fully equal partnership of the sexes, as part of the world-wide revolution of human rights now taking place within and beyond our national borders.

The purpose of NOW is to take action to bring women into full participation in the mainstream of American society now, exercising all the privileges and responsibilities thereof in truly equal partnership with men. . . .

NOW is dedicated to the proposition that women, first and foremost, are human beings, who, like all other people in our society, must have the chance to develop their fullest human potential. We believe that women can achieve such equality only by accepting to the full the challenges and responsibilities they share with all other people in our society, as part of the decision-making mainstream of American political, economic and social life.

We organize to initiate or support action, nationally, or in any part of this nation, by individuals or organizations, to break through the silken curtain of prejudice and discrimination against women in government, industry, the professions, the churches, the political parties, the judiciary, the labor unions, in education, science, medicine, law, religion and every other field of importance in American society.

Enormous changes taking place in our society make it both possible and urgently necessary to advance the unfinished revolution of women toward true equality, now. . . .

Despite all the talk about the status of American women in recent years, the actual position of women in the United States has declined, and is declining, to an alarming degree throughout the 1950's and 60's. . . . Working women are becoming increasingly—not less—concentrated on the bottom of the job ladder. As a consequence full-time women workers today earn on the average only 60% of what men earn, and that wage gap has been increasing over the past twenty-five years in every major industry group. . . .

Further, with higher education increasingly essential in today's society, too few women are entering and finishing college or going on to graduate or professional school. . . . And, increasingly, men are replacing women in the top positions in secondary and elementary schools, in social work, and in libraries—once thought to be women's fields.

Official pronouncements of the advance in the status of women hide not only the reality of this dangerous decline, but the fact that nothing is being done to stop it. . . . Until now, too few women's organizations and official spokesmen have been willing to speak out against these dangers facing women. Too many women have been restrained by the fear of being called "feminist." . . . The National Organization for Women must therefore begin to speak.

WE BELIEVE that the power of American law, and the protection guaranteed by the U.S. Constitution to the civil rights of all individuals, must be effectively applied and enforced to isolate and remove patterns of sex discrimination, to ensure equality of opportunity in employment and education, and equality of civil and political rights and responsibilities on behalf of women, as well as for Negroes and other deprived groups. . . .

WE DO NOT ACCEPT the token appointment of a few women to high-level positions in government and industry as a substitute for serious continuing effort to recruit and advance women according to their individual abilities. To this end, we urge American government and industry to mobilize the same resources of ingenuity and command with which they have solved problems of far greater difficulty than those now impeding the progress of women.

WE BELIEVE that this nation has a capacity at least as great as other nations, to innovate new social institutions which will enable women to enjoy the true equality of opportunity and responsibility in society, without conflict with their responsibilities as mothers and homemakers. . . . We do not accept the traditional assumption that a woman has to choose between marriage and motherhood, on the one hand, and serious participation in industry or the professions on the other. . . .

WE REJECT the current assumptions that a man must carry the sole burden of supporting himself, his wife, and family, and that a woman is automatically entitled to lifelong support by a man upon her marriage, or that marriage, home and family are primarily woman's world and responsibility—hers, to dominate—his to support. We believe that a true partnership between the sexes demands a different concept of marriage, an equitable sharing of the responsibilities of home and children and of the economic burdens of their support. We believe that proper recognition should be given to the economic and social value of homemaking and child-care. To these ends, we will seek to open a reexamination of laws and mores governing marriage and divorce, for we believe that the current state of "half-equity" between the sexes discriminates against both men and women, and is the cause of much unnecessary hostility between the sexes.

WE BELIEVE that women must now exercise their political rights and responsibilities as American citizens. They must refuse to be segregated on the basis of sex into separate-and-not-equal ladies' auxiliaries in the political parties, and they must demand representation according to their numbers in the regularly constituted party committees—at local, state, and national levels—and in the informal power structure, participating fully in the selection of candidates and political decision-making, and running for office themselves.

IN THE INTERESTS OF THE HUMAN DIGNITY OF WOMEN, we will protest, and endeavor to change, the false image of women now prevalent in the mass media, and in the texts, ceremonies, laws, and practices of our major social institutions. . . .

NOW WILL HOLD ITSELF INDEPENDENT OF ANY POLITICAL PARTY in order to mobilize the political power of all women and men intent on our goals. . . .

WE BELIEVE THAT women will do most to create a new image of women by acting now, and by speaking out in behalf of their own equality, freedom, and human dignity—not in pleas for special privilege, nor in enmity toward men, who are also victims of the current, half-equality between the sexes—but in an active, self-respecting partnership with men. By so doing, women will develop confidence in their own ability to determine actively, in partnership with men, the conditions of their life, their choices, their future and their society.

Glossary

auxiliaries: extra or subsidiary organizations

mores: social customs

token: symbolic; minimal

Short-Answer Questions

1. This document was written at a time when society expected women and men to occupy traditional roles (women as homemakers, men as breadwinners). How does this document suggest that society change those assumptions?

2. The civil rights movement had achieved important goals by 1966. How does NOW's Statement of Purpose recognize and build on the achievements of the civil rights movement, and why was that an important component of this document?

3. In a detailed response, consider how the authors make a case that the moment they occupied was the right time for NOW as an organization to form. Why was that the appropriate time for NOW? Is their argument convincing? Why or why not?

Loving v. Virginia

Author	Significance
Chief Justice Earl Warren	Major Supreme Court decision declaring interracial marriage protected by the U.S. Constitution's Fourteenth Amendment
Date	
1967	
Type	
Legal	

Overview

In *Loving v. Virginia*, Chief Justice Earl Warren wrote on behalf of a unanimous Supreme Court to declare antimiscegenation laws in violation of the Fourteenth Amendment to the U.S. Constitution. Laws against interracial marriage were widespread in the United States into the 1960s. An interracial couple, Richard Loving and Mildred Jeter, traveled to Washington, D.C., to get married and then returned to their home state of Virginia to take up life as Mr. and Mrs. Richard Loving. Police raided their home in 1958, jailed the couple, and took them to court for being married "against the peace and dignity of the Commonwealth." They were convicted in Virginia of the crime of marrying each other, but they were allowed to leave the state for Washington, D.C. From there, they appealed their convictions, and the case went to the Supreme Court. There, the Fourteenth Amendment was interpreted to declare unconstitutional all state laws against interracial marriage. States retained their authority over the law of marriage in other respects but no longer in regard to classification by race.

Loving v. Virginia proved to be the case that overturned the last laws supporting state-mandated segregation. Chief Justice Warren's decision to throw out the case against them can be seen as a crucial document, akin to President Harry S. Truman's Executive Order 9981 in 1948 against segregation in the armed forces, the Supreme Court's ruling in *Brown v. Board of Education of Topeka* in 1954, and the congressional passage of the Civil Rights Act of 1964 and the Voting Rights Act of 1965. *Loving v. Virginia* brought down the last of the Jim Crow laws that had segregated so much of American life for so long. The case would also set court precedent later for the decision in *Obergefell v. Hodges* striking down state-mandated laws in opposition to same-sex marriage.

The graves of Mildred and Richard Loving (Wikimedia Commons)

Document Text

This case presents a constitutional question never addressed by this Court: whether a statutory scheme adopted by the State of Virginia to prevent marriages between persons solely on the basis of racial classifications violates the Equal Protection and Due Process Clauses of the Fourteenth Amendment. For reasons which seem to us to reflect the central meaning of those constitutional commands, we conclude that these statutes cannot stand consistently with the Fourteenth Amendment. . . .

The State [of Virginia] argues that statements in the Thirty-ninth Congress about the time of the passage of the Fourteenth Amendment indicate that the Framers did not intend the Amendment to make unconstitutional state miscegenation laws. . . . There can be no question but that Virginia's miscegenation statutes rest solely upon distinctions drawn according to race. The statutes proscribe generally accepted conduct if engaged in by members of different races. Over the years, this Court has consistently repudiated "[d]istinctions between citizens solely because of their ancestry" as being "odious to a free people whose institutions are founded upon the doctrine of equality." *Hirabayashi v. United States*, 320 U.S. 81, 100 (1943). At the very least, the Equal Protection Clause demands that racial classifications, especially suspect in criminal statutes, be subjected to the "most rigid scrutiny," *Korematsu v. United States*, 323 U.S. 214, 216 (1944), and, if they are ever to be upheld, they must be shown to be necessary to the accomplishment of some permissible state objective, independent of the racial discrimination which it was the object of the Fourteenth Amendment to eliminate. Indeed, two members of this Court have already stated that they "cannot conceive of a valid legislative purpose . . . which makes the color of a person's skin the test of whether his conduct is a criminal offense." *McLaughlin v. Florida, supra*, at 198 (Stewart, J., joined by Douglas, J., concurring).

There is patently no legitimate overriding purpose independent of invidious racial discrimination which justifies this classification. The fact that Virginia prohibits only interracial marriages involving white persons demonstrates that the racial classifications must stand on their own justification, as measures designed to maintain White Supremacy. We have consistently denied the constitutionality of measures which restrict the rights of citizens on account of race. There can be no doubt that restricting the freedom to marry solely because of racial classifications violates the central meaning of the Equal Protection Clause. . . .

These statutes also deprive the Lovings of liberty without due process of law in violation of the Due Process Clause of the Fourteenth Amendment. The freedom to marry has long been recognized as one of the vital personal rights essential to the orderly pursuit of happiness by free men.

Marriage is one of the "basic civil rights of man," fundamental to our very existence and survival. *Skinner v. Oklahoma*, 316 U.S. 535, 541 (1942). . . . To deny this fundamental freedom on so unsupportable a basis as the racial classifications embodied in these statutes, classifications so directly subversive of the principle of equality at the heart of the Fourteenth Amendment, is surely to deprive all the State's citizens of liberty without due process of law. The Fourteenth Amendment requires that the freedom of choice to marry not be restricted by invidious racial discriminations. Under our Constitution, the freedom to marry, or not marry, a person of another race resides with the individual and cannot be infringed by the State.

These convictions must be reversed.

It is so ordered.

Glossary

Equal Protection and Due Process clauses of the Fourteenth Amendment: two sentences in Section 1 of the Fourteenth Amendment of the U.S. Constitution, passed in 1868, which reads: "All persons born or naturalized in the United States, and subject to the jurisdiction thereof, are citizens of the United States and of the State wherein they reside. No State shall make or enforce any law which shall abridge the privileges or immunities of citizens of the United States; nor shall any State deprive any person of life, liberty, or property, without due process of law; nor deny to any person within its jurisdiction the equal protection of the laws."

Glossary

Hirabayashi v. United States, **320 U.S. 81, 100 (1943)** . . . *Skinner v. Oklahoma,* **316 U.S. 535, 541 (1942):** references to other Supreme Court decisions from which Judge Warren was quoting

invidious: unjust, unfair

odious: repulsive

proscribe: prohibit

statutory scheme: a portion of the set of segregationist laws established in the state of Virginia, in this case dealing with interracial marriage; such laws were collectively referred to as "Jim Crow laws" throughout the southern states in the late nineteenth through mid-twentieth centuries

Short-Answer Questions

1. How did the state of Virginia argue that its laws against interracial marriage were legal, and how did Justice Warren counter those arguments?

2. At one point, Justice Warren notes that the state of Virginia banned interracial marriage only when a white person was involved in the marriage. Why? What did the state consider the purpose of marriage to be, and what about interracial marriage would subvert that purpose, in the state's opinion?

3. Several of the Supreme Court decisions that were central to the advance of the civil rights movement were based upon the principles of the Fourteenth Amendment to the U.S. Constitution. Yet if one reads the whole Constitution, those same principles were already established in the body of the Constitution and its first ten amendments, the Bill of Rights. Why do you think the Fourteenth Amendment would have been considered necessary to add to the Constitution in 1868, and why would so many of these civil rights–based Supreme Court cases have needed to refer to it as opposed to the rest of the Constitution?

Robin Morgan:
"No More Miss America!"

Author	Significance
Robin Morgan	Challenged society's beauty standards for women, generated significant media and public attention for the women's movement, and introduced the term "women's liberation" into the public consciousness
Date	
1968	
Document Type	
Essay, Reports, Manifestos; Speeches/Addresses	

Overview

New York Radical Women was established in New York City in 1967. Founded by Robin Morgan, Carol Hanisch, Shulmath Firestone, and Pam Allen, a group of friends in their twenties who had been active in the New Left movement, this feminist group garnered national attention for their role in organizing the Miss America Pageant protest in September 1968. Hoping to gain media attention for their movement, the New York Radical Women targeted the Miss America Pageant because of concerns about how beauty standards oppressed women. In a letter requesting a permit for the protest, Robin Morgan described the group's objection to the pageant's emphasis on physical appearance over intellect and on a standard of beauty valuing youth over maturity. She also denounced the commercial interests motivating the contest. Morgan served as the key organizer for the event, and she also wrote the press release announcing the protest.

This press release, published on August 22, 1968, invited women to take a public stance against the oppressive image of women propagated by the Miss America Pageant. The release included a list of events that would be included in the protest, including picket lines, distribution of women's liberation literature, lobbying, and street theater performances. They also announced the presence of a "Freedom Trash Can" into which women would be encouraged to dispose of items they viewed as oppressive to women, such as bras and makeup products, women's fashion magazines, and a range of kitchen and cleaning products. The day would culminate with a women's liberation rally at midnight, planned to correspond with the live broadcast of the crowning of Miss America on television. Male participation was not welcome. The press release also outlined ten specific points of contention that the organizers had with the pageant.

Historical accounts vary widely in their reports of attendance at the Miss America protest. Common estimates range from about 200 to 400 participants. In addition to the events held outside the venue, four protesters purchased tickets to the pageant and joined the audience. They famously displayed a banner with the words "Women's Liberation" on it from the balcony during the farewell speech of the former Miss America and shouted "women's liberation" and "no more Miss America" as the crowning ceremony continued. They were removed by police, but their words became rallying cries. Newspapers across the country covered the protest, drawing parallels between this event and anti–Vietnam War protests. The protest generated national attention and introduced the phrase "women's liberation" into the public consciousness.

Miss America candidates
(Library of Congress)

Document Text
August 22, 1968
New York City

NO MORE MISS AMERICA!
FOR IMMEDIATE RELEASE

On September 7th in Atlantic City, the Annual Miss America Pageant will again crown "your ideal." But this year, reality will liberate the contest auction-block in the guise of "genyoo-ine" de-plasticized, breathing women. Women's Liberation Groups, black women, high-school and college women, women's peace groups, women's welfare and social-work groups, women's job-equality groups, pro-birth control and pro-abortion groups—women of every political persuasion—all are invited to join us in a day-long boardwalk-theater event, starting at 1:00 p.m. on the Boardwalk in front of Atlantic City's Convention Hall. We will protest the image of Miss America, an image that oppresses women in every area in which it purports to represent us. There will be: Picket Lines; Guerrilla Theater; Leafleting; Lobbying Visits to the contestants urging our sisters to reject the Pageant Farce and join us; a huge Freedom Trash Can (into which we will throw bras, girdles, curlers, false eyelashes, wigs, and representative issues of *Cosmopolitan*, *Ladies' Home Journal*, *Family Circle*, etc.—bring any such woman-garbage you have around the house); we will also announce a Boycott of all those commercial products related to the Pageant, and the day will end with a Women's Liberation rally at midnight when Miss America is crowned on live television. Lots of other surprises are being planned (come and add your own!) but we do not plan heavy disruptive tactics and so do not expect a bad police scene. It should be a groovy day on the Boardwalk in the sun with our sisters. In case of arrests, however, we plan to reject all male authority and demand to be busted by policewomen only. (In Atlantic City, women cops are not permitted to make arrests—dig that!)

Male chauvinist-reactionaries on this issue had best stay away, nor are male liberals welcome in the demonstrations. But sympathetic men can donate money as well as cars and drivers. *We need cars* to transport people to New Jersey and back.

Male reporters will be refused interviews. We reject patronizing reportage. *Only newswomen will be recognized.*

Anyone interested in further information, and anyone willing to help with ideas, transportation, money, or anything, can write us at: P.O. Box 531, Peter Stuyvesant Station, New York, N.Y. 1009, or telephone (212) 475-8775 between 7:30 and 10:00 p.m. weeknights. Get a group of women together, come to the Miss America Pageant on Saturday, September 7th, and raise your voice for Women's Liberation. *We will reclaim ourselves for ourselves.* On to Atlantic City!

The Ten Points

We Protest:

1. *The Degrading Mindless-Boob-Girlie Symbol.* The Pageant contestants epitomize the roles we are all forced to play as women. The parade down the runway blares the metaphor of the 4-H Club county fair, where the nervous animals are judged for teeth, fleece, etc., and where the best "Specimen" gets the blue ribbon. So are women in our society forced daily to compete for male approval, enslaved by ludicrous "beauty" standards we ourselves are conditioned to take seriously.

2. *Racism with Roses.* Since its inception in 1921, the Pageant has not had one Black finalist, and this has not been for a lack of test-case contestants. There has never been a Puerto Rican, Alaskan, Hawaiian, or Mexican-American winner. Nor has there ever been a *true* Miss America—an American Indian.

3. *Miss America as Military Death Mascot.* The highlight of her reign each year is a cheerleader-tour of American troops abroad—last year she went to Vietnam to pep-talk our husbands, fathers, sons and boyfriends into dying and killing with a better spirit. She personifies the "unstained patriotic American womanhood our boys are fighting for." The Living Bra and the Dead Soldier. We refuse to be used as Mascots for Murder.

4. *The Consumer Con-Game.* Miss America is a walking commercial for the Pageant's sponsors. Wind her up and she plugs your product on promotion tours and TV—all in an "honest, objective" endorsement. What a shill.

5. *Competition Rigged and Unrigged.* We deplore the encouragement of an American myth that oppresses men as well as women: the win-or-you're-worthless competitive disease. The "beauty contest" creates only one winner to be "used" and forty-nine losers who are "useless."

6. *The Woman as Pop Culture Obsolescent Theme.* Spindle, mutilate, and then discard tomorrow. What is so ignored as last year's Miss America? This only reflects the gospel of our Society, according to Saint Male: women must be young, juicy, malleable—hence age discrimination and the cult of youth. And we women are brainwashed into believing this ourselves!

7. *The Unbeatable Madonna-Whore Combination.* Miss America and Playboy's centerfold are sisters over the skin. To win approval, we must be both sexy and wholesome, delicate but able to cope, demure yet titillatingly bitchy. Deviation of any sort brings, we are told, disaster: "You won't get a man!!"

8. *The Irrelevant Crown on the Throne of Mediocrity.* Miss America represents what women are supposed to be: inoffensive, bland, apolitical. If you are tall, short, over or under what weight The Man prescribes you should be, forget it. Personality, articulateness, intelligence, and commitment—unwise. Conformity is the key to the crown—and, by extension, to success in our Society.

9. *Miss America as Dream Equivalent To—?* In this reputedly democratic society, where every little boy supposedly can grow up to be President, what can every little girl hope to grow to be? Miss America. That's where it's at. Real power to control our own lives is restricted to men, while women get patronizing pseudo-power, an ermine cloak and

a bunch of flowers; men are judged by their actions, women by appearance.

10. *Miss America as Big Sister Watching You.* The pageant exercises Thought Control, attempts to sear the Image onto our minds, to further make women oppressed and men oppressors; to enslave us all the more in high-heeled, low-status roles; to inculcate false values in young girls; women as beasts of buying; to seduce us to our selves before our own oppression.

NO MORE MISS AMERICA

Glossary

"Big Sister Watching You": a reference to the slogan "Big Brother is watching you" from George Orwell's novel *1984*

4-H Club: a youth organization in which, among other activities, participants raise livestock for competition and for sale

shill: spokesperson, particularly one who promotes a cause or product without disclosing their relationship to the producer

spindle: small desktop spike on which notes or papers are impaled, to be filed or discarded later

"spindle, mutilate, and then discard": reference to the notation "Do not fold, spindle, or mutilate" on IBM punch cards, which would be rendered useless if they were damaged

---

Short-Answer Questions

1. Summarize the events that will be part of the protest.

2. Describe the author's view of men based on the content and tone of this piece. Use specific examples to support your claims.

3. Analyze one of the comparisons made in the "Ten Points" of protest between the Miss America Pageant and a social, political, or economic issues of the time period. How effective is this connection? What impact might it have on a reader?

Segregated Employment Ads

Author *Raleigh News and Observer* **Date** 1968 **Document Type** Advertisements	**Significance** Demonstrate the persistence of sex segregation in employment even after the passage of the Civil Rights Act of 1964, which made sex discrimination in employment illegal

Overview

Through the 1960s, it was common to see job advertisements with separate categories for "men wanted" and "women wanted." Passage of the Civil Rights Act of 1964, however, introduced questions about whether this practice was still acceptable. Title VII of the law prohibited employment discrimination based on race, color, religion, sex, or national origin. The specific question of job advertisements was addressed in Section 704(b), which prohibited "printing or publication of notices or advertisements indicating prohibited preference, limitation, specification, or discrimination . . . except that such a notice or advertisement may indicate a preference, limitation, specification, or discrimination . . . when religion, sex, or national origin is a bona fide occupational qualification for employment." This statement left many questioning whether it was permissible to continue publishing sex-segregated job advertisements. The issue was brought before the Equal Employment Opportunity

Commission (EEOC), which had been established to implement and enforce the new standards prohibiting employment discrimination.

In November 1965, the EEOC released a set of interpretive guidelines for sex-based help-wanted ads that allowed the practice to continue. Women's rights advocates took on the issue. The National Organization for Women (NOW) organized a demonstration outside the *New York Times* classified advertisement office to protest sex-segregated employment advertisements on August 30, 1967. Several hundred women participated, and it successfully focused public attention on the issue and prompted the EEOC to reopen its consideration of the practice.

After holding a series of public hearings in 1968, the EEOC published new guidelines in August 1968 stating that the separation of job advertisements under "male" and "female" headings violated Title VII. The ruling was challenged in court. While it was under review, newspapers across the nation continued to publish sex-segregated job advertisements. In June 1973, the Supreme Court's ruling in *Pittsburgh Press v. Pittsburgh Human Relations Committee* upheld the ban on sex-segregated job advertisements, effectively ending the practice.

Women workers at the U.S. Capitol switchboard (Library of Congress)

Document Text

The following segregated employment ads were published in the *Raleigh News and Observer* on December 1, 1968.

Male Help Wanted

• Office Supervisor: Wholesale distribution office offers rapid financial advancement to young man who learns over-all operation quickly. Start $400. Carolina Employment Agency, 201 First Federal, 200 S. Salisbury.

• Manager, trainee, degree, groom for upper management, $7,200 up. Dixie Personnel Agcy, 5. 2. Hargett ST, 833-2505

• Sales, college, public relations position, opportunity! To $8,400. Dixie Personnel Agcy, 5 W. Hargett St, 833-2505

• Personnel Manager—$9,500. Exper. Plus degree. Unlimited potential. American Personnel Agcy. 828-0761.

• Textile Engineer—$11,000. Degree necessary. 4yrs experience. American Personnel Agcy. 818-0716.

• WANTED experienced man to milk cows. Good salary, 6 room house with electric heat, also electric heat in milking parlor. Call (919) 275-1202 or write Hilltop Lane Dairy, McLeansville, N.C. Rt. 2

• Sales Representative. Several openings in Eastern Carolina for top level men from the selling field or executive group. Position carries very substantial income, group benefits and non-contributory pension plan if you qualify. Want men underpaid in their present field. Lifetime job in permanent industry. Write giving brief hist so that personal interview may be arranged. P.O. Box 10147, Wilson, N.C.

• WANTED young man to sell and manage residential heating and air conditioning. Experience necessary. Salary plus sharing profits. Write resume to P.O. Box 10147 Greensboro N.C.

• MARRIED MAN to assist branch manager, also to service our equipment and learn sales work. Could mean doubling your previous income. Earning opportunity $120 per week while learning. Call for personal interview, days 828-5405.

• PHARMACIST. Additional Pharmacist wanted for large independent Drug Store. $250wk, 45 hr. Week. Full day off per week. Work 1/2 day every other Sunday. 2 weeks paid vacation. Apply Westgate Pharmacy 1216 w. Front St. Statesville, N.C.

• BUILDING SUPERINTENDENT. Wanted Building Superintendent for office building in Raleigh. Must supervise 8 janitors and do minor mechanical work. Excellent working conditions and fringe benefits. Apply in person to J.V. Clifton, Dillon Supply Co. An Equal Opportunity Employer.

Female Help Wanted

• WAITRESS full or part time. Experience not necessary as we will train. Shoney's Big Boy, Downtown Blvd.

• WANTED, settled white lady to work nights in rest home. Some experience and transportation. 787-3320

• White waitress needed, salary $60 per wk. Very good tips. Contact Mr. Charlie J. Griffin, Charlie's Restaurant 2936 N. Blvd., Raleigh, N.C.

• Posting Machine Operator—$400. Free parking. Exper. Required. American Personal Agcy.

• Office Assistant—$325. NO shorthand. Some typing necessary. American Personnel Agcy.

• Admitting Clerk—$400. Public relations. Typing and filling. American Personnel Agcy.

• Bookkeeper, double entry, tax, P&L statements, full charge, $375.

• Bridal Consultant—$320. Challenging career. Exper. Needed. American Personnel Agcy. 828-0716.

• 1-Girl office: Type nicely, pleasing phone manner. $300. Carolina Employment Agency, 201 First Federal, 300 S. Salisbury.

• Timberlake Area: General Office "Gal Friday." type job for stable, personable lady in one girl office. Starting $80 week. CAREERS EMPLOYMENT AGENCY, Rm 98, Bldg. 828-0666.

• Dept. MGR'S SECY: Enjoy challenge of technical field and a Boss who warrants your respect. $434. Carolina Employment Agency, 201 First Federal, 300 S. Salisbury.

• LADIES WANTED EASTERN, N.C. Ladies over 35 with car and some ability who can work 20 or more hours a week. Representing a well established nationally known company. Earnings $2.80 per hour. Write P.O. Box 5001, Raleigh, N.C. 27607.

• UNDERWRITER—$7400. Trainee position, college grad. American Personnel Agcy. 818-0716

- CLERICAL—Sharp girl with no typing but good math aptitude. $330. Job Finders, Raleigh's most convenient employment agency. Phillips Bldg. Clark and Oberline, Cameron Village.

- Admissions Asst: 40hr wk but schedule is irregular. Nice typing, pleasing public contact personally. $400. Carolina Employment Agency. 201 First Federal, 300 S. Salisbury.

- Head Cashier—$430 Sec. Skills plus poise will get this top opportunity. Ambitious Personnel Agency, 501 Layers Bldg.

Male-Female Help Wanted
- MEDICAL LABORATORY TECHNICIAN. Salary and working conditions above average. Write N.C. Lisk, Administrator, Chattam Hospital, IN., Siller City, North Carolina 27344.
- Watchmaker—must be experienced. 5 days week, discount on purchases, hospitalization, and life insurance, profit sharing, vacation, holidays and sick pay. Apply Hudson Belk.

- TEACHER $5,600 Year 'round employment in specialized courses. P.E. Major will usually qualify. Think you're qualified? Call Linda Melton, 828-7232. Allied Personnel of Raleigh Agency. 610 Raleigh Bldg.

- Field Representative. The best position we've offered! Good pay, 1 mo. vacation, retirement, and liberal holiday, schedule. In Cumberland County. Call Linda Melton, 828-7238. Allied Personnel of Raleigh.

Glossary

Gal Friday: female assistant

posting machine: business machine used for accounting purposes

---

Short-Answer Questions

1. What patterns do you see in the advertisements in terms of the qualifications expected for jobs listed under the "Male Help Wanted" category? Under the "Female Help Wanted" category? Under the "Male-Female Help Wanted" category?

2. In addition to the categories based on sex, describe other kinds of discrimination you notice in these advertisements. Please be specific.

3. Analyze why you think the question about sex-segregated job advertisement became a focus for women's organizations. How does it fit into broader patterns of women's rights advocacy in the 1960s?

Ella Baker:
"The Black Woman in the Civil Rights Struggle"

Author
Ella Baker

Date
1969

Type
Speeches/Addresses

Significance
Pointed out the subordinate role traditionally assigned to Black women in the civil rights movement despite their importance in driving it

Overview

Ella Baker was part of the backbone of the civil rights movement. As a Black woman, she was sometimes excluded from woman's suffrage organizations, but she did not let this deter her from making a difference. She was a charismatic public speaker, although she spent most of her career working behind the scenes, helping to organize the National Association for the Advancement of Colored People (NAACP), the Southern Christian Leadership Conference (SCLC), the Student Nonviolent Coordinating Committee (SNCC), and other civil rights groups.

Much of what Baker said and wrote has been lost. She did not commit her speeches to paper, and the ones that survive have been reconstructed from notes or tapes made while she spoke. Although she gave many interviews in the 1970s and 1980s, only a few have been published. "The Black Woman in the Civil Rights Struggle," one of few remaining records of her many speeches, has historical significance as an example of her remarkable ability to galvanize audiences with her speeches. The topic of this speech, delivered December 31, 1969, was one on which she was asked to speak: the contributions of women to the civil rights movement.

Baker exposed the contributions of Black women to the civil rights movement. (Library of Congress)

Document Text

. . . I was a little bit amazed as to why the selection of a discussion on the role of Black women in the world. . . . I've always thought first and foremost of people as individuals . . . [but] wherever there has been struggle, Black women have been identified with that struggle. . . .

I would like to divide my remaining comments into two parts. First, the aspect that deals with the struggle to get into the society. . . . Second, the struggle for a different kind of society. . . .

[There was] an assumption that those who were trained were not trained to be *part* of the community, but to be *leaders* of the community . . . that your responsibility to the people was to *represent* them. . . . Later, in the 1960s, a different concept emerged: the concept of the right of the people to participate in the decisions that affected their lives. . . .

The struggle for being a part of the society also led to another major phase of the civil rights struggle. That was the period in which legalism or the approach to battling down the barriers of racial segregation through the courts was spearheaded by the National Association for the Advancement of Colored People. . . .

I think the period that is most important to most of us now is the period when we began to question whether we really wanted in. Even though the sit-in movement started off primarily as a method of getting in, it led to the concept of questioning whether it was worth trying to get in. . . . It was part of the struggle for full dignity as a human being. . . .

Around 1965 there began to develop a great deal of questioning about what is the role of women in the struggle. Out of it came a concept that Black women had to bolster the ego of the male. This implied that the Black male had been treated in such a manner as to have been emasculated both by the white society and Black women because the female was the head of the household. We began to deal with the question of the need of Black women to play the subordinate role. . . .

I don't think you could go through the Freedom Movement without finding that the backbone of the support of the Movement were women. . . .

What is the American society? Is it the kind of society that . . . permits people to grow . . . that gives them a sense of value. . . .

In order for us as poor and oppressed people to become a part of a society that is meaningful, the system under which we now exist has to be radically changed. This means that we are going to have to learn to think in radical terms. I use the term *radical* in its original meaning—getting down to and understanding the root cause. It means facing a system that does not lend itself to your needs and devising means by which you change the system. That is easier said than done. . . . We have to begin to think in terms of where do we really want to go and how we want to get there.

Finally, I think it is also to be said that it is not a job that is going to be done by all the people simultaneously. . . . We cannot lead a struggle that involves masses of people without getting the people to understand what their potentials are, what their strengths are.

Glossary

Freedom Movement: a reference to a volunteer campaign to register Blacks to vote in Mississippi in 1964

Short-Answer Questions

1. What two struggles does Ella Baker mention in her speech, and how does she differentiate between them?

2. Why do you think Baker stresses the importance of people needing "to participate in the decisions that affected their lives"? What decisions might these be?

3. How does Baker describe the woman's role in the struggle for equal civil rights?

Gloria Steinem:
"Living the Revolution"

Author Gloria Steinem **Date** 1970 **Document Type** Speeches/Addresses	**Significance** Highlighted the ways women were still facing oppression and being denied basic rights in the United States despite being granted the right to vote fifty years earlier

Overview

On May 31, 1970, Gloria Steinem delivered the commencement address to the graduating class of Vassar College. Vassar had been a women-only institution since its founding in 1861, but it admitted its first male students the year before Steinem was invited to give her speech. Steinem used her speech to talk about women's rights and the ways in which women, despite winning the right to vote fifty years earlier, were still oppressed and denied other basic rights.

Steinem was trained as a journalist and had worked for a variety of publications, often on women's issues. In 1962 she had published an article on women's access to contraception in *Esquire*, and the following year she

famously found work as a Playboy Bunny in New York's Playboy Club. The resulting article, "A Bunny's Tale," published in *Show* magazine, won her national attention—but it also made it difficult for her to find work; potential employers saw her as a model rather than a serious journalist.

In 1969 Steinem finally embraced the women's liberation movement, inspired by a meeting about abortion rights that she covered for *New York* magazine. Soon after, she earned a reputation as an advocate for women's reproductive freedoms and for the Equal Rights Amendment. Her Vassar commencement address looks at the ways in which cultural stereotypes, communicated through media, influence attitudes toward women both consciously and unconsciously.

Document Text

President Simpson, members of the faculty, families and friends, first brave and courageous male graduates of Vassar—and Sisters.

You may be surprised that I am a commencement speaker. . . . But this is the year of Women's Liberation. . . . The important thing is that we are spending this time together, considering the larger implications of a movement that some call "feminist" but should more accurately be called humanist; a movement that is an integral part of rescuing this country from its old, expensive patterns of elitism, racism, and violence.

The first problem for all of us, men and women, is not to learn, but to un-learn. We are filled with the Popular Wisdom of several centuries just past, and we are terrified to give it up. Patriotism means obedience, age means wisdom, woman means submission, Black means inferior—these are preconceptions imbedded so deeply in our thinking that we honestly may not know that they are there. . . .

I confess that, before some consciousness-changing of my own, I would have thought the Women's History courses springing up around the country belonged in the same cultural ghetto as home economics. The truth is that we need Women's Studies almost as much as we need Black Studies, and for exactly the same reason: too many of us have been allowed from a "good" education believing that everything from political power to scientific discovery was the province of white males. . . .

We believed, for instance, that the vote had been "given" to women. . . . We never learned about the long desperation of women's struggle, or about the strength and wisdom of the women who led it. We heard about the men who risked their lives in the Abolitionist Movement, but seldom about the women; even though women, as in many movements of social reform, had played the major role. . . .

Gloria Steinem in 1972
(Library of Congress)

Before we go on to other reasons why Women's Liberation is Man's Liberation, too—and why this incarnation of the women's movement is inseparable from the larger revolution—perhaps we should clear the air of a few more myths.

The myth that women are biologically inferior, for instance. In fact, an equally good case could be made for the reverse. Women live longer than men. . . . Men's hunting activities are forever being pointed to as proof of Tribal Superiority. But while they were out hunting, women built houses, tilled the fields, developed animal husbandry, and perfected language. . . . I don't want to prove the superiority of one sex to another. . . . The truth is that we're just not sure how many of our differences are biological, and how many are societal. . . . What we do know is that the differences between the two sexes, like the differences between races, are much less great than the differences to be found within each group. . . .

A second myth is that women are already being treated equally in this society. . . . The truth is that a woman with a college degree working full-time makes less than a Black man with a high school degree working full-time. And Black women make least of all. In many parts of the country . . . woman has no legally-guaranteed right to rent an apartment, buy a house, get accommodations in a hotel, or be served in a public restaurant. She can be refused simply because of her sex. In some states, women cannot own property, and get longer jail sentences for the same crime. Women on welfare must routinely answer humiliating personal questions; male welfare recipients do not. A woman is the last to be hired, the first to be fired. Equal pay for equal work is the exception. Equal chance for advancement, especially at upper levels or at any level with authority over men, is rare enough to be displayed in a museum. . . .

You may wonder why we have submitted to such humiliations all these years. . . . The answer lies in the psychology of second-classness. Like all such groups, we come to accept what society says about us. And that is the most terrible punishment of all. . . .

With women, the whole system reinforces this feeling of being a mere appendage. It's hard for a man to realize just how full of self-doubt we become as a result. Locked into suburban homes with the intellectual companionship of three-year-olds; locked into bad jobs, watching less-qualified men get promoted above us; trapped into poverty by a system that supposes our only identity is motherhood—no wonder we become pathetically grateful for small favors. . . .

Women have a special opportunity to live the revolution. By refusing to play their traditional role, they upset and displace the social structure around them. . . . The challenge to all of us, and to you men and women who are graduating today, is to live a revolution, not to die for one. . . . This revolution has to change consciousness, to upset the injustice of our current hierarchy by refusing to honor it, and to live a life that enforces a new social justice.

Because the truth is none of us can be liberated if other groups are not. Women's Liberation is a bridge between Black and white women, but also between the construction workers and the suburbanites, between Nixon's Silent Majority and the young people they hate and fear. . . . Women are sisters, they have many of the same problems, and they can communicate with each other. . . . Then we make the connection to other injustices in society. The Women's Movement is an important revolutionary bridge. And we are building it. . . .

I don't need to tell you what awaits you in this country. You know that much better than I. I will only say that my heart goes with you, and that I hope we will be working together. Divisions of age, race, class, and sex are old-fashioned and destructive.

One more thing, especially to the sisters, because I wish someone had said it to me. . . . You don't have to play one role in this revolutionary age above all others. If you're willing to pay the price for it, you can do anything you want to do. And the price is worth it.

Glossary

consciousness-changing: also called consciousness raising; the act of becoming aware of social structures, especially those that enforced sexism or racism

Silent Majority: a phrase that, when used by President Richard Nixon, referred to politically conservative citizens who did not engage in public protests

Short-Answer Questions

1. Describe how Steinem uses the term "women's liberation" throughout the speech.

2. Summarize one of the myths Steinem includes in the speech. Describe her proposed correction or refutation of the myth, and analyze the strength of her argument.

3. In a detailed response, analyze Steinem's claim that the movement should be considered "humanist" rather than "feminist."

Shirley Chisholm:
"For the Equal Rights Amendment"

Author Shirley Chisholm	**Significance** Explains key arguments given in support of the Equal Rights Amendment and responds to several of the claims made by those opposing it
Date 1970	
Document Type Speeches/Addresses; Legislative	

Overview

Shirley Chisholm was elected to Congress as a representative from New York in 1969. She championed the underdog against the privileged, was a critic of the establishment, and became an eloquent spokesperson for reform. Her public career was fueled by anger at the dismissive treatment she received at the hands of political leaders. Despite her strong record as an organizer and advocate, male colleagues seldom took her seriously. Chisholm often claimed that she met with more discrimination being a woman than she did being Black. At a time when the women's movement was beginning to gain national recognition, Chisholm emerged as one of its most prominent leaders. Her political career, especially her presidential candidacy, was an effort to convince the country that women deserved an equal voice in government. One of her first actions in Congress was to deliver her speech in favor of the Equal Rights Amendment, which she viewed as an avenue to extend equal opportunities to the nation's largest minority group.

Document Text

Mr. Speaker, House Joint Resolution 264, before us today, which provides for equality under the law for both men and women, represents one of the most clear-cut opportunities we are likely to have to declare our faith in the principles that shaped our Constitution. It provides a legal basis for attack on the most subtle, most pervasive, and most institutionalized form of prejudice that exists. Discrimination against women, solely on the basis of their sex, is so widespread that it seems to many persons normal, natural and right.

Legal expression of prejudice on the grounds of religious or political belief has become a minor problem in our society. Prejudice on the basis of race is, at least, under systematic attack. There is reason for optimism that it will start to die with the present, older generation. It is time we act to assure full equality of opportunity to those citizens who, although in a majority, suffer the restrictions that are commonly imposed on minorities, to women. . . .

The amendment is necessary to clarify countless ambiguities and inconsistencies in our legal system. For instance, the Constitution guarantees due process of law, in the 5th and 14th amendments. But the applicability of due process of sex distinctions is not clear. Women are excluded from some State colleges and universities. In some States, restrictions are placed on a married woman who engages in an independent business. Women may not be chosen for some juries. Women even receive heavier criminal penalties than men who commit the same crime. What would the legal effects of the equal rights amendment really be? The equal rights amendment would govern only the relationship between the State and its citizens—not relationships between private citizens. The amendment would be largely self-executing, that is, and Federal or State laws in conflict would be ineffective one year after date of ratification without further action by the Congress or State legislatures.

Opponents of the amendment claim its ratification would throw the law into a state of confusion and would result in much litigation to establish its meaning. This objection overlooks the influence of legislative history in determining intent and the recent activities of many groups preparing for legislative changes in this direction.

State labor laws applying only to women, such as those limiting hours of work and weights to be lifted, would become inoperative unless the legislature amended them to apply to men. As of early 1970 most States would have some laws that would be affected. However, changes are being made so rapidly as a result of Title VII of the Civil Rights Act of 1964, it is likely that by the time the equal rights amendment would become effective, no conflicting State laws would remain.

Shirley Chisholm
(Library of Congress)

In any event, there has for years been great controversy as to the usefulness to women of these State labor laws. There has never been any doubt that they worked a hardship on women who need or want to work overtime and on women who need or want better-paying jobs, and there has been no persuasive evidence as to how many women benefit from the archaic policy of the laws. . . .

Jury service laws not making women equally liable for jury service would have to be revised. The selective service law would have to include women, but women would not be required to serve in the Armed Forces where they are not fitted any more than men are required to serve. . . .

What would be the economic effects of the equal rights amendment? Direct economic effects would be minor. If any labor laws applying only to women still remained, their amendment or repeal would provide opportunity for women in better-paying jobs in manufacturing. More opportunities in public vocational and graduate schools for women would also tend to open up opportunities in better jobs for women.

Indirect effects could be much greater. The focusing of public attention on the gross legal, economic, and social discrimination against women by hearings and debates in the Federal and State legislatures would result in changes in attitude of parents, educators, and employers that would bring about substantial economic changes in the long run.

Sex prejudice cuts both ways. Men are oppressed by the requirements of the Selective Service Act, by enforced legal guardianship of minors, and by alimony laws. Each sex, I believe, should be liable when necessary to serve and defend this country. Each has a responsibility for the support of children.

There are objections raised to wiping out laws protecting women workers. No one would condone exploitation. But what does sex have to do with it? Working conditions and hours that are harmful to women are harmful to men; wages that are unfair for women are unfair for men. Laws setting employment limitations on the basis of sex are irrational, and the proof of this is their inconsistency from State to State. The physical characteristics of men and women are not fixed, but cover two wide spans that have a great deal of overlap. It is obvious, I think, that a robust woman could be more fit for physical labor than a weak man. The choice of occupation would be determined by individual capabilities, and the rewards for equal work should be equal.

This is what it comes down to: artificial distinctions between persons must be wiped out of the law. . . .

The time is clearly now to put this House on record for the fullest expression of that equality of opportunity which our founding fathers professed. They professed it, but they did not assure it to their daughters, as they tried to do for their sons.

The Constitution they wrote was designed to protect the rights of white, male citizens. As there were no black Founding Fathers, there were no founding mothers—a great pity, on both counts. It is not too late to complete the work they left undone. Today, here, we should start to do so.

Glossary

due process of law: the principle, guaranteed in the Fifth and Fourteenth Amendments, that an individual accused of a crime has a right to be formally charged and tried

Equal Rights Amendment: a proposed amendment to the U.S. Constitution to guarantee equal rights regardless of sex

ratification: the process whereby proposed amendments become law, as prescribed in Article 5 of the Constitution

selective service law: the requirement that men in the United States from 18 to 25 years old register with the Selective Service System, a government agency that tracks citizens eligible for military service

Title VII of the Civil Rights Act of 1964: prohibits employment discrimination based on race, color, religion, sex, and national origin

Short-Answer Questions

1. Summarize the author's claims about why the Equal Rights Amendment is necessary to clarify legal ambiguities and inconsistencies in the United States.

2. Who was the intended audience for this speech? How does this impact the author's argument and the examples she uses to support her claims?

3. Identify and analyze the potential economic, political, and social impact of the Equal Rights Amendment.

Phyllis Schlafly:
"What's Wrong with 'Equal Rights' for Women?"

<table>
<tr><td>

Author
Phyllis Schlafly

Date
1972

Document Type
Speeches/Addresses; Essays, Reports, Manifestos

</td><td>

Significance
Led directly to the creation of STOP ERA (Stop Taking Our Privileges ERA), a group concerned that feminism was a threat to motherhood and the family and claimed the ERA was not necessary because women's rights were already protected under the Constitution

</td></tr>
</table>

Overview

The Equal Rights Amendment (ERA) was originally proposed in Congress in 1923. Just three years after the Nineteenth Amendment guaranteed women the right to vote, this proposal aimed to secure full equality for women under the law. It did not receive congressional approval at the time, but the Equal Rights Amendment was reintroduced to Congress in 1971 during the second-wave feminist movement. In 1972, Congress officially passed the ERA, which stated, "Equality of rights under the law shall not be denied or abridged by the United States or by any state on account of sex. The Congress shall have the power to enforce, by appropriate legislation, the provisions of this article." It was then submitted to the states for ratification. Within a year, thirty states approved the ERA; it needed approval from thirty-eight states for ratification, which seemed imminent.

During this campaign, Phyllis Schlafly emerged as a prominent opponent to ratification, claiming that women's rights were already protected under the Constitution. Her argument was first presented in an article entitled "What's Wrong with Equal Rights for Women?" published in the February 1972 issue of *The Phyllis Schlafly Report*. Schlafly claimed that the ERA would undermine ways that women were already protected by the law, drawing attention to the possibility of women being susceptible to the military draft and financially vulnerable in the case of divorce or separation if the ERA was passed.

Schlafly's essay attracted other opponents of the amendment. It led to the formation of STOP ERA (Stop Taking Our Privileges ERA), a conservative grassroots organization that worked to block ratification and was made up primarily of middle-class, religious, married women with children who viewed the ERA and the feminist movement more broadly as a threat to traditional views of motherhood, family, and the home. Schlafly became the most public face of this movement, challenging feminist leaders to public debates and making media appearances on behalf of STOP ERA. The organization was also active in lobbying at the state level, with women often famously arriving to meetings with freshly baked cookies to appeal to the male congressmen they hoped to influence. Five states proved to be key battlegrounds: North Carolina, Missouri, Florida, Illinois, and Oklahoma. STOP ERA was successful in all of these states, effectively blocking the ERA from ratification. Following this victory, STOP ERA was renamed the Eagle Forum, a pro-family political interest group.

Document Text

Of all the classes of people who ever lived, the American woman is the most privileged. We have the most rights and rewards, and the fewest duties. Our unique status is the result of a fortunate combination of circumstances.

1. We have the immense good fortune to live in a civilization which respects the family as the basic unit of society. . . . It is based on the fact of life—which no legislation or agitation can erase—that women have babies and men don't. . . . Our Judeo-Christian civilization has developed the law and custom that, since women must bear the physical consequences of the sex act, men must be required to bear the other consequences and pay in other ways. These laws and customs decree that a man must carry his share by physical protection and financial support of his children and of the woman who bears his children, and also by a code of behavior which benefits and protects both the woman and the children. . . .

2. The second reason why American women are a privileged group is that we are the beneficiaries of a tradition of special respect for women which dates from the Christian Age of Chivalry. . . . It is not—as some youthful agitators seem to think—just a matter of opening doors for women, seeing that they are seated first, carrying their bundles, and helping them in and out of automobiles. Such good manners are merely the superficial evidences of a total attitude toward women which expresses itself in many more tangible ways, such as money. . . . In the states which follow the English common law, a wife has a dower right in her husband's real estate which he cannot take away from her during life or by his will. A man cannot dispose of his real estate without his wife's signature. . . .

Phyllis Schlafly in 1977
(Library of Congress)

Women fare even better in the states which follow the Spanish and French community-property laws. . . . The basic philosophy . . . is that a wife's work in the home is just as valuable as a husband's work at his job. Therefore, in community-property states, a wife owns one-half of all the property and income her husband earns during their marriage, and he cannot take it away from her. . . .

3. The third reason why American women are so well off is that the great American free enterprise

---

system has produced remarkable inventors who have lifted the backbreaking "women's work" from our shoulders. . . . Household duties have been reduced to only a few hours a day, leaving the American woman with plenty of time to moonlight. She can take a full or part-time paying job, or she can indulge to her heart's content in a tremendous selection of interesting educational or cultural or homemaking activities.

The Fraud of the Equal Rights Amendment

. . . New "women's liberation" organizations are popping up, agitating and demonstrating, serving demands on public officials, getting wide press coverage always, and purporting to speak for some 100,000,000 American women. It's time to set the record straight. The claim that American women are downtrodden and unfairly treated is the fraud of the century. The truth is that American women never had it so good. . . . The proposed Equal Rights Amendment states: "Equality of rights under the law shall not be denied or abridged by the United States or by any state on account of sex." So what's wrong with that? Well, here are a few examples of what's wrong with it. This Amendment will absolutely and positively make women subject to the draft. . . . Another bad effect of the Equal Rights Amendment is that it will abolish a woman's right to child support and alimony. . . .

What "Women's Lib" Really Means

. . . The women's libbers are radicals who are waging a total assault on the family, on marriage, and on children. Don't take my word for it—read their own literature and prove to yourself what these characters are trying to do. The most pretentious of the women's liberation magazines is called Ms., and subtitled "The New Magazine For Women." . . . It is anti-family, anti-children, and pro-abortion. It is a series of sharp-tongued, high-pitched whining complaints by unmarried women. They view the home as a prison, and the wife and mother as a slave. . . . The women's libbers don't understand that most women want to be wife, mother and homemaker—and are happy in that role. The women's libbers actively resent the mother who stays at home with her children and likes it that way. . . .

Another women's lib magazine, called Women, tells the American woman that she is a prisoner in the "solitary confinement" and "isolation" of marriage. The magazine promises that it will provide women with "escape from isolation . . . release from boredom," and that it will "break the barriers . . . that separate wife, mistress and secretary . . . heterosexual women and homosexual women."

These women's libbers do, indeed, intend to "break the barriers" of the Ten Commandments and the sanctity of the family. It hasn't occurred to them that a woman's best "escape from isolation and boredom" is—not a magazine subscription to boost her "stifled ego"—but a husband and children who love her. . . .

Women's Libbers Do Not Speak for Us

. . . Women's libbers do not speak for the majority of American women. American women do not want to be liberated from husbands and children. We do not want to trade our birthright of the special privileges of American women—for the mess of pottage called the Equal Rights Amendment. Modern technology and opportunity have not discovered any nobler or more satisfying or more creative career for a woman than marriage and motherhood. . . .

If the women's libbers want to reject marriage and motherhood, it's a free country and that is their choice. But let's not permit these women's libbers to get away with pretending to speak for the rest of us. Let's not permit this tiny minority to degrade the role that most women prefer. Let's not let these women's libbers deprive wives and mothers of the rights we now possess.

Tell your Senators NOW that you want them to vote NO on the Equal Rights Amendment. Tell your television and radio stations that you want equal time to present the case FOR marriage and motherhood.

Glossary

common law: a body of unwritten laws based on tradition or legal precedents

dower: a widow's share for life of her husband's estate

moonlight: to pursue a second occupation

pottage: stew; thick soup

Short-Answer Questions

1. Summarize the author's basic argument for why the ERA is not necessary.

2. Describe the tone of the author regarding "women's liberation" or "women's lib." What does that tell us about her point of view? Be specific.

3. In a detailed response, analyze the threat Phyllis Schlafly claimed the Equal Rights Amendment posed to the lives and status of women.

Equal Rights Amendment

Author	Significance
Alice Paul	Guaranteed full rights to women under the law but was defeated in the conservative era of the 1980s
Date	
1972	
Document Type	
Legislative	

Overview

The Equal Rights Amendment (ERA), originally written by Alice Paul in 1921 and first proposed to Congress in 1923, was intended to guarantee full rights for women under the law. Following the passage of the Nineteenth Amendment, which extended suffrage to women, in August 1920, some believed that the U.S. Constitution should be amended to guarantee full rights for women in all aspects of life, from employment to education to divorce to property ownership. In fact, not all feminists agreed that such a constitutional amendment was necessary. Nevertheless, Alice Paul and other members of the National Woman's Party (NWP) discussed language for the proposed ERA. In the ensuing years the fight over the amendment waxed and waned, with the proposed legislation being introduced to every session of Congress from 1923 onward but remaining bottled up in committees. Paul rewrote the ERA into the current language in 1943, aiming to echo the language of the Fifteenth Amendment (which bars governments from preventing a person from voting on the basis of race or previous slave status) and the Nineteenth Amendment. With the revitalization of the women's movement in the 1960s, the demand for the passage of the ERA gained new life. Feminists, male and female, recognized that inequities still existed under American law, despite the passage of such landmark legislation as the Equal Pay Act of 1963 and Title VII of the Civil Rights Act of 1964 (protecting people against discrimination in the workplace on the basis of race or national origin or gender). The revised version of the ERA was finally pushed through Congress and presented to the states for ratification on March 22, 1972. The amendment's proponents saw it as the culmination of the long struggle for women's rights that began with the American Revolution and the adoption of the U.S. Constitution.

Document Text

Section 1. Equality of rights under the law shall not be denied or abridged by the United States or by any State on account of sex.

Section 2. The Congress shall have the power to enforce, by appropriate legislation, the provisions of this article.

Section 3. This amendment shall take effect two years after the date of ratification.

Alice Paul
(Library of Congress)

Glossary

abridged: lessened, diminished, or curtailed

ratification: approval or confirmation; formal sanction

Short-Answer Questions

1. Compare and contrast the two versions of the ERA. Look at the context for both, consider the wording, and discuss the significance of the differences.

2. Imagine that you are a member of the International Ladies Garment Workers Union in 1925. Write an argument opposing the proposed ERA.

3. Why do you think the ERA is still not a part of the U.S. Constitution? Be specific and use examples in your answer.

Title IX Education Act of 1972

Author
U.S. Congress

Date
1972

Document Type
Legislative

Significance
Established the right of women to equal access to education and to all programs related to education

Overview

Title IX is a federal civil rights law that guarantees protection against sex-based discrimination in public schools or any other educational body that accepts funding from the federal government. It was passed on June 23, 1972, as part of the education amendments of 1972, themselves a series of laws meant to update the Civil Right Act of 1964. Although the Civil Rights Act banned some forms of discrimination, it did not explicitly address discrimination in education, and Title IX was introduced to fill that gap in its coverage. It is often invoked as a means of protecting women—whether in the educational workforce or as part of the student body—from bias, bigotry, and prejudice.

Although Title IX is often interpreted as a sports-oriented law, it is intended to protect women from all forms of discrimination, not just those in sports programs. The misunderstanding stemmed from a 1974 attempt by then-Congressman John Tower (a Republican from Texas) to amend the bill in a way that would have exempted school athletic programs from having to follow the anti-discrimination guidelines. The Tower Amendment was rejected by Congress, but the misunderstanding that Title IX primarily dealt with sports equity remained. The fight to remove women's sports from coverage under Title IX continued into the 1990s, until the Equity in Athletics Disclosure Act was passed in 1994.

Document Text
Sec. 1681. Sex
(a) Prohibition against discrimination; exceptions

No person in the United States shall, on the basis of sex, be excluded from participation in, be denied the benefits of, or be subjected to discrimination under any education program or activity receiving Federal financial assistance, except that:

(1) Classes of educational institutions subject to prohibition

in regard to admissions to educational institutions, this section shall apply only to institutions of vocational education, professional education, and graduate higher education, and to public institutions of undergraduate higher education;

(2) Educational institutions commencing planned change in admissions

in regard to admissions to educational institutions, this section shall not apply

(A) for one year from June 23, 1972, nor for six years after June 23, 1972, in the case of an educational institution which has begun the process of changing from being an institution which admits only students of one sex to being an institution which admits students of both sexes, but only if it is carrying out a plan for such a change which is approved by the Secretary of Education or

(B) for seven years from the date an educational institution begins the process of changing from being an institution which admits only students of only one sex to being an institution which admits students of both sexes, but only if it is carrying out a plan for such a change which is approved by the Secretary of Education, whichever is the later;

(3) Educational institutions of religious organizations with contrary religious tenets

Patsy Mink led efforts to protect Title IX after it was passed. (Library of Congress)

this section shall not apply to an educational institution which is controlled by a religious organization if the application of this subsection would not be consistent with the religious tenets of such organization;

(4) Educational institutions training individuals for military services or merchant marine

this section shall not apply to an educational institution whose primary purpose is the training of individuals for the military services of the United States, or the merchant marine;

(5) Public educational institutions with traditional and continuing admissions policy

in regard to admissions this section shall not apply to any public institution of undergraduate higher education which is an institution that traditionally and continually from its establishment has had a policy of admitting only students of one sex;

(6) Social fraternities or sororities; voluntary youth service organizations

this section shall not apply to membership practices—

(A) of a social fraternity or social sorority which is exempt from taxation under section 501(a) of title 26, the active membership of which consists primarily of students in attendance at an institution of higher education, or

(B) of the Young Men's Christian Association, Young Women's Christian Association, Girl Scouts, Boy Scouts, Camp Fire Girls, and voluntary youth service organizations which are so exempt, the membership of which has traditionally been limited to persons of one sex and principally to persons of less than nineteen years of age;

(7) Boy or Girl conferences

this section shall not apply to—

(A) any program or activity of the American Legion undertaken in connection with the organization or operation of any Boys State conference, Boys Nation conference, Girls State conference, or Girls Nation conference; or

(B) any program or activity of any secondary school or educational institution specifically for—

(i) the promotion of any Boys State conference, Boys Nation conference, Girls State conference, or Girls Nation conference; or

(ii) the selection of students to attend any such conference;

(8) Father-son or mother-daughter activities at educational institutions

this section shall not preclude father-son or mother-daughter activities at an educational institution, but if such activities are provided for students of one sex, opportunities for reasonably comparable activities shall be provided for students of the other sex; and

(9) Institution of higher education scholarship awards in "beauty" pageants

this section shall not apply with respect to any scholarship or other financial assistance awarded by an institution of higher education to any individual because such individual has received such award in any pageant in which the attainment of such award is based upon a combination of factors related to the personal appearance, poise, and talent of such individual and in which participation is limited to individuals of one sex only, so long as such pageant is in compliance with other nondiscrimination provisions of Federal law.

(b) Preferential or disparate treatment because of imbalance in participation or receipt of Federal benefits; statistical evidence of imbalance

Nothing contained in subsection (a) of this section shall be interpreted to require any educational institution to grant preferential or disparate treatment to the members of one sex on account of an imbalance which may exist with respect to the total number or percentage of persons of that sex participating in or receiving the benefits of any federally supported program or activity, in comparison with the total number or percentage of persons of that sex in any community, State, section, or other area: Provided, that this subsection shall not be construed to prevent the consideration in any hearing or proceeding under this chapter of statistical evidence tending to show that such an imbalance exists with respect to the participation in, or receipt of the benefits of, any such program or activity by the members of one sex.

(c) "Educational institution" defined

For purposes of this chapter an educational institution means any public or private preschool, elementary, or secondary school, or any institution of vocational, professional, or higher education, except that in the case of an educational institution composed of more than one school, college, or department which are administratively separate units, such term means each such school, college, or department.

Glossary

American Legion: an organization of American war veterans, formed after World War I to lobby on behalf of current and former servicepeople

Boys Nation/Girls Nation: a forum conducted annually by the American Legion and the American Legion Auxiliary designed to give selected high school juniors a better understanding of how the federal government works by attending a weeklong seminar in Washington, D.C.

Boys State/Girls State: two auxiliaries of the American Legion designed to give selected high school juniors experience in the way that American government and politics work

Short-Answer Questions

1. What is the deciding factor that separates programs that have to follow Title IX from programs that do not?

2. What kinds of schools are exempt from following Title IX? Why?

3. Why do you think Title IX does not apply to Boys State/Girls State and Boys Nation/Girls Nation?

Frontiero v. Richardson

Author William J. Brennan Jr.; Lewis F. Powell (concurrence)	**Significance** Held that the military's differing criteria for military spousal dependency based on whether the servicemember was male or female violated the Fifth Amendment's due process clause
Date 1973	
Document Type Legal	

Overview

The case of *Frontiero v. Richardson*, argued in January of 1973, brought to light a form of discrimination in the armed forces highlighted by the increasing numbers of female military personnel. Lieutenant Sharron Frontiero had sought to have a dependent's allowance for her husband, something that was automatically allowed for the wife of an active-duty servicemember. For a husband to qualify for the dependent's allowance, the active-duty member had to demonstrate that more than one-half of the spouse's support came from the pay and allowances of the mem-

ber of the armed forces. The government argued to the Court that the policy was designed in such a way as to "save money" as it was far more common for women to receive more than one-half of their support from their husband rather than the other way around, and the rule allowed the government to save time by not having to process every dependent claim to prove the one-half dependency rule. The Court disagreed with this position, responding that the statute itself discriminated against women, which violated the due process clause, and thus required the burden to be the same regardless of gender.

Document Text

A married woman Air Force officer (hereafter appellant) sought increased benefits for her husband as a "dependent." . . . Those statutes provide, solely for administrative convenience, that spouses of male members of the uniformed services are dependents for purposes of obtaining increased quarters allowances and medical and dental benefits, but that spouses of female members are not dependents unless they are in fact, dependent for over one-half of their support. When her application was denied for failure to satisfy the statutory dependency standard, appellant and her husband brought this suit in District Court, contending that the statutes deprived servicewomen of due process. From that Court's adverse ruling, they took a direct appeal.

Held: The judgment is reversed. . . .

The question before us concerns the right of a female member of the uniformed services to claim her spouse as a "dependent" for the purposes of obtaining increased quarters allowances and medical and dental benefits . . . on an equal footing with male members. Under these statutes, a serviceman may claim his wife as a "dependent" without regard to whether she is in fact, dependent upon him for any part of her support. . . . A servicewoman, on the other hand, may not claim her husband as a "dependent" under these programs unless he is in fact, dependent upon her for over one-half of his support. . . .

Thus, the question for decision is whether this difference in treatment constitutes an unconstitutional discrimination against servicewomen in violation of the Due Process Clause of the Fifth Amendment. A three-judge District Court for the Middle District of Alabama, one judge dissenting, rejected this contention and sustained the constitutionality of the provisions of the statutes making this distinction. . . .

I

. . . In essence, appellants asserted that the discriminatory impact of the statutes is twofold: first, as a procedural matter, a female member is required

Justice William Rehnquist dissented in **Frontiero v. Richardson.** (Library of Congress)

to demonstrate her spouse's dependency, while no such burden is imposed upon male members; and, second, as a substantive matter, a male member who does not provide more than one-half of his wife's support receives benefits, while a similarly situated female member is denied such benefits. Appellants therefore sought a permanent injunction against the continued enforcement of these statutes and an order directing the appellees to provide Lieutenant Frontiero with the same housing and medical benefits that a similarly situated male member would receive.

Although the legislative history of these statutes sheds virtually no light on the purposes underlying the differential treatment accorded male and female members, a majority of the three-judge District Court surmised that Congress might reasonably have concluded that, since the husband in our society is generally the "breadwinner" in the family— and the wife typically the "dependent" partner—"it would be more economical to require married female members claiming husbands to prove actual dependency than to extend the presumption of dependency to such members." . . . Indeed, given the fact that approximately 99% of all members of the uniformed services are male, the District Court speculated that such differential treatment might conceivably lead to a "considerable saving of administrative expense and manpower." . . .

II

At the outset, appellants contend that classifications based upon sex, like classifications based upon race, alienage, and national origin, are inherently suspect, and must therefore be subjected to close judicial scrutiny. We agree. . . .

[O]ur statute books gradually became laden with gross, stereotyped distinctions between the sexes, and, indeed, throughout much of the 19th century, the position of women in our society was, in many respects, comparable to that of blacks under the pre–Civil War slave codes. Neither slaves nor women could hold office, serve on juries, or bring suit in their own names, and married women traditionally were denied the legal capacity to hold or convey property or to serve as legal guardians of their own children. . . .

And although blacks were guaranteed the right to vote in 1870, women were denied even that right—which is itself "preservative of other basic civil and political rights"—until adoption of the Nineteenth Amendment half a century later.

It is true, of course, that the position of women in America has improved markedly in recent decades. Nevertheless, it can hardly be doubted that, in part because of the high visibility of the sex characteristic, women still face pervasive, although at times more subtle, discrimination in our educational institutions, in the job market and, perhaps most conspicuously, in the political arena. . . .

Moreover, since sex, like race and national origin, is an immutable characteristic determined solely by the accident of birth, the imposition of special disabilities upon the members of a particular sex because of their sex would seem to violate "the basic concept of our system that legal burdens should bear some relationship to individual responsibility." . . . And what differentiates sex from such nonsuspect statuses as intelligence or physical disability, and aligns it with the recognized suspect criteria, is that the sex characteristic frequently bears no relation to ability to perform or contribute to society. As a result, statutory distinctions between the sexes often have the effect of invidiously relegating the entire class of females to inferior legal status without regard to the actual capabilities of its individual members. . . .

[W]e can only conclude that classifications based upon sex, like classifications based upon race, alienage, or national origin, are inherently suspect, and must therefore be subjected to strict judicial scrutiny. Applying the analysis mandated by that stricter standard of review, it is clear that the statutory scheme now before us is constitutionally invalid. . . .

III

The sole basis of the classification established in the challenged statutes is the sex of the individuals involved. . . . Thus, to this extent, at least, it may fairly be said that these statutes command "dissimilar treatment for men and women who are . . . similarly situated." . . .

In any case, our prior decisions make clear that, although efficacious administration of governmental programs is not without some importance, "the Constitution recognizes higher values than speed and efficiency." . . . And when we enter the realm of "strict judicial scrutiny," there can be no doubt that "administrative convenience" is not a shibboleth, the mere recitation of which dictates constitutionality. . . . On the contrary, any statutory scheme which draws a sharp line between the sexes, solely for the purpose of achieving administrative convenience, necessarily commands "dissimilar treatment for men and women who are . . . similarly situated," and therefore involves the "very kind of arbitrary legislative choice forbidden by the [Constitution]." . . . We therefore conclude that, by according differential treatment to male and female members of the uniformed services for the sole purpose of achieving administrative convenience, the challenged statutes violate the Due Process Clause of the Fifth Amendment insofar as they require a female member to prove the dependency of her husband.

Glossary

appellant: person bringing a case on appeal to the Supreme Court

dependent: a person who relies on another person, particularly a family member, for financial or other support

due process clause: a portion of the Fifth and Fourteenth Amendments that states that a person must not be deprived of "life, liberty, or property, without due process of law"

permanent injunction: a court order requiring a party to do or to cease doing something

shibboleth: a saying used by adherents of a party, sect, or belief regarded by others as empty of real meaning

---

Short-Answer Questions

1. How did the rising feminist movement of the 1970s and America's growing distrust of the military system influence the Supreme Court's decision to hear the case and make the decision it did?

2. What effect might the decision of Frontiero v. Richardson have had on the civilian labor world in terms of women's competitiveness for jobs?

3. What effect might the outcome of this case have had on the passage (or failure to pass) of the Equal Rights Amendment? How might such an amendment have affected American views regarding gender and employment?

Shirley Chisholm: "The Black Woman in Contemporary America"

Author	Significance
Shirley Chisholm	Addressed the conflict that Black women faced in the 1970s between the women's rights movement and Black civil rights movement
Date	
1974	
Type	
Speeches/Addresses	

Overview

Selected as the keynote speaker for a national conference on Black women held at the University of Missouri in Kansas City, Shirley Chisholm enumerated the key issues facing African American women in her address "The Black Woman in Contemporary America." She pointedly reminded her audience that Black women were not interested in being addressed as "Ms." or in gaining access to all-male social clubs. Rather, African American women's top priority was the welfare of their families and communities. Black and white women, she asserted, should unite around issues such as improved day-care facilities and increased job opportunities. At the same time that Chisholm was criticizing white feminists, she chided African American spokesmen who suggested that Black women step aside to allow Black men to monopolize leadership positions. Only by working together as equals, she said, could Black men and women create the programs and policies needed by their communities. This speech typified

Chisholm's fighting spirit, her willingness to confront contentious issues head on, and her rousing oratorical style.

As the first African American woman elected to Congress and a candidate for the 1972 Democratic presidential nomination, Chisholm was the most prominent Black female political leader of the 1970s. An articulate and fiery public speaker, Chisholm was not afraid to challenge established power brokers or take a stand on controversial issues. Her arrival on the national stage coincided with growing African American political power and the emergence of the women's liberation movement. At a time when many women of color criticized white feminists for pursuing goals irrelevant to minority communities, Chisholm attempted to bridge the racial divide. She frequently claimed that she was more often discriminated against because she was a woman than because she was Black.

Shirley Chisholm (Library of Congress)

Document Text

. . . It is quite understandable why Black women in the majority are not interested in walking and picketing a cocktail lounge which historically has refused to open its doors a certain two hours a day when men who have just returned from Wall Street gather in said lounge to exchange bits of business transactions that occurred on the market. This is a middle-class white woman's issue. This is not a priority of minority women. Another issue that Black women are not overly concerned about is the "M-S" versus the "M-R-S" label. For many of us this is just the use of another label which does not basically change the fundamental inherent racial attitudes found in both men and women in this society. This is just another label, and Black women are not preoccupied with any more label syndromes. Black women are desperately concerned with the issue of survival in a society in which the Caucasian group has never really practiced the espousal of equalitarian principles in America.

An aspect of the women's liberation movement that will and does interest many Black women is the potential liberation, is the potential nationalization of daycare centers in this country. Black women can accept and understand this agenda item in the women's movement. It is important that Black women utilize their brainpower and focus on issues in any movement that will redound to the benefit of their people. . . .

The Black woman lives in a society that discriminates against her on two counts. The Black woman cannot be discussed in the same context as her Caucasian counterpart because of the twin jeopardy of race and sex which operates against her, and the psychological and political consequences which attend them. Black women are crushed by cultural restraints and abused by the legitimate power structure. To date, neither the Black movement nor women's liberation succinctly addresses itself to the dilemma confronting the Black who is female. And as a consequence of ignoring or being unable to handle the problems facing Black women, Black women themselves are now becoming socially and politically active.

Undoubtedly Black women are cultivating new attitudes, most of which will have political repercussions in the future. They are attempting to change their conditions. The maturation of the civil rights movement by the mid '60s enabled many Black women to develop interest in the American political process. From their experiences they learned that the real sources of power lay at the root of the political system. For example, Black sororities and pressure groups like the National Council of Negro Women are adept at the methods of participatory politics—particularly in regard to voting and organizing. . . .

Historically she has been discouraged from participating in politics. Thus she is trapped between the walls of the dominant white culture and her own subculture, both of which encourage deference to men. Both races of women have traditionally been limited to performing such tasks as opening envelopes, hanging up posters and giving teas. And the minimal involvement of Black women exists because they have been systematically excluded from the political process and they are members of the politically dysfunctional Black lower class. Thus, unlike white women, who escape the psychological and sociological handicaps of racism, the Black woman's political involvement has been a most marginal role.

But within the last six years, the Afro-American subculture has undergone tremendous social and political transformation and these changes have altered the nature of the Black community. . . . So obviously Black women who helped to spearhead the civil rights movement would also now, at this juncture, join and direct the vanguard which would shape and mold a new kind of political participation.

This has been acutely felt in urban areas, which have been rocked by sporadic rebellions. Nothing better illustrates the need for Black women to organize politically than their unusual proximity to the most crucial issues affecting Black people today. They have struggled in a wide range of protest movements to eliminate the poverty and injustice that permeates the lives of Black people. In New York City, for example, welfare mothers and mothers of schoolchildren have ably demonstrated the commitment of Black women to the elimination of the problems that threaten the well-being of the Black family. . . . Black women have a duty to move from the periphery of organized political activity into its main arena.

Glossary

label syndromes: related to the belief that a label defines who you are in society

National Council of Negro Women: an organization founded in 1935 to advance the opportunities and quality of life for African American women as well as their families

Short-Answer Questions

1. Why don't Black women associate with the larger women's rights movements, according to Shirley Chisholm? For which issues does Chisholm encourage Black women to unite with white women?

2. How have Black women been "doubly" repressed? How might this impact their drive not only to pursue racial equality but also gender equality?

3. How does Chisholm indicate that circumstances are improving for women's political activism? Why might that progress be met with resistance by Blacks who are also seeking racial equality? How might this division hamper the movement for desegregation?

Taylor v. Louisiana

Author	Significance
Byron R. White	Ruled that for a jury to be fully representative of the community, women could not be systematically excluded from jury service
Date	
1975	
Document Type	
Legal	

Overview

Until the ruling in *Taylor v. Louisiana* (1975), women in Louisiana were not required to sit on juries unless they volunteered. Billy Jean Taylor was arrested in September 1971 in St. Tammany Parish, Louisiana. He was charged on counts of kidnapping, robbery, and rape, and the trial was set to begin in April 1972. The day before the trial, Taylor filed a motion to disallow the jury for being unrepresentative of the population. Under Louisiana law, women could only serve on a jury if they had already actively registered to do so, whereas men did not have to register but were considered for duty automatically. In St. Tammany, only one in five women were registered for jury service despite making up over half of the individuals eligible. The 175 jury candidates selected before the trial were all men.

Taylor argued that because women were excluded from jury service by default and were not included as candidates, the jury chosen to try him was not made up of his peers. The trial court and, on appeal, the Louisiana Supreme Court both rejected Taylor's argument, citing that the different rules for men's and women's jury service did not violate federal law. The Supreme Court, however, determined that Louisiana's requirement that women (but not men) register for jury duty constituted the systematic exclusion of women and violated the Sixth Amendment's guarantee of a representative and impartial jury. Of other importance, the Court found that not overturning the Louisiana statute would possibly pave the way for other forms of exclusion of wome from other civic areas.

Document Text

II

The Louisiana jury selection system does not disqualify women from jury service, but, in operation, its conceded systematic impact is that only a very few women, grossly disproportionate to the number of eligible women in the community, are called for jury service. In this case, no women were on the venire from which the petit jury was drawn. The issue we have, therefore, is whether a jury selection system which operates to exclude from jury service an identifiable class of citizens constituting 53% of eligible jurors in the community comports with the Sixth and Fourteenth Amendments.

The State first insists that Taylor, a male, has no standing to object to the exclusion of women from his jury. But Taylor's claim is that he was constitutionally entitled to a jury drawn from a venire constituting a fair cross-section of the community, and that the jury that tried him was not such a jury by reason of the exclusion of women. Taylor was not a member of the excluded class, but there is no rule that claims such as Taylor presents may be made only by those defendants who are members of the group excluded from jury service. In *Peters v. Kiff* (1972), the defendant, a white man, challenged his conviction on the ground that Negroes had been systematically excluded from jury service. Six Members of the Court agreed that petitioner was entitled to present the issue, and concluded that he had been deprived of his federal rights. Taylor, in the case before us, was similarly entitled to tender and have adjudicated the claim that the exclusion of women from jury service deprived him of the kind of factfinder to which he was constitutionally entitled. . . .

IV

We are also persuaded that the fair cross-section requirement is violated by the systematic exclusion of women, who, in the judicial district involved here, amounted to 53% of the citizens eligible for jury service. This conclusion necessarily entails the judgment that women are sufficiently numerous and distinct from men, and that, if they are systematically eliminated from jury panels, the Sixth Amendment's fair cross-section requirement cannot be satisfied. This very matter was debated in *Ballard v. United States*. Positing the fair cross-section rule—said to be a statutory one—the Court concluded that the systematic exclusion of women was unacceptable. The dissenting view that an all-male panel drawn from various groups in the community would be as truly representative as if women were included, was firmly rejected:

"The thought is that the factors which tend to influence the action of women are the same as those which influence the action of men—personality, background, economic status—and not sex. Yet it is not enough to say that women when sitting as jurors neither act nor tend to act as a class. Men likewise do not act as a class. But, if the shoe were on the other foot, who would claim that a jury was truly representative of the community if all men were intentionally and systematically excluded from the panel? The truth is that the two sexes are not fungible; a community made up exclusively of one is different from a community composed of both; the subtle interplay of influence one on the other is among the imponderables. To insulate the courtroom from either may not, in a given case, make an iota of difference. Yet a flavor, a distinct quality, is lost if either sex is excluded. The exclusion of one may indeed make the jury less representative of the community than would be true if an economic or racial group were excluded."

In this respect, we agree with the Court in *Ballard*: If the fair cross-section rule is to govern the selection of juries, as we have concluded it must, women cannot be systematically excluded from jury panels from which petit juries are drawn. This conclusion is consistent with the current judgment of the country, now evidenced by legislative or constitutional provisions in every State and at the federal level qualifying women for jury service.

V

There remains the argument that women as a class serve a distinctive role in society and that jury service would so substantially interfere with that function that the State has ample justification for excluding women from service unless they volunteer, even though the result is that almost all jurors are men. It is true that *Hoyt v. Florida* (1961), held that such a system did not deny due process of law or equal protection of the laws because there was a sufficiently rational basis for such an exemption. But *Hoyt* did not involve a defendant's Sixth Amendment right to a jury drawn from a fair cross-section of the community and the prospect of depriving him of that right if women as a class are systematically excluded. The right to a proper jury cannot be overcome on merely rational grounds. There must be weightier reasons if a distinctive class representing 53% of the eligible jurors is for all practical purposes to be excluded from jury service. No such basis has been tendered here.

The States are free to grant exemptions from jury service to individuals in case of special hardship or incapacity and to those engaged in particular occupations the uninterrupted performance is critical to the community's welfare. *Rawlins v. Georgia* (1906). It would not appear that such exemptions would pose substantial threats that the remaining pool of jurors would not be representative of the community. A system excluding all women, however, is a wholly different matter. It is untenable to suggest these days that it would be a special hardship for each and every woman to perform jury service or that society cannot spare *any* women from their present duties. This may be the case with many, and it may be burdensome to sort out those who should be exempted from those who should serve. . . .

Glossary

Fourteenth Amendment: grants citizenship to all persons born in or naturalized in the United States regardless of gender, race, or religion and prohibits state and local governments from depriving persons of life, liberty, or property without a fair procedure, guaranteeing citizens and non-citizens equal protection under law

Sixth Amendment: guarantees criminal defendants nine different rights, including the right to a speedy and public trial by an impartial jury consisting of jurors from the state and district in which the crime was alleged to have been committed

---

Short-Answer Questions

1. The State of Louisiana asserted that Taylor, as a man, had no standing to object to the exclusion of women from his jury. Why did the state maintain this? The Supreme Court disagreed. What was the Supreme Court's reasoning?

2. In your view, how did the court use previous cases to interpret *Taylor v. Louisiana*?

3. This case comes during the era of second-wave feminism. How might this context have affected the ruling in this case or the arguments of those who favored overturning *Hoyt v. Florida*?

Audre Lorde:
"Poetry Is Not a Luxury"

Author
Audre Lorde

Date
1977

Type
Essays, Reports, Manifestos

Significance
Emphasized the need for Black women to find their voices and speak for themselves

Overview

Audre Lorde (1934–1992) was perhaps the best-known Black feminist lesbian poet and essayist working in America in the late twentieth century. She was the daughter of two Caribbean immigrants who had come to New York City and settled in Harlem. Lorde is especially well known for her collection *Sister Outsider: Essays and Speeches* (1984), which includes "Poetry Is Not a Luxury."

Lorde was a late speaker; she did not start talking until the age of five, and she began reading soon after. She began to write poems when she turned eight. She attended Catholic schools in New York, where her dark skin marked her as different from her classmates. In addition, her parents' relationship with her was distant most of the time. Those factors contributed to Lorde's sense of herself as an outsider, the theme that unifies the essays in *Sister Outsider*.

Lorde earned a master's degree in library science from Columbia University in 1961 and later served as writer-in-residence at Tougaloo College. She held professorships at Lehman College, John Jay College, Hunter College, and the Free University of Berlin. She won acclaim for her poetry beginning in the 1970s—she was named Poet Laureate of the state of New York in 1991—but she did not begin publishing her prose until the 1980s. By that time she had been diagnosed with cancer. She retired to St. Croix in the U.S. Virgin Islands and died there on November 17, 1992.

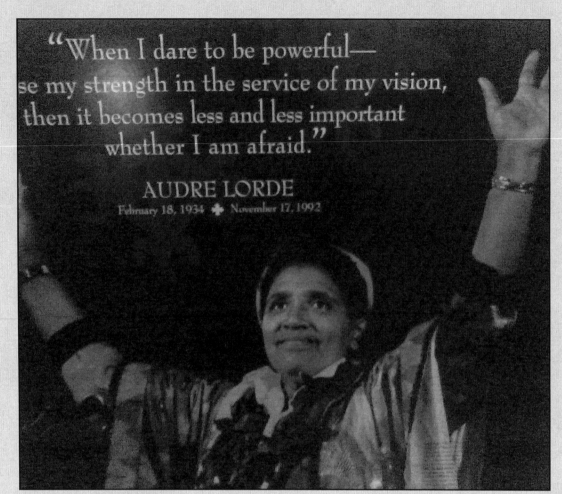

Audre Lorde (Sharon McKellar)

Document Text

As we learn to bear the intimacy of scrutiny and to flourish within it, as we learn to use the products of that scrutiny for power within our living, those fears which rule our lives and form our silences begin to lose their control over us.

For each of us as women, there is a dark place within, where hidden and growing our true spirit rises, "beautiful / and tough as chestnut / stanchions against (y)our nightmare of weakness /" and of impotence. . . .

When we view living in the european mode only as a problem to be solved, we rely solely upon our ideas to make us free, for these were what the white fathers told us were precious.

But as we come more into touch with our own ancient, noneuropean consciousness of living as a situation to be experienced and interacted with, we learn more and more to cherish our feelings, and to respect those hidden sources of our power from where true knowledge and, therefore, lasting action comes.

At this point in time, I believe that women carry within ourselves the possibility for fusion of these two approaches so necessary for survival, and we come closest to this combination in our poetry. I speak here of poetry as a revelatory distillation of experience, not the sterile word play that, too often, the white fathers distorted the word *poetry* to mean—in order to cover a desperate wish for imagination without insight.

For women, then, poetry is not a luxury. It is a vital necessity of our existence. It forms the quality of the light within which we predicate our hopes and dreams toward survival and change, first made into language, then into idea, then into more tangible action. Poetry is the way we help give name to the nameless so it can be thought. The farthest horizons of our hopes and fears are cobbled by our poems, carved from the rock experiences of our daily lives.

Sometimes we drug ourselves with dreams of new ideas. The head will save us. The brain alone will set us free. But there are no new ideas still waiting in the wings to save us as women, as human. There are only old and forgotten ones, new combinations, extrapolations and recognitions from within ourselves—along with the renewed courage to try them out. And we must constantly encourage ourselves and each other to attempt the heretical actions that our dreams imply, and so many of our old ideas disparage. In the forefront of our move toward change, there is only poetry to hint at possibility made real. Our poems formulate the implications of ourselves, what we feel within and dare make real (or bring action into accordance with), our fears, our hopes, our most cherished terrors.

For within living structures defined by profit, by linear power, by institutional dehumanization, our feelings were not meant to survive. Kept around as unavoidable adjuncts or pleasant pastimes, feelings were expected to kneel to thought as women were expected to kneel to men. But women have survived. As poets. And there are no new pains. We have felt them all already. We have hidden that fact in the same place where we have hidden our power. They surface in our dreams, and it is our dreams that point the way to freedom. Those dreams are made realizable through our poems that give us the strength and courage to see, to feel, to speak, and to dare.

If what we need to dream, to move our spirits most deeply and directly toward and through promise, is discounted as a luxury, then we give up the core—the fountain—of our power, our womanness; we give up the future of our worlds.

For there are no new ideas. There are only new ways of making them felt—of examining what those ideas feel like being lived on Sunday morning at 7 a.m., after brunch, during wild love, making war, giving birth, mourning our dead—while we suffer the old longings, battle the old warnings and fears of being silent and impotent and alone, while we taste new possibilities and strengths.

Glossary

adjuncts: extras; supplements to the main exercise

extrapolations: conclusions based on past evidence and trends rather than observations

stanchion: an upright structure that supports other structures

Short-Answer Questions

1. Why, according to Lorde, should ideas be less important than feelings?

2. What does Lorde say is the relationship between poetry and feelings? Why are they important for women?

3. Based on what Lorde says here, why is it important for women to embrace poetry as a means of reclaiming their voices?

Meritor Savings Bank v. Vinson

Author	Significance
William Rehnquist	Recognized sexual harassment as a violation of the Civil Rights Act of 1964 and set standards for appropriate workplace conduct, holding employers liable when violations occurred
Date 1986	
Document Type Legal	

Overview

Mechelle Vinson started working for Meritor Savings Bank (at the time called Capital City Federal Savings and Loan Association) in Washington, D.C., in 1974. Vinson alleged that after she had worked at the D.C. branch office for about a year, Sidney L. Taylor, her boss, started sexually harassing her at work, beginning what would be a three-year ongoing pattern. Vinson filed a lawsuit against the company in September 1978, charging that her employer created a "hostile working environment." Her charge stemmed from Taylor's inappropriate sexual advancements. Vinson stated that Taylor had coerced her into sex and demanded sexual favors from her. In particular, she testified that Taylor had engaged in inappropriate touching and other sexual acts at and outside the workplace and that he had raped her on multiple occasions. She testified that she had been forced to engage in about fifty sexual encounters with Taylor. Vinson was fired from her job in November 1978 for taking excessive sick leave.

The case raised the question of whether a hostile work environment created by sexual discrimination could be constituted as a form of unlawful discrimination under the Civil Rights Act. Up to this point, the Civil Rights Act only applied to economic discrimination as it pertained to the workplace. The ruling of the Supreme Court case was monumental, making sexual harassment an actionable offense.

William Rehnquist delivered the opinion of the Court. (Library of Congress)

Document Text

In 1974, respondent Mechelle Vinson met Sidney Taylor, a vice-president of what is now petitioner Meritor Savings Bank (bank) and manager of one of its branch offices. When the respondent asked whether she might obtain employment at the bank, Taylor gave her an application, which she completed and returned the next day; later that same day, Taylor called her to say that she had been hired. With Taylor as her supervisor, respondent started as a teller-trainee, and thereafter was promoted to teller, head teller, and assistant branch manager. She worked at the same branch for four years, and it is undisputed that her advancement there was based on merit alone. In September, 1978, respondent notified Taylor that she was taking sick leave for an indefinite period. On November 1, 1978, the bank discharged her for excessive use of that leave.

Respondent brought this action against Taylor and the bank, claiming that, during her four years at the bank, she had "constantly been subjected to sexual harassment" by Taylor in violation of Title

VII. She sought injunctive relief, compensatory and punitive damages against Taylor and the bank, and attorney's fees.

At the 11-day bench trial, the parties presented conflicting testimony about Taylor's behavior during respondent's employment. Respondent testified that, during her probationary period as a teller-trainee, Taylor treated her in a fatherly way and made no sexual advances. Shortly thereafter, however, he invited her out to dinner and, during the course of the meal, suggested that they go to a motel to have sexual relations. At first she refused, but out of what she described as fear of losing her job, she eventually agreed. According to the respondent, Taylor thereafter made repeated demands upon her for sexual favors, usually at the branch, both during and after business hours; she estimated that over the next several years she had intercourse with him some 40 or 50 times. In addition, respondent testified that Taylor fondled her in front of other employees, followed her into the women's restroom when she went there alone, exposed himself to her, and even forcibly raped her on several occasions. These activities ceased after 1977, respondent stated, when she started going with a steady boyfriend. Respondent also testified that Taylor touched and fondled other women employees of the bank, and she attempted to call witnesses to support this charge. But while some supporting testimony apparently was admitted without objection, the District Court did not allow her "to present wholesale evidence of a pattern and practice relating to sexual advances to other female employees in her case in chief, but advised her that she might well be able to present such evidence in rebuttal to the defendants' cases."

Respondent did not offer such evidence in rebuttal. Finally, respondent testified that, because she was afraid of Taylor, she never reported his harassment to any of his supervisors and never attempted to use the bank's complaint procedure.

Taylor denied respondent's allegations of sexual activity, testifying that he never fondled her, never made suggestive remarks to her, never engaged in sexual intercourse with her, and never asked her to do so. He contended instead that the respondent made her accusations in response to a business-related dispute. The bank also denied respondent's allegations, and asserted that any sexual harassment by Taylor was unknown to the bank and engaged in without its consent or approval.

The District Court denied relief, but did not resolve the conflicting testimony about the existence of a sexual relationship between respondent and Taylor. It found instead that

"[i]f [respondent] and Taylor did engage in an intimate or sexual relationship during the time of [respondent's] employment with [the bank], that relationship was a voluntary one having nothing to do with her continued employment at [the bank] or her advancement or promotions at that institution."

The court ultimately found that respondent "was not the victim of sexual harassment and was not the victim of sexual discrimination" while employed at the bank.

Although it concluded that respondent had not proved a violation of Title VII, the District Court nevertheless went on to address the bank's liability. After noting the bank's express policy against discrimination, and finding that neither respondent nor any other employee had ever lodged a complaint about sexual harassment by Taylor, the court ultimately concluded that "the bank was without notice, and cannot be held liable for the alleged actions of Taylor."

The Court of Appeals for the District of Columbia Circuit reversed. Relying on its earlier holding in *Bundy v. Jackson* (1981), decided after the trial in this case, the court stated that a violation of Title VII may be predicated on either of two types of sexual harassment: harassment that involves the conditioning of concrete employment benefits on sexual favors, and harassment that, while not affecting economic benefits, creates a hostile or offensive working environment. The court drew additional support for this position from the Equal Employment Opportunity Commission's Guidelines on Discrimination Because of Sex, which set out these two types of sexual harassment claims. Believing that "Vinson's grievance was clearly of the [hostile environment] type," and that the District Court had not considered whether a violation of this type had occurred, the court concluded that a remand was necessary.

The court further concluded that the District Court's finding that any sexual relationship between respondent and Taylor "was a voluntary one" did not obviate the need for a remand. "[U]ncertain as to precisely what the [district] court meant" by this finding, the Court of Appeals held that, if the evidence otherwise showed that "Taylor made Vinson's toleration of sexual harassment a condition of her employment," her voluntariness "had no materiality whatsoever."

Glossary

injunctive relief: a court order that prohibits an organization or an individual from taking a specific action

punitive damages: damages exceeding simple compensation and awarded to punish the defendant

respondent: defendant in a lawsuit

reversed: overturned an earlier ruling

Title VII: a portion of the Civil Rights Act of 1964 that prohibits employment discrimination based on race, color, religion, sex or national origin

Short-Answer Questions

1. What are the two types of sexual harassment identified by the Court of Appeals for the District of Columbia Circuit? How have these definitions of sexual harassment impacted the workplace?

2. After the ruling of the case, the reporting of sexual harassment incidents grew substantially. What might this reveal about gender dynamics in the workplace?

3. What does the District Court's ruling reveal about gender dynamics outside the workplace?

Jo Ann Gibson Robinson:
The Montgomery Bus Boycott and the Women Who Started It

Author
Jo Ann Gibson Robinson

Date
1987

Type
Essays, Reports, Manifestos

Significance
Illuminated the major role women played in the organization of the yearlong Montgomery Bus Boycott

---

Overview

In her 1987 memoir, *The Montgomery Bus Boycott and the Women Who Started It*, activist and educator Jo Ann Gibson Robinson writes about the 1956 Montgomery Bus Boycott for integration in transportation and the role the Women's Political Council, of which she was the president, played in organizing it. Martin Luther King Jr., perhaps the most recognizable name in relation to the bus boycott, acknowledged the vital role Robinson played in launching the boycott and making it a success. In this excerpt, Robinson describes the carpool system that was organized to take the place of the buses to transport Black workers during the 382-day boycott.

Document Text

The Montgomery carpool of 1955 was one of the most effectively planned mass transportation systems in American history. . . .

The bus boycott affected the entire city, and the MIA tried to cover every need. With few exceptions, the rides were free. . . . Each day some 325 private cars picked up passengers from 43 dispatch stations and 42 pickup stations. The dispatch stations were designated places where workers congregated in the early morning, beginning at 5 A.M., to be taken to work. From 5 A.M. until 10 A.M., dozens of cars left these points every ten minutes for anywhere within the working radius of Montgomery. The dispatch stations included

---

Rosa Parks's arrest ignited the Montgomery Bus Boycott. (Library of Congress)

most of the Negro churches, all of the Negro funeral homes, several clubhouses, stores and other key places. . . . By ten o'clock in the morning, most of the workers had been dispatched, so casual hourly pickups were scheduled during the rest of the day. . . .

The forty-two pickup stations became active around 1 P.M., when maids, cooks, nurses, and other domestic workers began getting off. From then until 8 P.M. this service continued. Many of the pickup places were in areas occupied pri-

marily by whites. Thus, grocery stores, churches, school corners, other centrally located corners, and downtown areas were common pickup stations. . . .

The two key downtown pickup spots were a Negro-owned parking lot on McDonough Street and Dean's Drugstore on Monroe. . . .

These two places were the central exchange points for transfers. . . . Because the sites were private property, authorities did not have authority to molest passengers or to question them there. . . . Had it not been for these two black-owned enterprises in the heart of downtown Montgomery, the carpool system could not have given the regular service it did. . . .

Very few black drivers ever passed a pedestrian walking along the street without stopping to give them a lift. Our "share-a-ride" slogan received a wonderful response. Even sympathetic whites, both men and women, stopped and picked up pedestrians. . . .

People who worked all day picked up during the early morning hours or late evenings. Those who worked nights picked up during certain hours of the day. From 5 A.M. until 8 A.M. and from 5 P.M. until 9 P.M., many working people could render volunteer service. . . .

During the first days of the boycott, people used their cars and furnished their own gas free of charge. But as it continued, collections were taken in churches . . . to furnish gasoline. The money was never paid to the drivers, but a certain number of gallons was supplied each driver daily from one of the eight black-owned filling stations. . . . Some people who drove never availed themselves of this free gasoline, donating it out of their own resources. . . .

After months of boycotting, individual drivers who had been picking up "walking people" on their way to and from work began to grow weary. To assist the walkers, all of us had driven before, in between, and after working at our own jobs. Exhausted, we were going to sleep at the dinner table. . . .

Then, like a miracle, money began to flow in to the MIA. When people across the country realized what the Montgomery black people were experiencing, . . . they sent more money to buy fuel for the motor vehicles. As money poured into the MIA treasury, the Finance Committee got busy paying its debts. . . . The MIA began to hire drivers to carry workers to their jobs, or to transfer places where other drivers would drive them to their destination. In addition to money, some people also sent station wagons to be used. . . . Several of the leading churches were given station wagons to transport their congregations to and from work. . . . Soon there were six station wagons with drivers paid to operate them. Eventually more than twelve churches either bought station wagons or received them from sympathetic people in various parts of the country.

When this money began coming in and bills had been paid, the boycotters took on great faith. They knew now that they would make it. At this point, . . . station wagons began to operate in large numbers from five in the morning to ten in the evenings. . . . New routes were mapped out, and a regular schedule was started that accommodated everyone. The system was operated efficiently and on schedule. No more walking to work now! . . . Now Montgomery black people settled down to a long year of boycotting.

Glossary

MIA: Montgomery Improvement Association, a civil rights organization formed to organize and maintain the bus boycott

Short-Answer Questions

1. How does Robinson illustrate that unification and organization were key elements in the success of the Montgomery Bus Boycott?

2. Toward the end of the excerpt, Robinson writes, "The system was operated efficiently and on schedule." According to Robinson, in addition to the MIA, what groups and individuals contributed to the success of the boycott?

3. Although Robinson's memoir highlights the Women's Political Council and "the women who started" the Montgomery Bus Boycott, this chapter about the boycott's logistics does not mention them. Why do you think Robinson does not mention their role in this chapter?

Bella Abzug:
"Women and the Fate of the Earth"

Author Bella Abzug	**Significance** Maintained that women were central to the environmental movement and needed to use their collective power to address climate issues
Date 1990	
Document Type Speeches/Addresses	

Overview

Bella Abzug (1920–1998) was a lifelong advocate for women's rights and the environment. An advocate of civil rights and a critic of McCarthyism, she devoted her life to helping others. In 1985 she organized a panel called "What If Women Ruled the World?" for the U.N. Women's Conference in Nairobi, Kenya. The outcome of the event was that she and other activists founded the Women's Environment and Development Organization (WEDO) in 1990. Related to this, she gave an address that year titled "Women and the Fate of the Earth" before the World Women's Congress for a Healthy Planet at the Center for Our Common Future in Vancouver, British Columbia, Canada. The speech stressed the importance of women's leadership in tackling pressing global concerns such as climate change and other environmental issues. Abzug argued that the women's rights and environmental justice movements were deeply intertwined. She encouraged women to be the leaders of environmental preservation and contended that to accomplish this, women need to be connected to Earth, define their roles and share their experiences with the environment, and take an international feminist approach.

Bella Abzug (Library of Congress)

Document Text

. . . I would like to focus your attention on Earth's most valuable and most neglected natural resource: women. We are more than half the world's population. In myth, tradition and history, we have been identified with Mother Nature, the nurturing female, creator of life, spirit of the Earth's bounty, capricious and unpredictable in her rule over natural forces. It is an image that has been pleasing to many male philosophers, writers and leaders because, by contrast, it assigns to the male sex dominion over the intellect, rationality, science and technology as well as the power—or should I say hubris—to tame and control nature in the name of progress for humankind.

As we now know, that has not worked out very well because much of what has been done in the name of progress and growth and development has been done without much regard for the effects on human beings—women, men and children—on water, air and soil, on our delicately balanced, intricately interconnected global ecology.

As a feminist and a mother, I fully value women's roles as creators of life and caretakers of family and home. These are not the only things we do, nor are they what every woman does. But almost everything we do is related to the trinity, or ABCs, of Our Common Future—environment, sustainable development and population.

All over the developing world, women interact most closely with the environment—as farmers, stock breeders, suppliers of fuel and water. They are the managers—and often the preservers—of natural resources. According to a UN estimate, women account for over half the food produced in developing countries, and for more than three-fourths of the family food supply in Africa. As many as one-third of rural households are headed by women, with women increasingly making decisions on production, land use, fertilizers, pesticides—that affect the environment in so many ways.

Women are not only land managers but innovators in crop use and monitors of plant species. Women are also primary users of water in agriculture. They have a compelling interest in the availability and good quality of water supplies. In many societies, women are also responsible for the care and maintenance of trees. They spend precious hours walking enormous distances to gather wood for fuel, for heating and cooking. Forests also provide them with fodder, medicinal plants, wild fruits, and raw materials. As major users of forests, women are sensitive to their value and aware of the need to limit the rate of exploitation so that forests can be regenerated and preserved for future generations.

In industrialized as well as developing economies, [where] factories, offices and communities are situated near toxic dumps, women are exposed to a variety of environmental hazards and pollutants. One constant is that their work is undervalued and underpaid. As a result, women and their children are the most numerous and poorest of the poor. They are victimized by hunger, illiteracy, poor health, scarce social and technical services and denial of birth control services to those who want and need them, although three different UN conferences have agreed that family planning is a human right. Because infant mortality in developing countries is ten times that of the industrialized nations, women in those countries have many more pregnancies to replace babies lost. Therefore, maternal mortality rates are two hundred times higher than those in developed countries. And every year fifteen million babies die from illnesses related to malnutrition, lack of sanitation or similar preventable situations.

Women, however, are not just victims. We are thinkers, organizers, and activists. We are part of a worldwide women's movement that has brought into every nation of the world, no matter how poor or oppressed, the message that women can work together to take control of our lives and to bring our collective experience, wisdom, and numbers into the areas where the policies and decisions are being made about the future of our planet. . . .

And that brings me to the crux of the matter. Women are both affected by and effectors of the environmental crisis. We must be part—a central part—of the solution. Our views on economic justice, human rights, reproduction and the achievement of peace—all elements of the environment/development crisis—must be heard at local, national, and international forums wherever policies and decisions are made that can affect the future of life on our planet. . . .

In 1989, the Women's Foreign Policy Council, of which I am co-chair, initiated a Women and the Environment Program. We circulated a Pledge of Allegiance to the Family of Earth and a Women's Declaration of Interdependence, saying that whenever and wherever people meet to decide the fate of the planet, it is women's intention to participate in an equal footing with full and fair representation, equivalent to our number and kind on Earth. We held briefings for leaders of major women's organizations on environmental issues, and sent a letter to President Bush signed by more than a hundred distinguished women leaders and environmental activists, asking that he meet with us to hear our views and offering our help. To date, there has been no response. . . .

At our World Women's Congress for a Healthy Planet, we will seek to bring together a broadly representative gathering of a thousand or more women, from every part of the globe. Briefly, we want to spotlight women's expertise, leadership skills, roles and need for support in environmental protection and sustainable development. We want to tell the world about the many women's "success stories" in safeguarding the environment and reaching self-sufficiency. We want to develop a Women's Environmental Action Agenda to present to the 1992 UN conference, parallel meetings—such as the proposed Congress of the People of Earth—and to official and unofficial policy-making groups for the rest of the decade. . . .

Some of you may have been at the UN Decade of Women conferences in Nairobi in 1985. That was where global feminism came of age—a symbol of sisterhood, of international women's networks, of our hopes for a better, fairer, safer world.

Glossary

developing countries: a poor agricultural country that is seeking to become more advanced economically and socially

fodder: food, especially dried hay or feed, for cattle and other livestock

Short-Answer Questions

1. Abzug argues that women need to lead the fight for environmental justice. How does she make that argument in this speech? What does she say women and the earth have in common, and how do those commonalities support her argument about women leading the environmental movement?

2. How does Abzug deal with the tension between women as "victims" of environmental injustices and her argument that women are the "thinkers, organizers, and activists" leading the environmental movement? Do you see any contradiction between those two views of the relationship between women and the environment? Can you resolve this contradiction? Please explain.

3. What do you think are some of the barriers that prevent people from coming together to address global issues like climate change? Do you think that Abzug's advocacy of ecofeminism, or global feminist activism on behalf of the environment, is an effective way to overcome some of these barriers? How so?

Sandra Day O'Connor: "Portia's Progress"

Author Sandra Day O'Connor **Date** 1991 **Document Type** Speeches/Addresses	**Significance** Illustrates how O'Connor viewed her role as the Supreme Court's first female justice and what influence she thought being a woman should have on judicial decision making

Overview

In 1981, Sandra Day O'Connor became the first woman appointed to the United States Supreme Court, where she served until 2006. Through her wide-ranging career, Justice O'Connor personally witnessed the evolution of the legal world from a time when a top Stanford Law School graduate could gain employment only as a legal secretary to one in which the law has more thoroughly protected women's rights. She also witnessed the development of what she identifies as a "new feminism," which, in contrast to traditional feminism, focuses less on seeking equality between the sexes and more on celebrating certain inherent differences between women and men. In this lecture, delivered on the 100th anniversary of New York University School

of Law's admission of women, Justice O'Connor outlines the Supreme Court's jurisprudence in the area of women's rights and takes on the "new feminism," calling it a throwback to the "myths we have struggled to put behind us." Justice O'Connor is critical of the insinuation that women practicing law, for example, will reach different verdicts or conclusions simply because they are women. This critique is outlined in her speech, in which she also notes the difficulties women faced in pursuing legal occupations and outlines their victories in helping eliminate sex-based discrimination. The title of the speech comes from Shakespeare's play *The Merchant of Venice*. Portia in the story is an intelligent woman who must camouflage herself as a man to practice law.

Sandra Day O'Connor (Library of Congress)

Document Text

Most of the women legal pioneers faced a profession and a society that espoused what has been called "The Cult of Domesticity," a view that women were by nature different from men. Women were said to be fitted for motherhood and home life, compassionate, selfless, gentle, moral, and pure. Their minds were attuned to art and religion, not logic. Men, on the other hand, were fitted by nature for competition and intellectual discovery in the world, battle-hardened, shrewd, authoritative, and tough-minded.

Women were thought to be ill-qualified for adversarial litigation because it required sharp logic and shrewd negotiation, as well as exposure to the unjust and immoral. In 1875, the Wisconsin Supreme Court told Lavinia Goodell that she could not be admitted to the state bar. The Chief Justice declared that the practice of law was unfit for the female character. To expose women to the brutal, repulsive, and obscene events of courtroom life, he said, would shock man's reverence for womanhood and relax the public's sense of decency. . . .

[In its jurisprudence], the Court has [come to look] with a somewhat jaundiced eye at the loose-fitting generalizations, myths, and archaic stereotypes that previously kept women at home. Instead, the Court has often asked employers to look to whether the particular person involved, male or female, is capable of doing the job, not whether women in general are more or less capable than men. . . .

The gender differences currently cited are surprisingly similar to stereotypes from years past. Women attorneys are more likely to seek to mediate disputes than litigate them. Women attorneys are more likely to focus on resolving a client's problem than on vindicating a position. Women attorneys are more likely to sacrifice career advancement for family obligations. Women attorneys are more concerned with public service or fostering community than with individual achievement. Women judges are more likely to emphasize context and deemphasize general principles. Women judges are more compassionate. And so forth.

This "New Feminism" is interesting, but troubling, precisely because it so nearly echoes the Victorian myth of the "True Woman" that kept women out of law for so long. It is a little chilling to compare these suggestions to Clarence Darrow's assertion that women are too kind and warmhearted to be shining lights at the bar. . . .

Today, while many women juggle both profession and home admirably, it is nonetheless true that time spent at home is time that cannot be billed to clients or used to make contacts at social or professional organizations. As a result, women still may face what has been called a "mommy track" or a "glass ceiling" in the legal profession—a delayed or blocked ascent to partnership or management status due to family responsibilities. Women who do not wish to be left behind sometimes are faced with a hard choice. Some give up family life in order to attain their career aspirations. Many talented young women lawyers decide that the demands of a career require delaying family responsibilities at the very time in their lives when bearing children is physically easiest. I myself chose to try to have and enjoy my family and to resume my career path somewhat later. . . .

The question of when equality requires accommodating differences is one with which the Court will continue to struggle. I think in recent cases the Court has acknowledged, along with the "New Feminism," that sometimes to treat men and women exactly the same is to treat them differently, at least with respect to pregnancy. Women do have the gift of bearing children, a gift that needs to be accommodated in the working world. However, in allowing for this difference, we must always remember that we risk a return to the myth of the "True Woman" that blocked the career paths of many generations of women.

I would hope that your generation of attorneys will find new ways to balance family and professional responsibilities between men and women, recognizing gender differences in a way that promotes equality and frees both women and men from traditional role limitations. You must reopen the velvet curtain between work and home that was drawn closed in the Victorian era. Not only women, but men too, have missed out through the division of work and home. As more women enjoy the challenges of a legal career, more men have blessings to garner from taking extra time to nurture and teach their children.

If we are to continue to find ways to repair the existing difference between professional women and men with regard to family responsibilities, however, we must not allow the "New Feminism" complete sway. For example, asking whether women attorneys speak with a "different voice" than men do is a question that is both dangerous and unanswerable. It again sets up the polarity between the feminine virtues of homemaking and the masculine virtues of breadwinning. It threatens, indeed, to establish new categories of "women's work" to which women are confined and from which men are excluded.

Instead, my sense is that as women continue to take on a full role in the professions, learning from those professional experiences, as from their experiences as homemakers, the virtues derived from both kinds of learning will meld. The "different voices" will teach each other. I myself have been thankful for the opportunity to experience a rich and fulfilling career as well as a close and supportive family life. I know the lessons I have learned in each have aided me in the other. As a result, I can revel both in the growth of my granddaughter and in the legal subtleties of the free exercise clause.

Do women judges decide cases differently by virtue of being women? I would echo the answer of my colleague, Justice Jeanne Coyne of the Supreme Court of Oklahoma, who responded that "a wise old man and a wise old woman reach the same conclusion." This should be our aspiration: that, whatever our gender or background, we all may become wise—wise through our different struggles and different victories, wise through work and play, profession and family.

Glossary

adversarial: involving two people or two sides who oppose each other

New Feminism: emphasizes the differences between women and men rather than their rights to equal treatment and opportunity

Short-Answer Questions

1. If "a wise old man and a wise old woman reach the same conclusion" when deciding a case, as Justice O'Connor suggested, why should it matter if there are female justices on the Supreme Court?

2. Is Justice O'Connor correct in saying that the idea that women and men might decide cases differently represents a threat to the political, social, and legal gains made by women in the twentieth century? Why or why not?

3. How does Justice O'Connor depict the "new feminism" and traditional gender role ideologies? Please explain.

Violence Against Women Act

Author Jack Brooks	**Significance** The first piece of federal legislation designed to end violence against women
Date 1994	
Document Type Legislative	

Overview

The Violence Against Women Act (VAWA) of 1994 was introduced to Congress in 1993 by Rep. Jack Brooks (D-TX). It received bipartisan support and was passed by both the House and the Senate that year. President Bill Clinton signed it into law in September 1994 as part of the Violent Crime Control and Law Enforcement Act of 1994, a set of laws commonly known as the 1994 Crime Bill.

VAWA marked the first federal legislation that was aimed at stopping violence targeting women. Women's groups had worked tirelessly to pressure Washington to pass much-needed legislation to protect women, and lobby groups had long been critical of state governments for failing to address the issue of violence toward women. Provisions under the act addressed rape and assault, among other issues. The act also focused on methods of prevention, included funding for victim services, and provided for educational services, including training for local officials about how to handle matters surrounding violent acts committed toward women. Every state was required to enforce protections made under the act.

President Bill Clinton signed the Violence Against Women Act into law in September 1994. (Wikimedia Commons)

Document Text

Violence Against Women Act of 1993—Title I: Safe Streets for Women—Safe Streets for Women Act of 1993—Subtitle A: Federal Penalties for Sex Crimes—Amends the Federal criminal code to: (1) authorize judges to increase sentences for repeat sex offenders to up to twice that otherwise authorized by statute; and (2) require the U.S. Sentencing Commission to implement such amendment by recommending to the Congress amendments, if appropriate, in the sentencing guidelines applicable to criminal sexual abuse. . . .

Subtitle B: Law Enforcement and Prosecution Grants to Reduce Violent Crimes Against Women—Amends the Omnibus Crime Control and Safe Streets Act of 1968 to require the Director of the Bureau of Justice Assistance to make grants to areas of high intensity crime against women. Authorizes the Director to make general grants to: (1) States to reduce violent crimes against women; and (2) Indian tribes to reduce violent crimes against women in Indian country.

Subtitle C: Safety for Women in Public Transit and Public Parks—Amends the Urban Mass Transportation Act of 1964 to direct the Secretary of Transportation, from funds authorized under existing provisions, to make capital grants for the prevention of crime and to increase security in existing and future public transportation systems. Authorizes the Secretary to make grants and loans to States and local public bodies to increase the safety of public transportation through lighting, camera surveillance, security phones, or other projects. Directs the Secretary to provide grants and loans to study ways to reduce violent crimes against women in public transit through better design or operation of public transit systems. . . .

Mandates that: (1) the alleged victim be given an opportunity to be heard regarding the danger posed by the defendant in proceedings to determine whether a defendant charged with committing such an offense shall be released pending trial or to determine conditions of such release; and (2) a court order restitution to the victim of such an offense.

Requires, provided certain conditions are met, that a protection order issued by the court of one State be accorded full faith and credit by the court of another State.

Subtitle C: Arrest in Spousal Abuse Cases—Amends the FVPSA to authorize the Secretary of HHS to make grants, with regard to spousal abuse, to: (1) implement pro-arrest programs and policies in police departments and improve case tracking; (2) centralize police enforcement, prosecution, or judicial responsibility for cases in one group of officers, prosecutors, or judges; (3) coordinate computer tracking systems to ensure communication between police, prosecutors, and both criminal and family courts; and (4) educate judges to improve judicial handling of cases.

Subtitle D: Domestic Violence, Family Support, and Shelter Grants—Directs the Secretary of HHS to make grants to support projects and programs relating to domestic violence and other criminal and unlawful acts that particularly affect women. Amends the FVPSA to authorize appropriations to carry out that Act. . . .

Title III: Civil Rights—Civil Rights Remedies for Gender-Motivated Violence Act—Declares that all persons within the United States shall have the right to be free from crimes of violence motivated by the victim's gender. Makes any person, including a person who acts under color of any statute, ordinance, regulation, custom, or usage of any State, who deprives another of such right, liable to the injured party in an action for compensatory and punitive damages, injunctive and declaratory relief, and such other relief as the court deems appropriate. Sets forth provisions regarding: (1) concurrent and pendent jurisdiction; and (2) limitations on removal. . . .

Title VI: Violence Against Women Act Improvements—Amends the Federal criminal code to provide for pretrial detention in sex offense cases.

(Sec. 602) Increases penalties for sex offenses against victims under age 16.

(Sec. 603) Amends: (1) the Victims' Rights and Restitution Act of 1990 to require the Attorney General to authorize the Director of the Office of Victims of Crime to provide for the payment of the cost of up to two tests for human immunodeficiency virus for a sexual assault victim in the 12 months following the assault and a counseling

session; and (2) the Federal criminal code to authorize the restitution of victims of sex offenses.

(Sec. 605) Provides for the enforcement of restitution orders through suspension of Federal benefits.

(Sec. 606) Adds a Federal Rule of Evidence that, in a criminal case in which a person is accused of a sex offense, evidence is not admissible to show that the alleged victim invited or provoked the commission of the offense.

(Sec. 607) Requires the Attorney General to provide for a national baseline study on campus sexual assault. Authorizes appropriations.

(Sec. 608) Directs the Attorney General to: (1) prepare a report on the status of battered women's syndrome as a medical and psychological condition and on its effect in criminal trials; (2) conduct a study of the means by which abusive spouses may obtain information concerning the addresses or locations of estranged or former spouses; and (3) complete a study of problems of recordkeeping of criminal complaints involving domestic violence.

(Sec. 611) Requires the Judicial Conference of the United States to: (1) review and make recommendations, and report to the Congress, regarding the advisability of creating Federal rules of professional conduct for lawyers in Federal cases involving sexual misconduct; and (2) complete a study of, and submit to the Congress recommendations for amending, Federal Rule of Evidence 404 as it affects the admission of evidence of a defendant's prior sex crimes in cases involving sexual misconduct.

(Sec. 613) Authorizes the Attorney General to award supplementary grants to States adopting effective laws relating to sexual violence. Authorizes appropriations.

Glossary

Omnibus Crime Control and Safe Streets Act of 1968: law passed by Congress to assist state and local governments in reducing the incidence of crime and to increase the effectiveness, fairness, and coordination of law enforcement and criminal justice systems at all levels of government

Urban Mass Transportation Act of 1964: law passed by Congress to provide additional assistance for the development of comprehensive and coordinated mass transportation systems, both public and private, in metropolitan and other urban areas, and for other purposes

Short-Answer Questions

1. Does the VAWA offer enough protection to individuals against gender-based violence? Why or why not?

2. In your opinion, are there any challenges or weaknesses that you can see that may make enforcing the VAWA difficult?

3. Covert violence is defined as violence that is kept hidden or is not acknowledged. Does the VAWA protect individuals from covert violence? Explain.

United States v. Virginia

Author	Significance
Ruth Bader Ginsburg	Recognized that the inherent gender discrimination in the Virginia Military Institute's male-only admission policy violated the Fourteenth Amendment, thus making a progressive step toward gender equality
Date	
1996	
Document Type	
Legal	

Overview

Ruth Bader Ginsburg's early commitment to women's rights and equality was perhaps forged when the dean of the Harvard Law School asked her and her eight female classmates why they were taking up seats at the school that rightly should be occupied by men. If that were not enough, she was unable to win a clerkship for a U.S. Supreme Court justice because of her gender, and she did not receive a job offer from the New York City firm where she clerked during the summer before her final year in law school. Then, after she took a teaching position at the Rutgers University Law School, she discovered that she was being paid less than male colleagues with the same rank.

These circumstances motivated Ginsburg's preoccupation with civil rights generally and the rights of women in particular. During her academic years, when she also served as counsel for the American Civil Liberties Union, she took on a number of sex discrimination cases with a view to seeing gender equality afforded the same protections as racial equality under the equal protection clause of the Fourteenth Amendment. Questions of sexual equality continued to face Ginsburg during her tenure on the Supreme Court. In *United States v. Virginia* (1996), the Court struck down the Virginia Military Institute's long-standing male-only admission policy. Writing for the majority, Ginsburg stated that the school had not offered a persuasive argument to justify its sex-based discrimination and therefore violated the equal protection clause.

Ruth Bader Ginsburg wrote the majority opinion.
(Supreme Court of the United States)

Document Text

Founded in 1839, VMI [Virginia Military Institute] is today the sole single-sex school among Virginia's 15 public institutions of higher learning. VMI's distinctive mission is to produce "citizen-soldiers," men prepared for leadership in civilian life and in military service. VMI pursues this mission through pervasive training of a kind not available anywhere else in Virginia. Assigning prime place to character development, VMI uses an "adversative method" modeled on English public schools and once characteristic of military instruction. VMI constantly endeavors to instill physical and mental discipline in its cadets and impart to them a strong moral code. . . .

In the two years preceding the lawsuit, the District Court noted, VMI had received inquiries from 347 women, but had responded to none of them. "[S]ome women, at least," the court said, "would want to attend the school if they had the opportunity." The court further recognized that, with recruitment, VMI could "achieve at least 10 percent female enrollment"—"a sufficient 'critical mass' to provide the female cadets with a positive educational experience." And it was also established that "some women are capable of all of the individual activities required of VMI cadets." In addition, experts agreed that if VMI admitted women, "the VMI ROTC experience would become a better training program from the perspective of the armed forces, because it would provide training in dealing with a mixed-gender army." . . .

The parties agreed that "some women can meet the physical standards now imposed on men," and the court was satisfied that "neither the goal of producing citizen soldiers nor VMI's implementing methodology is inherently unsuitable to women." The Court of Appeals, however, accepted the District Court's finding that "at least these three aspects of VMI's program—physical training, the absence of privacy, and the adversative approach—would be materially affected by coeducation." Remanding the case, the appeals court assigned to Virginia, in the first instance, responsibility for selecting a remedial course. The court suggested these options for the State: Admit women to VMI; establish parallel institutions or programs; or abandon state support, leaving VMI free to pursue its policies as a private institution. . . .

In 1971, for the first time in our Nation's history, this Court ruled in favor of a woman who complained that her State had denied her the equal protection of its laws. Since *Reed*, the Court has repeatedly recognized that neither federal nor state government acts compatibly with the equal protection principle when a law or official policy denies to women, simply because they are women, full citizenship stature—equal opportunity to aspire, achieve, participate in and contribute to society based on their individual talents and capacities.

Without equating gender classifications, for all purposes, to classifications based on race or national origin, the Court, in post-*Reed* decisions, has carefully inspected official action that closes a door or denies opportunity to women (or to men). To summarize the Court's current directions for cases of official classification based on gender: Focusing on the differential treatment or denial of opportunity for which relief is sought, the reviewing court must determine whether the proffered justification is "exceedingly persuasive." The burden of justification is demanding and it rests entirely on the State. The State must show "at least that the [challenged] classification serves 'important governmental objectives and that the discriminatory means employed' are 'substantially related to the achievement of those objectives.'" The justification must be genuine, not hypothesized or invented post hoc in response to litigation. And it must not rely on overbroad generalizations about the different talents, capacities, or preferences of males and females.

The heightened review standard our precedent establishes does not make sex a proscribed classification. Supposed "inherent differences" are no longer accepted as a ground for race or national origin classifications. Physical differences between men and women, however, are enduring: "[T]he two sexes are not fungible; a community made up exclusively of one [sex] is different from a community composed of both."

"Inherent differences" between men and women, we have come to appreciate, remain cause for celebration, but not for denigration of the members of either sex or for artificial constraints on an individual's opportunity. Sex classifications may be used to compensate women "for particular economic disabilities [they have] suffered," to "promot[e] equal employment opportunity," to advance full development of the talent and capacities of our Nation's people. But such classifications may not be used, as they once were, to create or perpetuate the legal, social, and economic inferiority of women.

Measuring the record in this case against the review standard just described, we conclude that Virginia has shown no "exceedingly persuasive justification" for excluding all women from the citizen-soldier training afforded by VMI. . . .

Single-sex education affords pedagogical benefits to at least some students, Virginia emphasizes, and that reality is uncontested in this litigation. Similarly, it is not disputed that diversity among public educational institutions can serve the public good. But Virginia has not shown that VMI was established, or has been maintained, with a view to diversifying, by its categorical exclusion of women, educational opportunities within the State. In cases of this genre, our precedent instructs that "benign" justifications proffered in defense of categorical exclusions will not be accepted automatically; a tenable justification must describe actual state purposes, not rationalizations for actions in fact differently grounded. . . .

VMI, too, offers an educational opportunity no other Virginia institution provides, and the school's "prestige"—associated with its success in developing "citizen-soldiers"—is unequaled. Virginia has closed this facility to its daughters and, instead, has devised for them a "parallel program," with a faculty less impressively credentialed and less well paid, more limited course offerings, fewer opportunities for military training and for scientific specialization. VMI, beyond question, "possesses to a far greater degree" than the VWIL program "those qualities which are incapable of objective measurement but which make for greatness in a . . . school," including "position and influence of the alumni, standing in the community, traditions and prestige." Women seeking and fit for a VMI-quality education cannot be offered anything less, under the State's obligation to afford them genuinely equal protection.

Glossary

equal protection principle: reference to the equal protection clause of the Fourteenth Amendment, which mandates that all people be treated equally according to the law

pervasive: spreading widely throughout an area or a group of people

Reed: reference to *Reed v. Reed* (1971), which marked the first time the Supreme Court applied the equal protection clause of the Fourteenth Amendment to strike down a law that discriminated against women

Short-Answer Questions

1. Taking into account the equal protection clause of the Fourteenth Amendment, how might the VMI adjust its program once women were admitted to make it more inclusive?

2. The VMI proposed a separate program for women. Looking at the majority ruling, why do you think that might violate the equal protection clause?

3. The majority ruling found that there were benefits to both single-sex education and diverse education. Taking into account the ruling, do you think an argument could be made for both at VMI and similar public institutions?

Patsy Mink:
Speech on the 25th
Anniversary of Title IX

Author Patsy Mink **Date** 1997 **Document Type** Speeches/Addresses	**Significance** Celebrates Title IX, which prohibits sex-based discrimination in any school or educational program that receives funding from the federal government

Overview

The Civil Rights Act of 1964 prohibited discrimination on the basis of race, sex, and religion, but only as it pertained to public accommodations and employment; it did not extend protections to people at educational institutions. Title IX of the Civil Rights Act was added in 1972 to fill in the gap. On Title IX's twenty-fifth anniversary, Congresswoman Patsy Mink of Hawaii gave this speech commemorating the historic law, which she was influential in expanding even after its initial passage.

Mink devoted her career to expanding the rights of women, especially related to educational freedom. In 1972, she

helped sponsor Title IX, which amended the Higher Education Act of 1965. The Patsy T. Mink Equal Opportunity in Education Act, as Title IX was renamed in 2002, was a symbol of the work Congresswoman Mink had advocated for and accomplished. Mink was also influential in introducing the Women's Educational Equity Act of 1974, which funded gender equity in schools. The act benefited women as it created new paths toward employment and education. It also tackled negative gender images that were common in schools at the time. Since its twenty-fifth anniversary in 1997, Title IX has gone through numerous changes and challenges, but at its core Title IX is still aimed at promoting equality and equity.

Patsy Mink in 1993
(Library of Congress)

Document Text

Today marks the 25th anniversary of Title IX of the Education Act Amendments of 1972 which prohibits sex discrimination in educational institutions receiving Federal funds. To commemorate the 25th anniversary of Title IX, the gentleman from Michigan [Mr. Bonior], the gentlewoman from New Jersey [Mrs. Roukema] and I along with 61 other cosponsors have introduced a concurrent resolution which celebrates the accomplishments of Title IX, supporting efforts to continue pursuing the goals of educational opportunity for women and girls. I will ask that the resolution be printed at the end of my special order this evening.

Since its enactment Title IX has opened the doors of educational opportunity to literally millions of girls and women across the Nation. Title IX helped tear down inequitable admission policies, increase opportunities for women in nontraditional fields of study such as math and science, law and medicine, improve vocational educational opportunities for women, reduce discrimination against pregnant students and teen mothers, protect female students from sexual harassment in our schools and increase athletic opportunities for girls and women.

As a member of the Education and Labor Committee in 1972, I helped to craft Title IX and worked diligently throughout the years to promote this law and fight against efforts to weaken its impact. I certainly consider Title IX one of my most significant accomplishments while I served in Congress from 1965 until 1977.

We have heard so much in recent years about the accomplishments of Title IX, particularly in the area of athletics, and many do not realize the history of this legislation and the battles that were fought to keep this law intact. On the occasion of the 25th anniversary of Title IX, I thought it would be appropriate to share this history and to recount its origins, its battles and its achievements.

The origins of Title IX began with a series of hearings on the House Education and Labor Committee beginning in the late 1960s and in 1970. In particular, there was a hearing conducted by Congresswoman Edith Green who was the chair then of the Special Subcommittee on Education which dealt with higher education matters.

In June of 1970 the subcommittee held a hearing on legislation introduced by the chair Edith Green, H.R. 16098 to amend Title VI of the Civil Rights Act of 1964, which included a prohibition against sex discrimination in any program or activity receiving Federal financial assistance.

We have to put this initiative in the context of the times. It was right around that time that there was this big push for ERA, the Equals Rights Amendment. The women's movement was very active, pursuing all avenues to gain equal rights and protections in the law. Representative Green's bill would have provided that protection under the Civil Rights Act.

At the hearing on July 3, 1970, Assistant Attorney General for Civil Rights Jerris Leonard testified before the subcommittee stating that, quote, "while we are not able to support this language, we suggest an alternative." He suggested that the committee should not amend Title VI of the Civil Rights Act, but enact separate legislation to prohibit sex discrimination in education only. This is the genesis of Title IX.

The House Education and Labor Committee had a large body of evidence of discrimination against girls and women in our educational system. Since the time I came to Congress in 1965 we began systematic hearings on textbooks to illustrate the discrimination against girls, women, and also the ethnic minorities.

We scrutinized the textbooks. We looked at the films and the books and other kinds of brochures that were being produced by, yes, our U.S. Department of Education, Office of Education. We scrutinized the admission policies and vocational education courses which taught girls home economics, and essentially there were cooking courses to prepare girls for homemakers, while the boys learned skills in order to enter into careers and to sustain their future ambitions. We had to fight in all areas to open up opportunities for women. We had to fight for equal participation in the poverty program, in the Job Corps Center.

So the proposal of the Assistant Attorney General to focus legislation to prohibit discrimination in education was a logical step for the committee to take. We had considerable debates. The Committee on Education finally reported the legislation in 1971, which then led to negotiations with the Senate and the conference committee that finally yielded Title IX, which is in its historic celebration today for its 25th anniversary.

Glossary

Education Act Amendments of 1972: legislation enacted in 1972 to amend the Vocational Education Act of 1963, the Higher Education Act of 1965, the Elementary and Secondary Education Act of 1965, the General Education Provisions Act, and related acts

scrutinized: examined or inspected closely and thoroughly

Short-Answer Questions

1. Explain how the women's movement influenced the passing of Title IX.

2. Are there limitations to Title IX? If there are any, what are they? How have these loopholes affected Title IX as a whole?

3. Think about modern-day arguments surrounding transgender students and school athletics. What influence might these issues have had on the scope of Title IX under the Civil Rights Amendment?

Billie Jean King: Commencement Address for University of Massachusetts, Amherst

Author	Significance
Billie Jean King	Recognized the impact of Title IX on women's sports and urged that the fight for equality in sports must be taken up by everyone
Date	
2000	
Document Type	
Speeches/Addresses	

Overview

As participants in the women's movement called attention to the societal inequalities between men and women in the early 1970s, one of the areas they addressed was women's sports. The years 1972 and 1973 were pivotal ones as *Roe v. Wade* was decided, making abortion legal in the United States; the Vietnam War was still ongoing; and Richard Nixon was under investigation in the Watergate scandal. In the midst of this was a tennis match between Billie Jean King and Bobby Riggs dubbed the Battle of the Sexes, in which King upset Riggs. For King and women in sports, the match had a personal meaning. It was about shifting the view of women not belonging in sports to that of women not only belonging in sports but deserving of equal treatment and pay as men.

In her commencement address, delivered in May 2000, King evokes the history of the University of Massachusetts, Amherst and its compliance with Title IX, which prohibits sex-based discrimination in any school that receives federal funding. Before Title IX was passed as part of the Education Amendments of 1972, the National Collegiate Athletic Association (NCAA) remained disinterested in women's sports and were not required to support it. Even after its passage, many colleges neglected to comply with Title IX, arguing that because they did not receive federal funds, they were not required to abide by the regulation. King argues in her speech that the fight for equality must continue until support for men's and women's sports is more equitable.

Billie Jean King in 1978
(Lynn Gilbert)

Document Text

June 23, 1972. Title IX. It was the first time a woman ever got an athletic scholarship to college. In 1972. Men had been getting them for over 100 years. You can be proud to be at the University of Massachusetts here at Amherst because you are among a handful of institutions that are fully compliant with Title IX. And the University achieves this in women's sports while not reducing any sports from the men's program. That is awesome, because only a handful of universities throughout this country are in compliance. So I thank you very much for that.

Without Title IX, our women would have never won the gold medals in the 1996 Olympics in Atlanta. We won softball. We won women's gymnastics. We won basketball. And we won soccer. And last year we won the World Cup in soccer for the women because of Title IX.

I'll fast forward. Now we're in 1973. We were just in 1972. Title IX, remember? Now we're in 1973. Let me set the stage. We're at the height of the women's movement. We were not burning bras, but wanting equal opportunity for women and men. Vietnam was finally calming down, we just passed *Roe v. Wade*, Watergate was heating up, we had no microwaves, we had no faxes, we had no cable TV, and personal computers? Forget it! Hadn't been thought of. Women were making 59 cents on the dollar in 1973, and the reason I played Bobby Riggs is because Margaret Port, the number-one player in the world that year, from Australia, had lost to him, on Mother's Day. It was called the Mother's Day Massacre. She lost so badly that I finally had to play the hustler Bobby Riggs, the former number-one tennis player in the world. And that match was not about tennis; it was about social change. It was about changing the hearts and minds of people to believe that women could chew gum and walk at the same time.

That we deserved an opportunity to compete, an opportunity to play. We deserved it. Now we're up to 75 cents on the dollar. Such a deal. We deserve a 25-cent discount every time we go shopping.

And the young men who experienced that match back in 1973, I call you the first generation of men of the women's movement. You are the first generation of men who insist that their daughters have equal opportunities with their sons. And the most important words that have helped me in life when things have gone right or when things have gone wrong are "accept responsibility."

"Accept responsibility."

And I'll give you an idea. Like in tennis, every ball that comes to me is a decision. Every ball that comes to me is a decision. Do I slice it, do I hit cross-court, do I hit topspin, do I hit sidespin, do I lob? What do I do? But I have to accept responsibility for that. And that's where sports teaches us to put it on the line, so to speak, and live it. And here remember one thing. It's everyone's responsibility to lead, to honor, and to fight, for everyone's basic rights, for equality. Regardless of our gender, our age, our race, our religion, our appearance, sexual orientation or our abilities.

So dream, act, and lead. And congratulations to you! Yes! Massachusetts, yes, you're the best! Yes! Go for it!

Glossary

faxes: devices that send and receive printed pages or images over telephone lines

Title IX: passed as part of the Education Amendments of 1972, which prohibits sex-based discrimination in any school or other education program that receives funding from the federal government

Watergate: a scandal involving the burglary of Democratic National Committee headquarters at the Watergate complex in Washington, D.C., in 1972 that was tied to President Richard Nixon and eventually led to his resignation

Short-Answer Questions

1. Explain how Billie Jean King uses sports as a conduit to evoke broader issues surrounding gender discrimination.

2. How does Billie Jean King situate the Mother's Day Massacre within the backdrop of what was occurring in the United States at the time?

3. Who is the intended audience for this speech? Why do you think so?

Chapter 10

Reproductive Rights in the United States

The history of women's reproductive rights in America is long and twisted, with many different branches and roots. The modern struggle, however, seems to have begun with the passage of the Comstock Act in 1873. Anthony Comstock (1844–1915) was a U.S. postal inspector in New York, a fervent and activist Christian—some would call him a fanatic—and one of the leaders of the New York Society for the Suppression of Vice. Comstock, a Civil War veteran, was fixated on eliminating obscene literature and pornography, but his definition of these categories was unusually broad. He took aim at all manner of items that could be considered sexual, but he also crusaded against birth control and extramarital sex, all of which had deep roots in American society. In 1873 Comstock began a concerted campaign in Congress for a law that would allow the federal government to police American sexuality. The key forces in this crusade would be the Post Office and the U.S. court system. The Comstock Act, which was revised and strengthened over the next two decades, eventually allowed postal inspectors the right to bar certain materials, including contraceptives or literature about contraceptive and sexual practices, from the mail, going as far as allowing postal inspectors to open private mail.

Margaret Sanger Advocates for Birth Control

This was the situation that confronted nurse Margaret Sanger (1879–1966) when she began working with poor women in the Lower East Side slums of New York City in 1912. The scenes of squalor she saw there led her to recognize that unplanned births significantly contributed to urban poverty, which she recorded years later in a chapter in her memoirs entitled "Awakening and Revolt" (1931). She began a long, concerted campaign to bring birth control information to these women, beginning in 1914. By 1919 she had already suffered arrest for her advocacy of birth control. In that year, she published "Birth Control and Racial Betterment" (1919), a controversial article that appeared in the *Birth Control Review* and that advocated for links between birth control and the then-popular eugenics movement. Eugenics was later discarded as a pseudoscience; thanks to Sanger's efforts, however, birth control remained a significant movement in American society.

Sanger not only wrote about birth control, but she also took action to bring devices and methods to women across the nation. In 1916 she opened the first public clinic in the United States dedicated to advising women on birth control and to making contraceptive devices available to them. In 1921 she founded the American Birth Control League, the forerunner of Planned Parenthood.

Right to Contraception

A woman's right to contraception was established by the Supreme Court in *Griswold v. Connecticut* (1965). The state of Connecticut had passed an anti-contraceptive law in 1879, but it was not challenged until eighty-five years later. A gynecologist at Yale, C. Lee Buxton, partnered with the state chapter of Planned Parenthood, led by Estelle Griswold, to open a birth control clinic in New Haven. They were arrested and convicted under the 1879 statute, but Griswold appealed the conviction to the Supreme Court. When the case came before the Court, the justices ruled 7–2 in favor of Griswold. The case established a constitutional right to reproductive counseling and access to contraception.

Sanger's brief involvement with the eugenics movement had darker consequences for women of color or women who were deemed mentally unfit to bear children. In various states, women who were regarded as mentally disabled were occasionally sentenced to undergo enforced sterilization. Occasionally one of these women sued, and eventually forced sterilizations came before the federal courts. One of the earliest was *Buck v. Bell* (1927), in which the state of Virginia sentenced Carrie Buck, a woman described by the state as "feeble-minded," to sterilization. Before the surgery could be carried out, however, a hearing had to be held in order to demonstrate due process of the law. The Court decided in favor of the defendant, with justice Oliver Wendell Holmes Jr. declaring ominously, "Three generations of imbeciles are enough."

In June 1973, two preteen Black girls from Montgomery, Alabama, Mary Alice Relf and Minnie Lee Relf, were sterilized without their consent by a federally funded clinic in the city. Their mother, who was illiterate, had signed paperwork that she could not read because she was under the impression that her daughters would receive contraceptive shots. Instead, the tubal ligation sterilization prevented either of the girls from being able to bear children. The Southern Poverty Law Center brought suit on the girls' behalf against the then-Secretary of Health, Education and Welfare Caspar Weinberger. The Court's decision in *Relf v. Weinberger* (1974) found that the secretary had violated the girls' right to procreate, a Constitutional right. In a case involving ten Mexican American women who had been sterilized without informed consent by a clinic in Los Angeles, *Madrigal v. Quilligan* (1978), the Supreme Court linked the right to procreate and to be informed about the consequences of sterilization to the right to an abortion, established four years earlier.

Access to Abortion Becomes a Flashpoint

It was the right to access a safe abortion that proved to be the most controversial legacy of Comstock's law and Sanger's crusade. Abortion rights came to define women's reproductive rights through the end of the twentieth and the beginning of the twenty-first century. In fact, as birth control became readily available throughout the second half of the twentieth century, abortion remained stubbornly illegal. Margaret Cerullo wrote about the dangers that accompanied her attempt to receive an abortion in *Hidden History: An Illegal Abortion in 1968* (1968). It was not until five years later, in the historic case of *Roe v. Wade* (1973), that the Supreme Court recognized access to abortion as a right protected by the Constitution.

Almost as soon as the decision in *Roe v. Wade* was handed down, anti-abortion protests began. In part these were fueled by conservative Christians who wanted to enshrine their vision of the sanctity of human life in law. By 1979 the opposition to *Roe v. Wade* was vocal enough that the International Campaign for Abortion Rights called for an International Day of Action, March 31, 1979, to protect women's reproductive rights and to call for those rights to be acknowledged and protected around the world.

Women's rights activists were correct to be concerned. From the 1980s into the 2020s a series of Supreme Court decisions began chipping away at the movement's foundational principles. In *Webster v. Reproductive Health Services* (1989), the Court found that the state of Missouri's restrictions on abortions were not unconstitutional—a decision that allowed those restrictions to stand. In *Planned Parenthood v. Casey* (1992), the Court found that the restrictions did not impose an undue burden on abortion clinics and physicians—and those restrictions were allowed to stand.

The End of the Roe Era

The end of the Roe era came with *Dobbs v. Jackson* (2022). That case pitted Thomas Dobbs, health officer for the state of Mississippi, against the only abortion-providing agency in the state, Jackson Women's Health Organization. The state of Mississippi had passed a law that prevented abortions after fifteen weeks of gestational age—which effectively meant the majority of abortions performed. Doctors at the Jackson clinic filed suit, challenging the law. The U.S. District Court that heard the case pointed out that there was no evidence that a fetus could survive outside the womb at fifteen weeks of age and therefore the law was unclear. When the case came before the Supreme Court in the summer of 2022, however, the justices ruled that the Constitution does not confer the right to an abortion—despite nearly fifty years of jurisprudence saying exactly the opposite. The decision effectively threw control of abortion back to the states. As of mid-2023, twenty-two states had banned abortion entirely or restricted it heavily.

Further Reading

Books

D'Emilio, John, and Estelle B. Freedman. *Intimate Matters: A History of Sexuality in America,* 2nd ed. Chicago: University of Chicago Press, 1997.

Kennedy, David M. *Birth Control in America: The Career of Margaret Sanger.* New Haven, CT: Yale University Press, 1970.

Kluchin, Rebecca M. *Fit to Be Tied: Sterilization and Reproductive Rights in America, 1950–1980.* New Brunswick, NJ: Rutgers University Press, 2009.

Regan, Leslie J. *When Abortion Was a Crime: Women, Medicine, and Law in the United States, 1867–1973.* Berkeley: University of California Press, 1997.

Solinger, Rickie. *Wake up Little Susie: Single Pregnancy and Race before* Roe v. Wade. New York: Routledge, 1992.

Weingarten, Karen. *Abortion in the American Imagination: Before Life and Choice, 1880–1940.* New Brunswick, NJ: Rutgers University Press, 2014.

Comstock Act

Author	Significance
U.S. Congress	Prohibited any so-called obscene or immoral material from being sent through the mail or the railroads, thereby restricting access to information about women's health, contraception, and abortion
Date	
1873	
Document Type	
Legislative	

Overview

The Comstock Act established the broad power of the federal government to regulate information or materials viewed as "obscene" or "immoral." Since there is no specific list of what makes something obscene or immoral, the law was interpreted and enforced very broadly. The power to enforce the Comstock Act fell under the umbrella of the U.S. Postal Service. Anything deemed obscene that was sent through the postal system—or was even *intended* to be mailed—could result in a substantial prison sentence or fine for the person who mailed it (or intended to do so). What are generally called the "Comstock laws" include the original Comstock Act plus the many similar state laws that followed.

This anti-obscenity law was named for Anthony Comstock, an anti-vice crusader in New York City in the late 1860s. Comstock began fighting against prostitution and pornography in New York by finding people and businesses to turn over to the police. He came to see "obscenity" in popular culture as a great problem, in particular contraception (methods of preventing pregnancy).

The Comstock Act defined anything aimed at preventing pregnancy as "obscene." That included not only the contraceptive devices themselves but also any information about them sent through the mail. Even distributing basic, scientific information about women's health and how women's reproductive systems work was considered obscene under this law. In the early 1900s, the Comstock Act was used to prosecute women for giving information to other women about reproductive health, including the birth control advocate Margaret Sanger.

After the Comstock Act was passed at the federal level, twenty-four states passed their own versions of the law, making the distribution of contraception or even information about contraception illegal. Connecticut passed the most extreme version in 1879, criminalizing methods of preventing pregnancy even when used by a married couple in the privacy of their own home. That law was in place until the Supreme Court overturned it in *Griswold v. Connecticut* in 1965. There was no birth control pill until almost a century after the passage of the Comstock Act, in part because of the limitations caused by the law.

The Comstock Act also forbade the distribution of any other materials deemed to be obscene, including pornography, sexual content in literature or films, and any information related to abortion. Some of what was viewed as pornography at the time would seem normal to Americans today, including photos of women wearing clothing that is commonplace in the twenty-first century. At the time the Comstock Act was passed, most people considered it obscene or immoral for women to wear pants, and even women's swimming clothes involved full-length skirts or pants that fully covered their legs. Similarly, some works of art and literature that are now considered great classics were prohibited in the United States by the Comstock Act.

The Comstock Act formed the foundation for the century of legal opposition to contraception and abortion that followed its passage in 1873. After landmark Supreme Court rulings like *Griswold v. Connecticut* and *Roe v. Wade* in the 1960s and 1970s, it was largely assumed that the Comstock Act was a relic of history. However, following the Supreme Court decision in 2022 in *Dobbs v. Jackson*, the Comstock Act has come back into play as anti-abortion activists seek to use it to prohibit sending abortion pills through the mail. The role of the Comstock Act in the twenty-first century is yet to be determined.

Anthony Comstock
(Library of Congress)

Document
An Act for the Suppression of Trade in, and Circulation of, obscene Literature and Articles of immoral Use.

That no obscene, lewd, or lascivious book, pamphlet, picture, paper, print, or other publication of an indecent character, or any article or thing designed or intended for the prevention of conception or procuring of abortion, nor any article or thing intended or adapted for any indecent or immoral use or nature, nor any written or printed card, circular, book, pamphlet, advertisement or notice of any kind giving information, directly or indirectly, where, or how, or of whom, or by what means either of the things before mentioned may be obtained or made, nor any letter upon the envelope of which, or postal-card upon which indecent or scurrilous epithets may be written or printed, shall be carried in the mail, and any person who shall knowingly deposit, or cause to be deposited, for mailing or delivery, any of the hereinbefore-mentioned articles or things, or any notice, or paper containing any advertisement relating to the aforesaid articles or things, and any person who, in pursuance of any plan or scheme for disposing of any of the hereinbefore-mentioned articles or things, shall take, or cause to be taken, from the mail any such letter or package, shall be deemed guilty of a misdemeanor, and, on conviction thereof, shall, for every offense, be fined not less than one hundred dollars nor more than five thousand dollars, or imprisoned at hard labor not less than one year nor more than ten years, or both, in the discretion of the judge.

Glossary

circular: a type of pamphlet, advertisement, or newsletter that comes out on a regular basis

obscene, lewd, or lascivious: adjectives that describe an expression of sexual desire that is seen as offensive, crude, disgusting, or indecent

scurrilous epithets: scandalous descriptions or insults; the use of foul language, curse words, or other sayings deemed to be scandalous or offensive

Short-Answer Questions

1. What did this law prevent people from legally doing in the 1870s through the mid-1900s?

2. What does this law tell you about how Americans thought about the role of women during this period?

3. How does the Comstock Act relate to the legal debates over reproductive rights in the twentieth and twenty-first centuries?

Margaret Sanger:
"Birth Control and Racial Betterment"

<table>
<tr><td>

Author
Margaret Sanger

Date
1919

Type
Essays, Reports, Manifestos

</td><td>

Significance
Advocated empowering women to decide for themselves whether and when to reproduce

</td></tr>
</table>

Overview

Margaret Sanger was a New York City nurse in 1912 when she began writing a series of articles for the *New York Call* that would be compiled into the 1916 book *What Every Girl Should Know*. By the time she wrote "Birth Control and Racial Betterment" in 1919, an article published in the monthly *Birth Control Review*, she had launched a new movement for birth control and women's empowerment. Her rhetoric changed as she grew more experienced and was exposed to different kinds of activism. She sought to expand the birth control movement beyond its radical base and draw support from broader segments of the population, first speaking to working-class women, then to middle-class and society women, and finally to an audience that included physicians, legislators, and eugenicists. The latter were scientists and others who advocated controlling hereditary characteristics and thereby preventing the birth of people deemed "unfit" for what they perceived as the betterment of humankind—even to the point of sterilizing poor people, immigrants, disabled people, and nonwhites. The philosophy was popular and even mainstream at the time but would taint the birth control movement in years to come.

Until the end of her long and active life, Sanger continued to refine her arguments and address new and different audiences on behalf of birth control, but she always maintained that birth control was fundamentally both the right and the responsibility of each woman.

Margaret Sanger (Library of Congress)

Document Text

Before eugenists and others who are laboring for racial betterment can succeed, they must first clear the way for Birth Control. Like the advocates of Birth Control, the eugenists, for instance, are seeking to assist the race toward the elimination of the unfit. . . .

Eugenists emphasize the mating of healthy couples for the conscious purpose of producing healthy children, the sterilization of the unfit to prevent their populating the world with their kind and they may, perhaps, agree with us that contraception is a necessary measure among the masses of the workers, where wages do not keep pace with the growth of the family and its necessities in the way of food, clothing, housing, medical attention, education and the like.

We who advocate Birth Control, on the other hand, lay all our emphasis upon stopping not only the reproduction of the unfit but upon stopping all reproduction when there is not economic means of providing proper care for those who are born in health. The eugenist also believes that a woman should bear as many healthy children as possible as a duty to the state. We hold that the world is already over-populated. Eugenists imply or insist that a woman's first duty is to the state; we contend that her duty to herself is her first duty to the state.

We maintain that a woman possessing an adequate knowledge of her reproductive functions is the best judge of the time and conditions under which her child should be brought into the world. We further maintain that it is her right, regardless of all other considerations, to determine whether she shall bear children or not, and how many children she shall bear. . . . To this end we insist that information in regard to scientific contraceptives be made open to all. We believe that if such information is placed within the reach of all, we will have made it possible to take the first, greatest step toward racial betterment. . . .

One fundamental fact alone, however, indicates the necessity of Birth Control if eugenics is to accomplish its purpose. Unless contraceptives are used, a child is likely to be born within a year of the last one. Even when the mother is exceptionally robust this frequent child-bearing is a heavy drain upon her system and nine times in ten, it is a drain upon the offspring. . . .

This principle asserts itself in all of the economic layers of society but its effects may be modified to a considerable extent by those women who have the means to provide adequate care of themselves during the ante-natal period and adequate care of the child after it is born. . . . Among the majority of wage-workers, the frequent arrival of children means not only the wrecking of the mother's health and the physical handicapping of the child, but often the disheartening and demoralization of the father, the stunting of the children through bad living conditions and early toil, and in that generation or the next, the contributing of morons, feeble-minded, insane and various criminal types to the already tremendous social burden constituted by these unfit.

While I personally believe in the sterilization of the feeble-minded, the insane and the syphiletic, I have not been able to discover that these measures are more than superficial deterrents when applied to the constantly growing stream of the unfit. . . . These measures do not touch those great masses, who through economic pressure populate the slums and there produce in their helplessness other helpless, diseased and incompetent masses, who overwhelm all that eugenics can do among those whose economic condition is better.

Birth Control, on the other hand, not only opens the way to the eugenist, but it preserves his work. Furthermore, it not only prepares the ground in a natural fashion for the development of a higher standard of motherhood and of family life, but enables the child to be better born, better cared for in infancy and better educated.

Birth Control of itself, by freeing the reproductive instinct from its present chains, will make a better race. . . .

Eugenics without Birth Control seems to us a house [built] upon the sands. It is at the mercy of the rising stream of the unfit. It cannot stand against the furious winds of economic pressure which have buffeted into partial or total helplessness a tremendous proportion of the human race. Only upon a free, self-determining motherhood can rest any unshakable structure of racial betterment.

Glossary

betterment: the act or process of improving something

contraceptive: method of preventing pregnancy

eugenist: eugenicist; person who believes the human species would improve through selective reproduction

race, racial: in this case, referring to the human race

syphiletic: syphilitic; person suffering from syphilis, a sexually transmitted disease

Short-Answer Questions

1. According to Sanger, how are birth control and human betterment connected?

2. According to Sanger, what are the consequences of women having too many children? Who else is affected by this, and how?

3. Why might Sanger's essay have been viewed as controversial in 1919? Why might her essay be viewed as controversial today?

Buck v. Bell

<table>
<tr><td>

Author
Oliver Wendell Holmes Jr.

Date
1927

Document Type
Legal

</td><td>

Significance
Affirmed that Virginia's state-enforced sterilization law did not violate the Fourteenth Amendment and legitimized eugenic sterilization laws throughout the United States

</td></tr>
</table>

Overview

Eugenics, the set of practices and beliefs that aimed to improve and protect certain groups by suppressing others, swept across the United States as a movement in the latter half of the nineteenth century and into the twentieth century. Eugenics theory and laws informed numerous policy areas, such as immigration (gatekeeping who should be allowed into the United States and who should not) and procreation (regulating who should be allowed to repopulate and who should not). Immigrant groups, people of color, and individuals with disabilities and mental health issues were all targeted for suppression. Such was the case in *Buck v. Bell*. In 1924, the superintendent of the Virginia State Colony for Epileptics and Feebleminded ordered that eighteen-year-old Carrie Buck be sterilized. The claim was that Buck had the mental age of nine years old and represented a genetic threat to so-

ciety. Buck, who was raped by her adoptive mother's nephew and gave birth, was deemed "promiscuous" and feeble-minded," as was Carrie Buck's biological mother, who suffered from a similar condition, had a record of sex work, and had given birth to three children, including Carrie. The State of Virginia determined that it was in the best interest of the state that both mother and daughter be sterilized. The Supreme Court upheld the decision and ruled that because of their disability, sterilizing did not violate the equal protection clause of the Fourteenth Amendment (". . . nor shall any State deprive any person of life, liberty, or property, without due process of law; nor deny to any person within its jurisdiction the equal protection of the laws"). The case paved the way for furthering eugenics studies and compulsory sterilization procedures and has yet to be repealed formally by the Supreme Court.

Document Text

Syllabus

1. The Virginia statute providing for the sexual sterilization of inmates of institutions supported by the State who shall be found to be afflicted with an hereditary form of insanity or imbecility, is within the power of the State under the Fourteenth Amendment.

2. Failure to extend the provision to persons outside the institutions named does not render it obnoxious to the Equal Protection Clause. . . .

Mr. JUSTICE HOLMES delivered the opinion of the Court.

. . . Carrie Buck is a feeble minded white woman who was committed to the State Colony above mentioned in due form. She is the daughter of a feeble minded mother in the same institution, and the mother of an illegitimate feeble minded child. She was eighteen years old at the time of the trial of her case in the Circuit Court, in the latter part of 1924. An Act of Virginia, approved March 20, 1924, recites that the health of the patient and the welfare of society may be promoted in certain cases by the sterilization of mental defectives, under careful safeguard, &c.; that the sterilization may be effected in males by vasectomy and in females by salpingectomy, without serious pain or substantial danger to life; that the Commonwealth is supporting in various institutions many defective persons who, if now discharged, would become a menace, but, if incapable of procreating, might be discharged with safety and become self-supporting with benefit to themselves and to society, and that experience has shown that heredity plays an important part in the transmission of insanity, imbecility, &c. The statute then enacts that, whenever the superintendent of certain institutions, including the above-named State Colony, shall be of opinion that it is for the best interests of the patients and of society that an inmate under his care should be sexually sterilized, he may have the operation performed upon any

Oliver Wendell Holmes Jr. wrote the majority opinion. (Library of Congress)

patient afflicted with hereditary forms of insanity, imbecility, &c., on complying with the very careful provisions by which the act protects the patients from possible abuse.

The superintendent first presents a petition to the special board of directors of his hospital or colony, stating the facts and the grounds for his opinion, verified by affidavit. Notice of the petition and of the time and place of the hearing in the institution is to be served upon the inmate, and also upon his guardian, and if there is no guardian, the superintendent is to apply to the Circuit Court of the County to appoint one. If the inmate is a minor, notice also is to be given to his parents, if any, with a copy of the petition. The board is to see to it that the inmate may attend the hearings if desired by him or his guardian. The evidence is all to be reduced to writing, and, after the board has made its order for or against the operation, the superintendent, or the inmate, or his guardian, may appeal to the Circuit Court of the County. The Circuit Court may consider the record of the board and the evidence before it and such other admissible evidence as may be offered, and may affirm, revise, or reverse the order of the board and enter such order as it deems just. Finally any party may apply to the Supreme Court of Appeals, which, if it grants the appeal, is to hear the case upon the record of the trial in the Circuit Court, and may enter such an order as it thinks the Circuit Court should have entered. There can be no doubt that, so far as procedure is concerned, the rights of the patient are most carefully considered, and, as every step in this case was taken in scrupulous compliance with the statute and after months of observation, there is no doubt that, in that respect, the plaintiff in error has had due process of law.

The attack is not upon the procedure, but upon the substantive law. It seems to be contended that in no circumstances could such an order be justified. It certainly is contended that the order cannot be justified upon the existing grounds. The judgment finds the facts that have been recited, and that Carrie Buck "is the probable potential parent of socially inadequate offspring, likewise afflicted, that she may be sexually sterilized without detriment to her general health, and that her welfare and that of society will be promoted by her sterilization," and thereupon makes the order. In view of the general declarations of the legislature and the specific findings of the Court, obviously we cannot say as a matter of law that the grounds do not exist, and, if they exist, they justify the result. We have seen more than once that the public welfare may call upon the best citizens for their lives. It would be strange if it could not call upon those who already sap the strength of the State for these lesser sacrifices, often not felt to be such by those concerned, in order to prevent our being swamped with incompetence. It is better for all the world if, instead of waiting to execute degenerate offspring for crime or to let them starve for their imbecility, society can prevent those who are manifestly unfit from continuing their kind. The principle that sustains compulsory vaccination is broad enough to cover cutting the Fallopian tubes. *Jacobson v. Massachusetts*. Three generations of imbeciles are enough.

But, it is said, however it might be if this reasoning were applied generally, it fails when it is confined to the small number who are in the institutions named and is not applied to the multitudes outside. It is the usual last resort of constitutional arguments to point out shortcomings of this sort. But the answer is that the law does all that is needed when it does all that it can, indicates a policy, applies it to all within the lines, and seeks to bring within the lines all similarly situated so far and so fast as its means allow. Of course, so far as the operations enable those who otherwise must be kept confined to be returned to the world, and thus open the asylum to others, the equality aimed at will be more nearly reached.

Judgment affirmed.

MR. JUSTICE BUTLER dissents.

Glossary

imbecility: term once used by psychiatrists to denote a category of people with moderate to severe intellectual disability

Jacobson v. Massachusetts: 1905 case that upheld the authority of states to enforce compulsory vaccination laws

obnoxious: antithetical; in opposition to

salpingectomy: a method of sterilizing females by removal of the fallopian tubes, which carry eggs from the ovary to the uterus

vasectomy: a method of sterilizing males by removing a small section of the vas deferens, the duct through which sperm cells flow

Short-Answer Questions

1. Why do you think this decision has never been overturned? Should it be overturned? Take into account our current understanding of intellectual disabilities, mental disorders, and trauma.

2. What role do you believe gender and gender stereotypes have to play in sterilization?

3. *Buck v. Bell* not only paved the way for the enacting of eugenics laws in other states but also served as a template for sterilization laws that were later enacted by the Nazi government in Germany during the 1930s. Knowing this, how would you describe the legacy of governmental treatment of disabled women during this period?

Griswold v. Connecticut

Author William O. Douglas (opinion); Hugo Black (dissent) **Date** 1965 **Document Type** Legal	**Significance** Paved the way for reproductive rights and established a constitutional right to privacy among married couples

Overview

During Associate Justice William O. Douglas's long tenure on the Supreme Court bench, from 1939 to 1975, a variety of cases came before the Court that affected American public life and the concepts of individual and civil rights. The mid-twentieth century was a tumultuous and pivotal time in American history that was marked by major international conflicts, such as World War II, the Cold War, and the Vietnam War, as well as major domestic movements, notably the civil rights movement. Douglas's opinions demonstrate his judicial priorities—protection of civil and individual rights, including the right to privacy; near-absolute deference to the First Amendment; and environmental protection. Douglas addressed cases not just from within the narrow confines of case-law precedent but also from what he saw as the social ramifications of the particular ques-

tions contested in the cases. The Supreme Court case *Griswold v. Connecticut* overturned the conviction of Estelle Griswold and C. Lee Buxton for violating an 1879 Connecticut law that prohibited the provision of contraceptive devices, medicines, or advice—even to married couples. The case definitively established a constitutional right to privacy among married couples.

Although Douglas found the Connecticut law offensive, in his dissent Hugo Black took issue with the concept that privacy was a right founded in any part of the Constitution. Although Black's dim view of unstated constitutional rights, such as the right to privacy he decries in *Griswold*, seemed out of step with the times in 1965, that opinion has since found favor with many who have been obliged to revisit one of the nation's most hotly contested issues: women's reproductive rights, including the right to abortion.

Document Text
William O. Douglas: Opinion

. . . The right to educate a child in a school of the parents' choice—whether public or private or parochial—is also not mentioned. Nor is the right to study any particular subject or any foreign language. Yet the First Amendment has been construed to include certain of those rights. . . .

In *NAACP v. Alabama*, we protected the "freedom to associate and privacy in one's associations," noting that freedom of association was a peripheral First Amendment right. . . . In other words, the First Amendment has a penumbra where privacy is protected from governmental intrusion. In like context, we have protected forms of "association" that are not political in the customary sense, but pertain to the social, legal, and economic benefit of the members. . . .

We have had many controversies over these penumbral rights of "privacy and repose." . . . These cases bear witness that the right of privacy which presses for recognition here is a legitimate one.

The present case, then, concerns a relationship lying within the zone of privacy created by several fundamental constitutional guarantees. And it concerns a law which, in forbidding the use of contraceptives, rather than regulating their manufacture or sale, seeks to achieve its goals by means having a maximum destructive impact upon that relationship. Such a law cannot stand in light of the familiar principle, so often applied by this Court, that a "governmental purpose to control or prevent activities constitutionally subject to state regulation may not be achieved by means which sweep unnecessarily broadly and thereby invade the area of protected freedoms [*NAACP v. Alabama*]."

Would we allow the police to search the sacred precincts of marital bedrooms for telltale signs of the use of contraceptives? The very idea is repulsive to the notions of privacy surrounding the marriage relationship.

William O. Douglas wrote the majority opinion. (Library of Congress)

We deal with a right of privacy older than the Bill of Rights—older than our political parties, older than our school system. Marriage is a coming together for better or for worse, hopefully enduring, and intimate to the degree of being sacred. It is an association that promotes a way of life, not causes; a harmony in living, not political faiths; a bilateral loyalty, not commercial or social projects. Yet it is an association for as noble a purpose as any involved in our prior decisions.

Hugo Black: Dissent

. . . The Court talks about a constitutional "right of privacy" as though there is some constitutional provision or provisions forbidding any law ever to be passed which might abridge the "privacy" of individuals. But there is not. There are, of course, guarantees in certain specific constitutional provisions which are designed in part to protect privacy at certain times and places with respect to certain activities. Such, for example, is the Fourth

Amendment's guarantee against "unreasonable searches and seizures." But I think it belittles that Amendment to talk about it as though it protects nothing but "privacy." To treat it that way is to give it a niggardly interpretation, not the kind of liberal reading I think any Bill of Rights provision should be given. The average man would very likely not have his feelings soothed any more by having his property seized openly than by having it seized privately and by stealth. He simply wants his property left alone. And a person can be just as much, if not more, irritated, annoyed and injured by an unceremonious public arrest by a policeman as he is by a seizure in the privacy of his office or home.

One of the most effective ways of diluting or expanding a constitutionally guaranteed right is to substitute for the crucial word or words of a constitutional guarantee another word or words, more or less flexible and more or less restricted in meaning. This fact is well illustrated by the use of the term "right of privacy" as a comprehensive substitute for the Fourth Amendment's guarantee against "unreasonable searches and seizures." "Privacy" is a broad, abstract and ambiguous concept which can easily be shrunken in meaning but which can also, on the other hand, easily be interpreted as a constitutional ban against many things other than searches and seizures. I have expressed the view many times that First Amendment freedoms, for example, have

suffered from a failure of the courts to stick to the simple language of the First Amendment in construing it, instead of invoking multitudes of words substituted for those the Framers used. . . .

. . . I repeat so as not to be misunderstood that this Court does have power, which it should exercise, to hold laws unconstitutional where they are forbidden by the Federal Constitution. My point is that there is no provision of the Constitution which either expressly or impliedly vests power in this Court to sit as a supervisory agency over acts of duly constituted legislative bodies and set aside their laws because of the Court's belief that the legislative policies adopted are unreasonable, unwise, arbitrary, capricious or irrational. The adoption of such a loose, flexible, uncontrolled standard for holding laws unconstitutional, if ever it is finally achieved, will amount to a great unconstitutional shift of power to the courts which I believe and am constrained to say will be bad for the courts and worse for the country. Subjecting federal and state laws to such an unrestrained and unrestrainable judicial control as to the wisdom of legislative enactments would, I fear, jeopardize the separation of governmental powers that the Framers set up and at the same time threaten to take away much of the power of States to govern themselves which the Constitution plainly intended them to have. . . .

Glossary

construing: interpreting

niggardly: stingy, small-minded

penumbra: body of rights considered to be guaranteed by implication

The Schlager Anthology of Women's History

Short-Answer Questions

1. According to Justice Douglas's majority opinion, how does the freedom to associate as held in *NAACP v. Alabama* relate to the privacy interests in *Griswold*?

2. How does Douglas's opinion discuss government action in the context of family privacy?

3. What are some of the ways family privacy rights set forth in *Griswold* can be applied to other individual privacy rights? Are there ways in which the state interferes with family privacy today?

Roe v. Wade

Author Harry Blackmun (majority opinion); William Rehnquist (dissent) **Date** 1973 **Document Type** Legal	**Significance** Established abortion as a fundamental right guaranteed in the U.S. Constitution

Overview

Abortion, or the deliberate termination of unwanted pregnancy, has occurred in some form in human society since ancient times. Nevertheless, amid the Victorian morals of the mid-nineteenth century, it became one of Western society's most contentious issues, sparking bitter religious and ethical debates that continued into the twenty-first century. In 1973 the Supreme Court case known as *Roe v. Wade* became the most pivotal moment for the issue in the history of the United States.

In *Roe v. Wade*, the Supreme Court established abortion as a fundamental right guaranteed in the U.S. Constitution, albeit with some qualifications. Regardless, the case brought a virtual end to illegal, unsanitary "back-alley" abortions and, in broader terms, established new parameters for the concept of a constitutional right to privacy.

Challenges to *Roe v. Wade* arose immediately after its passing, and in 2022 the case was overturned as a result of the ruling in the case of *Dobbs v. Jackson Women's Health Organization*. In that case, the Supreme Court reviewed whether Mississippi's Gestational Age Act was constitutional. The law banned most abortions after 15 weeks of pregnancy with certain exceptions. The Court upheld the Gestational Act, thereby overturning *Roe* and *Planned Parenthood v. Casey* (1992) and concluding that the Constitution does not guarantee abortion rights.

Norma McCorvey, "Jane Roe" of the Roe v. Wade *decision, shown in 1989 with attorney Gloria Allred.*
(Lorie Shaull)

Document Text
Justice Harry Blackmun, Majority Opinion

. . . This right of privacy, whether it be founded in the Fourteenth Amendment's concept of personal liberty and restrictions upon state action, as we feel it is, or, as the District Court determined, in the Ninth Amendment's reservation of rights to the people, is broad enough to encompass a woman's decision whether or not to terminate her pregnancy. The detriment that the State would impose upon the pregnant woman by denying this choice altogether is apparent. Specific and direct harm medically diagnosable even in early pregnancy may be involved. Maternity, or additional offspring, may force upon the woman a distressful life and future. Psychological harm may be imminent. Mental and physical health may be taxed by child care. There is also the distress, for all concerned, as-

sociated with the unwanted child, and there is the problem of bringing a child into a family already unable, psychologically and otherwise, to care for it. In other cases, as in this one, the additional difficulties and continuing stigma of unwed motherhood may be involved. All these are factors the woman and her responsible physician necessarily will consider in consultation. . . .

The Court's decisions recognizing a right of privacy also acknowledge that some state regulation in areas protected by that right is appropriate. [A] State may properly assert important interests in safeguarding health, in maintaining medical standards, and in protecting potential life. At some point in pregnancy, these respective interests become sufficiently compelling to sustain regulation of the factors that govern the abortion decision. The privacy right involved, therefore, cannot be said to be absolute. In fact, it is not clear to us that the claim . . . that one has an unlimited right to do with one's body as one pleases bears a close relationship to the right of privacy previously articulated in the Court's decisions. The Court has refused to recognize an unlimited right of this kind in the past.

We, therefore, conclude that the right of personal privacy includes the abortion decision, but that this right is not unqualified and must be considered against important state interests in regulation. . . .

This holding, we feel, is consistent with the relative weights of the respective interests involved, with the lessons and examples of medical and legal history, with the lenity of the common law, and with the demands of the profound problems of the present day. The decision leaves the State free to place increasing restrictions on abortion as the period of pregnancy lengthens, so long as those restrictions are tailored to the recognized state interests. The decision vindicates the right of the physician to administer medical treatment according to his professional judgment up to the points where important state interests provide compelling justifications for intervention. Up to those points, the abortion decision in all its aspects is inherently, and primarily, a medical decision, and basic responsibility for it must rest with the physician. . . .

Justice William Rehnquist, Dissent
. . . I have difficulty in concluding, as the Court does, that the right of "privacy" is involved in this case. Texas, by the statute here challenged, bars the performance of a medical abortion by a licensed physician on a plaintiff such as Roe. A transaction resulting in an operation such as this is not "private" in the ordinary usage of that word. Nor is the "privacy" that the Court finds here even a distant relative of the freedom from searches and seizures protected by the Fourth Amendment to the Constitution, which the Court has referred to as embodying a right to privacy.

If the Court means by the term "privacy" no more than that the claim of a person to be free from unwanted state regulation of consensual transactions may be a form of "liberty" protected by the Fourteenth Amendment, there is no doubt that similar claims have been upheld in our earlier decisions on the basis of that liberty. I agree with the statement of MR. JUSTICE STEWART in his concurring opinion that the "liberty," against deprivation of which without due process the Fourteenth Amendment protects, embraces more than the rights found in the Bill of Rights. But that liberty is not guaranteed absolutely against deprivation, only against deprivation without due process of law. The test traditionally applied in the area of social and economic legislation is whether or not a law such as that challenged has a rational relation to a valid state objective. . . . The Due Process Clause of the Fourteenth Amendment undoubtedly does place a limit, albeit a broad one, on legislative power to enact laws such as this. If the Texas statute were to prohibit an abortion even where the mother's life is in jeopardy, I have little doubt that such a statute would lack a rational relation to a valid state objective. . . . But the Court's sweeping invalidation of any restrictions on abortion during the first trimester is impossible to justify under that standard, and the conscious weighing of competing factors that the Court's opinion apparently substitutes for the established test is far more appropriate to a legislative judgment than to a judicial one. . . .

The fact that a majority of the States reflecting, after all the majority sentiment in those States, have had restrictions on abortions for at least a century is a strong indication, it seems to me, that the asserted right to an abortion is not "so rooted in the traditions and conscience of our people as to be ranked as fundamental." Even today, when society's views on abortion are changing, the very existence of the debate is evidence that the "right" to an abortion is not so universally accepted as the appellant would have us believe.

To reach its result, the Court necessarily has had to find within the scope of the Fourteenth Amendment a right that was apparently completely unknown to the drafters of the Amendment. As early as 1821, the first state law dealing directly with abortion was enacted by the Connecticut Legislature. . . . By the time of the adoption of the Fourteenth Amendment in 1868, there were at least 36 laws enacted by state or territorial legislatures limiting abortion. While many States have amended or updated their laws, 21 of the laws on the books in 1868 remain in effect today. Indeed, the Texas statute struck down today was, as the majority notes, first enacted in 1857, and "has remained substantially unchanged to the present time."

Glossary

abortion: the termination of a pregnancy, whether induced or naturally occurring, after or resulting in the death of the embryo or fetus

Due Process Clause of the Fourteenth Amendment: "No State shall make or enforce any law which shall abridge the privileges or immunities of citizens of the United States; nor shall any State deprive any person of life, liberty, or property, without due process of law . . ."

gestation: pregnancy

trimester: a period of three months

Short-Answer Questions

1. *Roe v. Wade* and *Brown v. Board of Education*, a 1954 ruling that ended racial segregation in public schools, are considered two of the Supreme Court's most significant landmark cases of the twentieth century. Compare and contrast the social impact of each. Which case do you think has had more importance in American society?

2. For centuries, philosophers and theologians have debated the question of when human life begins. The Supreme Court has examined the question of when human life is constitutionally protected on numerous occasions. In the modern era, scientific advancements have pushed the boundaries regarding what is considered a viable fetus (one able to survive outside the womb). Consider the perspectives from each of these realms of knowledge. When, in your view, does human life begin?

3. The Supreme Court is integral to the constitutional system of checks and balances instituted in the executive, legislative, and judicial branches of the U.S. government. Examine *Roe v. Wade* in the context of this system, and discusses the positions of each of the three branches of government on the abortion issue both before the decision and after the decision was handed down.

Relf v. Weinberger

Author	**Significance**
Gerhard Gesell	Established standards for informed consent and stated that federal dollars could not be used to fund forced sterilizations
Date	
1974	
Document Type	
Legal	

Overview

A significant number of women, especially Black women, who were on welfare during the 1970s were involuntary sterilized. The sterilization of African American women in the United States had been going on for decades. The practice was tied to eugenic proponents who supported the sterilization of Black women because of their race and economic class. Lower-class women did not have bodily autonomy; instead, state administrators, doctors and other medical professionals, and legal practitioners exerted control over poor women's health choices and reproductive systems. Many women were unable to choose their own form of birth control; some consented to sterilization due to the threats of loss of welfare assistance. In Alabama, the Relf sisters were both subjected to unwanted sterilization. Under the age of 18, the Relf sisters believed that their mother had volunteered them for birth control shots, but instead the two women were sterilized. A lawsuit filed on behalf of the sisters exposed how the federal government had been funding the involuntary sterilization of women for decades. The lawsuit led to the requirement that doctors obtain informed consent before performing sterilization procedures. *Relf v. Weinberger* (1974) ushered in the concept of reproductive freedom, eventually paving the way for women to choose for themselves whether and when to reproduce. The opinion was written by District Judge Gerhard Gesell for the U.S. District Court for the District of Columbia.

Document Text

MEMORANDUM OPINION

GESELL, District Judge.

Although Congress has been insistent that all family planning programs function on a purely voluntary basis, there is uncontroverted evidence in the record that minors and other incompetents have been sterilized with federal funds and that an indefinite number of poor people have been improperly coerced into accepting a sterilization operation under the threat that various federally supported welfare benefits would be withdrawn unless they submitted to irreversible sterilization. Patients receiving Medicaid assistance at childbirth are evidently the most frequent targets of this pressure, as the experiences of plaintiffs Waters and Walker illustrate. Mrs. Waters was actually refused medical assistance by her attending physician unless she submitted to a tubal ligation after the birth. Other examples were documented. . . .

These regulations provide that projects and programs receiving PHS [Public Health Service] or SRS [Supplementary Retirement Scheme] funds, whether for family planning or purely medical services, shall neither perform nor arrange for the performance of a non therapeutic sterilization unless certain procedures are carried out. These vary depending upon whether the patient is, under state law, a legally competent adult, a legally competent person under the age of 18, a legally incompetent minor, or a mental incompetent. . . .

Plaintiffs do not oppose the voluntary sterilization of poor persons under federally funded programs. However, they contend that these regulations are both illegal and arbitrary because they authorize *involuntary* sterilizations, without statutory or constitutional justification. They argue forcefully that sterilization of minors or mental incompetents is necessarily involuntary in the nature of things. Further, they claim that sterilization of competent adults under these regulations can be undertaken without ensuring that the request for sterilization is in actuality voluntary. The Secretary defends the regulations and insists that only "voluntary" sterilization is permitted under their terms.

For the reasons developed below, the Court finds that the Secretary has no statutory authority under the family planning sections of the Social Security or Public Health Services Acts to fund the sterilization of any person incompetent under state law to consent to such an operation, whether because of minority or of mental deficiency. It also finds that the challenged regulations are arbitrary and unreasonable in that they fail to implement the congressional command that federal family planning funds not be used to coerce indigent patients into submitting to sterilization. In short, federally assisted family planning sterilizations are permissible only with the voluntary, knowing and uncoerced consent of individuals competent to give such consent. This result requires an injunction against substantial portions of the proposed regulations and their revision to insure that all sterilizations funded under the family planning sections are voluntary in the full sense of that term and that sterilization of incompetent minors and adults is prevented. . . .

No person who is mentally incompetent can meet these standards, nor can the consent of a representative, however sufficient under state law, impute voluntariness to the individual actually undergoing irreversible sterilization. Minors would also appear to lack the knowledge, maturity and judgment to satisfy these standards with regard to such an important issue, whatever may be their competence to rely on devices or medication that temporarily frustrates procreation. This is the reasoning that provides the basis for the nearly universal common law and statutory rule that minors and mental incompetents cannot consent to medical operations. . . .

The statutory references to minors and mental incompetents do not contradict this conclusion, for they appear only in the context of family planning services in general. Minors, for example, are not legally incompetent for all purposes, and many girls of child-bearing age are undoubtedly sufficiently aware of the relevant considerations to use temporary contraceptives that intrude far less on fundamental rights. However, the Secretary has not demonstrated and the Court cannot find that Congress deemed such children capable of voluntarily consenting to an irreversible operation involving the basic human right to procreate. Nor can the Court find, in the face of repeated warnings concerning voluntariness, that Congress authorized the imposition of such a serious deprivation upon mental incompetents at the will of an unspecified "representative."

The regulations also fail to provide the procedural safeguards necessary to insure that even competent adults voluntarily request sterilization. Plaintiffs would require an elaborate hearing process prior to the operation to remedy this problem. The Secretary, however, has determined that the consent document procedure set forth in the existing regulations is adequate in most instances to insure a knowledgeable decision, and the Court finds that this determination is not unreasonable. In one respect, however, the consent procedure must be improved. Even a fully informed individual cannot make a "voluntary" decision concerning sterilization if he has been subjected to coercion from doctors or project officers. Despite specific statutory language forbidding the recipients of federal family planning funds to threaten a cutoff of program benefits unless the individual submits to sterilization and despite clear evidence that such coercion is actually being applied, the challenged regulations contain no clear safeguard against this abuse. Although the required consent document must state that the patient can *withdraw* his consent to sterilization without losing other program benefits, there is nothing to prohibit the use of such coercion to extract the initial consent. . . .

This controversy has arisen during a period of rapid change in the field of birth control. In recent years, through the efforts of dedicated proponents of family planning, birth control information and services have become widely available. Aided by the growing acceptance of family planning, medical science has steadily improved and diversified the techniques of birth prevention and control. Advancements in artificial insemination and in the understanding of genetic attributes are also affecting the decision to bear children. There are even suggestions in the scientific literature that the sex of children may soon be subject to parental control. And over this entire area lies the specter of overpopulation, with its possible impact upon the food supply, interpersonal relations, privacy, and the enjoyment of our "inalienable rights."

Glossary

arbitrary: based on random choice or personal whim, rather than any reason or system

Medicaid: a government program that provides health insurance for adults and children with limited income and resources

statutory: relating to laws or rules enacted by a legislative authority

Short-Answer Questions

1. In *Dobbs v. Jackson Women's Health Organization* (2022), which overturned *Roe v. Wade* (1973), issues concerning the Supreme Court's involvement in deciding matters concerning women's bodily autonomy have increased dramatically. How do the issues surrounding the *Relf* case compare or contrast to the *Dobbs* decision? Explain.

2. What does the *Relf* case reveal about the interconnectedness between race, gender, and class in the United States?

3. Black women in the United States are more at risk for adverse outcomes in health care, including maternal care, than white women or men. Despite the circumstances surrounding the *Relf* case and the ruling, why do you think these problems persist? Explain.

International Campaign for Abortion Rights: International Day of Action

Author	Significance
International Campaign for Abortion Rights	Called for protection of women's reproductive freedom worldwide

Date
1979

Document Type
Speeches/Addresses; Essays, Reports, Manifestos

Overview

Although the decision to recognize abortion as a constitutional right in *Roe v. Wade* in 1973 marked a turning point in the struggle for women to control their own bodies, it was really only the tip of the iceberg. *Roe v. Wade* only applied to women in the United States, and it still allowed restrictions to be placed on their rights to terminate pregnancies. In much of the world, including many Western societies, abortion was still illegal. Portugal, Spain, Italy, and Ireland all maintained laws that criminalized abortion throughout the 1970s. Even in countries that allowed abortions at that time, laws still placed restrictions—such as time limits, refusal of service to minors, and refusal of service because of a healthcare provider's personal objection to abortion—on the exercise of that right.

To bring attention to the abuses that women worldwide were subjected to in the name of health care, and to call for abortion as a universal right for women around the world, the International Campaign for Abortion Rights (ICAR) called for an International Day of Action on March 31, 1979. The ICAR was organized in 1977 following a European-wide feminist conference held in Vincennes, France. Its purpose was to campaign and petition for the right of women to control their fertility, their right to contraception, and their right to safe, legal abortion.

At the same time that the ICAR was organizing, a vocal minority that opposed abortion on the grounds that it was immoral and a kind of murder began agitating for the repeal of *Roe v. Wade* and restrictions on the right to abortion. In January 1979, one of the most vocal organizations opposed to abortion, Right to Life, organized a march on Washington to make their views heard in the most public way possible.

Document Text
International Day of Action March 31, 1979

On March 31st women from 17 countries will participate in an International Day of Action to demand the right to contraception and abortion and against all forced sterilisation.

The following actions will be taking place:

West Germany—CONDITION FOR ABORTION . . . UTERUS REMOVED

March 31—An event is being held in Berlin organised by the Women's Center. The demand will be for free abortion on demand and an end to force sterilisation and experimentation.

Although abortion is legal in West Germany, a woman must sign a form consenting to the removal of her uterus in case of "complications" in order to obtain one.

(1) 30% of women having abortions at the university women's clinic in Essen have "complications" and have their uteri removed.

(2) In Hamburg's Saint George's hospital, doctors remove the uteri of 25% of the women having an abortion.

(3) Doctors at the Tubingan University Women's Clinic removed the uteri of 20% of the women at the time of abortion.

This major surgical operation should only be performed 4 to 6 weeks *after* an abortion to lessen the possibilities of complications. Therefore, it is impossible not to conclude that *forced sterilisation* is being practiced in West Germany.

Columbia—STERILISATION FREE BUT ABORTION A CRIME . . .

On December 9th, 1978, over 300 women attended the first national women's conference in Colom-

A demonstration promoting legal abortion (Library of Congress)

bia. One of the resolutions passed was to support March 31st, the International Day of Action.

Abortion is illegal, with between 1,000 and 1,500 deaths and 250,000 backstreet abortions each year. Those doing or having abortions can go to prison for 1–6 years. The sentence is reduced by a third, or a state pardon given if the abortion was to save the family's "honor". No allowance is made for women whose lives are at risk.

The U.S.A. has invested 3 million dollars in Colombian Family Planning Institutes (Pro Familia) which carries out widespread sterilisation programs in 1,260 centers. In 1967, members of the Colombian government accused the Ford Foundation (U.S.A.) of sterilising 40,000 women in return for lipstick and artificial pearls. Birth control in Colombia is

---

not the result of a free decision, but a policy carried out [by] a U.S.A. backed government.

United States of America—ANTI-ABORTIONISTS ATTACK CONSTITUTION . . .

The right of American women to abortion has been under attack by anti-abortionists since legalisation in 1973. The latest attack is an attempt to amend the Constitution to protect the rights of the unborn. This move has no legal precedent and its possible effects could include the re-writing of the whole Constitution.

In an obscene gesture designed to shock the U.S.A. public, anti abortionists unrolled baby blankets containing supposed fetuses at a public meeting organised by the leaders of the National Organisation for Women (NOW) on February 15th. Recent fire bombings of abortion clinics led NOW president Ellie Smeal to plan this meeting to discuss areas of agreement excluding the abortion issue. Members of NOW strongly protested the action of their leadership at a time when women's rights are under severe attack, and Medicaid insurance has been withdrawn for abortion.

New Zealand—NO ABORTION FOR RAPE . . .

New Zealand has one of the most repressive abortion laws. Abortion is only permitted when:

(1) incest has taken place.

(2) there is *serious* danger to the woman's health.

(3) the pregnant woman is mentally retarded.

(4) the foetus is abnormal.

Rape and the woman's social and economic circumstances are *not* taken into account. Licensed consultants have to approve abortion, and liberal doctors are not being licensed by the Catholic

Minister of Health. Thousands of women now travel to Australia for abortions.

Spain—3000 DEATHS ANNUALLY FROM BACKSTREET ABORTIONS . . .

Abortion is a crime, and contraception which was recently legalised is not widely available. The only birth control clinics in existence are run by the women's movement in Barcelona and Madrid. A nation-wide campaign has been started by the women's movement to make abortion legal and contraception freely available.

Australia—STERILISATION PRACTICED ON ABORIGINAL WOMEN . . .

Abortion is illegal in all but one Australian state (South Australia). It is no longer available under the national health scheme. Medibank, and anti-abortionists have also tried to remove it as a claimable item under private health benefit schemes. Sterilisation is practiced on aboriginal women without their full knowledge. Women are demanding the repeal of all abortion laws, free safe abortions on demand, freely available contraception and no forced sterilisations.

Holland—WOMEN DEMAND THE RIGHT TO CHOOSE

March 31—There will be a demonstration with German women's groups in Groningen, North Holland, [and] a cycle demonstration passing the embassies of Colombia, Switzerland, S. Ireland, Spain and Italy in The Hague. A stall selling contraceptives will be set up outside the Irish embassy. [A] demonstration with [a] Belgian women's group will also be held in the south of Holland.

Abortion is a crime in Holland, but for the past ten years has been tolerated because of a militant campaign by the women's liberation movement. The pro-choice committee, "We Women Demand," is fighting a bill which will make abortion legal, but which gives the doctor, not the woman, right of decision. Abortion will remain in the Criminal Code. A woman will have to think over her request for abortion for 5 days before being given one. This clause will effectively stop thousands of foreign women from having abortions in Holland. "We Women Demand" want a woman's right to choose, decriminalisation of abortion, and abortion free on the Health Service.

Peru—60% OF WOMEN'S DEATHS CAUSED BY BACK STREET ABORTION . . .

Abortion is outlawed by both the civil and the criminal code. The number of illegal abortions has been estimated at 140,000 a year, but official estimates state 27,000. Many women die without safe, legal abortion and freely available contraception.

Brazil—BRAZILIAN WOMEN JOIN INTERNATIONAL MOVEMENT

Late April—a three day meeting will be held concerning the self appropriation of a woman's body.

Glossary

"fire bombings of abortion clinics": acts of domestic terrorism against abortion clinics and the people in them, about ten of which occurred in the United States during the 1970s

Ford Foundation: an original funder of Pro Familia

National Organisation for Women (NOW): founded in 1966 by second-wave feminist leaders Betty Friedan and Pauli Murray, a social welfare organization that lobbies the U.S. government for equality before the law, the prevention of violence against women, reproductive rights, LGBTQ+ rights, and racial justice

Pro Familia: also rendered as ProFamilia; a private nonprofit organization founded in 1964 by gynecologist Dr. Fernando Tamayo to promote reproductive rights and sexual health throughout the world

Short-Answer Questions

1. What are some of the rights protesters hope to gain for women?

2. What are the major points that participants in the International Day of Action are protesting?

3. Some of the laws International Day of Action participants are asked to protest actually legalize abortion. Why are those laws being protested?

Webster v. Reproductive Health Services

Author William Rehnquist	**Significance** Circumvented Roe v. Wade by upholding that Missouri measures to prevent abortion were not unconstitutiona
Date 1989	
Document Type Legal	

Overview

Webster v. Reproductive Health Services was a Missouri abortion case. After 1973, when the Court's landmark ruling in Roe v. Wade essentially legalized abortion, Americans were sharply divided on the issue. In the years that followed, the abortion-related cases the courts heard did not necessarily bear directly on the constitutionality of Roe v. Wade. Rather, they turned on the extent to which any state can impose restrictions on abortion by, for example, specifying at what stage in the life of an unborn fetus abortions might be obtained or whether government funds or facilities could be used to perform abortions.

State law in Missouri maintained that "unborn children have protectable interests in life, health, and wellbeing" and required Missouri to extend the same rights to fetuses ("unborn children") as it did to other persons and to prohibit any government-employed doctor from aborting any fetus the doctor believed to be viable (able to sustain life outside the womb). Further, the law prohibited doctors from using state facilities or the assistance of state employees to perform abortions and prohibited the use of public funding to provide abortion counseling. After a U.S. district court in Missouri struck down these provisions, the Eighth Circuit Court of Appeals affirmed, holding that the provisions of the Missouri law were inconsistent with Roe v. Wade and therefore unconstitutional. Missouri's attorney general, William Webster, appealed the case to the U.S. Supreme Court, where it was argued on April 25, 1989. The Court issued its decision on July 3 of that year. The majority decision was written by Chief Justice William Rehnquist, but various justices wrote dissents and concurrences—and in some cases both—to various portions of the opinion.

Pro-choice and anti-abortion demonstrators stage rallies during opening arguments in the **Webster v. Reproductive Health Services** *case.* (Library of Congress)

Document Text

CHIEF JUSTICE REHNQUIST announced the judgment of the Court and delivered the opinion of the Court with respect to Parts I, II-A, II-B, and II-C, and an opinion with respect to Parts II-D and III, in which JUSTICE WHITE and JUSTICE KENNEDY join.

This appeal concerns the constitutionality of a Missouri statute regulating the performance of abortions. The United States Court of Appeals for the Eighth Circuit struck down several provisions of the statute on the ground that they violated this Court's decision in *Roe v. Wade*, 410 U.S. 113 (1973), and cases following it. We noted probable jurisdiction, 488 U.S. 1003 (1989), and now reverse.

In June, 1986, the Governor of Missouri signed into law Missouri Senate Committee Substitute for House Bill No. 1596 (hereinafter Act or statute), which amended existing state law concerning unborn children and abortions. The Act consisted of 20 provisions, 5 of which are now before the Court. The first provision, or preamble, contains "findings" by the state legislature that "[t]he life of each human being begins at conception," and that "unborn children have protectable interests in life, health, and wellbeing." . . . The Act further requires that all Missouri laws be interpreted to provide unborn children with the same rights enjoyed by other persons, subject to the Federal Constitution and this Court's precedents. . . . Among its other provisions, the Act requires that, prior to performing an abortion on any woman whom a physician has reason to believe is 20 or more weeks pregnant, the physician ascertain whether the fetus is viable by performing

"such medical examinations and tests as are necessary to make a finding of the gestational age, weight, and lung maturity of the unborn child."

§ 188. 029. The Act also prohibits the use of public employees and facilities to perform or assist abortions not necessary to save the mother's life, and it prohibits the use of public funds, employees, or facilities for the purpose of "encouraging or counseling" a woman to have an abortion not necessary to save her life. . . .

In July, 1986, five health professionals employed by the State and two nonprofit corporations brought this class action in the United States District Court for the Western District of Missouri to challenge the constitutionality of the Missouri statute. Plaintiffs, appellees in this Court, sought declaratory and injunctive relief on the ground that certain statutory provisions violated the First, Fourth, Ninth, and Fourteenth Amendments to the Federal Constitution. App. A9. They asserted violations of various rights, including the "privacy rights of pregnant women seeking abortions"; the "woman's right to an abortion"; the "righ[t] to privacy in the physician-patient relationship"; the physician's "righ[t] to practice medicine"; the pregnant woman's "right to life due to inherent risks involved in childbirth"; and the woman's right to "receive . . . adequate medical advice and treatment" concerning abortions. . . .

Plaintiffs filed this suit

"on their own behalf and on behalf of the entire class consisting of facilities and Missouri licensed physicians or other health care professionals offering abortion services or pregnancy counseling and on behalf of the entire class of pregnant females seeking abortion services or pregnancy counseling within the State of Missouri."

. . . The two nonprofit corporations are Reproductive Health Services, which offers family planning and gynecological services to the public, including abortion services up to 22 weeks "gestational age," and Planned Parenthood of Kansas City, which provides abortion services up to 14 weeks gestational age. . . . The individual plaintiffs are three physicians, one nurse, and a social worker. All are "public employees" at "public facilities" in Missouri, and they are paid for their services with "public funds." . . . The individual plaintiffs, within the scope of their public employment, encourage and counsel pregnant women to have non therapeutic abortions. Two of the physicians perform abortions. . . .

Several weeks after the complaint was filed, the District Court temporarily restrained enforcement of several provisions of the Act. Following a 3-day trial in December, 1986, the District Court declared seven provisions of the Act unconstitutional and enjoined their enforcement. . . . These provisions included the preamble . . . ; the "informed consent" provision, which required physicians to inform the pregnant woman of certain facts before performing an abortion . . . ; the requirement that post-16-week abortions be performed only in hospitals . . . ; the mandated tests to determine viability . . . ; and the prohibition on the use of public funds, employees, and facilities to perform or assist non therapeutic abortions, and the restrictions on the use of public funds, employees, and facilities to encourage or counsel women to have such abortions. . . .

The Court of Appeals for the Eighth Circuit affirmed, with one exception not relevant to this appeal. . . . The Court of Appeals determined that Missouri's declaration that life begins at conception was "simply an impermissible state adoption of a theory of when life begins to justify its abortion regulations." . . . Relying on *Colautti v. Franklin*, 439 U.S. 379, 388–389 (1979), it further held that the requirement that physicians perform viability tests was an unconstitutional legislative intrusion on a matter of medical skill and judgment. . . . The Court of Appeals invalidated

Missouri's prohibition on the use of public facilities and employees to perform or assist abortions not necessary to save the mother's life. . . . It distinguished our decisions in *Harris v. McRae*, 448 U.S. 297 (1980), and *Maher v. Roe*, 432 U.S. 464 (1977), on the ground that

"[t]here is a fundamental difference between providing direct funding to effect the abortion decision and allowing staff physicians to perform abortions at an existing publicly owned hospital."

. . . The Court of Appeals struck down the provision prohibiting the use of public funds for "encouraging or counseling" women to have non therapeutic abortions, for the reason that this provision was both overly vague and inconsistent with the right to an abortion enunciated in *Roe v. Wade*. . . . The court also invalidated the hospitalization requirement for 16-week abortions . . . and the prohibition on the use of public employees and facilities for abortion counseling, . . . but the State has not appealed those parts of the judgment below.

Glossary

Colautti v. Franklin: 1979 ruling in which the Supreme Court held that the viability determination requirement and the standard of care requirement were unconstitutionally vague

non-therapeutic abortion: an abortion that is performed or induced when the life of the mother would not be endangered if the fetus were carried to term or when the pregnancy was not the result of rape or incest reported to a law enforcement agency

viability test: prenatal test to see if the baby has a chance to survive

Short-Answer Questions

1. What evidence did the Court consider to determine that the Missouri law restricting abortion was not unconstitutional? Consider how the court used the argument of when "life begins."

2. Public funds are used to provide a variety of services but are prohibited by federal and state governments from funding abortion. Knowing this, how do you think the ruling would influence future anti-abortion advocates in challenging state laws surrounding abortion?

3. The Missouri law required that all Missouri state laws be interpreted to provide "unborn children," or fetuses, with rights equal to those enjoyed by other persons. How does that influence the scope of the Fourteenth Amendment pertaining to citizenship laws?

Margaret Cerullo:
"Hidden History:
An Illegal Abortion in 1968"

Author
Margaret Cerullo

Date
1989

Document Type
Essays, Reports, Manifestos; Speeches/Addresses

Significance
Describes the author's experience obtaining an illegal abortion and suggests the ways demands for reproductive rights became an essential aspect of the American women's movement

Overview

The history of abortion in the United States is complicated, with the procedure being alternately accepted and contested by the public. Until the mid-1800s, abortion was regarded as a regular part of life for American women, and legislatures across the growing United States permitted the practice prior to "quickening," an archaic medical term for fetal movement. Historians have traced the development of attitudes about conception and childbearing and have found that, at conception and during the early stages of pregnancy, women did not believe that a human life existed. As a result, women could easily obtain abortions until roughly four months into their pregnancy. Medical literature, scientific opinion, and popular publications from the late 1700s until the late 1800s regularly referred to herbs and medications that could be used to induce abortions, and midwives and nurses advertised their services openly to the public. Abortion providers were con-

sidered to be trusted, essential medical professionals, and abortion was regarded as a fundamental and unremarkable aspect of reproductive health care.

This permissive state of affairs existed until the mid-1800s, when public opinion toward abortion began to shift. The medical establishment, supported by political and religious conservatives, pushed for bans on abortion. Abortion in the United States would become effectively criminalized by 1880. This did not mean that abortions stopped in the United States, however. Women with means were always able to obtain an abortion. Abortion businesses thrived, with some catering to an exclusive clientele of married, white, native-born Protestant women of the upper and middle classes. Some women left the country to obtain abortions. Poor and working-class women often resorted to more desperate measures, seeking out abortions from unlicensed and inexpert physicians or by inducing abortions themselves. Abortion was legalized in the United States in 1973 with the Supreme Court ruling *Roe v. Wade*, which the Court then reversed in 2002 with its *Dobbs v. Jackson* ruling. It remains a deeply contested political issue. Social and religious conservatives have aggressively pushed for the banning of abortion, and by the 2020s, many states effectively outlawed the procedure. As of 2023, 25 million women live in states with abortion bans or restrictions.

In Margaret Cerullo's account of her 1968 abortion, first presented at a speak-out at Hampshire College in 1989, she clearly explains the challenges associated with obtaining an illegal, underground abortion. In addition, her account shows that her experience was deeply formative for her and helped shape her political perspective. The rage she experienced at the injustice and indignity of her treatment became a foundational part of her identity. This account suggests how demands for reproductive rights became an integral part of the American women's movement.

Document Text

My story is not unusual. Like many women of my generation, women now in their late thirties and forties, my commitment to abortion rights drew its initial passion from my own illegal abortion, 21 years ago. . . .

In 1968 I was 20 years old and I was a student, a junior in college at the University of Pennsylvania. . . . Against my will, and much to my dismay, I was pregnant, a fact I discovered the Saturday before my final exams were going to begin. Not only was abortion illegal in 1968, so was birth control. In Philadelphia where I lived (not a backwater) you could only get the pill (the only form of birth control thought of) if you were married, had your parent's permission, or were 21 years of age. I was too young, and my parents were practicing Catholics. . . .

I was about nine or ten weeks pregnant by the time I figured out where I could get a pregnancy test, had one, and waited for the results. I really had very little idea how I was going to go about getting an abortion, but I was absolutely clear that I did not want to have a child. Like so many young women who get pregnant, I had not been sexually active for long. I felt I was only beginning to know the possibilities of my body, as I was only beginning to dream the possibilities of life.

I really cannot remember exactly how I found the phone numbers, but I suppose I got them through the various means of the underground student/political/counter-cultural scene. I began making calls all over the East Coast, very coded telephone calls. . . . You coded the relevant information about what you wanted and how serious the situation was. I made three or four of these calls from pay phones in between taking exams, and the person on the other end of each one hung up abruptly after I blurted out the critical information. Eventually, I found out there was a major crackdown in process, just a chance regular kind of repressive crackdown on illegal abortionists on the East Coast. . . .

Finally, I got the number of the "Clergymen's [sic] Council on Problem Pregnancies" and went to visit a clergyman in the Philadelphia suburbs. . . . It was explained to me that there was one place they thought it would be possible to have an illegal abortion very quickly, a place called Towson, Maryland, outside of Baltimore. I would have to appear with $600 in small bills.

It seemed an enormous amount of money then (I was living on $5 a week spending money) and not simple to find. . . . I was to appear in Townson at 2:00 in the afternoon outside the movie theater and wait until a man carrying a bag of groceries appeared at the theater and follow him. The clergyman with whom I spoke suggested that I think about the experience I was going to have as an act of civil disobedience against an unjust law. To call up righteous anger at a moment of terror was a great help to me.

. . . I encountered the man carrying a bag of groceries. He gestured and I went off with him to his car. There was another woman already there, another college student. She told me she got pregnant the first time she slept with her boyfriend. We stopped by the mall and picked up a third woman, then drove for about 45 minutes. The third woman, who was from near Towson, said that we had taken an amazingly circuitous route to arrive at a little cottage in the woods where the grocery bag man lived with his wife. . . .

As I rode in the back seat of the car through the Maryland countryside on my way to have an illegal abortion that day in May 1968, I came to a shocking realization. For the first time in my life, I understood that I was a woman, not a "human being," but a woman. For the first time, I understood something about what it meant to be a woman in this society—that the lives of women were not of value. And I realized, in an inchoate rage that is with me today as I recall this story, that in this society, *because I had sex, someone thought I deserved to die.*

Glossary

Clergymen's [sic] Council on Problem Pregnancies: a religious mission to assist women in finding safe abortions

inchoate: not yet completed or fully formed

practicing Catholics: faithful members of a church that considered contraception a sin

Short-Answer Questions

1. Describe the author's reasons for obtaining an illegal abortion, and outline the challenges she experienced in finding an abortion provider.

2. Describe the range of emotions experienced by the author during her narrative of securing an illegal abortion.

3. Analyze how the author's experience shaped her political consciousness. What factors likely contributed to the formative nature of this experience for her?

Planned Parenthood v. Casey

Author	Document Type
Sandra Day O'Connor, Anthony M. Kennedy, and David H. Souter (opinion); Antonin Scalia (partial dissent)	Legal
	Significance
Date	Reaffirmed women's right to an abortion while
1992	broadening the ability of states to regulate abortion

Overview

The debates surrounding the legality of abortion under *Roe v. Wade* (1973) and challenges to the federal law began almost immediately after the Supreme Court's ruling. Some states, such as Pennsylvania, passed laws requiring that women give informed consent before electing to have an abortion or even undergo a waiting period before seeking an abortion, during which time they were presented with certain information concerning abortion. Minors were required to obtain consent from a parent except in extreme cases, such as medical emergencies. In *Planned Parenthood v. Casey* (1992), the Supreme Court affirmed the ruling of *Roe v. Wade*, which prohibited states from banning most abortions. The Court did, however, also affirm most of Pennsylvania's restrictions, requiring only that such restrictions not place a "substantial obstacle in the path of a woman seeking an abortion before the fetus attains viability."

Planned Parenthood v. Casey, then, reaffirmed a woman's Fourteenth Amendment right to privacy and to protection from governmental interference before the fetus is viable (that is, before it can live outside the womb). Of significance in *Planned Parenthood v. Casey* is that although this ruling reaffirmed a woman's right to an abortion, it broadened the ability of states to regulate the practice.

Justice Sandra Day O'Connor was one of the authors of the standard of "undue burden." (Library of Congress)

Document Text

JUSTICE O'CONNOR, JUSTICE KENNEDY, and JUSTICE SOUTER announced the judgment of the Court.

It is conventional constitutional doctrine that where reasonable people disagree the government can adopt one position or the other. That theorem, however, assumes a state of affairs in which the choice does not intrude upon a protected liberty. Thus, while some people might disagree about whether or not the flag should be saluted, or disagree about the proposition that it may not be defiled, we have ruled that a State may not compel or enforce one view or the other.

Our law affords constitutional protection to personal decisions relating to marriage, procreation, contraception, family relationships, child rearing, and education. Our cases recognize "the right of the individual, married or single, to be free from unwarranted governmental intrusion into matters so fundamentally affecting a person as the decision whether to bear or beget a child." These matters, involving the most intimate and personal choices a person may make in a lifetime, choices central to personal dignity and autonomy, are central to the liberty protected by the Fourteenth Amendment. At the heart of liberty is the right to define one's own concept of existence, of meaning, of the universe, and of the mystery of human life. Beliefs about these matters could not define the attributes of personhood where they formed under compulsion of the State.

These considerations begin our analysis of the woman's interest in terminating her pregnancy but cannot end it, for this reason: though the abortion decision may originate within the zone of conscience and belief, it is more than a philosophic exercise. Abortion is a unique act. It is an act fraught with consequences for others: for the woman who must live with the implications of her decision; for the persons who perform and assist in the procedure; for the spouse, family, and society which must confront the knowledge that these procedures exist, procedures some deem nothing short of an act of violence against innocent human life; and, depending on one's beliefs, for the life or potential life that is aborted. Though abortion is conduct, it does not follow that the State is entitled to proscribe it in all instances. That is because the liberty of the woman is at stake in a sense unique to the human condition and so unique to the law. The mother who carries a child to full term is subject to anxieties, to physical constraints, to pain that only she must bear. That these sacrifices have from the beginning of the human race been endured by a woman with a pride that ennobles her in the eyes of others and gives to the infant a bond of love cannot alone be grounds for the State to insist she make the sacrifice. Her suffering is too intimate and personal for the State to insist, without more, upon its own vision of the woman's role, however dominant that vision has been in the course of our history and our culture. The destiny of the woman must be shaped to a large extent on her own conception of her spiritual imperatives and her place in society. . . .

JUSTICE SCALIA, with whom THE CHIEF JUSTICE, JUSTICE WHITE, and JUSTICE THOMAS join, concurring in the judgment in part and dissenting in part.

My views on this matter are unchanged from those I set forth in my separate opinions in *Webster v. Reproductive Health Services* (1989) (opinion concurring in part and concurring in judgment). The States may, if they wish, permit abortion on demand, but the Constitution does not require them to do so. The permissibility of abortion, and the limitations upon it, are to be resolved like most important questions in our democracy: by citizens trying to persuade one another and then voting. As the Court acknowledges, "where reasonable people disagree the government can adopt one position or the other." . . .

The Court's reliance upon stare decisis can best be described as contrived. It insists upon the necessity of adhering not to all of *Roe*, but only to what it calls the "central holding." It seems to me that stare decisis ought to be applied even to the doctrine of stare decisis, and I confess never to have heard of this new, keep-what-you-want-and-throw-away-the-rest version. . . .

The Court's description of the place of *Roe* in the social history of the United States is unrecognizable. Not only did *Roe* not, as the Court suggests, resolve the deeply divisive issue of abortion; it did more than anything else to nourish it, by elevating it to the national level where it is infinitely more difficult to resolve. National politics were not plagued by abortion protests, national abortion lobbying, or abortion marches on Congress before *Roe v. Wade* was decided. Profound disagreement existed among our citizens over the issue—as it does over other issues, such as the death penalty—but that disagreement was being worked out at the state level. As with many other issues, the division of sentiment within each State was not as closely balanced as it was among the population of the Nation as a whole, meaning not only that more people would be satisfied with the results of state-by-state resolution, but also that those results would be more stable. Pre-*Roe*, moreover, political compromise was possible.

Roe's mandate for abortion on demand destroyed the compromises of the past, rendered compromise impossible for the future, and required the entire issue to be resolved uniformly, at the national level. At the same time, *Roe* created a vast new class of abortion consumers and abortion proponents by eliminating the moral opprobrium that had attached to the act. ("If the Constitution guarantees abortion, how can it be bad?"—not an accurate line of thought, but a natural one.) Many favor all of those developments, and it is not for me to say that they are wrong. But to portray *Roe* as the statesmanlike "settlement" of a divisive issue, a jurisprudential Peace of Westphalia that is worth preserving, is nothing less than Orwellian. *Roe* fanned into life an issue that has inflamed our national politics in general, and has obscured with its smoke the selection of Justices to this Court in particular, ever since. And by keeping us in the abortion-umpiring business, it is the perpetuation of that disruption, rather than of any Pax Romana, that the Court's new majority decrees. The Imperial Judiciary lives.

Glossary

Orwellian: a political system in which the government tries to control every part of people's lives, similar to that described in George Orwell's novel *1984*

perpetuation: the continuation or preservation of a situation, idea, etc.

procreation: the production of offspring; reproduction

proscribe: forbid; ban

stare decisis: precedent; principles from earlier rulings

Short-Answer Questions

1. How do both the majority opinion and the dissenting minority opinion of the Court evoke the issue of humanity in their arguments?

2. How did *Planned Parenthood v. Casey* expand the ability of states to limit the right to an abortion?

3. The dissenting opinion describes the notion that *Roe v. Wade* settled the matter of abortion as "Orwellian." Do you agree with this characterization? Why or why not? Which ruling would you describe as more Orwellian: *Roe v. Wade* or *Planned Parenthood v. Casey*? Please explain.

Ruth Bader Ginsburg: Concurrence in *Stenberg, Attorney General of Nebraska, et al. v. Carhart*

Author Ruth Bader Ginsburg	**Significance** Reinforced a woman's constitutional right to an abortion
Date 2000	
Document Type Legal	

Overview

Ruth Bader Ginsburg (1933–2020) was a jurist and associate justice of the Supreme Court of the United States. Ginsburg's early commitment to women's rights and equality was perhaps forged when the dean of Harvard Law School asked her and her eight female classmates why they were taking up seats at the school that rightly should be occupied by men. If that were not enough, she was unable to win a clerkship for a U.S. Supreme Court justice because of her gender, and she did not receive a job offer from the New York City firm where she clerked during the summer before her final year in law school. Then, after she took a teaching position at the Rutgers University Law School, she discovered that she was being paid less than male colleagues with the same rank. These circumstances motivated Ginsburg's preoccupation with civil rights generally and the rights of women in particular.

Ginsburg cofounded the Women's Rights Project at the American Civil Liberties Union (ACLU), where she lit- igated gender discrimination cases before the Supreme Court. President Bill Clinton appointed her to the Court in 1993, making her the second female justice in history. During her tenure on the Court, Ginsburg consistently championed women's rights, LGBTQ+ rights, voting rights, and social justice, making her an iconic figure for many.

The case of *Stenberg, Attorney General of Nebraska, et al. v. Carhart* dealt with a Nebraska law that made it illegal to perform a second-trimester abortion, except where it was deemed necessary to save the life of the mother. Justice Stephen Breyer, writing for the majority, stated that any abortion law that imposed an undue burden on a woman's "right to choose" (abortion) was unconstitutional. Ginsburg sided with the majority in *Stenberg*, writing in her concurrence that the State of Nebraska was not interested in saving the life of the fetus but in limiting a woman's right to choose.

Ruth Bader Ginsburg (right), pictured with President Bill Clinton (National Archives)

Document Text

I write separately only to stress that amidst all the emotional uproar caused by an abortion case, we should not lose sight of the character of Nebraska's "partial birth abortion" law. As the Court observes, this law does not save any fetus from destruction, for it targets only "a method of performing abortion." Nor does the statute seek to protect the lives or health of pregnant women. Moreover, as Justice [John Paul] Stevens points out, the most common method of performing previability second trimester abortions is no less distressing or susceptible to gruesome description. Seventh Circuit Chief Judge Posner correspondingly observed, regarding similar bans in Wisconsin and Illinois, that the law prohibits the D&X procedure "not because the procedure kills the fetus, not because it risks worse complications for the woman than alternative procedures would do, not because it is a crueler or more painful or more disgusting method of termi-

nating a pregnancy." Rather, Chief Judge Posner commented, the law prohibits the procedure because the State legislators seek to chip away at the private choice shielded by *Roe v. Wade*, even as modified by *Casey*.

A state regulation that "has the purpose or effect of placing a substantial obstacle in the path of a woman seeking an abortion of a nonviable fetus" violates the Constitution. Such an obstacle exists if the State stops a woman from choosing the procedure her doctor "reasonably believes will best protect the woman in [the] exercise of [her] constitutional liberty." Again as stated by Chief Judge Posner, "if a statute burdens constitutional rights and all that can be said on its behalf is that it is the vehicle that legislators have chosen for expressing their hostility to those rights, the burden is undue."

Glossary

Casey: *Planned Parenthood v. Casey* (1992), a significant Supreme Court case that upheld the right to have an abortion, affirming and reinforcing the fundamental principle established by the landmark case of *Roe v. Wade* (1973)

D&X procedure: dilation and extraction, a procedure that involves the surgical removal of an intact fetus from the uterus; utilized in miscarriages and abortions occurring during the second and third trimesters of pregnancy

"partial birth abortion": a term coined by abortion opponents to refer to dilation and extraction (or D&X) in hopes of instigating a public and political backlash to it

Short-Answer Questions

1. According to Ginsburg's concurrence, what is the primary focus of Nebraska's "partial birth abortion" law?

2. According to Chief Judge Posner, why do similar bans on the D&X procedure exist in Illinois and Wisconsin?

3. According to the passage, when does a state regulation violate the Constitution in the context of abortion?

Dobbs v. Jackson Women's Health Organization

Author	Significance
Samuel Alito	Held that the U.S. Constitution does not provide a right to abortion, overturning the court's previous decision *Roe v. Wade* (1973)
Date	
2022	
Document Type	
Legal	

Overview

The Supreme Court's decision in 1973's *Roe v. Wade* proved to be one of its most contentious in the modern era. Reflecting the influence of the sexual revolution and the women's rights movement, *Roe* decriminalized abortion across the nation and protected the right to access abortion legally in all fifty states.

While a majority of Americans came to accept the right to an abortion as one protected by the Constitution, opponents of *Roe* devised various strategies intended to bring about its overturning. One of the most effective proved to be the appointment of anti-abortion judges and justices across the nation, including on the Supreme Court. By June 2022, when the Court was prepared to revisit *Roe* and determine its constitutionality, six of the nine justices were consistently conservative in their rulings, which indicated to anti-abortion activists that the moment had arrived.

The case that resulted in the overturning of *Roe*, *Dobbs v. Jackson Women's Health Organization*, centered on a challenge to a ban on most abortions at fifteen weeks of pregnancy that was passed by the Mississippi legislature in 2018. The law banned abortion roughly two months earlier in gestation than *Roe* and subsequent decisions allowed, but it failed to go into effect due to a swift legal challenge from the Jackson Women's Health Organization, the state's only abortion clinic. In response to the challenge, a federal appellate court blocked the new law's enforcement on the grounds that *Roe v. Wade* did not allow states to ban abortions before viability, and the state could not prove a fetus's viability at fifteen weeks. Mississippi waited until the fall of 2020 to appeal the lower court's ruling to the U.S. Supreme Court, which agreed in May 2021 to hear the case. By this time, Justice Anthony M. Kennedy, a moderate supporter of abortion rights, had retired, and Justice Ruth Bader Ginsburg, a staunch defender of abortion rights, had passed away. Their replacements, Brett Kavanaugh and Amy Coney Barrett, joined four other members of the Court in deciding that the Constitution failed to support the viability of *Roe*, and it was subsequently repealed.

In his opinion, Samuel Alito argues that *Roe* and *Planned Parenthood v. Casey* (1992) should be overruled based on the absence of any mention of abortion in the Constitution or explicit protection of the right to one. It rejects the arguments that link the right to an abortion to the due process clause of the Fourteenth Amendment, which guarantees some rights not stated in the Constitution that draw upon America's history and its traditions, as being inconsistent with the existing laws at the time of the amendment's adoption, when most states made abortion a crime. Alito condemns *Roe* as "egregiously wrong" with "exceptionally weak" reasoning from the start, and responsible for considerable damage in its aftermath.

Much of Alito's selective historical argument is based on mid-nineteenth century United States law, a period that saw a reduction in female agency and the begin-

ning of anti-abortion campaigns. Abortions, however, were a widespread and accepted medical procedure in colonial and eighteenth-century America. Benjamin Franklin even included an abortion recipe in a textbook he published. While there is no historical guarantee to an abortion, it was not a criminalized medical procedure at the nation's founding. While Alito emphasizes that there were many state laws outlawing abortion in the nineteenth century, it should be noted that those laws were entirely written by men and that women were not considered full and equal citizens at the time.

The Supreme Court's elimination of the federal constitutional right to abortion enabled numerous states to impose restrictions on abortion or outlaw the practice altogether. More than half of the fifty states may choose the latter option in coming years or have already done so; before the *Dobbs* case went before the court, thirteen states passed "trigger bans" designed to ban abortion when *Roe* was overturned. The impact of *Dobbs* will be felt most keenly by some the nation's most vulnerable populations, including rural inhabitants, African Americans, Indigenous Americans, individuals with disabilities, and those living in poverty.

Document Text

For the first 185 years after the adoption of the Constitution, each State was permitted to address this issue in accordance with the views of its citizens. Then, in 1973, this Court decided *Roe v. Wade.* Even though the Constitution makes no mention of abortion, the Court held that it confers a broad right to obtain one. It did not claim that American law or the common law had ever recognized such a right, and its survey ranged from the constitutionally irrelevant (e.g., its discussion of abortion in antiquity) to the plainly incorrect (e.g., its assertion that abortion was probably never a crime under the common law). After cataloging a wealth of other information having no bearing on the meaning of the Constitution, the opinion concluded with a numbered set of rules much like those that might be found in a statute enacted by a legislature.

Under this scheme, each trimester of pregnancy was regulated differently, but the most critical line was drawn at roughly the end of the second trimester, which, at the time, corresponded to the point in which a fetus was thought to achieve "viability," i.e., the ability to survive outside the womb. . . .

At the time of *Roe*, 30 States still prohibited abortion at all stages. In the years prior to that decision, about a third of States had liberalized their laws, but *Roe* abruptly ended that political process. It imposed the same highly restrictive regime on the entire Nation, and it effectively struck down the abortion laws of every single State.

Eventually, in *Planned Parenthood v. Casey*, the Court revisited *Roe*. . . . The opinion concluded that stare decisis, which calls for prior decisions

Demonstrators after the* Dobbs v. Jackson *decision (Wikimedia Commons)

to be followed in most instances, required adherence to what it called *Roe*'s "central holding"— that a State may not constitutionally protect fetal life before "viability"—even if that holding was wrong.

Casey threw out *Roe*'s trimester scheme and substituted a new rule of uncertain origin under which States were forbidden to adopt any regulation that imposed an "undue burden" on a woman's right to have an abortion. . . . The three Justices who authored the controlling opinion "call[ed] for the contending sides of a national controversy to end their national division" by treating the Court's decision as the final settlement of the question of the constitutional right to abortion.

As has become increasingly apparent in the intervening years, *Casey* did not achieve that goal. . . . 26 States have expressly asked this Court to overrule *Roe* and *Casey* and allow the States to regulate or prohibit pre-viability abortions.

Before us now is one such state law. The State of Mississippi asks us to uphold the constitutionality of a law that generally prohibits an abortion after the 15th week of pregnancy—several weeks before the point at which a fetus is now regarded as "viable" outside the womb. In defending this law, the State's primary argument is that we should reconsider and overrule *Roe* and *Casey* and once again allow each State to regulate abortion as its citizens wish. On the other side, respondents and the Solicitor General ask us to reaffirm *Roe* and *Casey*,

The Schlager Anthology of Women's History

and they contend that the Mississippi law cannot stand if we do so.

We hold that *Roe* and *Casey* must be overruled. The Constitution makes no reference to abortion, and no such right is implicitly protected by any constitutional provision, including the one on which the defenders of *Roe* and *Casey* now chiefly rely—the Due Process Clause of the Fourteenth Amendment. That provision has been held to guarantee some rights that are not mentioned in the Constitution, but any such right must be "deeply rooted in this Nation's history and tradition" and "implicit in the concept of ordered liberty."

The right to abortion does not fall within this category. Until the latter part of the 20th century, such a right was entirely unknown in American law. Indeed, when the Fourteenth Amendment was adopted, three quarters of the States made abortion a crime at all stages of pregnancy. The abortion right is also critically different from any other right that this Court has held to fall within the Fourteenth Amendment's protection of "liberty." . . .

We begin by considering the critical question of whether the Constitution, properly understood, confers a right to obtain an abortion. . . .

The Constitution makes no express reference to a right to obtain an abortion, and therefore those who claim that it protects such a right much show that the right is somehow implicit in the constitutional text. . . .

In interpreting what is meant by the Fourteenth Amendment's reference to "liberty," we must guard against the natural human tendency to confuse what the Amendment protects with our own ardent views about the liberty that Americans should enjoy. That is why the Court has long been reluctant to recognize rights that are not mentioned in the Constitution. . . . Instead, guided by the

history and tradition that map the essential components of our Nation's concept of ordered liberty, we must ask what the Fourteenth Amendment means by the term "liberty." When we engage in that inquiry in the present case, the clear answer is that the Fourteenth Amendment does not protect the right to an abortion. . . .

Not only was there no support for such a constitutional right until shortly before *Roe*, but abortion had long been a crime in every single State. At common law, abortion was criminal in at least some stages of pregnancy and was regarded as unlawful and could have very serious consequences at all stages. American law followed the common law until a wave of statutory restrictions in the 1800s expanded criminal liability for abortions. By the time of the adoption of the Fourteenth Amendment, three-quarters of the States had made abortion a crime at any stage of pregnancy, and the remaining States would soon follow. . . .

We do not pretend to know how our political system or society will respond to today's decision overruling *Roe* and *Casey*. And even if we could foresee what will happen, we would have no authority to let that knowledge influence our decision. We can only do our job, which is to interpret the law, apply longstanding principles of *stare decisis*, and decide this case accordingly.

We therefore hold that the Constitution does not confer a right to abortion. *Roe* and *Casey* must be overruled. . . .

We end this opinion where we began. Abortion presents a profound moral question. The Constitution does not prohibit the citizens of each State from regulating or prohibiting abortion. *Roe* and *Casey* arrogated that authority. We now overrule those decisions and return that authority to the people and their elected representatives.

Glossary

abortion: the ending of a pregnancy, whether induced or naturally occurring, after or resulting in the death of the embryo or fetus

due process clause: section 1, sentence 2 of the Fourteenth Amendment, which states, in part: "nor shall any State deprive any person of life, liberty, or property, without due process of law"

pre-viability abortions: abortions that take place before a fetus is able to survive outside the womb

stare decisis: the principle of honoring legal precedent

viability: the ability of a fetus to survive outside the womb

Short-Answer Questions

1. How did the Court's rulings in *Roe* and *Casey* impact the regulation of abortion across the United States?

2. According to the passage, what is the main argument presented by the State of Mississippi in defending its law that prohibits abortion after the fifteenth week of pregnancy?

3. According to Alito, what is the main argument against recognizing a constitutional right to abortion? How does he address the historical context of abortion laws in the United States?